Renwick Z. Willson.

October

1848.

COMMENTARIES

ON THE

TWELVE MINOR PROPHETS.

VOL. III.

JONAH, MICAH, NAHUM.

THE CALVIN TRANSLATION SOCIETY,

INSTITUTED IN MAY M.DCCC.XLIII.

FOR THE PUBLICATION OF TRANSLATIONS OF THE WORKS OF JOHN CALVIN.

COMMENTARIES

ON THE

TWELVE MINOR PROPHETS.

BY JOHN CALVIN.

NOW FIRST TRANSLATED FROM THE ORIGINAL LATIN

BY THE REV. JOHN OWEN,

VICAR OF THRUSSINGTON, LEICESTERSHIRE.

VOLUME THIRD.

JONAH, MICAH, NAHUM.

EDINBURGH:

PRINTED FOR THE CALVIN TRANSLATION SOCIETY.

M.DCCC.XLVII.

[Entered at Stationers' Hall.]

EDINBURGH:
THE EDINBURGH PRINTING COMPANY,
12, South St David Street.

TRANSLATOR'S PREFACE.

CONTAINED in this Volume, as in the last, are the Writings of *three* Prophets: and they are explained and elucidated in the Author's peculiar manner; every sentence being dissected and examined, and the meaning ascertained according to the context, without the introduction of any extraneous matters. The main object throughout seems to have been to exhibit the genuine sense and design of the Sacred Writers.

The Book of JONAH is a plain narrative, and no part is supposed to have been written in the style of poetry except the prayer in the second chapter.

Some things in this Book have furnished Infidels with objections, and have induced some learned men, bearing at least the name of believers, to indulge in inventions. To satisfy Infidels or themselves, they have endeavoured to prove, that this Book is either an historical allegory, or a parable, or a dream, or a moral fiction, or something else still more absurd and extravagant. But all these are mere vagrant conjectures, wholly groundless, rendered plausible only by a show of learning, and calculated to do tenfold more mischief than all the sneers and cavils of Infidels. THE BIBLE IS A BOOK OF MIRACLES as well as of PROPHECIES; and an attempt to divest it of its Miracles is an attempt to divest it of one of its distinctive properties. Its Prophecies, which are continued Miracles, capable in many instances of ocular demonstration, attest those Miracles which were confined to certain times and occasions, as these were also in some cases performed for the purpose of gaining credit at the time to what was predicted. But there are no Miracles recorded in Scripture, which involve as much exercise of divine power as the fulfilment of Prophecies, though less visible in its operation.[1]

The fact that Miracles of some sort form a part of the records of false religions and of superstitious times, is no reason for disbelieving the Miracles of Scripture. Almost all errors are imitations of truth, and superstition is man's substitute for true Religion. The existence of a false coin is no evidence that there is no genuine coin, but, on the contrary, proves that it exists. Independently of the general character of the Miracles recorded in Scripture, what has been just stated, their *connection* with indubitable Prophecies is an argument in their favour, which neither heathen nor Christian superstition is capable of adducing. Both must stand or fall together. If the truth of Prophecies be allowed, then the reality of Miracles cannot with any reason be denied. They are so connected together, that they cannot possibly be separated.

[1] "Prophecy is of a prodigious extent; it commenced from the fall of man, and reaches to the consummation of all things. So many illustrious events falling in, one after another, just as the word of prophecy foretold they should, must afford the most convincing proof that our Religion is, as it claims to be, of divine institution,—a *proof* the more convincing, because it is continually growing upon us; and the farther we are removed from the source of our religion, the clearer is the evidence of its truth."—*Bishop Hurd.*

Learned men, being driven back, as it were, by manifest and palpable absurdities, have sometimes resiliated beyond the limits of reason and truth; being disgusted, and justly so, by Heathen and Popish Miracles, they have often been imperceptibly led to doubt all Miracles, as when we are frequently deceived, we are tempted to conclude that there is no such a thing as honesty in the world. And hence has arisen the attempt to obliterate Miracles from Scripture; and various hypotheses have been suggested, and supported in some instances by no small measure of ingenuity and learning: but it is an attempt which ought in the strongest manner to be deprecated and condemned as being nothing less than a sacrilege, the robbing of God's Word of one of its peculiar characteristics, even of that by which God has visibly proved his supreme power; for by reversing and changing those laws of nature, which at the creation he had fixed and established, he has given a manifest demonstration of his Omnipotence and Sovereignty. He has made it known to the world by Miracles, that He who has constructed the wonderful mechanism of nature, can alter, change, and reconstruct it whenever He pleases.

"The opinion," says *Dr Henderson*, "which has been most generally entertained is that which accords to the Book a strictly historical character; in other words, which affirms that it is a relation of facts which actually took place in the life and experience of the Prophet. Nor can I view it in any other light while I hold fast an enlightened belief in the divine authority of the Books composing the Canon of the Old Testament, and place implicit reliance on the authority of the Son of God. Into the fixed and definite character of the Canon I need not here enter, having fully discussed the subject elsewhere; but assuming that all the Books contained in it possess the divine sanction, the test to which I would bring the question, and by which, in my opinion, our decision must be mainly formed, is the unqualified manner in which the personal existence, miraculous fate, and public ministry of JONAH are spoken of by our Lord. He not only explicitly recognises the prophetic office of the son of Amittai, (Ιωνα του πϱοφητου,) just as he does that of Elisha, Isaiah, and Daniel, but represents his being in the belly of the fish as a real miracle, (το σημειον,) grounds upon it, as a fact, the certainty of the future analogous fact in his own history; assumes the actual execution of the commission of the Prophet at NINEVEH; positively asserts that the inhabitants of that city repented at his preaching; and concludes by declaring respecting himself, "Behold! a greater than Jonah is here," (Matth. xii. 39–41; xvi. 4.) Now is it conceivable that all these historical circumstances would have been placed in this prominent light, if the person of the Prophet, and the brief details of his narrative, had been purely fictitious? On the same principle that the historical bearing of the reference in this case is rejected, may not that to the Queen of Sheba, which follows in the connection, be set aside, and the portion in the First Book of Kings, in which the circumstances of her visit to Solomon are recorded, be converted into an allegory, a moral fiction, or a popular tradition? The two cases, as adduced by our Lord, are altogether parallel; and the same may be affirmed of the allusion to Tyre and Sidon, and that to Sodom in the preceding chapter."

This reasoning is conclusive on the subject, and cannot be fairly evaded. Our learned author adds another consideration:—

"Certainly in no other instance in which our Saviour adduces passages out of the Old Testament for the purpose of illustrating or confirming his doctrines, can it be shown that any point or circumstance is thus employed which is not historically true. He uniformly quotes and reasons upon them as containing accounts of universally admitted facts, stamps them as such with the high sanction of his own authority, and transmits them for the confident belief of mankind in all future ages."

That the preservation of JONAH in the bowels of the fish was an impossibility according to the course and nature of things, as they now exist, is quite evident: but it was no greater reversion of nature than the parting of the Red Sea, or the dividing of the streams of Jordan, or the sustentation of life in Moses during his stay on the Mount for forty days. The laws of nature were equally suspended in all these instances; and to deny to Him, who made these laws to be what they are, the power of changing them, is an inconsistency which no reason can justify.

The next Prophet is MICAH; and his Book is especially interesting on account of the prediction it contains of the birth-place of our Saviour, and also of the establishment of his Kingdom, and the spread of his Gospel. The prophecy recorded in the fourth chapter is one of the most splendid in all the Writings of the Prophets. We find the same in the second chapter of ISAIAH; but it is fuller and given more at large by MICAH. The idea of borrowing seems not compatible with the fact, that each declares that what they delivered was conveyed to them by a vision: and there is nothing unreasonable in the thought, that the Divine Spirit communicated the very same things, to a certain extent, to two individual Prophets; and the fact that more, on the same subject, was revealed to one than to the other, seems to favour the notion, that the whole was communicated to each separately.

It is a subject worthy of being noticed,—that it was not the practice of the Prophets to refer to the testimony of one another, or even expressly to the commandments included in the Law of Moses. ISAIAH indeed once said, "To the Law and to the Testimony." Though the sins which generally prevailed were distinctly condemned in the Law, especially the idolatry which was so common, they yet never quoted the commandments, and brought them to bear on the reigning corruptions. This may appear singular: but the way to account for it seems to be this,—that the Prophets' authority was the same with that of Moses: Their communications proceeded from the same Author; and there was no necessity to confirm what they said by referring to what the Law sanctioned. The same God, who gave the Law by Moses, sent his messages to the people by his Prophets. And hence arises a strong, though, as it were, an incidental, proof of the Divine character of what they have written.

The style of MICAH much resembles, in some respects, the style of HOSEA. His transitions are sometimes abrupt, and the sudden change of persons is not unfrequent. *Lowth* in his Prelections describes him as "being brief in words, sententious, concise, pointed,—sometimes bordering on the obscurity of HOSEA,—in many parts lofty and fervid, and highly poetical."[1] *Marckius* says, that "his diction is elegant, not very unlike that of Isaiah."[2] *Henderson's* account is more extensive, but on the whole just, as well as discriminating,—"His style is concise, yet perspicuous,[3] nervous, vehement, and energetic; and, in many instances, equals that of ISAIAH in boldness and sublimity. He is rich and beautiful

[1] "Michas plerumque brevis est, pressus, concisus, acutus; nonnunquam ad Hoseæ obscuritatem propè accedens; in multis elatus et fervidus, valdèque poeticus."—Præl. xxi.

[2] "Dictio elegans, non admodum dissimilis isti Iesaiæ."

[3] This must be qualified; in most parts it is so, but in some, it borders, as *Lowth* says, on the obscurity of Hosea's style.

in the varied use of tropical language, indulges in paranomasias, preserves a pure and classical diction, is regular in the formation of parallelisms, and exhibits a roundness in the construction of his periods, which is not surpassed by his more celebrated contemporary. Both in administering threatenings and communicating promises, he evinces great tenderness, and shows that his mind was deeply affected by the subjects of which he treats. In his appeals he is lofty and energetic. His description of the character of Jehovah, chap. vii. 18–20, is unrivalled by any contained elsewhere in Scripture."

"Some of his prophecies," says *Newcome*, "are distinct and illustrious ones, as ii. 12, 13 ; iii. 12 ; iv. 1–4, 10 ; v. 2, 3, 4 ; vi. 13 ; vii. 8–10. We may justly admire the *beauty* and *elegance* of his manner,—ii. 12, 13 ; iv. 1, 2, 3, and particularly the two first lines of verse 4 ; his *animation*,—i. 5, lines 3, 4 ; ii. 7, 10, line 1 ; iv. 9 ; his *strength of expression*,—i. 6, 8 ; ii. 3, lines 3, 4 ; iii. 2, 3, 12 ; vii. 1, 2, 4, line 1, 19, line 2 ; his *pathos*,—i. 16 ; ii. 4 ; his *sublimity*,—i. 2, 3, 4 ; iii. 6, 12 ; iv. 12, lines 3, 13 ; v. 8 ; vi. 1, 9–16 ; vii. 16, 17."

The *three* first chapters are throughout comminatory, in which judgments are denounced on both nations, the Jews and the Israelites, and in which are also enumerated the various evils which prevailed, idolatry as the chief, and its accompanying sins—injustice, oppression, and cruelty.—The *fourth* and the *fifth* chapters are of an opposite character, being prophetic of blessings, appertaining more especially to the Kingdom of Christ, while at the same time the previous sufferings and trials of the Church are graphically described.—In the *sixth* chapter the people are summoned to a trial; the Lord had a controversy with them. Being proved guilty of ingratitude, ignorance, injustice, and idolatry, they are threatened with awful judgments.—In the *seventh* and last chapter the Prophet bewails the paucity of good men, deplores the faithlessness and perfidy of the people, turns to the Lord, entertains hope, foretells the restoration of the Church and the fall of its enemies, and ends with a rapturous exclamation, having been evidently favoured with a glimpse of the rich and abundant mercies which God had in reserve for his people.

The Prophet NAHUM has but one subject—the FALL OF NINEVEH—and he keeps to his subject without diverging to any other. In mentioning the sins of Nineveh, the first thing he states is a wicked design against the Lord, referring no doubt to the purpose formed of entirely destroying the Kingdom of JUDAH. In describing afterwards the vices of the people of Nineveh, he especially mentions their rapaciousness, deceit, injustice, oppression, and barbarous cruelty, and compares Nineveh to the den of lions.

The special design of the Prophet in the description he gives, at the beginning of the *first* chapter, of the character of the Almighty, was to delineate him as He is to his enemies, as the God of vengeance, who vindicates his own honour, and defends his own cause against profane and rebellious opponents. He only makes a transient allusion to his goodness towards his people. The other subject was that which was suitable to his purpose. He was going to denounce irrevocable judgment on God's adversaries; he therefore described Him as the God of vengeance: and the extremely awful character here presented to us by one who spoke, as he was inspired from above, ought to be well weighed and seriously considered, especially by all those who are not become God's friends, but still continue his enemies.

The *second* chapter contains a vivid description of the fierce assailants of NINEVEH, of their success, of the plunder of the city, and of the captivity of its people, with an exultation over the den of lions. To prevent, as it were, any hope of escape, the Prophet, in the *third* chapter, gives, according to CALVIN and many other Commentators, a graphic view of the ransack of the city, as though he were an eye-witness; then he states the reasons for this dreadful overthrow, reminds the Ninevites of what had happened to another powerful and well fortified city, shows the uselessness of resistance, and declares the doom of the city to be irrevocable and irremediable. How wonderfully exact has been the fulfilment of this Prophecy![1] Who can contemplate it without acknowledging that He who spoke by the Prophets is the supreme, who rules and overrules all the events of time?

The style of NAHUM has been admired by all critics. *Lowth* says, that "no one of the minor Prophets seems to equal the sublimity, the vehemence and the boldness of NAHUM: besides, his Prophecy is a complete and finished poem; his exordium is magnificent, and indeed majestic; the preparation for the destruction of Nineveh, and the description of its ruin, and its greatness, are expressed in most vivid colours, and possess admirable perspicuity and fulness."[2]

This Volume contains a very interesting portion of The Minor Prophets. The History of JONAH is in many respects

[1] Those who wish to see this proved at large, may consult Bishop *Newton* on the Prophecies. Vol. i. Diss. 9.

[2] "Verùm ex omnibus minoribus Prophetis nemo videtur æquare sublimitatem, ardorem et audaces spiritus Nahumi: adde quòd vaticinium integrum et justum est poema; exordium magnificum est et planè augustum; apparatus ad excidium Ninivæ, ejusque excidii descriptio et amplificatio, ardentissimis coloribus exprimatur, et admirabilem habet evidentiam et pondus."—Præl. xxi.

very instructive.[1] The Prophecies of MICAH are some of the most remarkable in the Old Testament. NAHUM exhibits in language the most awful the vengeance of the Almighty against the enemies of his Church. And readers will find that our Commentator continues to exercise his talents in that capacity with his wonted vigour, penetration, and judgment. An impartial consideration of his labours cannot fail to impress our minds with veneration for his character, and especially with gratitude to the only Giver of all good for having so richly endued his servant, and for having employed him in services so conducive to the interest of true religion. Such was the respect in which he was held by Bishop *Horsley*, whose learning and acuteness were not of an ordinary kind, that in quoting his comment on a portion of the eighteenth chapter of ISAIAH, he calls him "THE VENERABLE CALVIN."

J. O.

THRUSSINGTON, *July* 1847.

[1] It has been made the groundwork of a most interesting volume of Essays by the late Rev. Thomas *Jones* of Creaton, under the title of "Jonah's Portrait."

THE

COMMENTARIES OF JOHN CALVIN

ON THE

PROPHET JONAH.

PREFACE BY THE AUTHOR.

At what time Jonah discharged the office of a Teacher, we may in some measure learn from 2 Kings xiv.; for it is certain that he is the person there mentioned in Sacred history, as he is expressly called the son of Amittai.[1] It is said there that Jeroboam, the son of Joash, had enlarged the borders of his kingdom, from the entrance into Hamath to the sea of the desert, according to the word of Jonah, the servant of God, the son of Amittai, who came from Gath. It was then at that time, or shortly before, that Jonah prophesied. And it is certain that he was not only sent to the Ninevites, but that he also was counted a Teacher among the people of Israel. And the beginning also of his Book seems to intimate what I have said,—that he was an ordinary Prophet among the people of Israel, for it begins with a copulative, *And the word of the Lord came to Jonah.* Though the Holy Spirit does in other places speak sometimes in this manner, yet I doubt not but that Jonah intimates that he was recalled from the discharge of his ordinary office, and had a new charge committed to him,—to denounce, as we shall see, on the Ninevites a near destruction.

We must now then understand, that Jonah taught among

[1] "He was of Gath-hepher, in the tribe of Zebulun, a part of lower Galilee, Josh. xix. 13. He prophesied in the reign of Jeroboam the second, king of Israel, who began to reign 823 before Christ, and reigned in Samaria 41 years. See 2 Kings xiv. 23-25."—*Newcome.*

the people of Israel, but that he received a command to go to the Ninevites. Of this command we shall take notice in its proper place; but it is right that we should know that he was not then only made a Prophet, when he was given as a Teacher to the Ninevites, but that he was sent to the Ninevites after having for some time employed his labours for God and his Church.

This Book is partly historical and partly didactic. For Jonah relates what happened to him after he had attempted to avoid the call of God, and what was the issue of his prophecy: this is one thing. But at the same time he mentions the kind of doctrine which he was commanded to proclaim, and he also writes a Song of Thanksgiving. This last part contains doctrine, and is not a mere narrative.

I come now to the words.

COMMENTARIES

ON

THE PROPHET JONAH.

CHAPTER I.

Lecture Seventy-second.

1. Now the word of the Lord came unto Jonah, the son of Amittai, saying,

2. Arise, go to Nineveh, that great city, and cry against it; for their wickedness is come up before me.

1. Et fuit sermo Jehovæ ad Ionam, filium Amittai, dicendo,

2. Surge, vade Niniveh, ad urbem magnam, et clama contra eam; quia ascendit malitia eorum coram facie mea.

As I have before observed, Jonah seems here indirectly to intimate,[1] that he had been previously called to the office of

[1] *Calvin* lays no great stress on the circumstance of the Book commencing with a ו, but states what he thinks as its probable import. The fact that other Books, such as Joshua, Judges, 1 Samuel, Ezekiel, and other Books, begin thus, is no proof that the copulative here does not intimate what is here stated. *Marckius* and *Cocceius* think that it imports a connection between the different Books of Scripture; and if so, why may it not intimate a connection between this Book and the former Prophecy of Jonah? *Junius* and *Tremelius* render the ו "when," and connect it with "then" at the beginning of the third verse; and it may be so construed at the beginning of most of the other Books. Adopting this rendering, we may translate thus,—

[1] When the word of Jehovah came to Jonah, the son of Amittai, saying, [2] "Arise, go to Nineveh, that great city, and cry against her, for their wickedness has ascended before me." [3] Then Jonah arose to flee to Tarshish, from the presence of Jehovah, and went down to Joppa," &c.

This reads connected, and the passage admits of this construction, for

a teacher; for it is the same as though he had said, that he framed this history as a part of his ordinary function. The word of God then was not for the first time communicated to Jonah, when he was sent to Nineveh; but it pleased God, when he was already a Prophet, to employ him among other nations. It might have been then, that he was sent to Nineveh, that the Lord, being wearied with the obstinacy of his own people, might afford an example of pious docility on the part of a heathen and uncircumcised nation, in order to render the Israelites more inexcusable. They made a profession of true religion, they boasted that they were a holy people; circumcision was also to them a symbol and a pledge of God's covenant; yet they despised all the Prophets, so that their teaching among them was wholly useless. It is then probable that this Prophet was taken away from them, that the Ninevites by their example might increase the sin of Israel, for in three days they turned to God, after Jonah had preached to them: but among the Israelites and their kindred he had, during a long time, effected nothing, when yet his authority had been sufficiently ratified, and thus, as we have already said, in their favour: for Jonah had predicted, that the kingdom of Israel would as yet stand; and however much they deserved to perish, yet the Lord fulfilled what he had promised by the mouth of his servant. They ought then to have embraced his doctrine, not only because it was divine, but especially because the Lord had been pleased to show his love to them.

I do not indeed doubt, but that the ingratitude of the people was in this manner arraigned, since the Ninevites repented at the preaching of Jonah, and that for a short time, while the Israelites ever hardened themselves in their obstinacy. And hence some have refinedly expounded that passage in Matth. xii., 'This perverse generation seeketh a sign, and a sign shall not be given to it, except the sign of Jonah the Prophet,' as though this intimated, that the Gospel was to be preached to the Gentiles, inasmuch as Jonah was taken

the copulative ו in Hebrew, when repeated, may very frequently be thus rendered, the first by "when," and the second by "then."—*Ed.*

away from his own nation, and was given as a teacher to foreign and heathen nations. They therefore suppose, that we are to understand this as a prophecy respecting the future call of the Gentiles, as though Christ had said, that he would hereafter go to the Gentiles, after having found the wickedness of the chosen people past recovery. But as Christ expressly applies this comparison, we ought not to draw his words here and there.[1] He indeed confines the similitude to one particular thing, that is, "As Jonah had been three days in the whale's bowels, so also he would be three days in the bowels of the earth;" as though he had said, that in this he would be like to Jonah, for he would be a Prophet brought to life again. And this was said designedly by Christ, because he saw that he was despised by the Jews, and that his labours were in vain: "Since ye now hear me not, and regard me as nothing, know that I shall be hereafter a new Prophet, even after my resurrection; so at length I shall begin to speak more effectually both to the Jews and to the Gentiles, as Jonah converted Nineveh, after having returned again to life." This then is the simple meaning of the passage. Hence Jonah was not a type of Christ, because he was sent away unto the Gentiles, but because he returned to life again, after having for some time exercised his office as a Prophet among the people of Israel. They then who say that his going forth was a token of the call of the Gentiles, adduce indeed what is plausible, but it seems to be supported by no solid reason; for it was in fact an extraordinary thing. God, then, had not as yet openly showed what he would do at the coming of Christ. When Naaman the Syrian was converted to the faith, (2 Kings v. 15,) and a few others, God changed nothing in his ordinary proceedings: for there ever existed the special call of the race of Abraham, and religion was ever confined within the ancient limits; and it remained ever true, that God had not done to other nations as he had to the Jews, for he had revealed to them his judgments, (Ps. cxlvii. 20.) It was therefore God's will that the adop-

[1] *Marckius* wisely says on another subject, but on a similar occasion, "Extra Scripturam autem audacter hic sapiat nemo;"—"but let no one be here rashly wise beyond Scripture."—*Ed.*

tion of the race of Abraham should continue unaltered to the coming of Christ, so that the Jews might excel all other nations, and differ from them through a gratuitous privilege, as the holy and elect people of God.

Those who adopt the contrary opinion say, that the Ninevites were converted to the Lord without circumcision. This is true; but I know not whether that was a true and legitimate conversion, which is hereafter mentioned; and of this, the Lord being willing, I shall again speak more fully: but it seems more probable, that they were induced by the reproofs and threatenings of the Prophet, suppliantly to deprecate the impending wrath of God: hence God once forgave them; what took place afterwards does not clearly appear. It is certainly not probable that the whole city was converted to the Lord: for soon after that city became exceedingly hostile both to the Israelites and the Jews; and the Church of God was by the Ninevites continually harassed with slaughters. Since it was so, there is certainly no reason to think, that they had really and from the heart repented. But I put off a full discussion of this subject until we come to another passage. Let us go on now with our text.

Arise, go to Nineveh, to that great city. Nineveh is called a great city, and not without reason; for it was in circumference, as heathen writers say, 400 *stadia:* and we shall see that Jonah was three whole days in going through the squares and streets of the city.[1] It hence follows, that it

[1] There is some difference in the account given. *Diodorus Siculus*, as quoted by *Marckius*, says, that it was in form oblong; one side was 150 stadia, the other 90; so that its circumference must have been 480 stadia. A stadium is nearly equal to a furlong, eight of which make a mile. It must then have been in circuit about 60 miles. Its walls are reported to have been 100 feet *high*—33 yards and 1 foot, and so *broad* that three chariots might run abreast, and adorned by 1500 towers, the height of which were 200 feet. From the circumstance of having in it 120,000 not knowing the right hand from the left, supposed to be infants, some think that its population must have been above two millions. It was situated on the river *Tigris*, on the eastern side, not far from the present *Mosul.*

In building this city, as reported by *Bochart*, there were no less than 140 myriads of men for eight years. A myriad being ten thousand, the number must have been one million, four hundred thousand. Such a city none has ever built since, was the declaration of Diodorus: and there is not probably on record an account of such a city. That it had

was a very large city, and this all allow. Profane writers call it Ninus, and say that it is a name derived from its founder; for it was Ninus, the son of Belus, who built it. But more correct is their opinion, who think that נינוה, *Ninue*, is a Hebrew word: and hence what Herodotus and Diodorus, and others of the same class, say, is certainly fabulous, both as to the origin of the city and as to the whole progress of the kingdom, and their legends can easily be disproved by testimonies from holy Scripture. It is at the same time admitted by all, that Nineveh was a very large and a well fortified city. Babylon was afterwards built by Semiramis, who had been the wife of Belus: after her husband's death she wished to show that she also excelled in mind and industry, and that she had wisdom above her sex. But with regard to the founder of Nineveh, it is certain that the city was first built by Asshur: whether it was enlarged by Ninus, I know not: this, then, I leave as uncertain; for I wish not to contend about what is doubtful. But it is certain, from what Moses has said, that the founder of this city was Asshur, (Gen. x. 11.)

As to the largeness of the city, even if profane writers had not said a word, the testimony of Jonah ought to be sufficient to us. Now, since he is bidden to go and proceed to Nineveh, the Lord gives him some hope of success. He indeed wrought effectually by the hand of his servant, Nahum; who, though he continued at home, yet prophesied against the Ninevites; but with a different view, and for another end. For as the people were then miserably distressed, and saw the kingdom or monarchy of Assyria in a flourishing state, they must have despaired, had not some solace been afforded them. Hence Nahum showed that God would be a judge against the Ninevites; that though he for a time favoured and spared them, there was yet impending over them the dreadful judgment of which he speaks. Nahum, then, was not given as a teacher to the Ninevites, but was only a proclaimer, that the Jews might strengthen their faith by this comfort—that they were not wholly rejected by the

large gardens, and even fields, within its walls, there can be no doubt. —*Ed.*

Lord, as he would some time avenge their wrongs. The case with Jonah was different: for he was sent to the city itself, to exhort the Ninevites to repent. Now the Lord, by speaking expressly of the largeness of the city, intended thus to prepare him with firmness, lest he should be frightened by the splendour, wealth, and power of that city: for we know how difficult it is to take in hand great and arduous undertakings, especially when we feel ourselves destitute of strength. When we have to do with many and powerful adversaries, we are not only debilitated, but our courage wholly vanishes away. Lest, then, the greatness of Nineveh should fill Jonah with terror, he is here prepared and armed with firmness. "*Go* then to *Nineveh*, and let not the power of that monarchy prevent thee to fulfil what I command thee; which is, to show to the Ninevites their sins, and to denounce on them destruction, if they repent not."

We now then understand why Nineveh was called *a great city:* for had it not been for the reason just stated, it would not have been necessary that this should have been said to Jonah. The Israelites, I doubt not, knew well that it was a large city, and also possessed of strength and of a large number of men: but the Lord intended to set before his servant what might have been a hinderance to him in the discharge of his office; *Go* then *to this great city*. In short, God designed in this way to try Jonah, whether he would prefer his command to all the hinderances of this world. And it is a genuine proof of obedience when we simply obey God, however numerous the obstacles which may meet us and may be suggested to our minds, and though no escape may appear to us; yea, when we follow God, as it were with closed eyes, wherever he may lead us, and doubt not but that he will add strength to us, and stretch forth also his hand, whenever need may require, to remove all our difficulties. It was then the Lord's purpose to deal thus with Jonah; as though he had said to him, "Remember who I am, and be content with my authority; for I have ready at hand all resources; when any thing stands in your way, rely on my power, and execute what I command thee." This is the import of the passage. Whenever then God demands any service from us, and we at the same time see that what the discharge of our duty demands is either difficult or apparently impossible, let this come to our minds,—that there is not anything in the whole world which ought not to give way to God's command: we shall then gather courage and confidence, nor will anything be able to call us away from our duty and a right course, though the whole world were fighting against God.

It now follows, *Cry against her; for ascended has their wickedness before my presence.* Cry, he says, against her: it was an unpleasant undertaking to cry out against her immediately at the beginning. We indeed know that men take pride in their power: and as there was then but one monarchy in the world, the seat of which was at Nineveh, a teacher could hardly expect to obtain a patient hearing, though he excelled in gracefulness of manner, and had acquired reputation, and brought an agreeable message. But Jonah was a foreigner, one unknown, and destitute of authority; and still more, he was immediately to denounce destruction on the Ninevites, to cry aloud, to reprove, to make a vehement proclamation, to threaten. How difficult was all this? We hence see how hard a command it was when God charged his Prophet to cry against Nineveh.

It is now added, *For their wickedness has ascended to me.* By this clause God strengthens his servant Jonah; as though he said, "Thou wilt not, as an individual, have to contend with them, but I constitute thee as my herald, to summon them to my tribunal." And no doubt it must have served much to animate Jonah, that he had not to deal with the Ninevites as an individual, but as the messenger of God: and it might also have had an influence on their minds, to know, that though no mortal inflicted punishment for their crimes, they yet could not escape the vengeance of God. This then is the reason why the Lord here declares that he would be the judge of Nineveh. And at the same time he reminds us, that though the Ninevites felicitated themselves, and also gained the plaudits of the whole world on account of their power, yet all this was of no moment, because their wickedness and iniquity had ascended into heaven. When therefore we are reproved, there is no reason that we should turn our eyes here and there towards men; we ought instantly to present ourselves to the scrutiny of God; nay, we ought ourselves to take in hand that voluntary examination which God requires. By so doing, we shall not feed our vices by foolishly deceiving ourselves, as hypocrites do, who ever look around them to the right hand and to the left, and never raise up their thoughts to heaven. Let us go on—

3. But Jonah rose up to flee unto Tarshish from the presence of the Lord, and went down to Joppa; and he found a ship going to Tarshish: so he paid the fare thereof, and went down into it, to go with them into Tarshish from the presence of the Lord.

3. Et surrexit Jonas ad fugendum (ut fugeret) Tharsis à facie Jehovæ, et descendit Japho, et invenit navem, quæ transibat Tharsis, et dedit mercedem (*hoc est, naulum pretium vecturæ,*) et descendit in eam, ut iret cum ipsis (*nempe cum mercatoribus vel nautis*) in Tharsis à conspectu Jehovæ.

Jonah now relates how he sought hiding-places, that he might withdraw himself from the service of God; not that he deceived himself with such a gross notion, as that he would be no longer under the power of God, after having passed over the sea; but he intended to shun, as it were, the light of the present life, by proceeding to a foreign country. He was, no doubt, not only in a disturbed state of mind, when he formed such a purpose, but was utterly confused.

It may be asked, why Jonah thus avoided the command of God. The Jews, indulging in frigid trifles in divine things, say that he feared lest, when he came to Nineveh, he should be deprived of the prophetic spirit, as though he were not in the same danger by passing over the sea: this is very frivolous and puerile. And further, they blend things of no weight, when reasons sufficiently important present themselves to us.

It was first a new and unusual thing for Prophets to be drawn away from the chosen people, and sent to heathen nations. When Peter was sent to Cornelius, (Acts x. 17,) though he had been instructed as to the future call of the Gentiles, he yet doubted, he hesitated until he was driven as it were forcibly by a vision. What then must have come to the mind of Jonah? If only on account of one man the mind of Peter was disquieted, so as to think it an illusion, when he was sent a teacher to Cornelius, what must Jonah have thought, when he was sent to a city so populous? Hence novelty, doubtless, must have violently shaken the courage of the holy Prophet, and induced him to betake himself elsewhere, as one destitute of understanding. Again, doubt might have had an influence on him: for how could he have hoped that a people, who were notorious for their licentiousness, would be converted? He had indeed before an experience of the hardness of the chosen people. He had been faithfully engaged in his office, he had omitted nothing to confirm the worship of God and true religion among the people of Israel: but he had effected but little; and yet the Jews had been called from the womb. What then could he hope, when the Lord removed him to Nineveh? for unbridled licentiousness ruled there; there was also there extreme blindness, they had no knowledge of divine worship; in a word, they were sunk in extreme darkness, and the devil in every way reigned there. Doubt then must have broken down the spirit of Jonah, so that he disobeyed the command of God. Still further, the weakness of the flesh must have hindered him from following his legitimate call: "What then? even this,—I must go to the chief city of that monarchy, which at this day treads under its feet the whole earth; I must go there, a man obscure and despised; and then I must proclaim a message that will excite the greatest hatred, and instantly kindle the minds of men into rage; and what must I say to the Ninevites? 'Ye are wicked men, God can no longer endure your impiety; there is, therefore, a dreadful vengeance near at hand.' How shall I be received?" Jonah then, being still surrounded by the infirmities of the flesh, must have given way to fear, which dislodged the love of obedience.

And I have no doubt, in my own mind, but that Jonah discussed these things within himself, for he was not a log of wood. And doubtless it was not to no purpose, as I have already said, that he mentions that the city was great. God indeed sought to remove what might prove an hinderance, but Jonah, on the other hand, reasoned thus,—"I see that I am to have a fierce contest; nay, that such a number of people will fall on me, enough to overwhelm me a hundred times, as the Lord has not in vain foretold me that the city is great." And though he might have had some hope, if they had been chastised, that they would give God his due honour; yet he confesses, that this hinderance came to his mind, which prevented him to proceed in the course of his calling. Hence doubt, as well as the fear of the flesh, made Jonah to stumble, and novelty also, as I have already said, must have perplexed him; so that he preferred to go down, as it were, to the grave, than to undertake an office which apparently had no reason in its favour. For why were the Prophets sent, except to effect something by their labour, and to bring forth some fruit? but of this Jonah had no hope. Some authority was also allowed the Prophets, at least they were allowed the liberty of teaching; but Jonah thought that all entrance was closed up against him: and still more, Jonah thought that he was opposing the covenant of the Lord, who had chosen one people only; and he also thought that he was, as it were, fixed to his own land, when he was appointed a Teacher in his own country; he therefore could not remove elsewhere without feeling a great repugnance.

I hence think, that Jonah disobeyed the command of God, partly because the weakness of the flesh was an hinderance, partly because of the novelty of the message, and partly because he despaired of fruit, or of success to his teaching.

But he doubtless grievously transgressed: for the first rule, as to all our actions, is to follow the call of God. Though one may excel in heroic virtues, yet all his virtues are mere fumes, which shine before the eyes of men, except the object be to obey God. The call of God then, as I have said, holds the first place as to the conduct of men; and unless we lay this foundation, we do like him who would build a house in the air. Disordered then will be the whole course of our life, except God presides over and guides us, and raises up over us, as it were, his own banners. As then Jonah subverted the first and the only firm foundation of a right conduct, what could have remained for him? There is then no reason for us to extenuate his fault, for he could not have sinned more grievously than by forsaking God, in having refused to obey his call: it was, as it were, to shake off the yoke; and this he confesses himself.

They therefore very childishly write who wish to be his apologists, since he twice condemns himself—*Jonah rose up to flee from the presence of Jehovah—to go unto Tarshish from the presence of Jehovah.* Why does he the second time repeat, *from the presence of Jehovah?* He meant, no doubt, to express here more distinctly his fault: and the repetition is indeed very emphatical: and it also proves clearly that it was not a slight offence, when Jonah betook himself elsewhere when he was sent to Nineveh. He could not indeed have departed from the Lord, for God fills heaven and earth; and, as I have said already, he was not fascinated by so gross an error as to think, that when he became a fugitive, he was beyond the reach of God's hand. What then is to flee from the face of Jehovah, except it be that which he here confesses, that he fled from the presence of God, as though he wished, like run-away servants, to reject the government of God? Since then Jonah was carried away by this violent temptation, there is no reason why we should now try, by some vain and frivolous pretences, to excuse his sin. This is one thing.

With regard to the word *Tharsis,* or Tharsisa, I doubt not but that it means Cilicia. There are those who think that it is the city Tharsus; but they are mistaken, for it is the name of a country. They are also mistaken who translate it, Sea; for Jonah intended not only to go to sea, but also to pass over into Cilicia, which is opposite to the Syrian Sea. But the Jews called that the Sea of Tarshish, as it appears from many passages, because there was very frequent sailing to that place. As then that transmarine country was more known to them than any other, and as they carried there their merchandise, and in their turn purchased their goods, they called that the Sea of Tarshish, as it is well known, as being near it.

Jonah then intended to flee into Cilicia, when the Lord would have sent him to Nineveh. It is said, that he *rose up to flee*, and then, that he *went down to Joppa*, that he *found there a ship*, which was passing over to Tarshish, that he *paid the fare*, that he *went down* into the ship, *to go with them* into

Cilicia :[1] now by all those expressions Jonah intimates that he was wholly fixed in his purpose, and that it was necessary that he should have been brought back by a strong hand; for he was touched by no repentance during his journey. Many things may indeed come to our minds, when the call of God appears to us too burdensome. There is none of us, when service is to be performed to God, who does not roll this and that in his mind: "What will be the issue? how wilt thou reach the place where thou expectest to be? See what dangers await thee." For Satan always comes forth, whenever we resolve to obey God; but we are to struggle in this case, and then repel what we see to be contrary to our calling. But Jonah shows that he was obstinately fixed in his purpose of fleeing: for he not only intended to go into Tarshish, but he actually went down to the city Joppa, which was nigh to Judea; and, therefore, some think that Tarshish was Africa; but this is strained. Others divine it to be Thunetus or Carthage, as though indeed these cities were built at that time; but men are very bold in dreaming. But what need of giving a new meaning to this word against the most common usage of Scripture, when it is evident enough that Tarshish is Cilicia?

Now, when Jonah went down to Joppa, it was evident that he intended immediately to migrate from the land of Judah, and to pass over the sea: but by saying that he *paid the fare*, that he *went down* into the ship, that he might *go*,—by this gradual progress, he sets before us, as I have said, more fully his own perverseness; so that he

[1] On this success of Jonah in meeting with a ship, &c., *Marckius* has these appropriate remarks—

"God sometimes not only suffers the wicked to advance prosperously in their sins, but does not immediately restore the godly in their declensions; nay, he gives them every facility for a time in their downward course, in order that they may know themselves more, and that the glory of God may become thereby more manifest. Foolish then is the sinner, who, having begun life prosperously, concludes that the end will be equally happy."

Matthew Henry's remarks are of the same import, but still more striking—

"Providence seemed to favour his design, and gave him an opportunity to escape: we may be out of the way of duty, and yet may meet with a favourable gale. The ready way is not always the right way."

admits that he not only resolutely purposed to reject the call of God, but that he also confirmed himself in it: and though there were many things to be done, which might have sometimes forced him to stand still, he yet constantly followed where his perverse and blind impulse led him. There is no doubt, then, but that Jonah, in these distinct words, sets himself forth as a fugitive, not only by one act, but by many acts.

Now, as to his flight, we must bear in mind what I have before said—that all flee away from the presence of God, who do not willingly obey his commandments; not that they can depart farther from him, but they seek, as far as they can, to confine God within narrow limits, and to exempt themselves from being subject to his power. No one indeed openly confesses this; yet the fact itself shows, that no one withdraws himself from obedience to God's commands without seeking to diminish and, as it were, to take from him his power, so that he may no longer rule. Whosoever, then, do not willingly subject themselves to God, it is the same as though they would turn their backs on him and reject his authority, that they may no more be under his power and dominion.

It is deserving of notice, that as Jonah represents himself as guilty before the whole world, so he intended by his example to show how great and detestable a sin it is, not to submit to the commands of God, and not to undertake whatever he enjoins, but to evade his authority. That he might then enhance the atrocity of his sin, he shows by his own example that we cannot rebel against God, without seeking, under some pretence or another, to thrust him from his throne, and, at the same time, to confine him within certain limits, that he may not include heaven and earth within his empire.

PRAYER.

Grant, Almighty God, that as thou hast not sent a Jonah to us, when alienated from every hope of salvation, but hast given thy Son to be our Teacher, clearly to show to us the way of salvation, and not only to call us to repentance by threatenings and terrors, but also kindly to allure us to the hope of eternal life, and to be a pledge of thy paternal love,—O grant, that we may not reject so remarkable a favour offered to us, but willingly and from the heart obey thee; and though the condition which thou settest before us in thy Gospel may seem hard, and though the bearing of the cross is bitter to our flesh, yet may we never shun to obey thee, but present ourselves to thee as a sacrifice; and having overcome all the hinderances of this world, may we thus proceed in the course of our holy calling, until we be at length gathered into thy celestial kingdom, under the guidance of Christ thy Son, our Lord. Amen.

Lecture Seventy-third.

4. But the Lord sent out a great wind into the sea, and there was a mighty tempest in the sea, so that the ship was like to be broken.	4. Et Jehova emisit ventum magnum super mare, et facta est tempestas magna in mari, et navis cogitabit frangi.

Jonah declares here how he had been, as it were, by force brought back by the Lord, when he tried to flee away from his presence. He then says that a *tempest* arose *in the sea;* but he at the same time tells us, that this tempest did not arise by chance, as ungodly men are wont to say, who ascribe everything that happens to fortune. God, he says, *sent a strong wind on the sea.* Some give this rendering, "God raised up," deriving the verb from נטל, *nuthel;* but others derive it more correctly from טול, *thul:*[1] and we shall presently meet with the same word in the fifth verse. Now as to what took place, he says that there was so great a tempest, that the ship was not far from being broken. When he says, 'The ship thought to be broken,'[2] the expression corresponds with the idiom of

[1] This is no doubt its root. It is used when Saul is said to *cast* a javelin at David, 1 Sam. xviii. 11, and when the Lord threatens to *cast* out the people from his land, Jer. xvi. 13. It implies force and power. *Coverdale's* rendering, as quoted by *Henderson*, strikingly conveys its meaning, "But the Lord hurled a great wynde into the sea."—*Ed.*

[2] This perhaps can hardly be said to be a Hebrew idiom. *Marckius*, and also *Henderson*, think it to be a metonymy, the ship is mentioned, instead of the mariners: there is in Luke viii. 23 an opposite metonymy, the sailors are taken for the ship. *Newcome* renders the sentence, "and it was thought that the ship would be broken in pieces." If the metonymy be admitted, the rendering would be, "and the mariners thought that they should be shipwrecked."—*Ed.*

our language, *la navire cuidoit perir*. But some take the ship for the passengers or the sailors; but this is strained; and we know that our common language agrees in many of its phrases with the Hebrew.

Jonah then meant, that a tempest arose, not by chance, but by the certain purpose of God, so that being overtaken on the sea, he acknowledged that he had been deceived when he thought that he could flee away from God's presence by passing over the sea. Though indeed the Prophet speaks here only of one tempest, we may yet hence generally gather, that no storms, nor any changes in the air, which produce rain or stir up tempests on the sea, happen by chance, but that heaven and earth are so regulated by a Divine power, that nothing takes place without being foreseen and decreed. But if any one objects, and says that it does not harmonise with reason, that, for the fault of one man, so many suffered shipwreck, or were tossed here and there by the storm: the ready answer to this is,—that though God had a regard only, in a special manner, to the case of Jonah, yet there were hidden reasons why he might justly involve others in the same danger. It is probable that many were then sailing; it was not one ship only that was on that sea, since there were so many harbours and so many islands. But though the Lord may involve many men in the same punishment, when he especially intends to pursue only one man, yet there is never wanting a reason why he might not call before his tribunal any one of us, even such as appear the most innocent. And the Lord works wonderfully, while ruling over men. It would be therefore preposterous to measure his operations by our wisdom; for God can so punish one man, as to humble some at the same time, and to chastise others for their various sins, and also to try their patience. Thus then is the mouth of ungodly men stopped, that they may not clamour against God, when he so executes his judgments as not to comport with the judgment of our flesh. But this point I shall presently discuss more at large: there are indeed everywhere in Scripture, instances in which God inflicted punishment on a whole people, when yet one man only had sinned. But when some murmur and plead that they are innocent, there is ever to be found a reason why God cannot be viewed as dealing cruelly with them; nay, were he pleased, he might justly treat them with much greater severity: in a word, though God may appear to deal severely with men, he yet really spares them, and treats them with indulgence. Let us now proceed—

5. Then the mariners were afraid, and cried every one unto his god, and cast forth the wares that *were* in the ship into the sea, to lighten *it* of them. But Jonah was gone down into the sides of the ship; and he lay, and was fast asleep.	5. Et timuerunt nautæ et vociferati sunt quisque ad deum suum; et projecerunt vasa, quæ erant in navi, in mare, ut levaretur ab illis: Jonas autem descenderat in latera navis, et jacebat et dormiebat.

This narrative, in which Jonah relates in order so many circumstances, is not without its use; for, as we shall presently see, he intended to set forth his own insensibility, and to lay it before us as painted before our eyes: and the comparison, which is implied in the circumstances, greatly illustrates the supine and almost brutal security of Jonah.

He says first that *the mariners*[1] *were afraid*, and then, that each *cried*, that is, *to his god*, and that they *cast out into the sea the lading of the ship*. As then they were all so concerned, was it not marvellous that Jonah, on whose account the sea was stormy, was asleep? Others were busy, they ran here and there in the ship, and spoiled themselves of their goods, that they might reach the shore in safety: they indeed chose to strip themselves of all they had rather than to perish; they also cried to their gods. Jonah cared for nothing, nay, he lay asleep: but whence came such a carelessness as this, except that he was not only become torpid, but that he seemed also to have been deprived of all reason and common feeling? There is no doubt then but that Jonah, in order to show this to have been the case, has here enumerated so many circumstances.

He says that the *mariners were afraid*. We indeed know

[1] מלחים, from מלח, salt, "salt-men;" so "mariners," in our language, from *mare*, are literally sea-men; and sailors are sail-men. Nautæ, in Latin, and ναυται, in Greek, being from navis and ναυς, are, properly, ship-men.—*Ed.*

that sailors are not usually frightened by small or common storms; for they are a hardy race of men, and they are the less afraid, because they daily see various commotions in the air. When, therefore, he says that the sailors were afraid, we hence gather that it was not a moderate tempest, for such does not thus terrify men accustomed by long experience to all sorts of storms: they, then, who had been previously hardened, were disquieted with fear. He afterwards adds, that *they cried, each of them to his god.* Jonah certainly ought not to have slept so soundly, but that he might rouse himself at almost any moment, for he carried in his heart his own executioner, as he knew that he was a fugitive: for we have said before, that it was not a slight offence for Jonah to withdraw himself from the presence of God; he despised his call, and, as far as he could, cast off the yoke, so as not to obey God. Seeing, then, that Jonah was ill at ease with himself, ought he not to have trembled, even while asleep? But while others cried to their false gods, he either despised, or at least neglected the true God, to whom he knew he was disobedient, and against whom he rebelled. This is the point of the comparison, or of the antithesis.

But we at the same time see, how in dangers men are constrained to call on God. Though, indeed, there is a certain impression by nature on the hearts of men as to God, so that every one, willing or unwilling, is conscious that there is some Supreme Being; we yet by our wickedness smother this light, which ought to shine within us. We indeed gladly cast away all cares and anxieties; for we wish to live at ease, and tranquillity is the chief good of men. Hence it comes, that all desire to live without fear and without care; and hence we all naturally seek quietness. Yet this quietness generates contempt. Hence then it is, that hardly any religion appears in the world, when God leaves us in an undisturbed condition. Fear constrains us, however unwilling, to come to God. False indeed is what is said, that fear is the cause of religion, and that it was the first reason why men thought that there were gods: this notion is indeed wholly inconsistent with common sense and experience. But religion, which has become nearly extinct, or at least covered over in the hearts of men, is stirred up by dangers. Of this Jonah gives a remarkable instance, when he says that the sailors *cried, each of them to his god.* We know how barbarous is this race of men; they are disposed to shake off every sense of religion; they indeed drive away every fear, and deride God himself as long as they may. Hence that they cried to God, it was no doubt what necessity forced them to do. And here we may learn, how useful it is for us to be disquieted by fear; for while we are safe, torpidity, as it is well known, soon creeps over us. Since, then, hardly any one of himself comes to God, we have need of goads; and God sharply pricks us, when he brings any danger, so as to constrain us to tremble. But in this way, as I have already said, he stimulates us; for we see that all would go astray, and even perish in their thoughtlessness, were he not to draw them back, even against their own will.

But Jonah does not simply say, that each cried to God, but he adds, *to his own god.* As, then, this passage teaches, that men are constrained by necessity to seek God, so also, on the other hand, it shows, that men go astray in seeking God, except they are directed by celestial truth, and also by the Spirit of God. There is then some right desire in men, but it goes astray; for none will keep the right way except the Lord directs them, as it has been said, both by his word and his Spirit. Both these particulars we learn from the words of the Prophet: The sailors *feared;* men hardy and almost iron-hearted, who, like the Cyclops, despised God,—these, he says, were *afraid;* and they also *cried to God;* but they did not cry by the guidance of faith; hence it was, that every one cried to his own god.

When we read this, let it first come to our minds that there is no hope until God constrains us, as it were, by force; but we ought to anticipate extreme necessity by seeking him willingly. For what did it avail the sailors and other passengers, to call once on God? It is indeed probable that, shortly after, they relapsed into their former ungodly indifference; after having been freed from their danger, they probably despised God, and all religion was regarded by them with contempt. And so it commonly happens as to ungodly men, who never obey God except when they are constrained. Let therefore every one of us offer himself willingly to God, even now when we are in no danger, and enjoy full quietness. For if we think, that any pretext for thoughtlessness, or for error, or for ignorance, will serve as an excuse, we are greatly deceived; for no excuse can be admitted, since experience teaches us, that there is naturally implanted in all some knowledge of God, and that these truths are engraven on our hearts, —that God governs our life,—that he alone can remove us by death,—that it is his peculiar office to aid and help us. For how was it that these sailors cried? Had they any new teacher who preached to them about religion, and who regularly taught them that God was the deliverer of mankind? By no means: but these truths, as I have said, had been by nature impressed on their hearts. While the sea was tranquil, none of them called on their god; but danger roused them from their drowsiness. But it is hence sufficiently evident, that whatever excuses they may pretend, who ascribe not to God his glory, they are all frivolous; for there is no need of any law, there is no need of any Scriptures, in short, there is no need of any teaching, to enable men to know, that this life is in the hand of God, that deliverance is to be sought from him alone, and that nothing, as we have said, ought to be looked for from any other quarter: for invocation proves that men have this conviction respecting God; and invocation comes from nothing else but from some hidden instinct, and indeed from the guidance and teaching of nature, (*duce ac magistra naturâ.*) This is one thing.

But let us also learn from this passage, that when God is sought by us, we ought not to trust to our own understanding; for we shall in that case immediately go astray. God then must be supplicated to guide us by his word, otherwise every one will fall off into his own superstitions; as we here see, that each cried to his own god. The Prophet also reminds us that multiplicity of gods is no modern invention; for mankind, since the fall of Adam, have ever been prone to falsehood and vanity. We know how much corruption must occupy our minds, when every one invents for himself hideous and monstrous things. Since it is so, there is no wonder that superstitions have ever prevailed in the world; for the wit of man is the workshop of all errors (*quia ingenium hominis officina est omnium errorum.*) And hence also we may learn what I have lately touched upon,—that nothing is worse for us than to follow the impulses of our flesh; for every one of himself advances in the way of error, even without being pushed on by another; and at the same time, as is commonly the case, men draw on one another.

He now adds, that the *wares were cast out*, that is, the lading of the ship; and we know that this is the last resource in shipwrecks; for men, to save their lives, will deprive themselves willingly of all their goods. We hence see how precious is life to man; for he will not hesitate to strip himself of all he has, that he may not lose his life. We indeed shun want, and many seek death because extreme poverty is intolerable to them; but when they come to some great danger, men ever prefer their life to all their possessions; for what are the good things of this world, but certain additions to our life? But Jonah tells us for another purpose that the ship was lightened, even for this,—that we may know that the tempest was no ordinary commotion, but that the sailors, apprehensive of approaching death, adopted this as the last resource.

Another clause follows: *Jonah had gone down into the sides,*[1] or the side, *of the ship*. Jonah no doubt sought a retreat before the storm arose. As soon then as they sailed from the harbour, Jonah withdrew to some remote corner, that he might sleep there. But this was no excusable insensibility on his part, as he knew that he was a fugitive from the presence of God: he ought then to have been agitated by unceasing terrors; nay, he ought to have been to himself the taxer (*exactor*) of anxiety. But it often so happens, that when any one has sought hiding-places, he brings on himself a stupor almost brutal; he thinks of nothing, he cares for nothing, he is anxious for nothing. Such then was the insensibility which possessed the soul of Jonah, when he went

[1] "Sides," ירכתי, mean no doubt the lower parts. *Jerome* renders it, *ad interiora navis*; the Septuagint, εις την κοίλην του πλοίου—to the belly or cavity of the ship.—*Ed.*

down to some recess in the ship, that he might there indulge himself in sleep. Since it thus happened to the holy Prophet, who of us ought not to fear for himself? Let us hence learn to remind ourselves often of God's tribunal; and when our minds are seized with torpor, let us learn to stimulate and examine ourselves, lest God's judgment overwhelm us while asleep. For what prevented ruin from wholly swallowing up Jonah, except the mercy of God, who pitied his servant, and watched for his safety even while he was asleep? Had not the Lord then exercised such care over Jonah, he must have perished.[1]

We hence see that the Lord often cares for his people when they care not for themselves, and that he watches while they are asleep: but this ought not to serve to nourish our self-indulgence; for every one of us is already more indulgent to himself than he ought to be: but, on the contrary, this example of Jonah, whom we see to have been so near destruction, ought to excite and urge us, that when any of us has gone astray from his calling he may not lie secure in that state, but, on the contrary, run back immediately to God. And if God be not able to draw us back to himself without some violent means, let us at least follow in this respect the example of Jonah, which we shall in its own place notice. It follows—

6. So the shipmaster came to him, and said unto him, What meanest thou, O sleeper? Arise, call upon thy God, if so be that God will think upon us, that we perish not.	6. Et accessit ad eum magister funis, et dixit ei, Quid tibi, sopite? Surge, clama ad Deum tuum, si fortè serenum se exhibeat Deus nobis (*alii vertunt*, cogitet de nobis, *vel* gratificetur nobis,) et non pereamus.

Jonah relates here how he was reproved by the pilot or master of the ship,[2] inasmuch as he alone slept, while all the

[1] "We see in this instance the great danger in which unconscious sinners are often involved, that the solace sought by them departs from them, that a dead sleep remains, and even increases under God's judgment, and that in the performance of duty the godly are sometimes more slothful than the ungodly."—*Marckius.*

[2] רב החבל, the master of the rope or roping: ὁ πρωρευς, the prowman, the boatswain.—*Sept.* *Nauclerus*, pilot, is the word used by *Calvin.* —*Ed.*

rest were in anxiety and fear. *What meanest thou, fast sleeper?* The pilot no doubt upbraids Jonah for his sleepiness, and reproves him for being almost void of all thought and reflection. "*What meanest thou, sleeper?*"[1] he says; "when thou seest all the rest smitten with alarm, how canst thou sleep? Is not this unnatural? *Rise*, then, and *call on thy God*."

We see that where there is no rule of faith a liberty is commonly taken, so that every one goes astray here and there. Whence was it, that the pilot said to Jonah, *Call on thy God*, and that he did not confine him to any certain rule? Because it had been customary in all ages for men to be satisfied with some general apprehension of God; and then every one according to his own fancy formed a god for himself: nor could it have been otherwise, as I have said, while men were not restrained by any sacred bond. All agree as to this truth, that there is some God, and also that no dead idol can do anything, but that the world is governed by the providence and power of God, and further, that safety is to be sought from him. All this has been received by the common consent of all; but when we come to particulars, then every one is in the dark; how God is to be sought they know not. Hence every one takes his own liberty: "For the sake of appeasing God I will then try this; this shall be my mode of securing his favour; the Lord will regard this service acceptable; in this way shall all my iniquity be expiated, that I may obtain favour with God." Thus each invents for themselves some tortuous way to come to God; and then every one forms a god peculiar to himself. There can therefore be no stability nor consistency in men, unless they are joined together by some bond, even by some certain rule of religion, so that they may not vacillate, and

[1] מה־לך נרדם, "τί σὺ ῥέγχεις—why dost thou snore?"—*Sept.* "Quid tu sopore deprimeris—why art thou oppressed with deep sleep?"—*Jerome.* "Quid dormis—why sleepest thou?"—*Dathius.* "How is it, thou art fast asleep?"—*Henderson.* "What ails thee? sleeping!"—*Benjoin.* The first part is well rendered by the last author, but not the other; for נרדם, only found as a verb in Niphal, ever means a *deep* sleep. It is applied to Sisera, in Jael's tent, Judges iv. 21, and to the sleep of death, Ps. lxxvi. 6. The rendering then ought to be, "What ails thee? being fast asleep."—*Ed.*

not be in doubt as to what is right to be done, but be assured and certainly persuaded, that there is but one true God, and know what sort of God he is, and then understand the way by which he is to be sought.

We then learn from this passage, that there is an awful license taken in fictitious religions, and that all who are carried away by their fancy are involved in a labyrinth, so that men do nothing but weary and torment themselves in vain, when they seek God without understanding the right way. They indeed run with all their might, but they go farther and farther from God. But that they, at the same time, form in their minds an idea of some God, and that they agree on this great principle, is sufficiently evident from the second clause of this verse, *If so be that God will be propitious* to us. Here the pilot confines not his discourse to the God of Jonah, but speaks simply of a God; for though the world by their differences divide God, and Jonah worshipped a God different from the rest, and, in short, there was almost an endless number of gods among the passengers, yet the pilot says, *If so be that God*, &c.: now then he acknowledges some Supreme God, though each of them had his own god. We hence see that what I have said is most true,—that this general truth has ever been received with the consent of all,—that the world is preserved by the providence of God, and hence that the life and safety of men are in his hand. But as they are very far removed from God, and not only creep slowly, but are also more inclined to turn to the earth than to look up to heaven, and are uncertain and ever change, so they seek gods which are nigh to them, and when they find none, they hesitate not to invent them.

We have elsewhere seen, that the Holy Spirit uses this form of speaking, *If so be*, when no doubt, but difficulty alone is intended. It is however probable, that the pilot in this case was perplexed and doubtful, as it is usual with ungodly men, and that he could determine nothing certain as to any help from God; and as his mind was thus doubtful, he says, that every means of relief were to be tried. And here, as in a mirror, we may see how miserable is the condition of all those who call not on God in sure faith: they indeed cry to

God, for the impulse of nature thus leads them; but they know not whether they will obtain any thing by their cries: they repeat their prayers; but they know not whether they pass off into air or really come to God. The pilot owns, that his mind was thus doubtful, *If so be* that God will be *propitious to us, call thou* also *on thy God.* Had he been so surely convinced, as to call on the true God, he would have certainly found it to have been no doubtful relief. However, that nothing might be left untried, he exhorted Jonah, that if he had a God, to call upon him. We hence see, that there are strange windings, when we do not understand the right way. Men would rather run here and there, a hundred times, through earth and heaven, than come to God, except where his word shines. How so? because when they make the attempt, an insane impulse drives them in different ways; and thus they are led here and there: "It may be, that this may be useful to me; as that way has not succeeded, I will try another." God then thus punishes all the unbelieving, who obey not his word; for to the right way they do not keep: He indeed shows how great a madness it is, when men give loose reins to their imaginations, and do not submit to celestial truth.

As to the words, interpreters translate them in different ways. Some say, "If so be that God will think of us;" others, "If so be that God will favour us." עשת, *oshit,* is properly to shine; but when put as here in the conjugation Hithpael, it means to render one's self clear or bright: and it is a metaphor very common in Scripture, that the face of God is cloudy or dark, when he is not propitious to us; and again, God is said to make bright his face and to appear serene to us, when he really shows himself kind and gracious to us. As then this mode of speaking altogether suits this place, I wonder that some seek extraneous interpretations.[1]

[1] Calvin is quite right here. The verb יתעשת occurs only here in Hithpael; and once as a verb in Kal, Jer. v. 28, עשתו, they "shine," applied to fat men, and once as a participle, applied to iron, ברזל עשות, "bright iron," or iron brightened, or made to shine, Ezek. xxvii. 19. It occurs as a noun in three other places, עשת, Cant. v. 14, עשתות in Job xii. 5, and עשתנת in Ps. cxlvi. 4. The idea of shining, brightness, or splendour, comports better with the context than that of thought, as given in our version in the two last places. It occurs once in its Chaldee

He afterwards adds, *Lest we perish*. Here the pilot clearly owns, that he thought the life of man to be in the power of God; for he concluded, that they must perish, unless the Lord brought aid. Imprinted then in the minds of all is this notion or προληψις, that is, preconception, that when God is angry or adverse, we are miserable, and that near destruction impends over us; and another conviction is found to be in the hearts of men,—that as soon as the Lord looks on us, his favour and goodwill brings to us immediate safety. The Holy Spirit does not speak here, but a heathen, and we know too how great is the impiety of sailors, and yet he declares this by the impulse of nature, and there is here no feigning; for God, as I have already said, extorts by necessity a confession from the unbelieving, which they would gladly avoid.

Now what excuse can we have, if we think our safety to be in our own hands, if we depend not wholly on God, and if we neglect him in prosperity, as though we could be safe without his help? These words then, spoken by the sailor, ought to be weighed by us, 'If so be that God's face may appear bright to us, and that we perish not.'[1] It now follows—

7. And they said every one to his fellow, Come and let us cast lots, that we may know for whose cause	7. Et dixit vir (*hoc est*, quisque) ad socium suum, Venite et jaciamus sortes, ut sciamus ob quam causam[2]

form in Dan. vi. 3, and there, no doubt, it means thought, or intention, or design. Following the usual import of the Hithpael conjugation, we may render the word here, "It may be, that God will himself shine upon us;" which means, "will show himself gracious to us." The Septuagint gives the sense, but not the ideal meaning of the verb, διασωσῃ, *may save*, and so does *Pagninus*, placeatur—*may* be *pacified*. Both *Newcome* and *Henderson* are wrong here: they follow our common version. *Dathius* retains the right idea, "se nobis clementem exhibeat."—*Ed.*

[1] "The servants of God are sometimes surpassed, reproved, and stimulated, by those far below them, yea, even by brute animals: a salutary admonition, from whatever quarter it may come, ought never to be despised."—*Marchius.*

"If the professors of religion do an ill thing, they must expect to hear of it from those who make no such profession."—*M. Henry.*

[2] בשלמי, this is a singular combination, two relatives with two prepositions—"through what—for what." It is in a more complete form in the next verse, באשר למי; ש in the first instance stands for אשר, what. The first may be rendered consistently with the context, "through whom—for whom:" but the context in the eighth verse requires it to be "through what—for what."—*Ed.*

this evil *is* upon us. So they cast lots, and the lot fell upon Jonah.

malum hoc nobis: et jecerunt sortes, et cecidit sors super Jonam.

Jonah did not without reason mention this,—that the passengers consulted together about casting lots; for we hence learn, that it was no ordinary tempest: it appeared then to be a token of God's wrath. For if strong wind arose, it would not have been so strange, for such had been often the case; and if a tempest followed, it would not have been a thing unusual. It must then have been something more dreadful, as it filled men's minds with alarm, so that they were conscious that God was present as an avenger: and we know, that it is not common with ungodly men to recognise the vengeance of God, except in extreme dangers; but when God executes punishment on sins in an unusual manner, then men begin to acknowledge God's vengeance.

This very thing Jonah now bears witness to, *They said* then *each to his friend, Come, let us cast lots.* Was it not an accustomed thing for them to cast lots, whenever a tempest arose? By no means. They had recourse, no doubt, to this expedient, because they knew, that God had not raised up that tempest without some very great and very serious cause. This is one thing: but I cannot now pursue the subject, I must therefore defer it until to-morrow.

PRAYER.

Grant, Almighty God, that though we are here disquieted in the midst of so many tossings, we may yet learn with tranquil minds to recumb on thy grace and promise, by which thou testifiest that thou wilt be ever near us, and not wait until by a strong hand thou drawest us to thyself, but that we may be, on the contrary, ever attentive to thy providence: may we know that our life not only depends on a thread, but also vanishes like the smoke, unless thou protectest it, so that we may recumb wholly on thy power; and may we also, while in a cheerful and quiet state, so call on thee, that relying on thy protection we may live in safety, and at the same time be careful, lest torpor, which draws away our minds and thoughts from meditating on the divine life, should creep over us, but may we, on the contrary, so earnestly seek thee, morning and evening, and at all times, that we may through life advance towards the mark thou hast set before us, until we at length reach that heavenly kingdom, which Christ thy Son hath obtained for us by his own blood. Amen.

Lecture Seventy-fourth.

We said in yesterday's lecture, that it was a proof of extreme fear, that the sailors and the rest cast lots; for this is not usually done, except men see themselves to be destitute of judgment and counsel.

But it must at the same time be observed, that through error they cast lots: for they did not know, that if God intended to punish each of them, they were worthy even of heavier punishment. They would not indeed have thrown the blame on one man, if each had well considered what he deserved before God. When a calamity happens, it is the duty of every one to examine himself and his whole life before God: then every one, from the first to the last, must confess that he bears a just judgment. But when all demand together who is guilty before God, they thus exonerate themselves, as though they were innocent. And it is an evil that prevails at this day in the world, that every one is disposed to cast the blame on others, and all would have themselves to be innocent before God; not that they can clear themselves of every fault, but they extenuate their sins, as though God could not justly pursue them with so much severity. As for instance,—When any one perceives that he has, in various ways, done wrong, he will indeed confess in words that he is a sinner; but were any person to enumerate and bring forward each of his sins, he would say, "This is a light offence, that is a venal sin; and the Lord deals not with us with so much strict justice, that he means to bring on us instantly extreme punishment." When there is a slight offence, it is immediately referred to by every one. Thus acted the sailors, of whom Jonah now speaks. Had any one asked, whether they were wholly without fault, every one, no doubt, would have confessed that he was a sinner before God; but yet they cast lots, as though one only was exposed to God's judgment.

How so? because they did not think that their own sins deserved so heavy a punishment. How much soever they might have offended,—and this they really felt and were convinced of,—they yet did not make so much of their sins as to think that they deserved any such judgment. This then is the reason why they come to the lot; it was, because every one seemed to himself to be blameless, when he came to examine himself.

This passage, then, shows what is even well known by common experience,—that men, though they know themselves to be guilty before God, yet extenuate their sins and promise themselves pardon, as though they could make an agreement with God, that he should not treat them with strict justice, but deal with them indulgently. Hence, then, is the hope of impunity, because we make light offences of the most grievous sins. Thus we find under the Papacy, that various modes are devised, by which they absolve themselves before God and wipe away their stains: the sprinkling of holy water cleanses almost all sins; except a man be either an adulterer, or a murderer, or a sorcerer, or ten times perjured, he hardly thinks himself to be guilty of any crime. Then the expiations which they use, avail, as they think, to obliterate all iniquities. Whence is this error? Even because they consider God to be like themselves, and think not their sins to be so great abominations before God. But this is no new thing; for we see what happened in the time of Jonah; and from profane histories also we may learn, that this error possessed everywhere the minds of all. They had then daily expiations, as the Papists have their masses, their pilgrimages, their sprinklings of holy water, and similar playthings (*nugas*—trifles, fopperies:) but as under the Papacy there are reserved cases, so also in former times, when any one had killed a father or mother, when any one had committed incest, he stood in need of some extraordinary expiation; and if there was any one of great renown on the earth, they applied to him, that he might find out some new kind of expiation. An example of this error is set before us here, when they said, *Let us cast lots.* For except they thought that one only was guilty, and not all, every one would have publicly confessed his sins, and would then have acknowledged that such was the mass of them as to be enough to fill heaven and earth; but this they did not. One man must have been the offender; but no one came forward with such a confession: hence they cast lots.

It may now be inquired, whether this mode of seeking out the truth was lawful; as they knew not through whose fault the tempest arose, was it right to have recourse to lots? Some have been too superstitious in condemning lots; for they have plainly said, that all lots are wicked. Hence has come the name, lot-drawers, (*sortilegi;*) and they have thought that lot-drawers differ nothing from magicians and enchanters. This has proceeded from ignorance, for we know that the casting of lots has been sometimes allowed. And Solomon certainly speaks, as of a common rule, when he says of lots being cast into the bosom, and of the issue being from Jehovah, (Prov. xvi. 33.) Solomon speaks not there of the arts of magic, but says that when lots are cast, the event is not by chance but by God's providence. And when Matthias was chosen in the place of Judas, it was done by lot, (Acts i. 26.) Did the Apostles use this mode presumptuously? No, the Holy Spirit presided over this election. There is then no doubt but that God approved of that casting of lots. So also Joshua had recourse to the lot when the cause of God's displeasure was unknown, though it was evident that God was angry with the people. Joshua, being perplexed by what was unknown, did cast lots; and so Achan was discovered and his sacrilege. That lot no one will dare condemn. Then what I have said is clear enough, that those have been too superstitious who have condemned all casting of lots without exception. But we must yet remember that lots are not to be used indiscriminately. It is a part of the civil law, that when a common inheritance is divided, it is allowed to cast lots: as it belongs not to this or that person to choose, each must take the part which the lot determines. So again it is lawful to cast lot in great undertakings, when men are anywhere sent: and when there is a division of labour, to prevent jealousy when one wishes to choose a certain part for himself, the lot will remove all contentions. A lot of this kind is allowed both by the word of God and by civil laws. But when any one adopts the lot without any reason, he is no doubt superstitious, and differs not much from the magician or the enchanter. As for instance, when one intends to go a journey, or to take anything in hand, if he throws into his hat a white and a black lot, and says, "I will see whether my going out to-day will be prosperous;" now this is of the devil; for Satan by such arts deludes wretched men. If then any one makes use of the lot without any just reason, he is, as I have said, without excuse.

But as to the other lots, such as we have now noticed, they ought not to be viewed as precedents. For though Joshua used the lot to bring to light the cause for which God was angry with his people, it is not yet right for us to imitate what he did; for Joshua was no doubt led by some peculiar influence to adopt this measure. So also as to Saul, when he cast lots, and his son Jonathan was discovered as the one who had tasted honey, it was an especial example. The same thing must be also said of the lot mentioned here; for as the sailors were trembling, and knew not the cause why the tempest arose, and the fear of shipwreck seized them, they had recourse to the lot. Were we continually to imitate such examples, such a liberty would not certainly be pleasing to God, nor consistent with his word. We must therefore bear in mind, that there were some peculiar influences, (*instinctus*—movements,) whenever God's servants used the lot in doubtful and extreme cases.[1] This then is shortly the answer to the question—Was it lawful for the sailors to cast lots, that they might find out the person on account of whom they were in so much danger? I now proceed to what follows—

8. Then said they unto him, Tell us, we pray thee, for whose cause this evil *is* upon us: what *is* thine occupation? and whence comest thou? what *is* thy country? and of what people *art* thou?	8. Et dixerunt ei, Narra nunc nobis quare malum hoc nobis contingerit, quodnam opus tuum et unde venias, quæ sit patria tua, et ex quo populi sis?

[1] Similar is the view given by *Jerome.* "We ought not, for this example, to put implicit confidence in lots, nor to connect with it the instance recorded in the Acts, when Matthias was chosen an Apostle by lot, since privileges granted to individuals cannot make a common rule, (*cum privilegia singulorum non possint legem* facere communem.")

9. And he said unto them, I *am* an Hebrew; and I fear the Lord, the God of heaven, which hath made the sea and the dry *land*.

10. Then were the men exceedingly afraid, and said unto him, Why hast thou done this? For the men knew that he fled from the presence of the Lord, because he had told them.

9. Et dixit ad eos, Hebræus ego sum, et Jehovam Deum cœlorum ego timeo, qui fecit mare et aridam.

10. Et timuerunt viri timore magno, et dixerunt ei, Quare hoc fecisti? quia noverant viri quòd à facie Jehovæ ipse fugeret; nam ipsis narraverat.

After the lot fell on Jonah, they doubted not but that he was the guilty person, any more than if he had been a hundred times proved to be so: for why did they cast lots, except that they were persuaded that all doubt could thus be removed, and that what was hid could thus be brought to the light? As then this persuasion was fixed in their minds, that the truth was elicited, and was in a manner drawn out of darkness by the lot, they now inquire of Jonah what he had done: for they took this as allowed, that they had to endure the tempest on his account, and also, that he, by some detestable crime, had merited such a vengeance at God's hand. We hence see that they cast lots, because they fully believed that they could not otherwise find out the crime on account of which they suffered, and also, that lots were directed by the hidden purpose of God: for how could a certain judgment be found by lot, except God directed it according to his own purpose, and overruled what seemed to be especially fortuitous? These principles then were held as certain in a manner by men who were heathens,—that God can draw out the truth, and bring it to the light,—and also, that he presides over lots, however fortuitous they may be thought to be.

This was the reason why they now asked what Jonah *had done. Tell us*, then, *why has this evil happened to us, what is thy work?* &c. By work here I do not mean what is wrong, but a kind of life, or, as they say, a manner of living. They then asked how Jonah had hitherto employed himself, and what sort of life he followed. For it afterwards follows, *Tell us, whence comest thou, what is thy country*, and from what people art thou? They made inquiries, no doubt, on each particular in due order; but Jonah here briefly records the questions.

I now come to his answer, *He said to them, I am an Hebrew; and I fear Jehovah the God of heaven, who has created the sea and the dry land.*[1] Here Jonah seemed as yet to evade, yea, to disown his crime, for he professed himself to be the worshipper of the true God. Who would not have said, but that he wished here to escape by a subterfuge, as he set up his own piety to cover the crime before-mentioned? But all things are not here in the first verse related; for shortly after, it follows, that the sailors knew of Jonah's flight; and that he had himself told them, that he had disobeyed God's call and command. There is then no doubt but that Jonah honestly confessed his own sin, though he does not say so. But we know, that it is a mode of speaking common among the Hebrews, to add in the last place what had been first said; and grammarians say, that it is ὕστερον πρότερον, (last first,) when anything is left out in its proper place and then added as an explanation. When therefore Jonah says that he was *an Hebrew*, and worshipper of the true God,—this tended to aggravate his fault or crime rather than to excuse it: for had he said only, that he was conscious of having done wrong in disobeying God, his crime would not have appeared so atrocious; but when he begins by saying, that known to him was the true God, the framer of heaven and earth, the God of Israel, who had made himself known by a law given and pub-

[1] This answer reverses the order of the questions. He answers the last question first. "Whence comest thou, and what is thy country?" The answer is, "I am an Hebrew." The previous question was, "What is thy work," or occupation? To this he answers, "I fear Jehovah," &c. This was his calling, his work, his occupation. "Fear," of course, includes worship and service. This ought to be the work and occupation of all. But to the first question, as to what evil he had done, he gives no answer. *Calvin* supposes that the whole is not here related, but is to be gathered from what follows. It is, however, probable that he had previously told them, that is, before the storm arose, that he was fleeing from the presence of the Lord: he therefore left them to conclude what evil it was which he had done.

It may be inquired why he said that he was "an Hebrew," and not, that he was an Israelite, as the case really was, for he belonged to the ten tribes, and not to the kingdom of Judah; and Israelites, and not Hebrews, seem to have been then the common name of the ten tribes. The reason may be, that as the Israelites were then for the most part idolatrous, he wished to show that he was a true descendant of the patriarchs, who were God's faithful servants, real Hebrews, passengers, sojourners, and pilgrims, as the word imports, on the earth.—*Ed.*

lished,—when Jonah made this introduction, he thereby removed from himself all pretences as to ignorance and misconception. He had been educated in the law, and had, from childhood, been taught who the true God was. He could not then have fallen through ignorance ; and further, he did not, as the others, worship fictitious gods ; he was an Israelite. As then he had been brought up in true religion, his sin was the more atrocious, inasmuch as he had fallen away from God, having despised his command, and, as it were, shaken off the yoke, and had become a fugitive.

We now then perceive the reason why Jonah called himself here an Hebrew, and testified that he was the worshipper of the true God. First, by saying that he was an Hebrew, he distinguished the God of Abraham from the idols of the Gentiles: for the religion of the chosen people was well known in all places, though disapproved by universal consent; at the same time, the Cilicians and other Asiatics, and also the Grecians, and the Syrians in another quarter,—all these knew what the Israelites gloried in,—that the true God had appeared to their father Abraham, and then made with him a gratuitous covenant, and also had given the law by Moses;—all this was sufficiently known by report. Hence Jonah says now, that he was an Hebrew, as though he had said, that he had no concern with any fictitious god, but with the God of Abraham, who had formerly appeared to the holy Fathers, and who had also given a perpetual testimony of his will by Moses. We see then how emphatically he declared, that he was an *Hebrew:* secondly, he adds, *I fear Jehovah, the God of heaven.* By the word fear is meant worship : for it is not to be taken here as often in other places, that is, in its strict meaning; but fear is to be understood for worship : "I am not given," he says, "to various superstitions, but I have been taught in true religion ; God has made himself known to me from my childhood : I therefore do not worship any idol, as almost all other people, who invent gods for themselves ; but I worship God, the creator of heaven and earth." He calls him *the God of heaven,* that is, who dwells alone as God in heaven. While the others thought heaven to be filled with a great number of gods, Jonah here sets up against them the one true God, as though he said, "Invent according to your own fancy innumerable gods, there is yet but one, who possesses the highest authority in heaven; for it is he who *made the sea and the dry land.*"[1]

We now then apprehend what Jonah meant by these words: he shows here that it was no wonder that God pursued him with so much severity; for he had not committed a slight offence, but a fatal sin. We now see how much Jonah had profited since the Lord had begun severely to deal with him: for inasmuch as he was asleep, yea, and insensible in his sin, he would have never repented, had it not been for this violent remedy. But when the Lord roused him by his severity, he then not only confessed that he was guilty, or owned his guilt in a formal manner, (*defunctoriè*—as ridding one's self of a business, carelessly;) but also willingly testified, as we see, before men who were heathens, that he was the guilty man, who had forsaken the true God, in whose worship he had been well instructed. This was the fruit of true penitence, and it was also the fruit of the chastisement which God had inflicted on him. If then we wish God to approve of our repentance, let us not seek evasions, as for the most part is the case; nor let us extenuate our sins, but by a free confession testify before the whole world what we have deserved.

It then follows, that the men feared with great fear, and said, *Why hast thou done this?*[2] *for they knew that he had fled from the presence of Jehovah, for he had told them.* And this is not unimportant—that *the sailors feared with great fear:* for Jonah means that they were not only moved by what he said, but also terrified, so that they gave to the true God his

[1] "Non Deos quos invocatis, et qui salvare non possunt, sed Deum cœli qui mare fecit et aridam, mare in quo fugio, aridam de qua fugio," &c.—*Jerome.*

[2] מה־זאת עשית,—"What this thou hast done?" "τί τουτο εποίησας,—what this thou hast done?"—*Sept.* "Quid (*i.e.*, cur) hoc fecisti—why hast thou done this?"—*Marckius;* so *Jerome*, and *Drusius*, and *Dathius.* "What is this thou hast done?"—*Henderson.* It is not a question, requiring a reason for what he had done, but rather an exclamation—"What an evil is this which thou hast done!" They judged of it by the effects; for they knew before that he had fled from the presence of the Lord; and now they perceived how great an evil it was.—*Ed.*

glory. We indeed know that superstitious men almost trifle with their own idols. They often entertain, it is true, strange fears, but afterwards they flatter themselves, and in a manner cajole their own hearts, so that they can pleasantly and sweetly smile at their own fancies. But Jonah, by saying here that they *feared with great fear*, means that they were so smitten, that they really perceived that the God of Israel was a righteous judge, and that he was not such as other nations fancied him to be, but that he was capable of affording dreadful examples whenever he intended to execute his vengeance. We hence see what Jonah means, when he speaks of great fear. At the same time, two things ought to be noticed,—that they feared, because it was easy for them to conclude from the Prophet's words, that the God of Israel was the only creator of heaven and earth,—and then, that it was a great fear, which, as I have said, must be considered as serious dread, since the fear which the unbelieving have soon vanishes.

But with regard to the reproof which the sailors and other passengers gave to Jonah, the Lord returned to him this as a reward which he had deserved. He had fled from the presence of God; he had thus, as we have said, taken away from God his supreme power: for what becomes of God's authority when any one of us rejects his commands and flees away from his presence? Since Jonah then sought to shun God, he was now placed before men. There were present heathens, and even barbarians, who rebuked him for his sin, who were his censors and judges. And the same thing we see happening often. For they who do not willingly obey God and his word, afterwards abandon themselves to many flagrant sins, and their baseness becomes evident to all. As, then, they cannot bear God to be their Master and Teacher, they are constrained to bear innumerable censors; for they are branded by the reproaches of the vulgar, they are pointed at every where by the finger, at length they are conducted to the gallows, and the executioner becomes their chief teacher. The case was similar, as we see, with Jonah: the pilot had before reproved his torpor, when he said, "Do thou also call on thy God; what meanest thou, O sleeper? thou liest down here like a log of wood, and yet thou seest us perplexed and in extreme danger." As, then, the pilot first so sharply inveighed against Jonah, and then all reproved him with one mouth, we certainly find that he was made subject to the condemnation of all, because he tried to deprive God of his supreme power. If at any time the same thing should happen to us, if God should subject us to the reproaches of men when we seek to avoid his judgment, let us not wonder. But as Jonah here calmly answers, and raises no clamour, and shows no bitterness, so let every one of us, in the true spirit of meekness, acknowledge our own sins; when charged with them, were even children our condemners, or were even the most contemptible of the people to rise up against us, let us patiently bear all this; and let us know that these kinds of censors befall us through the providence of God. It now follows—

11. Then said they unto him, What shall we do unto thee, that the sea may be calm unto us? for the sea wrought, and was tempestuous.

12. And he said unto them, Take me up, and cast me forth into the sea; so shall the sea be calm unto you: for I know that for my sake this great tempest *is* upon you.

11. Et dixerunt ad eum, Quid faciemus tibi ut resideat mare à nobis? quia mare ibat (*id est*, commovebatur,) et erat tempestuosum.

12. Et dixit illis, Tollite me, et projicite me in mare, et residebit mare à vobis; quia novi ego, quòd propter me tempestas magna hæc contingerit super vos (*hoc est*, sit super vos.)

The sailors asked counsel of Jonah; and hence it appears that they were touched with so much fear as not to dare to do any thing to him. We hence see how much they had improved almost in an instant, since they spared an Israelite, because they acknowledged that among that people the true God was worshipped, the supreme King of heaven and earth: for, without a doubt, it was this fear that restrained them from throwing Jonah immediately into the sea. For since it was certain that through his fault God was displeased with them all, why was it that they did not save themselves by such an expiation? That they then delayed in so great a danger, and dared not to lay hold instantly on Jonah, was an evident proof that they were restrained, as I have said, by the fear of God.

They therefore inquire what was to be done, *What shall we do to thee, that the sea may be still to us?*[1] *for the sea was going*, &c. By going Jonah means, that the sea was turbulent: for the sea is said to rest when it is calm, but when it is turbulent, then it is going, and has various movements and tossings. *The sea*, then, *was going and very tempestuous.*[2] We hence see that God was not satisfied with the disgrace of Jonah, but he purposed to punish his offence still more. It was necessary that Jonah should be led to the punishment which he deserved, though afterwards he was miraculously delivered from death, as we shall see in its proper place.

Jonah then answers, *Take me, and throw me into the sea, and it will be still to you.* It may be asked, whether Jonah ought to have of his own accord offered himself to die; for it seemed to be an evidence of desperation. He might, indeed, have surrendered himself to their will; but here he did, as it were, stimulate them, "*Throw me into the sea*," he says; "for ye cannot otherwise pacify God than by punishing me." He seemed like a man in despair, when he would thus advance to death of his own accord. But Jonah no doubt knew that he was doomed to punishment by God. It is uncertain whether he then entertained a hope of deliverance, that is, whether he confidently relied at this time on the grace of God. But, however it may have been, we may yet conclude, that he gave himself up to death, because he knew

[1] Literally, "that the sea may cease from upon us." The waves were rolling over them; hence מעלינו, from upon us. That the sea may be calm *around* us, is to give a meaning to the word which it never has.—*Ed.*

[2] כי הים הולך וסער, "*ὅτι η θαλασσα επορευετο και εξηγειρε μαλλον κλυδωνα*—for the sea went and more raised the swell."—*Sept.* "Quia mare ibat et intumescebat;—for the sea did go and swell."—*Jerome*, *Grotius*, and the *Vulgate*. "For the sea grew more and more tempestuous."—*Newcome*. The verb הולך, connected as here with another verb, does not always mean increase, but continuance. See Gen. viii. 3; Esth. ix. 4. Literally it is, "For the sea *was* going on, and was tempestuous," that is, it continued to be tempestuous. An increase of violence seemed not to have been hardly possible, for a shipwreck was previously dreaded. *Jerome*, in a strain rather imaginary, but striking, says, "*For the sea went and did swell*,—it *went*, as it had been commanded,—it went, to manifest the vengeance of its Lord,—it went, to prosecute a runaway Prophet; and it *swelled* at every moment, and rose, as it were, in larger billows, while the mariners were delaying, to show that they could not put off the vengeance of its Creator."—*Ed.*

and was fully persuaded that he was in a manner summoned by the evident voice of God. And thus there is no doubt but that he patiently submitted to the judgment which the Lord had allotted to him. *Take me*, then, *and throw me into the sea.*

Then he adds, *The sea will be to you still.* Here Jonah not only declares that God would be pacified by his death, because the lot had fallen upon him, but he also acknowledges that his death would suffice as an expiation, so that the tempest would subside : and then the reason follows—*I know*, he says, *that on my account is this great tempest come upon you.* When he says that *he* knew this, he could not refer to the lot, for that knowledge was common to them all. But Jonah speaks here by the prophetic spirit : and he no doubt confirms what I have before referred to,—that the God of Israel was the supreme and only King of heaven and earth. This certainty of knowledge, then, of which Jonah speaks, must be referred to his own conscience, and to the teaching of that religion in which he had been instructed.

And now we may learn from these words a most useful instruction : Jonah does not here expostulate with God, nor contumeliously complain that God punished him too severely, but he willingly bears his charged guilt and his punishment, as he did before, when he said, "I am the worshipper of the true God." How could he confess the true God, whose great displeasure he was then experiencing ? But Jonah, we see, was so subdued, that he failed not to ascribe to God his just honour ; though death was before his eyes, though God's wrath was burning, we yet see, that he gave to God, as we have said, the honour due to him. So the same thing is repeated in this place, *Behold*, he says, *I know that on my account has this great tempest happened.* He who takes to himself all the blame, does not certainly murmur against God. It is then a true confession of repentance, when we acknowledge God, and willingly testify before men that he is just, though, according to the judgment of our flesh, he may deal violently with us. When, however, we give to him the praise due to his justice, we then really show our penitence ; for unless God's wrath brings us down to this humble state of mind, we shall be always full of bitterness; and, however silent we may be for a time, our heart will be still perverse and rebellious. This humility, then, always follows repentance,—the sinner prostrates himself before God, and willingly admits his own sin, and tries not to escape by subterfuges.

And it was no wonder that Jonah thus humbled himself; for we see that the sailors did the same: when they said that lots were to be cast, they added at the same time, "Come ye and let us cast lots, that we may know why this evil has happened to us." They did not accuse God, but constituted him the Judge; and thus they acknowledged that he inflicted a just punishment. And yet every one thought himself to have been innocent; for however conscience might have bitten them, still no one considered himself to have been guilty of so great a wickedness as to subject him to God's vengeance. Though, then, the sailors thought themselves exempt from any great sin, they yet did not contend with God, but allowed him to be their Judge. Since then they, who were so barbarous, confined themselves within these bounds of modesty, it was no wonder that Jonah, especially when he was roused and began to feel his guilt, and was also powerfully restrained by God's hand,—it was no wonder that he now confessed that he was guilty before God, and that he justly suffered a punishment so heavy and severe. We ought then to take special notice of this,—that he *knew* that on his account the storm happened, or that the sea was so tempestuous against them all. The rest we defer until to-morrow.

PRAYER.

Grant, Almighty God, that as thou urgest us daily to repentance, and each of us is also stung with the consciousness of his own sins,—O grant, that we may not grow stupid in our vices, nor deceive ourselves with empty flatteries, but that each of us may, on the contrary, carefully examine his own life, and then with one mouth and heart confess that we are all guilty, not only of light offences, but of such as deserve eternal death, and that no other relief remains for us but thine infinite mercy, and that we may so seek to become partakers of that grace which has been once offered to us by thy Son, and is daily offered to us by his Gospel, that, relying on him as our Mediator, we may not cease to entertain hope even in the midst of thousand deaths, until we be gathered into that blessed life, which has been procured for us by the blood of thy only Son. Amen.

Lecture Seventy-fifth.

13. Nevertheless the men rowed hard to bring *it* to the land; but they could not: for the sea wrought, and was tempestuous against them.

14. Wherefore they cried unto the Lord, and said, We beseech thee, O Lord, we beseech thee, let us not perish for this man's life, and lay not upon us innocent blood: for thou, O Lord, hast done as it pleased thee.

13. Et quærebant (*vel*, moliebantur, *propriè est* fodiebant) viri ut reducerent navem, et non poterant; quia mare ibat et turbulentum erat super eos.

14. Et clamaverunt ad Jehovam, et dixerunt, Obsecro, Jehova, ne, quæso, pereamus propter animam viri hujus, et ne des super nos (*hoc est*, ne ponas) sanguinem innocentem; quia, tu Jehova, sicuti placitum tibi est, fecisti.

This verse shows that the sailors and the rest were more inclined to mercy, when they saw that the holy Prophet was willing to undergo the punishment which he had deserved. When, therefore, he confessed that he was guilty, and refused not to be punished, they became anxious to spàre his life, though they were heathens, and also for the most part barbarians: and as each of them could not but be frightened with his immediate danger, the wonder is increased, that they had such regard for the life of one who alone was in fault, and who had now freely confessed this. But the Lord so turned their hearts, that they now saw more clearly how grievous a sin it was to flee away from the call of God, and not to yield obedience, as we have before observed, to his command. Many think that this is a light offence, and readily indulge themselves in it: but it is not in the power of men to weigh sins; the balance is deceitful when men estimate their sins according to their own judgment. Let us then learn to ascribe to God his own honour,—that he alone is Judge, and is far above us, and can alone determine how grievous or how slight any sin is. But common sense, except when men wilfully deceive themselves by vain flatteries, clearly teaches this,—that it is no light offence when we evade the command of God; for, as we have stated, men do thus take away from God his supreme authority; and what is left to God, when he governs not the creatures whom he has formed, and whom he sustains by his power? The Lord, then, designed to show here, that his displeasure could not be otherwise pacified than by drowning Jonah in the sea; though, as we shall presently see, he had something greater in view. But, in the meantime, this is worthy of being observed,—that the Lord intended to make Jonah an example, that all may now know that he is not to be trifled with, but that he ought to be obeyed as soon as he commands any thing.

The word which the Prophet uses has been variously explained by interpreters. חתר, *chetar*, is properly, to dig; so that some think it to be a metaphorical expression, as rowers seem to dig the sea; and this sense is not unsuitable. Others carry the metaphor still higher,—that the sailors searched out or sought means by which they might drive the ship to land. But the other metaphor, as being less remote, is more to be approved. The Latins call it to toil, (*moliri*,) when the rowers not only apply gently their oars, but when they make a greater effort. *The sailors*, then, *toiled to bring back the ship*.[1] But for what purpose? To spare the life of the man who had already confessed that he was guilty before God, and that the storm, which threatened them all with a shipwreck, had arisen through his fault: but he says, that they *could not, for the sea was tempestuous*, as we have already seen in our yesterday's lecture.

I come now to the second verse. *They cried*, he says, *to Jehovah, and said, We beseech*,[2] *Jehovah, let us not perish, we pray, on account of the life of this man, and give not*, that is, lay not, *innocent blood upon us*.[3] The Prophet now expresses

[1] Literally, "And the men laboured to return to dry land." The ideal meaning of חתר is to dig, or to dig through, Job xxiv. 16; Ezek. xii. 7: but it is here in its secondary sense of labouring or toiling. להשיב, to return, must be taken here intransitively, though generally it bears in Hiphil a transitive sense. "Καί παρεβιαζοντο οι ανδρες του επιστρεψαι προς την γην—And the men strove to return to land."—*Sept.* "And the men rowed hard to regain the land."—*Henderson.*—*Ed.*

[2] אנה and נא are particles of entreaty or exclamation, and may be rendered, "I, or, we pray," according to the context. Here they should be, "We pray." They are sometimes rendered, Oh! alas! now.—*Ed.*

[3] "Hoc est, ne nobis imputes cædem viri justi—Impute not unto us

more fully why the sailors toiled so much to return to port, or to reach some shore,—they were already persuaded that Jonah was a worshipper of the true God, and not only this, but that he was a Prophet, inasmuch as he had told them, as we have seen, that he had fled from the presence of God, because he feared to execute the command which we have noticed. It was therefore pious fear (*reverentia*) that restrained the sailors, knowing, as they did, that Jonah was the servant of the true God. They, at the same time, saw, that Jonah was already standing for his sin before God's tribunal, and that punishment was demanded. This they saw; but yet they wished to preserve his life.

Now this place shows, that there is by nature implanted in all an abhorrence of cruelty; for however brutal and sanguinary many men may be, they yet cannot divest themselves of this feeling,—that the effusion of human blood is hateful. Many, at the same time, harden themselves; but they apply a searing iron: they cannot shake off horror, nay, they feel that they are detested by God and by men, when they thus shed innocent blood. Hence it was that the sailors, who in other respects hardly retained a drop of humanity, fled as suppliants to God, when the case was about the death of man; and they said, אנה יהוה, *ane Ieve*, 'We beseech Jehovah:' and the expression is repeated; which shows that the sailors earnestly prayed that the Lord would not impute this as a sin to them.

We hence see that though these men had never known the doctrine of the law, they were yet so taught by nature that they knew that the blood of man is dear and precious in the sight of God. And as to us, we ought not only to imitate these sailors, but to go far beyond them: for not only ought the law of nature to prevail among us, but also the law of God; for we hear what God had formerly pronounced with his own mouth, 'Whosoever sheddeth man's blood, shed shall his blood be,' (Gen. ix. 6.) And we know also the reason why God undertakes to protect the life of men,

the slaughter of a just man."—*Marckius*. See Judges ix. 24; Matth. xxvii. 24.—*Ed.*

and that is, because they have been created in his image. Whosoever then uses violence against the life of man, destroys, as far as he can, the image of the eternal God. Since it is so, ought not violence and cruelty to be regarded by us with double horror? We ought also to learn another thing from this doctrine: God proves by this remarkable testimony what paternal feeling he manifests towards us by taking our life under his own guardianship and protection; and he even proves that we are really the objects of his care, inasmuch as he will execute punishment and vengeance when any one unjustly injures us. We then see that this doctrine on the one side restrains us, that we may not attempt anything against the lives of our brethren; and, on the other side, it assures us of the paternal love of God, so that being allured by his kindness we may learn to deliver up ourselves wholly to his protection.

I now come to the last clause of the verse, *For thou, Jehovah, hast done as it hath pleased thee.* The sailors clearly prove here that they did not willingly shed innocent blood. How then can these two things agree,—that the blood was innocent, and that they were blameless? They adopted this excuse,—that they obeyed God's decree, that they did nothing rashly or according to their own inclinations, but followed what the Lord had prescribed: though, indeed, God had not spoken, yet what he required was really evident; for as God demanded an expiation by the death of Jonah, so he designed to continue the tempest until he was thrown into the deep. These things the sailors now put forward. But we must notice, that they did not cast the blame on God, as blasphemers are wont to do, who, while they seek to exempt themselves from blame, find fault with God, or at least put him in their own place: "Why then," they say, "does he sit as a judge to condemn us for that of which he is himself the author, since he has so decreed?" At this day there are many fanatics who thus speak, who obliterate all the difference between good and evil, as if lust were to them the law. They at the same time make a covert of God's providence. Jonah wished not that such a thing should be thought of the sailors; but as they well understood that God governed the world justly, though his counsels be secret and cannot be comprehended by us,—as, then, they were thus convinced, they thus strengthened themselves; and though they gave to God the praise due to his justice, they at the same time trembled lest they should be guilty of innocent blood.

We now then see how reverently these men spoke of God, and that so much religious fear possessed them, that they did not rob God of his praise, *Thou Jehovah*, they said, *hast done as it has pleased thee.*[1] Do they here accuse God of tyranny, as though he confounded all things without any cause or reason? By no means. They took this principle as granted,—that the will of God is right and just, yea, that whatever God has decreed is beyond doubt just. Being then thus persuaded, they took the will of God as the rule for acting rightly: "As *thou, Jehovah, hast done as it seemed good to thee*, so we are blameless." But at the same time it is proper also to add, that the sailors do not vainly talk here of the secret providence of God in order to impute murder to him, as ungodly men and profane cavillers do at this day: but as the Lord made known his purpose to them, they show that the storm and the tempest could not be otherwise calmed and quieted than by drowning Jonah: they therefore took this knowledge of God's purpose as a certain rule to follow. At the same time they fled, as I have said, to God, and supplicated his mercy, lest in a matter so perplexed and difficult

[1] Some render this sentence in the present tense, as *Marckius*, "Tu enim Jehovah sicut vis facis—for thou, Jehovah, doest as thou willest." The verbs are in the past tense, but this tense in Hebrew includes often both times,—"Thou hast done and doest, as thou hast willed and willest:" and this seems to be the full import of the passage. *Mercerius*, quoted by Poole, gives this paraphrase,—"All these things have taken place through thine appointment,—that Jonah came to the ship, that a storm has been raised, that the lot has fallen on Jonah, and that he has confessed his sin: we unwillingly do this dreadful deed, but this is understood to be thy will." *Drusius* took the words as referring to the time then present, for he expresses the meaning thus: "Tu vis ut in mare dejeciatur: fiat igitur quod vis; nam voluntati tuæ quis resistat? Thou willest that he should be cast into the sea: be then that done which thou willest; for who can resist thy will?" According to this view, it is an expression of acquiescence in God's will respecting Jonah. But both *Newcome* and *Henderson* retain our common version. *Dathius* reads, "Tu enim, O Jova, pro arbitratu tuo agis.—For thou, O Jehovah, doest according to thine own will."—*Ed.*

he should involve them in the same punishment, as they were constrained to shed innocent blood. We now then apprehend the meaning of this passage. Now it follows—

15. So they took up Jonah, and cast him forth into the sea; and the sea ceased from her raging.

15. Et sustulerunt Jonam, et projecerunt in mare; et stetit mare à fervore suo.

Jonah shows here that the tempest arose through his fault; for the issue proved this with certainty. The sailors had not only cast lots, but after Jonah was thrown into the sea the storm calmed, and the sea became still,—this sudden change sufficiently proved that Jonah was the only cause why they were so nearly shipwrecked. For if the sea had not calmed immediately, but after some interval of time, it might have been ascribed to chance: but as the sea instantly rested, it could not be otherwise said than that Jonah was condemned by the judgment of God. He was indeed cast into the sea by the hands of men; but God so presided, that nothing could be ascribed to men, but that they executed the judgment which the Lord had openly demanded and required from them. This, then, is the import of this verse. He now adds—

16. Then the men feared the Lord exceedingly, and offered a sacrifice unto the Lord, and made vows.

16. Et timuerunt viri timore magno Jehovam, et sacrificarunt sacrificium Jehovæ, et voverunt vota.

Jonah now declares what fruit followed; and first, he says, that the sailors feared the true God. He uses here the proper name of God, Jehovah; for, as we have already seen, they were addicted to their own superstitions, as each of them cried to his own god: but it was a false notion; for they went astray after their own superstitions. The Prophet now points out the difference,—that they began to fear the true God. At the same time it may have been, that they afterwards relapsed into their own errors; yet it ought not to be overlooked that the Lord constrained them to entertain such a fear. The Hebrews, as it has been already said, sometimes take fear in a general sense, as meaning worship. It is said in 2 Kings xvii., of the new inhabitants of the land of Canaan, who had been removed from Persia, that they "feared God," that is, that they imitated the legal rite in sacrifices while worshipping God. But there is an addition in this place, which shows that the meaning is more restricted, for it is said to have been a *great fear*. Then Jonah means that the sailors and the passengers were not only touched with the fear of God, but that they also had the impression that the God of Israel was the supreme King of heaven and earth, that he held all things under his hand and government. This fear no doubt led them to true knowledge, so as to know that they were previously deluded, and that whatever the world had invented was mere delusion, and that the gods devised by the fancies of men were nothing else but mere idols. We now then perceive what Jonah means.

But we must here say somewhat more at large of the fear of God. When the Scripture speaks of the fear of God, it sometimes means the outward worship, and sometimes true piety. When it designates the outward worship, it is no great thing; for hypocrites usually perform their ceremonies, and thus testify that they worship God: but yet, as they obey not God with sincerity of heart, nor bring faith and repentance, they do nothing but trifle. But the fear of God is often taken for true piety; and then it is called the beginning or the chief point of wisdom, or even wisdom itself, as it is in Job xxix. 28. The fear of God, then, or that pious regard (*reverentia*) by which the faithful willingly submit themselves to God, is the chief part of wisdom.

But it also often happens that men are touched by servile fear, so as to have a desire to satisfy God, while, at the same time, they have even a wish to draw him down from his throne. This servile fear is full of perverseness; for they, at the same time, champ the bridle, as they cannot exempt themselves from his power and authority. Such was this fear of which Jonah speaks; for all those whom he mentions were not suddenly so changed as to devote themselves to the true God: they had not indeed made such a progress as this; it was not such real and thorough conversion of the soul as changed them into new men. How, then, is it said that they feared? even because the Lord extorted from them a confession at the time: it may have been that some of them afterwards made a greater progress; but I speak now generally of the whole. Because then it is said that they feared God, we are not hence to conclude that they really repented, so as to become wholly devoted to the God of Israel. But yet they were constrained to know and to confess that the God of Israel was the only and the true God. How so? because that dreadful judgment filled them with terror, so that they perceived that he alone was God who had heaven and earth under his command.

We now then see how that fear is to be viewed, of which Jonah speaks. If they afterwards made no farther progress, it only served to condemn them, that these sailors, having perceived by a sure evidence who the only true God was, mingled with the worship of him their wicked and ungodly superstitions, as many do even in our day. The Papists hold this truth in common with us,—that there is one true God, the framer of heaven and earth, yea, they come still nearer, and say that the only-begotten Son of God is our Redeemer; but yet we see how they contaminate the whole worship of God, and turn his truth to a lie; for they blend the worship of God with that of idols, so that there is nothing pure among them. But this main truth is however of great service, when the Lord stretches forth his hand to miserable men; for if there was no conviction of this under the Papacy —that the word of God is to be believed, and that Christ the Son of God is the King and Head of the Church, we must have had to employ against them a long circuitous argument; but now an access to them is easy: when we bring against them the Law, and the Prophets, and the Gospel, they are restrained by some measure of reverence, and dare not to reject the authority of the Supreme God. We then see, that this fear is in itself of no great value, if men remain fixed in their own mire; but when it is the Lord's purpose afterwards to call them, this fear opens for them the door to true godliness. So it may have been, as I have said, that some of these sailors and passengers had afterwards made better progress. But this fear of itself could have done nothing more than to convict them, so that no excuse could avail them before God's tribunal; for a proof had been given them, by which they might know that there was no other God than He who was then worshipped by the chosen people.

He afterwards adds, that they *sacrificed a sacrifice to Jehovah.*[1] They were accustomed before to offer sacrifices to their idols; but now they testified that they worshipped the God of Israel; for this is what sacrifices signify. But it must at the same time be observed, that they thereby expressed this confession, that God confirmed the truth of his word. When, therefore, they perceived that this whole affair was ordered by the will of God, they were constrained to bear witness that he was the true God: this was the end and design of sacrifices.

It may, however, be inquired, whether that sacrifice pleased God. It is certain that whenever men bring forward their own devices, whatever is otherwise worthy of approbation in what they do, it cannot but be corrupted and vitiated by such a mixture; for God, as it is well known, allows of no associate. And we must remember that which is said in Ezekiel, 'Go ye, sacrifice to the devil, and not to me!' God there repudiates all the sacrifices which were wont to be offered by the people of Israel, because superstitions were blended with them. God then shows that such a mixture is so disapproved by him, that he chooses rather that the superstitious should wholly give themselves up to the devil, than that his holy name should be thus profaned. Hence this sacrifice of itself was not lawful, nor could it have pleased God; but it was, so to speak, by accident and extrinsically

[1] "The first," says *Adam Clarke*, "that perhaps was ever offered on board a vessel, since the ark floated on the waters of the great deluge."

How uselessly have learned men often employed their talents, trying to improve what is simply and plainly related. *Jerome* allegorises this act of the mariners, and says that their sacrifice was that of praise. A Jewish Rabbi, *Jonathan*, makes an addition to the sentence—that they *said* that they would sacrifice to Jehovah; and *Grotius* adopts his addition. Another Rabbi, *Elieser*, has fabricated a fine tale, that they returned immediately to Joppa, went up to Jerusalem, and were circumcised! The fact is alone stated here, as to when and where we know nothing, and it signifies nothing to us; only that the most obvious import of the narrative is, that they *did* offer a sacrifice on board the vessel, immediately after the storm ceased.—*Ed.*

that this sacrifice pleased God,—because he designed thus to make known his glory. Though, then, he repudiated the sailors themselves, yet it was his will that this act should bear a testimony to his glory: as, for instance, a deed is often vicious with regard to men, and yet in an accidental way it tends to set forth the glory of God.

And this ought to be carefully borne in mind: there is at this day a dispute, yea a fierce contest, about good works: and the Sophists ever deceive themselves by false reasoning, (παραλογισμῷ—sophistry;) for they suppose that works morally good are either preparatory to the obtaining of grace, or meritorious towards attaining eternal life. When they speak of works morally good, they refer only to the outward deeds; they regard not the fountain or motive, nor even the end. When the heart of man is impure, unquestionably the work which thence flows is also ever impure, and is an abomination before God. When the end also is wrong, when it is not man's purpose to worship God in sincerity of heart, the deed, however splendid it may appear, is filth in the presence of God. Hence the Sophists are greatly deceived, and are very childish, when they say, that works morally good please God, and are preparatory to grace and meritorious of salvation. But can this be, that a work does not please God, and yet avails to set forth his glory? I answer, that these two things are perfectly consistent, and are in no way so contrary that they cannot be easily reconciled. For God by accident, as I have said, accommodates to his own glory what is in itself vicious; I say, in itself, that is, with respect to men. Thus even under the Papacy the Christian name serves to the glory of God, for there ever remains some remnant. And how has it happened, that at this time the light of the Gospel has shone forth, and that true religion has been restored at least in many places? Even because the Lord has never suffered true religion to be extinguished, though it has been corrupted: for baptism under the Papacy, the very name of Christ as well as of the Church, and the very form of religion—all these have become wholly useless; but they have accidentally, as I have said, been of great service. When, therefore, we regard the priests (*sacrificos*—the sacrificers) as well as the people, we find nothing but a perverted worship of God; they presumptuously and indiscriminately add their own superstitions and devices to the word of God, and there is nothing pure among them. Since then they thus blend together heaven and earth, they do nothing but provoke God's wrath against themselves.

We now then understand why Jonah says that the sailors and passengers offered sacrifices. We must, at the same time, remember what I have lately said, that sacrifice was, as it were, a symbol of Divine worship: for even from the beginning this notion prevailed among all, that sacrifices were to be offered to none but to God; and heathens in all ages had no other opinion of sacrifices, but that they thus manifested their piety towards their gods. Since then sacrifices have been from the beginning offered to God alone, it follows, that they at this day are wholly inexcusable who join associates to God, and offer their sacrifices to mortals or to angels. How can this be borne in Christians, since heathens have ever confessed that they regarded those as gods to whom they were wont to offer their sacrifices? Now then, since God declares that the chief sacrifice to him is invocation, as we read in Ps. l., the whole of religion under the Papacy must be perverted, as they pray not only to God but even to creatures: for they hesitate not to flee to Peter or to Paul, yea, to their own saints, real and fictitious, in the same manner as to the only true God. Inasmuch, then, as they rob God of this chief right, we see that they tread under foot the whole of religion by this sacrilege. Since, then, heathen men testified that they worshipped Jehovah, the God of Israel, by their external sacrifice, let us learn at this day not to transfer the rightful honour of God to creatures; but let this honour of being alone prayed to, be wholly and entirely reserved for him; for this, as we have said, is the chief and the most valuable sacrifice which he demands and approves.

But Jonah also adds, that the sailors *vowed vows to God.* This is a part of thanksgiving; for we know that the object, not only of the holy fathers, but also of the superstitious, in making vows, has ever been this—to bind themselves to God, and also to express their gratitude, and to make it evident, that they owed to him both their life and every favour bestowed on them. This then has in all ages been the reason for making vows. When, therefore, the sailors vowed a vow to God, they renounced their own idols. They cried before to their gods; but now they understand that they had cried in vain, and without any benefit, as they had to no purpose uttered their cries in the air. Now then they made their vows to the only true God; for they knew that their lives were in his hand.

And here we may easily learn how foolishly the Sophists of our day heap together all passages of Scripture which make any mention of vows; for they think that we are to be overwhelmed by that term alone, when we condemn their false vows. But no one of us has ever denied, or does deny, that it is lawful to vow, provided it be done according to what the Law and the Gospel prescribes. What we hold is,—that men are not thoughtlessly to obtrude on God what comes uppermost, but that they are to vow what he approves, and also, that they regard a right and just end in vowing, even to testify their gratitude to God. But in common vows which are made, there are the grossest errors, as also in the whole of the Papal worship; for they vow this and that to God indiscriminately, and regard not what the Lord requires or approves: one, on certain days, abstains from meat; another combs not his head: and a third trots away on some pilgrimage. All these things, we know, are rejected by God. And further, when they vow nothing but what God approves, it is yet done for a wrong purpose: for they seek in this way to bind God to themselves, and the diabolical conceit of merits ever possesses their minds. And, lastly, they consider not what they can do; they vow perpetual celibacy, when at the same time incontinency burns them; and thus we see that, like the giants, they fight with God himself; and, in the meantime, they allow themselves an unbridled liberty as to whatever they vow.

Let us then know, that whenever the Scripture speaks of vows, we are to take for granted these two principles,—that vows, as they appertain to the worship of God, ought not to be taken without any discretion, according to men's fancy, but ought to be regulated and guided by God's rule, so that men may bring nothing to God, except what they know to be approved by his word,—and then, that they are to keep in view the right end, even to show by this symbol their gratitude to God, to testify that they are preserved by his kindness, as was the case with these sailors, who made a vow because they thought that none but God was their deliverer; and so they testified, that when they came safe to shore, they would make it known that the God of Israel had showed mercy to them. It follows—

17. Now the Lord had prepared a great fish to swallow up Jonah. And Jonah was in the belly of the fish three days and three nights.

17. Et paravit Jehova piscem magnum ad vorandum Jonam; et fuit Jonas in visceribus piscis tribus diebus et tribus noctibus.

What the Prophet here briefly relates ought to be carefully weighed by us. It is easily passed over, when we read in a few words that Jonah was swallowed up by a fish, and that he was there three days and three nights: but though Jonah neither amplified or illustrated in a rhetorical manner what is overlooked by us, nor adopted any display of words, but spoke of the event as though it were an ordinary thing, we yet see what the event itself really was: Jonah was cast into the sea. He had been previously not only a worshipper of the true God, but also a Prophet, and had no doubt faithfully discharged his office; for God would not have resolved to send him to Nineveh, had he not conferred on him suitable gifts; and he knew him to be qualified for undertaking a burden so great and so important. As Jonah then had faithfully endeavoured to serve God, and to devote himself to him through the whole of his past life, now that he is cast into the sea as one unworthy of the common light, that he is cut off from the society of men, and that he seems unworthy of undergoing a common or an ordinary punishment, but is exiled, as it were, from the world, so as to be deprived of light and air, as parricides, to whom formerly, as it is well-known, this punishment was allotted—as then Jonah saw that he was thus dealt with, what must have been the state of his mind?

Now that he tells us that he was three whole days in the inside of the fish, it is certain that the Lord had so awakened him, that he must have endured continual uneasiness. He was asleep before he was swallowed by the fish; but the Lord drew him, as it were, by force to his tribunal, and he must have suffered a continual execution. He must have every moment entertained such thoughts as these, "Why does he now thus deal with thee? God does not indeed slay thee at once, but intends to expose thee to innumerable deaths." We see what Job says, that when he died, he would be at rest and free from all evils, (Job xiv. 6.) Jonah no doubt continually boiled with grief, because he knew that God was opposed to and displeased with him: he doubtless said to himself, "Thou hast to do, not with men, but with God himself, who now pursues thee, because thou hast become a fugitive from his presence." As Jonah then must have necessarily thus thought within himself of God's wrath, his case must have been harder than hundred deaths, as it had been with Job and with many others, who made it their chief petition that they might die. Now as he was not slain, but languished in continual torments, it is certain that no one of us can comprehend, much less convey in words, what must have come into the mind of Jonah during these three days. But I cannot now discuss what remains; I must therefore defer it to the next lecture.

PRAYER.

Grant, Almighty God, that as thou settest before us this day thy holy Prophet as an awful example of thy wrath against all who are rebellious and disobedient to thee,—O grant, that we may learn so to subject all our thoughts and affections to thy word, that we may not reject any thing that pleases thee, but so learn both to live and to die to thee, that we may ever regard thy will, and undertake nothing but what thou hast testified is approved by thee, so that we may fight under thy banners, and through life obey thy word, until at length we reach that blessed rest which has been obtained for us by the blood of thy only-begotten Son, and is laid up for us in heaven through the hope of his Gospel. Amen.

Lecture Seventy-sixth.

In yesterday's lecture we began to explain the last verse of the first chapter, in which Jonah said, that *a fish was prepared by the Lord.* We stated that it could not have been otherwise but that Jonah, when he was in the inside of the fish, must have felt the most grievous agonies, as though he had been doomed to perpetual death, as long as he was deprived of the enjoyment of God's favour: and this fact will be further explained when his song comes under our consideration.

But now there is a question to be considered, and that is, whether God created a fish to receive Jonah. The expression, that God *prepared*[1] *a fish*, seems indeed to mean this; for if the fish had already been swimming in the sea, the Prophet might have adopted another mode of speaking, and said, that the Lord caused the fish to meet him, or that God had sent a fish; for so the Scripture usually speaks: but a fish is said to have been prepared. This doubt may be thus removed,—that though God may not have created the fish, he had yet prepared him for this purpose; for we know that it was not according to the course of nature that the fish swallowed Jonah, and also, that he was preserved uninjured in his inside for three days and three nights. I therefore

[1] The verb מנה does not necessarily include the idea of creation, but its meaning is, to distribute, to arrange, to order, to provide, to prepare; and yet this preparation may involve the exercise of a creative power, as in the case of the gourd mentioned in the fourth chapter, for it is the same verb. Though it might be an indigenous plant, yet to provide it so quickly in one night was the act of Divine power. So also as to this fish, it might or it might not have been one usually found in that part of the sea. To provide it, by bringing it to the spot, was as much a miracle as to provide it by a new act of creation. To allow the one and to deny the other, is wholly unreasonable. The whole was clearly miraculous: and the discovery of any such fish now does not in the least render the transaction less miraculous. Every part of it must be ascribed to a Divine interposition; and let those stumble who are resolved to stumble.

It has been supposed to have been the "whale," because the word κητος is used in the reference made to Jonah in Matth. xii. 40: but that word is a general term applied to a large fish, and does not necessarily mean the whale. κητος, says *Ribera*, in his comment on Jonah, non certæ speciei, sed generis nomen est, et piscem quemvis magnum significat.—*Ed.*

refer what is said here, that a *fish was prepared*, to the preservation of Jonah: for it is certain that there are some fishes which can swallow men whole and entire. And William Rondelet, who has written a book on the fishes of the sea, concludes that in all probability it must have been the *Lamia*. He himself saw that fish, and he says that it has a belly so capacious, and a mouth so wide, that it can easily swallow up a man; and he says that a man in armour has sometimes been found in the inside of the *Lamia*. Therefore, as I have said, either a whale, or a Lamia, or a fish unknown to us, may be able to swallow up a man whole and entire; but he who is thus devoured cannot live in the inside of a fish. Hence Jonah, that he might mark it out as a miracle, says that the fish was prepared by the Lord; for he was received into the inside of the fish as though it were into an hospital; and though he had no rest there, yet he was as safe as to his body, as though he were walking on land. Since then the Lord, contrary to the order of nature, preserved there his Prophet, it is no wonder that he says that the *fish was prepared by the Lord*. I come now to thė second chapter.

CHAPTER II.

1. Then Jonah prayed unto the Lord his God out of the fish's belly,	1. Et oravit Jonas ad Jehovam Deum suum è ventre piscis;
2. And said, I cried by reason of mine affliction unto the Lord, and he heard me; out of the belly of hell cried I, *and* thou heardest my voice.	2. Et dixit, Clamavi in angustia mea ad Jehovam, et exaudit me (*vel*, respondit mihi;) è ventre sepulchri vociferatus sum, audivisti vocem meam.[1]

[1] It is remarkable that several sentences in this prayer, as it has been observed by *Marckius* and *Henderson*, are exactly the same, not only in sense, but also, in most instances, in words, with passages in the Psalms. The first clause of this verse is found in Ps. cxx. 1, only the words are differently arranged. The last clause of the third verse, both in words and order, is the same with a distich in Ps. xlii. 7. The beginning of the fourth verse agrees nearly with Ps. xxxi. 22; and so does the fifth verse with a line in Ps. lxix. 1, one word being different. The first clause of the seventh verse is found in the very same words in Ps. cxlii. 3; and the first line in the eighth verse in Ps. xxxi. 6, with the exception of one letter; and the last words of the ninth verse are to be met with in Ps. iii. 8, only the order is reversed. "On the supposition," says *Henderson*, "that Jonah was familiar with the Psalms, it was very na-

When Jonah says that he *prayed from the bowels of the fish*, he shows first with what courage of mind he was endued. He had then put on a new heart; for when he was at liberty he thought that he could in a manner escape from God, he became a fugitive from the Lord: but now, while inclosed within narrow bounds, he begins to pray, and of his own accord sets himself in God's presence.

This is a change worthy of being noticed: and hence we may learn how much it profits us to be drawn back often as it were by cords, or to be held tied up with fetters, because when we are free we go astray here and there beyond all limits. Jonah, when he was at liberty, became, as we have seen, wanton; but now, finding himself restrained by the mighty hand of God, he receives a new mind, and prays from the bowels of the fish.[1] But how was it that he directed his petitions then to God, by whose hand he saw that he was so heavily pressed? For God most rigidly handled him; Jonah was in a manner doomed to eternal ruin; the bowels of the fish, as we shall hereafter see, were indeed to him as it were hell or the grave. But in this state of despair Jonah even gathered courage, and was able to betake himself directly to God. It was a wonderful and almost incredible example of faith. Let us then learn to weigh well what is here said; for when the Lord heavily afflicts us, it is then a legitimate and seasonable time for prayer. But we know that the greater part despond, and do not usually offer their prayers freely to God, except their minds be in a calm state; and yet God then especially invites us to himself when we are reduced to extremities. Let this, then, which Jonah declares

tural for him to incorporate sentences taken from them with his own language."—*Ed.*

[1] "No place amiss for prayer, *I will that men pray everywhere;* wherever God casts us we may find a way open heavenwards, if it be not our own fault. Jonah was now in the bottom of the sea, yet out of the depths he cries to God."—*M. Henry.* "It may be asked, How could Jonah either pray or breathe in the stomach of a fish? Very easily, if God so willed it. And let the reader keep this constantly in view: the whole is a *miracle*, from Jonah's being swallowed by the fish, till he was cast ashore by the same animal. It was God that had *prepared* the great fish; it was the Lord that *spake* to the fish, and *caused* it to vomit Jonah on the dry land. ALL is miracle."—*Adam Clarke.*—*Ed.*

of himself, come to our minds,—that he cried to God from hell itself: and, at the same time, he assures us that his prayer proceeded from true faith; for he does not simply say that he prayed to *Jehovah,* but he adds that he was *his God;* and he speaks with a serious and deeply-reflective mind. Though Jonah then was not only like one dead, but also on the confines of perdition, he yet believed that God would be merciful if he fled to him. We hence see that Jonah prayed not at random, as hypocrites are wont to take God's name in their mouths when they are in distress, but he prayed in earnest; for he was persuaded that God would be propitious to him.

But we must remember that his prayer was not composed in the words which are here related; but Jonah, while in the bowels of the fish, dwelt on these thoughts in his mind. Hence he relates in this song how he thought and felt; and we shall see that he was then in a state of distraction, as our minds must necessarily be tossed here and there by temptations. For the servants of God do not gain the victory without great struggle. We must fight, and indeed strenuously, that we may conquer. Jonah then in this song shows that he was agitated with great trouble and hard contests: yet this conviction was firmly fixed in his heart,—that God was to be sought, and would not be sought in vain, as he is ever ready to bring help to his people whenever they cry to him.

Then he says, *I cried, when I had trouble, to Jehovah, and he answered me.* Jonah no doubt relates now, after having come forth from the bowels of the fish, what had happened to him, and he gives thanks to the Lord.[1] This verse then

[1] He relates here, as it appears from the preceding, "and he said," the prayer he offered when in the fish's bowels, and not a prayer offered after his deliverance. Some have entertained the latter opinion, because some of the verbs here are in the past tense: but this circumstance only shows that he continued to pray from the time when he was swallowed by the fish to the time when he was delivered. It was a continued act. It is the same as though he said, "I have called, and do call on Jehovah." *Marckius,* and also *Dathius,* render the verbs in the present tense, "I call," &c. The following is a translation according to this view of the prayer,—

3. I call in my distress on Jehovah, and he will answer me;

contains two parts,—that Jonah in his trouble fled to God, —and the latter part contains thanksgiving for having been miraculously delivered beyond what flesh could have thought. *I cried*, he says, *in my distress, to Jehovah; I cried out from the bowels of hell, thou hast heard my voice.* Jonah, as we shall hereafter see, directed his prayers to God not without great struggle; he contended with many difficulties; but however great the impediments in his way, he still persevered and ceased not from praying. He now tells us that he had not prayed in vain; and, that he might amplify the grace of God, he says, *from the bowels of the grave.* He mentioned *distress* (*angustiam*—straitness) in the first clause; but here he more clearly expresses how remarkable and extraordinary had been the kindness of God, that he came forth safe from the bowels of the fish, which were like the bowels of the grave. שאול, *shaul,* derived from corruption, is called the grave by the Hebrews and the Latin translator has almost

From the belly of the grave I cry,—thou hearest my voice.
4. When thou didst send me to the deep, into the midst of the waters,
And the flood surrounded me,—
Thy billows and waves over me passed;
5. Then I said, I am banished from the sight of thine eyes;—
Yet I will again look towards the temple of thy holiness.
6. Encompass me do the waters to the soul,
The deep surrounds me,
The sedge is wrapped around my head:
7. To the cuttings off of the mountains have I descended;
The earth! its bars *are* continually around me:
But thou wilt bring from destruction my life,
O Jehovah, my God.
8. When overwhelmed within me was my soul,
Jehovah did I remember;
And come to thee shall my prayer—
To the temple of thy holiness.
9. They who regard idols of vanity,
Their own mercy forsake:
10. But I, with the voice of praise, will sacrifice to thee,
What I have vowed will I fulfil:
Salvation *belongs* to Jehovah.

"The cuttings off," in verse 7, says *Parkhurst*, were those parts which were *cut off* from the mountains at the deluge. The Septuagint has σχισμας—rents—clefts. Roots, bottoms, foundations, have been adopted by some, but not consistently with the meaning of the original word.—"The bars or bolts" of the earth convey the idea of impediments in his way to return to the earth. They were "around" him, or literally "upon" him, בעדי, that is, they were, as it were, closed upon him.—*Ed.*

everywhere rendered it hell, (*infernum;*) and שאול, *shaul*, is also sometimes taken for hell, that is, the state of the reprobate, because they know that they are condemned by God: it is, however, taken more frequently for the grave; and I am disposed to retain this sense,—that the fish was like the grave. But he means that he was so shut up in the grave, that there was no escape open to him.

What are the bowels of the grave? Even the inside or the recess of the grave itself. When Jonah was in this state, he says, that he was heard by the Lord. It may be proper to repeat again what I have already slightly touched,—that Jonah was not so oppressed, though under the heaviest trial, but that his petitions came forth to God. He prayed as it were from hell, and not simply prayed, for he, at the same time, sets forth his vehemence and ardour by saying, that he cried and cried aloud. Distress, no doubt, extorted from Jonah these urgent entreaties. However this might have been, he did not howl, as the unbelieving are wont to do, who feel their own evils and bitterly complain; and yet they pour forth vain howlings. Jonah here shows himself to be different from them by saying, that he cried and cried aloud to God. It now follows—

3. For thou hadst cast me into the deep, in the midst of the seas; and the floods compassed me about: all thy billows and thy waves passed over me.

3. Atqui projeceras me in profundum, in cor marium, et fluvius circumdedit me; omnes conflictus tui (*sed hac voce intelligit undas quæ inter se confligunt; scimus enim esse varias collisiones, ideò vertunt aliqui*, contritiones tui, *nam* שבר *significat propriè confligere et frangere; perinde est igitur ac si diceret*, omnes fracturæ tuæ et collisiones super me transierunt, *et explicat quid velit, quum dicit*) fluctus tui super me transierunt.

In this verse are set forth his difficulties: for Jonah, for the sake of amplifying, refers to his condition. It was a great thing that he cried to God from the bowels of the fish; but it was far more difficult for him to raise up his mind in prayer, when he knew or thought God to be angry with him: for had he been thrown into extreme evils, he might yet call upon God; but as it came to his mind that all the evil he suffered was inflicted by God, because he tried to shun his call, how was it possible for him to penetrate into heaven when such an obstacle stood in his way? We hence see the design of these words, *But thou hadst cast me into the gulf, into the heart of the sea; the flood surrounded me, all thy billows and waves passed over me.*

In short, Jonah shows here what dreadful temptations presented themselves to him while he was endeavouring to offer up prayers. It came first to his mind that God was his most inveterate enemy. For Jonah did not then think of the sailors and the rest who had cast him into the sea, but his mind was fixed on God: this is the reason why he says, THOU, Lord, *hadst cast me into the deep, into the heart of the sea;* and then, THY *billows,* THY *waves.*[1] He does not here regard the nature of the sea; but he bestows, as I have already said, all his thoughts on God, and acknowledges that he had to do with him; as though he said, "Thou, Lord, in pursuing me, drivest me away; but to thee do I come: thou showest by dreadful proofs that thou art offended with me, but yet I seek thee; so far is it that these terrors drive me to a distance from thee, that now, being subdued as it were by thy goads, I come willingly to thee; for nowhere else is there for me any hope of deliverance." We now then see how much avails the contrast, when Jonah sets the terrible punishment which he endured in opposition to his prayer. Let us now proceed—

4. Then I said, I am cast out of thy sight; yet I will look again toward thy holy temple.	4. Tunc ego dixi, (*nam copula resolvi debet in adverbium temporis,*) Expulsus sum à conspectu oculorum tuorum; vèrum adjiciam aspicere ad templum sanctitatis tuæ.

In the first clause of this verse Jonah confirms again what I have said,—that when he sought to pray, not only the door was closed against him, but there were mountains, as it were, intervening, so that he could not breathe a prayer to God: for he did not so much think of the state in which he was; nay, but he chiefly considered his own case, how he had pro-

[1] "He calls them God's billows and his waves, not because he made and rules them, but because he had now commissioned them against Jonah, and ordered them to afflict and terrify, but not to destroy him. These words are plainly quoted by Jonah from Ps. xlii. 7. What David spoke figuratively and metaphorically, Jonah applies to himself as literally fulfilled."—*M. Henry.*

voked the wrath of God. Hence he says, *I have said, I am cast away from the sight of thine eyes.* Some give this frigid exposition, that he had been only expelled from his own country, that he might not behold the temple. But I have no doubt but that Jonah tells us here that he suffered extreme agonies, as though every hope of pardon had been cut off from him: "What! shall I yet hope that God will be propitious? It is not to be hoped." This then is the casting away of which he speaks: for it is said that God casts us away, when he allows us no access to him. Hence Jonah thought that he was wholly alienated from God. Were any to object and say, that then his faith must have been extinct; the obvious answer is,—that in the struggle of faith there are internal conflicts; one thought is suggested, and then another of an opposite character meets it; there would indeed be no trial of our faith, except there were such internal conflicts; for when, with appeased minds, we can feel assured that God is propitious to us, what is the trial of faith? But when the flesh tells us that God is opposed to us, and that there is no more hope of pardon, faith at length sets up its shield, and repels this onset of temptation, and entertains hope of pardon: whenever God for a time appears implacable, then faith indeed is tried. Such then was the condition of Jonah; for, according to the judgment of the flesh, he thought that he was utterly cast away by God, so that he came to him in vain. Jonah, then, having not yet put off flesh and blood, could not immediately lay hold on the grace of God, but difficulties met him in his course.

The latter clause is differently explained by interpreters. Some take it negatively, "I shall no more look towards the temple of thy holiness:" but the words admit not of this explanation. אך, *ak*, means in Hebrew, truly, nevertheless; and it means also, certainly; and sometimes it is taken dubitatively, perhaps. The greater part of expounders render the clause thus, "But I shall see the temple of thy holiness;" as though Jonah here reproved his own distrust, which he had just expressed, as the case is with the faithful, who immediately check themselves, when they are tempted to entertain any doubt: "What! dost thou then cast away hope, when yet God will be reconciled to thee if thou wilt come to him?" Hence interpreters think that it is a sort of correction, as though Jonah here changed his mind, and retracted what he had previously taken up, as a false principle derived from the judgment of the flesh. He had said then that he had been cast away from the presence of the Lord; but now, according to these expositors, he repels that temptation, "But I shall see thy holy temple; though I seem now to be rejected by thee, thou wilt at last receive me into favour." We may, however, explain this clause, consistently with the former, in this way, At least, or, *but, I would again see*, &c., as an expression of a wish. The future then may be taken for the optative mood, as we know that the Hebrews are wont thus to use the future tense, either when they pray or express a wish. This meaning then best agrees with the passage, that Jonah as yet doubtingly prays, *At least*, or, *but, I would again, O Lord, see the temple of thy holiness.* But since the former explanation which I have mentioned is probable, I do not contend for this. However this may be, we find that Jonah did not wholly despair, though the judgment of the flesh would drive him to despair; for he immediately turned his address to God. For they who murmur against God, on the contrary, speak in the third person, turning themselves, as it were, away from him: but Jonah here sets God before his eyes, *I have been cast away*, he says, *from the sight of thine eyes.* He does not remonstrate here with God, but shows that he was seeking God still, though he thought that he was cast far away.

Then he adds, *I would at least see again the temple of thy holiness.* And by speaking of the temple, he no doubt set the temple before him as an encouragement to his faith. As then he had been cast away, he gathers everything that might avail to raise up and confirm his hope. He had indeed been circumcised, he had been a worshipper of God from his childhood, he had been educated in the Law, he had exercised himself in offering sacrifices: under the name of temple he now includes briefly all these things. We hence see that he thus encouraged himself to entertain good hope in his extreme necessity. And this is a useful admonition; for when every access to God seems closed up against us, nothing is more useful than to recall to mind, that he has adopted us from our very infancy, that he has also testified his favour by many tokens, especially that he has called us by his Gospel into a fellowship with his only-begotten Son, who is life and salvation ; and then, that he has confirmed his favour both by Baptism and the Supper. When, therefore, these things come to our minds, we may be able by faith to break through all impediments. Let us go on—

5. The waters compassed me about, *even* to the soul: the depth closed me round about, the weeds were wrapped about my head.	5. Obsederunt me aquæ usque ad animam, abyssus undique circumdedit me, juncus alligatus fuit capite meo :
6. I went down to the bottoms of the mountains ; the earth with her bars *was* about me for ever : yet hast thou brought up my life from corruption, O Lord my God.	6. Ad radices (*propriè*, excisuras ; *nam* קצב *significat excidere ; alii vertunt*, ad fines extremos ; ad radices *igitur*) montium descendi ; terra cum vectibus suis circum me in seculum : et ascendere fecisti vitam meam è sepulchro (*est aliud nomen quàm* שאול, *nempe*, שחת ; *alii vertunt*, à corruptione, *vel*, interitu,) Jehova, Deus mi.

Here in many words Jonah relates how many things had happened to him, which were calculated to overwhelm his mind with terror and to drive him far from God, and to take away every desire for prayer. But we must ever bear in mind what we have already stated,—that he had to do with God : and this ought to be well considered by us. The case was the same with David, when he says in Ps. xxxix., 'Thou hast yet done it ;' for, after having complained of his enemies, he turned his mind to God : " What then do I? what do I gain by these complaints ? for men alone do not vex me ; thou, God, he says, hast done this." So it was with Jonah ; he ever set before him the wrath of God, for he knew that such a calamity had not happened to him but on account of his sins.

He therefore says that *he was by waters beset*, and then, that he was *surrounded by the deep ;* but at length he adds, that God *made his life to ascend*, &c. All these circumstances tend to show that Jonah could not have raised up his mind to God except through an extraordinary miracle, as his life was in so many ways oppressed. When he says that he was *beset with waters even to the soul*, I understand it to have been to the peril of his life; for other explanations seem frigid and strained. And the Hebrews say, that to be pressed to the soul, is to be in danger of one's life; as the Latins, meaning the same thing, say that the heart, or the inside, or the bowels, are wounded. So also in this place the same thing is meant, 'The waters beset me even to the soul,' and then, 'the abyss surrounds me.' Some render סוף, *suph*, sedge; others, sea-weed; others, bulrush: but the sense amounts to the same thing. No doubt סוף, *suph*, is a species of sedge; and some think that the Red Sea was thus called, because it is full of sedges or bulrushes. They think also that bulrushes are thus called, because they soon putrify. But what Jonah means is certain, and that is, that weed enveloped his head, or that weed grew around his head: but to refer this to the head of the fish, as some do, is improper. Jonah speaks metaphorically when he says that he was entangled in the sedge, inasmuch as there is no hope when any one is rolled in the sedge at the bottom of the sea. How, indeed, can he escape from drowning who is thus held, as it were, tied up? It is then to be understood metaphorically; for Jonah meant that he was so sunk that he could not swim, except through the ineffable power of God.

According to the same sense he says, *I descended to the roots of the mountains.* But he speaks of promontories, which were nigh the sea; as though he had said, that he was not cast into the midst of the sea, but that he had so sunk as to be fixed in the deep under the roots of mountains. All these things have the same design, which was to show that no deliverance could be hoped for, except God stretched forth his hand from heaven, and indeed in a manner new and incredible.

He says that *the earth with its bars was around him.* He means by this kind of speaking, that he was so shut up, as if the whole earth had been like a door. We know what sort of bars are those of the earth, when we ascribe bars to it: for when any door is fastened with bolts, we know how small a portion it is. But when we suppose the earth itself to be like a door, what kind of things must the bolts be? It is the same thing then as though Jonah had said, that he was so hindered from the vital light, as if the earth had been set against him to prevent his coming forth to behold the sun: *the earth*, then, *was set against me, and that for ever.*

He afterwards comes to thanksgiving, *And thou, Jehovah, my God, hast made my life to ascend from the grave.* Jonah, after having given a long description, for the purpose of showing that he was not once put to death, but that he had been overwhelmed with many and various deaths, now adds his gratitude to the Lord for having delivered him, *Thou*, he says, *hast made my life to ascend from the grave, O Jehovah.* He again confirms what I have once said,—that he did not pour forth empty prayers, but that he prayed with an earnest feeling, and in faith: for he would not have called him his God, except he was persuaded of his paternal love, so as to be able to expect from him a certain salvation. *Thou* then *Jehovah, my God*, he says; he does not say, "Thou hast delivered me," but, "Thou hast brought forth my life from the grave." Then Jonah, brought to life again, testifies here that he was not only delivered by God's aid from the greatest danger, but that he had, by a certain kind of resurrection, been raised from the dead. This is the meaning of this mode of speaking, when he says that his life had been brought forth from the grave, or from corruption itself. It follows—

7. When my soul fainted within me I remembered the Lord; and my prayer came in unto thee, into thine holy temple.	7. Quum deficeret in me anima mea (*vel*, dum se convolveret supra me anima mea,) Jehovæ recordatus sum, et ingressa est oratio mea ad templum sanctitatis tuæ.

Here Jonah comprehends in one verse what he had previously said,—that he had been distressed with the heaviest troubles, but that he had not yet been so cast down in his mind, as that he had no prospect of God's favour to encourage him to pray. He indeed first confesses that he had suffered some kind of fainting, and that he had been harassed by anxious and perplexing thoughts, so as not to be able by his own efforts to disengage himself.

As to the word עטף, *otheph*, it means in Hebrew to hide,

to cover; but in Niphal and Hithpael (in which conjugation it is found here) it signifies to fail: but its former meaning might still be suitably retained here; then it would be, 'My soul hid or rolled up itself,' as it is in Ps. cii., 'The prayer of the afflicted, when he rolled up himself in his distress.' They who render it, "he multiplied prayers," have no reason to support them. I therefore doubt not but that Jonah here means, either that he had been overcome by a swoon, or that he had been so perplexed as not to be able without a violent struggle to raise up his mind to God. However it may have been, he intended by this word to express the anxiety of his mind. While then we are tossed about by divers thoughts, and remain, as it were, bound up in a hopeless condition, then our soul may be said to roll or to fold up itself within us. When therefore the soul rolls up itself, all the thoughts of man in perplexity recoil on himself. We may indeed seek to disburden ourselves, while we toss about various purposes, but whatever we strive to turn away from us, soon comes back on our own head; thus our soul recoils upon us. We now perceive what Jonah meant by this clause, *When my soul infolded itself*, or failed within me, *I remembered*, he says, *Jehovah*. We hence learn that Jonah became not a conqueror without the greatest difficulties, not until his soul, as we have said, had fainted: this is one thing. Then we learn, also, that he was not so oppressed with distresses but that he at length sought God by prayer. Jonah therefore retained this truth, that God was to be sought, however severely and sharply he treated him for a time; for the remembering, of which he speaks, proceeded from faith. The ungodly also remember Jehovah, but they dread him, for they look on him as a judge; and whenever a mention is made of God, they expect nothing but destruction: but Jonah applied the remembrance of God to another purpose, even as a solace to ease his cares and his anxieties.

For it immediately follows, *that his prayer had penetrated unto God*, or entered before him.[1] We then see that Jonah

[1] "Here prayer is *personified*, and is represented as a *messenger* going from the *distressed* and entering into the temple of God, and standing before him. This is a very fine and delicate image."—*Adam Clarke*.

so remembered his God, that by faith he knew that he would be propitious to him; and hence was his disposition to pray. But by saying that his prayer entered into his temple, he no doubt alludes to a custom under the law; for the Jews were wont to turn themselves towards the temple whenever they prayed: nor was this a superstitious ceremony; for we know that they were instructed in the doctrine which invited them to the sanctuary and the ark of the covenant. Since then this was the custom under the law, Jonah says that his prayer entered into the temple of God; for that was a visible symbol, through which the Jews might understand that God was near to them; not that they by a false imagination bound God to external signs, but because they knew that these helps (*adminicula*) had not in vain been given to them. So then Jonah not only remembered his God, but called also to mind the signs and symbols in which he had exercised his faith, as we have just said, through the whole course of his life; for they who view him as referring to heaven, depart wholly from what the Prophet meant. We indeed know that the temple sometimes means heaven; but this sense suits not this place. Then Jonah meant that though he was far away from the temple, God was yet near to him; for he had not ceased to pray to that God who had revealed himself by the law which he gave, and who had expressed his will to be worshipped at Jerusalem, and also had been pleased to appoint the ark as the symbol of his presence, that the Jews might, with an assured faith, call upon him, and that they might not doubt but that he dwelt in the midst of them, inasmuch as he had there his visible habitation.

PRAYER.

Grant, Almighty God, that as thou hast once given us such an evidence of thy infinite power in thy servant Jonah, whose mind, when he was almost sunk down into hell, thou hadst yet raised up to thyself, and hadst so supported with firm constancy, that he ceased not to pray and to call on thee,—O grant, that in the trials by which we must be daily exercised, we may raise upwards our minds to thee, and never cease to think that thou art near us; and that when the signs of thy wrath appear, and when our sins thrust themselves before our eyes, to drive us to despair, may we still constantly struggle, and never surrender the hope of thy mercy, until, having finished all our contests, we may at length freely and fully give thanks to thee, and praise thy infinite goodness, such as we daily experience, that being conducted through continual trials, we may at last come into that blessed rest which is laid up for us in heaven, through Christ our Lord. Amen.

Lecture Seventy-seventh.

8. They that observe lying vanities forsake their own mercy.

9. But I will sacrifice unto thee with the voice of thanksgiving; I will pay *that* that I have vowed. Salvation *is* of the Lord.

8. Qui observant vanitates mendaces, misericordiam suam (*vel*, clementiam) derelinquent (*hoc est*, derelinquunt.)

9. Ego autem in voce laudis sacrificabo tibi, quæ vovi reddam : salus est Jehovæ.

Here Jonah says first, that men miserably go astray, when they turn aside to vain superstitions, for they rob themselves of the chief good: for he calls whatever help or aid that is necessary for salvation, the mercy of men. The sense then is, that as soon as men depart from God, they depart from life and salvation, and that nothing is retained by them, for they wilfully cast aside whatever good that can be hoped and desired. Some elicit a contrary meaning,—that the superstitious, when they return to a sound mind, relinquish their own reproach; for חסד, *chesad*, sometimes means reproach. They then think that the way of true penitence is here described,—that when God restores men from their straying to the right way, he gives them at the same time a sound mind, so that they rid themselves from all their vices. This is indeed true, but it is too strained a meaning. Others confine this to the sailors, who vowed sacrifices to God; as though Jonah had said, that they would soon relapse to their own follies, and bid adieu to God, who in his mercy had delivered them from shipwreck; so they explain their mercy to be God; but this is also too forced an explanation.

I doubt not, therefore, but that Jonah here sets his own religion in opposition to the false inventions of men; for it immediately follows, *But I with the voice of praise will sacrifice to thee.* Jonah, then, having before confessed that he would be thankful to God, now pours contempt on all those inventions which men foolishly contrive for themselves, and through which they withdraw themselves from the only true God, and from the sincere worship of him. For he calls all those devices, by which men deceive themselves, *the vanities of falsehood;*[1] for it is certain that they are mere fallacies, which men invent for themselves without the authority of God's word; for truth is one and simple, which God has revealed to us in his word. Whosoever, then, turns aside the least, either on this or on that side, seeks, as it were designedly, some imposture or another, by which he ruins himself. *They*, then, *who follow* such vanities, says Jonah, *forsake their own mercy*,[2] that is, they reject all happiness:

[1] הבלי־שוא, "Idols of vanity or falsehood," *i. e.*, false, or deceitful, or vain idols. הבל means vapour, smoke, breath, vanity, inanity: but in the plural number it is applied for the most part to idols. See Deut. xxxii. 21; 1 Kings xvi. 13, 26. שוא is a lie, which is vain—useless, and false—deceptive. *Marckius* renders the words, "Vanitates inanitatis—vanities of inanity;" *Junius* and *Tremelius*, "Vanitates mendaces—mendacious vanities;" *Septuagint*, "ματαια και ψευδη—vain and false things." "He thus calls idols," says an author in Poole's Syn., "and all those things in which any one, excluding God, trusts; which are nothing, and can do nothing, and which deceive their worshippers." This is true, that is, that all other things, as well as idols, are, apart from God, vain, and worthless, and deceptive; but the reference here no doubt is to idols. They are not only empty, but deceptive.—*Ed.*

[2] חסדם יעזבו, "Their mercy or goodness they forsake," that is, the mercy exhibited and offered to them by God; or, if we render it goodness, it means their chief good, which is God. The Psalmist calls God his goodness in Ps. cxliv. 2, חסדי, "my goodness," the giver of all his goodness, or his chief good. *Dathius* gives very correctly the meaning of the two lines in these words—

"Qui vana idola colunt,
Felicitatis suæ auctorem deserunt—

They who worship vain idols,
Desert the author of their own happiness."

More literally—

"They who attend on the idols of vanity,
Their own goodness forsake."

There is a contrast between vain idols and their own goodness, that is, the goodness received by them from God. *Grotius* gives this para-

for no aid and no help can be expected from any other quarter than from the only true God.

But this passage deserves a careful notice; for we hence learn what value to attach to all superstitions, to all those opinions of men, when they attempt to set up religion according to their own will: for Jonah calls them lying or fallacious vanities. There is then but one true religion, the religion which God has taught us in his word. We must also notice, that men in vain weary themselves when they follow their own inventions; for the more strenuously they run, the farther they recede from the right way, as Augustine has well observed. But Jonah here adopts a higher principle,—that God alone possesses in himself all fulness of blessings: whosoever then truly and sincerely seeks God, will find in him whatever can be wished for salvation. But God is not to be sought but by obedience and faith: whosoever then dare to give themselves loose reins, so as to follow this or that without the warrant of God's word, recede from God, and, at the same time, deprive themselves of all good things. The superstitious do indeed think that they gain much when they toil in their own inventions; but we see what the Holy Spirit declares by the mouth of Jonah. The Lord says the same by Jeremiah, 'They have forsaken me, the fountain of living water, and cisterns have they digged for themselves,' (Jer. ii. 13.) There the Lord complains of his chosen people, who had gone astray after wicked superstitions. Hence, when men wander beyond the word of God, they in a manner renounce God, or say adieu to him; and thus they deprive themselves of all good things; for without God there is no salvation and no help to be found.

Jonah therefore rightly adds, *But I, with the voice of praise, will sacrifice to thee;* as though he said, "While men as it were banish themselves from God, by giving themselves up to errors, I will sacrifice to thee, and to thee alone, O Lord."

phrase, "They who worship idols are vain; for they forsake their own mercy, that is, God, who is able to help them in their distress." *Henry* suggests another view, "They who follow their own inventions, as Jonah had done, when he fled from the presence of the Lord to go to Tarshish, forsake their own mercy, that mercy which they may find in God."—*Ed.*

And this ought to be observed by us; for as our minds are prone to falsehood and vanity, any new superstition will easily lay hold on us, except we be restrained by this bond, except we be fully persuaded,—that true salvation dwells in God alone, and every aid and help that can be expected by us: but when this conviction is really and thoroughly fixed in our hearts, then true religion cannot be easily lost by us: though Satan should on every side spread his allurements, we shall yet continue in the true and right worship of God. And the more carefully it behoves us to consider this passage, because Jonah no doubt meant here to strengthen himself in the right path of religion; for he knew that, like all mortals, he was prone to what was false; he therefore encouraged himself to persevere: and this he does, when he declares that whatever superstition men devise, is a deprivation of the chief good, even of life and salvation. It will hence follow, that we shall abominate every error when we are fully persuaded that we forsake the true God whenever we obey not his word, and that we at the same time cast away salvation, and every thing good that can be desired. Then Jonah says, *I will sacrifice to thee with the voice of praise.*

It must be noticed here farther, that the worship of God especially consists in praises, as it is said in Ps. l.: for there God shows that he regards as nothing all sacrifices, except they answer this end—to set forth the praise of his name. It was indeed his will that sacrifices should be offered to him under the law; but it was for the end just stated: for God cares not for calves and oxen, for goats and lambs; but his will was that he should be acknowledged as the Giver of all blessings. Hence he says there, 'Sacrifice to me the sacrifice of praise.' So also Jonah now says, 'I will offer to thee the sacrifice of praise,' and he might have said with still more simplicity, "Lord, I ascribe to thee my preserved life." But if this was the case under the shadows of the law, how much more ought we to attend to this, that is,—to strive to worship God, not in a gross manner, but spiritually, and to testify that our life proceeds from him, that it is in his hand, that we owe all things to him, and, in a word, that he is the

Source and Author of salvation, and not only of salvation, but also of wisdom, of righteousness, of power?

And he afterwards mentions his vows, *I will pay*, he says, *my vows.* We have stated elsewhere in what light we are to consider vows. The holy Fathers did not vow to God, as the Papists of this day are wont to do, who seek to pacify God by their frivolous practices; one abstains for a certain time from meat, another puts on sackcloth, another undertakes a pilgrimage, and another obtrudes on God some new ceremony. There was nothing of this kind in the vows of the holy Fathers; but a vow was the mere act of thanksgiving, or a testimony of gratitude: and so Jonah joins his vows here with the sacrifice of praise. We hence learn that they were not two different things; but he repeats the same thing twice. Jonah, then, had declared his vow to God for no other purpose but to testify his gratitude.

And hence he adds, *To Jehovah is*, or belongs, *salvation;* that is, to save is the prerogative of God alone; Jehovah is here in the dative case, for prefixed to it is ל, *lamed.* It is then to Jehovah that salvation belongs; the work of saving appertains to no other but to the Supreme God. Since it is so, we see how absurd and insane men are, when they transfer praises to another, as every one does who invents an idol for himself. As, then, there is but the one true God who saves, it behoves us to ascribe to him alone all our praises, that we may not deprive him of his right. This is the import of the whole. It follows—

10. And the Lord spake unto the fish, and it vomited out Jonah upon the dry *land.*	10. Et dixit Jehovah pisci (*hoc est*, præcepit;) et evomuit Jonam super aridam.

The deliverance of Jonah is here in few words described; but how attentively ought we to consider the event? It was an incredible miracle, that Jonah should have continued alive and safe in the bowels of the fish for three days. For how was it that he was not a thousand times smothered or drowned by waters? We know that fish continually draw in water: Jonah could not certainly respire while in the fish; and the life of man without breathing can hardly continue for a minute. Jonah, then, must have been preserved beyond the power of nature. Then how could it have been that the fish should cast forth Jonah on the shore, except God by his unsearchable power had drawn the fish there? Again, who could have supernaturally opened its bowels and its mouth? His coming forth, then, was in every way miraculous, yea, it was attended with many miracles.

But Jonah, that he might the more extol the infinite power of God, adopted the word *said*. Hence we learn that nothing is hard to God, for he could by a nod only effect so great a thing as surpasses all our conceptions. If Jonah had said that he was delivered by God's kindness and favour, it would have been much less emphatical, than when he adopts a word which expresses a command, *And Jehovah spake*, or said, *to the fish*.

But as this deliverance of Jonah is an image of the resurrection, this is an extraordinary passage, and worthy of being especially noticed; for the Holy Spirit carries our minds to that power by which the world was formed and is still wonderfully preserved. That we may then, without hesitation and doubt, be convinced of the restoration which God promises to us, let us remember that the world was by him created out of nothing by his word and bidding, and is still thus sustained. But if this general truth is not sufficient, let this history of Jonah come to our minds,—that God commanded a fish to cast forth Jonah: for how was it that Jonah escaped safe and was delivered? Even because it so pleased God, because the Lord commanded; and this word at this day retains the same efficacy. By that power then, by which he works all things, we also shall one day be raised up from the dead. Now follows—

CHAPTER III.

1. And the word of the Lord came unto Jonah the second time, saying,	1. Et factum fuit verbum Jehovæ ad Jonam secundò, dicendo,—
2. Arise, go unto Nineveh, that	2. Surge, proficiscere Nineven in

great city, and preach unto it the preaching that I bid thee.

urbem magnam, et prædica ad eam prædicationem quam ego mando tibi.

There is here set before us a remarkable proof of God's grace,—that he was pleased to bestow on Jonah his former dignity and honour. He was indeed unworthy of the common light, but God not only restored him to life, but favoured him again with the office and honour of a prophet. This, as I have said, Jonah obtained through the wonderful and singular favour of God. As he had previously fled, and by disobedience deprived himself in a manner of all God's favour, the recovery of his prophetic office was certainly not obtained through his own merit.

It must, in the first place, be observed, that this phrase, *The word of Jehovah came the second time*, ought to be noticed; for the word of God comes to men in different ways. God indeed addresses each of us individually; but he spoke to his Prophets in a special manner; for he designed them to be witnesses and heralds of his will. Hence, whenever God sets a man in some peculiar office, his word is said to come to him: as the word of God is addressed to magistrates, because they are commanded to exercise the power committed to them; so also the word of God ever came to the Prophets, because it was not lawful for them to thrust in themselves without being called.

The command now follows, *Arise, go to Nineveh, to that great city, and preach there the preaching which I command thee.*[1] God again repeats what we have observed at the be-

[1] Literally, "And proclaim to or against her the proclamation which I declare to thee." The Septuagint is, "Και κηρυξον εν αυτη κατα το κηρυγμα το εμπροσθεν, ὃ εγω ελαλησα προς σε—And preach in it the former preaching which I have spoken to thee." עָלֶיהָ in five MSS., as in chap. i. 2, "against her," and not אליה, "to her." אשר אנכי דבר אליך, "which I *am* speaking or declaring to thee." דבר is a participle; being preceded by a nominative, it will admit of an auxiliary verb either in the past, present, or future tense, according to the context; though it is often used to express the present time.

Newcome renders the sentence thus—"And cry unto her *in* the words which I *shall* speak unto thee;" *Henderson* more paraphrastically thus—"And make the proclamation to it which I order thee;" and *Adam Clarke* gives this version—"And cry the cry that I bid thee;" and adds the following remarks,—"Be my herald, and faithfully deliver my message. The word κηρυξ in Greek answers to the Hebrew קורא, *kore*, both signi-

ginning,—that Nineveh was a great city, that Jonah might provide himself with an invincible courage of mind, and come there well prepared: for it often happens, that many boldly undertake an office, but soon fail, because difficulties had not been sufficiently foreseen by them. Hence, when men find more hardships than they thought of at the beginning, they nearly faint, at least they despond. The Lord, therefore, expressly foretold Jonah how difficult would be his employment; as though he said, "I send thee, a man unknown, and of no rank, and a stranger, to denounce ruin on men, not a few in number, but on a vast multitude, and to carry on a contest with the noblest city, and so populous, that it may seem to be a region of itself."

We now then understand why this character of the city was added; it was, that Jonah might gird up himself for the contest, that he might not afterwards fail in the middle of his course. This fear indeed frightened him at the beginning, so that he shunned the call of God; but he is not now moved in any degree by the greatness of the city, but resolutely follows where the Lord leads. We hence see, that faith, when once it gains the ascendancy in our hearts, surmounts all obstacles, and despises all the greatness of the world; for it is immediately added—

3. So Jonah arose, and went unto Nineveh, according to the word of the Lord. Now Nineveh was an exceeding great city of three days' journey.

3. Et surrexit Jonah et profectus est Nineven, secundum mandatum Jehovæ: Nineveh autem erat urbs magna Dei (Deo, *ad verbum*) itinere trium dierum.

Jonah, by saying that he went to Nineveh according to God's command, proves in the first place, as I have said, how great was the power and energy of his faith; for though

fying a *crier*, a *herald*, a *preacher;* one that makes proclamation with a *loud* and *earnest* cry. Such was John Baptist, Isa. xl. 3; such was Jesus Christ, John vii. 18-37; and such were all his apostles. And such earnestness becomes a ministry that has to do with immortal souls, asleep and dead in sin, hanging on the brink of perdition, and insensible of their state. The soft-speaking, gentle-toned, unmoved preacher, is never likely to awaken souls."

Henry considers that the commission was not specifically explained to him then. "Jonah must go," he says, "with implicit faith: he shall not know till he comes thither what message he must deliver."—*Ed.*

Jonah had considered the greatness and pride of the city, he seems to have forgotten that he was an obscure man, alone, and unarmed; but he had laid hold on weapons capable of destroying all the power of the world, for he knew that he was sent from above. His conviction was, that God was on his side; and he knew that God had called him. Hence then it was, that with a high and intrepid mind he looked down on all the splendour of the city Nineveh. Hence John does not without reason say, that the victory, by which we overcome the world, proceeds from faith, (1 John v. 4.) Jonah also proves, at the same time, how much he had improved under God's scourges. He had been severely chastised; but we know that most of the unbelieving grow hardened under the rod, and vomit forth their rage against God; Jonah, on the contrary, shows here that chastisement had been useful to him, for he was subdued and led to obey God.

He went, then, *according to the command of Jehovah;* that is, nothing else did he regard but to render obedience to God, and to suffer himself to be wholly ruled by him. We hence learn how well God provides for us and for our salvation, when he corrects our perverseness; though sharp may be our chastisements, yet as this benefit follows, we know that nothing is better for us than to be humbled under God's hand, as David says in Ps. cxix. This change then, *he went*, is to us a remarkable example; and this is what the Lord has ever in view whenever he roughly handles us; for he cannot otherwise subdue either the haughtiness or the rebellion, or the slowness and indolence of our flesh. We must now also take notice how Jonah attained so much strength; it was, because he had found by experience in the bowels of the fish, that even amidst thousand deaths there is enough in God's protection to secure our safety. As then he had by experience known that the issues of death are at the will and in the hand of God, he is not now touched with fear so as to shun God's command, even were the whole world to rise up against him. Hence the more any one has found the kindness of God, the more courageously he ought to proceed in the discharge of his office, and confidently to commit to God his life and his safety, and resolutely to surmount all the perils of the world.

He then says, *that Nineveh was a great city,*[1] *even a journey of three days.* Some toil much in untying a knot, which at last is no knot at all; for it seems to them strange that one city should be in compass about thirty leagues according to our measure. When they conceive this as being impossible, then they invent some means to avoid the difficulty,—that no one could visit the whole city so as to go through all the alleys, all the streets, and all the public places, except in three days; nay, they add, that this is not to be understood as though one ran or quickly passed through the city, but as though he walked leisurely and made a stay in public places: but these are mere puerilities. And if we believe profane writers, Nineveh must have been a great city, as Jonah declares here: for they say that its area was about four hundred *stadia;* and we know what space four hundred *stadia* include. A *stadium* is one hundred and twenty-five paces; hence eight *stadia* make a mile. Now if any one will count he will find that there are twelve miles in a hundred *stadia;* there will then be in four hundred *stadia* forty-eight miles. This account well agrees with the testimony of Jonah. And then Diodorus and Herodotus say that there were 1500 towers around the city. Since it was so, it could not certainly be a smaller city than what it is represented here by Jonah. Though these things may seem to exceed what is commonly believed, writers have not yet reported them without some foundation: for however false are found to be many things in Diodorus and Herodotus, yet as to Babylon and

[1] The original is, "And Nineveh was a city great to God"—עיר־גדולה לאלהים. The remark of *Henry* is, "So the Hebrew phrase is, meaning no more than as we render it, *exceeding great;* this honour that language doth to the great God, that great things derive their denomination from him." Though the form of the expression here is different from what we find in other places, when God is taken in this sense, as in Ps. lxxx. 10, ארזי־אל, cedars of God, that is, tall or great cedars,—yet there is no other sense that comports with this place. This is the view of *Dathius, Drusius, Newcome,* and many others. Some render it, *great through God,* and *Grotius* seems to have taken it in this sense, for he explains it by "Deo eam augente—God having increased it." *Henderson* considers ל here in the sense of לפני, *before,* and refers to Gen. x. 9. But this has hardly a meaning in this connection.—*Ed.*

Nineveh they could not have dared to say what was untrue; for the first was then standing and known to many; and the ruins of the other were still existing, though it had been for some time destroyed. We shall farther see about the end of the book that this city was large, and so populous, that there were there 120,000 children. If any one receives not this testimony, let him feed on the lies of the devil. But since there were so many children there, what else can we say but that the circumference of the city was very great?

But this seems inconsistent with what immediately follows; for Jonah says, that when he entered the city, he performed a journey in the city for one day and preached. The answer is this,—that as soon as he entered the city, and began to proclaim the command of God, some conversions immediately followed: so Jonah does not mean that he went through the city in one day. He then in the first day converted a part of the city; he afterwards continued to exhort each one to repentance: thus the conversion of the whole city followed; but not in the second or the third day, as it may be easily gathered. Let us now proceed to what remains—

4. And Jonah began to enter into the city a day's journey, and he cried, and said, Yet forty days, and Nineveh shall be overthrown.	4. Et cœpit Jonah ingredi in urbem itinere diei unius, et clamavit et dixit, Adhuc quadraginta dies et Nineveh subversa.

Jonah here relates what had briefly been said before,—that he went to Nineveh according to the command of God. He shows then how faithfully he executed the duty enjoined on him, and thus obeyed the word of God. Hence Jonah came and began to enter the city and to preach on the first day. This promptness proves clearly how tractable Jonah had become, and how much he endeavoured to obey God in discharging his office: for had there been still a timidity in his heart, he would have inspected the city, as careful and timid men are wont to do, who inquire what is the condition of the place, what are the dispositions of the people, and which is the easiest access to them, and what is the best way, and where is the least danger. If Jonah then had been still entangled by carnal thoughts, he would have waited two or three days, and then have begun to exercise his office as a Prophet. This he did not, but entered the city and cried. We now then see how prompt he was in his obedience, who had before attempted to pass over the sea: he now takes hardly a moment to breathe, but he begins at the very entrance to testify that he had come in obedience to God.

We hence see with what emphasis these words ought to be read. The narrative is indeed very simple; Jonah uses here no rhetorical ornaments, nor does he set forth his entrance with any fine display of words. *Jonah*, he says, *entered into the city*. He who is not well versed in Scripture might say that this is frigid: but when we weigh the circumstances, we see that this simple way of speaking possesses more force and power than all the displays of orators.

He entered then the city *a day's journey, and cried and said*, &c. By saying that he cried, he again proves the courage of his soul; for he did not creep in privately, as men are wont to do, advancing cautiously when dangers are apprehended. He says that he cried: then this freedom shows that Jonah was divested of all fear, and endued with such boldness of spirit, that he raised himself up above all the hinderances of the world. And we ought, in the meantime, to remember how disliked must have been his message: for he did not gently lead the Ninevites to God, but threatened them with destruction, and seemed to have given them no hope of pardon. Jonah might have thought that his voice, as one says, would have to return to his own throat, "Can I denounce ruin on this populous city, without being instantly crushed? Will not the first man that meets me stone me to death?" Thus might Jonah have thought within himself. No fear was, however, able to prevent him from doing his duty as a faithful servant, for he had been evidently strengthened by the Lord. But it will be better to join the following verse—

5. So the people of Nineveh believed God, and proclaimed a fast, and put on sackcloth, from the greatest of them even to the least of them.	5. Et crediderunt viri Ninevæ Deo, et indixerunt jejunium, et induerunt saccos à magno eorum usque ad parvum eorum.

One thing escaped me in the third verse: Jonah said that Nineveh was a city *great to God*. This form of speech is common in Scripture: for the Hebrews call that Divine, whatever it be, that is superior or excellent: so they say, the cedars of God, the mountains of God, the fields of God, when they are superior in height or in any other respect. Hence a city is called the city of God, when it is beyond others renowned. I wished briefly to allude to this subject, because some, with too much refinement and even puerility, say, that it was called the city of God, because it was the object of God's care, and in which he intended to exhibit a remarkable instance of conversion. But, as I have said, this is to be taken as the usual mode of speaking in similar cases.

I now return to the text: Jonah says, that the citizens of Nineveh *believed God*.[1] We hence gather that the preaching of Jonah was not so concise but that he introduced his discourse by declaring that he was God's Prophet, and that he did not proclaim these commands without authority; and we also gather that Jonah so denounced ruin, that at the same time he showed God to be the avenger of sins, that he re-

[1] ויאמינו···באלהים, "And they believed in God. The verb אמן in Hiphil is ever followed by ב or ל, except in one instance by את in Judges xi. 20. When followed by ב, it seems to mean, to give credit to what is said, to believe one's testimony, or the truth of what is referred to. To believe then in God is to believe the truth of what he declares, to believe his word. Hence in 2 Chron. xx. 20, Jehoshaphat said to the people, "Believe in the Lord your God," האמינו ביהוה אלהיכם; and he adds, "Believe [in] his Prophets," האמינו בנביאיו. It is the word of God, and the word of the Prophets, which was the same, or the truth or veracity of God and of his Prophets, that they were exhorted here to believe. This view throws light on an expression in Ps. cxix. 66, "For I have believed [in] thy commandments," במצותיך, that is, in the truth of thy commandments.—When the verb in Hiphil is followed by ל, the idea of reliance or dependance is more especially conveyed, though in many instances there is hardly a difference to be recognized, except the context be minutely observed.

Among other passages, the verb in its Hiphil form is followed by ב, in Gen. xv. 6, Exod. xiv. 31, Num. xx. 12, 2 Kings xvii. 14, Prov. xxvi. 25, Jer. xii. 6;—and by ל in Exod. iv. 1-8, Deut. ix. 23, 1 Kings x. 7, Ps. cvi. 24, Isa. xliii. 10, Jer. xl. 14.

The Septuagint renders believing *in* God by επίστευσαν τω θεω: so does Paul in Rom. iv. 3, Gal. iii. 6; but he retains the Hebrew form in Rom. iv. 5, πιστευοντι επι τον, &c. *Calvin* here conveys the same meaning by "crediderunt Deo—believed God:" that is, the Ninevites gave credit to what God declared by Jonah, they believed God's word.—*Ed.*

proved the Ninevites, and, as it were, summoned them to God's tribunal, making known to them their guilt; for had he spoken only of punishment, it could not certainly have been otherwise, but that the Ninevites must have rebelled furiously against God; but by showing to them their guilt, he led them to acknowledge that the threatened punishment was just, and thus he prepared them for humility and penitence. Both these things may be collected from this expression of Jonah, that the Ninevites believed God; for were they not persuaded that the command came from heaven, what was their faith? Let us then know, that Jonah had so spoken of his vocation, that the Ninevites felt assured that he was a celestial herald: hence was their faith: and further, the Ninevites would never have so believed as to put on sackcloth, had they not been reminded of their sins. There is, therefore, no doubt but that Jonah, while crying against Nineveh, at the same time made known how wickedly the men lived, and how grievous were their offences against God. Hence then it was that they put on sackcloth, and suppliantly fled to God's mercy: they understood that they were deservedly summoned to judgment on account of their wicked lives.

But it may be asked, how came the Ninevites to believe God, as no hope of salvation was given them? for there can be no faith without an acquaintance with the paternal kindness of God; whosoever regards God as angry with him, must necessarily despair. Since then Jonah gave them no knowledge of God's mercy, he must have greatly terrified the Ninevites, and not have called them to faith. The answer is, that the expression is to be taken as including a part for the whole; for there is no perfect faith when men, being called to repentance, do suppliantly humble themselves before God; but yet it is a part of faith; for the Apostle says, in Heb. xi., that Noah through faith feared; he deduces the fear which Noah entertained on account of the oracular word he received, from faith, showing thereby that it was faith in part, and pointing out the source from which it proceeded. At the same time, the mind of the holy Patriarch must have been moved by other things besides threatenings, when he built an ark for himself, as the means of safety. We may thus, by taking a part for the whole, explain this place,—that the Ninevites believed God; for as they knew that God required the deserved punishment, they submitted to him, and, at the same time, solicited pardon: but the Ninevites, no doubt, derived from the words of Jonah something more than mere terror: for had they only apprehended this—that they were guilty before God, and were justly summoned to punishment, they would have been confounded and stunned with dread, and could never have been encouraged to seek forgiveness. Inasmuch then as they suppliantly prostrated themselves before God, they must certainly have conceived some hope of grace. They were not, therefore, so touched with penitence and the fear of God, but that they had some knowledge of divine grace: thus they believed God; for though they were aware that they were most worthy of death, they yet despaired not, but betook themselves to prayer. Since then we see that the Ninevites sought this remedy, we must feel assured that they derived more advantage from the preaching of Jonah than the mere knowledge that they were guilty before God: this ought certainly to be understood. But we shall speak more on the subject in our next lecture.

PRAYER.

Grant, Almighty God, that as there is so much timidity in us, that none of us is prepared to follow where thou mayest call us, we may be so instructed by the example of thy servant Jonah, as to obey thee in every thing, and that though Satan and the world may oppose us with all their terrors, we may yet be strengthened by a reliance on thy power and protection, which thou hast promised to us, and may go on in the course of our vocation, and never turn aside, but thus contend against all the hinderances of this world, until we reach that celestial kingdom, where we shall enjoy thee and Christ thy only begotten Son, who is our strength and our salvation: and may thy Spirit quicken us, and strengthen all our faculties, that we may obey thee, and that at length thy name may be glorified in us, and that we may finally become partakers of that glory to which thou invitest us through Christ our Lord. Amen.

Lecture Seventy-eighth.

6. For word came unto the king of Nineveh; and he arose from his throne, and he laid his robe from him, and covered *him* with sackcloth, and sat in ashes.

7. And he caused *it* to be proclaimed and published through Nineveh by the decree of the king and his nobles, saying, Let neither man nor beast, herd nor flock, taste any thing; let them not feed, nor drink water:

8. But let man and beast be covered with sackcloth, and cry mightily unto God; yea, let them turn every one from his evil way, and from the violence that *is* in their hands.

6. Et pervenit verbum (sermo, *vel*, res) ad regem Nineveh; et surrexit è solio suo, et abjecit splendidam suam vestem à seipso, et induit saccum, et sedit super pulverem:

7. Et promulgavit ac dixit per Nineven ex consilio regis et magnatum ejus, dicendo, Homo et jumentum (*vel*, bestia,) bos et ovis, ne gustent quidpiam, ne pascantur, et ne aquas bibant;

8. Et induantur saccis homo et bestia, et clament ad Deum in fortitudine; et revertatur quisque à via sua mala, et à rapacitate quæ est in manibus eorum.

It is uncertain whether Jonah had preached for some days in the city before it was known to the king. This is indeed the common opinion; for interpreters so expound the verse, which says that word was brought to the king, as though the king himself knew, that the whole city was in commotion through the preaching of Jonah: but the words admit of a different sense, that is, that the preaching of Jonah immediately reached the king; and I am disposed to take this view, as Jonah seems here to explain how the Ninevites were led to put on sackcloth. He had before spoken briefly on the subject, but he now explains what took place more fully; and we know that it was commonly the manner of the Hebrews—to relate the chief points in few words, and then to add an explanation. As then Jonah had said in the last verse that the Ninevites had put on sackcloth, and proclaimed a fast, so he now seems to express more distinctly how this happened, that is, through the royal edict. And it is by no means probable that a fast was proclaimed in the royal city by the mere consent of the people, as the king and his counsellors were there present. Inasmuch then as it appears more reasonable that the edict respecting the fast had proceeded from the king, I am therefore inclined so to connect the two verses, as that the first briefly mentions the fruit which followed the preaching of Jonah, and that the second is added as an explanation, for it gives a fuller account of what took place.

Jonah then now says, that a fast was proclaimed by the Ninevites, for the king and his council had so appointed: and I regard the verb ויגע, *uigo,* as being in the pluperfect tense, *When word had come to the king;*[1] for Jonah now states the reason why the Ninevites proclaimed a fast; it was because the king had been apprised of the preaching of Jonah, and had called together his counsellors. It was then a public edict, and not any movement among the people, capriciously made, as it sometimes happens. He says, that it was an edict published by the authority of the king and his council, or his nobles. At the same time, some take טעם, *thom,* as meaning reason or approbation. טעם, *thom,* means to taste, and Jonah afterwards uses the verb in this sense; but it is to be taken here in a metaphorical sense for counsel; and I think this meaning is more suitable to this passage. I come now to the subject.

It is worthy of being noticed, that the king of so splendid a city,[2] nay, at that time the greatest monarch, should have rendered himself so submissive to the exhortation of Jonah: for we see how proud kings are; as they think themselves exempt from the common lot of men, so they carry themselves above all laws. Hence it comes, that they will have all things to be lawful for them; and while they give loose

[1] *Grotius*, as well as *Junius* and *Tremelius*, had the same view of this verse, by rendering the verb in the tense here proposed. *Quia pervenerat* is the version of the former; and the version of the latter is, *Quum enim pervenisset.* Our own version and that of *Newcome* seem also to favour this view, by rendering ו, "for," as giving a reason for what is said in the preceding verse: but *Henderson* has "and," and *Marckius* the same, and also the Septuagint. What *Calvin* states as to the manner of speaking often adopted in Hebrew, is no doubt true. But *Henry* thinks that the people "led the way," and that what they commenced was afterwards enforced and made general by the order of the king and his nobles.—*Ed.*

[2] Who this king was is a matter of conjecture. "About thirteen years," says *Newcome*, "after the death of Jeroboam II., king of Israel, Pul, king of Assyria, invaded Israel. So that Pul, or his predecessor, may have been the king here mentioned." Others think that he was Sardanapalus, a character notorious in history for his luxurious, effeminate, and debauched life.—*Ed.*

reins to their lusts they cannot bear to be admonished, even by their equals. But Jonah was a stranger and of a humble condition: that he therefore so touched the heart of the king, must be ascribed to the hidden power of God, which he puts forth through his word whenever he pleases. God does not indeed work alike by the preaching of his word, he does not always keep to the same course; but, when he pleases, he so efficaciously touches the hearts of men, that the success of his word exceeds all expectation, as in the memorable example presented to us here. Who could have said that a heathen king, who had ever lived according to his own will, who had no feeling as to true and genuine religion, would have been thus in an instant subdued? For he put aside his royal dress, laid himself in the dust, and clothed himself in sackcloth. We hence see that God not only spoke by the mouth of Jonah, but added power to his word.

We must also bear in mind what Christ says, that the men of Nineveh would rise up in judgment against that generation, as they had repented at the preaching of Jonah; and "Behold," he said, "a greater than Jonah is here," (Matth. xii. 41.) Christ, at this day, proclaims the voice of his Gospel; for though he is not here in a visible form among us, he yet speaks by his ministers. If we despise his doctrine, how can our obstinacy and hardness be excused, since the Ninevites, who had no knowledge of the true doctrine of religion, who were imbued with no religious principles, were so suddenly converted by the preaching of Jonah? And that their repentance was sincere we may conclude from this circumstance—that the preaching of Jonah was severe, for he denounced destruction on a most powerful city; this might have instantly inflamed the king's mind with rage and fury; and that he was calmly humbled, was certainly a proof of no common change. We have then here a remarkable instance of penitence,—that the king should have so forgotten himself and his dignity, as to throw aside his splendid dress, to put on sackcloth, and to lie down on ashes.

But as to fasting and sackcloth, it is very true, as we have observed in our remarks on Joel, that repentance consists not in these external things: for God cares not for outward rites, and all those things which are resplendent in the sight of men are worthless before him; what, indeed, he requires, is sincerity of heart. Hence what Jonah here says of fasting, and other outward performances, ought to be referred to their legitimate end,—that the Ninevites intended thus to show that they were justly summoned as guilty before God's tribunal, and also, that they humbly deprecated the wrath of their judge. Fasting then and sackcloth were only an external profession of repentance. Were any one to fast all his life, and to put on sackcloth, and to scatter dust on himself, and not to connect with all this a sincerity of heart, he would do nothing but mock God.[1] Hence these outward performances are, in themselves, of small or of no value, except when preceded by an interior feeling of heart, and men be on this account led to manifest such outward evidences. Whenever then Scripture mentions fasting, and ashes, and sackcloth, we must bear in mind that these things are set before us as the outward signs of repentance, which, when not genuine, do nothing else but provoke the wrath of God; but when true, they are approved of God on account of the end in view, and not that they avail, of themselves, to pacify his wrath, or to expiate sins.

If now any one asks whether penitence is always to be accompanied with fasting, ashes, and sackcloth, the answer is at hand,—that the faithful ought through their whole life to repent: for except every one of us continually strives to renounce himself and his former life, he has not yet learned what it is to serve God; for we must ever contend with the flesh. But though there is a continual exercise of repentance, yet fasting is not required of us always. It then follows that fasting is a public and solemn testimony of repentance, when there appears to be some extraordinary evidence of God's wrath. Thus have we seen that the Jews were by Joel called to lie

[1] *Ου τη νηστεια προσεσχεν, αλλα τη αποχη των κακων*—"He [God] did not regard fasting, but abstinence from evils."—*Theodoret.* "It is not enough," says *Henry*, "to fast for sin, but we must fast from sin, and, in order to the success of our prayers, must no more regard iniquity in our hearts. . . The work of a fast-day is not done with the day; no, then the hardest and most needful part of the work begins, which is to turn from sin and to live a new life, and not to return with the dog to his vomit."—*Ed.*

in ashes, and to put on sackcloth, because God had come forth, as it were, armed against them; and all the Prophets had declared that destruction was nigh the people. In the same manner the Ninevites, when terrified by this dreadful edict, put on sackcloth, proclaimed a fast, because this was usually done in extremities. We now then perceive why the king, having himself put on sackcloth, enjoined on the whole people both fasting and other tokens of repentance.

But it seems strange, and even ridiculous, that the king should bid animals, as well as men, to make a confession of repentance; for penitence is a change in man, when he returns to God after having been alienated from him: this cannot comport with the character of brute animals. Then the king of Nineveh acted foolishly and contrary to all reason in connecting animals with men when he spoke of repentance. But, in answer to this, we must bear in mind what I have before said—that destruction had been denounced, not only on men, but also on the whole city, even on the buildings: for as God created the whole world for the sake of men, so also his wrath, when excited against men, includes the beasts, and trees, and every thing in heaven and on earth. But the question is not yet solved; for though God may punish animals on account of men's sins, yet neither oxen nor sheep can pacify the wrath of God. To this I answer—that this was done for the sake of men: for it would have been ridiculous in the king to prohibit food and drink to animals, except he had a regard to men themselves. But his object was to set before the Ninevites, as in a mirror or picture, what they deserved. The same was done under the law; for, whenever they slew victims, they were reminded of their own sins; for it ought to have come to their minds, that the sheep or any other animal sacrificed was innocent, and that it stood at the altar in his stead who had sinned. They therefore saw in the ox, or the lamb, or the goat, a striking emblem of their own condemnation. So also the Ninevites, when they constrained the oxen, the asses, and other animals, to fast, were reminded of what grievous and severe punishment they were worthy: inasmuch as innocent animals suffered punishment together with them. We hence see that no expiation was sought for by the king, when he enjoined a fast on brute animals, but that, on the contrary, men were roused by such means seriously to acknowledge the wrath of God, and to entertain greater fear, that they might be more truly humbled before him, and be displeased with themselves, and be thus more disposed and better prepared and moulded to seek pardon.

We now then see that this must be considered as intended to terrify the consciences of men, that they, who had long flattered themselves, might by such a remedy be roused from their insensibility. The same was the intention of different washings under the law, the cleansing of garments and of vessels; it was, that the people might know that every thing they touched was polluted by their filth. And this ought to be especially observed; for the Papists, wedded as they are to external rites, lay hold on anything said in Scripture about fasting, and ashes, and sackcloth, and think that the whole of religion consists in these outward observances: but bodily exercise, as Paul says, profiteth but little, (1 Tim. iv. 8.) Therefore this rule ought ever to be our guide—that fasting and such things are in themselves of no value, but must be estimated only by the end in view. So then, when the animals were constrained by the Ninevites to suffer want, the men themselves, being reminded of their guilt, learned what it was to dread God's wrath; and on this account it was that fasting was approved by God.

Now, if any one objects and says, that nothing ought to be done in the worship of God beyond what his word warrants, the answer is—that the king of Nineveh had not appointed any kind of expiation, neither did he intend that they should thus worship God, but regarded only the end which I have mentioned; and that end fully harmonises with the word of God and his command. Hence the king of Nineveh attempted nothing that was inconsistent with the word of God, since he had in every thing this in view—that he and his people might go humbly before God's tribunal, and with real penitential feelings solicit his forgiveness. This then is an answer sufficiently plain.

When therefore Jonah afterwards subjoins,[1] that the king commanded both the people and the beasts to put on sackcloth, let us know, that if any one now were to take this as an example, he would be nothing else but a mountebank; for this reason ought ever to be remembered,—that the king sought aids by which he might lead himself and his people to true repentance. But the disposition of man is prone to imitate what is evil: for we are all very like apes; we ought therefore always to consider by what spirit those were actuated whom we wish to imitate, lest we should be contented with the outward form and neglect the main thing.

Jonah afterwards adds, *And they cried mightily*[2] *to God.* This must be confined to men; for it could not have been applied to brute animals. Men then, as well as the beasts, abstained from meat and drink, and they cried to God. This crying could not have proceeded except from fear and a religious feeling: hence, as I have said, this cannot be applied indiscriminately to the beasts as well as to men.[3] But it deserves to be noticed, that the king of Nineveh commanded the people to cry mightily to God; for we hence learn that they were really frightened, inasmuch as he speaks not here of ordinary crying, but he adds mightily, as when we say, with all our power, or as we say in French, *A force*, or, *fort et ferme.* Jonah then expresses something uncommon and

[1] *Calvin* has omitted to notice the words at the beginning of the seventh verse. His version is, *Et promulgavit ac dixit*, &c., but this rendering comports not with what follows. The verbs are evidently in future Niphal, preceded by a ו conversive, and ought to be rendered impersonally, "And it was proclaimed and published," &c. And so *Newcome* renders them; and this is in conformity with the Septuagint, *Και εκηρυχθη και ερρεθη εν τη Νινευη*—"And it was proclaimed and published in Nineveh." *Henderson* gives a paraphrase, "And a proclamation was made through Nineveh."—*Ed.*

[2] בחזקה, with vigour. "*Εκτενῶς*—intensely, earnestly."—*Sept.* "*Vehementer*—vehemently."—*Grotius.* "*Totis viribus*—with all their powers."—*Mercerius.* "*Cum intensione valida*—with strong intensity."—*Marckius.* "In prayer," says *Henry*, "we must cry mightily, with a fixedness of thought, firmness of faith, and fervour of pious and devout affections."—*Ed.*

[3] Yet *Henry* does in a manner apply this mighty crying to the beasts. "Let even the brute creatures do it according to their capacity; let their cries and moans for want of food be graciously construed as cries to God; as the cries of young ravens are, Job xxxviii. 41; and of the young lions, Ps. civ. 21."—*Ed.*

extraordinary, when he tells us that it was contained in the king's edict, that men should cry mightily to God; for it was the same as though he said, "Let all men now awake and shake off their indifference; for every one of us have hitherto greatly indulged ourselves in our vices: it is now time that fear should possess our minds, and also constrain us to deprecate the wrath of God." And it is also worthy of being observed, that the king proposes no other remedy, but that the people should have recourse to prayer. It might indeed have been, that Jonah exhorted the Ninevites to resort to this duty of religion, &c. We may, however, undeniably conclude that it is a feeling implanted in us by nature, that when we are pressed by adversities, we implore the favour of God. This then is the only remedy in afflictions and distresses, to pray to God. But when we, taught by the Law and by the Gospel, use not this remedy, whenever God warns us and exhorts us to repentance, what shadow of excuse can we have, since heathens, even those who understood not a syllable of true religion, yet prayed to God, and the king himself commanded this with the consent of his nobles? Hence this edict of the king ought to fill us with more shame than if one adduced the same doctrine only from the word of God: for though the authority of that king is not the same with that of God, yet when that miserable and blind prince acknowledged through the dictates of nature, that God is to be pacified by prayer, what excuse, as I have said, can remain for us?

But Jonah shows more clearly afterwards, that it was no feigned repentance when the Ninevites put on sackcloth, and abstained also from meat and drink; for it follows in the king's edict, *And let every one turn from his own wicked way, and from the plunder which is in their hands.* Here the heathen king shows for what purpose and with what design he had given orders respecting fasting and other things; it was done that the Ninevites might thus more effectually stimulate themselves to fear God; for he here exhorts them to turn from their evil way. By *way* the Scripture usually means the whole course or manner of man's life; it was as though he said, "Let every one of you change his disposition and his conduct; let us all become new creatures." And this is true penitence, the conversion of man to God; and this the heathen king meant. The more shameful then is their dulness who seek to pacify God by frivolous devices, as the Papists do; for while they obtrude on God trifles, I know not what, they think that these are so many expiations, and they tenaciously contend for them. They need no other judge than this heathen king, who shows that true penitence is wholly different, that it then only takes place when men become changed in mind and heart, and wholly turn to a better course of life.

Let every one then *turn*, he says, *from his evil way, and from the plunder*[1] *which is in their hand.* One kind of evil is here subjoined, a part being stated for the whole; for plunders were not the only things which stood in need of amendment among the Ninevites, as it is probable that they were polluted by other vices and corruptions. In a city so large, drunkenness probably prevailed, as well as luxury, and pride, and ambition, and also lusts. It cannot indeed be doubted, but that Nineveh was filled with innumerable vices: but the king, by mentioning a part for the whole, points out here the principal vice, when he says, *Let every one turn from his evil way*, and *from his rapacity*. It was the same as though he had said that the principal virtue is equity or justice, that is, when men deal with one another without doing any hurt or injury: and well would it be were this doctrine to prevail at this day among all those who falsely assume the Christian name. For the Papists, though they accumulate expiations,

[1] *A rapacitate*, from robbery, extortion, plunder, מן־החמס, from violence, outrage, or injustice done by force or violence: it means tyrannical injustice. "Απο της αδικιας—from injustice," wrong, iniquity.—*Sept.* But as it is said to be in their hands, it means, by a metonymy, the plunder got by injustice, exercised tyrannically.

Marckius observes that the similitude here is first taken from the feet, and then from the hands. The feet are not to go in the evil way, nor the hands employed in doing what is unjust. *Henry* explains the passage very fully and yet concisely, "*Let them turn every one from his evil way* —the evil way he hath chosen—the evil way he is addicted to and walks in—the evil way of his heart—and the evil way of his conversation; and particularly *from the violence that is in their hands*, —let them restore what they have unjustly taken, and make reparation for the wrong they have done,—and let them not any more oppress those they have power over, or defraud those they have dealings with."—*Ed.*

pass by charity; and in the whole course of life equity has hardly any place. Let them then learn, from the mouth of a heathen king, what God principally requires from men, and approves of in their life, even to abstain from plunder and from the doing of any injury. We now then perceive why rapacity was especially mentioned. But we must bear in mind that the king, as yet a novice, and hardly in a slight degree imbued with the elements of religion, through hearing what Jonah preached, gave orders to his people according to the measure of his faith and knowledge: but if he made such progress in so short a time, what excuse can we pretend, whose ears have been stunned by continual preaching for twenty or thirty years, if we yet come short of the noviciate of this king? These circumstances ought then to be carefully observed by us. Let us now proceed—

9. Who can tell *if* God will turn and repent, and turn away from his fierce anger, that we perish not?

9. Quis novit an convertatur et pœnitentia ducatur Deus, et revertatur à furore iræ suæ, ut non pereamus?

The mind and design of the king are here more distinctly stated,—that he thus endeavoured to reconcile himself and the people to God. Some give a rendering somewhat different, "He who knows will turn and be led by penitence," &c.; they read not interrogatively; but this rendering cannot stand. There is in the meaning of the Prophet nothing ambiguous, for he introduces the king here as expressing a doubt, *Who knows whether God will be reconciled to us?* We hence see that the king was not overwhelmed with despair, for he still thought of a remedy; and this is the purport of the verse.

But this may seem contrary to the nature of faith; and then if it be opposed to faith, it follows that it must be inconsistent with repentance; for faith and repentance are connected together, as we have observed in other places; as no one can willingly submit to God, except he has previously known his goodness, and entertained a hope of salvation; for he who is touched only with fear avoids God's presence; and then despair prevails, and perverseness follows. How then was it that the king of Nineveh had seriously and undissemblingly repented, while yet he spoke doubtfully of the favour of God? To this I answer, that it was a measure of doubt, which was yet connected with faith, even that which does not directly reject the promise of God, but has other hinderances: as for instance, when any one, cast down with fear, afterwards receives courage from the hope of pardon and salvation set before him, he is not yet immediately freed from all fear; for as long as he looks on his sins, and is entangled by various thoughts, he vacillates, he fluctuates. There is, therefore, no doubt but that the king of Nineveh entertained hope of deliverance; but at the same time his mind was perplexed, both on account of the sermon of Jonah and on account of the consciousness of his own sins: there were then two obstacles, which deprived the king's mind of certainty, or at least prevented him from apprehending immediately the mercy of God, and from perceiving with a calm mind that God would be gracious to him. The first obstacle was the awful message,—that Nineveh would be destroyed in forty days. For though Jonah, as we have said, might have added something more, yet the denunciation was distinct and express, and tended to cast down the minds of all. The king then had to struggle, in order to overcome this obstacle, and to resist this declaration of Jonah as far as it was found to be without any comfort. And then the king, while considering his own sins, could not but vacillate for some time. But yet we see that he strove to emerge, though he had these obstacles before his eyes, for he says, *Who knows whether God will turn from the fury of his wrath, and repent?* We hence see that the king was in a hard struggle; for though Jonah seemed to have closed the door and to shut out the king from any hope of deliverance, and though his own conscience held him fast bound, he yet perseveres and encourages himself; in short, he aspires to the hope of pardon.

And it must be further noticed, that this form of expression expresses a difficulty rather than a mistrust. The king then here asks, as it were doubtingly, "Who knows whether God will turn?" for it was a difficult thing to be believed, that

God, after a long forbearance, would spare the wicked city. Hence the king expresses it as a difficulty; and such an interrogation was no proof of the absence of faith. A similar expression is found in Joel, "Who knows," &c.? We then stated several things in explaining that passage: but it is enough here briefly to state, that the king here does not betray a mistrust, but sets forth a difficulty. And it was an evidence of humility that he acknowledged himself and his people to be sunk, as it were, in the lowest hell, and yet ceased not to entertain some hope: for it is a strong proof of hope, when we still entertain it, though this be contrary to the whole order of nature, and wholly inconsistent with human reason. We now then see the meaning of the words. Of the repentance of God we shall speak hereafter, either to-morrow or the day after.

Lest we perish, he says. We see how a heathen king thought of redeeming himself from destruction; it was by having God pacified. As soon then as any danger threatens us, let us bear this in mind, that no deliverance can be found except the Lord receives us into favour; such was the conviction of the king of Nineveh, for he concluded that all things would be well as soon as God should be propitious. We hence see how much this new and untrained disciple had improved; for he understood that men cannot escape miseries until God be pacified towards them, and that when men return into favour with him, though they ought to have perished a hundred times before, they yet shall be delivered and made safe; for the grace or the favour of God is the fountain of life and salvation, and of all blessings. It afterwards follows—

10. And God saw their works, that they turned from their evil way; and God repented of the evil that he had said that he would do unto them; and he did *it* not.

10. Et vidit Deus opera eorum, quòd conversi essent à via sua mala; et pœnituit Deum super malo, quod pronuntiaverat se facturum illis, et non fecit.

Jonah now says, that the Ninevites obtained pardon through their repentance: and this is an example worthy of being observed; for we hence learn for what purpose God daily urges us to repentance, and that is, because he desires to be reconciled to us, and that we should be reconciled to him. The reason then why so many reproofs and threatenings resound in our ears, whenever we come to hear the word of God, is this,—that as God seeks to recover us from destruction he speaks sharply to us : in short, whatever the Scripture contains on repentance and the judgment of God ought to be wholly applied for this purpose—to induce us to return into favour with him ; for he is ready to be reconciled, and is ever prepared to embrace those who without dissimulation turn to him. We then understand by this example that God has no other object in view, whenever he sharply constrains us, than that he may be reconciled to us, provided only we be our own judges, and thus anticipate his wrath by genuine sorrow of heart, provided we solicit the pardon of our guilt and sin, and loathe ourselves, and confess that we are worthy of perdition.

But Jonah seems to ascribe their deliverance to their repentance, and also to their works : for he says that the Ninevites obtained pardon, because God looked on their works.

We must first see what works he means, that no one may snatch at a single word, as hypocrites are wont to do ; and this, as we have said, is very commonly the case under the Papacy. *God had respect to their works*—what works ? not sackcloth, not ashes, not fasting ; for Jonah does not now mention these ; but he had respect to their works—because they turned from their evil way. We hence see that God was not pacified by outward rites only, by the external profession of repentance, but that he rather looked on the true and important change which had taken place in the Ninevites, for they had become renewed. These then were their works, even the fruits of repentance. And such a change of life could not have taken place, had not the Ninevites been really moved by a sense of God's wrath. The fear of God then had preceded ; and this fear could not have been without faith. We hence see that he chiefly speaks here not of external works, but of the renovation of men.

But if any one objects and says, that still this view does

not prevent us from thinking that good works reconcile us to God, and that they thus procure our salvation: to this I answer—that the question here is not about the procuring cause of forgiveness. It is certain that God was freely pacified towards the Ninevites, as he freely restores his favour daily to us. Jonah then did not mean that satisfactions availed before God, as though the Ninevites made compensations for their former sins. The words mean no such thing; but he shows it as a fact which followed, that God was pacified, because the Ninevites repented. But we are to learn from other parts of Scripture how God becomes gracious to us, and how we obtain pardon with him, and whether this comes to us for our merits and repentance, or whether God himself forgives us freely. Since the whole Scripture testifies that pardon is gratuitously given us, and that God cannot be otherwise propitious to us than by not imputing sins, there is no need, with regard to the present passage, anxiously to inquire why God looked on the works of the Ninevites, so as not to destroy them: for this is said merely as a consequence. Jonah then does not here point out the cause, but only declares that God was pacified towards the Ninevites, as soon as they repented. But we shall speak more on this subject.

PRAYER.

Grant, Almighty God, that as we are loaded with so many vices, and so many sins, yea, and scandalous crimes break out daily among us,—O grant, that we may not be hardened against so many exhortations, by which thou invitest us to thyself, but that being made contrite in spirit, whenever thou denouncest on us thy wrath, we may be really humbled, and so place ourselves before thy tribunal, that we may, by a true confession and genuine fear, anticipate the judgment which would otherwise have been prepared for us; and that in the meantime relying on Christ our Mediator, we may entertain such a hope of pardon as may raise us up to thee, and not doubt but that thou art ready to embrace us, when we shall be moved by a true and real feeling of fear and penitence, since it is a proof of thy favour, when thou art pleased to anticipate us, and by thy Spirit testifiest that thou art a Father to us; and, in a word, may we be so cast down in ourselves, as to raise up our hope even to heaven, through Jesus Christ our Lord. Amen.

Lecture Seventy-ninth.

We stated yesterday how God remitted to the Ninevites the punishment which he had threatened by the mouth of Jonah, and that the remission both of the punishment and of the guilt was gratuitous. For whenever God sets forth pardon to sinners, the condition of repentance is at the same time added: it does not yet follow that repentance is the procuring cause of obtaining pardon; for God offers it freely, nor is he otherwise induced than by his own mere bounty. But as he would not have men to abuse his indulgence and forbearance, he lays down this condition,—that they must repent of their former life and change for the better. So then he regards the works of those who testify that they hate sin, and who, with a sincere and real desire, flee to his mercy; and no man from the heart desires God to be propitious to him, but he who loathes himself on account of his sin. This is the reason why Isaiah also says, that God would be merciful to the remnants of his people, even because every one would turn away from his iniquity. God does not certainly mean by these words, that repentance, as already stated, is the cause of our salvation; but he requires a change for the better, for no one will really seek grace, except he loathes himself on account of his sins.

Now as to what Jonah adds, *that God was led to repent*, it is a mode of speaking that ought to be sufficiently known to us. Strictly speaking, no repentance can belong to God: and it ought not to be ascribed to his secret and hidden counsel. God then is in himself ever the same, and consistent with himself; but he is said to repent, when a regard is had to the comprehension of men: for as we conceive God to be angry, whenever he summons us to his tribunal, and shows to us our sins; so also we conceive him to be placable, when he offers the hope of pardon. But it is according to our perceptions that there is any change, when God forgets his wrath, as though he had put on a new character. As then we cannot otherwise be terrified, that we may be humbled before God and repent, except he sets forth before us his wrath, the Scripture accommodates itself to the grossness of our understanding. But, on the other hand, we cannot confidently call on God, unless we feel assured that he is placable. We hence see that some kind of change appears to us, whenever God either threatens or gives hope of pardon and reconciliation: and to this must be referred this mode of speaking which Jonah adopts, when he says, that God repented.

We hence see that there is a twofold view of God,—as he sets himself forth in his word,—and as he is as to his hidden counsel. With regard to his secret counsel, I have already said that God is always like himself, and is subject to none of our feelings: but with regard to the teaching of his word, it is accommodated to our capacities. God is now angry with us, and then, as though he were pacified, he offers pardon, and is propitious to us. Such is the repentance of God.

Let us then remember that it proceeds from his word, that God is said to repent; for the Ninevites could form no other opinion but that it was God's decree that they were to be destroyed,—how so? because he had so testified by his word. But when they rose up to an assurance of deliverance, they then found that a change had taken place, that is, according to the knowledge of their own faith: and the feelings both of fear and of joy proceeded from the word: for when God denounced his wrath, it was necessary for the wretched men to be terrified; but when he invited them to a state of safety by proposing reconciliation to them, he then put on a new character; and thus they ascribed a new feeling to God. This is the meaning. Let us now proceed—

CHAPTER IV.

1. But it displeased Jonah exceedingly, and he was very angry.

1. Et displicuit Jonæ dolore magno, et succensuit apud se.[1]

[1] The two verbs used here are evidently to be construed as impersonals. The most literal rendering would be thus,—

"And it was an evil to Jonah, a great evil; and wrath was to him," or, "he was wroth."

Jerome commends this grief of Jonah, and compares it to the holy zeal of Paul when he wished himself to be an anathema for his brethren, (Rom. ix. 3 :) for he denies that he grieved because God had showed mercy to so illustrious a city; but because the conversion of the Gentiles was a certain presage of the destruction of the chosen people. As then Jonah perceived as in a mirror the near ruin of Israel, he on this account grieved, if we believe Jerome : but this notion is extremely frivolous; for, immediately after, God reproved Jonah. What then will the foolish and puerile apology of Jerome avail the Prophet, since God has declared that he acted perversely in grieving? Nay, the dulness of Jerome is thus become evident; (thus indeed do I speak of a man, who, though learned and laborious, has yet deprived himself of that praise, which otherwise he might have justly earned.) His wayward disposition everywhere betrayed itself; and he is evidently disproved in this very context, where Jonah shows clearly that the cause of his grief was another, even this,—that he was unwilling to be deemed a false or a lying prophet : hence was his great grief and his bitterness. And this, we see, had

Evil means often grief or distress, and so it is here : but the verb חרה, properly rendered in our version, "very angry," seldom, if ever, means grief. It is sometimes rendered "grieved" in our version ; but in every instance that I can find, it means the grief of anger or displeasure. It occurs twice in Gen. iv. in exactly similar form as we find it here, followed by the preposition ל, ויחר לקין מאד, "and Cain was very wroth," or literally, "and there was wrath to Cain very much," ver. 5. And then in the following verse we have the like form, למה חרה לך, "Why art thou wroth?" or, "Why is wrath to thee?" The phrase here is, ויחר לו, "and wrath was to him." What seems to have made some commentators to change wrath or anger to grief, has been a desire to screen the guilt of Jonah. But the whole narrative clearly shows that he was so displeased as to be angry. His pettish request to die is a sufficient proof of this. Calvin was not a man to trifle with the word of God for this purpose, or for any other : nor was he at a loss to account for the sin of Jonah, without denying his piety. It is only shallow Christians, and such as have only the outward shell of religion, who are reduced to this dilemma.

Marckius very justly observes, "That though all the works of God are altogether blameless (irreprehensibilia,) yet there is hardly any thing which is not sometimes blamed by our most foolish flesh (carne insipientissima.) Thus not only the world, God's enemy, sins against him ; but even his own people, who honour him, openly show, one while, that his severity, and at another time that his kindness, displease them, as though they were not befitting."—*Ed.*

God not expressed his mind, was unjust and inconsistent with every reason.

We may then conclude that Jonah was influenced by false zeal when he could not with resignation bear that the city of Nineveh should have been delivered from destruction : and he also himself amplifies the greatness of his sin. He might have said, in one word, that it displeased Jonah ; but not satisfied with this simple form, he adds, that he felt great displeasure or grief; and he afterwards adds, that he was very angry. Though the beginning may not have been wrong, yet excess was sinful. But he confesses that there was excess, and want of moderation in his grief: since then he accuses himself in plain words, what good is it, by false and invented pretences, to cover what we clearly see cannot be excused ? But that it may be more evident why the deliverance of the city of Nineveh displeased Jonah, let us go on with the context—

2. And he prayed unto the Lord, and said, I pray thee, O Lord, *was* not this my saying when I was yet in my country? Therefore I fled before unto Tarshish: for I knew that thou *art* a gracious God, and merciful, slow to anger, and of great kindness, and repentest thee of the evil.

2. Et oravit ad Jehovam et dixit, Obsecro Jehova, an non hic sermo meus, quum adhuc essem in terra mea? Propterea festinavi fugere in Tharsis, quia noveram quòd tu sis Deus propitius (*vel*, plenus gratiæ,) et misericors, tardus ad iram, multus clementiâ, et qui pœnitentiâ duceris super malo.

It seems by no means befitting that Jonah should have said here that he prayed ; for prayer ought to be calm ; but he confesses that his mind was in a state of excitement. As then anger was burning within the Prophet, how could he come before God and utter a suitable prayer ? And further, what is the end of praying, but to confess that whatever good is to be obtained resides in God, and is to be sought humbly from him ? But Jonah here, on the contrary, expostulates and clamours against God ; for he seems in a manner to be contending that he had a just reason for his flight, and also that God ought not to have pardoned the Ninevites. He then accuses God, that he might free himself from every blame. But all this is foreign and remote from what is required in prayer. How then must we understand this passage, in which he says that he prayed? My answer is—that the faithful often in a disturbed state of mind approach God with a desire to pray, and that their prayers are not wholly rejected, though they are not altogether approved and accepted. And hence also it appears more evident how the works of the godly are regarded by God, though they are sprinkled with many stains. Whenever the Papists read that any work has pleased God, they imagine that all was perfection and cleanness: but there is no work which is not infected with some pollution, unless it be purified by a free pardon. This I say is evident to us in this prayer, which was not so rejected by God, as though it retained not the character of prayer: and yet it is certain that Jonah was by no means rightly influenced when he prayed so clamorously, finding fault, as it were, with God, and retaining still some portion of his own obstinacy; for he boasted of his flight. But this flight, as we have stated, was a proof of manifest rebellion, since, by shaking off the yoke, he despised the call of God.

We must therefore acknowledge that there was some piety in this prayer of Jonah, as well as many faults. It was an act of piety that he addressed his complaints to God. For though hypocrites may pray to God, they yet are wholly averse to him, and freely give vent to their bitterness against God: but Jonah, while he here complains, and observes no moderation, but is carried away by a blind and perverse impulse, is yet prepared to submit to God, as we shall hereafter see. This is the reason why he says that he prayed: for he would not have been ashamed to confess any grievous sin of which he might have been conscious. He did not then extenuate his fault by using the word prayer as hypocrites are wont to do, who ever set up some pretences or veils when they seek to cover their own baseness: such was not the object of Jonah. When therefore he says that he prayed, he declares generally that he did not so speak against God, but that he still retained some seed of piety and obedience in his heart. *Jonah* then *prayed.* Hence it follows, as I have before stated, that many of the prayers of the saints are sinful (*vitiosas*—faulty,) which, when tried by the right rule, deserve to be rejected. But the Lord, according to his own mercy, pardons their defects, so that these confused and turbulent prayers yet retain their title and honour.

Now he says, *I pray thee, Jehovah, is not this what I said?* Here Jonah openly declares why he bore so ill the deliverance of Nineveh from destruction, because he was thus found to have been false and lying. But it may seem strange that the Prophet had more regard for his own reputation than for the glory of God; for in this especially shines forth the glory of God, that he is reconcilable as soon as men return to the right way, and that he offers himself to them as a father. Ought then Jonah to have preferred his own honour to the glory of God? I answer,—that the Prophet was not so devoted to himself, but that a concern for the glory of God held the first place in his soul; this is certain. For he connected, and justly so, his own ministry with the glory of God; as it proceeded from his authority. When Jonah entered Nineveh, he cried not as a private man, but avowed that he was sent by God. Now if the preaching of Jonah is found to be false, reproach will recoil on the author of his call, even on God. Jonah then no doubt could not bear that the name of God should be exposed to the reproaches of the Gentiles, as though he had spoken dissemblingly, now opening hell, then heaven: and there is nothing so contrary to the glory of God as such a dissimulation. We hence see why Jonah was seized with so much grief; he did not regard himself; but as he saw that an occasion would be given to ungodly blasphemers, if God changed his purpose, or if he did not appear consistent with his word, he felt much grieved.

But however specious this reason may be, we yet learn of how much avail are good intentions with God. Whatever good intention can be imagined, it was certainly a good intention in Jonah, worthy of some praise, that he preferred dying a hundred times rather than to hear these reproachful blasphemies—that the word of God was a mere sport, that his threatenings were no better than fables, that God made this and that pretence, and transformed himself into various characters. This was certainly the very best intention, if it be estimated by our judgment. But we shall presently see that it was condemned by the mouth of God himself. Let us hence learn not to arrogate to ourselves judgment in matters which exceed our capacities, but to subject our minds to God, and to seek of him the spirit of wisdom, (*discretionis*—of discretion, of prudence.) For whence was it that Jonah so fretted against God, except that he burned with a desire for his glory? But his zeal was inconsiderate, for he would be himself the judge and arbitrator, while, on the contrary, he ought to have subjected himself altogether to God. And the same rule ought to be observed also by us. When we see many things happening through a Divine interposition, that is, through the secret providence of God, and things which expose his name to the blasphemies of the ungodly, we ought indeed to feel grief; but in the meantime let us ask of the Lord to turn at length these shameful reproaches to his own glory; and let us by no means raise an uproar, as many do, who immediately begin to contend with God, when things are otherwise ordered than what they wish or think to be useful. Let us learn by the example of Jonah not to measure God's judgments by our own wisdom, but to wait until he turns darkness into light. And at the same time let us learn to obey his commands, to follow his call without any disputing: though heaven and earth oppose us, though many things occur which may tend to avert us from the right course, let us yet continue in this resolution,—that nothing is better for us than to obey God, and to go on in the way which he points out to us.

But by saying that he *hastened to go to Tarshish*, he does not altogether excuse his flight; but he now more clearly explains, that he did not shun trouble or labour, that he did not run away from a contest or danger, but that he only avoided his call, because he felt a concern for the glory of God. The import, then, of Jonah's words is,—that he makes God here, as it were, his witness and judge, that he did not withdraw himself from obedience to God through fear of danger, or through idleness, or through a rebellious spirit, or through any other evil motive, but only because he was unwilling that his holy name should be profaned, and would not of his own accord be the minister of that preaching, which would be the occasion of opening the mouth of ungodly and profane men, and of making them to laugh at God himself. "Since then I cannot hope," he says, "for any other issue to my preaching than to make the Gentiles to deride God, yea, and to revile his holy name, as though he were false and deceitful, I chose rather to flee to Tarshish." Then Jonah does not here altogether clear himself; for otherwise that chastisement, by which he ought to have been thoroughly subdued, must have failed in its effect. He had been lately restored from the deep, and shall we say that he now so extols himself against God, that he wishes to appear wholly free from every blame? This certainly would be very strange: but, as I have said, he declares to God, that he fled at the beginning for no other reason, but because he did not expect any good fruit from his preaching, but, on the contrary, feared what now seemed to take place,—that God's name would be ridiculed.

For he immediately adds, *For I know that thou art a God full of grace, and merciful, slow to wrath,* &c. It is a wonder that Jonah withdrew from his lawful call; for he knew that God was merciful, and there is no stronger stimulant than this to stir us on, when God is pleased to use our labour: and we know that no one can with alacrity render service to God except he be allured by his paternal kindness. Hence no one will be a willing Prophet or Teacher, except he is persuaded that God is merciful. Jonah then seems here to reason very absurdly when he says, that he withdrew himself from his office, because he knew that God was merciful. But how did he know this? By the law of God; for the passage is taken from Exod. xxxiii., where is described that remarkable and memorable vision, in which God offered to Moses a view of himself: and there was then exhibited to the holy Prophet, as it were, a living representation of God; and there is no passage in the law which expresses God's nature more to the life; for God was then pleased to make himself known in a familiar way to his servant.

As then Jonah had been instructed in the doctrine of the law, how could he discharge the office of a Prophet among his own people? And why did not this knowledge discourage his mind, when he was called to the office of a

Teacher? It is then certain that this ought to be confined to the sort of preaching, such as we have before explained. Jonah would not have shrunk from God's command, had he been sent to the Ninevites to teach what he had been ordered to do among the chosen people. Had then a message been committed to Jonah, to set forth a gracious and merciful God to the Ninevites, he would not have hesitated a moment to offer his service. But as this express threatening, "Nineveh shall be destroyed," was given him in charge, he became confounded, and sought at length to flee away rather than to execute such a command. Why so? Because he thus reasoned with himself, "I am to denounce a near ruin on the Ninevites; why does God command me to do this, except to invite these wretched men to repentance? Now if they repent, will not God be instantly ready to forgive them? He would otherwise deny his own nature: God cannot be unlike himself, he cannot put off that disposition of which he has once testified to Moses. Since God, then, is reconcilable, if the Ninevites will return to the right way and flee to him, he will instantly embrace them: thus I shall be found to be false in my preaching."

We now then perceive how this passage of Jonah is to be understood, when he says that he fled beyond the sea, at least that he attempted to do so, because he knew that God was gracious; for he would not have deprived God of his service, had not this contrariety disturbed and discouraged his mind, "What! I shall go there as God's ambassador, in a short time I shall be discovered to be a liar: will not this reproach be cast on the name of God himself? It is therefore better for me to be silent, than that God, the founder of my call, should be ridiculed." We see that Jonah had a distinct regard to that sort of preaching which we have already referred to. And it hence appears that Jonah gave to the Ninevites more than he thought; for he supposed that he was sent by God, only that the Ninevites might know that they were to be destroyed: but he brought deliverance to them; and this indeed he partly suspected or knew before; for he retained this truth—that God cannot divest himself of his mercy, for he remains ever the same. But when he went forth to execute the duty enjoined on him, he certainly had nothing to expect but the entire ruin of the city Nineveh. God in the meantime employed his ministry for a better end and purpose. There is indeed no doubt but that he exhorted the Ninevites to repentance; but his own heart was as it were closed up, so that he could not allow them the mercy of God. We hence see that Jonah was seized with perplexities, so that he could not offer deliverance to the Ninevites, and it was yet offered them by God through his instrumentality.

We now then understand how God often works by his servants; for he leads them as the blind by his own hand where they think not. Thus, when he stirs up any one of us, we are sometimes ὀλιγόπίστοι—very weak in faith; we think that our labour will be useless and without any fruit, or at least attended with small success. But the Lord will let us see what we could not have expected. Such was the case with Jonah; for when he came to Nineveh, he had no other object but to testify respecting the destruction of the city; but the Lord was pleased to make him the minister of salvation. God then honoured with remarkable success the teaching of Jonah, while he was unworthy of so great an honour; for, as we have already said, he closed up in a manner every access to the blessing of God. We now then apprehend the meaning of this passage, in which Jonah says that he fled from the call of God, because he knew that God was ready to be gracious and merciful.

I come now to the great things which are said of God. חנון, *chenun*, properly means a disposition to show favour, as though it was said, that God is gratuitously benevolent; we express the same in our language by the terms, *benin, gratieux, debonnaire*. God then assumes to himself this character; and then he says, *merciful;* and he adds this that we may know that he is always ready to receive us, if indeed we come to him as to the fountain of goodness and mercy. But the words which follow express more clearly his mercy, and show how God is merciful,—even because he is abundant in compassion and slow to wrath. God then is inclined to kindness; and though men on whom he looks are unworthy, he is yet merciful; and this he expresses by the word רחום, *rechum.*

It is at the same time necessary to add these two sentences —that he is *abundant in compassion and slow to wrath,*—why so? For we ever seek in ourselves some cause for God's favour; when we desire God to be kind to us, we inquire in ourselves why he ought to favour us: and when we find nothing, all the faith we before had respecting God's grace at once vanishes. The Lord therefore does here recall us to himself, and testifies that he is kind and merciful, inasmuch as he is abundant in compassion; as though he said, "I have in myself a sufficient reason, why I should be accessible to you, and why I should receive you and show you favour." Hence the goodness of God alone ought to be regarded by us, when we desire his mercy, and when we have need of pardon. It is as though he had said, that he is not influenced by any regard for our worthiness, and that it is not for merits that he is disposed to mercy when we have sinned, and that he receives us into favour; but that he does all this because his goodness is infinite and inexhaustible. And it is also added, that he is *slow to wrath.* This slowness to wrath proves that God provides for the salvation of mankind, even when he is provoked by their sins. Though miserable men provoke God daily against themselves, he yet continues to have a regard for their salvation. He is therefore slow to wrath, which means, that the Lord does not immediately execute such punishment as they deserve who thus provoke him. We now then see what is the import of these words.

Let us now return to this—that Jonah thrust himself from his office, because he knew that God was slow to wrath, and merciful, and full of grace: he even had recourse to this reasoning, "Either God will change his nature, or spare the Ninevites if they repent: and it may be that they will repent; and then my preaching will be found to be false; for God will not deny himself, but will afford an example of his goodness and mercy in forgiving this people." We may again remark, that we act perversely, when we follow without discrimination our own zeal: it is indeed a blind fervour which then hurries us on. Though then a thousand inconsistencies meet us when God commands any thing, our eyes ought to be closed to them, and we ought ever to follow the course of our calling; for he will so regulate all events, that all things shall redound to his glory. It is not for us in such a case to be over-wise; but the best way is, to leave in God's hand the issue of things. It becomes us indeed to fear and to feel concerned; but our anxiety ought, at the same time, to be in submission to God, so that it is enough for us to pray. This is the import of the whole.

Now as to what he says that God *repents of the evil*, we have already explained this: it means, that though God has already raised his hand, he will yet withdraw it, as soon as he sees any repentance in men; for *evil* here is to be taken for punishment. The Lord then, though he might justly inflict extreme punishment on men, yet suspends his judgment, and when they come to him in true penitence he is instantly pacified. This is God's repentance; he is said to repent when he freely forgives whatever punishment or evil men have deserved, whenever they loathe themselves.[1] It now follows—

[1] Added here shall be *Marckius*' excellent explanation of this passage, as given in Joel ii. 13. It corresponds materially with that of *Calvin*,—"Ipse est חנון, *gratiosus*, apud LXX., et Hieronymum, ελεημων, *benignus*, h. e. ut voces junctas sic distinguamus commodè, in creaturas præter omne earum meritum *beneficus;* deinde רחום, *misericors*, apud LXX., οικτίρμων, h. e. tenerrimo amore motus in miseros ad illis succurrendum et indulgendum; tum ארך אפים, *longanimis*, apud LXX., et Hieronymum, μακροθυμος, *patiens*, h. e. tardus ad iram, seu judicia sua satis facilè et satis diu differens; adhuc רב־חסד, *amplus benignitate*, apud LXX., et Hieronymum, πολυελεος, *multæ misericordiæ*, h. e. bonitatem demonstrans intensissime, latissime et diutissime, inter homines; tandem quod aliis vocibus in Exodo exprimitur, נחם על הרעת, non *consolabilis*, sed *pœnitens super malo*, apud LXX., μετανοων επὶ ταις κακιαις, apud Hieronymum, *præstabilis super malitia*, sive *pœnitens*,—h. e. malum, non culpæ ab hominibus commissum, sed pœnæ, seu afflictionis, juxta Hieronymum, coll. Matth. vi. 34, à se immittendum aut immissum homini, ad hujus resipiscentiam facilè arcens vel auferens, adeoque *placabilis*, juxta propositum suum immutabile et promissa generalia, Jer. xviii. 7, 8; xxvi. 3, &c., et finem judicii omnis, qui est, malum peccati dedocere. Quomodo pœnitentia Deo, respectu mutati operis sui, et verbi sui absque explicita conditione antea propositi, sæpe tribuitur, Gen. vi. 6; Exod. xxxii. 14; 1 Sam. xv. 11, &c.; alias respectu decreti longissimi ab eo arcenda, Num. xxiii. 19; 1 Sam. xv. 29; Jac. i. 17, &c.; notante dudum *Theodoreto*, et præeunte *Jonathane*, apud quem dicitur, *revocens verbum suam ab inducendo malo*. Ita hæc boni-

3. Therefore now, O Lord, take, I beseech thee, my life from me; for *it is* better for me to die than to live.

3. Et tu Jehova, tolle, quæso, animam meam à me; quia melius mori meum quàm vivere.

We here see how angry Jonah was in his zeal: for this prayer cannot certainly be ascribed to his faith, as some think, who say that Jonah took a flight as it were in his soul to heaven, when he made this prayer, as though he dreaded not death, but having been divested of all fear, being free and disengaged, he presented himself to God. I do not think that the mind of Jonah was so heroic. There is indeed no doubt, as I have already said, but that he still retained some seed of piety; and this, I said, is sufficiently proved by the word prayer; for if Jonah had burst out in the strain of one in despair, it would not have been a prayer. Since then he prayed by thus speaking, it follows that it was not the cry of despair, but of too much displeasure, which Jonah did not restrain. In short, this prayer proceeded from a pious and holy zeal; but Jonah sinned as to its measure or excess; for he had in a manner forgotten himself, when he *preferred death to life.*

Thou, Jehovah, he says, *take me away.* He was first not free from blame in hastily wishing to die; for it is not in our power to quit this world; but we ought with submissive minds to continue in it as long as God keeps us in the station in which we are placed. Whosoever, then, hastens to death with so great an ardour no doubt offends God. Paul knew that death was desirable in his case, (Philip. i. 22;) but when he understood that his labour would be useful to the Church, he was contented with his lot, and preferred the will of God to his own wish; and thus he was prepared both to live and to die, as it seemed good to God. It was otherwise with Jonah, "Now," he says, "take away my life." This was one fault; but the other was,—that he wished to die, because God spared the Ninevites. Though he was touched with some grief, he ought not yet to have gone so far as this, or rather to rush on, so as to desire death on account of the weariness of his life.

tatis nomina Deo, per Scripturæ testimonia et clarissima rerum documenta, verissimè competunt."—*Ed.*

But we hence learn to what extremes men are carried, when once they give loose reins to inconsiderate zeal. The holy Prophet Jonah, who had been lately tamed and subdued by so heavy a chastisement, is now seized and carried away by a desire to die,—and why? because he thought that it was hard that he denounced destruction on the Ninevites, and that still their city remained safe. This example ought to check us, that we express not too boldly our opinion respecting the doings of God, but, on the contrary, hold our thoughts captive, lest any presumption of this kind be manifested by us; for there is none of us who does not condemn Jonah, as also he condemned himself; for he does not here narrate his own praise, but means to show how foolishly he had judged of God's work. Jonah then confesses his own folly; and therefore his experience is to us an evidence that there is nothing more preposterous than for us to settle this or that according to our own wisdom, since this is alone true wisdom, to submit ourselves wholly to the will of God.

Now if any one raises a question here,—whether it is lawful to desire death; the answer may be briefly this,—that death is not to be desired on account of the weariness of life; this is one thing: and by the weariness of life I understand that state of mind, when either poverty, or want, or disgrace, or any such thing, renders life hateful to us: but if any, through weariness on account of his sins and hatred to them, regrets his delay on earth, and can adopt the language of Paul, "Miserable am I, who will free me from the body of this death!" (Rom. vii. 24,)—he entertains a holy and pious wish, provided the submission, to which I have referred, be added, so that this feeling may not break forth in opposition to the will of God; but that he who has such a desire may still suffer himself to be detained by his hand as long as he pleases. And further, when any one wishes to die, because he fears for himself as to the future, or dreads to undergo any evil, he also struggles against God; and such was the fault of Jonah; for he says that death was better to him than life,—and why? because the Lord had spared the Ninevites. We hence see how he was blinded, yea, carried away by a mad impulse to desire death.

Let us then learn so to love this life as to be prepared to lay it down whenever the Lord pleases: let us also learn to desire death, but so as to live to the Lord, and to proceed in the race set before us, until he himself lead us to its end. Now follows the reproof of God—

4. Then said the Lord, Doest thou well to be angry?	4. Et dixit Jehova, An bene facis excandescendo apud te?[1]

There is no doubt but that God by thus reproving Jonah condemns his intemperate warmth. But since God alone is a fit judge of man's conduct, there is no reason for us to boast that we are influenced by good intentions; for there is nothing more fallacious than our own balances. When therefore we weigh facts, deeds, and thoughts, by our own judgment, we deceive ourselves. Were any disposed rhetorically to defend

[1] This clause has been variously rendered. The original words are these, ההיטב חרה לך. It is not to the point to say, as *Dr Henderson* does, that the first word is sometimes rendered adverbially, as meaning "greatly," &c.; for in other places it is rendered as a verb, "to be good," or "to do good." It depends wholly on the form of the sentence what rendering is the most suitable. Both the construction of the words and the connection of the passage seem to favour the literal rendering. The first ה is the *an* of the Latin, *whether*, it is an interrogation. Then the rendering is, "Whether is it good," or, "Is it good?" Jonah had said before, that it was "good" for him to die rather than to live; for it is the same word in a different form—כי טוב מותי מחיי, "for good my death rather than my life." Then the question to him is, "Is it good *that* thou art wrathful," or literally, "*that* wrath is to thee?" the verb חרה, as in the first verse, is to be construed impersonally.

The rendering, "Art thou much vexed?" is pointless and vapid. It is indeed countenanced by the Septuagint; but we must remember that on some points there is a wrong leaning in that version, and this is one of those points. As in the case of Jerome and the early Fathers, there was a disposition and an attempt to lessen and even to obliterate all the faults and defects of the ancient saints, so it was evidently with the authors of this version. Superstition and Pharisaism must have all their saints perfect, while the word of God represents all true saints as imperfect in the present state, but aiming at, and longing for, perfection, and fully expecting to enjoy it hereafter.

The version of *Newcome* is, "Doest thou well that *thine anger* is kindled?" Kindling or heat, that is, of anger or wrath, is the ideal meaning of the verb. *Junius* and *Tremelius*, as well as *Dathius*, consider that anger, and not grief, is meant. *Dr Adam Clarke's* version is this, "Is anger good for thee?" which is certainly very literal; or, as the verb is in the causative mood, it might be rendered, "Can anger do good to thee?" It may be doubted whether here, and in the ninth verse, where the same phrase twice occurs, this rendering is the most obvious and natural.—*Ed.*

the conduct of Jonah, he might certainly muster up many specious pretences; and were any one inclined to adduce excuses for Jonah, he might be made to appear to us altogether innocent: but though the whole world absolved him, what would it avail, since he was condemned by the mouth of God himself, who alone, as I have already stated, is the judge? We ought then to feel assured, that Jonah had done foolishly, even if no reason was apparent to us; for the authority of the Supreme Judge ought to be more than sufficient.

Now God expressly condemns his wrath. Had Jonah modestly expostulated, and unburdened his griefs into the bosom of God, it would have been excusable; though his ardour would not have been free from blame, it might yet have been borne with. But now, when he is angry, it is past endurance; for wrath, as one says, is but short madness; and then it blinds the perceptions of men, it disturbs all the faculties of the soul. God then does not here in a slight manner condemn Jonah, but he shows how grievously he had fallen by allowing himself to become thus angry. We must at the same time remember, that Jonah had sinned not only by giving way to anger; he might have sinned, as we have said, without being angry. But God by this circumstance—that he thus became turbulent, enhances his sin. And it is certainly a most unseemly thing, when a mean creature rises up against God, and in a boisterous spirit contends with him: this is monstrous; and Jonah was in this state of mind.

We hence see why an express mention is made of his anger,—God thus intended to bring conviction home to Jonah, that he might no more seek evasions. Had he simply said, "Why! how is it that thou dost not leave to me the supreme right of judging? If such is my will, why dost not thou submissively acknowledge that what I do is rightly done? Is it thy privilege to be so wise, as to dictate laws to me, or to correct my decisions?"—had the Lord thus spoken, there might have remained still some excuse; Jonah might have said, "Lord, I cannot restrain my grief, when I see thy name so profaned by unseemly reproaches; can I witness this with a calm mind?" He might thus have still sought some coverings for his grief; but when the Lord brought forward his anger, he must have been necessarily silenced; for what could be found to excuse Jonah, when he thus perversely rebelled, as I have said, against God, his Judge and Maker? We now then understand why God expressly declares that Jonah did not do well in being thus angry.

But I wonder how it came into Jerome's mind to say that Jonah is not here reproved by the Lord, but that something of an indifferent kind is mentioned. He was indeed a person who was by nature a sophister, (*cavillator*—a caviller;) and thus he wantonly trifled with the work of falsifying Scripture: he made no conscience of perverting passages of holy writ. As, for instance, when he writes about marriage, he says that they do not ill who marry, and yet that they do not well. What a sophistry is this, and how vapid! So also on this place, "God," he says, "does not condemn Jonah, neither did he intend to reprove his sin; but, on the contrary, Jonah brings before us here the person of Christ, who sought death that the whole world might be saved; for when alive he could not do good to his own nation, he could not save his own kindred; he therefore preferred to devote himself and his life for the redemption of the world." These are mere puerilities; and thus the whole meaning of this passage, as we clearly see, is distorted. But the question is more emphatical than if God had simply said, "Thou hast sinned by being thus angry;" for an affirmative sentence has not so much force as that which is in the form of a question.

God then not only declares as a Judge that Jonah had not done well, but he also draws from him his own confession, as though he said, "Though thou art a judge in thine own cause, thou canst not yet make a cover for thy passion, for thou art beyond measure angry." For when he says לך, *lak*, *with*, or, *in thyself*, he reminds Jonah to examine his own heart, as though he said, "Look on thyself as in a mirror: thou wilt see what a boisterous sea is thy soul, being seized as thou art by so mad a rage." We now then perceive not only the plain sense of the passage, but also the emphasis, which is contained in the question, which Jerome has turned to a meaning wholly contrary. I will not proceed farther;[1] for what remains will be sufficient for to-morrow's lecture.

PRAYER.

Grant, Almighty God, that as thou seest us implicated in so many errors, that we often fall through want of thought, and as thou also seest that the violent emotions of our flesh wholly blind whatever reason and judgment there is in us,—O grant, that we may learn to give up ourselves altogether to obey thee, and so honour thy wisdom as never to contend with thee, though all things may happen contrary to our wishes, but patiently to wait for such an issue as it may please thee to grant; and may we never be disturbed by any of the hinderances which Satan may throw in our way, but ever go on towards the mark which thou hast set before us, and never turn aside from thee, until, having gone through all dangers and overcome all impediments, we shall at length reach that blessed rest, which has been obtained for us by the blood of thy Son. Amen.

Lecture Eightieth.

5. So Jonah went out of the city, and sat on the east side of the city, and there made him a booth, and sat under it in the shadow, till he might see what would become of the city.	5. Et egressus est Jonas ex urbe, et sedit ab oriente contra urbem, et fecit sibi illic tabernaculum, et sedit sub eo in umbra, quousque videret quid fieret in urbe.

It may be here doubted whether Jonah had waited till the forty days had passed, and whether that time had arrived; for if we say that he went out of the city before the fortieth day, another question arises, how could he have known what would be? for we have not yet found that he had been informed by any oracular communication. But the words which we have noticed intimate that it was then known by the event itself, that God had spared the city from destruction; for in the last lecture it was said, that God had

[1] Appended here is this note in the margin,—"Putavit, cessante horologio, se ante tempus finire;"—"He thought that, through the clock stopping, he had finished before the time."—*Ed.*

repented of the evil he had declared and had not done it. It hence appears that Jonah had not gone out of the city until the forty days had passed. But there comes again another question, what need had he to sit near the city, for it was evident enough that the purpose of God had changed, or at least that the sentence Jonah had pronounced was changed? he ought not then to have seated himself near the city as though he was doubtful.

But I am inclined to adopt the conjecture, that Jonah went out after the fortieth day, for the words seem to countenance it. With regard to the question, why he yet doubted the event, when time seemed to have proved it, the answer may be readily given: though indeed the forty days had passed, yet Jonah stood as it were perplexed, because he could not as yet feel assured that what he had before proclaimed according to God's command would be without its effect. I therefore doubt not but that Jonah was held perplexed by this thought, "Thou hast declared nothing rashly; how can it then be, that what God wished to be proclaimed by his own command and in his own name, should be now in vain, with no corresponding effect?" Since then Jonah had respect to God's command, he could not immediately extricate himself from his doubts. This then was the cause why he sat waiting: it was, because he thought that though God's vengeance was suspended, his preaching would not yet be in vain, but that the ruin of the city was at hand. This therefore was the reason why he still waited after the prefixed time, as though the event was still doubtful.

Now that this may be more evident, let us bear in mind that the purpose of God was hidden, so that Jonah understood not all the parts of his vocation. God, then, when he threatened ruin to the Ninevites, designed to speak conditionally: for what could have been the benefit of the word, unless this condition was added,—that the Ninevites, if they repented, should be saved? There would otherwise have been no need of a Prophet; the Lord might have executed the judgment which the Ninevites deserved, had he not intended to regard their salvation. If any one objects by saying that a preacher was sent to render them inexcusable,—this would have been unusual; for God had executed all his other judgments without any previous denunciation, I mean, with regard to heathen nations: it was the peculiar privilege of the Church that the Prophets ever denounced the punishments which were at hand; but to other nations God made it known that he was their Judge, though he did not send Prophets to warn them. There was then included a condition, with regard to God's purpose, when he commanded the Ninevites to be terrified by so express a declaration. But Jonah was, so to speak, too literal a teacher; for he did not include what he ought to have done,—that there was room for repentance, and that the city would be saved, if the Ninevites repented of their wickedness. Since then Jonah had learned only one half of his office, it is no wonder that his mind was still in doubt, and could not feel assured as to the issue; for he had nothing but the event, God had not yet made known to him what he would do. Let us now proceed—

6. And the Lord God prepared a gourd, and made *it* to come up over Jonah, that it might be a shadow over his head, to deliver him from his grief. So Jonah was exceeding glad of the gourd.

6. Et paravit Jehova Deus cucurbitam (*vel*, hederam,) et ascendere fecit ad Jonam, ut esset umbra super caput ejus, atque liberaret eum à molestia sua; et gavisus est Jonas super hedera (*vel*, cucurbita) gaudio magno.

7. But God prepared a worm when the morning rose the next day, and it smote the gourd that it withered.

7. Et paravit Deus vermem quum ascenderet aurora postridie, qui percussit hederam et exaruit.

8. And it came to pass, when the sun did arise, that God prepared a vehement east wind; and the sun beat upon the head of Jonah, that he fainted, and wished in himself to die, and said, *It is* better for me to die than to live.

8. Et accidit, quum exoriretur sol, ut pararet Deus ventum impetuosum (*qui obsurdescere facit homines; חריש significat obsurdescere; alii vertunt*, ventum arationis, *quia verbum illud etiam significat arare; et intelligunt*, ventum siccum et frigidum, *qualis grassari solet arationis tempore*,) et percussit sol super caput Jonæ, et defecit; et optavit pro anima sua, ut moreretur; et dixit, Melior mors mea quam vita.

Before I proceed to treat on the contents of these verses, I will say a few things on the word קיקיון, *kikiun;* for there were formerly some disputes respecting this word. Some render it, a gourd, (*cucurbitam;*) others think it to have been a cucumber. Free conjectures are commonly made respecting obscure and unknown things. However, the first rendering has been the received one: and Augustine says, that a tumult arose in some church, when the Bishop read the new interpretation of Jerome, who said that it was the ivy. Those men were certainly thoughtless and foolish who were so offended for a matter so trifling; for they ought to have more carefully inquired which version was the best and most correct. And Augustine did not act so very wisely in this affair; for superstition so possessed him, that he was unwilling that the received version of the Old Testament should be changed. He indeed willingly allowed Jerome to translate the New Testament from the Greek original; but he would not have the Old Testament to be touched; for he entertained a suspicion of the Jews,—that as they were the most inveterate enemies of the faith, they would have tried to falsify the Law and the Prophets. As then Augustine had this suspicion, he preferred retaining the common version. And Jerome relates that he was traduced at Rome, because he had rendered it ivy instead of gourd; but he answered Augustine in a very severe and almost an angry manner; and he inveighed in high displeasure against some Cornelius and another by the name of Asinius Polio, who had accused him at Rome as one guilty of sacrilege, because he had changed this word. I cannot allege in excuse, that they peevishly rejected what was probable. But as to the thing itself, I would rather retain in this place the word gourd, or cucumber, than to cause any disturbance by a thing of no moment. Jerome himself confesses, that it was not ivy; for he says, that it was a kind of a shrub, and that it grows everywhere in Syria; he says that it was a shrub supported by its own stem, which is not the case with ivy; for the ivy, except it cleaves to a wall or to a tree, creeps on the ground. It could not then have been the ivy; and he ought not to have so translated it. He excuses himself and says, that if he had put down the Hebrew word, many would have dreamt it to have been a beast or a serpent. He therefore wished to put down something that was known. But he might also have caused many doubts: "Why! ivy is said to have ascended over the head of Jonah, and to have afforded him a shade; how could this have been?" Now I wonder why Jerome says in one place that the shrub was called in his time Cicion in the Syriac language; and he says in another place in his Commentaries, that it was called in the same language Elkeroa; which we see to be wholly different from the word קיקיון, *kikiun*. Now when he answered Augustine, I doubt not but that he dissembled; for he knew that Augustine did not understand Hebrew: he therefore trifled with him as with a child, because he was ignorant. It seems to have been a new gloss, I know not what, invented at the time for his own convenience: I doubt not but that he at the moment formed the word, as there is some affinity between קיקיון, kikiun and cicion. However it may have been, whether it was a gourd or a shrub, it is not necessary to dispute much how it could have grown so soon into so great a size. Jerome says, that it was a shrub with many leaves, and that it grew to the size of a vine. Be it so; but this shrub grows not in one day, nor in two, nor in three days.

It must have therefore been something extraordinary. Neither the ivy, nor the gourd, nor any shrub, nor any tree, could have grown so quickly as to afford a cover to the head of Jonah: nor did this shrub alone give shelter to Jonah's head; for it is more probable, that it was derived also from the booth which he had made for himself. Jonah then not only sheltered himself under the shrub, but had the booth as an additional cover, when he was not sufficiently defended from the heat of the sun. Hence God added this shrub to the shade afforded by the booth: for in those regions, as we know, the sun is very hot; and further, it was, as we shall see, an extraordinary heat.

I wished to say thus much of the word ivy; and I have spoken more than I intended; but as there have been contentions formerly on the subject, I wished to notice what may be satisfactory even to curious readers. I come now to what is contained in this passage.

Jonah tells us that a gourd, or a cucumber, or an ivy, was

prepared by the Lord. There is no doubt but that this shrub grew in a manner unusual, that it might be a cover to the booth of Jonah. So I view the passage. But God, we know, approaches nature, whenever he does anything beyond what nature is: this is not indeed always the case; but we generally find that God so works, as that he exceeds the course of nature, and yet from nature he does not wholly depart. For when in the desert he intended to collect together a great quantity of quails, that he might give meat to the people, he raised wind from the east, (Num. xi. 31.) How often the winds blew, without bringing such an abundance of birds? It was therefore a miracle: but yet God did not wholly cast aside the assistance of nature; hence he made use of the wind; and yet the wind could not of itself bring these birds. So also in this place, God had chosen, I have no doubt, a herb, which soon ascended to a great height, and yet far surpassed the usual course of nature. In this sense, then, it is that God is said to have prepared the קִיקָיוֹן, *kikiun*,[1] and to have made it to ascend over Jonah's head, that it might be for a shade to his head and free him from his distress.

But it is said afterwards that *a worm was prepared.* We see here also, that what seemed to happen by chance was yet directed by the hidden providence of God. Should any one say, that what is here narrated does not commonly happen, but what once happened; to this I answer,—that though God then designed to exhibit a wonderful example, worthy of being remembered, it is yet ever true that the gnawings even of worms are directed by the counsel of God, so that neither a herb nor a tree withers independently of his purpose. The same truth is declared by Christ when he says, that without the Father's appointment the sparrows fall

[1] Much has been written on the character of this plant. Modern critics have pretended to determine that it was the *Ricinus*, commonly called *Palma Christi.* It matters not what it was: its growth was doubtless miraculous. It may have been an indigenous plant, it may have been such a plant as never grew before or after. Two things are evident—God prepared it, and prepared it to shelter Jonah. In a translation it would have been better either to retain the original name, or to give it the general name of a plant or shrub. To call it a gourd, an ivy, or a cucumber, is to convey an incorrect idea.—*Ed.*

not on the ground, (Matth. x. 29.) Thus much as to the worm.

It is now added, *that when the sun arose the day following, a wind was prepared.* We here learn the same thing,—that winds do not of themselves rise or by chance, but are stirred up by a Divine power. There may indeed be found causes in nature why now the air is tranquil, and then it is disturbed by winds; but God's purpose regulates all these intermediate causes, (*has omnes medias causas gubernat Dei consilium;*) so that this is ever true—that nature is not some blind impulse, but a law settled by the will of God. God then ever regulates by his own counsel and hand whatever happens. The only difference is, that his works which flow in the usual course have the name of nature; and they are miracles and retain not the name of nature, when God changes their wonted course; but yet they all proceed from God as their author. Therefore with regard to this wind, we must understand that it was not usual or common; and yet that winds are daily no less stirred up by God's providence than this wind of which Jonah speaks. But God wrought then, so to speak, beyond the usual course of nature, though he daily preserves the regular order of nature itself.

Let us now see why this whole narrative has been set down. Jonah confesses that he *rejoiced with great joy,* when he was sheltered from the extreme heat of the sun: but when the shrub withered, he was touched with so much grief that he wished to die. There is nothing superfluous here; for Jonah shows, with regard to his joy and his grief, how tender he was and how susceptible of both. Jonah here confesses his own sensibility, first by saying that he greatly rejoiced, and then by saying that he was so much grieved for the withered shrub, that through weariness of life he instantly desired death. There is then here an ingenuous confession of weakness; for Jonah in a very simple manner has mentioned both his joy and his grief. But he has distinctly expressed the vehemence of both feelings, that we might know that he was led away by his strong emotions, so that in the least things he was either inflamed with anger, or elated with joy beyond any bounds. This then was the case with him in his grief as well as in his joy. But he does not say that he prayed as before; but he adopts the word שׁאל, *shal,* which signifies to desire or wish. *He desired,* it is said, *for his soul that he might die.* It is hence probable that Jonah was so overwhelmed with grief that he did not lift up his heart to God; and yet we see that he was not neglected by God; for it immediately follows—

9. And God said to Jonah, Doest thou well to be angry for the gourd? And he said, I do well to be angry, *even* unto death.	9. Et dixit Deus ad Jonam, An bene facis excandescendo apud te super cucurbitam? et dixit, Bene facio irascendo apud me usque ad mortem.

We see here that God had concealed himself for a time, but did not yet forsake his servant. He often looks on us from behind; that is, though we think that he has forgotten us, he yet observes how we go on, that he may in due time afford help: and hence it is that he recovers and raises up the falling, before we perceive that he is near. This was his manner with Jonah, when he began to address him: for, as we have said, grief had so oppressed the mind of the holy Prophet, that it could no longer be raised up to God. Hence he desired to die; and still God did not forsake him. This was no common example of the invaluable mercy of God, with which he favours his own people, even when they precipitate themselves into ruin: such was the case with Jonah, who rushed headlong into a state of despair, and cared not for any remedy. God then did not wait until he was sought, but anticipated miserable Jonah, who was now seeking destruction to himself.

He says, *Doest thou well that thou art thus angry for the gourd?* As though he had said, that he was too violently disturbed for a matter so trifling. And we must ever bear that in mind, of which we spoke more fully yesterday,—that God did not merely reprove his servant, because he did not patiently bear the withering of the gourd—what then? but because he became angry; for in anger there is ever an excess. Since then Jonah was thus grieved beyond measure, and without any restraint, it was justly condemned by God as a fault. I will not now repeat what I said yesterday respecting the enhancing of the crime, inasmuch as Jonah not only murmured on account of the withering of the shrub, but also disregarded himself, and boiled over with displeasure beyond all due limits.

And the answer of Jonah confirms this, *I do well,* he says, *in being angry even to death.* We here see how obstinately the holy Prophet repelled the admonition of God, by which he ought to have been restored to a right mind. He was not ignorant that God spoke. Why then was he not smitten with shame? Why was he not moved by the authority of the speaker, so as immediately to repress the fierceness of his mind? But thus it commonly happens, when the minds of men are once blinded by some wrong feeling; though the Lord may thunder and fulminate from heaven, they will not hear, at least they will not cease violently to resist, as Jonah does here. Since then we find such an example of perverseness in this holy man, how much more ought every one of us to fear? Let us hence learn to repress in time our feelings, and instantly at the beginning to bridle them, lest if they should burst forth to a greater extent, we become at last altogether obstinate. I do well, he says, in being angry even to death. God charged his servant Jonah with the vice of anger; Jonah now indulges himself in his own madness, so that he says that desperation is not a vice: "I do not sin," he says, "though I am despairing; though I abandon myself to death as with mad fury, I do not yet sin."

Who could have thought that the holy Prophet could have been brought into this state of mind? But let us be reminded, as I have already said, by this remarkable example, how furious and unreasonable are the passions of our flesh. There is, therefore, nothing better than to restrain them, before they gather more strength than they ought; for when any one feeds his vices, this obstinacy and hardness always follow. But to be angry, or to be in a fume even to death, is to feel such a weariness of life, as to give ourselves up of our own accord to death. It was not indeed the design of Jonah to lay violent hands on himself; but though he abstained from violence, he yet, as to the purpose of his mind, procured death to himself; for he submitted not to God, but was carried away by a blind impulse, so that he wished to throw away his life. It now follows—

10. Then said the Lord, Thou hast had pity on the gourd, for the which thou hast not laboured, neither madest it grow; which came up in a night, and perished in a night:

11. And should not I spare Nineveh, that great city, wherein are more than sixscore thousand persons that cannot discern between their right hand and their left hand; and *also* much cattle?

10. Et dixit Jehova, Tu pepercisti cucurbitæ, in qua non laborasti, et quam non extulisti; filia noctis fuit, et filia noctis transiit (*hoc est, nata fuit, vel, exorta una nocte, et nocte etiam una emarcuit.*)

11. Et ego non parcerem Nineveh urbi magnæ, in qua sunt duodecies decem millia hominum, quorum quisque non novit inter dexteram suam et sinistram suam, et animalia etiam multa?

Here God explains the design he had in suddenly raising up the gourd, and then in causing it to perish or wither through the gnawing of a worm; it was to teach Jonah that his conduct towards the Ninevites was very inhuman. Though we find that the holy Prophet had become a prey to dreadful feelings, yet God, by this exhibition, does in a manner remind him of his folly; for, under the representation of a gourd, he shows how unkindly he desired the destruction of so populous a city as Nineveh.

Yet this comparison may appear ill suited for the purpose. Jonah felt sorry for the gourd, but he only regarded himself: hence he was displeased, because the relief with which he was pleased was taken away from him. As then this inconvenience had driven Jonah to anger, the similitude may not seem appropriate when God thus reasons, "Thou wouldest spare the gourd, should I not spare this great city?" Nay, but he was not concerned for the gourd itself: if all the gourds of the world withered, he would not have been touched with any grief; but as he felt the greatest danger, being scorched by the extreme heat of the sun, it was on this account that he was angry. To this I answer,—that though Jonah consulted his own advantage, yet this similitude is most suitable: for God preserves men for the purpose for which he has designed them. Jonah grieved for the withering of the gourd, because he was deprived of its shade: and God does not create men in vain; it is then no wonder that he wishes them to be saved. We hence see that Jonah was not unsuitably taught by this representation, how inhumanly he conducted himself towards the Ninevites. He was certainly but one individual; since then he made such an account of himself and the gourd only, how was it that he cast aside all care for so great and so populous a city? Ought not this to have come to his mind, that it was no wonder that God, the Creator and Father, had a care for so many thousands of men? Though indeed the Ninevites were alienated from God, yet as they were men, God, as he is the Father of the whole human race, acknowledged them as his own, at least to such an extent as to give them the common light of day, and other blessings of earthly life. We now then understand the import of this comparison: "Thou wouldest spare," he says, "the gourd, and should I not spare this great city?"

It hence appears how frivolous is the gloss of Jerome,—that Jonah was not angry on account of the deliverance of the city, but because he saw that his own nation would, through its means, be destroyed: for God repeats again that Jonah's feeling was quite different,—that he bore with indignity the deliverance of the city from ruin. And less to be endured it is still, that Jerome excuses Jonah by saying that he nobly and courageously answered God, that he had not sinned in being *angry even to death.* That man dared, without any shame or discernment, to invent a pretence that he might excuse so disgraceful an obstinacy. But it is enough for us to understand the real meaning of the Prophet. Here then he shows, according to God's representation, that his cruelty was justly condemned for having anxiously desired the destruction of a populous city.

But we ought to notice all the parts of the similitude, when he says, *Thou wouldest have spared,* &c. There is an emphasis in the pronoun אתה, *ate;* for God compares himself with Jonah; "Who art thou? Doubtless a mortal man is not so inclined to mercy as I am. But thou takest to thyself this right—to desire to spare the gourd, even thou who art made of clay. Now this gourd is not thy work, *thou hast not laboured for it,* it has not proceeded from thy culture or toil; and further, *thou hast not raised it up,* and further still, *it was the daughter of a night, and in one night it perished:* it was an evanescent shrub or herb. If then thou regardest the nature of the gourd, if thou regardest thyself, and joinest together all the other circumstances, thou wilt find no reason for thy hot displeasure. But should not I, who am God, in whose hand are all things, whose prerogative and whose constant practice it is mercifully to bear with men—should not I spare them, though they were worthy of destruction ? and should not I spare a great city? The matter here is not concerning a little plant, but a large number of people. And, in the last place, it is a city, *In which there are a hundred and twenty thousand men who know not how to distinguish between their right hand and the left.*"

We now then see how emphatical are all the parts of this comparison. And though God's design was to reprove the foolish and sinful grief of Jonah, we may yet further collect a general instruction by reasoning in this manner,—"We feel for one another, and so nature inclines us, and yet we are wicked and cruel. If then men are inclined to mercy through some hidden impulse of nature, what may not be hoped from the inconceivable goodness of God, who is the Creator of the whole world, and the Father of us all? and will not he, who is the fountain of all goodness and mercy, spare us?"

Now as to the number, Jonah mentions here twelve times ten thousand men, and that is, as we have said, one hundred and twenty thousand. God shows here how paternally he cares for mankind. Every one of us is cherished by him with singular care: but yet he records here a large number, that it might be more manifest that he so much regards mankind that he will not inconsiderately fulminate against any one nation. And what he adds, that they could not distinguish between the right hand and the left, is to be referred, I have no doubt, to their age; and this opinion has been almost universally received. Some one, however, has expressed a fear lest the city should be made too large by allowing such a number of men: he has, therefore, promiscuously included the old, as well as those of middle age and infants. He says that these could not distinguish between the right hand and the left, because they had not been taught in the school of God, nor understood the difference between right and wrong; for the unbelieving, as we know, went astray in their errors. But this view is too strained; and besides, there is no reason for this comment; for that city, we know, was not only like some great cities, many of which are at this day in Europe, but it surpassed most of the principal cities at this day. We know that in Paris there are more than four hundred thousand souls: the same is the case with other cities. I therefore reject this comment, as though Jonah was here speaking of all the Ninevites. But God, on the contrary, intended to show, that though there was the justest reason for destroying entirely the whole city, there were yet other reasons which justified the suspension of so dreadful a vengeance; for many infants were there who had not, by their own transgressions, deserved such a destruction.

God then shows here to Jonah that he had been carried away by his own merciless zeal. Though his zeal, as it has been said, arose from a good principle, yet Jonah was influenced by a feeling far too vehement. This God proved, by sparing so many infants hitherto innocent. And to infants he adds the brute animals. Oxen were certainly superior to shrubs. If Jonah justly grieved for one withering shrub, it was far more deplorable and cruel for so many innocent animals to perish. We hence see how apposite are all the parts of this similitude, to make Jonah to loathe his folly, and to be ashamed of it; for he had attempted to frustrate the secret purpose of God, and in a manner to overrule it by his own will, so that the Ninevites might not be spared, who yet laboured by true repentance to anticipate the divine judgment.

PRAYER.

Grant, Almighty God, that as thou hast, in various ways, testified, and daily continuest to testify, how dear and precious to thee are mankind, and as we enjoy daily so many and so remarkable proofs of thy goodness and favour,—O grant, that we may learn to rely wholly on thy goodness, many examples of which thou settest before us, and which thou wouldest have us continually to experience, that we may not only pass through our earthly course, but also confidently aspire to the hope of that blessed and celestial life which is laid up for us in heaven, through Christ our Lord. Amen.

END OF THE COMMENTARIES ON JONAH.

THE

COMMENTARIES OF JOHN CALVIN

ON THE

PROPHET MICAH.

CALVIN'S PREFACE TO MICAH.

Among the Minor Prophets, Micah comes next, who is commonly called Micaiah.[1] But he was the second, as they say, of this name; for the first was the Micaiah who had a contest with that wicked king Ahab; and he then exercised his Prophetic office. But the second was in the same age with Isaiah, perhaps a little later: at least Isaiah had been performing his office some years before Micah had been called. It appears then that he was added to Isaiah, that he might confirm his doctrine; for that holy man had to do with an untoward people, and of a hardened neck, yea, and so wicked, that they were wholly irreclaimable. That their doctrine therefore might be more entitled to credit, it pleased God that Isaiah and Micah should deliver their message at the same time, as it were, with one mouth, and avow their consent, that all the disobedient might be proved guilty.

But I will now come to his words: for the contents of this Book suggest what is useful for our instruction.[2]

---

[1] The confusion of the name has been through the Septuagint, in which *Michaiah*, the son of Imlah, about a hundred years before, is rendered Μιχαίας, as well as this Prophet. The son of Imlah in Hebrew is מיכיהו while our Prophet is מיכה.—*Ed.*

[2] "This Book," says *Henderson*, "may be divided into two parts: the first consisting of chapters i.–v.; and the second, the two remaining chapters, which are more general and didactic in their character."

CALVIN'S PREFACE TO MICAH.

AMONG the Minor Prophets, MICAH comes next, who is commonly called MICAIAH.[1] But he was the second, as they say, of this name; for the first was the Micaiah who had a contest with the wicked king Ahab; and he then exercised his Prophetic office. But the second was in the same age with ISAIAH, perhaps a little later: at least Isaiah had been performing his office some years before Micah had been called. It appears then that he was added to Isaiah, that he might confirm his doctrine; for that holy man had to do with ungodly men, with men of a hardened neck, yea, and so wicked, that they were wholly irreclaimable. That their doctrine therefore might be more entitled to credit, it pleased God that ISAIAH and MICAH should deliver their message at the same time, as it were, with one mouth, and avow their consent, that all the disobedient might be proved guilty.

But I will now come to his words: for the contents of this Book suggest what is useful for our instruction.[2]

[1] The confusion of the name has been through the Septuagint, in which *Michaiah*, the son of Imlah, about a hundred years before, is rendered Μιχαιας, as well as this Prophet. The son of Imlah in Hebrew is מיכיה, while our Prophet is מיכה.—*Ed.*

[2] "This Book," says *Henderson*, "may be divided into two parts: the first consisting of chapters i.—v.; and the second, the two remaining chapters, which are more general and didactic in their character."

COMMENTARIES

ON

THE PROPHET MICAH.

Lecture Eighty-first.

CHAPTER I.

1. The word of the Lord that came to Micah the Morasthite in the days of Jotham, Ahaz, *and* Hezekiah, kings of Judah, which he saw concerning Samaria and Jerusalem.

1. Sermo Jehovæ qui factus est (*vel*, directus) ad Michah Morasthitem, diebus Jotham, Achaz, Jehizkiæ, regum Judæ, quem vidit super Samariam et Jerusalem.

This inscription, in the first place, shows the time in which Micah lived, and during which God employed his labours. And this deserves to be noticed: for at this day his sermons would be useless, or at least frigid, except his time were known to us, and we be thereby enabled to compare what is alike and what is different in the men of his age, and in those of our own: for when we understand that Micah condemned this or that vice, as we may also learn from the other Prophets and from sacred history, we are able to apply more easily to ourselves what he then said, inasmuch as we can view our own life as it were in a mirror. This is the reason why the Prophets are wont to mention the time in which they executed their office.

But how long Micah followed the course of his vocation we cannot with certainty determine. It is, however, probable that he discharged his office as a Prophet for thirty years:

it may be that he exceeded forty years; for he names here three kings, the first of whom, that is Jotham, reigned sixteen years; and he was followed by Ahaz, who also reigned as many years. If then Micah was called at the beginning of the first reign, he must have prophesied for thirty-two years, the time of the two kings. Then the reign of Hezekiah followed, which continued to the twenty-ninth year: and it may be, that the Prophet served God to the death, or even beyond the death, of Hezekiah.[1] We hence see that the number of his years cannot with certainty be known; though it be sufficiently evident that he taught not for a few years, but that he so discharged his office, that for thirty years he was not wearied, but constantly persevered in executing the command of God.

I have said that he was contemporary with Isaiah: but as Isaiah began his office under Uzziah, we conclude that he was older. Why then was Micah joined to him? that the Lord might thus break down the stubbornness of the people. It was indeed enough that one man was sent by God to bear witness to the truth; but it pleased God that a testimony should be borne by the mouth of two, and that holy Isaiah should be assisted by this friend and, as it were, his colleague. And we shall hereafter find that they adopted the very same words; but there was no emulation between them, so that one accused the other of theft, when he repeated what had been said. Nothing was more gratifying to each of them than to receive a testimony from his colleague; and what was committed to them by God they declared not only in the same sense and meaning, but also in the same words, and, as it were, with one mouth.

Of the expression, that the *word was sent to him*, we have elsewhere reminded you, that it ought not to be understood of private teaching, as when the word of God is addressed to individuals; but the word was given to Micah, that he might be God's ambassador to us. It means then that he came fur-

[1] It is probable that the greater part of his Prophecy was written in the days of this king; for a portion of what is contained in the *third* chapter is referred to in Jeremiah, ch. xxvi. 18, 19, as having been delivered "in the days of Hezekiah."—*Ed.*

nished with commands, as one sustaining the person of God himself; for he brought nothing of his own, but what the Lord commanded him to proclaim. But as I have elsewhere enlarged on this subject, I now only touch on it briefly.

This vision, he says, was given him against two cities, *Samaria* and *Jerusalem*.[1] It is certain that the Prophet was specifically sent to the Jews; and Maresah, from which he arose, as it appears from the inscription, was in the tribe of Judah: for Morasthite was an appellative, derived from the place Maresah.[2] But it may be asked, why does he say that visions had been given him against Samaria? We have said elsewhere, that though Hosea was specifically and in a peculiar manner destined for the kingdom of Israel, he yet by the way mingled sometimes those things which referred to the tribe or kingdom of Judah: and such was also the case with our Prophet; he had a regard chiefly to his own kindred, for he knew that he was appointed for them; but, at the same time, he overlooked not wholly the other part of the people; for the kingdom of Israel was not so divided from the tribe of Judah that no connection remained: for God was unwilling that his covenant should be abolished by their defection from the kingdom of David. We hence see, that though Micah spent chiefly his labours in behalf of the Jews, he yet did not overlook or entirely neglect the Israelites.

But the title must be restricted to one part of the book; for threatenings only form the discourse here. But we shall find that promises, full of joy, are also introduced. The inscription then does not include all the contents of the book; but as his purpose was to begin with threatenings, and to

[1] "He mentions Samaria first," says *Marckius*, "not because it was superior to Jerusalem, or more regarded by the Prophet, but because it would be first in undergoing judgment, as it had been first in transgression." The preposition על is rendered by some, "against," and not "concerning." *Calvin* renders it in his version *super*, and in his comment, *contra*.—*Ed.*

[2] It was a village, according to *Eusebius* and *Jerome*, west of Jerusalem, near Eleutheropolis, not far from the borders of the Philistines. See Josh. xv. 44; 1 Chron. iv. 21; 2 Chron. xi. 8; xiv. 10. There is another circumstance, besides that of his birth in the land of Judah, which tends to prove his special mission to the Jews,—he mentions in the first verse only the kings of Judah.—*Ed.*

terrify the Jews by setting before them the punishment that was at hand, this inscription was designedly given. There is, at the same time, no doubt but that the Prophet was ill received by the Jews on this account; for they deemed it a great indignity, and by no means to be endured, to be tied up in the same bundle with the Israelites; for Samaria was an abomination to the kingdom of Judah; and yet the Prophet here makes no difference between Samaria and Jerusalem. This was then an exasperating sentence: but we see how boldly the Prophet performs the office committed to him; for he regarded not what would be agreeable to men, nor endeavoured to draw them by smooth things: though his message was disliked, he yet proclaimed it, for he was so commanded, nor could he shake off the yoke of his vocation. Let us now proceed—

2. Hear, all ye people; hearken, O earth, and all that therein is; and let the Lord God be witness against you, the Lord from his holy temple.	2. Audite populi omnes, ausculta terra et plenitudo ejus, et sit Dominus Jehova vobis (*vel*, inter vos, *vel*, contra vos, *potius*) in testem, et Dominus è palatio (*vel*, templo) sanctitatis tuæ.

The Prophet here rises into an elevated style, being not content with a simple and calm manner of speaking. We hence may learn, that having previously tried the disposition of the people, he knew the stubbornness of almost all classes: for except he was persuaded that the people would be rebellious and obstinate, he would certainly have used some mildness, or have at least endeavoured to lead them of their own accord rather than to drive them thus violently. There is then no doubt but that the obstinacy of the people and their wickedness were already fully known to him, even before he began to address one word to them. But this difficulty did not prevent him from obeying God's command. He found it necessary in the meantime to add vehemence to his teaching; for he saw that he addressed the deaf, yea, stupid men, who were destitute of every sense of religion, and who had hardened themselves against God, and had not only fallen away through want of thought, but had also become immersed in their sins, and were wickedly and abominably obstinate in them. Since then the Prophet saw this, he makes here a bold beginning, and addresses not only his own nation, for whom he was appointed a Teacher; but he speaks to the whole world.

For what purpose does he say, *Hear, all ye people?*[1] It was not certainly his object to proclaim indiscriminately to all the truth of God for the same end: but he summons here all nations as witnesses or judges, that the Jews might understand that their impiety would be made evident to all, except they repented, and that there was no reason for them to hope that they could conceal their baseness, for God would expose their hidden crimes as it were on an open stage. We hence see how emphatical are the words, when the Prophet calls on all nations, and would have them to be witnesses of the judgment which God had resolved to bring on his people.

He afterwards adds, *Let also the earth give ear and its fulness.* We may take the earth, by metonymy, for its inhabitants; but as it is added, *and its fulness,* the Prophet, I doubt not, meant here to address the very earth itself, though it be without reason. He means that so dreadful would be the judgment of God, as to shake created things which are void of sense; and thus he more severely upbraids the Jews with their stupor, that they heedlessly neglected the word of God, which yet would shake all the elements by its power.

He then immediately turns his discourse to the Jews: after having erected God's tribunal and summoned all the

[1] שמעו עמים כלם, "Hear, ye peoples, all of them." Were it not for a similar anomaly as to number in the following line, "Give ear, thou earth, and its fulness," we might think that כלם is here a mistake for כלכם, as it is evidently the case in 1 Sam. vi. 4, and Job xvii. 10; for in these two places there are several MSS. which have כלכם, though here there is no variety. Some, to get rid of the difficulty, have suggested that כלם here is to be construed as an adverb, "universally," regarding it as assuming the same form with חנם, "gratuitously," and ריקם, "vainly." But such irregularity is common in Hebrew; there is therefore no need of having recourse to such expedients.

The word עמים, peoples, may be rendered nations: for, notwithstanding the dissent of *Drusius*, what *Horsley* says seems to be correct, that עם in the plural number designates the heathen nations, as distinguished from the people of Israel. The verse literally is this,—

Hear, ye nations,—all of them;
Give ear, thou earth,—even its fulness;
And the Lord Jehovah shall be against you a witness,
The Lord from the temple of his holiness. —*Ed.*

nations, that they might form as it were a circle of a solemn company, he says, *There will be for me the Lord Jehovah against you for a witness—the Lord from the temple of his holiness.* By saying that God would be as a witness for him, he not only affirms that he was sent by God, but being as it were inflamed with zeal, he appeals here to God, and desires him to be present, that the wickedness and obstinacy of the people might not be unpunished; as though he said, "Let God, whose minister I am, be with me, and punish your impiety; let him prove that he is the author of this doctrine, which I declare from his mouth and by his command; let him not suffer you to escape unpunished, if ye do not repent."

We now then perceive the meaning of the Prophet, when he says that God would be for him a witness; as though he had said, that there was no room here to trifle; for if the Jews thought to elude God's judgment they greatly deceived themselves; inasmuch as when he has given a command to his servants to treat with his people, he is at the same time present as a judge, and will not suffer his word to be rejected without immediately undertaking his own cause.

Nor is this addition superfluous, *The Lord from the temple of his holiness:* for we know how thoughtlessly the Jews were wont to boast that God dwelt in the midst of them. And this presumption so blinded them that they despised all the Prophets; for they thought it unlawful that any thing should be said to their disgrace, because they were the holy people of God, his holy heritage and chosen nation. Inasmuch then as the Lord had adopted them, they falsely boasted of his favours. Since then the Prophet knew that the people insolently gloried in those privileges, with which they had been honoured by God, he now declares that God would be the avenger of impiety from his temple; as though he said, "Ye boast that God is bound to you, and that he hath so bound up his faith to you as to render his name to you a sport: he indeed dwells in his temple; but from thence he will manifest himself as an avenger, as he sees that you are perverse in your wickedness." We hence see that the Prophet beats down that foolish arrogance, by which the Jews were inflated; yea, he turns back on their own heads what they were wont boastingly to bring forward. After having made this introduction, to awaken slumbering men with as much vehemence as he could, he subjoins—

3. For, behold, the Lord cometh forth out of his place, and will come down, and tread upon the high places of the earth.	3. Quia ecce Jehova egreditur è loco suo, et descendet, et calcabit super excelsa terræ:
4. And the mountains shall be molten under him, and the valleys shall be cleft, as wax before the fire, *and* as the waters *that are* poured down a steep place.	4. Et liquefient montes sub eo, et solventur (*vel*, dehiscent) valles; sicut cera à conspectu ignis, sicut aquæ in locum inferiorem actæ.

The Prophet pursues the same subject; and he dwells especially on this—that God would be a witness against his people from his sanctuary. He therefore confirms this, when he says that *God would come from his place.* Some interpreters do at the same time take this view—that the temple would hereafter be deprived of God's presence, and would hence become profane, according to what Ezekiel declares. For as the Jews imagined that God was connected with them as long as the temple stood, and this false imagination proved to them an allurement, as it were, to sin, as on this account they took to themselves greater liberty,—this was the reason why the Prophet Ezekiel declares that God was no longer in the temple; and the Lord had shown to him by a vision that he had left his temple, so that he would no longer dwell there. Some, as I have said, give a similar explanation of this passage; but this sense does not seem to suit the context. I therefore take another view of this sentence—that God would go forth from his place. But yet it is doubted what place the Prophet refers to: for many take it to be heaven, and this seems probable, for immediately after he adds, *Descend shall God, and he will tread on the high places of the earth.* This descent seems indeed to point out a higher place: but as the temple, we know, was situated on a high and elevated spot, on mount Zion, there is nothing inconsistent in saying that God descended from his temple to chastise the whole of Judea as it deserved. Then the going forth of God is by no means ambiguous in its meaning, for he means that God would at length go forth, as it were, in a visible form. With regard then to the place, I am inclined to refer it to the temple; and this clause, I have no doubt, has proceeded from the last verse.

But why is going forth here ascribed to God? Because the Jews had abused the forbearance of God in worshipping him with vain ceremonies in the temple; and at the same time they thought that they had escaped from his hand. As long then as God spared them, they thought that he was, as it were, bound to them, because he dwelt among them. Besides, as the legal and shadowy worship prevailed among them, they imagined that God rested in their temple. But now the Prophet says, "He will go forth: ye have wished hitherto to confine God to the tabernacle, and ye have attempted to pacify him with your frivolous puerilities; but ye shall know that his hand and his power extend much farther: he shall therefore come and show what that majesty is which has been hitherto a derision to you." For when hypocrites set to sale their ceremonies to God, do they not openly trifle with him, as though he were a child? and do they not thus rob him of his power and authority? Such was the senselessness of that people. The Prophet therefore does not say without reason that God would go forth, that he might prove to the Jews that they were deluded by their own vain imaginations, when they thus took away from God what necessarily belonged to him, and confined him to a corner in Judea and fixed him there, as though he rested and dwelt there like a dead idol.

The particle, *Behold*, is emphatical: for the Prophet intended here to shake off from the Jews their torpidity, inasmuch as nothing was more difficult to them than to be persuaded and to believe that punishment was nigh at hand, when they flattered themselves that God was propitious to them. Hence that they might no longer cherish this wilfulness, he says, *Behold, come shall the Lord, forth shall he go from his place.* Isaiah has a passage like this in an address to the people, chap. xxvi.; but the object of it is different; for Isaiah intended to threaten the enemies of the Church and heathen nations: but here Micah denounces war on the chosen people, and shows that God thus dwelt in his temple, that the Jews might perceive that his hand was opposed to them, as they had so shamefully despised him, and, by their false imaginations, reduced, as it were, to nothing his power.

He shall tread, he says, *on the high places of the earth.* By the high places of the earth I do not understand superstitious places, but those well fortified. We know that fortresses were then fixed, for the most part, on elevated situations. The Prophet then intimates, that there would be no place into which God's vengeance would not penetrate, however well fortified it might be: "No inclosures," he says, "shall hinder God from penetrating into the inmost parts of your fortresses; he shall tread on the high places of the earth." At the same time, I doubt not but that he alludes, by this kind of metaphor, to the chief men, who thought themselves exempted from the common lot of mankind; for they excelled so much in power, riches, and authority, that they would not be classed with the common people. The Prophet then intimates, that those, who were become proud through a notion of their own superiority, would not be exempt from punishment.

And he afterwards adds, that this going forth of God would be terrible, *Melt*, he says, *shall the mountains under him.* It hence appears, that the Prophet did not speak in the last verse of the departure of God, as though he was going to forsake his own temple, but that he, on the contrary, described his going forth from the temple, that he might ascend his tribunal and execute punishment on the whole people, and thus, in reality, prove that he would be a judge, because he had been very daringly despised. Hence he says, *Melt shall the mountains under him, the valleys shall be rent*, or cleave, *as wax before the fire, as waters rolling into a lower place.*[1] The Prophets do not often describe God in a manner so awful;

[1] These two similes, as observed by *Marckius* and others, refer not to the same thing, but to the two things previously mentioned,—the wax, to the mountains,—and the waters, to the valleys. This kind of order, in a sentence, is common in Hebrew. The *Septuagint* presents an instance, not uncommon, of an attempt to reconcile what, from not apprehending the sense, appeared incongruous; for *motion* is ascribed to the mountains—σαλευθησεται τα ορη, and *melting* to the valleys—τακησονται,

but this representation is to be referred to the circumstance of this passage, for he sets forth God here as the judge of the people: it was therefore necessary that he should be exhibited as furnished and armed with power, that he might take such vengeance on the Jews as they deserved. And other similar passages we shall hereafter meet with, and like to those which we found in Hosea. God then is said to melt the mountains, and he is said to strike the valleys with such terror that they cleave under him; in short, he is said so to terrify all elements, that the very mountains, however stony they may be, melt like wax or like waters which flow,—because he could not otherwise produce a real impression on a people so obstinate, and who, as it has been said, so flattered themselves even in their vices.

We may further easily learn what application to make of this truth in our day. We find the Papists boasting of the title Church, and, in a manner, with vain confidence, binding God to themselves, because they have baptism, though they have adulterated it with their superstitions; and then, they think that they have Christ, because they still retain the name of a Church. Had the Lord promised that

quite contrary to the meaning of the words in Hebrew. *Newcome* renders the last line thus,—

"As waters poured down a steep place."

Henderson renders the last word, "a precipice;" and *Marckius*, *declive*—"a declivity." I would give this version of the whole verse,—

For, behold, Jehovah shall go forth from his place;
Yea, he shall descend and tread on the high places of the land;
And dissolve shall the mountains under him,
And the valleys shall burst forth;
Like the wax before the fire,
Like waters rolling down a declivity.

The verb בקע is applied to express the bursting out of waters from a fountain, of the young when emerging from the egg, and of light dispelling darkness. It is here in Hithpael, and only in one other place, Joshua ix. 13; where it means the bursting of wine bottles, made of leather. The word מורד is going down, descent, declivity; *καταβασις*, *Sept.* See Joshua x. 11; Jer. xlviii. 5.

"Do men trust to the height and strength of mountains, as if they were sufficient to bear up their hopes and bear off their fears? They shall be *molten* under him.—Do they trust to the fruitfulness of the valleys and their products? They shall be cleft, or rent,—and be wasted away as the ground is by the waters that are poured down a steep place."—*Henry*.

his dwelling would be at Rome, we yet see how foolish and frivolous would be such boasting: for though the temple was at Jerusalem, yet the Lord went forth thence to punish the sins of the people, yea, even of the chosen people. We further know, that it is folly to bind God now to one place, for it is his will that his name should be celebrated without any difference through the whole world. Wheresoever, then, the voice of the Gospel sounds, God would have us to know that he is present there. What the Papists then proudly boast of—that Christ is joined to them—will turn out to their own condemnation;—why so? Because the Lord will prove that he is the avenger of so impious and shameful a profanation, as they not only presumptuously lay claim to his name, but also tear it in pieces, and contaminate it with their sacrilegious abominations.

Again, since God is said to melt the mountains with his presence, let us hence learn to rouse up all our feelings whenever God comes forth, not that we may flee to a distance from him, but that we may reverently receive his word, so that he may afterwards appear to us a kind and reconciled Father. For when we become humble, and the pride and height of our flesh is subdued, he then immediately receives us, as it were, into his gentle bosom, and gives us an easy access to him, yea, he invites us to himself with all possible kindness. That the Lord then may thus kindly receive us, let us learn to fear as soon as he utters his voice: but let not this fear make us to flee away, but only humble us, so that we may render true obedience to the word of the Lord. It follows—

5. For the transgression of Jacob *is* all this, and for the sins of the house of Israel. What *is* the transgression of Jacob? *is it* not Samaria? And what *are* the high places of Judah? *Are they* not Jerusalem?

5. Propter scelus[1] Jacob totum hoc, et propter transgressiones domus Israel: quod scelus Jacob? Annon Samaria? Et quæ excelsa Jehudah? Annon Jerusalem?

[1] פשע, rendered *scelus*—wickedness, by *Calvin*, means evidently *defectio*—defection—apostacy, as rendered by *Junius* and *Tremelius*. חטאות, *transgressiones*—transgressions, rather, sins. Several MSS. and the Septuagint have חטאת, *sin;* but the plural is more suitable to this place, to correspond with the high places at the end of the verse. It is evident, from the context, that *Jacob* means Samaria or the ten tribes, and that

The Prophet teaches, in this verse, that God is not angry for nothing; though when he appears rigid, men expostulate with him, and clamour as though he were cruel. That men may, therefore, acknowledge that God is a just judge, and that he never exceeds moderation in punishments, the Prophet here distinctly states that there was a just cause, why God denounced so dreadful a judgment on his chosen people,—even because not only a part of the people, but the whole body had, through their impiety, fallen away; for by the house of Jacob, and by the house of Israel, he means that impiety had everywhere prevailed, so that no part was untainted. The meaning then is,—that the contagion of sin had spread through all Israel, that no portion of the country was free from iniquity, that no corner of the land could bring an excuse for its defection; the Lord therefore shows that he would be the judge of them all, and would spare neither small nor great.

We now then understand the Prophet's object in this verse: As he had before taught how dreadful would be God's vengeance against all the ungodly, so now he mentions their crimes, that they might not complain that they were unjustly treated, or that God employed too much severity. The Pro-

the *house*, or family of *Israel*, means what is not usual, the tribe of Judah. (See 2 Chron. xxviii. 19.) Israel seems here to be taken as a special distinction of God's people. Judah was still in name the true Israel, while the ten tribes were apostates from the faith.

It is better to adopt the future tense in this verse, that it may correspond with the preceding. When the auxiliary verb is supplied, it must ever be regulated as to its tense by the context. Then the first line should be,—

For the defection of Jacob *shall* all this *be*.

Or, it may be rendered, "*shall* all these things *be*," כל־זאת; for זאת is plural as well as singular; and παντα ταυτα is the rendering of the Septuagint.

Grotius and some others give this version of the four last lines,—

What is *the origin* of the defection of Jacob?
Is it not Samaria?
What is *the origin* of the high places of Judah?
Is it not Jerusalem?

Who, or what is the defection of Jacob? no doubt means, Who is the author, or what is the cause or origin of his defection? It is the same form of expression, as when it is said, that God is our salvation, that is, the author of it.—*Ed.*

phet then testifies that the punishment, then near at hand, would be just.

He now adds, *What is the wickedness of Jacob?* The Prophet, no doubt, indirectly reproves here the hypocrisy which ruled dominant among the people. For he asks not for his own satisfaction or in his own person; but, on the contrary, he relates, by way of imitation, (μιμητικῶς—imitatively,) what he knew to be ever on their lips, "Oh! what sort of thing is this sin? Why! thou assumest here a false principle,—that we are wicked men, ungodly and perfidious: thou doest us a grievous wrong." Inasmuch, then, as hypocrites thought themselves pure, having wiped, as it were, their mouths, whenever they eluded reproofs by their sophistries, the Prophet borrows a question, as it were, from their own lips, "Of what kind is this wickedness? Of what sort is that transgression?" As though he said, "I know what ye are wont to do, when any one of the Prophets severely reproves you; ye instantly contend with him, and are ready with your objections: but what do you gain? If you wish to know what your wickedness is, it is Samaria; and where your high places are, they are at Jerusalem." It is the same as if he had said, "I do not here contend with the common people, but I attack the first men: my contest then is with the princes themselves, who surpass others in dignity, and are, therefore, unwilling to be touched."

But it sometimes happens that the common people become degenerated, while some integrity remains among the higher orders: but the Prophet shows that the diseases among the people belonged to the principal men; and hence he names the two chief cities, Jerusalem and Samaria, as he had said before, in the first verse, that he proclaimed predictions against these: and yet it is certain, that the punishment was to be in common to the whole people. But as they thought that Jerusalem and Samaria would be safe, though the whole country were destroyed, the Prophet threatens them by name: for, relying first on their strength, they thought themselves unassailable; and then, the eyes of nearly all, we know, were dazzled with empty splendour, power, and dignity: thus the ungodly wholly forget that they are men, and what they owe to God, when elevated in the world. So great an arrogance could not be subdued, except by sharp and severe words, such as the Prophet, as we see, here employs. He then says, that the *wickedness of Israel* was *Samaria;* the fountain of all iniquities was the royal city, which yet ought to have ruled the whole land with wisdom and justice: but what any more remains, when kings and their counsellors tread under foot all regard for what is just and right, and having cast away every shame, rise up in rebellion against God and men? When therefore kings thus fall from their dignity, an awful ruin must follow.

This is the reason why the Prophet says that the wickedness of Israel was Samaria, that thence arose all iniquities. But we must at the same time bear in mind, that the Prophet speaks not here of gross crimes; but, on the contrary, he directs his reproof against ungodly and perverted forms of worship; and this appears more evident from the second clause, in which he mentions transgressions in connection with the high places. We hence see, that all sins in general are not here reproved, but their vicious modes of worship, by which religion had been polluted among the Jews as well as the Israelites. But it might seem very unjust, that the Prophet should charge with sin those forms of worship in which the Jews laboriously exercised themselves with the object of pacifying God. But we see how God regards as nothing whatever men blend with his worship out of their own heads. And this is our principal contest at this day with the Papists; we call their perverted and spurious modes of worship abominations: they think that what is heavenly is to be blended with what is earthly. "We diligently labour," they say, "for this end—that God may be worshipped." True; but, at the same time, ye profane his worship by your inventions; and it is therefore an abomination. We now then see how foolish and frivolous are those delusions, when men follow their own wisdom in the duty of worshipping God: for the Prophet here, in the name of God, fulminates, as it were, from heaven against all superstitions, and shows that no sin is more detestable, than that preposterous caprice with which idolaters are inflamed, when they observe such forms of worship as they have themselves invented.

Now with regard to the *high places*, we must notice, that there was a great difference between the Jews and the Israelites at that time as to idolatry. The Israelites had so fallen, that they were altogether degenerated; nothing could be seen among them that had an affinity to the true and legitimate worship of God: but the Jews had retained some form of religion, they had not thus abandoned themselves; but yet they had a mixture of superstitions; such as one would find, were he to compare the gross Popery of this day with that middle course which those men invent, who seem to themselves to be very wise, fearing, forsooth, as they do, the offences of the world; and hence they form for us a mixture, I know not what, from the superstitions of the Papacy and from the Reformation, as they call it. Something like this was the mixture at Jerusalem. We however see, that the Prophet pronounces the same sentence against the Jews and the Israelites, and that is, that God will allow nothing that proceeds from the inventions of men to be joined to his word. Since then God allows no such mixtures, the Prophet here says, that there was no less sin on the high places of Judea, than there was in those filthy abominations which were then dominant among the people of Israel. But the remainder we must defer until to-morrow.

PRAYER.

Grant, Almighty God, that, since to a perverse, and in every way a rebellious people, thou didst formerly show so much grace, as to exhort them continually to repentance, and to stretch forth thy hand to them by thy Prophets,—O grant, that the same word may sound in our ears; and when we do not immediately profit by thy teaching, O cast us not away, but, by thy Spirit, so subdue all our thoughts and affections, that we, being humbled, may give glory to thy majesty, such as is due to thee, and that, being allured by thy paternal favour, we may submit ourselves to thee, and, at the same time, embrace that mercy which thou offerest and presentest to us in Christ, that we may not doubt but thou wilt be a Father to us, until we shall at length enjoy that eternal inheritance, which has been obtained for us by the blood of thine only-begotten Son. Amen.

Lecture Eighty-second.

6. Therefore I will make Samaria as an heap of the field, *and* as plantings of a vineyard; and I will pour down the stones thereof into the valley, and I will discover the foundations thereof.

6. Et ponam Samariam (*hoc est*, ideo; ו *enim hic sumitur pro illativa particula;* ponam *igitur* Samariam) in acervum agri, in plantationes vinæ; et devolvam in vallem lapides ejus, et fundamenta ejus retegam.

Though Micah intended especially to devote his services to the Jews, as we have said yesterday, he yet, in the first place, passes judgment on Samaria; for it was his purpose afterwards to speak more fully against Jerusalem and the whole of Judea. And this state of the case ought to be borne in mind; for the Prophet does not begin with the Israelites, because he directs his discourse peculiarly to them; but his purpose was briefly to reprove them, and then to address more especially his own people, for it was for this purpose that he was called. Now, as he threatens destruction to Samaria and the whole kingdom of Israel on account of their corrupted forms of worship, we may hence learn how displeasing to God is superstition, and that he regards nothing so much as the true worship of his name. There is no reason here for men to advance this position—that they do not designedly sin; for God shows how he is to be worshipped by us. Whenever, then, we deviate in any thing from the rule which he has prescribed, we manifest, in that particular, our rebellion and obstinacy. Hence the superstitious ever act like fools with regard to God, for they will not submit to his word, so as to be thereby alone made wise.

And he says, *I will set Samaria as an heap of the field*, that is, such shall be the ruins, that they shall differ nothing from the heaps of the fields: for husbandmen, we know, when they find stones in their fields, throw them into some corner, that they may not be in the way of the plough. Like such heaps, then, as are seen in the fields, Samaria would be, according to what God declares. He then says, that the place would be empty, so that *vines* would be *planted* there; and, in the third place, that its *stones* would be *scattered* through the *val-*

ley: as when one casts stones where there is a wide plain, they run and roll far and wide; so would be the scattering of Samaria according to what the Prophet says, it was to be like the rolling of stones in a wide field. He adds, in the fourth place, *I will uncover her foundations*, that is, I will entirely demolish it, so that a stone, as Christ says, may not remain on a stone, (Matth. xxiv. 2.) We now perceive the import of the words; and we also perceive that the reason why the Prophet denounces on Samaria so severe a judgment was, because it had corrupted the legitimate worship of God with its own inventions; for it had devised, as we well know, many idols, so that the whole authority of the law had been abolished among the Israelites. It now follows—

7. And all the graven images thereof shall be beaten to pieces, and all the hires thereof shall be burned with the fire, and all the idols thereof will I lay desolate: for she gathered *it* of the hire of an harlot, and they shall return to the hire of an harlot.

7. Et omnia sculptilia[1] ejus diruentur, et omnes mercedes ejus exurentur igne (*alii transferunt*, donaria,) et omnia idola ejus ponam in vastitatem; quia è mercede meretricis congregavit, et ad mercedem meretricis revertentur.

The Prophet goes on with the same subject, and says, that the ruin of Samaria was at hand, so that its idols would be broken, and also, that its wealth would be destroyed, which she had gathered by illegitimate means, and which she thought to be the reward of her idolatry. But God mentions idols here expressly by his Prophet, in order to confirm what we noticed yesterday—that the cause of vengeance was, because Samaria had abandoned itself to ungodly forms of wor-

[1] פסילים, from פסל, to chip or cut with a tool. They were graven or carved images, made of wood, and overlaid with gold or silver.

"The *graven* image," says *Bishop Horsley*, "was not a thing wrought in metal by the tool of the workman we should now call an engraver; nor was the *molten* image an image made of metal. In fact, the graven image and the molten image are the same thing under different names. The images of the ancient idolaters were first cut out of wood by the carpenter, as is very evident from the Prophet Isaiah. This figure of wood was overlaid with plates, either of gold or of silver, or, sometimes perhaps, of an inferior metal. And, in this finished state, it was called a graven image, *i.e.*, a carved image, in reference to the inner solid figure of wood, and a molten, *i.e.*, an overlaid or covered image, in reference to the outward metalline case or covering: and sometimes both epithets are applied to it at once, 'I will cut off the graven and molten image,' Nah. i. 14." See also Deut. vii. 25; Isa. xxx. 22.—*Ed.*

ship, and had departed from the Law. That the Israelites might then understand the cause for which God would so severely punish them, the Prophet here makes express mention of their graven images and idols. God is not indeed angry with stones and wood; but he observes the abuse and the perversion of them, when men pollute themselves by wickedly worshipping such things. This is the reason why God says here that the graven images of Samaria would be broken in pieces, and that its idols would be destroyed.

With regard to the *wages*, the Prophet no doubt designed to stamp with disgrace all the wealth of Samaria. אתנן, *atanen*, is properly a gift or a present. But as he twice repeats it, and says, that what Samaria possessed was the *reward of an harlot*, and then, that it would *return to the reward of an harlot*, he, in the first place, I have no doubt, upbraids the Israelites, because they, after the manner of harlots and strumpets, had heaped together their great riches: and this was done by Jeroboam, who constructed a new form of worship, in order to secure his own kingdom. The Israelites then began to flourish; and we also know how wealthy that kingdom became, and how proud they were on account of their riches. As, then, the Israelites despised the kingdom of Judah, and thought themselves in every way happy, and as they ascribed all this, as we have seen in Hosea, to their superstitions, Micah speaks here according to their view of things, when he says, "Idolatry has been gainful to you, this splendour dazzles your eyes; but your rewards I have already doomed to the burning: they shall then be burnt, and thus perish." Hosea also, as we have seen, made use of the same comparison,—that the children of Israel felicitated themselves in their impiety, like a harlot, who, while she gains many presents from those who admire her beauty, seems not conscious of her turpitude and baseness: such were the Israelites. The Prophet, therefore, does not say, without reason, *Behold, your rewards, by burning, shall perish*, or, be consumed with fire. Why so? Because ye have gathered them, he says, from the reward of an harlot, and all this shall return to the reward of an harlot.

This last clause ought to be restricted to the gifts or wealth of Samaria; for it cannot properly be applied to idols or graven images. The import of the whole then is, that God would be the avenger of idolatry with regard to the city of Samaria and the whole kingdom of Israel. Besides, as the Israelites boasted that their ungodly forms of worship turned out to their happiness and prosperity, God declares that the whole of this success would be evanescent, like that of the harlot, who amasses great wealth, which soon vanishes away: and we see that thus it commonly happens.

Some explain the passage thus,—that the gifts, with which the Israelites adorned their temples, would return to be the reward of an harlot, that is, would be transferred to Chaldea, and that the Babylonians would, in their turn, adorn with them their idols. But this view is not suitable to the place; for the Prophet does not say that what Samaria had gathered would be a prey or a spoil to enemies, but that it would perish by fire.[1] He speaks, therefore, proverbially, when he says that the produce, from the reward of an harlot, would return to be the reward of an harlot, that is, that it would become nothing; for the Lord sets a curse on such riches as strumpets gain by their baseness, while they prostitute themselves. Since, then, the whole of such wealth is under the curse of God, it must necessarily soon pass away like smoke: and this, in my view, is the real meaning of the Prophet. It now follows—

8. Therefore I will wail and howl; I will go stripped and naked: I will make a wailing like the dragons, and mourning as the owls.	8. Super hoc plangam et ululabo; incedam spoliatus et nudus; faciam planctum tanquam draconum, et luctum tanquam filiarum struthionis:[2]

[1] The view given above is the one embraced by *Henderson;* but the reason here given renders it improbable. *Newcome* mentions the above, and also the following, "She imputed her wealth to her spiritual idolatry, and her conquerors shall distribute it as the reward of harlots in the literal sense." But inasmuch as it is said, that her rewards would be burnt, it is more consistent to take the last clause as a proverbial expression, signifying the destruction of all the wealth that was ascribed to idolatry as its source.

"It is common," says *Henry,* "that what is squeezed out by one lust, is squandered away by another."—*Ed.*

[2] All the verbs in this verse are in the Septuagint in the third person, κοψεται—"she will mourn," &c. The whole is applied to Samaria. The Hebrew will admit of this sense, if the verbs be considered to be, as

9. For her wound *is* incurable; for it is come unto Judah: he is come unto the gate of my people, *even* to Jerusalem.	9. Quia acerbæ sunt plagæ ejus (*est mutatio numeri;*) quia venit usque ad Jehudam; accessit ad portam populi mei, ad Jerusalem.

The Prophet here assumes the character of a mourner, that he might more deeply impress the Israelites; for we have seen that they were almost insensible in their torpidity. It was therefore necessary that they should be brought to view the scene itself, that, seeing their destruction before their eyes, they might be touched both with grief and fear. Lamentations of this kind are everywhere to be met with in the Prophets, and they ought to be carefully noticed; for we hence gather how great was the torpor of men, inasmuch as it was necessary to awaken them, by this form of speech, in order to convince them that they had to do with God: they would have otherwise continued to flatter themselves with delusions. Though indeed the Prophet here addresses the Israelites, we ought yet to apply this to ourselves; for we are not much unlike the ancient people: for however God may terrify us with dreadful threatenings, we still remain quiet in our filth. It is therefore needful that we should be severely treated, for we are almost void of feeling.

they may be, in Hiphil, the omission of the י is not uncommon. Then the rendering of the two verses will be the following:—

8. I will therefore make her to moan and to howl,
I will cause her to go stripped and naked;
I will make her to moan like the whales,
And to wail like the ostriches:
9. For grievous *will be* her stroke;
Yea, it *will* come even to Judah,
Reaching to the gate of my people—to Jerusalem.

תנים, rendered "dragons" in our common version, and by Calvin, and by many others, is rendered "foxes" by *Newcome*, "wolves" by *Henderson*, but by *Bochart*, "whales," or those species called "dolphins;" and *Professor Lee*, in his Notes on Job xl. 25, seems to be of the same opinion. The mournful groans of the dolphins, when taken, are said to be extremely distressing; their doleful moanings, too, in the night, when at liberty, have been testified by historians.—בנות יענה, "owls" in our version, is rendered both by *Calvin* and *Newcome*, "daughters of the ostrich," and by *Henderson*, "ostriches." The Septuagint has θυγατερων σειρηνων—"the daughters of sea-monsters:" στρουθοκαμηλων—"camel-sparrows—ostriches," is the rendering of *Aquila* and *Symmachus*. The literal expression is, "the daughters of the ostrich," meaning evidently the females. *Dr Shaw*, as quoted by *Newcome*, says, "During the lonesome part of the night, they often make a very doleful and hideous noise. I have often heard them groan, as if they were in the greatest agonies; an action beautifully alluded to by the Prophet Micah."—*Ed.*

But the Prophets sometimes assumed mourning, and sometimes they were touched with real grief: for when they spoke of aliens and also of the enemies of the Church, they introduce these lamentations. When a mention is made of Babylon or of Egypt, they sometimes say, "Behold, I will mourn, and my bowels shall be as a timbrel." The Prophets did not then really grieve; but, as I have said, they transferred to themselves the sorrows of others, and ever with this object,—that they might persuade men that God's threatenings were not vain, and that God did not trifle with men when he declared that he was angry with them. But when the discourse was respecting the Church and the faithful, then the Prophets did not put on grief. The representation here is then to be taken in such a way as that we may understand that the Prophet was in real mourning, when he saw that a dreadful ruin was impending over the whole kingdom of Israel. For though they had perfidiously departed from the Law, they were yet a part of the holy race, they were the children of Abraham, whom God had received into favour. The Prophet, therefore, could not refrain from mourning unfeignedly for them. And the Prophet does here these two things,—he shows the fraternal love which he entertained for the children of Israel, as they were his kindred, and a part of the chosen people,—and he also discharges his own duty; for this lamentation was, as it were, the mirror in which he sets before them the vengeance of God towards men so extremely torpid. He therefore exhibits to them this representation, that they might perceive that God was by no means trifling with men, when he thus denounced punishment on the wicked and such as were apostates.

Moreover, he speaks not of a common lamentation, but says, *I will wail and howl,* and then, *I will go spoiled.* The word שׁוֹלָל, *shulal,* some take as meaning one out of his mind or insane, as though he said, "I shall be now as one not possessed of a sound mind." But as this metaphor is rather unnatural, I prefer the sense of being spoiled; for it was the custom with mourners, as it is well known, to tear and to throw away their garments from them. *I will* then *go spoiled and naked;* and also, I will *make wailing,* not like that of men, but like the wailing *of dragons:* I will mourn, he says, as the ostriches are wont to do. In short, the Prophet by these forms of speech intimates, that the coming evil would by no means be of an ordinary kind: for if he adopted the usual manner of men, he could not have set forth the dreadfulness of God's vengeance that was impending.

He afterwards subjoins, that the wounds would be grievous; but he speaks as of what was present, *Grievous,* he says, *are the wounds. Grievous* means properly full of grief; others render it desperate or incurable, but it is a meaning which suits not this place; for אנושה, *anushe,* means what we express in French by *douloureuse. The wounds,* then, *are full of grief: for it came,* (something is understood; it may suitably be referred to the enemy, or, what is more approved, to the slaughter)—*It came* then, that is, th slaughter,[1] *to Judah; it hath reached to the gate of my people,* even *to Jerusalem itself.* He says first, *to Judah,* speaking of the land; and then he confines it to the cities; for when the gates are closed up against enemies, they are forced to stop. But the Prophet says, that the cities would be no hinderance to the enemies to approach the very gates and even the chief city of Judah, that is, Jerusalem; and this, we know, was fulfilled. It is the same then as though he said, that the whole kingdom of Israel would be so laid waste, that their enemies would not be content with victory, but would proceed farther, and besiege the holy city: and this Sennacherib did. For after having subverted the kingdom of Israel, as though it was not enough to draw the ten tribes into exile, he resolved to take possession of the kingdom of Judah; and Jerusalem, as Isaiah says, was left as a tent. We hence see that the threatenings of the Prophet Micah were not in vain. It now follows—

[1] Or rather the stroke before mentioned; for the true reading is no doubt מכתה, her wound or her stroke, in the singular. Though there are but two MSS. which have this reading, yet the previous participial noun, אנושה, being singular, and the following verbs or participles being in the same number, favour this supposition. The corresponding word in the Septuagint is also in the singular number—ἡ πληγη ἀυτης, her stroke, stripe, or scourge.—*Ed.*

10. Declare ye it not at Gath, weep ye not at all: in the house of Aphrah roll thyself in the dust.	10. In Gath ne annuntietis, flendo ne fleatis;[1] propter domum Aphrah pulvere te involve (*vel*, voluta te in pulvere.)

The Prophet seems here to be inconsistent with himself: for he first describes the calamity that was to be evident to all; but now he commands silence, lest the report should reach the enemies. But there is here nothing contradictory; for the evil itself could not be hid, since the whole kingdom of Israel would be desolated, the cities demolished or burnt, the whole country spoiled and laid waste, and then the enemies would enter the borders of Judah: and when Jerusalem should have been nearly taken, how could it have been concealed? No, this could not have been. There is no wonder then that the Prophet had referred here to a solemn mourning. But he now speaks of the feeling of those who were desirous of hiding their own disgrace, especially from their enemies and aliens: for it is an indignity which greatly vexes us, when enemies taunt us, and upbraid us in our misfortunes; when no hope remains, we at least wish to perish in secret, so that no reproach and disgrace should accompany our death; for dishonour is often harder to be borne, and wounds us more grievously, than any other evil. The Prophet then means that the Israelites would not only be miserable, but would also be subject to the reproaches and taunts of their enemies. We indeed know that the Philistines were inveterate in their hatred to the people of God; and we know that they ever took occasion to upbraid them with their evils and calamities.

This then is the meaning of the Prophet, when he says, *In Gath declare it not, by weeping weep not;* as though he said, "Though extreme evils shall come upon you, yet seek to perish in silence; for you will find that your enemies will gape for the opportunity to cut you with their taunts, when they shall see you thus miserable." He then forbids the

[1] *Henderson* renders this clause, "weep not in Acco," and mentions *Gesenius* and others, who consider that בכו is put here for בעכו, and Ocu or Acco was a town in the tribe of Asher; see Judges i. 31. The Septuagint favours this rendering, at least in one copy, for it has εν ακειμ, though in Judges the name is Ακχω.—*Ed.*

people's calamities to be told *in Gath;* for the Philistines usually desired nothing more than the opportunity to torment the people of God with reproaches.

It now follows, *In the house of Aphrah, in dust roll thyself.* There is here an alliteration which cannot be conveyed in Latin: for עפרה, *ophre,* means dusty, and עפר, *opher,* is dust. That city attained its name from its situation, because the country where it was, was full of dust; as if a city were called Lutosa, muddy or full of clay; and indeed many think that Lutetia (Paris) had hence derived its name. And he says, *Roll thyself in dust, in the house full of dust;* as though he had said, that the name would be now most suitable, for the ruin of the city would constrain all neighbouring cities to be in mourning, to cast themselves in the dust; so great would be the extremity of their evils.

But we must ever bear in mind the object of the Prophet: for he here rouses the Israelites as it were with the sharpest goads, who entertained no just idea of the dreadfulness of God's vengeance, but were ever deaf to all threatenings. The Prophet then shows that the execution of this vengeance which he denounced was ready at hand; and he himself not only mourned, but called others also to mourning. He speaks of the whole country, as we shall see by what follows. I shall quickly run over the whole of this chapter; for there is no need of long explanation, as you will find.

11. Pass ye away, thou inhabitant of Saphir, having thy shame naked: the inhabitant of Zaanan came not forth in the mourning of Beth-ezel; he shall receive of you his standing.

11. Transi pariter (*ad verbum,* transi vobis[1]) habitatrix Saphir, nuda probrosè; non egredietur habitatrix Zaanan in luctu Beth-Aezel, sumet à vobis stationem suam (*alii vertunt,* substantiam; *sed malè, meo judicio.*)

[1] עברי לכם, pass over or migrate, as to you. One MS. has לך, as to thee; but the anomaly of number is common through all the Prophets. "The inhabitant" here is a poetical noun of number, including the whole people. What usage has thus sanctioned in one language, cannot at all times be retained in another. We must in the present instance make "Inhabitant" in our language plural, or לכם, "as to you, or, yea, you," singular. The latter is the best mode. Then as to the peculiar form of לכם or לך after an imperative, we have similar instances; see Gen. xii. 1; Jer. v. 5; Hosea vii. 12. It is an emphatic mode of speaking. The sentence here may be thus expressed, "Pass thou over, yea, thou, O inhabitant of Saphir." Amaziah said to Amos, ברח לך, "Flee, yea, thou," &c. Or to give to ל its most usual meaning, we may suppose "I say" to be understood; then it would be, "Flee, *I say,* to thee."—*Ed.*

The Prophet here addresses the cities which were on the borders of the kingdom of Israel, and through which the enemy would pass in entering the kingdom of Judah. He therefore bids the inhabitants of the city Saphir to pass over, and says, that the city would be ashamed, or in a shameful manner naked. The word שפיר, *Shaphir*, means splendid. He then says, "Thou art now beautiful, but the Lord will discover thy shame, so that thy nakedness shall be a shame to all, and the greatest disgrace to thyself." There is a correspondence in the words, though not an alliteration. Hence the Prophet says, that though the city was called splendid, it would yet be deformed, so that no one would deign to look on it, at least without feeling shame. There is the same correspondence in the word Zaanan; for צעה, *tsoe*, means to transfer, as צען, *tson*, is to migrate. Hence the Prophet says, *Go forth shall not the inhabitant of Zaanan for the mourning of Beth-Aezel;* that is, he will remain quiet at home: this he will do contrary to what will be natural; for whence is the name of the city? even from removing, for it was a place of much traffic. But he will remain, he says, at home: though he may see his neighbours dragged into exile, he will not dare to move from his place.

He now adds, *Take will the enemy from you his station.* The verb עמד, *omad*, means to stand; nor is there a doubt but that when the Prophet says, He will take from you his standing, he speaks of the standing or station of the enemy: but interpreters however vary here. Some understand, that when the enemy had continued long in the land, they would not depart before they possessed the supreme power; as though he said, "Ye will think that your enemy can be wearied out with delay and tediousness, when not able soon to conquer your cities: this, he says, will not be the case; for he will resolutely persevere, and his expectation will not disappoint him; for he will receive the reward of his station, that is, of his delay." But some say, "He will receive his station from you." They explain the verb לקח, *lakech*, metaphorically, as meaning to receive instruction from hand to hand; as though the Prophet had said, "Some," that is, "your neighbours, will learn their own position from you." What does this mean? Zaanan will not go forth on account of the mourning of its neighbouring city Aezel: others will afterwards follow this example. How so? For Zaanan will be, as it were, the teacher to other cities; as it will not dare to show any sign of grief for its neighbours, being not able to succour them; so also, when it shall be taken in its turn into exile, that is, its citizens and inhabitants, its neighbours will remain quiet, as though the condition of the miserable city was no object of their care. "They shall then learn from you their standing;" that is, "Ye will remain quiet and still, when your neighbours will be destroyed; the same thing will afterwards happen to you." But as this bears but little on the main subject, we may take either of these views.[1] It afterwards follows—

[1] This verse is variously rendered; by *Newcome* thus,—

Pass on, thou inhabitress of Saphir, naked and in confusion.
The inhabitants of Zanan went not forth to wailing.
O Beth-Ezel, he shall receive of you *the reward of* his station *against you.*

By *Henderson* thus,—

Pass on, thou inhabitant of Shaphir, naked and ashamed;
The inhabitant of Zanan goeth not forth;
The wailing of Beth-Ezel will take away continuance from you.

It seems more consistent to take all the verbs in this and the preceding verse as imperatives, though they be not in the same person. Those in the second are evidently so; and I would render such as are in third person as imperatives too. That Saphir, Zaanan, &c., as well as those which follow, are not appellatives, but proper names of places within or on the borders of Judah, is what is allowed by most, though not by all, especially by some of the ancient commentators, at least with regard to some of the names. I offer the following version of the tenth and eleventh verses,—

10. In Gath declare ye it not, in Acco weep not;
In Beth-Ophrah, roll thyself in dust:
11. Pass thou over, yea, thou, O inhabitant of Saphir,
Naked *and* in shame;
Let not the inhabitant of Zaanan go forth wailing;
Let Beth-Azel take from you its position;
that is, follow your example.

The last word, עמדתו, presents the greatest difficulty. It is found here alone in this form. It occurs as עמד, a pillar, a station, עמוד, a stand, stage, and as מעמד, a standing, and also a state, Isa. xxii. 19. *Buxtorf* gives the same meaning to the last with the one in the text, *constitutio*, constitution, a fixed order of things. The verb עמד signifies to stand, to stand erect, to remain the same, either in motion or at rest, to continue. Hence it may rightly signify a position, a standing, that is taken and maintained.—*Ed.*

12. For the inhabitant of Maroth waited carefully for good; but evil came down from the Lord unto the gate of Jerusalem.

12. Quia doluit propter bonum (*alii*, expectavit ad bonum; *alii*, infirmata est) habitatrix Maroth; quia descendit malum à Jehova ad portam Jerusalem.

The Prophet joins here another city, even *Maroth*, and others also in the following verses. But in this verse he says, that Maroth would be in sorrow for a lost good. The verb חול, *chul*, means to grieve; and it has this sense here; for the Marothites, that is, the inhabitants of that city, would have to grieve for losing their property and their former happy condition. But as the verb means also to expect, some approve of a different exposition, that is,—that the inhabitants of the city Maroth would in vain depend on an empty and fallacious expectation, for they were doomed to utter destruction. In vain then will the inhabitant of Maroth expect or entertain hope; for *an evil descends from Jehovah to the gate of the city.* This view is the most suitable, that is, that its hope will disappoint Maroth, since even the city of Jerusalem shall not be exempted. For though God had then by a miracle delivered the chief city, and its siege was raised through the intervention of an angel, when a dreadful slaughter, as sacred history records, took place; yet the city Maroth was not then able to escape vengeance. We now see the reason why this circumstance was added. Some give a harsher explanation,—that the citizens of Maroth were to be debilitated, or, as it were, demented. As this metaphor is too strained, I embrace the other,—that the citizens of Maroth *would grieve for* the loss *of good*,[1] or that they would vainly expect or hope, since they were already doomed to utter ruin, without any hope of deliverance.

But we must notice, that *evil was nigh at hand from Jehovah*, for he reminds them, that though the whole country would be desolated by the Assyrians, yet God would be the chief

[1] *Grieving* is the idea commonly given to the verb here used. "Dolebit, will grieve," *Grotius*,—"Parturit, travails," *Marckius*,—"Pineth," *Henderson*. *Newcome*, following the mere conjecture of *Houbigant* changes the original, and substitutes למות for לטוב, and gives this version,—"is sick unto death." Not only is this wholly unwarranted, but it destroys the evident contrast there is in the verse—the good and the evil. —*Ed.*

leader, since he would employ the work of all those who would afflict the people of Israel. That the Jews then, as well as the Israelites, might know that they had to do, not with men only, but also with God, the celestial Judge, the Prophet distinctly expresses that all this would proceed from Jehovah. He afterwards adds—

13. O thou inhabitant of Lachish, bind the chariot to the swift beast: she *is* the beginning of the sin to the daughter of Zion; for the transgressions of Israel were found in thee.

13. Alliga currum ad camelum (*vel*, dromedarium; *alii vertunt*, equos celeres) habitatrix Lachis: principium sceleris ipsa est filiæ Zion; quia in te inventæ sunt transgressiones Israel.

By bidding the citizens of Lachish to tie their chariots to dromedaries, he intimates that it would not be now safe for them to remain in their city, and that nothing would be better for them than to flee elsewhere and to carry away their substance. "Think," he says, "of flight, and of the quickest flight." The word רכש, *recash*, which I render dromedary or camel, is of an uncertain meaning among the Hebrews; some render it swift horses: but we understand the Prophet's meaning; for he intimates that there would be no time for flight, except they made great haste, for the enemies would come upon them quickly.

And he then subjoins, that that city had been the beginning of sin to the Jews; for though he names here the daughter of Zion, he still includes, by taking a part for the whole, all the Jews. And why he says that Lachish had been the beginning of sin to the citizens of Jerusalem, we may collect from the next clause, *In thee*, he says, *were found the transgressions of Israel.* The citizens of Lachish were then, no doubt, the first who had embraced the corruptions of Jeroboam, and had thus departed from the pure worship of God. When, therefore, contagion had entered that city, it crept, by degrees, into neighbouring places, until at length, as we find, the whole kingdom of Judah had become corrupt: and this is what the Prophet repeats more fully in other places. It was not then without reason that he denounces desolation here on the citizens of Lachish; for they had been the authors of sin to their own kindred. However alienated the ten tribes had become from pure faith and pure worship, the kingdom of Judah remained still upright, until Lachish opened the door to ungodly superstitions; and then its superstitions spread through the whole of Judea. She therefore suffered the punishment which she deserved, when she was drawn away into distant exile, or, at least, when she could not otherwise escape from danger, than by fleeing into some far country, and that very swiftly. *She is the beginning*, he says, *of sin to the daughter of Zion.* How so? For *in thee*—(it is more emphatical when the Prophet turns his discourse to Lachish itself)—*in thee*, he says, *were found the transgressions of Israel.* It follows—

14. Therefore shalt thou give presents to Moresheth-gath: the houses of Achzib *shall be* a lie to the kings of Israel.	14. Propterea mittes dona super Moreseth (*vel*, propter Moreseth-) Gath, filiis Achzib in mendacium regibus Israel.

Here the Prophet alludes to another thing,—that they would attempt to pacify their enemies with gifts, and would try to redeem themselves and their neighbours. But the Prophet expressly mentions this, that the event might teach them that nothing happens without a design; for it ought to work a greater conviction in blind and obstinate men, when they see that they really find that to be true which had been long before predicted. This, then, is the reason why the Prophet enumerates here various particulars; it was, that the hand of God might be more evident and conspicuous, when he would begin, in an especial manner, to fulfil all the things which he now in words foretells, *Thou*, he says, *wilt send a gift for Moreseth-gath;* that is, for a neighbouring city. And he calls it Moreseth-gath, to distinguish it from another city of the same name. *Thou wilt* then *send gifts for Moreseth-gath to the sons of Achzib for a lie.* אכזיב, *aczib*, is a word derived from one which means a lie. There is, therefore, a striking alliteration, when he says, Thou wilt send gifts to the sons of אכזיב, *Aczib*, for a lie, לאכזב, *laaczeb;* that is, Thou wilt send gifts to the sons of a lie, for a lie. The city had obtained its name from its fallacies or guiles. And he says, *for a lie to the kings of Israel;* because it profited the children of Israel nothing to pacify them with gifts, or to attempt to draw them to their side, as they hired the services of one another. So then he says, that they would be for a lie to the kings of Israel, for they would gain nothing by having many auxiliaries. Some take the words actively,—that the kings of Israel had first deceived the citizens of Achzib: but this view is less probable; I am therefore disposed to adopt the other,—that though the citizens of Lachish tried to conciliate their neighbours with a great sum of money, especially the people of Achzib, this would be yet to no purpose; for it would be a lie to the people of Israel: or, it may be, that the Prophet's meaning is this,—that the citizens of Achzib had already wished to bring aid, but in vain, to the kings of Israel; for Lachish was one of the first cities which the Assyrians conquered; but it was within the kingdom of Judah, or on its borders. It is then probable that the kings of Israel had recourse to the aid of this people, and were not assisted. Now, as the citizens of Lachish also endeavoured to extricate themselves from the hand of their enemies by such aid, the Prophet derides such a folly, inasmuch as they did not become wise by experience, having seen, with their own eyes, that such an help had been useless and deceptive to the kings of Israel: they ought then to have tried some other means, rather than to expose themselves to the same deceptions.[1] I cannot finish the chapter to-day.

PRAYER.

Grant, Almighty God, that, being warned by so many examples, the record of which thou hast designed to continue to the end of the world, that we may learn how dreadful a judge thou art to the perverse,—O grant, that we may not, at this day, be deaf to thy teaching, which is conveyed to us by the mouth of thy

[1] The two lines of this verse are improperly connected, and the word "sons" is substituted for "houses," בתי, and there are no various readings, and the Septuagint has "houses." The literal rendering is this,—

Therefore thou wilt send presents to Moresheth-gath:
The houses of Achzib will be a lie (*i. e.*, false) to the kings of Israel.

Henderson, after Cocceius, gives a different meaning to "presents," שלוחים; and he renders it "divorce," and says that it signifies letters of repudiation, and that it is to be taken here metaphorically for the breaking up of connection. The word only occurs in two other places, that is, in Exod. xviii. 2, and 1 Kings ix. 16; and in neither does it mean what is alleged.—*Ed.*

Prophet, but that we may strive to be so reconciled to thee, that, passing by all men, we may present ourselves unreservedly to thee, so that, relying on thy mercy alone which thou hast promised to us in Christ, we may not doubt but thou wilt be propitious to us, and be so touched with the spirit of true penitence, that, if we have been to others a bad example and an offence, we may lead others to the right way of salvation, and each of us may so endeavour to assist our neighbours in a holy life, that we may together attain that blessed and celestial life, which thine only-begotten Son has procured for us by his own blood. Amen.

Lecture Eighty-third.

15. Yet will I bring an heir unto thee, O inhabitant of Mareshah: he shall come unto Adullam the glory of Israel.

15. Adhuc possessorem mittam,[1] tibi habitatrix Maresah; usque ad Adullam veniet gloria Israel.

The Prophet here threatens his own birth place, as he had done other cities; for, as we have stated, he sprung from this city. He does not now spare his own kindred: for as God is no respecter of persons, so also God's servants ought, as with closed eyes, to deal impartially with all, so as not to be turned here and there either by favour or by hatred, but to follow, without any change, whatever the Lord commands them. We see that Micah was endued with this spirit, for he reproved his own kindred, as he had hitherto reproved others.

There is a peculiar meaning in the word, Maresah, for it is derived from ירש, *iresh,* and it means possession. The Prophet now says, *I will send to thee* הורש, *euresh,* a possessor; the word is from the same root. But he means, that the Morasthites would come into the power of their enemies no less than their neighbours, of whom he had spoken before. He says, *to Adullam.* This was also a city in the tribe of Judah, as it is well known. But some would have "enemy"

[1] אבי, there is א left out, which is supplied in several MSS. It ought to be אביא, which means, I will bring, rather than, I will send.

[2] The instances of paranomasia or alliteration in this passage, including this line and the five preceding verses, are unparalleled in any other parts of the Prophets; and when there is no coincidence of sound in the words, there is sometimes a direct contrast in the ideas, as good and evil in verse 12.—*Ed.*

to be here understood, and they put כבוד, *cabud*, in the genitive case: "The enemy of the glory of Israel shall come to Adullam;" but this is strained. Others understand the passage thus, that the glory of Israel would come to disgrace; for Adullam, we know, was a cave. Since then it was an obscure place, the Prophet here, as they think, declares that the whole glory of Israel would be covered with dishonour, because the dignity and wealth, in which they gloried, would lose their pristine state, so that they would differ nothing from an ignoble cave. If any approve of this meaning, I will not oppose them. Yet others think that the Prophet speaks ironically, and that the Assyrian is thus called, because the whole glory and dignity of Israel would by him be taken away. But there is no need of confining this to enemies; we may then take a simpler view, and yet regard the expression as ironical,—that the glory, that is, the disgrace or the devastation of Israel, would come to Adullam. But what if we read it, in apposition, "He shall come to Adullam, the glory of Israel?" For Adullam was not obscure, as those interpreters imagine, whom I have mentioned, but it is named among the most celebrated cities after the return and restoration of the people. When, therefore, the whole country was laid waste, this city, with a few others, remained, as we read in the eleventh chapter of Nehemiah. It might then be, that the Prophet called Adullam the glory of Israel; for it was situated in a safe place, and the inhabitants thought that they were fortified by a strong defence, and thus were not open to the violence of enemies. This meaning also may be probable; but still, as the glory of Israel may be taken ironically for calamity or reproach, if any one approves more of this interpretation, it may be followed. I am, however, inclined to another,—that the Prophet says, that the enemy would come to Adullam, which was the glory of Israel,[1]

[1] Of all the various renderings of this clause, this is the most satisfactory, which is that of our own version. The substitution of "honour' for "glory," on the mere authority of the Targum, as is done by *Newcome*, is wholly indefensible.

Εως Οδαλαμ ἥξει την δοξην Ισραηλ, *Symmachus*. At the same time, the most obvious and natural construction of the clause is the following, though its meaning is obscure: To Adullam shall come the glory of Israel.—*Ed.*

because that city was as it were in the recesses of Judea, so that an access to it by enemies was difficult. It may be also that some may think, that the recollection of its ancient history is here revived; for David concealed himself in its cave, and had it as his fortress. The place no doubt had, from that time, attained some fame; then this celebrity, as I have said, may be alluded to, when Adullam is said to be the glory of Israel. It follows—

16. Make thee bald, and poll thee for thy delicate children; enlarge thy baldness as the eagle; for they are gone into captivity from thee.

16. Decalvare et tondeas te super filiis delitiarum tuarum; dilata calvitium sicut aquila, quoniam migrarunt abs te.

The Prophet at length concludes, that nothing remained for the people but lamentation; for the Lord had resolved to desolate and destroy the whole country. Now they were wont in mourning, as we have seen in other places, to shave and even tear off their hair: and some think that the verb קרחי, *korechi*, implies as much as though the Prophet said, "Pluck, tear, pull off your hair." When afterwards he adds גזי, *regizi*, they refer it to shaving, which is done by a razor. However this may be, the Prophet here means, that the condition of the people would be so calamitous, that nothing would be seen anywhere but mourning.

Make bald, he says, *for the children of thy delicacies.*[1] The Prophet here indirectly upbraids those perverse men, who after so many warnings had not repented, with the neglect of God's forbearance: for whence did those delicacies proceed, except from the extreme kindness of God in long sparing the Israelites, notwithstanding their disobedience? The Prophet then shows here that they had very long abused the patience of God, while they each immersed themselves in their delicacies. Now, he says, *Enlarge thy baldness as the eagle.* Eagles are wont to cast off their feathers; and hence he compares here bald men to eagles, as though he called them, Hairless.

[1] Or, "children of thy indulgences or luxuries," *i. e.*, luxurious children, rather than "darling children," as rendered by *Henderson.* The Septuagint has τα τεκνα τα τρυφερα σου—"thy voluptuous children." The version of Newcome is, "thy delicate children." What seems to be intended is, their indulgence in pleasures and luxuries.—*Ed.*

As then the eagles are for a certain time without feathers, until they recover them; so also you shall be hairless, even on account of your mourning. He says, *For they have migrated from thee.* He intimates that the Israelites would become exiles, that the land might remain desolate. Now follows—

CHAPTER II.

1. Woe to them that devise iniquity, and work evil upon their beds! when the morning is light, they practise it, because it is in the power of their hand.

1. Væ cogitantibus iniquitatem et fabricantibus malitiam super cubilibus suis! quum illuxerit mane, exequentur eam, quia est ad potentiam manus ipsorum.

The Prophet does not here speak only against the Israelites, as some think, who have incorrectly confined this part of his teaching to the ten tribes; but he, on the contrary, in discharging his office, addresses also the Jews. He refers not here to idolatry, as in the last chapter; but inveighs against sins, condemned in the second table. As then the Jews had not only polluted the worship of God, but also gave loose reins to many iniquities, so that they dealt wrongfully with their neighbours, and there was among them no attention to justice and equity, so the Prophet inveighs here, as we shall see, against avarice, robberies, and cruelty: and his discourse is full of vehemence; for there was no doubt such licentiousness then prevailing among the people, that there was need of severe and sharp reproofs. It is at the same time easy to perceive that his discourse is mainly directed against the chief men, who exercised authority, and turned it to wrong purposes.

Woe, he says, *to those who meditate on iniquity, and devise*[1]

[1] Literally, work; but פעל means to work not only with the hands, but also with the mind; and hence, to contrive, to devise, to machinate. *Henderson* has "fabricate," while *Newcome*, less suitably, retains the word, "work." *Marckius* justly observes, that the working here is not external but internal, the framing, the setting in order, the preparation of evil in the mind. The Prophet points out here the source from which outward evils proceed. What numberless schemes, both good and evil, are concocted and arranged by men on their beds! "They set their wits on work to invent ways of accomplishing their desire. They devise

evil on their beds, that, when the morning shines, they may execute it. Here the Prophet describes to the life the character and manners of those who were given to gain, and were intent only on raising themselves. He says, that in their beds they were meditating on iniquity, and devising wickedness. Doubtless the time of night has been given to men entirely for rest; but they ought also to use this kindness of God for the purpose of restraining themselves from what is wicked: for he who refreshes his strength by nightly rest, ought to think within himself, that it is an unbecoming thing and even monstrous, that he should in the meantime devise frauds, and guiles, and iniquities. For why does the Lord intend that we should rest, except that all evil things should rest also? Hence the Prophet shows here, by implication, that those who are intent on devising frauds, while they ought to rest, subvert as it were the course of nature; for they have no regard for that rest, which has been granted to men for this end,—that they may not trouble and annoy one another.

He afterwards shows how great was their desire to do mischief, *When it shines in the morning,* he says, *they execute it.* He might have said only, "They do in the daytime what they contrive in the night:" but he says, *In the morning;* as though he had said, that they were so heated by avarice, that they rested not a moment; as soon as it shone, they were immediately ready to perpetrate the frauds they had thought of in the night. We now then apprehend the import of the Prophet's meaning.

He now subjoins, *For according to their power is their hand.* As אל, *al,* means God, an old interpreter has given this rendering, "Against God is their hand:" but this does not suit the passage. Others have explained it thus, "For strength is in their hand:" and almost all those well-skilled in Hebrew agree in this explanation. Those who had power, they think, are here pointed out by the Prophet,—that as they had strength, they dared to do whatever they pleased. But the Hebrew phrase is not translated by them; and I greatly

iniquity with a great deal of cursed art and policy; they plot how to do it effectually, and yet so as not to expose themselves. This is called working evil; they are working it in their heads."—*Henry.*

wonder that they have mistaken in a thing so clear: for it is not, "There is power in their hand;" but "their hand is to power." The same mode of speaking is found in the third chapter of Proverbs, and there also many interpreters are wrong; for Solomon there forbids us to withhold from our neighbour his right, "When thine hand," he says, "is for power;" some say, "When there is power to help the miserable." But Solomon means no such thing; for he on the contrary means this, "When thine hand is ready to execute any evil, abstain." So also the Lord says in Deut. xxviii., "When the enemy shall take away thy spoils, thy hand will not be for power;" that is, "Thou wilt not dare to move a finger to restrain thy enemies; when they will plunder thee and rob thee of thy substance, thou wilt stand in dread, for thy hand will be as though it were dead." I come now to the present passage, "Their hand is for power:"[1] the Prophet means, that they dared to try what they could, and that therefore their hand was always ready; whenever there was hope of lucre or gain, the hand was immediately prepared. How so? Because they were restrained neither by the fear of God nor by any regard for justice; but their hand was for power, that is, what they could, they dared to do. We now then see what the Prophet means, as far as I can judge. He afterwards adds—

2. And they covet fields, and take *them* by violence; and houses, and take *them* away: so they oppress a man and his house, even a man and his heritage.	2. Et concupiverunt agros et rapiunt; et domos, et auferunt; et vexant virum et domum ejus, virum et hæreditatem ejus.

Micah confirms here what is contained in the former verse; for he sets forth the alacrity with which the avaricious were led to commit plunder; nay, how unbridled was their cupi-

[1] The original is, כי יש־לאל ידם. *Marckius* after having referred to *Calvin's* version, says, that he prefers that of *Junius* and *Tremelius* which is as follows: "Quum est in potestate manus ipsorum—When it is in the power of their hand," כי is taken as an adverb of time. The phrase is found in four other places,—Gen. xxxi. 29; Deut. xxviii. 32; Neh. v. 5; and Prov. iii. 27. So that to render אל here "God," as it is done by the Septuagint, Theodoret, and Jerome, and some others, must be wrong. כי is rendered "because" both by *Newcome* and *Henderson*, but not so suitably as to the sense.—*Ed.*

dity to do evil. As soon as they have coveted any thing, he says, they take it by force. And hence we gather, that the Prophet, in the last verse, connected wicked counsels with the attempt of effecting them; as though he had said, that they indeed carefully contrived their frauds, but that as they were skilful in their contrivances, so they were not less bold and daring in executing them.

The same thing he now repeats in other words for a further confirmation, *As soon as they have coveted fields, they seize them by force; as soon as they have coveted houses, they take them away;* they oppress a man and his house together;[1] that is, nothing escaped them: for as their wickedness in frauds was great, so their disposition to attempt whatever they wished was furious. And well would it be were there no such cruel avarice at this day; but it exists every where, so that we may see, as in a mirror, an example of what is here said. But it behoves us carefully to consider how greatly displeasing to God are frauds and plunders, so that each of us may keep himself from doing any wrong, and be so ruled by a desire of what is right, that every one of us may act in good faith towards his neighbours, seek nothing that is unjust, and bridle his own desires: and whenever Satan attempts to allure us, let what is here taught be to us as a bridle to restrain us. It follows—

3. Therefore thus saith the Lord, Behold, against this family do I devise an evil, from which ye shall not remove your necks; neither shall ye go haughtily: for this time *is* evil.	3. Propterea sic dicit Jehova, Ecce ego cogitans super familiam hanc malum, quod non submovebitis ab illo *(sic est ad verbum;* à quo submovebitis) colla vestra, et non ambulabitis in altitudine; quia tempus malum hoc.

[1] This verse presents an instance of parallelism not uncommon, in which the first and the last line correspond, and the second and the third; as will be seen in the following version:—

And they covet fields and forcibly seize *them*,
And houses, and they take *them* away;
Yea, they oppress the young man and his house,
And the old man and his inheritance.

There must be some distinction between גבר, which I render, "the young man," and איש, rendered above, "the old man." The first means, robust, strong; and the second is a common term for man, but sometimes signifies a husband, and also a man in years. We may, indeed, in har-

The Prophet shows now that the avaricious were in vain elevated by their frauds and rapacity, because their hope would be disappointed; for God in heaven was waiting his time to appear against them. Though they had anxiously heaped together much wealth, yet God would justly dissipate it altogether. This is what he now declares.

Behold, he says, *thus saith Jehovah, I am meditating evil against this family.*[1] There is here a striking contrast between God and the Jews, between their wicked intentions and the intentions of God, which in themselves were not evil, and yet would bring evil on them. God, he says, thus speaks, Behold, I am purposing; as though he said, "While ye are thus busying yourselves on your beds, while ye are revolving many designs, while ye are contriving many artifices, ye think me to be asleep, ye think that I am all the while meditating nothing; nay, I have my thoughts too, and those different from yours; for while ye are awake to devise wickedness, I am awake to contrive judgment." We now then perceive the import of these words: it is God that declares that he meditates evil, and it is not the Prophet that speaks to these avaricious and rapacious men; and the evil is that of punishment, inasmuch as it is the peculiar office of God to repay to all what they deserve, and to render to each the measure of evil they have brought on others.

Ye shall not, he says, *remove your necks from under it.* Since hypocrites always promise to themselves impunity, and lay hold on subterfuges, whenever God threatens them, the Prophet here affirms, that though they sought every escape, they would yet be held bound by God's hand, so that they could not by any means shake off the burden designed for them. And this was a reward most fully deserved by those who had withdrawn their necks, when God called them to

mony with the passage, consider the first as meaning a householder, and the latter as signifying a husbandman. The fields in the first line are the same with the inheritance in the last: and houses and a house are mentioned in the two intervening lines.—*Ed.*

[1] The word משפחה, family, no doubt designates the people of Israel, so called, either for their descent from the same father, or for their adoption by God as his people, designed to live in subjection to him as a family to its head.—*Ed.*

obedience. They then who refuse to obey God, when he requires from them a voluntary service, will at length be drawn by force, not to undergo the yoke, but the burden which will altogether overwhelm them. Whosoever then will not willingly submit to God's yoke, must at length undergo the great and dreadful burden prepared for the untameable.

Ye will not then be able to withdraw your necks, and *ye shall not walk in your height.* He expresses still more clearly what I have referred to,—that they were so elated with pride, that they despised all threatenings and all instruction: and this presumption became the cause of perverseness; for were it not that a notion of security deceived men, they would presently bend, when God threatens them. This then is the reason why the Prophet joins this sentence, *ye shall no more walk in your height;* that is, your haughtiness shall then surely be made to succumb; *for it will be a time of evil.* He means, as I have said, that those who retain a stiff and unbending neck towards God, when he would lay on them his yoke, shall at length be made by force to yield, however rebellious they may be. How so? For they shall be broken down, inasmuch as they will not be corrected. The Prophet then adds—

4. In that day shall *one* take up a parable against you, and lament with a doleful lamentation, *and* say, We be utterly spoiled: he hath changed the portion of my people: how hath he removed *it* from me! turning away he hath divided our fields.

4. In die illo tollent super eos parabolam, et lugebunt (*sunt quidem verba singularis numeri,* ישא *et* נהה; *cæterum indefinita est locutio; nam qui subaudiunt conductios homines, quibus solebat injungi hæc provincia, ut lugubres cantus conciperent ad cladem aliquam, nescio an assecuti sint mentem Prophetæ: tamen hoc relinquo in medio, quia alibi vidimus fuisse tunc cantores in luctu, quemadmodum etiam alibi erunt Præficæ, hoc est, mulieres lamentatrices; cæterum malo indefinitè accipere;* Tollent *igitur* super vos parabolam et lugebunt) luctu lamentabili (*vel,* lamento lamenti,) dicendo, Vastando vastati sumus; partem populi mei mutavit; quomodo tollent à nobis ad restituendum? Agros nostros dividèt.

The verse is in broken sentences; and hence interpreters vary. But the meaning of the Prophet appears to me to be simply this, *In that day they shall take up a proverb against you;* that is, it will not be an ordinary calamity, but the report concerning it will go forth every where, so that the Jews will become to all a common proverb. This is one thing. As to the word משל, *meshil*, it is taken, we know, for a weighty saying, and in the plural, weighty sayings, called by the Latins, sentences *(sententias)* or sayings (*dicta*,) and by the Greeks, apophthegms (αποφθεγματα.) But these sayings were thus called weighty by the Hebrews, because he who elevated his style, made use especially of figurative expressions, to render his discourse nobler and more splendid.[1] Hence many render this word, enigmas, (αινιγματα.) It accords well with the Prophet's meaning, to suppose, that proverbial sayings would spread every where respecting the Jews, especially as calamities were usually described in a plaintive song. *They shall* then *mourn over you with lamentable mourning*. But this ought to be referred to the fact,—that the calamity would be every where known. It yet seems that this sentence is applied afterwards to the Jews themselves, and not unsuitably. But it is an indefinite mode of speaking, since the Prophet speaks not of one or two men, but of the whole people.

They shall then mourn in this manner, *Wasted, we have been wasted: the portion of my people hath he changed*—(it is the future instead of the past)—*He hath* then *changed the portion of my people*. This may be applied to God as well as to the Assyrians; for God was the principal author of this calamity; he it was who changed the portion of the people: for as by his blessing he had long cherished that people, so afterwards he changed their lot. But as the Assyrians were the ministers of God's vengeance, the expression cannot be unsuitably applied to them. The Assyrian then has taken away *the portion of my people*. And then he says, *How hath he made to depart*, or hath taken away, or removed *from me*, (literally, *to me*,) *to restore*,—though שבב, *shibeb*, may be from

[1] Very similar is the description of משל by *Lowth* in his Prælections; he describes it as that style which is sententious, figurative, and sublime —*Sententiosum, figuratum, et sublime docendi genus*. He says also that the word means often a saying, an axiom, a short sentence compactly formed—*est quævis sententia sive axioma scite gravitaque dictum, paucis concinnatum, et ad γνωμων firmam compositum*, 1 Sam. xxiv. 14, Præl. iv. And this is evidently its meaning here,—a common saying, everywhere known.—*Ed.*

the root שׁוּב, *shub*, it yet means the same,—*How* then *hath he taken away from us to restore our fields he divides*, that is, which he hath divided; for the relative אשר, *asher*, is understood, and there is also a change of time. Now as the discourse, as I have said, is in broken sentences, there are various interpretations. I however think that the Prophet simply means this—*How as to restoring hath he taken away our fields, which he hath divided?* that is, How far off are we from restitution? for every hope is far removed, since the Lord himself has divided among strangers our land and possession; or since the enemies have divided it among themselves; for it is usual after victory, for every one to seize on his own portion. Whether then this be understood of the Assyrians, or rather be referred to God, the meaning of the Prophet seems clearly to be this,—that the Jews were not only expelled from their country, but that every hope of return was also taken away, since the enemies had parted among themselves their inheritance, so that they who had been driven out, now in vain thought of a restitution.[1] But I read this in the pre-

[1] Most commentators agree as to the general meaning of this verse, which is clearly stated here: but their versions differ. *Newcome*, following the Septuagint, renders the verbs in the first and second lines in a passive sense, but *Henderson* gives them an active meaning, supplying "one" as the nominative case, *i. e.*, the person, who utters the lamentation afterwards mentioned. The two last lines are the most difficult. *Marckius* has this version,—

Quomodo subtraxit mihi!
Avertenti agros nostros distribuit!

That of *Junius* and *Tremelius* is essentially the same, only the verbs are put in the present tense. *Newcome's* rendering is this,—

How hath he departed from me,
To bring again *him* that divided our fields!

Meaning by "him" the Assyrian. *Henderson's* version seems wide of the mark,—

How hath he withdrawn it from me!
To an apostate he hath divided our fields!

To call the king of Babylon an apostate, seems incongruous, as it cannot be applied to any one but who has turned away from true religion. The most obvious and literal rendering is that given by *Marckius*, with the exception of the tense. I offer the following version of the whole verse, with no alteration in the text, except the supplying of a ו before אמר, which is found in several MSS.,—

In that day shall be taken up concerning you a proverb,
And lament a lamentation will the oppressed,
And say will the desolate,—"We are destroyed,

sent time; for the Prophet introduces here the Jews as uttering this lamentation,—"It is now all over with us, and there is no remedy for this evil; for not only are we stripped of all our property and ejected from our country, but what has been taken away by our enemies cannot be restored to us, inasmuch as they have already parted our possessions among themselves, and every one occupies his own portion and his own place, as though it were his own inheritance. We have therefore to do, not only with the Assyrians in general, but also with every individual; for what every one now occupies and possesses he will defend, as his rightful and hereditary possession."

Some conjecture from this verse, that the discourse belongs rather to the Israelites, who were banished without any hope of return; but no necessity constrains us to explain this of the Israelites; for the Prophet does not declare here what God would do, but what would be the calamity when considered in itself. We have indeed said already in many places, that the Prophets, while threatening, speak only of calamities, desolations, deaths, and destructions, but that they afterwards add promises for consolation. But their teaching is discriminative: when the Prophets intend to terrify hypocrites and perverse men, they set forth the wrath of God only, and leave no hope; but when they would inspire with hope those who are by this means humbled, they draw forth comfort to them even from the goodness of God. What is here said then may fitly and really be applied to the Jews. It follows—

5. Therefore thou shalt have none that shall cast a cord by lot in the congregation of the Lord.	5. Itaque non erit tibi projiciens funiculum ad sortem in cœtu Jehovæ.

Here the Prophet concludes his discourse respecting God's design to cleanse Judea from its perverse and wicked inha-

> The portion of my people he changes;
> How he takes away from me!
> To the alienator of my fields he divides *them!*"

It is a proverb, a common saying, and a lament, that would be uttered, as the Prophet foretells, at the time of the expulsion of the people from the land, when it would be taken possession of by their enemies.—*Ed.*

bitants, that it might no longer be the inheritance of one people. For the land, we know, had been given to the posterity of Abraham, on the condition, that it was to be held by them as an heritage: and we also know, that a line was determined by lot whenever the year of Jubilee returned, that every one might regain his own possession. The Prophet now testifies that this advantage would be taken away from the Jews, and that they would hereafter possess the land by no hereditary right; for God, who had given it, would now take it away.

There shall not then *be one to cast a line by lot in the assembly of Jehovah.* And he seems here to touch the Jews, by calling them the assembly of Jehovah. He indeed adopted them, they were the people of God: but he intimates that they were repudiated, because they had rendered themselves unworthy of his favour. He therefore, by calling them ironically *the assembly of Jehovah*, denies that they rightly retained this name, inasmuch as they had deprived themselves of this honour and dignity. It now follows—

6. Prophesy ye not, *say they to them that* prophesy: they shall not prophesy to them, *that* they shall not take shame.	6. Ne stilletis; stillabunt; non stillabunt illis (*hoc est*, super eos;) non apprehendet ignominias (*sic est ad verbum.*)

Here the conciseness of the expressions has made interpreters to differ in their views. Some read thus, *Distil ye not,—they will distil;* that is, the Jews speak against the prophets, and with threats forbid them, as with authority, to address them. The Hebrew word, distil, means the same as to speak; though at the same time it is applied more commonly to weighty addresses than to such as are common and ordinary. If any understands, *they will distil*, or speak, of the Jews, then the Prophet points out their arrogance in daring to contend with God's prophets, and in trying to silence and force them to submission. We indeed find that ungodly men act thus, when they wish to take away the liberty of teaching from God's prophets; for they resist as though they themselves were doubly and trebly prophets. So also in this place, *Distil ye not*, that is, the Jews say, "Let not the servants of God prophesy." But some think that a relative is understood, *Distil ye not* ~~to those~~ who distil; as though he had said, that ungodly men would not bear God's prophets, and thus would prevent and restrain them, as much as they could, from speaking. Others make this distinction, *Distil ye not,—they shall distil;* as though the Jews said the first, and God the second. *Distil ye not,*— this was the voice of the ungodly and rebellious people, who would cast away from them and reject every instruction: but God on the other side opposed them and said, *Nay, they shall distil;* ye forbid, but it is not in your power; I have sent them: though ye may rage and clamour a hundred times, it is my will that they should proceed in their course.

We hence see how various are the explanations: and even in the other part of the verse there is no more agreement between interpreters: *They shall not distil;* respecting this clause, it is sufficiently evident, that God here intimates that there would be now an end to all prophecies. How so? Because he would not render his servants a sport, and subject them to reproach. This is the true meaning: and yet some take another view, as though the Prophet continued his sentence, *They shall not distil,* lest the people should receive reproaches; for the ungodly think, that if they close the mouths of the prophets, all things would be lawful to them, and that their crimes would be hid, in short, that their vices would not be called to an account; as though their wickedness was not in itself sufficiently reproachful, were God to send no prophets, and no reproof given. No doubt, profane men are so stupid as to think themselves free from every reproach, when God is silent, and when they put away from themselves every instruction. Hence some think, that this passage is to be understood in this sense. But I consider the meaning to be that which I have stated; for he had before said, *Distil ye not who distil;* that is, "Ye prophets, be no longer troublesome to us; why do you stun our ears? We can no longer bear your boldness; be then silent." Thus he expressly introduced the Jews as speaking with authority, as though it was in their power to restrain the prophets from doing their duty. Now follows, as I think, the answer of God, *They shall not distil,* that he may not get reproaches: "Since I see that my doctrine is intolerable to you, since I find a loathing so great and so shameful, I will take away my prophets from you: I will therefore rest, and be hereafter silent."—Why? "Because I effect nothing; nay, I subject my prophets to reproaches; for they lose their labour in speaking, they pour forth words which produce no fruit; for ye are altogether irreclaimable. Nay, as they are reproachfully treated by you, their condition is worse than if they were covered with all the disgrace of having been criminal. Since then I subject my prophets to reproach, I will not allow them to be thus mocked by you. They shall therefore give over, they shall prophesy no longer."[1]

But the Lord could not have threatened the Jews with any thing worse or more dreadful than with this immunity,

[1] *Newcome*, apparently on the authority of the Septuagint, joins a part of the last verse to this, and gives this rendering,—

In the congregation of Jehovah prophesy not, O ye that prophesy:
They shall not prophesy to these:
For he shall remove *from himself* reproaches.

The last line he applies to the true prophet, that he would not subject himself to disgrace by exercising his office. *Henderson's* version is the following:—

Prophesy not; thou shalt prophesy
Who will not prophesy of these things:
Reproaches are incessant.

This is viewed as being altogether the language of the people, interdicting the true prophets, specifying those whom they approved, and deprecating the reproaches cast upon them by the true prophets. Another version, which is materially adopted by *Calvin*, is admitted by our Author as not unsuitable, but he prefers the one given above. The main objection is to the last line, which in the original is this,—

לא יסג כלמות

The last word is plural, and means reproaches; and the verb יסג is in the third person of the future tense, and may be derived either from סוג, to recede, to depart, or from נסג, to remove, both in a transitive and intransitive sense. Having an objective case, it cannot be the first verb, and must be the second in its transitive meaning. Then the rendering is, He will not, or let him not, or let none remove reproaches. This being the literal rendering of this sentence, we must now consider what version of the former part will correspond best with it. It is that no doubt adopted by Calvin, though the last clause cannot admit of the meaning he attaches to it. The people say, "Prophesy ye not who prophesy;" God answers, "They shall not prophesy to thee;" and then the Prophet adds, speaking of God, "He will not remove reproaches;" that is, he will not remove them by his prophets with the view of amending their reproachful conduct.

The last clause is evidently viewed as an anomalous construction by *Henderson;* for he renders it as though the plural noun were the nominative case to the verb in the singular number, and this because the latter precedes the former. There may be instances of this in Hebrew, but it is

—that they should no more hear anything which might disturb them: for it is an extreme curse, when God gives us loose reins, and suffers us, with unbridled liberty, to rush as it were headlong into evils, as though he had delivered us up to Satan, to be his slaves. Since it is so, let us be assured that it is an awful threatening, when he says, *They shall not distil*, lest they should hereafter become objects of reproach.

PRAYER.

Grant, Almighty God, that as thou art pleased to try our patience by requiring mutual justice and the offices of love and benevolence,—O grant, that we may not be wolves one to another, but show ourselves to be really thy children, by observing all those duties of justice and kindness which thou commandest, and thus follow what is right and just through the whole course of our life, that we may at length enjoy that blessedness which is laid up for us in heaven, through Christ our Lord. Amen.

Lecture Eighty-fourth.

7. O *thou that art* named the house of Jacob, is the Spirit of the Lord straitened? *are* these his doings? do not my words do good to him that walketh uprightly?

7. Qui diceris domus Jacob, an reductus est in angustias Spiritus Jehova? (*alii vertunt,* an imminutus est Spiritus Jehovæ; קצר *significat coarctare, significat etiam imminuere apud Hebræos; sed melius quadrat sensus ille quem reddidi.*) An hæc sunt opera ejus? Annon verba mea bona sunt cum eo (*hoc est*, apud eum) qui rectus ambulat?

The Prophet now reproves the Israelites with greater severity, because they attempted to impose a law on God and on his prophets, and would not endure the free course of instruction. He told us in the last verse, that the Israelites were inflated with so much presumption, that they wished to make terms with God: "Let him not prophesy," they said, as though it were in the power of man to rule God: and the

by no means a common usage; though it be so in the *Welsh* language, which in many of its peculiarities is very much like Hebrew. This sort of construction is the ordinary one in that language: a plural noun has commonly a verb in the singular number, when placed before it. This sentence in Welsh would be exactly the same as in Hebrew—*Nid ymadawa gwaradwyddiadau.* The noun in the plural number is the nominative case to the preceding verb, which is in the singular number, and the verb too is in the future tense, and is yet understood as having the meaning of the present tense.—*Ed.*

Prophet now repeats, *Is the Spirit of Jehovah straitened?* as though he said, "Ye see the intent of your presumption, and how far it proceeds; for ye wish to subject God's Spirit to yourselves and to your own pleasure." The prophets doubtless did not speak of themselves, but by the bidding and command of God. Since then the prophets were the organs of the Holy Spirit, whosoever attempted to silence them, usurped to himself an authority over God himself, and in a manner tried to make captive his Spirit: for what power can belong to the Spirit, except he be at liberty to reprove the vices of men, and condemn whatever is opposed to God's justice? When this is taken away, there is no more any jurisdiction left to the Holy Spirit. We now then see what the Prophet means in this place: he shows how mad a presumption it was in the Israelites to attempt to impose silence on the prophets, as though they had a right to rule the Spirit of God, and to force him to submission.

Is the Spirit of Jehovah straitened? And this mode of speaking ought to be noticed, for it possesses no ordinary emphasis; inasmuch as the Prophet, by this reproof, recalls the attention of these perverse men to the author of his teaching; as though he had said, that the wrong was not done to men, that war was not carried on with them, when instruction is prohibited, but that God is robbed of his own right, and that his liberty is taken away, so that he is not allowed to execute his judgment in the world by the power of his Spirit.

And farther, the Prophet here ironically reproves the Israelites, when he says, *O thou who art called the house of Jacob, is the Spirit of Jehovah reduced to straits?* For if heathens, who have never known the teaching of religion, and to whom no heavenly mysteries have been revealed, had said, that they would have nothing to do with the prophets, it would have been much more endurable; for what wonder would it be for ignorant men to repudiate all instruction? But it was monstrous for the Israelites, who gloried in the name of God, to dare to rise up so rebelliously against the prophets: they always boasted of their own race, as though they surpassed all the rest of the world, and were a holy nation, separated from all others. Hence the Prophet says, "Ye wish to be called the house of Jacob; what is your excellency and dignity, except that you have been chosen by God to be his peculiar people? If then you have been habituated to the teaching of God, what fury and madness it is, that you cannot bear his prophets, but wish to close their mouths?" We now then see the point of this irony, when the Prophet says that they were *called the house of Jacob*. He seems at the same time to intimate, in an indirect way, that they were a spurious race. As they were called by other prophets, Amorites and Sodomites: even so in this place the Prophet says, "Ye are indeed the house of Jacob, but it is only as to the name." They were in reality so degenerated, that they falsely pretended the name of the holy patriarch; yea, they falsely and mendaciously boasted of their descent from holy men, though they were nothing else, but as it were rotten members. Inasmuch then as they had so departed from the religion of Abraham and of other fathers, the Prophet says, "Thou art indeed called what thou art not."

He afterwards adds, *Are these his works?* Here he brings the Israelites to the proof, as though he said, "How comes it, that the prophets are so troublesome and grievous to you, except that they sharply reprove you, and denounce on you the judgment of God? But God is in a manner forced, except he was to change his nature, to treat you thus sharply and severely. Ye boast that you are his people, but how do you live? *Are these his works?* that is, do you lead a life, and form your conduct according to the law laid down by him? But as your life does not in any degree correspond with what God requires, it is no wonder that the prophets handle you so roughly. For God remains the same, ever like himself; but ye are perfidious, and have wholly repudiated the covenant he has made with you. Then this asperity, of which ye are wont to complain, ought not to be deemed unjust to you."

He then subjoins, *Are not my words good to him who walks uprightly?* Here the Prophet more distinctly shows, why he had before asked, Whether their works were those of the Lord; for he compares their life with the doctrine, which on account of its severity displeased them; they said that the words of the prophets were too rigid. God here answers, that his words were gentle and kind, and therefore pleasant, that is, to the pious and good; and that hence the fault was in them, when he treated them less kindly than they wished. The import of the whole then is, that the word of God, as it brings life and salvation to man, is in its own nature gracious, and cannot be either bitter, or hard, or grievous to the pious and the good, for God unfolds in it the riches of his goodness.

We hence see that God here repudiates the impious calumny that was cast on his word; as though he had said, that the complaints which prevailed among the people were false; for they transferred the blame of their own wickedness to the word of God. They said that God was too severe: but God here declares that he was gentle and kind, and that the character of his word was the same, provided men were tractable, and did not, through their perverseness, extort from him anything else than what he of himself wished. And the same thing David means in Psalm xviii., when he says that God is perverse with the perverse: for in that passage he intimates, that he had experienced the greatest goodness from God, inasmuch as he had rendered himself docile and obedient to him. On the contrary, he says, God is perverse with the perverse; that is, when he sees men obstinately resisting and hardening their necks, he then puts on as it were a new character, and deals perversely with them, that is, severely, as their stubbornness deserves; as for a hard knot, according to a common proverb, a hard wedge is necessary. We now then perceive the meaning of this passage, that *God's words are good to those who walk uprightly;* that is, they breathe the sweetest odour, and bring nothing else but true and real joy: for when can there be complete happiness, except when God embraces us in the bosom of his love? But the testimony respecting this love is brought to us by his word. The fault then is in us, and ought to be imputed to us, if the word of God is not delightful to us.

Some expound this whole passage differently, as though the Prophet relates here what was usually at that time the boast of the Israelites. They hence think that it is a narrative in which he represents their sentiments, (*narrationem esse mimiticam;*) as though the Prophet introduced here the ungodly and the rebellious, animating one another in their contempt of God's word, *O thou who art called the house of Jacob, is the Spirit of Jehovah straitened?* Hypocrites, we know, are so blind and intoxicated by a false confidence, that they hesitate not heedlessly to abuse all the favours of God. As then God had conferred a great excellency on his people, they thus emboldened one another,—"Are we not the children and posterity of Abraham? What will it avail us to be a holy and chosen race, and the peculiar people of God, and a royal priesthood, if we are to be thus unkindly treated? We find that these prophets shamefully reprove us: where is our dignity, except we show that we have more privileges than other nations?" These interpreters therefore think the meaning to be this,—that they make a show of their own privileges, that they might with more liberty reject every instruction, and shake off every yoke. And when it is said, *Is the Spirit of God diminished?* these interpreters regard this as meaning, that they were satisfied with the solemn promise of God, and that as they were a holy race, they now superciliously despised all the prophets,—"Is the Spirit of God dead, who was formerly the interpreter of the everlasting covenant, which God made with us? Has he not testified that we should be to him a holy and elect people? Why then do ye now attempt to reduce to nothing this sacred declaration of the Holy Spirit, which is inviolable?" It is then added, *Are these his works?* "Ye talk of nothing but of threats and destruction; ye denounce on us numberless calamities: but God is beneficent and kind in his nature, patient and merciful; and ye represent him to us as a tyrant; but this view is wholly inconsistent with the nature of God." And, in the last place, God subjoins, as these interpreters think, an exception,—"All these are indeed true, if faithfulness exists among you, and the authority of my word continues; for *my words are good*, but not to all without any difference: be upright and sincere, and ye shall find me dealing kindly, gently, tenderly, and pleasantly with you: then my rigour will cease, which now through my word so much offends and exasperates you."

This meaning may in some measure be admitted; but as it is hard to be understood, we ought to retain the former, it being more easy and flowing. There is nothing strained in the view, that the Prophet derides the foolish arrogance of the people, who thought that they were sheltered by this privilege, that they were the holy seed of Abraham. The Prophet answers, that this titular superiority did not deprive God of his right, and prevent him to exercise his power by the Spirit. "*O thou* then *who art called the house of Jacob;* but only as far as the title goes: the Spirit of God is not reduced to straits. But if thou boastest thyself to be the peculiar people of God, are these thy works the works of God? Does thy life correspond with what he requires? There is no wonder then that God chastises you so severely by his word, for there is not in you the spirit of docility, which allows the exercise of his kindness."[1]

But though the Prophet here upbraids the ancient people with ingratitude, yet this truth is especially useful to us, which God declares, when he says, that his word is good and sweet to all the godly. Let us then learn to become submissive to God, and then he will convey to us by his word nothing but sweetness, nothing but delights; we shall then find nothing more desirable than to be fed by this spiritual food; and it will ever be a real joy to us, whenever the Lord will open his mouth to teach us. But when at any time the word of the Lord goads and wounds, and thus exasperates us, let us know that it is through our own fault. It follows—

[1] *Newcome*, adopting האמר, as found in four MSS., renders the first part of the verse as the language of the people, though not in the sense of those referred to by Calvin. His version is as follows:—

Doth the house of Israel [Jacob] say,
"Is the Spirit of Jehovah straitened?
Are these his doings?"

"Straitened," *i. e.*, confined to a few, such as Micah. And by "doings," he means the judgments before announced. *Henderson* regards the "doings," or, as he renders them, "operations," in the same light, though he views the words as spoken by the Prophet, and renders the first line thus,—

What language, O house of Jacob!

The first word, האמור, as it is in our text, is viewed by *Henderson*, as well as by *Marckius*, as a passive participle, signifying *what is said* or *spoken*, and the ה prefixed is considered as a note of exclamation. But the objection made to our common version is not valid, that אמר in Niphael, when it means *being called* or *named*, has uniformly an ל after it, for we have an instance to the contrary in Jer. vii. 32, ולא־יאמר עוד התפת, "and it shall no more be called Tophet."—*Ed.*

8. Even of late my people is risen up as an enemy: ye pull off the robe with the garment from them that pass by securely as men averse from war.	8. Et qui antehac populus meus, quasi in hostem surrexit ex adverso; vestem decoris (*alii vertunt*, pallium et tunicam; *sed nulla est copula, et* אדר *significat decorem, ideo possumus vertere vestem decoris*) prædati estis à transeuntibus cum fiducia, perinde ac si reverterentur à prælio.

As the words of the Prophet are concise, they contain some obscurity. Hence interpreters differ. First, as to the word אתמול, *atmul*, some think it to be one word, others divide it into את, *at*, and מול, *mul*, which means, over against, opposite; and they regard it of the same import with ממול, which immediately follows. But as the repetition would be frigid, the Prophet no doubt intended that it should be taken here in its proper sense, and its meaning is yesterday. But this time is not strictly taken by the Hebrews, for they take yesterday as meaning the past time, even when many years have elapsed. I have therefore rendered it *formerly*, which suits this place. There is also another difference as to the sense of the text, for some think that this אתמול, *atmul*, is to be joined to the verb קומם, *kumem;* but it is rather to be connected with the word עמי, *omi*, *My people formerly*. There is another diversity, that is, as to the term אויב, *avib*, for some apply it to God, and others to the people; that they rose up or stood one against another. For this verb is explained in two ways: some view it as a verb neuter, "They stand against the enemy;" and others render it, "They rise up against the enemy;" and this second meaning is most approved, and harmonizes best with the context.

I will now refer to what I consider to be the real meaning. The Prophet, in the first place, says, that the people were formerly under the power and government of God, but that now they were become wholly alienated from him. *Formerly*, then, *it was my people*, as though God now renounced all friendship with them. "I have hitherto owned you as my people, but hereafter I shall have nothing to do with you, for the whole authority of my word is by you entirely abolished; ye have violated your faith: in short, as you have destroyed my covenant, ye have ceased to be my people; for whatever favour I have conferred on you, you have deprived yourselves of it by your wickedness; and though I have adopted you, yet your wickedness now strips you of this privilege." This is one thing.

It then follows, *They have risen up as against an enemy.* I consider a note of likeness to be here understood. The Prophet says simply, *Against an enemy have they risen up*; but I regard the meaning to be, that they had risen up as against an enemy; that is, that they had made God, their best father, their enemy, inasmuch as they had by their crimes provoked his displeasure.[1] He then confirms this truth by saying, that they practised robberies among themselves. We indeed know that hypocrites ever hide themselves under their religious rites, and spread them forth as their shield whenever they are reproved. Hence the Prophet says, that they were not to be deemed the people of God for spending their labours on sacrifices, for they were at the same time robbers, and plundered innocent men.

The garment of comeliness, he says, or, the garment and the cloak, (about such words I do not labour much,) *they take away from those who pass by securely*;[2] that is, from all who are peaceable. For when there is a suspicion of war, or when a traveller does any mischief, he rightly deserves to be punished. But the Prophet says here, that they were robbed, who passed by securely as though they were in a safe country. "When travellers fear nothing, ye strip them of their garments, as though they were returning from war: as they are wont, when war is over, to seize on spoils wherever found,

[1] *Newcome* gives the same meaning to this part of the line, though another to the former part,—

But of old my people hath risen up as an enemy.

Henderson's version is the same. The word rendered "of old" means "yesterday," and expresses often past time indefinitely. It is once rendered "of old," Isa. xxx. 33; but in other places, "heretofore," "in times past;" but "formerly," or "of late," would be the most suitable expression in this passage.—*Ed.*

[2] The literal rendering of these two lines may be given thus:—

From off the garment the mantle ye strip
From those who pass by securely, returning from war.

Or, the last words, שובי מלחמה, "averters of war," may designate people of a peaceable disposition, and "war" may be taken for strife or contention; then the rendering would be, "who turn away from contention." *Newcome*, on the authority of one MS., which has שבי, gives this version, "captives of war," which seems unsuitable to this passage *Marckius* renders the phrase thus, *aversi belli*, seu, *a bello*, "turning away from war," or, "shy of war." This view evidently comports best with the context.—*Ed.*

and no one can keep his own ; so now, during peace, ye take to yourselves the same liberty, as though all things were exposed to plunder, and ye were in a hostile country, lately the scene of warfare."

We now then perceive the meaning of the Prophet. He first intimates that the people were now rejected by God, for they had rendered themselves, by their most abandoned life, wholly unworthy of his benefits ; and at the same time he reproves their ingratitude, that having been the people of God, they choose to make war with him rather than to observe the covenant which he had made for their safety ; for it was a most shameful wickedness in them, since they had been chosen from the whole world to be a peculiar people, to prefer going to war with God rather than to live quietly under his protection. And that they did rise up against God he proves, for they gave themselves up to robberies ; they plundered, even during times of peace, which circumstance greatly aggravated their wickedness. It now follows—

9. The women of my people have ye cast out from their pleasant houses ; from their children have ye taken away my glory for ever.	9. Mulieres populi mei expulistis è domo delectationum ipsarum, (*est quidem mutatio numeri, sed hoc nihil ad rem;*) à parvulis earum abstulistis decus (*vel*, ornamentum) meum perpetuò.

He proceeds with the same subject, that they refrained from no acts of injustice. It was indeed a proof of extreme barbarity not to spare women and children, for they are both weak and helpless. Their sex exempts women from violence, and their age, children.[1] Even in wars, women, and also children, escape in safety. We hence see that the Pro-

[1] This verse presents several anomalies. We have "women" and the verbs in the plural, and then "house," "*her* delights," and "*her* children." It may be thus rendered,—

The women of my people ye drive away,
Each from the house of her delights ;
From off her children ye take away my ornament for ever.

The word rendered in our version "glory," is הדר, which means ornament, beauty. *Piscator* says, *pulchras vestes quas Deus illis donavit*—"the beautiful garments which God gave them." God claimed the land of Canaan and all its blessings as his own. They took these away without restoring them according to the law. *Henderson* justly observes, that "ornament" is to be taken "collectively for the ornamental clothes which they wore, and with which they had been provided by Jehovah."—*Ed.*

phet, by stating a part for the whole, proves here that the people had addicted themselves to cruelty really barbarous; they were not restrained from exercising it, no, not even on women and children. Since it was so, it follows, that their boast of being the chosen people was vain and fallacious.

House of delights he ascribes to the women, who, being the weaker sex, prefer being at home and in the shade, rather than going abroad. The more necessary it was that their recesses should remain safe to them. Now, what was taken away from the children, God calls it *his ornament;* for his blessing, poured forth on children, is the mirror of his glory: he therefore condemns this plunder as a sacrilege. The word לעולם, *laoulam*, designates the continuance of their crimes, as though he had said, that they were cruel without ever showing any repentance. Now it follows—

10. Arise ye, and depart; for this *is* not *your* rest: because it is polluted, it shall destroy *you*, even with a sore destruction.	10. Surgite, abite, quia non est hæc requies; quoniam polluta est; dissipavit dissipatione violenta (*interponitur copula*, et dissipatione; ideo *poterimus commode vertere*, dissipavit et quidem dissipatione violenta, [*vel*, roborata; *id enim significat verbum* נמרץ.)

Here again the Prophet checks the foolish confidence of the people. The land of Canaan, we know, had been honoured by God with the distinction of being a rest; yea God called it, not only the rest of the people, but also his own rest, 'I have sworn in my wrath, if they shall enter into my rest,' (Ps. xcv. 12.) The land of Canaan then was a sort of nest, hidden under the wings of God; for the Lord had assigned it as an inheritance to his chosen people. As God then dwelt in that land, and had also given it to the children of Abraham, that they might rest there in safety, and as this was also one of the blessings contained in the Law, hypocrites said, pursuing their usual course of falsely and groundlessly claiming to themselves the favours of God, that they could not be thence expelled, and that those Prophets were falsifiers who dared to change any thing in God's covenant. This is the reason why the Prophet now says,

Arise, depart; this is not your rest. "False confidence," he says, "deceives you, as ye think that ye are inseparably fixed in your habitation. God indeed has made such a promise, but this condition was added,—If ye will stand faithful to his covenant. Now ye are become covenant-breakers : ye think that he is fast bound to you ; all the cords are loosened; for as ye have perfidiously departed from the law of God, there is now no reason for you to think that he is under any obligation to you. There is then no ground for you to boast of being a holy people ; you have indeed the name, but the reality has ceased to be : therefore *arise and depart :* but to sit still securely and proudly will avail you nothing, for God will now drive you afar off : and I now declare to you that you must arise and depart, for ye cannot rest in this land against the will of God : and God will now thrust you out of it." We now perceive the real meaning of the Prophet.

He afterwards adds, *For it is polluted ; he will scatter you with violent scattering.*[1] Here again he vindicates God from their calumny and ungodly murmurings. We indeed know how difficult it was to bring down that people, who were steeped in so great a perverseness. And we find that the Prophet had a hard contest with the hypocrites, for the multitude had ever this language in their mouths,—"What ! is it of no moment that God has favoured us with so many and so re-

[1] The original is תחבל וחבל נמרץ, which, according to Parkhurst, is, "It is bound;" that is, bound over to punishment, "and the bond is grievous ;" or, as it may be rendered, strong ; which is only found in Niphal in two other places, 1 Kings ii. 8 ; Job vi. 25. In the first it is rendered, grievous,—"a grievous crime," and in the second, forcible,—"How forcible are right words ! "

But most others attach the idea of corruption and destruction to חבל : and *Newcome* takes the verb here in a passive sense, and gives this rendering of the distich,—

"Because it is polluted, it shall be destroyed,
And the destruction *shall be* great."

Some render the verb actively, "It," *i. e.*, the land, "shall destroy you," a reference being made, as it is thought, to what is said in Lev. xviii. 25. The version of Marckius is this,—

"Quando quidem impuritas corrumpet,
Et corruptio acris."—
Seeing that impurity will destroy *it*,
And a violent destruction.

The previous word טמאה is here taken as a noun. But the most literal, and the most satisfactory, is the rendering of *Newcome.*—*Ed.*

markable promises? Is our adoption nothing but a mockery? Has he in vain given us this land by an hereditary right?" Since then hypocrites thus brought forward their privileges in opposition to God, and yet abused them, it was necessary to convince them to the contrary, and this is what the Prophet does here,—"Ye call," he says, "this land your rest, but how do you rest in it? God has commanded you to observe the Sabbath, for he dwells among you to sanctify you: but ye live disorderly, and carry on war with God himself: have not your pollutions obliterated that holy rest, which has been enjoined on you by God? Ye then see that this change has happened through your fault, that is, that God has ceased to call this land, as he was wont formerly to do, your and his own rest. *It is not* then *your rest;* he will therefore *scatter* you *with violent* or strong *scattering:* Ye in vain promise to yourselves rest in this land, since ye carry on war with God, and cease not to provoke his wrath against you." It follows—

11. If a man walking in the spirit and falsehood do lie, *saying*, I will prophesy unto thee of wine and of strong drink; he shall even be the prophet of this people.	11. Si vir ambulans in spiritu et falaciter mentiens, stillem tibi pro vino et pro sicera, tunc erit stillans populi hujus (*hoc est*, hic demum erit Propheta populi hujus: *sicut etiam priore membro propriè vertendum est*, si prophetem.)

The Prophet points out here another vice by which the people were infected—that they wished to be soothed with flatteries: for all the ungodly think that they are in a manner exempt from God's judgment, when they hear no reproof; yea they think themselves happy, when they get flatterers, who are indulgent to their vices. This is now the disease which the Prophet discovers as prevailing among the people. Jerome sought out a meaning quite different here, as in the former verses; but I will not stop to refute him, for it is enough to give the real meaning of the Prophet. But as before he rendered women, princes, and thus perverted entirely the meaning, so he says here, "I would I were a vain Prophet, that is, walking in vanity, and mendacious;" as though Micah said, "I wish I were false in denouncing on you the calamities of which I speak; for I would rather announce to you something joyful and favourable: but I cannot do this, for the Lord commands what is different." But there is nothing of this kind in the words of the Prophet. Let us then return to the text.

If a man walks in the spirit, and deceitfully lies,[1] *&c.* Almost all interpreters agree in this,—that to walk in the spirit, is to announce any thing proudly and presumptuously; and they take spirit for wind or for deceits. But I doubt not, but that to walk in the spirit was then a common mode of speaking, to set forth the exercise of the prophetic office. When therefore any one was a Prophet, or one who discharged that office, or sustained the character of a teacher, he professed himself to have been sent from above. The Prophets were indeed formerly called the men of the spirit, and for this reason,—because they adduced nothing from themselves or from their own heads; but only delivered faithfully, as from hand to hand, what they had received from God. To walk in the spirit then means, in my view, the same thing as to profess the office of a teacher. When therefore any one professed the office of a teacher, what was he to do? "If I," says Micah, "being endued with the Spirit, and called to teach, wished to ingratiate myself with you, and preached that there would be an abundant increase of wine and strong drink, all would applaud me; for if any one promises these things, he becomes *the prophet of this people.*"

[1] Perhaps the more literal rendering would be thus,—

If a man, the follower of the spirit and of deception,
Speaks falsely, "I will prophesy to thee of wine and of strong drink,"
He then becomes the prophet of this people.

To walk after, or to follow, "the wind," as some render רוח, seems by no means proper. The phrase means the same as "the man of the spirit" in Hosea ix. 7. *Newcome* changes the whole form of the passage, though not the meaning, except in one instance. Guided by the Syriac version, Houbigant and the Septuagint, without the sanction of any MS., he gives this version,—

If a man, walking *in* the spirit of falsehood and lies,
Prophesy unto thee for wine and for strong drink,
He shall be the prophet of this people.

He puts "*for* wine," &c., and not "*of* wine:" but the latter rendering is much more suitable to the context.—*Ed.*

In short, Micah intimates that the Israelites rejected all sound doctrine, for they sought nothing but flatteries, and wished to be cherished in their vices ; yea, they desired to be deceived by false adulation to their own ruin. It hence appears, that they were not the people they wished to be deemed, that is, the people of God : for the first condition in God's covenant was,—that he should rule among his people. Inasmuch then as these men would not endure to be governed by Divine power, and wished to have full and unbridled liberty, it was the same as though they had banished God far from them. Hence, by this proof, the Prophet shows that they had wholly departed from God, and had no intercourse with him. If there be then any man walking in the spirit, let him, he says, keep far from the truth ; for he will not otherwise be borne by this people.—How so ? Because they will not have honest and faithful teachers. What is then to be done ? Let flatterers come, and promise them plenty of wine and strong drink, and they will be their best teachers, and be received with great applause : in short, the suitable teachers of that people were the ungodly ; the people could no longer bear the true Prophets ; their desire was to have flatterers who were indulgent to all their corruptions.

PRAYER.

Grant, Almighty God, that since we cannot otherwise really profit by thy word, than by having all our thoughts and affections subjected to thee, and offered to thee as a sacrifice,—O grant, that we may suffer thee, by the sound of thy word, so to pierce through every thing within us, that being dead in ourselves, we may live to thee, and never suffer flatteries to become our ruin, but that we may, on the contrary, patiently endure reproofs, however bitter they may be, only let them serve to us as medicine, by which our inward vices may be cleansed, until at length being thoroughly cleansed and formed into new creatures, we may, by a pious and holy life, really glorify thy name, and be received into that celestial glory, which has been purchased for us by the blood of thy only-begotten Son, our Lord Jesus Christ. Amen.

Lecture Eighty-fifth.

12. I will surely assemble, O Jacob, all of thee; I will surely gather the remnant of Israel; I will put them together as the sheep of Bozrah, as the flock in the midst of their fold: they shall make great noise by reason of *the multitude of* men.	12. Congregans congregabo te totum Jacob; colligens colligam residuum Israel; simul ponam eum tanquam oves Bosra, tanquam gregem in medio ovilis sui; tumultuabuntur præ hominibus (*id est*, propter hominum multitudinem.)
13. The breaker is come up before them: they have broken up, and have passed through the gate, and are gone out by it; and their king shall pass before them, and the Lord on the head of them.	13. Ascendet effractor coram ipsis; frangent et transibunt portam, et egredientur per ipsam; et transibit rex ipsorum coram ipsis; et Jehova in capite ipsorum.

The exposition of this passage is twofold. The greater part of interpreters incline to this view,—that God here promises some alleviation to the Israelites, after having sharply reproved them, and threatened them with utter ruin. They therefore apply this passage to the kingdom of Christ, as though God gave hope of a future restoration. But when I narrowly weigh every thing, I am, on the contrary, forced to regard these two verses as a commination, that is, that the Prophet here denounces God's future vengeance on the people. As, however, the former opinion is almost universally received, I will briefly mention what has been adduced in its favour, and then I shall return to state the other meaning, which I prefer.

It is suitable to the kingdom of Christ to say, that a people who had been dispersed should be gathered under one head. We indeed know how miserable a dispersion there is in the world without him, and that whenever the Prophets speak of the renovation of the Church, they commonly make use of this form of expression, that is, that the Lord will gather the dispersed and unite them together under one head. If then the passage be referred to the kingdom of Christ, it is altogether proper to say, that God *by gathering will gather the whole of Jacob.* But a restriction is afterwards added, that no one may extend this restoration to the whole race of Abraham, or to all those who, according to the flesh, derived their descent from Abraham as their father: hence the word

שארית, *sharit,* is laid down. Then the whole of Jacob is not that multitude, which, according to the flesh, traced their origin from the holy Patriarchs, but only their residue. It then follows, *I will set them together as the sheep of Bozrah,* that is, I will make them to increase into a large, yea, into an immense number; for they shall make a tumult, that is, a great noise will be made by them, as though the place could not contain so large a number. And they explain the next verse thus,—*A breaker shall go before them,* that is, there shall be those who, with a hand, strong and armed, will make a way open for them; inasmuch as Christ says that the kingdom of heaven suffereth violence, (Matth. xi. 12:) they then mean that the people will have courageous leaders, whom nothing will stop from breaking through, and that they will also lead the whole people with them. They shall therefore go forth through the gate, and their king shall pass through. This also well agrees with the kingdom of Christ. For whenever God declares that he will be propitious to his Church, he at the same time adds, that he will give a king to his people; for their safety had been placed in that kingdom, which had been erected by the authority and command of God himself. It is therefore a common thing, and what occurs everywhere in the Prophets, that God would give a king from the seed of David to his people, when it would be his will to favour them with complete happiness. Thus they understand that a king shall pass on before them, which is the office of a leader, to show them the way. *And Jehovah shall be at their head;* that is, God himself will show himself to be the chief king of his people, and will ever defend by his help and grace those whom he adopts as his people.

But I have already said that I more approve of another exposition: for I see not how the Prophet could pass so suddenly into a different strain. He had said in the last verse that the people could endure no admonitions, for they only desired flatteries and adulation. He now joins what I have lately referred to respecting the near judgment of God, and proceeds, as we shall see, in the same strain to the end of the third chapter: but we know that the chapters were not divided by the Prophets themselves. We have therefore a discourse continued by the Prophet to the third chapter; not that he spoke all these things in one day; but he wished to collect together what he had said of the vices of the people; and this will be more evident as we proceed. I will now come to the words.

Gathering, I will gather thee, the whole of Jacob; collecting, I will collect the remnant of Israel. God has two modes of gathering; for he sometimes gathers his people from dispersion, which is a singular proof of his favour and love. But he is said also to gather, when he assembles them together to devote and give them up to destruction, as we say in French, *Trousser;* and this verb is taken elsewhere in the same sense, and we have already met with an instance in Hosea. So, in the present passage, God declares that there would be a gathering of the people,—for what purpose? Not that being united together they might enjoy the blessings of God, but that they might be destroyed. As then the people had united together in all kinds of wickedness, so God now declares, that they should be gathered together, that the one and the same destruction might be to them all. And he adds, *the remnant of Israel;* as though he said, "Whatever shall remain from slaughters in wars and from all other calamities, such as famine and pestilence, this I will collect, that it may be wholly destroyed." He mentions the remnant, because the Israelites had been worn out by many evils, before the Lord stretched forth his hand at last to destroy them.

He afterwards subjoins, *I will set them together as the sheep of Bozrah;* that is, I will cast them into one heap. Bozrah was a city or a country of Idumea; and it was a very fruitful place, and had the richest pastures: hence Isaiah, chap. xxxiv., in denouncing vengeance on the Idumeans, alludes at the same time to their pastures, and says, "God will choose for himself fat lambs and whatever is well fed, and will also collect fatness, for the Lord has a sacrifice in Bozrah." So also, in this place, the Prophet says, that the Jews, when collected together as it were into a bundle, shall be like *the sheep of Bozrah.* And he further adds, *as the sheep in the middle of the sheepfolds,* though some render it, *leading:* דבר, *daber,* sometimes means to lead; but I see no reason why it should be drawn so far from its meaning in this connection. I take it as signifying a sheepfold, because sheep are there collected together. Some interpreters consider that a siege is referred to here, that is, that God would confine the whole people within cities, that they might not be open to the incursions of enemies; but I extend the meaning much wider, namely, that God would gather the people, in order at last to disperse them. *I will* then *gather them*, as I have already said, *Je vous trousserai, as the sheep of Bozrah in the middle of the sheepfold; and there shall be a noise on account of their number;* that is, "Though ye now glory in your number, this will avail you nothing; for I shall be able to reduce you all to a strait, so that you may, as ye deserve, perish together."

It follows, *Ascend shall a breaker before them;* that is, they shall be led in confusion; and the gate shall also be broken, that they may go forth together; for the passage would not be large enough, were they, as is usually done, to go forth in regular order; but the gates of cities shall be broken, that they may pass through in great numbers and in confusion. By these words the Prophet intimates, that all would be quickly taken away into exile. *And they shall go forth,* he says, *through the gate, and their king shall pass on before them.* The Prophet means here, that the king would be made captive; and this was the saddest spectacle: for some hope remained, when the dregs of the people had been led into Chaldea; but when the king himself was led away a captive, and cast into prison, and his eyes pulled out, and his children slain, it was the greatest of misery. They were wont to take pride in their king, for they thought that their kingdom could not but continue perpetually, since God had so promised. But God might for a time overturn that kingdom, that he might afterwards raise it anew, according to what has been done by Christ, and according to what had been also predicted by the Prophets. "Crosswise, crosswise, crosswise, (*transversa*,) let the crown be, until its lawful possessor comes." We then see that this, which the Prophet mentions respecting their king, has been added for the sake of amplifying.

He afterwards adds, *Jehovah shall be at the head of them;* that is, He will be nigh them, to oppress and wholly to overwhelm them. Some consider something to be understood, and of this kind, that Jehovah was wont formerly to rule over them, but that now he would cease to do so: but this is too strained; and the meaning which I have stated seems sufficiently clear, and that is,—that God himself would be the doer, when they should be driven into exile, and that he would add courage to tyrants and their attendants, in pursuing the accursed people, in order to urge on more and more and aggravate their calamities, and thus to show that their destruction would happen through his righteous judgment. We now then understand the real meaning of the Prophet.[1] Now follows—

CHAPTER III.

1. And I said, Hear, I pray you, O heads of Jacob, and ye princes of the house of Israel; *Is it* not for you to know judgment?	1. Et dixi, Audite quæso principes Jacob et gubernatores domus Israel; annon vestrum est (*vel*, ad vos spectat) scire judicium?
2. Who hate the good, and love the evil; who pluck off their skin from off them, and their flesh from off their bones;	2. Atqui oderunt bonum et diligunt malum, rapiunt pellem ab ipsis, et carnem ab ossibus eorum;
3. Who also eat the flesh of my people, and flay their skin from off them; and they break their bones and chop them in pieces, as for the pot, and as flesh within the caldron.	3. Et tunc vorant carnem populi mei, et pellem ipsorum ab ipsis excoriant; et ossa eorum frangunt, et comminuunt; sicuti ad ollam (*vel*, ac si destinata essent ollæ,) et carnem eorum in medio aheni.

[1] *Calvin* is not singular in his view of this passage. *Scott* takes the same view, while *Henry* regards the passage as containing a promise, and so do *Marckius*, *Newcome*, and *Henderson*. But some have considered the words as those of the false prophets, referred to in the eleventh verse, and that Micah answers them in the next chapter. There is no sufficient ground for this opinion. Of those who regard the passage as including a promise, some apply it to the restoration from the Babylonian captivity, and others to spiritual restoration by the gospel. But the passage, viewed in itself, and in its connection with the next chapter, bears evidently the appearance of a commination: there are especially two words which manifestly favour this view,—תהימנה and הפרץ; both are taken generally, if not uniformly, in a bad sense. The first means to tumultuate, to be turbulent and riotous, to be clamorous and noisy; the second signifies to demolish, to break through, to destroy, and in every instance in which it is found as a personal noun, it means a destroyer or a robber.—See Ps. xvii. 4; Ezek. xviii. 10; Dan. xi. 14. The first is a verb in the second person plural of the future tense, and in the feminine gender, because of the comparison made in the former lines to sheep and a flock. The verbs in the 12th verse are all in the future tense, and the two first in the 13th are in the past, according to what is

The Prophet in this chapter assails and severely reproves the chief men as well as the teachers; for both were given to avarice and cruelty, to plunder, and, in short, to all other vices. And he begins with the magistrates, who exercised authority among the people; and briefly relates the words in which he inveighed against them. We have said elsewhere, that the Prophets did not record all that they had spoken, but only touched shortly on the heads or chief points: and this was done by Micah, that we might know what he did for forty or more years, in which he executed his office. He could have related, no doubt, in half-an-hour, all that exists of his writings: but from this small book, however small it is, we may learn what was the Prophet's manner of teaching, and on what things he chiefly dwelt. I will now return to his words.

He says that the chief men of the kingdom had been reproved by him. It is probable, that these words were addressed to the Jews; for though at the beginning he includes the Israelites, we yet know that he was given as a teacher to the Jews, and not to the kingdom of Israel. It was as it were accidental, that he sometimes introduces the ten tribes together with the Jews. This address then was made, as I think, to the king as well as to his counsellors and other judges, who then ruled over the people of Judah.

Hear this, I pray, he says. Such a preface betokens carelessness in the judges; for why does he demand a hearing from them, except that they had become so torpid in their vices, that they would attend to nothing? Inasmuch then

common in prophecies, but must be rendered as futures. I propose the following version of the passage,—

12. Gathering, I will gather Jacob, the whole of thee;
Assembling, I will assemble the residue of Israel;
Together will I set them as the sheep of Bozrah,
As a flock in the midst of its fold;—
Ye shall be more noisy than men.
13. Ascend *shall* the breaker in the sight of them,—they shall break through,
And pass the gate, yea, they shall go forth through it,
And pass shall their king before them,
And Jehovah *shall be* at their head,
or, for their leader.—*Ed.*

as so brutal a stupor had seized on them, he says, *Hear now ye chiefs*, or heads, *of Jacob, and ye rulers*[1] *of the house of Israel.* But why does he still speak of the house of Israel? Because that name was especially known and celebrated, whenever a mention was made of the posterity of Abraham: and the other Prophets, even while speaking of the kingdom of Judah, often make use of this title, "ye who are called by the name of Israel;" and they did this, on account of the dignity of the holy Patriarch; and the meaning of the word itself was no ordinary testimonial of excellency as to his whole race. And this is what is frequently done by Isaiah. But the name of Israel is not put here, as elsewhere, as a title of distinction: on the contrary, the Prophet here amplifies their sin, because they were so corrupt, though they were the chief men among the chosen race, being those whom God had honoured with so much dignity, as to set them over his Church and elect people. It was then an ingratitude, not to be endured, to abuse that high and sacred authority, which had been conferred on them by God.

Does it not belong to you, he says, *to know judgment?* Here he intimates that rectitude ought to have a place among the chief men, in a manner more especial than among the common people; for it behoves them to excel others in the knowledge of what is just and right: for though the difference between good and evil be engraven on the hearts of all, yet they, who hold supremacy among the people, and excel in power, are as it were the eyes of the community; as the eyes direct the whole body, so also they, who are placed in any situation of honour, are thus made eminent, that they may show the right way to others. Hence by the word, to *know*, the Prophet intimates that they wickedly subverted the whole order of nature, for they were blind, while they ought to have been the luminaries of the whole people. *Is it not for you*, he says, *to know judgment* and equity? But why was this said, especially to the chief men? Because they, though they of themselves knew what was right, having the law en-

[1] קצינים, from קצה, to cut off, to sever, to separate: they were those who were *separated* from others, as leaders of an army, rendered in our version, captains, rulers, Jos. x. 24; Isa. xxii. 3.—*Ed.*

graven within, ought yet as leaders to have possessed superior knowledge, so as to outshine others. It is therefore your duty to know judgment. We hence learn that it is not enough for princes and magistrates to be well disposed and upright; but it is required of them to know judgment and wisdom, that they may discern matters above the common people. But if they are not thus endued with the gift of understanding and wisdom, let them ask of the Lord. We indeed know, that without the Spirit of God, the acutest men are wholly unfit to rule; nor is it in vain, that the free Spirit of God is set forth, as holding the supreme power in the world; for we are thus reminded, that even they who are endued with the chief gifts are wholly incapable of governing, except the Spirit of God be with them. This passage then shows that an upright mind is not a sufficient qualification in princes; they must also excel in wisdom, that they may be, as we have already said, as the eyes are to the body. In this sense it is that Micah now says, that it belonged to the leaders of the people to know judgment and justice.[1]

He afterwards subjoins, *But they hate good, and love evil, and pull off the skin*[2] *from my people, the flesh from their bones;* that is, they leave nothing, he says, sound and safe, their ra-

[1] Some, such as *Marckius*, and also *Grotius*, take another view of this sentence: Is it not for you, who judge and punish others, to know the judgment of God, which awaits you? But most agree in the view given here.—*Ed.*

[2] *Their* skin, literally. The antecedent (which is not unusual in Hebrew) is mentioned afterwards: it is the word, people, which follows.

The idea of sheep or flock, to which the people are compared in the last chapter, is still retained here. *Adam Clarke* quotes from *Suetonius* a striking answer of Tiberius, the Emperor, to some governors, who solicited him to increase the taxes,—" It is the property of a good shepherd to shear his sheep, not to *skin* them"—*Boni pastoris esse tondere pecus, non deglubere.*

To " hate good, and to love evil," in the former sentence, betokens a character dreadful in the extreme; for good here, טוב, means kindness, benevolence, the doing of good to others; this they *hated:* and evil, רעה, means wrong, mischief, injury, the doing of harm, of wrong, and of injustice to others; and this they *loved.* How transmuted they were in their spirit into that of very fiends! " They hate to do good, hate to have any good done, and hate those that are good; and they love the evil, delight in mischief, and in those that do mischief." These words of *Henry,* no doubt, convey a correct view of the sentence. It might therefore be rendered, " Haters of benevolence, and lovers of mischief."—*Ed.*

pacity being so furious. The Prophet conveys first a general reproof,—that they not only perverted justice, but were also given to wickedness and hated good. He means then that they were openly wicked and ungodly, and also that they with a fixed purpose carried on war against every thing just and right. We hence learn how great and how abominable was the corruption of the people, when they were still the peculiar possession and heritage of God. Inasmuch then as the state of this ancient people had become so degenerated, let us learn to walk in solicitude and fear, while the Lord governs us by pious magistrates and faithful pastors: for what happened to the Jews might soon happen to us, so that wolves might bear rule over us, as indeed experience has proved even in this our city. The Prophet afterwards adds the kinds of cruelty which prevailed; of which he speaks in hyperbolical terms, though no doubt he sets before our eyes the state of things as it was. He compares the judges to wolves or to lions, or to other savage beasts. He says not that they sought the property of the people, or pillaged their houses; but he says that they devoured their flesh even to the very bones; he says that they pulled off their skin: and this he confirms in the next verse.

They devour, he says, *the flesh of my people, and their skin they strip off from them, and their bones they break in pieces and make small, as that which into the pot is thrown, and which is in the midst of the caldron.*[1] For when any one throws meat into the pot, he does not take the whole ox, but cuts it into pieces, and having broken it, he then fills with these pieces his pot or his caldron. The Prophet then enhances the cruelty of the princes; they were not content with one kind of oppression, but exercised every species of barbarous cruelty towards the people, and were in every respect like bears, or wolves, or lions, or some other savage beasts, and that they were also like gluttons. We now then perceive the Prophet's meaning.

[1] "Under the similitude of butchers the Prophet sets forth their savage cruelty: 1. they take off the skin; 2. they eat the flesh; 3. they break the bones, to pick out the marrow. The insatiable avarice of the princes is described."—*Cocceius.*

Now this passage teaches us what God requires mainly from those in power,—that they abstain from doing injustice: for as they are armed with power, so they ought to be a law to themselves. They assume authority over others ; let them then begin with themselves, and restrain themselves from doing evil. For when a private man is disposed to do harm, he is restrained at least by fear of the laws, and dares not to do any thing at his pleasure ; but in princes there is a greater boldness; and they are able to do greater injustice : and this is the reason why they ought to observe more forbearance and humanity. Hence lenity and paternal kindness especially become princes and those in power. But the Prophet here condemns the princes of his age for what deserved the highest reprehension ; and their chief crime was cruelty or inhumanity, inasmuch as they spared not their own subjects.

We now see that the Prophet in no degree flattered the great, though they took great pride in their own dignity. But when he saw that they wickedly and basely abused the power committed to them, he boldly resisted them, and exercised the full boldness of the Spirit. He therefore not only calls them robbers or plunderers of the people ; but he says, that they were cruel wild beasts; he says, that they devoured the flesh, tore and pulled it in pieces, and made it small; and he says all this, that he might convey an idea of the various kinds of cruelty which they practised. Now follow threatenings—

4. Then shall they cry unto the Lord, but he will not hear them ; he will even hide his face from them at that time, as they have behaved themselves ill in their doings.	4. Tunc clamabunt ad Jehovam, et non respondebit illis ; sed abscondet faciem suam ab ipsis tempore illo, quemadmodum perversè egerunt in factis suis.

Micah now denounces judgment on the chief men, such as they deserved. He says, *They shall cry then to Jehovah*. The adverb אז, *az*, is often put indefinitely in Hebrew, and has the force of a demonstrative, and may be taken as pointing out a thing, (δεικτικως—demonstratively,) *then*, or there, as though the Prophet pointed out by his finger things which could be seen, though they were far away from the sight of men. But in this place, the Prophet seems rather to pursue the subject to which I have already referred : for he had before stated that God would take vengeance on that people. This adverb of time then is connected with the other comminations, which have been already explained.[1] If, however, any one prefer a different meaning, namely, that the Prophet meant here to hold them in suspense, as to the nearness of God's vengeance, I do not oppose him, for this sense is not unsuitable. However this may be, the Prophet here testifies that the crimes of the chief men would not go unpunished, though they did not think themselves to be subject either to laws or to punishment. As then the princes and magistrates regarded themselves as exempt, by some imaginary privilege, from the lot of other people, the Prophet declares here expressly, that a distress was nigh at hand, which would extort a cry from them : for by the word, cry, he means the miseries which were nigh at hand. *They shall* then *cry* in their distress. I have now explained the design of the Prophet.

We indeed see how at this day those who are in high stations swell with arrogance ; for as they abound in wealth, and as honour is as it were an elevated degree, so that being propped up by the shoulders of others they seem eminent, and as they are also feared by the rest of the people, they are on these accounts led to think that no adversity can happen to them. But the Prophet says, that such would be their distress, that it would draw a cry from them.

They shall then *cry, but* Jehovah *will not hear ;* that is, they shall be miserable and without any remedy. Jehovah *will not answer them,* but *will hide from them his face, as they have done perversely ;* that is, God will not hear their complaints; for he will return on their own heads all the injuries with which he now sees his own people to be afflicted. And thus God

[1] There is nothing in the context to which אז, then, or at that time, can be referred, except to the two concluding verses of the last chapter, which ought not to have been separated from this. And this connection confirms the view, that these two verses contain not a promise but a threatening. The same time is meant by אז as by בעת ההיא in the following part of the verse ; for it is usual with the Prophets to express generally or indefinitely at first what they afterwards more distinctly specify.—*Ed.*

will show that he was not asleep, while they were with so much effrontery practising all kinds of wrong.

It may however be asked here, how it is that God rejects the prayers and entreaties of those who cry to him? It must first be observed, that the reprobate, though they rend the air with their cries, do not yet direct their prayers to God; but if they address God himself, they do this clamorously; for they expostulate with him, and contend with him, yea, they vomit out their blasphemies, or at least they murmur and complain of their evils. The ungodly then cry, but not to the Lord; or if they address their cries to God, they are, as it has been said, full of clamour. Hence, except one is guided by the Spirit of God, he cannot pray from the heart. And we know that it is the peculiar office of the Spirit to raise up our hearts to heaven: for in vain we pray, except we bring faith and repentance: and who is the author of these but the Holy Spirit? It appears then that the ungodly so cry, that they only violently contend with God: but this is not the right way of praying. It is therefore no wonder that God rejects their clamours. The ungodly do indeed at times pour forth a flood of prayers and call on God's name with the mouth; but at the same time they are, as we have said, full of perverseness, and they never really humble themselves before God. Since then they pour forth their prayers from a bitter and a proud heart, this is the reason why the Prophet says now, that the Lord *would not then hear, but hide his face from them at that time, inasmuch as they acted perversely.*[1]

He shows here that God would not be reconciled to men wholly irreclaimable, who could not be restored by any means to the right way. But when any one falls [and repents] he will ever find God propitious to him, as soon as he cries to him; but when with obstinate minds we pursue our own course, and

[1] Literally, "As they have rendered evil their deeds," or, to coin a corresponding word, As they have evilized their deeds. To render their deeds evil was to render them afflictive, injurious, and oppressive to others, according to what has been previously described. Hence the following version of *Henderson* is incorrect,—

Because they have corrupted their doings.—*Ed.*

give no place to repentance, we close up the door of mercy against ourselves; and so what the Prophet teaches here necessarily takes place,—the Lord hides his face in the day of distress. And we also hear what the Scripture says,—that judgment will be without mercy to those who are not merciful, (James ii. 11.) Hence if any one be inexorable to his brethren, (as we see at this day many tyrants to be, and we also see many in the middle class to be of the same tyrannical and wholly sanguinary disposition,) he will at length, whoever he may be, meet with that judgment which Micah here denounces. The sentence then is not to be taken in a general sense, as though he had said, that the Lord would not be reconciled to the wicked; but he points out especially those irreclaimable men, who had wholly hardened themselves, so that they had become, as we have already seen, altogether inflexible. The Prophet now comes to his second reproof.

5. Thus saith the Lord concerning the prophets that make my people err, that bite with their teeth, and cry, Peace; and he that putteth not into their mouths, they even prepare war against him:

5. Sic dicit Jehova super (*vel*, ad) prophetas, qui decipiunt populum meum, et mordent dentibus suis, et clamant, Pax; et si quis non dederit in os ipsorum, edicunt contra eum prœlium:

Micah accuses here the Prophets, in the first place, of avarice and of a desire for filthy lucre. But he begins by saying that he spoke by God's command, and as it were from his mouth, in order that his commination might have more weight and power. *Thus* then *saith Jehovah against the Prophets:* and he calls them the deceivers of the people: but at the same time he points out the source of the evil, that is, why or by what passion they were instigated to deceive, and that was, because the desire of gain had wholly possessed them, so that they made no difference between what was true and what was false, but only sought to please for the sake of gain. And he shows also, on the other hand, that they were so covetous of gain, that they *declared war*, if any one did not feed them. And God repeats again the name of his people: this had escaped my notice lately in observing on the words of Micah, that the princes devoured the flesh of

God's people; for the indignity was increased when this wrong was done to the people of God. Had the Assyrians, or the Ethiopians, or the Egyptians, been pillaged by their princes, it would have been more tolerable; but when the very people of God were thus devoured, it was, as I have said, less to be borne. So when the people of God were deceived, and the truth was turned to a lie, it was a sacrilege the more hateful.

This then was the reason why he said, *Who deceive my people*:[1] "This people is sacred to me, for I have chosen them for myself; as then they are destroyed by frauds and deceptions, is not my majesty in a manner dishonoured—is not my authority lessened?" We now then see the reason why the Prophet says, *They deceive my people.* It is indeed certain, that the Jews were worthy of such deceptions; and God elsewhere declares, that whenever he permitted false prophets to come among them, it was to try them to see what sort of people they were, (Deut. xiii.) It was then their just reward, when liberty was given to Satan to prevent sound doctrine among the people. And no one is ever deceived, except through his own will. Though their own simplicity seems to draw many to destruction, yet there is ever in them some hypocrisy. But it does not extenuate the sin of false teachers, that the people deserve such a punishment: and hence the Prophet still goes on with his reproof and says, that they were the people of God,—in what respect? By adoption. Though then the Jews had rendered themselves unworthy of such an honour, yet God counts them his people, that he might punish the wickedness of the false teachers, of which he now accuses them. It now follows, that they did *bite with their teeth.* But I cannot finish to-day.

[1] "Who deceive my people," is better than, "Who cause my people to err," according to *Newcome* and *Henderson;* for what is referred to is the "peace," promised by the false prophets. *Marckius'* version is, "Who seduce my people," and he makes this remark,—that the people had three seducers,—the devil, their own deceitful hearts, and the false prophets.—*Ed.*

PRAYER.

Grant, Almighty God, that as thou wouldest have the image of thy justice to shine in princes, and whom thou armest with the sword, that they might rule in thy name, and be really thy ministers,—O grant, that this thy blessing may openly appear among us, and that by this evidence thou mayest testify that thou art not only propitious to us, but hadst also a care for our safety, and watchest over our welfare and well-being: and do thou so shine by thy word, that it may never be obscured or clouded among us through any depraved cupidity, but ever retain its own clear purity, so that we may proceed in the right path of salvation, which thou hast discovered and prescribed, until we be at length gathered into thy celestial kingdom, to enjoy that eternal inheritance, which has been procured for us by the blood of thy only-begotten Son. Amen.

Lecture Eighty-sixth.

LET us proceed to explain that sentence of the Prophet, in which he shows the cause why the teachers deceived the people and turned the truth of God to a lie; and this was, because they were greedy of gain, and were wholly given to avarice. We hence see, according to the testimony of Paul, that avarice affords a cause to all evils, (1 Tim. vi. 10;) and that wherever this contagion comes, all things necessarily fall into decay: for when avarice reigns in the hearts of men, the truth of God especially is ever adulterated.

But Micah adduces two evidences of avarice,—that they *cried, Peace,* when well fed and filled,—and that they proclaimed war, when they were hungry. Then as to the first point, he says, הנשכים בשניהם וקראו שלום, *enushikim besheniem ukrau shelum,* that is, " who bite with their teeth,[1]

[1] The expression, " to bite with the teeth," is singular, when understood to signify voraciousness, as evidently it does here; for the corresponding words in the next distich, " who put not into their mouth," seem to require this meaning. Almost all critics, except some of the Greek Fathers, who followed the Septuagint, agree in attaching this import to the sentence. The paraphrase of Rabbi *Jonathan* is, " To him who offers to them a feast of meat, they prophesy peace." *Jerome's* view is the same. *Dathius* gives this paraphrase, *dum illis datur quod edunt*—" while is given them something to eat."

and cry, Peace." But the sentence is to be so understood, that when they did bite well, they announced peace with full confidence: for by the word, *bite*, the Prophet means their gormandizing; for they who, under the guise of God's name, sought only their own advantage, were not satisfied with a moderate support, inasmuch as they were like hungry dogs. They therefore devoured, and gorged themselves, without any limits or moderation. This is the reason why he says that they did bite: for he compares them either to lions or to bears; and we know that wild beasts are not satiated with a small quantity of food, but that they gnash as it were their teeth except they are always pampered. So also Micah says, that the false teachers of his age were voracious men, who demanded a large proportion of food. We see the same thing in our day as to the monks under the Papacy, especially those who, under the name of mendicity, devour the substance of all people. Except they are pampered, they always murmur; nay, they are not content with murmurs, they proclaim war, as the Prophet says here. We indeed see at the same time, that they are insatiable; for when they come to tables well furnished, no one would say that they are men, but beasts, for they devour every thing. We now then understand the Prophet's meaning.

But it is not voracity alone that is reprehended: he says, that they sold their blessings, when they were well filled and had their stomach well supplied. In the same manner the monks also are wont to pronounce peace when they are well fed,—" O! ye do good, when ye take care of the brethren; for they are careful of you: when ye sleep in your beds, they watch, and their prayers make you rich; for how could the world stand, were it not that the brethren make amends for it?

Henry's comment is much to the purpose,—" They will flatter and compliment those who will feed them with good bits, will give them something to eat; but as for those who put not into their mouths, who are not continually cramming them, they look upon them as their enemies; to them they do not cry, Peace, but even prepare war against them; against them they denounce the judgments of God: they preach either comfort or terror to men, not according as they are to God, but as they are to them; as the crafty priests of the Church of Rome, in some places, make their image either to smile or to frown upon the offerer, according as his offering is."—*Ed.*

As then ye are so kind to our community, all things shall turn out well and prosperously to you, and God also will bless you." This then is the practice of those who for reward sell their blessings; they cry, Peace, that is, they confidently declare that all things shall be well, they make God propitious, provided such liberality towards their order be ever continued.

But, on the other hand, he also says, *If any one gives not to their mouth, they instantly sanctify war against you:*[1] but I give a different rendering, as the passage requires,—that they *proclaim war;* though the word is literally, to sanctify. But we have seen in Joel, chap. ii., that the word is used to designate any solemn proclamation,—"Sanctify a fast," that is, Proclaim a fast. So also in this place, They sanctify war, that is, they proclaim war, when any one does not feed them, nor satisfy their gormandizing; for they could not bear want. In short, the Prophet shows, that these false teachers were so blinded by avarice, that they discerned not the difference between right and wrong; but only praised those who fed them: and, on the other hand, when they found that they and their stomach were not cared for nor satisfied, they cursed, fulminated, and uttered nothing but anathemas; as we see to be done at this day by the monks under the Papacy. The Prophet now says—

6. Therefore night *shall be* unto you, that ye shall not have a vision; and it shall be dark unto you, that ye shall not divine; and the sun shall go down over the prophets, and the day shall be dark over them;

7. Then shall the seers be ashamed, and the diviners confounded: yea, they shall all cover their lips; for *there is* no answer of God.

6. Propterea nox vobis erit à visione (*vel,* pro visione, *vel,* propter visionem; *dicemus postea de sensu,*) et tenebræ vobis à divinatione (*vel,* propter divinationem,) et occumbet sol super prophetas, et obtenebrabitur super eos dies;

7. Et pudefient videntes (*hoc est,* prophetæ,) et erubescent divini, et velabunt (*hoc est,* velum opponent) super labium suum omnes; quia non erit responsum Dei.

God declares here to the false teachers by the mouth of

[1] The original may be thus rendered,—

But whosoever will not put into their mouth,
Even against him they will proclaim war.—*Ed.*

Micah, that he would inflict punishment on them, so that they should be exposed to the reproach of all. Hence the kind of punishment of which the Prophet speaks is—that he would strip the false teachers of all their dignity, so that they should hereafter in vain put on an appearance, and claim the honourable name which they had so long abused. We indeed know, when ungodly and profane men clothe themselves with the dignified titles of being the princes, or bishops, or prelates of the Church, how audaciously they pervert every thing, and do so with impunity. There is then no other remedy, except God pulls off the mask from them, and openly discovers to all their baseness. Of this punishment Micah now speaks.

There shall be to you a night from vision; so is the phrase literally, but the particle מ, *mem,* means often, for, or, on account of; and we can easily see that the Prophet represents night as the reward for vision, and darkness for divination. "As then my people have been deceived by your fallacies, for your visions and divinations have been nothing but lies and deceits, I will repay you with the reward which you have deserved: for instead of a vision you shall have night, and instead of divination you shall have thick darkness."[1] It is indeed certain, that the false teachers, even when they were, as they say, in great reputation, that is, when they retained the honour and the title of their office, were blind and wholly destitute of all light: but the Prophet here declares, that as their baseness did not appear to the common people, God would cause it to be made at length fully evident. As for instance, there is nothing at this day more stupid and

[1] That this is the meaning is evident from the two last lines of the verse. It is a kind of parallelism, in which the four lines contain the same idea or ideas, announced in the two first lines in one form, and in the two last in another, with more clearness, and sometimes with something additional. The preposition מ has sometimes the meaning of *rather than*, but here, *instead of.* I would render the verse thus,—

> Therefore night shall be to you instead of vision,
> And darkness shall be to you instead of divination:
> Yea, set shall the sun upon the Prophets,
> And darken upon them shall the day.

Piscator gives the sense when he says, *Visio vestra mutabitur in noctem* —"Your vision shall be changed into night."—*Ed.*

senseless than the bishops of the Papacy: for when any one draws from them any expression about religion, they instantly betray not only their ignorance, but also their shameful stupidity. With regard to the monks, though they be the most audacious kind of animals, (*audacissimum animalium genus,*) yet we know how unlearned and ignorant they are. Therefore at this time the night has not yet passed away, nor the darkness, of which Micah speaks here.

We now then understand what the Holy Spirit teaches here, and that is,—that God would at length strip those false teachers of that imaginary dignity, on account of which no one dared to speak against them, but received as an oracle whatever they uttered. *Night*, then, *shall be to you instead of a vision;* that is, "The whole world shall understand that you are not what you boast yourselves to be: for I will show that there is not in you, no, not a particle of the prophetic spirit, but that ye are men as dark as night, and darkness shall be to you instead of divination. Ye boast of great acuteness and great perspicuity of mind; but I will discover your baseness, so that the very children may know that ye are not endued with the Spirit."

To the same purpose is what he adds, *Go down shall the sun upon you, and darkened over you shall be the day;* that is, such will be that darkness, that even at noon they will see nothing; the sun will shine on all, but they shall grope as in the dark; so that God's vengeance would be made so manifest, that it might be noticed by all, from the least to the greatest.

He confirms the same thing in the next verse, *And ashamed shall be the seers, and confounded the diviners,*[1] *and they shall cover their lip;* that is, they will put veils on their mouths. In short, he means, that they would become a reproach to all, so that they would be ashamed of themselves, and no more dare to boast with so much confidence of their name and of the prophetic office.

As to this form of expression, ועטו על־שפם, *uothu ol she-*

[1] רסמים, μαντεις, Sept. *fatidici*, soothsayers, diviners. It is used generally in a bad sense, while חזים, seers, is commonly used in a good sense; but here both words denote pretenders, the false prophets.—*Ed.*

phim, some think that the practice of mourners is referred to; but this interpretation is frigid. I have therefore no doubt but that Micah intimates that the mouths of the false teachers would be closed. There is nearly the same denunciation mentioned by Zechariah; for speaking of the restoration of the Church, he says,—They who before went about boasting greatly, and gloried in the name of Prophets, shall cast away their mantle, and will no longer dare to show themselves; yea, when they shall come abroad, they shall be as it were herdsmen or private persons, and shall say, "I am not a prophet, nor the son of a prophet, I am chastised by my father;" that is, they shall profess themselves unworthy of being called prophets; but that they are scholars under discipline, (Zech. xiii. 5.) So also in this place, "They deceive at this day my people," saith the Lord; "I will reward them as they deserve; I will fill them with disgrace and contempt. They shall not then dare hereafter to show themselves as they have been wont to do; they shall not presume boastingly to profess themselves to be the pillars of the Church, that the whole world may be made subject to them; they shall not dare with tyrannical force to oppress the common and ignorant portions of society." *Veil*, then, *shall they their mouth;* that is, "I will cause their mouth to be closed, so that they shall not dare hereafter to utter even a word."[1]

It follows, *For there will be no answer from God.* Some so explain this sentence, as though the Prophet upbraided them with their old deceits, which they boasted were the words of God: as then they were not faithful to God, but lied to miserable men, when they said, that they were sent from above, and brought messages from heaven, while they only uttered their own inventions or fables, they should on these accounts be constrained to cover their mouth. But different is the meaning of the Prophet, and it is this,—that they were to be deprived of any answer, so that their want of knowledge might be easily perceived even by the most ignorant:

[1] The version of Newcome is, "They shall cover the mouth;" that is, as he adds in a note, "with part of the long eastern vesture. This action was a sign of being put to silence, of disgrace and dejection, Lev. xiii. 45; Ezek. xxiv. 17, 22." There is no reason to render mouth, beard, as some have done.—*Ed.*

for false teachers, though they possess nothing certain, yet deceive the simple with disguises, and render plausible their absurdities, that they may seem to be the interpreters of God; and they further add great confidence: and then the stupidity of the people concedes to them such great power, according to what is said by Jeremiah in chapter v., where he says, that the priests received gifts, and that for gifts the Prophets divined, and that the people loved such depravations. But Micah declares here that such delusions would no longer be allowed, for God would dissipate them. It will then be made evident, that *you have no answer from God;* that is, "All will perceive that you are void and destitute of every celestial truth, and that you were formerly but gross cheats, when ye passed yourselves as God's servants, though you had no ground for doing so."

We now perceive what the Prophet means. But this punishment might have then contributed to the benefit of the people: for as it is a cause of ruin to the world, when there is no difference made between light and darkness; so when the baseness of those is discovered, who abuse God's name and adulterate his pure truth, there is then a door open to repentance. Rightly then is this commination addressed to false prophets. It now follows—

8. But truly I am full of power by the Spirit of the Lord, and of judgment, and of might, to declare unto Jacob his transgression, and to Israel his sin.

8. Atqui verê ego repletus sum virtute à Spiritu Jehovæ, et judicio, et fortitudine, ad annuntiandum Jacob scelus suum, et Israeli peccatum suum.

Here Micah, in a courageous spirit, stands up alone against all the false teachers, even when he saw that they were a large number, and that they appealed to their number, according to their usual practice, as their shield. Hence he says, *I am filled with power by the Spirit of Jehovah.*[1] This confi-

[1] *Jerome* renders "the Spirit of Jehovah" in the genitive case, which in meaning amounts to the same thing; but *Newcome* puts the words in apposition with "power." The את before Spirit seems to betoken a difference in its connection with "filled." It appears to be here a preposition, *ab*, by. The "power," כח, is the δυναμις of the New Testament; and "judgment," משפט, is discernment or discrimination; and "might" or courage, גבורה, is "an intrepid firmness of mind," as *Marckius* observes, "against all opposing evils and hinderances."—*Ed.*

dence is what all God's servants should possess, that they may not succumb to the empty and vain boastings of those who subvert the whole order of the Church. Whenever, then, God permits his pure truth to be corrupted by false teachers, and them to be popular among those high in honour, as well as the multitude, let this striking example be remembered by us, lest we be discouraged, lest the firmness and invincible power of the Holy Spirit be weakened in our hearts, but that we may proceed in the course of our calling, and learn to oppose the name of God to all the deceptions of men, if indeed we are convinced that our service is approved by him, as being faithful. Since, then, Micah says, that he was *filled with power*, he no doubt stood, as it were, in the presence of the whole people, and alone pitched his camp against the whole multitude; for there were then false teachers going about every where, as the devil sows always seed enough, whenever God lets loose the reins. Though then their number was not small, yet Micah hesitated not to go forth among them: *I*, he says; there is stress to be laid on the pronoun אנכי, *anki*,—"Ye despise me, being one man, and ye despise a few men; ye may think that I alone serve the Lord; but I am a match for a thousand, yea, for an innumerable multitude; for God is on my side, and he approves of my ministry, as it is from him, nor do I bring any thing to you but what he has commanded: It is then *I*."

He further expresses a fuller confidence by using the word אולם, *aulam*;[1] *Verily*, he says, *I am filled with power*. This *verily* or truly is opposed to those lofty boastings, by which the false prophets were ever wont to attain a name and honour among the people. But Micah intimates, that all that they uttered was only evanescent: "Ye are," he says, "wonderful prophets; nay, ye are superior to the angels, if you are to be believed; but show that you are so in reality; let there be some proof by which your calling can be confirmed. There is no proof. It then follows, that ye are only men of wind, and not really spiritual: but there is really in

[1] *Marckius* renders it the same, *verè*, and says, that it is of the same import with *Amen, Amen*, so often used by our Saviour. *Truly* is adopted by *Newcome* and *Henderson*.—*Ed.*

me what ye boast of with your mouths." And he says, that he was *filled*, that he might not be thought one of the common sort: and Micah no doubt shows here, on account of the necessity of the occasion, that he was not supplied with ordinary or usual power; for, according as God employs the labours of his servants, so is he present with them, and furnishes them with suitable protection. When any one is not exercised with great difficulties in discharging his office of teaching, a common measure of the Spirit is only necessary for the performance of his duties ; but when any one is drawn into arduous and difficult struggles, he is at the same time especially strengthened by the Lord : and we see daily examples of this; for many simple men, who have never been trained up in learning, have yet been so endued by the celestial Spirit, when they came to great trials, that they have closed the mouths of great doctors, who seemed to understand all oracles. By such evidences God openly proves at this day, that he is the same now as when he formerly endued his servant Micah with a power so rare and so extraordinary. This then is the reason why he says, that he was *filled with power*.

He afterwards adds, *By the Spirit of Jehovah*. Here the Prophet casts aside every suspicious token of arrogance ; lest he should seem to claim anything as his own, he says, that this power was conferred on him from above: and this circumstance ought to be particularly noticed. Though Micah rightly and justly claimed to himself the name of a teacher, he yet had nothing different from others before the world; for all his opponents discharged the same office, and obtained the same honour: the office was common to both parties. Micah was either alone, or connected with Isaiah and a few others. Since then he here dares to set up himself, we see that his call alone must be regarded ; for we know how great is the propensity of Satan to oppose the kingdom of Christ, and also how proud and fierce are false teachers. Since then the rage of Satan is well known and the presumption of false teachers, there is no reason why the faithful should make much of mere naked titles: and when they, who lived at that time, declared, as Papists do at this day, that they had no discrimination nor judgment to know, whether of them ought to have been deemed impostors or the ministers of God, inasmuch as Micah was alone and they were many, and also that the others were prophets, that at least they had the name and repute of being so,—what was to be done? This was the reason why I have said, that this circumstance was worthy of special notice,—that though their vocation was common, yet as they had acted perfidiously, and Micah alone, or with few others, had faithfully performed what the Lord had commanded, he alone is to be deemed a Prophet and a teacher: in short, there is no reason for false prophets to set up against us a mere covering, when they cannot prove that they are endued with the Spirit of God. Whosoever then desires to be deemed a servant of God, and a teacher in his Church, must have this seal which Micah here adduces; he must be endued with the Spirit of God; honour then will be given to God. But if any one brings nothing but the name, we see how vain before God it is.

He afterwards subjoins, *With judgment and courage* (*fortitudine.*) By judgment, I have no doubt, he understands discernment, as this is also the common meaning of the word. He then adds *courage*. These two things are especially necessary for all ministers of the word,—that is, to excel in wisdom, to understand what is true and right, and to be also endued with inflexible firmness, by which they may overcome both Satan and the whole world, and never turn aside from their course, though the devil may in all ways assail them. We hence see what these two words import. He had put כח, *kech*, first, power; but now he mentions גבורה, *gebure*, courage or magnanimity. By the term, power, he meant generally all the endowments, with which all who take upon them the office of teaching ought to be adorned. This qualification is then first required, and it is a general one: but Micah divides this power of the prophets into two kinds, even into wisdom or judgment, and into courage; and he did this, that they might understand what God intended: Let them excel in doctrine; and then that they may be confirmed, let them not yield to any gales that may blow, nor be overcome by threats and terrors; let them not bend here and there to please the world; in a word, let them not succumb to any corruptions: it is therefore necessary to add courage to judgment.

He then adds, *To declare to Jacob his wickedness,*[1] *and to Israel his sin.* We here see that the Prophet did not hunt for the favour of the people. Had he courted their approbation, he must have soothed with flatteries those who sought flatteries; and were already seized with such hatred and malignant feelings, that they had rejected Micah. He must then have spoken softly to them, to please them; but this he did not do. "On the one hand," he says, "these men sell to you their blessings and deceive you with the hope of peace; and, on the other, they denounce war, except their voracity is satisfied; and thus it is that they please you; for so ye wish, and ye seek such teachers as will promise you wine and strong drink: but I am sent to you for another purpose; for the Lord has not deposited flatteries with me, such as may be pleasant to you; but he has deposited reproofs and threatenings. I shall therefore uncover your crimes, and will not hesitate to condemn you before the whole world, for ye deserve to be thus treated." We now perceive why the Prophet says, that he was endued with power to *declare his wickedness to Jacob, &c.*

But we hence learn how necessary it is for us to be supported by celestial firmness, when we have to do with insincere and wicked men; and this is almost the common and uniform lot of all God's servants; for all who are sent to teach the word are sent to carry on a contest. It is therefore not enough to teach faithfully what God commands, except we also contend: and though the wicked may violently

[1] *Scelus*, פשע; it means defection, apostacy, rebellion, a wilful transgression, and a proud contempt of divine law and institutions; it is *ανομια*—lawlessness, as it is sometimes rendered by the Septuagint. But "sin," חטאה, is a deviation from what is right through delusion, mistaken views, error, ignorance, or infirmity. The first included idolatry and gross acts of imposture and oppression; the second, the superstition of the people, and their common vices. *Muis*, as quoted by *Leigh*, says that פשע is "defection from God or rebellion, and prevarication towards God,"—*defectio à Deo seu rebellio, ac prævaricatio in Deum.* And he quotes also *Mollerius* as describing חטאה as including not only sins of error, ignorance, and infirmity, but also those of omission,—*Ea potissimum peccata significat, quæ vel errore, vel per ignorantiam, vel per infirmitatem carnis, committuntur; item peccata omissionis.*—*Ed.*

rise up against us, we must yet put on a brazen front, as it is said in Ezek. iii. 8, 9; nor must we yield to their fury, but preserve invincible firmness. Since then we have a contest with the devil, with the world, and with all the wicked, that we may faithfully execute our office, we must be furnished with this courage, of which Micah speaks.

As I have already shown that God's servants ought courageously to break through all those obstacles by which Satan may attempt either to delay or to force them backward; so also the doctrine taught here ought to be applied to all the godly: they ought wisely to distinguish between the faithful servants of God and impostors, who falsely pretend his name. Then no one, who desires truly and from the heart to obey God, will be deceived; for the Lord will ever give the spirit of judgment and discrimination. And the reason why at this day many miserable souls are led to endless ruin is, because they either shut their eyes, or wilfully dissemble, or designedly involve themselves in such subterfuges as these,—"I cannot form any judgment; I see on both sides learned and celebrated men, at least those who are in some repute and esteem: some call me to the right hand, and others to the left, where am I to betake myself? I therefore prefer to close my mouth and my ears." Thus many, seeking a cloak for their sloth, often manifest their ignorance: for we see that the eyes must be opened when the Lord exercises and tries our faith: and he suffers discords and contentions to arise in the Church, that some may choose this, and others that. Though God then relaxes the reins of Satan, that contests and turmoils of this kind may be excited in the Church, there is yet no excuse for us, if we follow not what the Lord prescribes; for he will ever guide us by his Spirit, provided we foster not our own slothfulness. It follows—

9. Hear this, I pray you, ye heads of the house of Jacob, and princes of the house of Israel, that abhor judgment, and pervert all equity.	9. Audite hoc, quæso, principes domus Jacob, et gubernatores domus Israel, qui abominantur (*est mutatio personæ*) judicium, et rectitudinem omnem pervertunt;
10. They build up Zion	10. Qui ædificat[1] (*nunc est mutatio*

[1] It is בנה, in the singular number, with no variation as to number in the MSS. The Septuagint gives it as a plural participle, οἱ οικοδομουντες.

with blood, and Jerusalem with iniquity. *numeri)* Sionem in sanguinibus, et Jerusalem in iniquitate.

The Prophet begins really to prove what he had stated,—that he was filled with the power of the Holy Spirit: and it was, as they say, an actual proof, when the Prophet dreaded no worldly power, but boldly addressed the princes and provoked their rage against him, *Hear,* he says, *ye heads,* ye rulers *of the house of Jacob,* ye men who are cruel, bloody, and iniquitous. We then see that the Prophet had not boasted of what he did not without delay really confirm. But he began with saying, that he was filled with the Spirit of God, that he might more freely address them, and that he might check their insolence. We indeed know that the ungodly are so led on headlong by Satan, that they hesitate not to resist God himself: but yet the name of God is often to them a sort of a hidden chain. However much then the wicked may rage, they yet become less ferocious when the name of God is introduced. This is the reason why the Prophet had mentioned the Spirit of God; it was, that there might be a freer course to his doctrine.

When he now says, *Ye heads of the house of Jacob, ye rulers of the house of Israel,* it is by way of concession, as though he had said, that these were indeed splendid titles, and that he was not so absurd as not to acknowledge what had been given them by God, even that they were eminent, a chosen race, being the children of Abraham. The Prophet then concedes to the princes what belonged to them, as though he had said, that he was not a seditious man, who had no care nor consideration for civil order. And this defence was very necessary, for nothing is more common than for the ungodly to charge God's servants with sedition, whenever they use a freedom of speech as it becomes them. Hence all who govern the state, when they hear their corruptions reproved, or their avarice, or their cruelty, or any of their other crimes, immediately cry out,—"What! if we suffer these things, every thing will be upset: for when all

It may be rendered as a participial noun, "The building of Zion *is* by blood," &c.; for ה, when radical, does not always turn into ת, when in *regimine.—Ed.*

respect is gone, what will follow but brutal outrage? for every one of the common people will rise up against the magistrates and the judges." Thus then the wicked ever say, that God's servants are seditious, whenever they boldly reprove them. This is the reason why the Prophet concedes to the princes and judges of the people their honour; but a qualifying clause immediately follows,—"Ye are indeed the heads, ye are rulers; but yet *they hate judgment*:" he does not think them worthy of being any longer addressed. He had indeed bidden them to hear as with authority; but having ordered them to hear, he now uncovers their wickedness, *They hate*, he says, *judgment, and all rectitude pervert*:[1] each of them *builds Zion by blood, and Jerusalem by iniquity*; that is, they turn their pillages into buildings: "This, forsooth, is the splendour of my holy city, even of Zion! where I designed the ark of my covenant to be placed, as in my only habitation, even there buildings are seen constructed by blood and by plunder! See, he says, how wickedly these princes conduct themselves under the cover of their dignity!"[2]

[1] It often happens, as in the present case, that the relative ה, in Hebrew, prefixed to a participle, has after it a verb in the future connected by ו, and in person different from that to which the relative refers. The relative here refers to a noun in the second, and the verb connected with the participle is in the third person. It is an idiom, of which there are frequent instances. We find the same to be the case with the relative אשר, in the third verse. It refers to the chiefs, who are addressed, and must therefore be viewed as in the second person, and all the verbs which follow it are in the third. Some render the participle, "who hate," which is in Hiphil, in a causative sense. See Amos v. 7; vi. 12. The distich may then be rendered thus,—

Who render judgment hateful, (or, abominable,)
And distort every thing that is right, *or more literally*,
And make crooked every thing that is straight.—*Ed.*

[2] "They pretend," says *Henry*, "in justification of their extortion and oppressions, that they build up Zion and Jerusalem; they add new streets and squares to the holy cities and adorn them; they establish and advance the public interests both in church and state, and think therein they do God and Israel good service; but it is with blood and with iniquity, and therefore it cannot prosper; nor will their intentions of good to the city of God justify their contradictions to the law of God." A flaming zeal for a good cause can never consecrate extortion, injustice, and murder.

It may be asked, What is the difference between *Zion* and *Jerusalem*? Zion was the church, Jerusalem was the state; or it may be, that, according to the usual style of the Prophets, the more limited idea is given first, and the more extensive one is added to it.—*Ed.*

We now see that the word of God is not bound, but that it puts forth its power against the highest as well as the lowest; for it is the Spirit's office to arraign the whole world, and not a part only. 'When the Spirit shall come,' says Christ, 'it will convince the world,' (John xvi. 8.) He speaks not there of the common people only, but of the whole world, of which princes and magistrates form a prominent part. Let us then know, that though we ought to show respect to judges, (as the Lord has honoured them with dignified titles, calling them his vicegerents and also gods,) yet the mouths of Prophets ought not to be closed; but they ought, without making any difference, to correct whatever is deserving of reproof, and not to spare even the chief men themselves. This is what ought in the first place to be observed.

Then when he says, that Zion *was built by blood, and Jerusalem by iniquity*, it is the same as though the Prophet had said, that whatever the great men expended on their palaces had been procured, and, as it were, scraped together from blood and plunder. The judges could not have possibly seized on spoils on every side, without being bloody, that is, without pillaging the poor: for the judges were for the most part corrupted by the rich and the great; and then they destroyed the miserable and the innocent. He then who is corrupted by money will become at the same time a thief; and he will not only extort money, but will also shed blood. There is then no wonder that Micah says, that Zion was *built by blood*. He afterwards extends wider his meaning and mentions *iniquity*, as he wished to cast off every excuse from hypocrites. The expression is indeed somewhat strong, when he says, that Zion was built by blood. They might have objected and said, that they were not so cruel, though they could not wholly clear themselves from the charge of avarice. "When I speak of blood," says the Prophet, "there is no reason that we should contend about a name; for all iniquity is blood before God: if then your houses have been built by plunder, your cruelty is sufficiently proved; it is, as though miserable and innocent men had been slain by your own hands." The words, *Zion* and *Jerusalem*, enhance their sin;

for they polluted the holy city and the mount on which the temple was built by the order and command of God.

PRAYER.

Grant, Almighty God, that as thou wouldest have us to be ruled by the preaching of thy word,—O grant, that those who have to discharge this office may be really endued with thy celestial power, that they may not attempt any thing of themselves, but with all devotedness spend all their labours for thee and for our benefit, that through them we may be thus edified, so that thou mayest ever dwell among us, and that we through our whole life may become the habitation of thy Majesty, and that finally we may come to thy heavenly sanctuary, where thou daily invitest us, as an entrance there has been once for all opened to us by the blood of thy only-begotten Son. Amen.

Lecture Eighty-seventh.

11. The heads thereof judge for reward, and the priests thereof teach for hire, and the prophets thereof divine for money: yet will they lean upon the Lord, and say, *Is* not the Lord among us? none evil can come upon us.	11. Principes ejus pro munere judicant, et sacerdotes ejus mercede docent, et prophetæ ejus pecunia divinant, et super Jehova nituntur, dicendo, Annon Jehova in medio nostri? non veniet super nos malum.
12. Therefore shall Zion for your sake be plowed *as a* field, and Jerusalem shall become heaps, and the mountain of the house as the high places of the forest.	12. Itaque propter vos Sion ut ager arabitur, et Jerusalem acervus erit, et mons domus in excelsa sylvæ.[1]

The Prophet shows here first, how gross and supine was the hypocrisy of princes as well as of the priests and prophets: and then he declares that they were greatly deceived in thus soothing themselves with vain flatteries; for the Lord would punish them for their sins, since he had in his forbearance spared them, and found that they did not repent. But he does not address here the common people or the multitude, but he attacks the chief men: for he has previously told us,

[1] "As the *Masoretes*, in their division of the Bible, reckon the *Twelve Minor Prophets* but as *one* Book, they mark this verse (*twelfth* of chap. iii.) the *middle* verse of these Prophets."—*Adam Clarke.*

that he was endued with the spirit of courage. It was indeed necessary for the Prophet to be prepared with invincible firmness, that he might freely and boldly declare the judgment of God, especially as he had to do with the great and the powerful, who, as it is well known, will not easily, or with unruffled minds, bear their crimes to be exposed; for they wish to be privileged above the ordinary class of men. But the Prophet not only does not spare them, but he even arraigns them alone, as though the blame of all evils lodged only with them, as indeed the contagion had proceeded from them; for though all orders were then corrupt, yet the cause and the beginning of all the evils could not have been ascribed to any but to the chief men themselves.

And he says, *Princes for reward judge, priests teach for reward,*[1] *the prophets divine for money:* as though he had said, that the ecclesiastical as well as the civil government was subject to all kinds of corruptions, for all things were made matters of sale. We know that what the Holy Spirit declares elsewhere is ever true,—that by gifts or rewards the eyes of the wise are blinded, and the hearts of the just are corrupted,

[1] *Calvin* has *mercede* in both instances. The first in Hebrew is שחר, a gift, a bribe; this was given to the princes: and the second is מחיר, commutation, barter, price, something in exchange; this was given to the priests: and then what was given to the prophets is literally silver, כסף; but it often means money in general. The Septuagint renders the first, μετα δωρων—for gifts; the second, μετα μισθου—for reward; and the last, μετα αργυριου—fo money. The princes decided matters according to the bribes given them; the priests, not satisfied with the regular allowance given them according to the law, did not teach except they were paid, had something in exchange, a reward for their trouble. And while the true prophets, who were extraordinary teachers sent by God, delivered their messages freely, without any pay, as they received them; the false prophets, who pretended that they came from God, required money for performing their office; see Jer. vi. 13. And notwithstanding all their gains, all things were done badly. Money was extracted for doing wrong. The princes determined cases unjustly, the priests taught erroneous doctrine, and the prophets prophesied falsely: and yet for all these evils, money was required! How ignorant and infatuated the people must have been!

Cocceius enumerated *six* things as chargeable on the persons mentioned in this verse; 1. Avarice—the seeking of wealth instead of doing God's will; 2. A mercenary disposition, influenced by gain and not by sense of duty; 3. The exacting of unlawful reward; 4. The doing, even for reward, of what was evil and wicked; 5. A false pretence of trust in God; and, 6. The tying of God's favour to external privileges.—*Ed.*

(Eccles. xx. 29,) for as soon as judges open a way for rewards, they cannot preserve integrity, however much they may wish to do so. And the same is the case with the priests: for if any one is given to avarice, he will adulterate the pure truth: it cannot be, that a complete liberty in teaching should exist, except when the pastor is exempt from all desire of gain. It is not therefore without reason that Micah complains here, that the princes as well as the priests were hirelings in his day; and by this he means, that no integrity remained among them, for the one, as I have said, follows from the other. He does not say, that the princes were either cruel or perfidious, though he had before mentioned these crimes; but in this place he simply calls them mercenaries. But, as I have just said, the one vice cannot be separated from the other; for every one who is hired will pervert judgment, whether he be a teacher or a judge. Nothing then remains pure where avarice bears rule. It was therefore quite sufficient for the Prophet to condemn the judges and the prophets and the priests for avarice; for it is easy hence to conclude, that teaching was exposed to sale, and that judgments were bought, so that he who offered most money easily gained his cause. *Princes* then *judge for reward*, and *priests* also *teach for reward*.

We can learn from this place the difference between prophets and priests. Micah ascribes here the office or the duty of teaching to the priests, and leaves divination alone to the prophets. We have said elsewhere, that it happened through the idleness of the priests, that prophets were added to them; for prophesying belonged to them, until being content with the altar, they neglected the office of teaching: and the same thing, as we find, has taken place under the Papacy. For though it be quite evident for what reason pastors were appointed to preside over the Church, we yet see that all, who proudly call themselves pastors, are dumb dogs. Whence is this? Because they think that they discharge their duties, by being only attentive to ceremonies; and they have more than enough to occupy them: for the priestly office under the Papacy is laborious enough as to trifles and scenic performances (*ritus histrionicos*—stage-playing rites:) but at the same time they neglect the principal thing—to feed the Lord's flock with the doctrine of salvation. Thus degenerated had the priests become under the Law. What is said by Malachi ought to have been perpetuated,—that the law should be in the mouth of the priest, that he should be the messenger and interpreter of the God of hosts, (Mal. ii. 7;) but the priests cast from them this office: it became therefore necessary that prophets should be raised up, and as it were beyond the usual course of things, while yet the regular course formally remained. But the priests taught in a cold manner; and the prophets divined, that is, professed that oracles respecting future things were revealed to them.

This distinction is now observed by the Prophet, when he says, *The priests teach for reward*, that is, they were mercenaries, and hirelings in their office: and the *prophets divined for money*. It then follows, that they yet *leaned on Jehovah*, and said, *Is not Jehovah in the midst of us? Come then shall not evil upon us.* The Prophet shows here, as I have said at the beginning, that these profane men trifled with God: for though they knew that they were extremely wicked, nay, their crimes were openly known to all; yet they were not ashamed to lay claim to the authority of God. And it has, we know, been a common wickedness almost in all ages, and it greatly prevails at this day,—that men are satisfied with having only the outward evidences of being the people of God. There was then indeed an altar erected by the command of God; there were sacrifices made according to the rule of the Law; and there were also great and illustrious promises respecting that kingdom. Since then the sacrifices were daily performed, and since the kingdom still retained its outward form, they thought that God was, in a manner, bound to them. The same is the case at this day with the great part of men; they presumptuously and absurdly boast of the external forms of religion. The Papists possess the name of a Church, with which they are extremely inflated; and then there is a great show and pomp in their ceremonies. The hypocrites also among us boast of Baptism, and the Lord's Supper, and the name of Reformation; while, at the same time, these are nothing but mockeries, by which the name of God and the whole of religion are profaned, when no real piety flourishes in the heart. This was the reason why Micah now expostulated with the prophets and the priests, and the king's counsellors; it was, because they falsely pretended that they were the people of God.[1]

But by saying, that *they relied on Jehovah*, he did not condemn that confidence which really reposes on God; for, in this respect, we cannot exceed the bounds: as God's goodness is infinite, so we cannot trust in his word too much, if we embrace it in true faith. But the Prophet says, that hypocrites leaned on Jehovah, because they flattered themselves with that naked and empty distinction, that God had adopted them as his people. Hence the word, *leaning* or recumbing, is not to be applied to the real trust of the heart, but, on the contrary, to the presumption of men, who pretend the name of God, and so give way to their own wills, that they shake off not only all fear of God, but also thought and reason. When, therefore, so great and so supine thoughtlessness occupies the minds of men, stupidity presently follows: and yet it is not without reason that Micah employs this expression, for hypocrites persuade themselves that all things will be well with them, as they think that they have God propitious to them. As then they feel no anxiety while they have the idea that God is altogether at peace with them, the Prophet declares, by way of irony, that they *relied on Jehovah;* as though he had said, that they made the name of God their support: but yet the Prophet speaks in words contrary to their obvious meaning, (*καταχρηστικῶς loquitur*—speaks catachrestically;) for it is certain that no one relies on Jehovah except he is humbled in himself. It is penitence that leads us to God; for it is when we are cast down that we recumb on him; but he who is inflated with self-confidence flies in the air, and has nothing solid in him. And our Pro-

[1] In unison with the foregoing are these striking remarks of *Henry*,—"Many are rocked asleep in a fatal security by their church privileges, as if these would protect them in sin and shelter them from punishment, which are really, and will be, the greatest aggravations both of their sin and of their punishment. If men's having the Lord among them will not restrain them from doing evil, it can never secure them from suffering evil for so doing; and it is very absurd for sinners to think that their impudence will be their impunity."—*Ed.*

phet, as I have said, intended indirectly to condemn the false security in which hypocrites sleep, while they think it enough that the Lord had once testified that they would be his people; but the condition is by them disregarded.

He now recites their words, *Is not Jehovah in the midst of us? Come will not evil upon us.* This question is a proof of a haughty self-confidence; for they ask as of a thing indubitable, and it is an emphatic mode of speaking, by which they meant to say, that Jehovah was among them. He who simply affirms a thing, does not show so much pride as these hypocrites when they set forth this question, "Who shall deny that Jehovah dwells in the midst of us?" God had indeed chosen an habitation among them for himself; but a condition was interposed, and yet they wished that he should be, as it were, tied to the temple, though they considered not what God required from them. They hence declared that Jehovah was in the midst of them; nay, they treated with disdain any one who dared to say a word to the contrary: nor is there a doubt but that they poured forth blasts of contempt on the Prophets. For whenever any one threatened what our Prophet immediately subjoins, such an answer as this was ever ready on their lips,—"What! will God then desert us and deny himself? Has he in vain commanded the temple to be built among us? Has he falsely promised that we should be a priestly kingdom? Dost thou not make God a covenant-breaker, by representing him as approving of the terrors of thy discourse? But he cannot deny himself." We hence see why the Prophet had thus spoken; it was to show that hypocrites boasted, so to speak, of their proud confidence, because they thought that God could not be separated from them.

Now this passage teaches us how preposterous it is thus to abuse the name of God. There is indeed a reason why the Lord calls us to himself, for without him we are miserable; he also promises to be propitious to us, though, in many respects, we are guilty before him: he yet, at the same time, calls us to repentance. Whosoever, then, indulges himself and continues sunk in his vices, he is greatly deceived, if he applies to himself the promises of God; for, as it has been said, the one cannot be separated from the other.[1] But when God is propitious to them, they rightly conclude, that all things will be well with them, for we know that the paternal favour of God is a fountain of all felicity. But in this there was a vitious reasoning,—that they promised to themselves the favour of God through a false imagination of the flesh, and not through his word. Thus we see that there is ever in hypocrisy some imitation of piety: but there is a sophistry (*paralogismus*) either in the principle itself or in the argument.

Now follows a threatening, *Therefore, on your account, Zion as a field shall be plowed, and Jerusalem a heap shall be, and the mount of the house as the high places of a forest.* We here see how intolerable to God hypocrites are; for it was no ordinary proof of a dreadful vengeance, that the Lord should expose to reproach the holy city, and mount Zion, and his own temple. This revenge, then, being so severe, shows that to God there is nothing less tolerable than that false confidence with which hypocrites swell, for it brings dishonour on God himself; for they could not boast that they were God's people without aspersing him with many reproaches. What then is the meaning of this, "God is in the midst of us," except that they thereby declared that they were the representatives (*vicarios*) of God, that the kingdom was sacred and also the priesthood? Since then they boasted that they did not presumptuously claim either the priesthood or the regal power, but that they were divinely appointed, we hence see that their profanation of God's name was most shameful. It is then no wonder that God was so exceedingly displeased with them: and hence the Prophet says, *For you shall Zion as a field be plowed;* as though he said, "This is like something monstrous, that the temple should be subverted, that the holy mount and the whole city should be entirely demolished, and that nothing should remain but a horrible desolation,—who can believe all this? It shall, however, take place, and it shall take place on your account; you will have to bear the blame of this so monstrous a change." For it

[1] That is, the promise from repentance.—*Ed.*

was as though God had thrown heaven and earth into confusion; inasmuch as he himself was the founder of the temple; and we know with what high encomiums the place was honoured. Since then the temple was built, as it were, by the hand of God, how could it be otherwise, but that, when destroyed, the waste and desolate place should be regarded as a memorable proof of vengeance? There is therefore no doubt but that Micah intended to mark out the atrocity of their guilt, when he says, *For you shall Zion as a field be plowed, Jerusalem shall becôme a heap of stones;* that is, it shall be so desolated, that no vestige of a city, well formed and regularly built, shall remain.

And the mount of the house, &c. He again mentions Zion, and not without reason: for the Jews thought that they were protected by the city Jerusalem; the whole country rested under its shadow, because it was the holy habitation of God. And again, the city itself depended on the temple, and it was supposed, that it was safe under this protection, and that it could hardly be demolished without overthrowing the throne of God himself: for as God dwelt between the cherubim, it was regarded by the people as a fortress incapable of being assailed. As then the holiness of the mount deceived them, it was necessary to repeat what was then almost incredible, at least difficult of being believed. He therefore adds, *The mount of the house* shall be *as the high places of a forest;* that is, trees shall grow there.

Why does he again declare what had been before expressed with sufficient clearness? Because it was not only a thing difficult to be believed, but also wholly inconsistent with reason, when what the Lord had said was considered, and that overlooked which hypocrites ever forget. God had indeed made a covenant with the people; but hypocrites wished to have God, as it were, bound to them, and, at the same time, to remain themselves free, yea, to have a full liberty to lead a wicked life. Since then the Jews were fixed in this false opinion,—that God could not be disunited from his people, the Prophet confirms the same truth, that the mount of the house would be as the high places of a forest. And, by way of concession, he calls it the mount of the house, that is, of the temple; as though he said, "Though God had chosen to himself a habitation, in which to dwell, yet this favour shall not keep the temple from being deserted and laid waste; for it has been profaned by your wickedness."

Let us now see at what time Micah delivered this prophecy. This we learn from the twenty-sixth chapter of Jeremiah; for when Jeremiah prophesied against the temple, he was immediately seized and cast into prison; a tumultuous council was held, and he was well nigh being brought forth unto execution. All the princes condemned him; and when now he had no hope of deliverance, he wished, not so much to plead his own cause, as to denounce a threatening on them, that they might know that they could effect no good by condemning an innocent man. "Micah, the Morasthite," he said, "prophesied in the days of Hezekiah, and said thus, 'Zion as a field shall be plowed, Jerusalem shall be a heap, and the mount of the house as the high places of a forest.'" Did the king and the people, he said, consult together to kill him? Nay, but the king turned, and so God repented; that is, the Lord deferred his vengeance; for king Hezekiah humbly deprecated the punishment which had been denounced. We now then know with certainty the time.

But it was strange that under such a holy king so many and so shameful corruptions prevailed, for he no doubt tried all he could to exercise authority over the people, and by his own example taught the judges faithfully and uprightly to discharge their office; but he was not able, with all his efforts, to prevent the Priests, and the Judges, and the Prophets, from being mercenaries. We hence learn how sedulously pious magistrates ought to labour, lest the state of the Church should degenerate; for however vigilant they may be, they can yet hardly, even with the greatest care, keep things (as mankind are so full of vices) from becoming very soon worse. This is one thing. And now the circumstance of the time ought to be noticed for another purpose: Micah hesitated not to threaten with such a judgment the temple and the city, though he saw that the king was endued with singular virtues. He might have thought thus with himself, "King Hezekiah labours strenuously in the execution of his high office: now, if a reproof so sharp and so severe will reach his ears, he will either despond, or think me to be a man extremely rigid, or, it may be, he will become exasperated against sound doctrine." The Prophet might have weighed these things in his mind; but, nevertheless, he followed his true course in teaching, and there is no doubt but that his severity pleased the king, for we know that he was oppressed with great cares and anxieties, because he could not, by all his striving, keep within proper bounds his counsellors, the priests and the prophets. He therefore wished to have God's servants as his helpers. And this is what pious magistrates always desire, that their toils may in some measure be alleviated by the aid of the ministers of the word; for when the ministers of the word only teach in a cold manner, and are not intent on reproving vices, the severity of the magistrates will be hated by the people. "Why, see, the ministers say nothing, and we hence conclude that they do not perceive so great evils; and yet the magistrates with the drawn sword inflict new punishments daily." When, therefore, teachers are thus silent, a greater odium no doubt is incurred by the magistrates: it is hence, as I have said, a desirable thing for them, that the free reproofs of teachers should be added to the punishments and judgments of the law.

We further see how calm and meek was the spirit of the king, that he could bear the great severity of the Prophet: *Behold*, he said, *on your account*, &c.: "Thou oughtest at least to have excepted me." For the king was not himself guilty. Why then did he connect him with the rest? Because the whole body was infected with contagion, and he spoke generally; and the good king did not retort nor even murmur, but, as we have recited from Jeremiah, he humbly deprecated the wrath of God, as though a part of the guilt belonged to him. Now follows—

CHAPTER IV.

1. But in the last days it shall come to pass, *that* the mountain of the house of the Lord shall be established in the top of the mountains, and it shall be exalted above the hills; and people shall flow unto it.

2. And many nations shall come, and say, Come, and let us go up to the mountain of the Lord, and to the house of the God of Jacob; and he will teach us of his ways, and we will walk in his paths: for the law shall go forth of Zion, and the word of the Lord from Jerusalem.

1. Accidet ultimis diebus, ut sit mons domus Jehovæ dispositus in capite montium, et extolletur ipse præ sublimitatibus; et venient ad eum populi:

2. Et proficiscentur gentes multæ et dicent, Venite, et ascendemus ad montem Jehovæ, et ad domum Dei Jacob; et docebit nos de viis suis, et ambulabimus in semitis ejus; quia ex Sion prodibit lex, et verbum Jehovæ ex Jerusalem.

Here Micah begins his address to the faithful, who were a remnant among that people; for though the infection had nearly extended over the whole body, there were yet a few, we know, who sincerely worshipped God. Hence Micah, that he might not dishearten God's children by extreme terror, reasonably adds what we have now heard,—that though for a time the temple would be demolished and laid waste, it would yet be only for a season, for the Lord would be again mindful of his covenant. When, therefore, the Prophet had hitherto spoken of God's dreadful vengeance, he directed his discourse to the whole people and to the princes; but now, especially, and as it were apart, addresses the pious and sincere servants of God; as though he said, "There is now a reason why I should speak to the few: I have hitherto spoken of the near judgment of God on the king's counsellors, the priests and the prophets; in short, on the whole community, because they are all become wicked and ungodly; a contempt of God and an irreclaimable obstinacy have pervaded the whole body. Let them therefore have what they have deserved. But now I address the children of God by themselves, for I have something to say to them."

For though the Prophet publicly proclaimed this promise, there is yet no doubt but that he had regard only to the children of God, for others were not capable of receiving this consolation; nay, he had shortly before condemned the extreme security of hypocrites, inasmuch as they leaned upon God; that is, relied on a false pretence of religion, in thinking that they were redeemed by a lawful price when they had offered their sacrifices. And we know that we meet with the same thing in the writings of the Prophets, and that it is a practice common among them to add consolations to threatenings, not for the sake of the whole people, but to sustain the faithful in their hope, who would have despaired had not a helping hand been stretched forth to them: for the faithful, we know, tremble, as soon as God manifests any token of wrath; for the more any one is touched with the fear of God, the more he dreads his judgment, and fears on account of his threatenings. We hence see how necessary it is to moderate threatenings and terrors, when prophets and teachers have a regard to the children of God; for, as I have said, they are without these fearful enough. Let us then know that Micah has hitherto directed his discourse to the wicked despisers of God, who yet put on the cloak of religion; but now he turns his address to the true and pious worshippers of God. And he further so addresses the faithful of his age, that his doctrine especially belongs to us now; for how has it been, that the kingdom of God has been propagated through all parts of the earth? How has it been, that the truth of the gospel has come to us, and that we are made partakers with the ancient people of the same adoption, except that this prophecy has been fulfilled? Then the calling of the Gentiles, and consequently our salvation, is included in this prophecy.

But the Prophet says, *And it shall be in the extremity of days,*[1] *that the mount of the house of Jehovah shall be set in order*[2] *on the top of mountains.* The extremity of days the

[1] *In extremitate dierum*, באחרית הימים, in the posteriority or postremity of the days; επ' εσχατων των ημερων, in the last days.—*Sept.* "In the latter days," or, "in the end of days."—*Newcome.* "In the last of the days."—*Henderson.* See Jer. xxiii. 20; xxx. 24; Ezek. xxxviii. 8; Dan. x. 14; Hos. iii. 5. *Kimchi*, as quoted by *Lowth*, says, "Whenever the latter days are mentioned in Scripture, the days of the Messiah are always meant."—*Ed.*

[2] *Dispositus*, נכון—*constitutus*, constituted—*præparatus*, prepared—*firmatus*, made firm—are the words by which the term is commonly ex-

Prophet no doubt calls the coming of Christ, for then it was that the Church of God was built anew; in short, since it was Christ that introduced the renovation of the world, his advent is rightly called a new age; and hence it is also said to be the extremity of days: and this mode of expression very frequently occurs in Scripture; and we know that the time of the gospel is expressly called the last days and the last time by John, (1 John ii. 18,) as well as by the author of the Epistle to the Hebrews, (Heb. i. 2,) and also by Paul, (2 Tim. iii. 1;) and this way of speaking they borrowed from the prophets. On this subject some remarks were made on the second chapter of Joel. Paul gives us the reason for this mode of speaking in 1 Cor. x. 11: "Upon whom," he says, "the ends of the world are come." As Christ then brought in the completion of all things at his coming, the Prophet rightly says that it would be the last days when God would restore his Church by the hand of the Redeemer. At the same time, Micah no doubt intended to intimate that the time of God's wrath would not be short, but designed to show that its course would be for a long time.

It shall then *be in the last of days;* that is, when the Lord shall have executed his vengeance by demolishing the temple, by destroying the city, and by reducing the holy place into a solitude, this dreadful devastation shall continue, not for one year, nor for two; in a word, it will not remain only for forty or fifty years, but the Lord will let loose the reins of his wrath, that their minds may long languish, and that no restoration may be evident. We now then understand the Prophet's design as to the last days.

He calls the mount, *the mount of the house of Jehovah,*[1] in a

pressed. It comes from כון, which, *Leigh* justly says, means "aptly and timely to frame, and likewise to make firm and sure;" and he adds, "The word noteth *the ordering*, *perfecting*, and *fast establishing* of any thing." How suitably then it is here used: it is a mountain (which means evidently the Church) that is fitly framed, ordered, and firmly established.—*Ed.*

[1] *Marckius* adduces the opinions of the ancients as to the signification of this "mount." Some, such as *Tertullian*, *Jerome*, and *Augustine*, interpret it of Christ; while others, namely, *Origen*, the two *Cyrils*, and *Chrysostom*, regard it as signifying the Church; and with the latter most modern commentators agree. Here the consent of moderns exceeds that of the ancients; and it is no doubt sounder and wiser.—*Ed.*

sense different from what he did before; for then it was, as we have stated, by way of concession; and now he sets forth the reason why God did not wish wholly to cast aside that mount; for he commanded his temple to be built there. It is the same, then, as though he said,—"This ought not to be ascribed to the holiness of the mountain, as if it excelled other mountains in dignity; but because there the temple was founded, not by the authority of men, but by a celestial oracle, as it is sufficiently known."

The mount then *of the house of Jehovah shall be set in order on the top of the mountains*, that is, it shall surpass in height all other mountains; *and it shall be raised*, he says, *above the highest summits, and assemble*[1] *there shall all nations*. It is

[1] *Convenient*, ונהרו, literally, "and flow;" σπευσουσι—hasten, *Sept.* It is flowing like that of a river, or of a strong current, and implies copiousness and spontaneity. "There shall be," says Henry, "a constant stream of believers flowing in from all parts into the Church, as the people of the Jews flowed into the temple, while it was standing, to worship there."

Kimchi says, that this word means to "run to what is pleasing or delightful,"—*currere ad beneplacitum, hoc est, ad id quod cupias*. An old author, quoted by *Leigh*, says, that it implies abundance and celerity—*affluentiam cum celeritate*. It is rendered "flow together" in Jer. li. 44.

Instead of "peoples," עמים, Isaiah has כל הגוים, "all the nations." One MS. has the same here, and three have כל before עמים, and this seems to be the correct reading. עם, in the plural number, is synonymous with גוים, meaning nations. The rest of this verse is exactly the same in the two Prophets, except that נכון, "prepared," is differently placed, and הוא, "it," is added by Micah after נשא, "exalted."

In the second verse, which is the third in Isaiah, there is a complete verbal identity, except that גוים and עמים are reversed, and that ו before אל is wanting in Isaiah; but it is supplied in several MSS.

In the third, the fourth in Isaiah, there are verbal varieties in the two first lines, the four remaining are exactly the same with the exception of a paragogic ן, *nun*, added to a verb by Micah, and the verb ישאו is singular in Isaiah. In the two lines referred to, there is also an addition of עד רחוק, "afar of," in Micah.

Isaiah.

4. ושפט בין הגוים
והוכיח לעמים רבים

And he shall judge among the nation
And shall convince many peoples.

Micah.

3. ושפט בין עמים רבים
והוכיח לגוים עצמים עד רחוק

And he shall judge among many peoples,
And shall convince strong nations afar off.

certain, that by these words of the Prophet is to be understood no visible eminence of situation: for that mount was not increased at the coming of Christ; and they who lived in the time of the Prophet entertained no gross idea of this kind. But he speaks here of the eminence of dignity,—that God would give to mount Zion a distinction so eminent, that all other mountains would yield to its honour. And how was this done? The explanation follows in the next verse. Lest, then, any one thought that there would be some visible change in mount Zion, that it would increase in size, the Prophet immediately explains what he meant, and says, at the end of the verse, Come shall nations to God. It is now easy to see what its elevation was to be,—that God designed this mount to be, as it were, a royal seat. As under the monarchy of the king of Persia, the whole of the east, we know, was subject to one tower of the Persian; so also, when mount Zion became the seat of sovereign power, God designed to reign there, and there he designed that the whole world should be subject to him; and this is the reason why the Prophet said that it would be higher than all other mountains. Hence his meaning, in this expression, is sufficiently evident.

There follows, however, a fuller explanation, when he says, that *many nations would come*. He said only before that nations would come: but as David, even in his age, made some nations tributary to himself, the Prophet here expresses something more,—that *many nations would come;* as if he had said, "Though David subjugated some people to himself, yet the borders of his kingdom were narrow and confined, compared with the largeness of that kingdom which the Lord will establish at the coming of his Messiah: for not a few

With this verse the passage ends in Isaiah; Micah adds another: and this, with the two other circumstances—that the passage is fuller and more connected with the context here than in Isaiah, may seem to favour the opinion that Isaiah, and not Micah, was the copyist; but the words, with which the passage is introduced in Isaiah, forbid such a supposition.

"Bishop Lowth, on Isaiah ii. 2, thinks that Micah took this passage from Isaiah. It is true that he has improved it after the manner of imitators. Or, the Spirit may have inspired both with this prediction: or both may have copied some common original, the words of a Prophet well known at the time."—*Newcome.*

nations but many shall assemble to serve him, and *shall say,*" *&c.* The Prophet now shows that it would be a spiritual kingdom. When David subdued the Moabites and the Amorites, and others, he imposed a certain tribute to be paid annually, but he was not able to establish among them the pure and legitimate worship of God, nor was he able to unite them in one faith. Then the Moabites and other nations, though they paid a tribute to David, did not yet worship the true God, but continued ever alienated from the Church. But our Prophet shows that the kingdom, which God would set up at the coming of the Messiah, would be spiritual.

For they shall say,[1] *Let us go and ascend to the mount of Jehovah, and to the house of the God of Jacob; and he will teach us of his ways, and we will walk in his paths: for*[2] *go forth shall a law from Zion, and the word of Jehovah from Jerusalem.* Throughout this passage the Prophet teaches us, that people are not to be constrained by an armed force, or by the power of the sword, to submit to David's posterity, but that they are to be really and thoroughly reformed, so that they submit themselves to God, unite with the body of the Church, and become one people with the children of Abraham; for they will yield a voluntary service, and embracing the teaching of the Law, they will renounce their own superstitions. This then is the Prophet's meaning. But the remainder we shall defer till to-morrow.

[1] *Marckius* says, "*corde, ore, et opere*—with the heart, mouth, and in deed."

[2] כִּי, *ki*, for, or because: what follows contains the reason for the preceding promise. How could it be, that the mount of the house of Jehovah should be firmly fixed on the top of mountains, &c.? The answer is here given, "for go forth shall a law from Zion," &c. And this was literally fulfilled at the commencement of the Gospel; it was first preached at Jerusalem: in consequence of this, the mount of Jehovah's house, or the Church, was formed; and what is here predicted was in part fulfilled, and will no doubt be hereafter more completely fulfilled.

It is said, "on the top of the mountains," not of a mountain. The Church was not to be confined to one place, but was to be pre-eminent throughout the earth. It was to be co-extensive with the word that was to go forth from Zion.—*Ed.*

PRAYER.

Grant, Almighty God, that as thou hast been pleased to erect the throne of thy Son among us, we may rely on his protection, and learn to resign ourselves wholly to thee, and never turn aside here and there, but with true obedience so submit ourselves to the King who has been appointed by thee, that he may own us as his legitimate people, and so glorify thy name, that we may not at the same time profane it by an ungodly and wicked life, but testify by our works that we are really thy subjects, and that thou attainest full authority over us, so that thy name may be sanctified and thy Spirit may really guide us, until at length thy Son, who has gathered us when we were awfully gone astray, gather us again to that kingdom, which he has purchased for us by his own blood. Amen.

Lecture Eighty-eighth.

We began yesterday to explain the prophecy, in which Micah promises the restoration of the Church. We have said that this promise cannot be understood except of Christ's kingdom, for it refers to the last days. And it was also added, that the superiority and eminence of mount Zion, of which he speaks, cannot be otherwise understood than of God's spiritual kingdom; for the explanation follows, when he says, that many nations would come to be taught in the ways of the Lord. We hence see that an earthly empire is not what is here predicted, but what exists through the word and celestial doctrine. But each particular ought to be considered by us. We yesterday said, that in the distinct mention made of many nations, there is to be understood a contrast; for till that time God was only known by one people. Since God then had chosen the race of Abraham alone, there is here pointed out a future change, when he shall gather his Church from various nations, so as to do away with the difference between the Gentiles and the Jews.

It now follows, *They shall say, Come, and let us ascend to the mount of Jehovah.* The Prophet shows in these words, that not only each one would be obedient to God, when called, but that they would also encourage one another: and this ardour is what is justly required in the faithful; they ought to animate and stir on one another; for it is not enough for each of us himself to obey God, but this zeal ought to be added, by which we may strive to produce a mutual benefit. This concern then is what the Prophet now refers to, when he says, "Come, that we may ascend to the mountain of the Lord." He might have said, that people would come, and there close his sentence; but he wished to join the two clauses,—that they, who had before despised the God of Israel, would come from all parts,—and also that they would become exhorters to one another. Come then that we may ascend. But the manner of the exhortation deserves to be noticed; for each one offers himself as a companion in the journey. We indeed see that many are prompt enough, when others are to be stimulated in their duty; but they at the same time lie still; their whole fervour is consumed in sending others, and they themselves move not, no, not a finger; so far are they from running with alacrity in company with others. The Prophet shows here, that the faithful will be so solicitous about the salvation of their brethren that they will strenuously run themselves, and that they will prescribe nothing to others but what they themselves perform. "Come then that we may ascend;" they say not, "Go, ascend to the mount of Jehovah;" but, "Let us go together." It is then the right way of encouraging, when we really show that we require nothing from our brethren but what we desire to do ourselves.

The circumstance of time must now be noticed; for what the Prophet says respecting the nations coming into mount Zion, as it was to be reduced to a waste, might have appeared a fable; for what had he shortly before predicted? That Zion would be plowed as a field, and that trees would grow there, that it would become a wild forest. How then could it be, that many nations would flow to it as to a most renowned place, as it was to be reduced to a dreadful desolation? But the Prophet here extols the wonderful power of God,—that in this wild and desert place there would at length be raised a noble and a celebrated temple, where God would show mercy to his own people. Hence he promises what this mount of Jehovah would be, which was for a time to be forsaken; and that there would be, as formerly, a noble temple in the place, where desolation had for a season existed.

It afterwards follows, *And he will teach us of his ways.*[1] Here the Prophet in a few words defines the legitimate worship of God: for it would not be sufficient for the nations to come together into one place to profess the one true God, unless true obedience followed, which rests on faith, as faith does on the word. It ought then to be especially noticed, that the Prophet sets here the word of God before us, in order to show that true religion is founded on the obedience of faith, and that God cannot be truly worshipped, except when he himself teaches his people, and prescribes to them what is necessary to be done. Hence when the will of God is revealed to us, we then can truly worship him. When the word is again taken away, there will indeed be some form of divine worship; but there will be no genuine religion, such as is pleasing to God. And hence we also learn, that there is no other way of raising up the Church of God than by the light of the word, in which God himself, by his own voice, points out the way of salvation. Until then the truth shines, men cannot be united together, so as to form a true Church.

Since it is so, it follows, that where the truth is either corrupted or despised, there is no religion, at least such as is approved by God. Men may indeed boast of the name with their lips: but there is no true religion before God, except it be formed according to the rule of his word. It hence also follows, that there is no Church, except it be obedient to the word of God, and be guided by it: for the Prophet defines here what true religion is, and also how God collects a Church for himself. *He will* then *teach us of his ways.* And a third particular may be added,—that God is robbed of his right and of his honour, when mortals assume to themselves the authority to teach; for it is to God alone that this office

[1] Both *Newcome* and *Henderson* render the ו, *vau*, here, *that*, "that he may teach us," &c.: but it is better to retain the most common meaning as a simple copulative, as it is done in our version, and by *Calvin*, and by *Lowth* in Isaiah. The passage thus runs better, and more emphatically expresses the language of faith.—*Ed.*

of teaching his people can strictly be ascribed (*propriè tribuitur.*) There were then priests and prophets, yet Micah here brings them down to their proper state, and shows that the right and the office of teaching would be in the power of the only true God. We hence see that God claims this office for himself, that we may not be tossed to and fro, and led astray by various teachers, but continue in simple obedience to his word, so that he alone may be the Supreme. In short, God is not the God and Head of the Church, except he be the chief and the only Teacher.

What he now says, " He will teach us of his ways," ought to be thus understood,—He will teach us what his ways are; as though the Prophet had said, that the perfect wisdom of men is to understand what pleases God, and what is his will: for there is nothing farther to be learnt.

It follows, *And we will walk in his paths.* By this clause we are reminded, that the truth of God is not, as they say, speculative, but full of energizing power. God then not only speaks to the end that every one may acknowledge that to be true which proceeds from him, but at the same time he demands obedience. Hence we shall then only be the disciples of God, when we walk in his ways: for if we only nod with our ears, as asses are wont to do, and assent to what God says with our mouth and lips, it is extremely vain and absurd. It is therefore then only that men really profit under the teaching of God, when they form their life according to his doctrine, and be prepared with their feet to walk, and to follow whithersoever he may call them. *We will* then *walk in his paths.*

Micah has hitherto related only what the faithful would do; he now himself confirms the same truth, *For from Zion shall go forth a law,*[1] *and the word of Jehovah from Jerusalem.*

[1] So *Newcome* renders it; *Lowth* and *Henderson* read the same with our version, " the law." The absence of the definite article is certainly no objection, as it is but seldom used in Hebrew. But " a law " is better, except we render the copulative before " word," even; and then we shall destroy the distinct character of the line. It appears that, according to the usual style of the Prophets, what the first line states indefinitely, is in the second specified, as being the " word of Jehovah."

The word תורה, law, in Hebrew, is more comprehensive than the word law, in our language. It is derived from the Hiphil of ירה, which

Here is a reason given why many nations would come to the temple of the Lord; and that is, because a doctrine would be then promulgated, which had been before heard only in one place. We indeed know that the Jews came to the temple, not only to worship, but also to be instructed in the Law of God. The Law then had, at that time, as it were, its habitation in Zion: there was the sanctuary of celestial wisdom. But what does our Prophet say? A law shall go forth from Zion, that is, it shall be proclaimed far and wide: the Lord will show, not only in one corner, what true religion is, and how he seeks to be worshipped, but he will send forth his voice to the extreme limits of the earth. *A law* then *shall go forth from Zion*, according to what is said in Ps. cx., 'The sceptre of thy power the Lord will send forth from Zion.' In that passage the doctrine of Christ is metaphorically called a sceptre, or is compared to a royal sceptre; for Christ does not otherwise rule among us, than by the doctrine of his Gospel: and there David declares, that this sceptre would be sent far abroad by God the Father, that Christ might have under his rule all those nations which had been previously aliens. Such is the meaning in this place, *A law from Zion shall go forth*. Then it follows, *The word of Jehovah from Jerusalem*. This is a repetition of the same sentiment, which is often the case. Then by תורה, *ture*, the Prophet means no other thing than doctrine: but, by another term, he confirms the same thing, that is, that God would be heard not only at Jerusalem and in Judea, but that he would make his word to be proclaimed everywhere. It now follows—

3. And he shall judge among many people, and rebuke strong nations afar off; and they shall beat their swords into plowshares, and their spears into pruninghooks: nation shall not lift up a sword against nation, neither shall they learn war any more.

3. Et judicabit inter populos multos, et arguet (*vel*, corripiet) gentes robustos usque in longinquum, et concident gladios suos in vomeres, et lanceas suas in falces: non tollent gens contra gentem gladium, et non assuescent ultrà prælio.

means to direct, to appoint, to instruct, to teach. Hence the noun, תורה, may be rendered, directory, institution, law, teaching, or doctrine. "It doth," says *Leigh*, "not only signify strictly what is to be done, but it denoteth largely any heavenly doctrine, whether it be promise or precept." It means often the whole of God's revealed word, as in Ps. i. 2; cxix. 174, &c. See Josh. i. 8.—*Ed.*

The Prophet here describes the fruit of Divine truth,—that God would restore all nations to such gentleness, that they would study to cultivate fraternal peace among themselves, and that all would consult the good of others, having laid aside every desire for doing harm. As then he has lately showed, that the Church of God could not be otherwise formed than by the Word, and that the legitimate worship of God cannot be set up and continued, except where God is honoured with the obedience of faith; so now he shows that Divine truth produces this effect,—that they, who before lived in enmity towards one another and burned with the lust of doing harm, being full of cruelty and avarice, will now, having their disposition changed, devote themselves wholly to acts of kindness. But, before the Prophet comes to this subject, he says,—

He will judge[1] *among many people, and will reprove strong nations.* The word judge, in Hebrew, means the same as to rule or govern. It is certain that God is spoken of here: it is then the same as though the Prophet had said, that though the nations had not hitherto obeyed God, they would now own him as king and submit to his government. God has indeed ever governed the world by his hidden providence, as he does still govern it: for how much soever the devil and the ungodly may rage; nay, how ever much they may boil with unbridled fury, there is no doubt but that God restrains and checks their madness by his hidden bridle. But the Scripture speaks of God's kingdom in two respects. God does indeed govern the devil and all the wicked, but not by his word, nor by the sanctifying power of his Spirit: it is so done, that they obey God, not willingly, but against their will.

[1] There is a difference of opinion as to the nominative case to the verb "judge;" whether it be Jehovah in the preceding line, or the word of Jehovah. The most natural construction is the last supposition. *Jerome* and *Cyril*, as quoted by *Marckius*, refer it to the word of Jehovah, taking the word for Christ: but this cannot be admitted, as the law and the word seem to mean the same thing, and must be considered as the word of the Gospel; and *Justin Martyr* and *Irenæus*, when referring to this passage, regard it as such. And this is the view which *Marckius* seems to prefer. The rendering then would be,—

And it shall judge among many people,
And convince strong nations afar off.

The peculiar government of God is that of his Church only, where, by his word and Spirit, He bends the hearts of men to obedience, so that they follow him voluntarily and willingly, being taught inwardly and outwardly,—inwardly by the influence of the Spirit,—outwardly by the preaching of the word. Hence it is said in Ps. cx., 'Thy willing people shall then assemble.' This is the government that is here described by the Prophet; God then *shall judge;* not as he judges the world, but he will, in a peculiar manner, make them obedient to himself, so that they will look for nothing else than to be wholly devoted to him.

But as men must first be subdued before they render to God such obedience, the Prophet expressly adds, *And he will reprove (corripiet)* or convince (*arguet*) *many people.* And this sentence ought to be carefully noticed; for we hence learn, that such is our innate pride, that not one of us can become a fit disciple to God, except we be by force subdued. Truth then would of itself freeze amidst such corruption as we have, except the Lord proved us guilty, except he prepared us beforehand, as it were, by violent measures. We now then perceive the design of the Prophet in connecting reproof with the government of God: for the verb יכח, *ikech,* signifies sometimes to expostulate, to convince, and sometimes to correct or reprove.[1] In short, the wickedness and perversity of our flesh are here implied; for even the best of us would never offer themselves to God, without being first subdued, and that by God's powerful correction. This, then, is the beginning of the kingdom of Christ.

But when he says, that *strong nations* would be reproved, he hereby eulogises and sets forth the character of the kingdom

[1] The two verbs here used are שפט, to judge, and הוכיח, in Hiphil, to reprove. The first is to decide what is right and wrong, and also to defend the right and to punish the wrong; hence it means to arbitrate, and also to vindicate as well as to punish. The first sense is most suitable to this place.—The other verb does not occur in Kal, but in Hiphil, it means to make manifest, or show, by facts or by words, or by action; and hence it signifies to demonstrate, to convince, to reprove, to chastise. The Septuagint often renders it by ελεγχειν, which, Parkhurst says, means, in its primary sense, to demonstrate by convincing reasons or arguments. *Lowth's* version in Isaiah is, "And shall work conviction," &c. *Newcome* renders it "convince." The rendering of *Henderson,* "give decision," is not to be approved. See John xvi. 8.—*Ed.*

of which he speaks: and we hence learn the power of truth,—that strong men, when thus reproved, shall offer themselves, without any resistance, to be ruled by God. Correction is indeed necessary, but God employs no external force, nor any armed power, when he makes the Church subject to himself: and yet he collects strong nations. Hence then is seen the power of truth: for where there is strength, there is confidence and arrogance, and also rebellious opposition. Since then the word, without any other helps, thus corrects the perverseness of men, we hence see with what inconceivable power God works, when he gathers his own Church. It is to be added, that there is not the least doubt, but that this is to be applied to the person of Christ. Micah speaks of God, without mentioning Christ by name; for he was not yet manifested in the flesh: but we know that in his person has this been fulfilled,—that God has governed the universe, and subjected to himself the people of the whole world. We hence conclude that Christ is true God; for he is not only a minister to the Father, as Moses, or any one of the Prophets; but he is the supreme King of his Church.

Before I proceed to notice the fruit, the expression, עד רחוק, *od rechuk*, "afar off," must be observed. It may intimate a length of time as well as distance of place. Jonathan applies it to a long continuance of time,—that God would convince men to the end of the world. But the Prophet, I doubt not, intended to include the most distant countries; as though he had said, that God would not be the king of one people only, or of Judea alone, but that his kingdom would be propagated to the extremities of the earth. *He will* then *convince* people *afar off*.

He afterward adds, with respect to the fruit, *They shall beat their swords into plowshares, and their spears into pruning-hooks*. I have already briefly explained the meaning of the Prophet: he in fact shows, that when the nations should be taught by the word of God, there would be such a change, that every one would study to do good, and to perform the duties of love towards his neighbours. But by speaking of swords and spears, he briefly intimates, that men, until they are made gentle by the word of the Lord, are ever intent on iniquitous tyranny and oppression; nor can it be otherwise, while every one follows his own nature; for there are none who are not wedded to their own advantages, and the cupidity of men is insatiable. As then all are thus intent on gain, while every one is blinded by self-love, what but cruelty must ever break forth from this wicked principle? Hence then it is, that men cannot cultivate peace with one another; for every one seeks to be the first, and draws every thing to himself; no one will willingly give way: then dissensions arise, and from dissensions, fightings. This is what the Prophet intimates. And then he adds, that the fruit of the doctrine of Christ would however be such, that men, who were before like cruel wild beasts, would become gentle and meek. *Forge* then *shall they their swords into plowshares, and their spears into pruninghooks.*

Raise, he says, *shall not a nation a sword against a nation, and accustom themselves they shall no more to war.* He explains here more fully what I have before said,—that the Gospel of Christ would be to the nations, as it were, a standard of peace: as when a banner is raised up, soldiers engage in battle, and their fury is kindled; so Micah ascribes a directly opposite office to the Gospel of Christ,—that it will restore those to the cultivation of peace and concord, who before were given to acts of hostility. For when he says, 'Raise a sword shall not a nation against nation,' he intimates, as I have already stated, that wherever Christ does not reign, men are wolves to men, for every one is disposed to devour all others. Hence as men are naturally impelled by so blind an impulse, the Prophet declares, that this madness cannot be corrected, that men will not cease from wars, that they will not abstain from hostilities, until Christ becomes their teacher: for by the word למד, *lamed*, he implies, that it is a practice which ever prevails among mankind, that they contend with one another, that they are ever prepared to do injuries and wrongs, except when they put off their natural disposition. But gentleness, whence does it proceed? Even from the teaching of the Gospel.

This passage ought to be remembered; for we here learn, that there is not growing among us the real fruit of the

Gospel, unless we exercise mutual love and benevolence, and exert ourselves in doing good. Though the Gospel is at this day purely preached among us, when yet we consider how little progress we make in brotherly love, we ought justly to be ashamed of our indolence. God proclaims daily that he is reconciled to us in his Son; Christ testifies, that he is our peace with God, that he renders him propitious to us, for this end, that we may live as brethren together. We indeed wish to be deemed the children of God, and we wish to enjoy the reconciliation obtained for us by the blood of Christ; but in the meantime we tear one another, we sharpen our teeth, ourdispositions are cruel. If then we desire really to prove ourselves to be the disciples of Christ, we must attend to this part of divine truth, each of us must strive to do good to his neighbours. But this cannot be done without being opposed by our flesh; for we have a strong propensity to self-love, and are inclined to seek too much our own advantages. We must therefore put off these inordinate and sinful affections, that brotherly kindness may succeed in their place.

We are also reminded that it is not enough for any one to refrain from doing harm, unless he be also occupied in doing good to his brethren. The Prophet might indeed have said only, "They shall break their swords and their spears;" so that they shall hereafter abstain from doing any hurt to others: this only is not what he says; but, "They shall forge," or beat, "their swords into plowshares, and their spears into pruninghooks;" that is, when they shall abstain from all injuries, they will seek to exercise themselves in the duties of love, consistently with what Paul says, when he exhorts those who had stolen to steal no more, but to work with their own hands, that they might relieve others, (Eph. iv. 28.) Except then we endeavour to relieve the necessities of our brethren, and to offer them assistance, there will not be in us but one part of true conversion, as the case is with many, who are not indeed inhuman, who commit no plunder, who give no occasion for complaint, but they live to themselves, and enjoy unprofitable leisure. This indolence the Prophet here indirectly condemns, when he speaks of the plowshares and the pruninghooks.

Again, a question may be here asked,—Was this fulfilled at the coming of Christ? It seems that the Prophet does not describe here the state of the Church for a time, but shows what would be the kingdom of Christ to the end. But we see, that when the Gospel was at first preached, the whole world boiled with wars more than ever; and now, though the Gospel in many parts is clearly preached, yet discords and contentions do not cease; we also see that rapacity, ambition, and insatiable avarice, greatly prevail; and hence arise contentions and bloody wars. And at the same time it would have been inconsistent in the Prophet to have thus spoken of the kingdom of Christ, had not God really designed to perform what is here predicted. My answer to this is,—that as the kingdom of Christ was only begun in the world, when God commanded the Gospel to be everywhere proclaimed, and as at this day its course is not as yet completed; so that which the Prophet says here has not hitherto taken place; but inasmuch as the number of the faithful is small, and the greater part despise and reject the Gospel, so it happens, that plunders and hostilities continue in the world. How so? Because the Prophet speaks here only of the disciples of Christ. He shows the fruit of his doctrine, that wherever it strikes a living root, it brings forth fruit: but the doctrine of the Gospel strikes roots hardly in one out of a hundred.[1] The measure also of its progress must be taken to the account; for so far as any one embraces the doctrine of the Gospel, so far he becomes gentle and seeks to do good to his neighbours. But as we as yet carry about us the relics of sin in our flesh, and as our knowledge of the Gospel is not yet perfect, it is no wonder, that not one of us has hitherto wholly laid aside the depraved and sinful affections of his flesh.

It is also easy hence to see, how foolish is the conceit of those, who seek to take away the use of the sword, on account of the Gospel. The Anabaptists, we know, have been tur-

[1] "All these predictions must be confined to the nations converted by the word of Jehovah, and brought into Zion, that is, such as truly repent and believe, and must not be extended to all nations indiscriminately, or to all who embrace the Christian name, who are often as far as possible from the kingdom of Christ, inasmuch as they neither learn nor follow his doctrine."—*Marckius.*

bulent, as though all civil order were inconsistent with the kingdom of Christ, as though the kingdom of Christ was made up of doctrine only, and that doctrine without any influence. We might indeed do without the sword, were we angels in this world ; but the number of the godly, as I have already said, is small ; it is therefore necessary that the rest of the people should be restrained by a strong bridle ; for the children of God are found mixed together, either with cruel monsters or with wolves and rapacious men. Some are indeed openly rebellious, others are hypocrites. The use of the sword will therefore continue to the end of the world.

We must now understand that at the time our Prophet delivered this discourse, Isaiah had used the very same words, (Isa. ii. 4 :) and it is probable that Micah was a disciple of Isaiah. They, however, exercised at the same time the Prophetic office, though Isaiah was the oldest. But Micah was not ashamed to follow Isaiah and to borrow his words ; for he was not given to self-ostentation, as though he would not adduce any thing but what was his own ; but he designedly adopted the expressions of Isaiah, and related verbally what he had said, to show that there was a perfect agreement between him and that illustrious minister of God, that his doctrine might obtain more credit. We hence see how great was the simplicity of our Prophet, and that he did not regard what malevolent and perverse men might say : " What ! he only repeats the words of another." Such a calumny he wholly disregarded ; and he thought it enough to show that he faithfully declared what God had commanded. Though we have not the words, עד רחוק, *od rechuk*, in Isaiah, yet the meaning is the same : in all other things they agree. It now follows—

4. But they shall sit every man under his vine and under his fig tree ; and none shall make *them* afraid : for the mouth of the Lord of hosts hath spoken *it*.

4. Et sedebunt *(hoc est,* quiescent, *vel,* quieti habitabunt) quisque sub vite sua et sub ficu sua ; et nemo erit qui exterreat ; quia os Jehovæ exercituum loquutum est.

Micah goes on here with the same subject,—that when the minds of men shall be disposed to acts of kindness, every one shall enjoy God's blessing without being disturbed. There seems indeed to be two things here included,—that acts of hostility shall cease,—and that real happiness cannot exist among men, except Christ rules among them by the doctrine of his Gospel. And the same thing the prophets teach elsewhere, that is, that every one shall live without fear; and this they do, in order to show that men ever live in a miserable dread, except when they are safe under the protection of God. It is the same thing as though the Prophet had said, that the life of men is most miserable, where the doctrine of the Gospel is not had, inasmuch as when they are disturbed by continual disquietude, every one fears for himself, every one suffers constant terrors. There is nothing more miserable than such a state of things, for peace is the chief good.

We now then understand the meaning of the Prophet to be,—that under the reign of Christ, the faithful shall enjoy true and full happiness, as they shall be exempt from trembling and fear; hence he names the vine and the fig-tree. He might have said, "Every one shall live securely at home;" but he says, *Every one shall rest under his own fig-tree and under his own vine;* that is, though exposed to thieves, he shall yet fear no violence, no injury; for those who were thieves shall observe what is just and right; those who were bloody shall study to do good. Hence when no one closes the door of his house, yea, when he goes out into the fields and sleeps in the open air, he will still be safe and secure. We now then see why the Prophet mentions here the fig-tree and the vine, rather than the dwelling-house.

And there will be no one to terrify them. What the Prophet designed to express is here more clearly specified,—that there would be no danger, and that there would therefore be no need of hiding-places or of any defences. Why? Because the very fields, he says, will be free from every thing that may hurt, as there will be none to cause fear. And the Prophet seems to allude to the blessing promised in the Law, for Moses used nearly the very same words: and the Prophets, we know, drew many things from the Law; for their design was to retain the people in its doctrine, and to render it as familiar as possible to them. As then Moses promised, among other things, this security, 'Ye shall sleep, and none shall terrify you,' (Lev. xxvi. 6 ;) so the Prophet also, in speaking here of the kingdom of Christ, shows that this blessing would be then fully accomplished.

He now at last subjoins, *The mouth of Jehovah hath thus spoken*, that he might confirm what seemed incredible : for, as I have already said, since he had shortly before predicted the devastation of mount Zion and the ruin of the temple, it seemed very improbable that the nations would come there to worship God. But he declares that the mouth of God had thus spoken, that the faithful might overcome all obstacles and struggle against despair ; though they saw the temple destroyed, the mount Zion desolated, though they saw a horrible waste and wild beasts occupying the place of men; they were yet to continue to entertain firm hope.—How so ? Because Jehovah has made a promise and he will fulfil it : for when mention is made of God's mouth, his omnipotence is to be understood, by which will be executed whatever he has promised.

PRAYER.

Grant, Almighty God, that since, at the coming of Christ thy Son, thou didst really perform what thy servants, the Prophets, had previously so much foretold, and since thou daily invitest us to the unity of faith, that with united efforts we may truly serve thee,—O grant, that we may not continue torn asunder, every one pursuing his own perverse inclinations, at a time when Christ is gathering us to thee ; nor let us only profess with the mouth and in words, that we are under thy government, but prove that we thus feel in real sincerity : and may we then add to the true and lawful worship of thy name brotherly love towards one another, that with united efforts we may promote each other's good, and that our adoption may thus be proved and be more and more confirmed, that we may ever be able with full confidence to call on thee as our Father, through Christ our Lord. Amen.

Lecture Eighty-ninth.

5. For all people will walk every one in the name of his god, and we will walk in the name of the Lord our God for ever and ever.

5. Quia omnes populi ambulabunt, quisque in nomine dei sui ; nos autem ambulabimus in nomine Jehovæ Dei nostri in seculum et usque.

Micah, after having spoken of the restoration of the Church, now confirms the same truth, and shows that the faithful would have reason enough to cleave constantly to their God, and to despise all the superstitions of the world, and that though they may be tossed here and there by contrary opinions, they will yet continue in true religion. This verse then is connected with the kingdom of Christ; for until we are gathered, and Christ shines among us and rules us by his word, there can be in us no constancy, no firmness. But when under the auspices of Christ, we join together in one body, the Church, such then becomes the constancy of our faith, that nothing can turn us from the right course, though new storms were at any time to arise, by which the whole world might be shaken, and though it were to happen that the universe should be agitated or pass away. We now understand what the Prophet means.

He therefore says, *All nations shall walk every one in the name of his god.* This sentence must be thus explained,—"Though nations be divided into various sects, and each be addicted to their own superstitions, yet we shall continue firm in the pure worship of God and in unity of faith." But this question occurs, How could the Prophet say that there would be such discords in the world, when he had shortly before spoken of the Church being gathered and united together? for he had said, "Come shall all nations, and each will say, Come, let us ascend into the mount of Jehovah." There seems to be here some sort of inconsistency,—that all nations would come to mount Zion, and yet that every people would have their own gods. But the solution is not difficult: the Prophet in this verse strengthens the faithful, until Christ should be revealed to the world: nor is there any doubt but the Prophet intended to sustain the confidence of the godly, who might have otherwise been overwhelmed a hundred times with despair. When the children of Israel were driven into exile, when their inheritance was taken away from them, when the temple had been demolished, when, in a word, no visible religion existed, they might, as I have said, have desponded, had not this promise come to their minds,—that God would restore mount Zion, and gather a Church from the whole world. But there was also need of some confirmation, and this is what the Prophet now subjoins. Hence he says, "Since the Lord gives you hope of so glorious a restoration, you ought to feel confidence, and, in reliance on his promise, to continue in his true worship, how much soever the Gentiles may serve their own idols, and boast that they have the true God. However, then, every one of the nations may take pride in their superstitions, you ought not to fluctuate, nor turn here and there, like reeds, which are tossed to and fro, as the wind changes; but ye shall continue firm and steady in your course; for ye know that God is true, who has once for all adopted you, and has promised that your salvation will be the object of his care, even when the world shall think you to be ruined and lost."

We hence see that what the Prophet had in view was to raise up into confidence the minds of the godly in the midst not only of troubles, but of utter confusion. *All nations* then *shall walk*, that is, when the temple and the city shall be demolished, and the people be led into distant exile, the ungodly will, at the same time, triumph, every one will extol his own gods: though our God should not then appear, there will yet be no reason why we should be discouraged; but we ought to recumb on his word. *We shall* then *walk in the name of our God, and that for ever and ever;* that is, though it should happen that the world should a hundred times be turned and turned over again, there shall yet be no change in our minds: for as the truth of God is eternal, so also our faith ought to be constant and never to vary. Now the difficulty is removed, and we see how these two things agree,—that all nations shall come and with one consent worship God,—and yet that to each of them there would be their own gods: for the diversity of time must be here regarded, when all nations would walk every one in the name of his god.[1]

By saying, איש בשם אלהיו, *aish beshem Aleiu*, he touches, in an indirect way, on that variety which exists among men. Though all of them pertinaciously follow and defend their own superstitions, yet each one fabricates a god for himself. Thus it happens, that nothing is certain, for they follow only their own inventions. But this the Prophet meant only to touch by the way. His main object was that which I have stated,—that though the Church of God would be small, and should find a great multitude opposed to it, it ought not yet to succumb. We know how violent a thing is public consent; for when the majority conspire together, the small number, who entertain a different opinion, are, as it were, instantly swallowed up. It is not then without reason that the Prophet exhorts the faithful here to an invincible firmness of mind, that they might triumph over all the nations. How-

[1] *Marckius* views this passage differently. He considers that the converted Gentiles are meant here,—that when turned from their idols and their superstitions, they shall profess the true God, as revealed in the Gospel, and that each nation will regard him as its own God: however various in outward circumstances, they shall yet acknowledge the God revealed in his Word as their own. This view most certainly harmonises better with the context than that of *Calvin*, which is commonly adopted. There is another, which is the same nearly in meaning, but founded on a different rendering of the words. The Jewish commentator *Abarbanel*, as quoted by *Marckius*, gives this version:—

"Nam omnes populi, qui ambulabant quisque in nomine dei sui, et nos ambulabimus in nomine Jehovæ Dei nostri."

The words will no doubt admit of this construction; for it is often the case in Hebrew, that אשר, who, is understood before a verb in the future tense, especially when it has the meaning of the present, as here, for the preceding "ambulabant," might be rendered "ambulant," without any inconsistency in the meaning. I would therefore render the verse thus,—

For all the nations,
Who walk each in the name of its god,
And we ourselves,
Shall walk in the name of Jehovah our God,
For ever and ever.

The nations were then walking in the name of their multiplied gods; but at the time alluded to, both Gentiles and Jews would walk together in the name of Jehovah. There is thus an entire correspondence between all the parts of this remarkable passage, which extends from the first verse to the seventh inclusive; a part of which, extending only to the end of the third verse, is to be found in Isaiah.—*Ed.*

ever small, then, might be the faithful in number, the Prophet wished them to look down, as it were, from a higher place, not only on a large multitude, but on all mankind. *Though* then *all nations walk, &c.:* nor is the word כל, *cal,* all, superfluous,—though *all nations shall walk, &c.* There was then but one nation, the offspring of Abraham, among whom true religion existed; and it was a dreadful devastation, when God suffered the royal city and the temple to be pulled down, and the whole body of the people to be torn asunder, to be driven away here and there, so that no kingdom and no kind of civil community remained. Hence the Prophet intimates here, that though the faithful should find that in number and dignity they were far surpassed by their enemies, they yet should not despair. "Though then all the nations walked, every one in the name of their god,—though every people set up their superstitions against you, and all conspired against you together, yet stand ye firm and proceed in your course, and this not for a short time, but for ever and ever."[1]

Now this passage shows that faith depends not on the suffrages of men, and that we ought not to regard what any one may think, or what may be the consent of all; for the truth of God alone ought to be deemed sufficient by us. How much soever, then, the whole world may oppose God, our faith ought not to be changeable, but remain firm on this strong foundation,—that God, who cannot deceive, hath spoken. This is one thing. Then, in the second place, it must be added, that this firmness ought to be perpetual. Though then Satan may excite against us new troubles, since we have hitherto stood firm as to our faith in God's word, let us proceed in the same course to the end. And the Prophet designedly added this verse; because he saw that the people

[1] לעולם ועד, "for ages and perpetually." עולם means most commonly an indefinite, rather than an infinite time. The verb signifies to be hidden or concealed; and so the noun means an undefined and unknown period. "For ages," would perhaps be its best version; whether these ages be limited or unlimited must depend on the context. Here עד is added to show that these ages would be endless, or to the end of time: for עד is "still," unceasing futurity, that which is perpetual, still the same. The Levitical dispensation was לעולם, "for ages;" but the new state of things promised here is to be, not only for ages, but also perpetually, that is, to the end of time, while the world lasts.—*Ed.*

would be subject to various and long-continued temptations. It was a long captivity: hence languor might have, as it were, wasted away all the confidence which the people then had. And further, after they returned from exile, we know how often and how grievously their faith was tried, when all their neighbours inimically assailed them, and when they were afterwards oppressed by cruel tyranny. This was the reason why the Prophet said that the children of God are to *walk perpetually and to the end in his name.*

Though he gives the name of gods to the idols of the nations, he yet shows that there is a great and striking difference; for the nations worship their own gods, which they had invented: or how did they derive their majesty and their power, except from the false imagination of men? But the Prophet says, *We will walk in the name of Jehovah our God.* He hence shows that the power and authority of God is not founded on any vain device of men, for he of himself exists, and will exist, though he were denied by the whole world. And this also confirms what I have already stated,—that the faithful ought thus to embrace the word of God, as they know that they have not to do with men, the credit of whom is doubtful and inconstant, but with him who is the true God, who cannot lie, and whose truth is immutable. Let us proceed—

6. In that day, saith the Lord, will I assemble her that halteth, and I will gather her that is driven out, and her that I have afflicted;	6. In die illa, inquit Jehova, colligam claudam, et ejectam congregabo, et quam malis afflixi;
7. And I will make her that halted a remnant, and her that was cast far off a strong nation: and the Lord shall reign over them in mount Zion from henceforth, even for ever.	7. Et ponam claudam in reliquias, et ultrà ejectam in gentem robustam; regnabit Jehova super eos in monte Sion ex nunc usque in seculum.

The Prophet pursues the same subject. But we must ever remember what I have previously reminded you of,—that the trials would be so grievous and violent, that there would be need of strong and uncommon remedies; for the faithful might have been a hundred times sunk, as it were, in the deepest gulfs, except they had been supported by various means. This then is the reason why the Prophet confirms so fully the truth which we have noticed respecting the restoration of the Church.

In that day, he says, *I will gather the halting*. This metaphor is not only found here; for David says that his own affliction was like that of halting. The word צלעה, *tsaloe*, means the side: hence they metaphorically call those halters who walk only on one side: it is the same as though he had said, that they were maimed or weak.[1] He then adds, *I will assemble the ejected, whom I have afflicted*. In the next verse he repeats the same, *I will make the halting*, he says, *a remnant;* that is, I will make her who is now halting to remain alive, and her who is cast afar off, *a strong nation*. Some explain הנהלאה,[2] *enelae*, in a more refined manner, and say that it means, "She who is gone before;" as though the Prophet said, "God will sustain the halting, and to those who are lively he will add strength." But this exposition is too strained. We see that the context will not admit it; for the Prophet brings forward the Church here as afflicted by the hand of God, and nigh utter ruin: and then, on the other hand, he intimates, that it was to be restored by God's power, and that it would thereby gather new strength, and flourish as before: he therefore calls the Church as one cast far away, as in the previous verse; and the other verse clearly shows, that the Prophet's design was no other but to point out the twofold state of the Church.

Now, in the first place, we must observe, that the Prophet meets the trial then present, which must have otherwise depressed the hearts of the godly. He saw that they were in a manner broken down; and then their dispersion was as it were a symbol of final ruin. If then the faithful had their minds continually fixed on that spectacle, they might have a hundred times despaired. The Prophet therefore comes here

[1] It means, doubtless, no more here; some refer it to halting between two opinions, between idols and God: but such an idea is foreign to the drift of this passage. It is the depressed, weak, or afflicted and miserable state of the Church that is here set forth.—*Ed.*

[2] It is a Niphal participle from הלא, and corresponds in meaning with הנדחה, "the ejected," in the last verse; only it is a stronger term, as it means one cast to a distance, while the latter signifies one cast or driven away. The first, as rendered by *Junius* and *Tremelius*, is *procul disjecta*, and the other is *depulsa.—Ed.*

seasonably to their help, and reminds them, that though they were now halting, there was yet in God new vigour; that though they were scattered, it was yet in God's power to gather those who had been driven afar off. The meaning briefly is, that though the Church differed nothing for a time from a dead man, or at least from one that is maimed, no despair ought to be entertained; for the Lord sometimes raises up his people, as though he raised the dead from the grave: and this fact ought to be carefully noticed, for as soon as the Church of God does not shine forth, we think that it is wholly extinct and destroyed. But the Church is so preserved in the world, that it sometimes rises again from death: in short, the preservation of the Church, almost every day, is accompanied with many miracles.

But we ought to bear in mind, that the life of the Church is not without a resurrection, nay, it is not without many resurrections, if the expression be allowed. This we learn from the words of the Prophet, when he says, 'I will then gather the halting, and assemble the driven away;' and then he adds, 'and her whom I have with evils afflicted.' And this has been expressly said, that the faithful may know, that God can bring out of the grave those whom he has delivered to death. For if the Jews had been destroyed at the pleasure of their enemies, they could not have hoped for so certain a remedy from God: but when they acknowledged that nothing happened to them except through the just judgment of God, they could entertain hope of restoration. How so? Because it is what is peculiar to God to bring forth the dead, as I have already said, from the grave; as it is also his work to kill. We then see that what the Prophet promised, respecting the restoration of the Church, is confirmed by this verse: "I am he," says God, "who has afflicted; cannot I again restore you to life? For as your death is in my hand, so also is your salvation. If the Assyrians or the Chaldeans had gained the victory over you against my will, there would be some difficulty in my purpose of gathering you; but as nothing has happened but by my command, and as I have proved that your salvation and your destruction is in my power, there is no reason for you to think that it is difficult for me to gather you, who have through my judgment been dispersed."

He then adds, *I will make the halting a remnant.* By remnant he understands the surviving Church. Hence the metaphor, halting, is extended even to destruction ; as though he said, " Though the Jews for a time may differ nothing from dead men, I will yet cause them to rise again, that they may become again a new people." It was difficult to believe this at the time of exile : no wonder, then, that the Prophet here promises that a posterity would be born from a people that were dead. For though Babylon was to them like the grave, yet God was able to do such a thing as to bring them forth as new men, as it really happened.

He afterwards subjoins, *And the driven afar off, a strong nation.* When the Jews were scattered here and there, how was it possible that God should from this miserable devastation form for himself a new people, and also a strong people ? But the Prophet has put the contrary clauses in opposition to one another, that the Jews, amazed at their own evils, and astonished, might not cast away every consolation. As then he had dispersed them, he would again gather them, and would not only do this, but also make them a strong nation.

He then adds, *Reign shall Jehovah over them on mount Zion, henceforth and for ever.* The Prophet no doubt promises here the new restoration of that kingdom which God himself had erected ; for the salvation of the people was grounded on this—that the posterity of David should reign, as we shall hereafter see. And it is a common and usual thing with the prophets to set forth the kingdom of David, whenever they speak of the salvation of the Church. It was necessary then that the kingdom of David should be again established, in order that the Church might flourish and be secure. But Micah does not here name the posterity of David, but mentions Jehovah himself, not to exclude the kingdom of David, but to show that God would become openly the founder of that kingdom, yea, that he himself possessed the whole power. For though God governed the ancient people by the hand of David, by the hand of Josiah and of Hezekiah, there was yet, as it were, a shade intervening, so that God reigned not then visibly. The Prophet then mentions here some difference between that shadowy kingdom and the latter new kingdom, which, at the coming of the Messiah, God would openly set up. *Jehovah himself shall* then *reign over them;* as though he said, "Hitherto indeed, when the posterity of David held the government, as God himself created both David and his sons, and as they were anointed by his authority and command, it could not have been thought but that the kingdom was his, though he governed his people by the ministry and agency of men: but now God himself will ascend the throne in a conspicuous manner, so that no one may doubt but that he is the king of his people." And this was really and actually fulfilled in the person of Christ. Though Christ was indeed the true seed of David, he was yet at the same time Jehovah, even God manifested in the flesh. We hence see, that the Prophet here in lofty terms extols the glory of Christ's kingdom; as though he had said, that it would not be a shadowy kingdom as it was under the Law. *Jehovah* then *shall reign over you.*

He then subjoins, *on mount Zion.* We know that the seat of the kingdom of Christ has not been continued on mount Zion; but this verse must be connected with the beginning of this chapter. The Prophet has previously said, "From Zion shall go forth a law, and the word of Jehovah from Jerusalem." If then the interpretation of this place be asked, that is, how Jehovah showed himself the king of his people, and erected his throne on mount Zion, the answer is, that from thence the law went forth; from that place, as from a fountain flowed the doctrine of salvation, to replenish the whole world. As then the Gospel, which God caused to be promulgated through the whole world, had its beginning on mount Zion, so the Prophet says that God would reign there. But we must at the same time observe, that through the defection and perfidy of the people it has happened, that mount Zion is now only an insignificant corner of the earth, and not the most eminent in the world, as also the city Jerusalem, according to the prediction of Zechariah. Mount Zion then is now different from what it was formerly; for wherever the doctrine of the Gospel is preached, there is God really worshipped, there sacrifices are offered; in a word, there the spiritual temple exists. But yet the commencement of the Gospel must be taken to the account, if we would understand the real meaning of the Prophet, that is, that Christ, or God in the person of Christ, began to reign on mount Zion, when the doctrine of the Gospel from thence went forth to the extremities of the world. It now follows—

8. And thou, O tower of the flock, the stronghold of the daughter of Zion, unto thee shall it come, even the first dominion; the kingdom shall come to the daughter of Jerusalem.

8. Et tu turris gregis, arx filiæ Sion, ad te veniet; perveniet principatus primus, regnum filiæ Jerusalem.

Micah still continues the same subject,—that the miserable calamities of the people, or even their ruin, will not prevent God to restore again his Church. *Thou tower of the flock,* he says, *the fortress of the daughter of Zion,* "doubt not but that God will again restore to thee thy ancient kingdom and dignity from which thou seemest now to have entirely fallen." But interpreters take "the tower of the flock" in various senses. Some think that the devastation of the city Jerusalem is pointed out, because it became like a cottage, as it is said in Isaiah; and עפל, *ophil,* they render "obscure," for its root is to cover. But another explanation is simpler,—that the holy city is called "the tower of the flock," because God had chosen it for himself, to gather his people there; for we know that they had there their holy assemblies. *Thou,* then, *the tower of the flock,* and then, *the fortress of the daughter of Zion, to thee shall come the former kingdom.*[1] If, however, the former sense be more approved, I will not contend; that is, that Jerusalem is here called the tower of the flock on account of its devastation, as it was reduced as it were into a cottage. As to the main import of the passage, there is no

[1] "I think the temple is meant, or Jerusalem; the place where the *flock,* the whole *congregation* of the people, assembled to worship God. *Newcome* retains the Hebrew word עדר, *eder,* a tower in or near Bethlehem, Gen. xxxv. 21, or as some think, a tower near the sheep gate in Jerusalem. I believe Jerusalem, or the temple, or both, are meant; for these were considered the *stronghold of the daughter of Zion,* the fortress of the Jewish people."—*Adam Clarke.* What especially confirms this view is, that the two clauses are in apposition, the latter is explanatory of the former.—*Ed.*

ambiguity; for the Prophet here strengthens the minds of the godly: they were not to regard the length of time, nor to allow their thoughts to be occupied with their present calamity, but to feel assured, that what God had promised was in his power, that he could, as it were, raise the dead, and thus restore the kingdom of David, which had been destroyed.

Do then, he says, firmly hope.—Why? because *come to thee, come to thee shall the former kingdom.*[1] Here the breaking off of the sentence is to be noticed, when the Prophet speaks of the ancient kingdom and dignity. It is not indeed to be doubted, but that the people of God had become objects of mockery, and that hypocrites and heathens thought that what David had testified respecting the perpetuity of his kingdom was a mere delusion. 'Behold thy kingdom,' he said, 'shall continue as long as the sun and the moon,' (Ps. lxxii.:) but soon after the death of Solomon, a small portion only was reserved for his posterity, and at length the kingdom itself and its dignity disappeared. This is the reason that the Prophet now says, that the former kingdom would come. *Come,* he says, *to thee, daughter of Zion, come shall the former kingdom.* There is indeed no doubt, but that by the former kingdom he understands its most flourishing condition, recorded in Scripture, under David and Solomon.

The kingdom, he says, *to the daughter of Jerusalem shall come.* He expressly mentions the daughter of Jerusalem, because the kingdom of Israel had obscured the glory of the true kingdom. Hence the Prophet testifies here that God was not unmindful of his promise, and that he would restore to Jerusalem the dignity which it had lost, and unite the whole people into one body, that they might be no more divided,

[1] *Calvin* observes the order of the original, which is not done in our version. The whole verse may be thus rendered,—

> And thou tower of the flock,
> The fortress of the daughter of Zion!
> To thee it shall return;
> Yea, come shall the former dominion,
> The kingdom to the daughter of Jerusalem.

The verb אתה, which I render "return," means mostly, to come, to come near, to approach, to happen.—*Ed.*

but that one king would rule over the whole race of Abraham. But this was not fulfilled, we are certain, at the coming of Christ, in a manner visible to men: we must therefore bear in mind what Micah has previously taught,—that this kingdom is spiritual; for he did not ascribe to Christ a golden sceptre, but a doctrine, "Come, and let us ascend unto the mount of Jehovah, and he will teach us of his ways;" and then he added, "From Zion shall go forth a law, and the word of Jehovah from Jerusalem." This, then, ought ever to be remembered,—that God has not rendered Jerusalem glorious in the sight of men, as it was formerly, nor has he enriched it with influence and wealth and earthly power; but he has yet restored the sovereign authority; for he has not only subjected to himself the ten tribes which had formerly revolted, but also the whole world. Let us go on—

9. Now why dost thou cry out aloud? *is there* no king in thee? is thy counsellor perished? for pangs have taken thee as a woman in travail.

10. Be in pain, and labour to bring forth, O daughter of Zion, like a woman in travail: for now shalt thou go forth out of the city, and thou shalt dwell in the field, and thou shalt go *even* to Babylon; there shalt thou be delivered; there the Lord shall redeem thee from the hand of thine enemies.

9. Nunc quare vociferaris vociferatione? Rex nullus in te? An conciliarius tuus periit? quià te occupavit dolor quasi parturientem.

10. Dole et ingemisce, filia Sion, quasi parturiens; quia[1] exibis è civitate, et habitabis in agro; et venies Babylonem usque; illic liberaberis, illic redimet te Jehova è manu hostium tuorum.

The Prophet blends here things in their nature wholly contrary,—that the Jews were for a time to be cut off,—and that afterwards they were to recover their former state. Why, he says, *dost thou cry out with crying?* We must notice the Prophet's design. He did not intend to overturn what he had before stated; but as the minds of the godly might have fainted amidst so many changes, the Prophet here gives them support, that they might continue firm in their faith; and hence he says, *Why dost thou cry aloud with loud crying?* That is, "I see that grievous troubles will arise capable of

[1] *Tunc*, הת, is left out; nor is it restored in the comment. It should be, "For now thou shalt go forth from the city."—*Ed.*

shaking even the stoutest hearts: time will be changeable; it will often be, that the faithful will be disturbed and degraded; but though various tumults may arise, and tempests throw all things into confusion, yet God will redeem his people." We now then see what the Prophet means by saying, Why dost thou now cry? Why dost thou make an uproar? for the verb here properly means, not only to cry out, but also, to sound the trumpet; as though he said, Why do the Jews so much torment themselves? There is, he says, no doubt, a good reason.

And he adds, *Is there no king among thee?* This was doubtless the reason why the Jews so much harassed themselves; it was, because God had deprived them of their kingdom and of counsel: and we know what Jeremiah has said, 'Christ,' that is, the anointed of the Lord, 'by whose life we breathe, is slain,' (Lam. iv. 20.) Since, then, the whole Church derived as it were its life from the safety of its king, the faithful could not be otherwise than filled with amazement, when the kingdom was upset and abolished; for the hope of salvation was taken away. *Is there*, then, *not a king among thee? and have thy counsellors perished?* Some think that the unfaithfulness of the people is here indirectly reproved, because they thought themselves to be destitute of the help of God and of his Christ, as though he said,—"Have ye forgotten what God has promised to you, that he would be your king for ever, and would send the Messiah to rule over you? nay, has he not promised that the kingdom of David would be perpetual? Whence, then, is this fear and trembling, as though God no longer reigned in the midst of you, and the throne of David were hopelessly overturned?" These interpreters, in confirmation of this opinion, say, that Christ is here distinguished by the same title as in Isa. ix.; where he is called יועץ, *ivots*, a counsellor. But as in this verse, it is the Prophet's design to terrify, and to reprove rather than to alleviate the grievousness of evils by consolation; it is more probable, that their own destitution is set before the people; as though Micah said, "What cause have you for trembling? Is it because your king and all his counsellors have been taken away?" But what immediately follows proves that this sorrow arose from a just cause; it was because they were stripped of all those things which had been till that time the evidences of God's favour.

Why then *hath pain laid hold on thee as on one in travail? Be in pain*, he says, *and groan;*[1] that is, I will not prevent thee to grieve and to mourn; as though he said, "Certainly even the strongest cannot look on calamities so dreadful, without suffering the heaviest sorrow; but though God may for a time subject his children to the greatest tortures, and expose them to the most grievous evils, he will yet restore them at length from their exile." *Thou shalt depart*, he says, *from the city, and dwell in the field: thou shalt come even to Babylon; but there thou shalt be delivered; there shall Jehovah redeem thee from the hand of thy enemies.* The import of the whole is, that though God would have a care for his people, as he had promised, there was yet no cause for the faithful to flatter themselves, as though they were to be exempt from troubles; but the Prophet, on the contrary, exhorts them to prepare themselves to undergo calamities, as they were not only to be ejected from their country, and to wander in strange lands like vagrants, but were to be led away into Babylon as to their grave.

But to strengthen the minds of the faithful to bear the cross, he gives them a hope of deliverance, and says, that God would *there deliver* them, and *there redeem* them from the hand of their *enemies*. He repeats the adverb, שם, *shem*, there, twice, and not without cause: for the faithful might have excluded every hope of deliverance, as though the gate of God's power had been closed. And this is the reason why the Prophet repeats twice, *there, there;* even from the grave he will deliver and redeem thee: "Extend then your hope, not only to a small measure of favour, as though God could deliver you only from a state of some small danger, but even to death itself. Though then ye lay, as it were, in your graves, yet doubt not but that God will stretch forth his hand to you,

[1] *Ingemisce*, groan, mourn, or sigh and sob. גחי, burst forth, or break out; that is, into tears or mourning. "Bring forth," as it is rendered by *Newcome* and *Henderson*, seems not to be the import of the word here. It may be rendered, as *Parkhurst* proposes, "labour to bring forth."—*Ed.*

for he will be your deliverer. God then, in whose power is victory, can overcome many and innumerable deaths."

PRAYER.

Grant, Almighty God, that since under the guidance of thy Son we have been united together in the body of thy Church, which has been so often scattered and torn asunder,—O grant, that we may continue in the unity of faith, and perseveringly fight against all the temptations of this world, and never deviate from the right course, whatever new troubles may daily arise: and though we are exposed to many deaths, let us not yet be seized with fear, such as may extinguish in our hearts every hope; but may we, on the contrary, learn to raise up our eyes and minds, and all our thoughts, to thy great power, by which thou quickenest the dead, and raisest from nothing things which are not, so that though we may be daily exposed to ruin, our souls may ever aspire to eternal salvation, until thou at length really showest thyself to be the fountain of life, when we shall enjoy that endless felicity, which has been obtained for us by the blood of thy only-begotten Son our Lord. Amen.

Lecture Ninetieth.

11. Now also many nations are gathered against thee, that say, Let her be defiled, and let our eye look upon Zion.

12. But they know not the thoughts of the Lord, neither understand they his counsel: for he shall gather them as the sheaves into the floor.

13. Arise and thrash, O daughter of Zion: for I will make thine horn iron, and I will make thy hoofs brass; and thou shalt beat in pieces many people: and I will consecrate their gain unto the Lord, and their substance unto the Lord of the whole earth.

11. Et nunc congregatæ sunt contra se gentes multæ (*vel*, robustæ,) dicentes, Damnata erit; et aspiciet in Sion oculus noster.

12. Ipsi vero non noverunt cogitationes Jehovæ, et non intellexerunt consilium ejus; quia congregabis eos quasi manipulum in aream.

13. Surge, et tritura filia Sion; quia cornu tuum ponam ferrum, et ungulas tuas ponam chalybem; et conteres populos robustos; et dicabis Jehovæ opes ipsorum, et substantiam eorum Dominatori universæ terræ.

The Prophet's object here is to give some alleviation to the faithful, lest they should succumb under their calamities; for, as we have stated, there were most grievous evils approaching, sufficient to overwhelm the minds of the godly. The

Prophet then raises up here, with the most suitable comfort, those who would have otherwise fainted under their calamities; and the sum of the whole is this,—that the faithful were not to be confounded on finding the ungodly proudly triumphing, as they are wont to do, when they seem to have gained their wishes. Since, then, the wicked show a petulant spirit beyond all bounds, the Prophet exhorts the faithful to sustain themselves by God's promises, and not to care for such insolence. He then subjoins a promise,—that God would assemble all the forces of their enemies, as when one gathers many ears of corn into a bundle, that he may thrash them on the floor. I will come now to the words of the Prophet.

Assemble, he says, *against thee do nations*, or strong nations: for, by saying, גוים רבים, *guim rebim*, he intimates one of two things, either that they were strong, or that they were large in number: as to the subject there is no great difference. The Prophet had this in view,—that though the Church of God may be pressed by a great multitude of enemies, it yet ought not to be broken down in mind: for the ungodly, while they cruelly domineer, do not understand the design of God. *Assemble*, then, *against thee do many nations*. He sets the thing before them, to heal them of terror: for when we are beyond the reach of harm, we, for the most part, too heedlessly despise all dangers; and then, when we come to a real struggle, we tremble, or even fall and become wholly weak. This is the reason why the Prophet sets before the Jews their prospects, and shows that the time was near when they were to endure a siege, as enemies would, on all sides, surround them. Assemble then do nations, and strong or many nations: he shows here that the Jews had no reason to despond, though their enemies would far exceed them in number, and in forces, and in courage; for it was enough for them to be under the protection of God.

Who say, condemned now shall be Zion.[1] The verb חנף,

[1] *Jam damnata erit.* *Newcome* renders the distich thus,—

Who say, Let her be defiled,
And let our eye see *its desire* on Zion.

Profaned, or defiled, is no doubt the meaning of the verb. But it is better to retain the future tense here, though it may often, in the third person, be rendered as an imperative. To look on, is a Hebrew idiom, and *chenaph*, means to act wickedly and perversely. It may then be literally rendered, 'profane (scelerata) shall be Zion; and on it shall our eye look:' but this word is often taken metaphorically for condemnation. The meaning then is, 'Zion is now condemned:' and the Prophet, no doubt, intended to intimate here, that the enemies would so triumph, as though Zion were not under the guardianship of God; as when any one, who has rendered himself hateful by his vices, is left and forsaken by his patrons. So, then, the Prophet here arms the faithful against the arrogance of their enemies, that they might not despair, when they found that they were condemned by the consent of all men, and that this was the opinion of all,—that they were forsaken by God.

Consolation follows, *But they know not the thoughts of Jehovah, nor understand his counsel:* for verbs in the past tense have the meaning of the present. Here the Prophet recalls the attention of the godly to a subject the most suitable to them: for when the wicked rise up so cruelly against us, we are apt to think that all things are allowed to them, and then their reproaches and slanders immediately take possession of our minds and thoughts, so that we in a manner measure God's judgment by their words. Hence, when the ungodly deride our faith, and boast that we are forsaken by God, we succumb, being as it were filled with amazement: and nothing is easier than to shake off from us faith and the memory of God's promises, whenever the ungodly are thus insolent. The Prophet then does not without cause apply a remedy, which ought to be carefully observed by us. *Who say, condemned is Zion;* but they are like the blind when judging of colours, *for they understand not the counsel of Jehovah, and his thoughts they know not.* We now then see what the Prophet had in view, which was to show,—that the faithful would be unwise and foolish, if they formed an opinion of God's judg-

means often to triumph or exalt over another, or to gain the upper hand. See Ps. xxii. 17; cxviii. 7. Several copies have the word for "eyes" in the singular number, as the verb is so: but anomalies of this kind often occur, as it is the case in Greek with respect to plural nouns in the neuter gender, and in Welsh, when the verb precedes its nominative, almost in all instances. I offer the following version,—

Who say, "Defiled shall she be,
And look on Zion shall our eyes."—*Ed.*

ment according to the boasting of the ungodly: for Satan carries them away in a furious manner; and when the Lord gives them liberty to do evil, they think that they shall be conquerors to the end. As then the ungodly are thus inebriated with foolish confidence, and despise not only men, but God himself, the Prophet here holds up and supports the minds of the godly that they might ascend higher, and thus understand that the design of God was not the same as what the wicked thought, who neither belonged to nor approached God.[1]

It is especially needful to know this truth. Some at the first sight may think it frigid, "O! then, what does the Prophet mean? he says that what these declare is not the design of Jehovah; and this we know." But were all to examine the subject, they would then confess with one mouth, that nothing could have been more seasonable than this consolation. Now we are wounded by reproaches, and this very often happens to ingenuous men; and then, while the ungodly vomit forth their slanders, we think that God rests indifferently in heaven; and one of their words, like a cloud, obscures the judgment of God. As soon as any one of the wicked derides us, and laughs at our simplicity, threatens ferociously, and spreads forth his terrors, his words, as I have said, are like a cloud intervening between us and God. This is the reason why the Prophet says here, that the thoughts of Jehovah are different, and that his counsel is different: in short, the Prophet's object is to show, that whenever the ungodly thus proudly despise us, and also reproachfully threaten and terrify us, we ought to raise our thoughts to heaven.—Why so? Because the design of God is another. Their boastings then will vanish, for they arise from nothing, and they shall come to nothing, but the purpose of God shall stand.

But let us now see why the Prophet spoke here of the design and thoughts of God: for if only these two words are brought before us, there is certainly but little solid comfort,

[1] The beginning of these two lines is very emphatic: I would give this rendering,—

> But they—they know not the purposes of Jehovah,
> And they understand not his counsel.

It has been rendered, "But, as for them;" but this is flat, and too prosaic.—*Ed.*

and nothing that has much force or power. There is then another principle to be understood,—that the thoughts of God are known to us, who are taught in his school. The counsel of God then is not hidden, for it is revealed to us in his Word. Consolation therefore depends on a higher and a more recondite doctrine; that is, that the faithful, in their miseries, ought to contemplate the counsel of God as in a mirror. And what is this? that when he afflicts us, he holds a remedy in his hand, and that when he throws us into the grave, he can restore us to life and safety. When, therefore, we understand this design of God,—that he chastens his Church with temporal evils, and that the issue will ever be most salutary,—when this is known by us, there is then no reason why the slanders of the ungodly should deject our minds; and when they vomit forth all their reproaches, we ought to adhere firmly to this counsel of God. But that the ungodly are thus proud is no matter of wonder; for if they raise their horns against God, why should they not despise us also, who are so few in number, and of hardly any influence, at least not equal to what they possess? The Church is indeed contemptible in the eyes of the world; and it is no wonder if our enemies thus deride us, and load us with ridicule and contempt, when they dare to act so frowardly towards God. But it is enough for us to know, that they do not understand the counsel of God. We now then see the Prophet's meaning, and an explanation follows,—

For thou shalt assemble them, he says, *as a sheaf*[1] *to the floor*. The Prophet adds this clause as an explanation, that we may know what the counsel of God is, which he has mentioned, and that is, that God will collect the enemies as a sheaf. What is a sheaf? It is a small quantity of corn, it may be three hundred or a thousand ears of corn: they are ears of corn, and carried in a man's hand. And then, what is to be done with the sheaf? It is to be thrashed on the floor. It was indeed difficult to believe, that enemies, when thus collected together on every side, would be like a sheaf. If an

[1] *Manipulum*, a handful, a bundle of fruit; עמיר, a sheaf,—a poetical singular for the plural—sheaves.—*Ed.*

army assembled against us, not only ten or twenty thousand, but a much larger number, who would think, according to the judgment of the flesh, that they would be like a sheaf? They shall be as so many deaths and graves: even the thought of God ought to be to us of more account than the formidable power of men. Whenever, therefore, our enemies exceed us in strength and number, let us learn to arise to that secret counsel of God, of which our Prophet now speaks; and then it will be easy for us to regard a vast multitude to be no more than a handful. And he says, that our enemies are to be gathered to a floor, that they may be thrashed there. They assemble themselves for another purpose; for they think that we shall be presently in their power, that they may swallow us up; but when they thus collect themselves and their forces, the Lord will frustrate their purpose and cause them to be thrashed by us. It follows,—

Arise and thrash, daughter of Zion; for I have made thy horn[1] *iron, and thy hoofs brass.* The Prophet here confirms what he had previously said: and he exhorts the daughter of Zion to arise; for it was necessary for her to have been cast down, so as to lie prostrate on the ground. God did not indeed restore at once his Church, but afflicted her for a time, so that she differed nothing from a dead man. As then a dead body lies on the ground without any feeling, so also did the Church of God lie prostrate. This is the reason why the Prophet now says, *Arise, daughter of Zion;* as though God, by his voice, roused the dead. We hence see, that the word קומי, *kumi,* is emphatical; for the Prophet reminds us, that there is no reason for the faithful wholly to despair, when they find themselves thus cast down, for their restoration is in the hand and power of God, as it is the peculiar office of God to raise the dead. And this same truth ought to be applied for our use, whenever we are so cast down, that no

[1] *Horn,* in Scripture, means often elevation, dignity, power, strength. It means evidently the last here. Zion was made strong to thrash the nations, and supplied with strong hoofs to tread on them. The Paraphrase of Rabbi Jonathan is to the purpose, *Fortes sicut ferrum, et robusti sicut æs*—"Strong as iron, and robust as brass." And that this is the meaning is proved by what follows, *Thou shalt beat in pieces,* or beat small, or thrash out, *strong nations.—Ed.*

strength, no vigour, remains in us. How then can we rise again? By the power of God, who by his voice alone can restore us to life, which seemed to be wholly extinct.

He afterwards subjoins, *Thrash, for I have made thy horn iron, and thy hoofs brass.* A mode of thrashing, we know, was in use among the Jews, the same with that in Italy, and at this day in French Provence. We here thrash the corn with flails; but there by treading. The Prophet speaks here of this custom, and compares the Church of God to oxen; as though he said, "The Jews shall be like oxen with iron horns and brazen hoofs, that they may lay prostrate under them the whole strength of the nations. However much then the nations may now excel, I will subject them under the feet of my people, as if sheafs were thrashed by them."

He then adds,[1] *And thou shalt separate* or consecrate *their wealth to Jehovah, and their substance*[2] *to the Lord of the whole earth.* Here the Prophet specifies the end for which God had purposed to subject the heathen nations to his chosen people,—that he might be glorified. This is the meaning. But they have refined too much in allegories, who have thought that this prophecy ought to be confined to the time of Christ: for the Prophet no doubt meant to extend consolation to the whole kingdom of Christ, from the beginning to the end.

[1] It is not often that Calvin passes over a sentence without noticing it, but he does so here; and it is this, *and thou shalt tear in pieces strong nations.* The verb is הדקות, thou shalt beat small, or thrash out; see Isa. xxviii. 28; perhaps the latter sense is most suitable to the passage. The meaning is, that a complete subjugation will take place. To thrash and to thrash out, is to conquer and to bring thoroughly under subjection.—*Ed.*

[2] The Hebrew word for this is חיל, and for "wealth" בצע. The latter means gain, spoil, or what is often unjustly got, or what is scraped together and constitutes the wealth of the covetous; חיל is properly substance, including possessions of all kinds, land, cattle, &c. בצע serves to include money, silver and gold; and חיל, every thing else which makes up wealth.

The verb, "consecrate," is in Hebrew in the first person, as it is in our version. There is no different reading; but the Septuagint and the earlier versions put it in the second person, to correspond with the previous verb, "Thou shalt beat in pieces." There will be no difference in the sense, if we render it according to the Hiphil form, in which it is found,—"I will cause thee to consecrate." *Jerome, Theodoret, Marckius, Dathius, Newcome,* and *Henderson,* adopt the second person.—This construction renders the passage no doubt more uniform.—*Ed.*

Others, not more correctly, say, that this is to be referred to the Babylonian captivity, because then Daniel and some others thrashed the people, when heathen kings were induced through their teaching to restore the temple, and also to offer some worship to the God of Israel. But on this point they are both mistaken, because they take the word thrashing in a different sense from the Prophet; for it commonly means that heathen nations are to be subjected to the Church of God: and this takes place, whenever God stretches forth his hand to the faithful, and suffers not the ungodly to exercise their cruelty as they wish; yea, when he makes them humbly to supplicate the faithful. This often happens in the world, as it is written of Christ, 'thy enemies shall lick the earth,' (Ps. lxxii. 9.) But this prophecy shall not be fulfilled until the last coming of Christ. We indeed begin to tread on our enemies whenever God by his power destroys them, or at least causes them to tremble and to be cast down, as we find that they dread whenever any change takes place; and then they blandly profess that they desire to serve God. So at this day it has happened both in France and in Italy. How many hypocrites, for the sake of an earthly advantage, have submitted themselves to God? and how many such England produced when the Gospel flourished there? All the courtiers, and others who were unwilling to incur the displeasure of the king, professed themselves to be the very best lovers of religion, (*optimos pietatis cultores*,—the best observers of piety.) But yet this is ever the case, 'Aliens have been false to thee,' (Ps. xviii. 44.)

We hence see what the Prophet means when he speaks of thrashing: he intimates, that the Lord would often cause that the enemies of the Church should be bruised, though no one crushed them: but, as I have said, we must look forward to the last day, if we wish to see the complete fulfilment of this prophecy.

He afterwards adds, *Thou shalt consecrate their wealth to Jehovah, and their substance to the Lord of the whole earth.* The Prophet shows here, that the dominion is not to be hoped for by the children of God, that they may abound in worldly pleasures, and appropriate every thing to themselves and also abuse their power, as ungodly men are wont to do; but that all is to be applied to the worship and the glory of God. For what purpose, then, does God design his Church to become eminent? That he himself may alone shine forth, and that the faithful may rightly enjoy their honour, and not become thereby proud. There is, therefore, nothing more alien to the power of the Church than pride, or cruelty or avarice. This, then, that is said ought to be carefully observed, *Their wealth thou shalt consecrate to Jehovah.* He had spoken before of power, "Thou shalt bind strong people, thou shalt thrash them, and thou shalt tread them under thy feet;" but lest the faithful should turn all this to a purpose the Lord had not designed, a most suitable correction is immediately added, and that is, that this power shall not be exercised according to the will of men, but according to the will of God: *Thou shalt* then *consecrate*, &c.; and he uses the word חרם, *cherem*, which means to make a thing an anathema or an offering;[1] as though he said, "God will raise his Church, that it may rule over its enemies; but let the faithful at the same time take heed, that they rule not tyrannically; for God designs ever to reign alone: therefore the whole excellency, the whole dignity, the whole power of the Church ought to be applied for this end,—that all things may become subject to God, and every thing among the nations may be altogether sacred to him, so that the worship of God may flourish among the conquerors, as well as among the conquered." We now perceive the Prophet's object in speaking of consecrating the wealth of the nations. Now follows—

[1] The word is very emphatic; it means to devote a thing to a purpose for ever, so as to be unchangeably settled. חרם, says *Parkhurst*, "is any thing *separated* absolutely from its common condition and *devoted* to Jehovah, so as to be incapable of redemption. See Lev. xxvii. 21, 28, 29. As a verb in Hiph. *to separate* or *devote* thus to Jehovah. Lev. xxvii. 28, 29; Micah iv. 12." It is therefore a sacrilege to take merely to our own use what ought to be, or what we have, thus consecrated to the Lord.—*Ed.*

CHAPTER V.

1. Now gather thyself in troops, O daughter of troops: he hath laid siege against us; they shall smite the judge of Israel with a rod upon the cheek.

2. But thou, Beth-lehem Ephratah, *though* thou be little among the thousands of Judah, *yet* out of thee shall he come forth unto me *that is* to be ruler in Israel; whose goings forth *have been* from of old, from everlasting.

1. [1]Nunc colligas te (*vel*, obsidione cingeris, *ut alii vertunt*) filia congregationis (*hoc est*, turmæ;) obsidionem posuit contra nos; in virga percutient ad maxillam judicem Israel.

2. Et tu Beth-lehem Ephrata, parva ad essendum (*ut ita loquar*) inter millia Jehudah; ex te mihi egredietur ad essendum dominatorem (*sic transfero durius*, ut sit dominator) in Israel: et egressus ejus ab initio, à diebus seculi.

To encourage the faithful to patience, the Prophet again reminds them that hard and severe time was nigh; for it was needful to put them in mind often of the approaching calamity, lest terror should wholly discourage them. As then there was danger from despair, the Prophet often repeats what he has already said of God's judgment, which was then suspending over the people of Israel. And this mode and order of teaching ought to be observed. When the Prophets threaten us, or denounce the punishment we have deserved, we either become torpid, or grow angry with God, and murmur: but when they set forth any thing of comfort, we then indulge ourselves and become too secure. It is therefore necessary to connect threatenings with promises, so that we may be always ready to endure temporal evils, and that our minds, sustained by hope, may, at the same time, depend on the Lord, and recumb on him. It was for this reason that the Prophet again mentions what he had already several times stated,—that the Jews would be surrounded by a siege. How do these two things agree,—that the enemies, assembled together, would be like sheaves which are taken to the floor to be trodden by the feet of animals,—and that the Jews would be besieged? I answer, that these things harmonize, because

[1] *Calvin* has, in this division, followed the Septuagint, and so have the translators of our version. This verse, in Hebrew, belongs to the last chapter. *Marckius*, *Dathius*, and *Henderson*, follow the Hebrew division; *Junius*, and *Tremelius*, and *Newcome*, that of our version.

the temporary punishment, which God would inflict on his Church, would not prevent him to restore it again whenever it pleased him. Lest, therefore, security should creep over the minds of the godly, the Prophet designed often to remind them of that dreadful calamity which might have entirely upset them, had no support been afforded them, that is, had not God sustained them by his word.

Now then *thou shalt assemble thyself*, he says, *O daughter of a troop*. The verb התגדדי, *etgaddi*, and the noun גדוד, *gadud*, sound alike; as though he said, "Thou shalt be collected, O daughter of collection." The Prophet addresses Jerusalem: but we must see why he calls her the daughter of collection. Some think that by this word is designated the splendid and wealthy state of Jerusalem; as though the Prophet said,—"This city has been hitherto populous, but now it shall be reduced to such straits that none shall dare to go forth beyond its gates, for they shall on every side be surrounded." But the Prophet calls Jerusalem the daughter of a troop in another sense,—because they were wont to occasion great troubles: as thieves agree together, and meet in troops for the purpose of committing plunder; so also the Prophet calls Jerusalem the daughter of a troop, for its citizens were wont wilfully to do great evils, and like robbers to use violence. *Thou* then, he says, *shalt now be collected;* that is, thou shalt not send forth thy troops, but enemies shall assemble thee together by a severe siege, so that thou shalt contract thyself like a bundle.

There are, then, two clauses in this verse,—that though the Lord resolved to help his Church, he would yet straiten her for a time,—and then the Prophet shows the reason, lest they complained that they were too severely treated: "You have been hitherto," he says, "without a cause oppressive to others: the time then is come when the Lord will return to you your recompense." As Isaiah says, 'Woe to thee, plunderer! Shalt thou not also be exposed to plunder?' Isa. xxxiii. 1; so also in this place,—"Ye have assembled in troops, that ye might pillage innocent men; therefore other troops shall now encircle you; nay, ye shall be beset by your own fear." The verb is in Hithpael: he says not, "Thou daughter of a troop shalt be now encircled;" but he says, "Thou shalt gather thyself."

He then adds, *A siege hath he set against thee.* This may refer to God; but it must be understood only of enemies: for the Prophet immediately adds, *They shall strike with the rod, &c.*, in the plural number,—*They shall* then *strike with the rod the cheek of the judge of Israel.* He means that the Jews would be subdued by their enemies, that their judges and governors would be exposed to every kind of contumely and dishonour; for to strike on the cheek is to offer the greatest indignity; as indeed it is the greatest contempt, as Demosthenes says, and is so mentioned by the lawyers. We now then perceive, that the Prophet's object was to show,—that the Jews in vain boasted of their kingdom and civil constitution, for the Lord would expose the governors of that kingdom to extreme contempt. The enemies then *shall strike their judges even on the cheek.*[1]

But there follows immediately a consolation: we hence see that the Prophet, at one time, humbles the children of God and prepares them for enduring the cross; and then he mitigates all sorrow; yea, and makes them to rejoice in the midst of their evils. For this purpose he adds what follows—

[1] This verse has been variously interpreted. It is considered by most as connected with the last chapter. Some, as *Marckius*, consider it as an address to the Roman power; some, to the Babylonian; and others, to Jerusalem. The construction of it is the main point. The first verb, תתגדדי, is found in six other places, and rendered in all, except in Jer. v. 7, to cut one's self; but its other meaning, as in Jer. v. 7, and evidently here, is to troop or to band together; and the noun גדוד, which follows, commonly means a band or a troop. The participle שם, in the next clause, can refer to nothing in the text but to "the daughter of a troop." The obvious and natural rendering of the verse would be the following,—

Band thyself together, thou daughter of a band,
Laying against us a siege:—
With the rod shall they strike on the cheek
The judge of Israel.

The daughter of a band or a troop means a military power, which collects bands or troops for warlike purposes. It is certainly more obvious to apply this to the Babylonian power than to Jerusalem, especially as the next line, "Laying against us a siege," necessarily refers to the latter.

"The judge" is, as Calvin seems to take it, a poetical singular for the plural. No particular person is meant, as *Newcome* and others seem to think, but judges in general.—*Ed.*

Thou, Bethlehem Ephratah, art small, that thou shouldest be among the thousands of Judah. As Matthew quotes this passage differently, some think that it ought to be read as a question, "And thou, Bethlehem Ephratah, art thou the least among the provinces of Judah?" Matthew says, "Thou art by no means the least," thou excellest.[1] But what need there is of distorting the words of the Prophet, as it was not the design of the Evangelist to relate the expressions of the Prophet, but only to point out the passage. As to the words, Matthew had regard to the condition of the town Bethlehem, such as it was at the coming of Christ. It then, indeed, began to be eminent: but the Prophet represents here how ignoble and mean a place Bethlehem then was, *Thou,* he says, *art the least among the thousands of Judah.* Some, not very wisely, give this explanation,—*Thou art the least among the thousands of Judah;* that is, "Though there might be a thousand towns in the tribe of Judah, yet thou couldest hardly have a place among so great a number." But this has been said through ignorance of a prevailing custom: for

[1] This does not follow; for to say that it was "not the least," is not to deny that it was "small." There is, in fact, no contradiction in the expressions. Matthew quotes literally neither the Hebrew nor the Septuagint version. The latter, in this case, agrees with the former. He gives the sense, but not the words, even in two instances besides this. Instead of "Ephratah," he has, "in the land of Judah;" and instead of "Ruler," he has, "Governor that shall rule," or feed. The meaning in these three instances is the same, though the words are different. The place was, in former times, called Bethlehem-Judah, and also Ephratah. See Gen. xxxv. 19; Judges xvii. 7; and Ruth iv. 11.

The attempt by a question to produce similarity of expressions in the second line, according to what is done by *Marckius* and *Newcome*, is by no means to be approved. The literal rendering is the following:—

And thou, Bethlehem Ephratah!
Small to be among the thousands of Judah,—
From thee shall *one* to me come forth,
To be a Ruler in Israel:
And his going forth *has been*
From of old, from the days of ages.

The word for "going forth" is plural, which, as Calvin says, is sometimes used for the singular; but two MSS. have it in the singular number, מצאתו. The last line in the Septuagint is as follows,—*απ' αρχης, εξ ημερων αιωνος.*

"In every age, from the foundation of the world, there has been some manifestation of the Messiah. He was the hope, as he was the salvation, of the world, from the promise to Adam in paradise, to his manifestation in the flesh *four thousand* years after."—*Adam Clarke.—Ed.*

the Jews, we know, were wont to divide their districts into thousands or chiliads. As in the army there are centurions, so also in the divisions of every nation there are hundreds; there are also in an army tribunes, who preside over a thousand men. Thus the Prophet calls them thousands, that is, tribunes; for the districts were so arranged, that the town, which, with its villages, could bring forth three thousand men, had three prefectures; and it had three tribunes, or four or five, if it was larger. The Prophet then, in order to show that this town was small and hardly of any account, says, "Thou, Bethlehem, art hardly sufficient to be one province." And it was a proof of its smallness, that hardly a thousand men could be made up from Bethlehem and its neighbouring villages. There were not, we know, many towns in the tribe of Judah; and yet a large army could be there collected. Since then the town of Bethlehem was so small, that it could hardly attain the rank of a province, it is hence no doubt evident that it was but a mean town. We now perceive what the Prophet had in view.

Thou, Bethlehem, he says, *art small among the cities of Judah;* yet *arise,* or go forth, *for me shall* one *from thee, who is to be a Ruler in Israel.* He calls it Bethlehem Ephratah; for they say that there was another Bethlehem in the tribe of Zebulon, and we know that Ephratah in meaning is nearly the same with Bethlehem; for both designate an abundance of fruit or provisions: and there David was born.

I will now proceed to the second clause, *From thee shall go forth for me* one *who is to be a Ruler.* Here the Prophet introduces God as the speaker, *go forth,* he says, *shall* one *for me.* God declares in this passage that it was not his purpose so to destroy his people, but that he intended, after a season, to restore them again. He therefore recalls the attention of the faithful to himself and to his eternal counsel; as though he said,—"I have thus for a time cast you away, that I may yet manifest my care for you." *For me* then *shall go forth one who is to be a Ruler in Israel.* Now there is no doubt but that the Prophet at the same time recalls the attention of the faithful to the promise which had been given to David. For whence arises the hope of salvation to the chosen people, except from the perpetuity of that kingdom? The Prophet now says,—"There is indeed a reason, according to the perception of the flesh, why the faithful should despond; for whence does their confidence arise, except from the kingdom of David? and from what place is David to arise? Even from Bethlehem; for Bethlehem has been called the city of David; and yet it is an obscure and a small town, and can hardly be considered a common province. Since it is so, the minds of the faithful may be depressed; but this smallness shall be no hinderance to the Lord, that he should not bring forth from thence a new king."

Even before the time of David Bethlehem was a small town, and one of the most common provinces. Who could have expected that a king would have been chosen from such a hamlet, and then, that he should come from a hut? for David belonged to a pastoral family; his father was a shepherd, and he was the least among his brethren. Who then could have thought that light would have arisen from such a corner, yea, from so mean a cottage? This was done contrary to the expectations of men. Hence the Prophet sets here before the faithful a similar expectation for their comfort; as though he said,—"Has not God once formed a most perfect state of things by making David a king, so that the people became in every respect happy and blessed? And whence did David come? It was from Bethlehem. There is then no reason why your present miseries should over-much distress you; for God can again from the same place bring forth a king to you, and he will do so."

Thou then *Bethlehem, small art thou, &c.* The Prophet doubtless intended here that the faithful should consider of what kind was the beginning of that most perfect state, when David was chosen king. David was a shepherd, a man in humble life, without reputation, without influence, and even the humblest among his brethren. Since then God had drawn light out of darkness, there was no cause for the faithful to despair of a future restoration, considering what had been the beginning of the previous happy condition of the people. We now understand the Prophet's meaning. But the rest I cannot finish to-day; I must therefore defer it till to-morrow.

PRAYER.

Grant, Almighty God, that as we cease not to provoke thy wrath against us, and as it is needful for us to be often chastised by thy hand, that we may be humbled and learn to submit ourselves to thee in true and willing obedience,—O grant, that we faint not under thy scourges, but ever raise up our minds to the hope of deliverance, which thou givest to us through our Mediator, whom thou hast once for all sent into the world, that thou mightest through him reconcile us to thyself, and through whom also thou bringest help whenever we need it: and may we at the same time learn to rely on thy only-begotten Son, so that with courageous minds we may pass through all the miseries of this world, and never at any time grow weary, until having at length obtained the victory, we come to that blessed rest and enjoy the fruit of our victory, through the same Christ our Lord. Amen.

Lecture Ninety-first.

WE began yesterday to explain the promise by which our Prophet designed to sustain the minds of the faithful, lest they should despair in their heavy trial. He reminds them, as it has been stated, of the commencement of the kingdom: as David had been raised as it were from nothing, and God had given in him an example of his wonderful grace, the Prophet reminds the godly, that the same is now to be expected, that God will again raise up the fallen kingdom. *Go forth* then *from Bethlehem*, he says, *shall* one *who is to be a Ruler in Israel*, though it was but a mean town. He calls him a Ruler in Israel; for he had before declared that there would be such a dreadful judgment, that the enemy would strike with the hand the face of the judge; and this was the same as though the Prophet had said, that no honour would be shown to the people, for the chief himself would be beaten. He therefore now promises a new Ruler, he promises that there would be again some civil order to be found among the people; for a governor could not have been struck on the cheek, except all authority and honour had departed. We then see what the Prophet intended by mentioning the word, Ruler; it was to show, that God would again cause that a new Prince would arise to govern the people. It was therefore a remedy to their devastation.

But the Prophet subjoins, *His going forth is from the beginning*, or from far antiquity, *and from the days of ages*, that is, from the days of eternity. He intimates here, that it would not be a sudden thing, that a prince should arise to govern the people; for it had been already long ago determined by God. This is the plain meaning. Some, I know, pertinaciously maintain, that the Prophet speaks here of the eternal existence of Christ; and as for myself, I willingly own that the divinity of Christ is here proved to us; but as this will never be allowed by the Jews, I prefer taking the words simply as they are,—that Christ will not come forth unexpectedly from Bethlehem, as though God had previously determined nothing respecting him. *His goings forth* then *are from the beginning*. But others bring a new refinement,—that the Prophet uses the plural number, his goings forth, to designate the twofold nature of Christ: but there is in this an absurdity; for the Prophet could not properly nor wisely mention the human nature of Christ with the divine, with reference to eternity. The Word of God, we know, was eternal; and we know, that when the fulness of time came, as Paul says, Christ put on our nature, (Gal. iv. 4.) Hence the beginning of Christ as to the flesh was not so old, if his existence be spoken of: to set them together then would have been absurd. It is a common thing in Hebrew to use the plural for the singular number. He says then, that the going forth of Christ is from eternity; for he will not go forth suddenly from Bethlehem, as one who rises unexpectedly to bring help, when things are in a hopeless state, and so rises, when nothing had been foreseen. But the Prophet declares that the going forth of Christ would be different,—that God had from the beginning determined to give his people an eternal king.

At the same time, we must repudiate that gloss with which the Rabbins are pleased; for they say that the Messiah was created before the creation of the world, and also the throne of eternity, and the Law, and other things ; but these are insipid fables. The Prophet shows simply, that even before the world was made Christ was chief, as he is also called the First-born of every creature, for by him all things were created, (Col. i. 15 :) and the same Word of God, by whom the world was created, is to be the Head of the Church, and by him what has been lost is to be recovered. We now then comprehend what the Prophet meant by saying, *the goings forth* of Christ *are from eternity*. But I would not concede to the Jews, that only by the perpetual appointment of God the going forth of Christ has been from the beginning, or from all ages : but two things must be noticed by us,—that Christ, who was manifested in the flesh that he might redeem the Church of God, was the eternal Word, by whom the world was created,—and then, that he was destined by the eternal counsel of God to be the first-born of every creature, and especially to be the Head of the Church, that he might restore a fallen world by his grace and power.

We now then see the reason why the Prophet connects together these two things,—that there would go forth one from Bethlehem who would rule among Israel,—and yet that his goings forth have been from eternity : for if he had only said what I explained yesterday, an objection might easily have been made, and this might have come into the mind of some,—"Why dost thou say that one will come from Bethlehem who will govern the chosen people, as though God were to contrive a new remedy on seeing that it is all over with respect to the deliverance of his Church?" The Prophet here anticipates this objection, and reminds us, that his goings forth have been from eternity, that they have been already decreed, even from the beginning ; for with God there is nothing new, so that he should stand in need of holding any unlooked for consultation ; as is the case with us when any thing happens which we in no degree apprehended ; we then find it necessary to devise some new measures. The Prophet shows that nothing of this kind can happen to God : but all this,—that people are reduced to nothing,—and that they are again restored by Christ,—all this is overruled by his secret and incomprehensible providence. *His goings* forth then *are from the beginning, and from the days of eternity.* Let us proceed—

3. Therefore will he give them up, until the time *that* she which travaileth hath brought forth; then the remnant of his brethren shall return unto the children of Israel.

3. Propterea[1] dabit eos (*hoc est*, ponet eos, *vel*, relinquet) usque ad tempus quo parturiens pariet; et revertentur ad filios Israel residuum fratrum ejus.

The Prophet here again so moderates his words, that the Jews might understand, that they were to endure many evils before God relieved their miseries. He wished then here to prepare the minds of the godly to bear evils, that they might not despair in great troubles, nor be depressed by extreme fear. He then states these two things,—that the people, as they deserved, would be heavily afflicted,—and then that God, notwithstanding such severe punishment, would be mindful of his covenant, so as to gather at length some remnants, and not to suffer his people to be wholly destroyed. He therefore promises a middle course between a prosperous state and destruction. The people, says the Prophet, shall not continue entire.—How so? For God will cut off the kingdom and the city; and yet he will afford relief to the miserable: When they shall think that they are given up to entire ruin, he will stretch forth his hand to them. This is the sum of the whole.

He then says, that they shall be delivered up, that is, forsaken by God, *until she who is in travail bringeth forth.*[2] There are those who apply this to the blessed Virgin; as though Micah had said, that the Jews were to look forward to the

[1] לכן, *Grotius* renders it *certè*—surely: but *nevertheless*, as proposed by *Scott*, is the most suitable particle here. *Dathius* gives this paraphrase—*Verùm quidem est*—True indeed it is.—*Ed.*

[2] Until the time the begetting shall beget, (יולדה ילדה,)
And the remnant of his brethren shall be converted
Together with the children of Israel.

Newcome gives this explanation of the verse,—"The sense is: God will not fully vindicate and exalt his people, till the Virgin-mother shall have brought forth her Son; and till Judah and Israel, and all the true sons of Abraham among their brethren, the Gentiles, be converted to Christianity."—*Ed.*

time when the Virgin would bring forth Christ: but all may easily see that this is a forced interpretation. The Prophet, I have no doubt, in using this similitude, compares the body of the people to a woman with child. The similitude of a woman in travail is variously applied. The wicked, when they promise to themselves impunity, are suddenly and violently laid hold on: thus their destruction is like the travail of a woman with child. But the meaning of this passage is different; for the Prophet says, that the Jews would be like pregnant women, for this reason,—that though they would have to endure the greatest sorrows, there yet would follow a joyful and happy issue. And Christ himself employs this example for the same purpose, 'A woman,' he says, 'has sorrow when she brings forth, but immediately rejoices when she sees a man born into the world,' (John xvi. 21.) So Micah says in this place, that the chosen people would have a happy deliverance from their miseries, for they would bring forth. There shall indeed be the most grievous sorrows, but their issue will be joy, that is, when they shall know that they and their salvation had been the objects of God's care, when they shall understand that their chastisements had been useful to them. *Until* then *she who is in travail bringeth forth, God,* he says, *will forsake them.*

There are then two clauses in this verse;—the first is, that the Jews were for a time to be forsaken, as though they were no longer under the power and protection of God;—the other is, that God would be always their guardian, for a bringing forth would follow their sorrows. The following passage in Isaiah is of an opposite character; 'We have been in sorrow, we have been in travail, and we brought forth wind,' (Isa. xxvi. 18.) The faithful complain there that they had been oppressed with the severest troubles, and had come to the birth, but that they brought forth nothing but wind, that is, that they had been deceived by vain expectation, for the issue did not prove to be what they had hoped. But the Lord promises here by Micah something better, and that is, that the end of all their evils would be the happy restoration of the people, as when a woman receives a compensation for all her sorrow, when she sees that a child is born.

And he confirms this sentence by another, when he says, *So the children of Israel shall return,* or be converted, *the residue of his brethren.*[1] The Prophet then intimates that it could not be otherwise, but that God would not only scatter, but tread under foot his people, so that their calamity would threaten an unavoidable destruction. This is one thing; but in the meantime, he promises that there would be some saved. But he speaks of a *remnant,* as we have observed elsewhere, lest hypocrites should think that they could escape unpunished, while they trifled with God. The Prophet then shows, that there would come such a calamity as would nearly extinguish the people, but that some would be preserved through God's mercy, and that beyond ordinary expectation.[2] We now perceive the intention of the Prophet. It now follows—

4. And he shall stand and feed in the strength of the Lord, in the majesty of the name of the Lord his God; and they shall abide: for now shall he be great unto the ends of the earth.

4. Et stabit et pascet in virtute Jehovæ, in magnificentia nominis Jehovæ Dei sui; et habitabunt, quia nunc magnificabitur usque ad fines terræ.

[1] By this arrangement of the sentence, *Calvin* evidently meant, that "his," before "brethren," refers to "Israel." In the original, the latter clause is before the former, but in Hebrew, as well as in other languages, the antecedent sometimes comes after its pronoun.—*Ed.*

[2] Most commentators differ from Calvin in their view of this verse, regarding it as a distinct prophecy of the Saviour's birth. There are difficulties on both sides: but taking the whole context, especially the following verse, we can hardly resist the conclusion, that Christ, born of a Virgin, is the subject. Indeed, the whole of this chapter, notwithstanding the reference to the Assyrian, is not capable of a satisfactory explanation, without applying what is said to Christ and his Church. Some things, no doubt, in the history of the Jews, may be alluded to, or incidentally mentioned; but the full accomplishment must be looked for in the new dispensation. And it is a splendid prophecy, in words often derived from customs and incidents among the Jews, of the birth of the Saviour, and of the character and extent, and blessedness of his kingdom, and of the destruction of his enemies.

Newcome and *Adam Clarke* propose to divide the chapter after the first line in verse 5, thinking that a new subject is there introduced: but evidently the same subject, the Gospel dispensation, is continued to the end of the chapter. The Assyrian, the especial enemy of the ancient Church, designates the enemies of the Christian Church in all ages.

"As Sennacherib's invasion," says *Scott,* "was not repelled by the ruler or chieftains of Israel; nor did the Jews ever invade or waste the Assyrian dominions; it seems evident, that these expressions must be understood as mystically intending other enemies and persecutors of the

There is no doubt but that the Prophet continues here to speak of Christ; and though the Jews shamelessly pervert the whole Scripture, they yet cannot deny that Micah calls here the attention of all the godly to the coming of Christ, yea, of all who hope or desire to obtain salvation. This is certain. Let us now see what the Prophet ascribes to Christ.

He shall stand, he says, *and feed in the power of Jehovah.* The word, *stand*, designates perseverance, as though he had said, that it would not be for a short time that God would gather by Christ the remnant of the people; that it would not be, as it often happens, when some rays of joy shine, and then immediately vanish. The Prophet shows here that the kingdom of Christ would be durable and permanent. It will then proceed; for Christ will not only rule his Church for a few days, but his kingdom will continue to stand through unbroken series of years and of ages. We now then understand the Prophet's object.

He adds, in the second place, *He shall feed in the strength of Jehovah, in the greatness of the name of Jehovah his God;* by which words he means, that there would be sufficient power in Christ to defend his Church. The Church, we know, is in this world subject to various troubles, for it is never without enemies; for Satan always finds those whom he induces, and whose fury he employs to harass the children of God. As then the Church of God is tossed by many tempests, it has need of a strong and invincible defender. Hence this distinction is now ascribed by our Prophet to Christ,—that *he shall feed in the strength of Jehovah, and in the majesty of his God.* As to the word, *feed*, it no doubt expresses what Christ is to his people, to the flock committed to him and to his care. Christ then rules not in his Church as a dreaded tyrant, who distresses his subjects with fear; but he is a Shepherd who gently deals with his flock. Nothing therefore can exceed the kindness and gentleness of Christ towards the faithful, as he performs the office of a Shepherd: and he prefers to be

Church, who should be of the same spirit with Sennacherib and the Assyrians." *Henry*, who is a much more learned critic and much profounder divine than what is commonly thought, agrees with *Scott*, and many others, in the interpretation of this chapter.—*Ed.*

adorned with this title, rather than to be called and deemed a king, or to assume authority to himself. But the Prophet, on the other hand, shows that the power of Christ would be dreadful to the ungodly and wicked. *He shall feed*, he says,—with regard to his flock, Christ will put on a character full of gentleness; for nothing, as I have said, can imply more kindness than the word shepherd: but as we are on every side surrounded by enemies, the Prophet adds,—

He shall feed *in the power of Jehovah, and in the majesty of the name of Jehovah;* that is, as much power as there is in God, so much protection will there be in Christ, whenever it will be necessary to defend and protect the Church against her enemies. Let us hence learn that no less safety is to be expected from Christ, than there is of power in God. Now, since the power of God, as we confess, is immeasurable, and since his omnipotence far surpasses and swallows up all our conceptions, let us hence learn to extend both high and low all our hopes.—Why so? Because we have a King sufficiently powerful, who has undertaken to defend us, and to whose protection the Father has committed us. Since then we have been delivered up to Christ's care and defence, there is no cause why we should doubt respecting our safety. He is indeed a Shepherd, and for our sake he thus condescended and refused not so mean a name; for in a shepherd there is no pomp nor grandeur. But though Christ, for our sake, put on the character of a Shepherd, and disowns not the office, he is yet endued with infinite power.—How so? Because he governs not the Church after a human manner, but *in the majesty of the name of his God.*[1]

Now, that he subjects Christ to God, he refers to his human nature. Though Christ is God manifested in the flesh, he is yet made subject to God the Father, as our Mediator and the Head of the Church in human nature: he is indeed the middle Person between God and us. This then is the reason

[1] "The Prophets prefaced their messages with, *Thus saith the Lord;* but Christ spoke not as a servant, but as a Son, *Verily, verily, I say unto you:* this was feeding in the majesty of the name of the Lord his God; all power was given him in heaven and earth, a power over all flesh, by the virtue of which he still rules in the majesty of the name of the Lord his God."—*Henry.*

why the Prophet now says, that Christ has power, as it were, at the will of another; not that Christ is only man, but as he appears to us in the person of man, he is said to receive power from his Father; and this, as it has been said, with respect to his human nature. There is yet another reason why the Prophet has expressly added this,—that we may know that Christ, as the protector of the Church, cannot be separated from his Father: as then God is God, so Christ is his minister to preserve the Church. In a word, the Prophet means that God is not to be viewed by the faithful, except through the intervening Mediator; and he means also that the Mediator is not to be viewed, except as one who receives supreme power from God himself, and who is armed with omnipotence to preserve his people.

He afterwards adds, *They shall dwell; for he shall now be magnified to the extremities of the earth.* He promises a secure habitation to the faithful; for Christ shall be extolled to the utmost regions of the world. We here see that he is promised to foreign nations: for it would have been enough for Christ to exercise his supreme power within the borders of Judea, had only one nation been committed to his safe keeping. But as God the Father intended that he should be the Author of salvation to all nations, we hence learn that it was necessary that he should be extolled to the utmost borders of the earth. But with regard to the word *dwell,* it is explained more fully in the next verse, when the Prophet says—

5. And this *man* shall be the peace, when the Assyrian shall come into our land: and when he shall tread in our palaces, then shall we raise against him seven shepherds, and eight principal men.

5. Et erit hic pax: Assur quum venerit in terram nostram, et quum calcaverit in palatiis nostris, tunc constituemus super eum septem pastores et octo principes hominum.

Micah, as I have said, confirms his former statement. By the word *dwell,* he no doubt meant a quiet and peaceable inhabitation; as though he had said, that the children of God would, under Christ, be safe and secure. Now he adds, *And he shall be our peace.* It might have been asked, "Whence will come this secure dwelling? For the land has been very often wasted, and the people have been at length driven to exile. How then can we now venture to hope for what thou promisest, that we shall be quiet and secure?" Because, he says, *He shall be our peace;* and we ought to be satisfied with the protection of the King whom God the Father has given us. Let his shadow, then, suffice us, and we shall be safe enough from all troubles. We now see in what sense the Prophet calls Christ the Peace of his people or of his Church; he so calls him because he will drive far away all hurtful things, and will be armed with strength and invincible power to check all the ungodly, that they may not make war on the children of God, or to prevent them in their course, should they excite any disturbances.

We further know, that Christ is in another way our peace; for he has reconciled us to the Father. And what would it avail us to be safe from earthly annoyances, if we were not certain that God is reconciled to us? Except then our minds acquiesce in the paternal benevolence of God, we must necessarily tremble at all times, though no one were to cause us any trouble: nay, were all men our friends, and were all to applaud us, miserable still would be our condition, and we should toil with disquietude, except our consciences were pacified with the sure confidence that God is our Father. Christ then can be our peace in no other way than by reconciling God to us. But at the same time the Prophet speaks generally,—that we shall lie safely under the shadow of Christ, and that no evil ought to be feared,—that though Satan should furiously assail us, and the whole world become mad against us, we ought yet to fear nothing, if Christ keeps and protects us under his wings. This then is the meaning, when it is said here that Christ is our peace.

He afterwards subjoins, *When the Assyrian shall come into our land, and when he shall tread in our palaces, then we shall raise up against him*, or on him, *seven shepherds and eight princes of the people.*[1] The Prophet intimates that the Church of

[1] The order of the words in Hebrew is not strictly observed in this instance. There is here an example, not unfrequent in the Prophets, of the nominative case absolute,—

And he shall be *our* peace:
The Assyrian—when he shall come into our land, &c.

God would not be free from troubles, even after the coming of Christ: for I am disposed to refer this to the intervening time, though interpreters put another construction on the words of the Prophet. But this meaning is far more suitable,—that while the help which God promised was expected and yet suspended, the Assyrians would come, who would pass far and wide through the land of Israel. Hence he says, that though Assur should come to our land, and break through with such force and violence that we could not drive him out, we shall yet set up for ourselves shepherds and princes against him. It must at the same time be observed, that this prophecy is not to be confined to that short time; for the Prophet speaks generally of the preservation of the Church before as well as after the coming of Christ; as though he said, —"I have said that the king, who shall be born to you, and shall go forth from Bethlehem, shall be your peace; but before he shall be revealed to the world, God will gather his Church, and there shall emerge as from a dead body Princes as well as Shepherds, who will repel unjust violence, nay, who will subdue the Assyrians."

We now see what the Prophet had in view: After having honoured Christ with this remarkable commendation—that he alone is sufficient to give us a quiet life, he adds, that God would be the preserver of his Church, so as to deliver it from its enemies. But there is a circumstance here expressed which ought to be noticed: Micah says, that when the Assyrians shall pass through the land and tread down all the palaces, God would then become the deliverer of his people. It might have been objected, and said, "Why not sooner? Would it have been better to prevent this? Why! God now looks as it were indifferently on the force of the enemies, and loosens the reins to them, that they plunder the whole land,

And when he shall tread in our palaces,
Then raise shall we against him
Seven shepherds and eight anointed men.

נסיכי אדם, literally, anointed of men; but it is a phrase signifying men in authority, princes or sovereigns. נסיכים is rendered *dukes* in Joshua xiii. 21, and *princes* in Ps. lxxxiii. 11, and Ezek. xxxii. 30. It is not necessary to say "eight princes of men," but, "eight princes," or "eight anointed men."—*Ed.*

and break through to the very middle of it. Why then does not God give earlier relief?" But we see the manner in which God intends to preserve his Church: for as the faithful often need some chastisement, God humbles them when it is expedient, and then delivers them. This is the reason why God allowed such liberty to the Assyrians before he supplied assistance. And we also see that this discourse is so moderated by the Prophet, that he shows, on the one hand, that the Church would not always be free from evils,—the Assyrians shall come, they shall tread down our palaces,—this must be endured by God's children, and ought in time to prepare their minds to bear troubles; but, on the other hand, a consolation follows; for when the Assyrians shall thus penetrate into our land, and nothing shall be concealed or hidden from them, then the Lord will cause new shepherds to arise.

The Prophet means that the body of the people would be for some time mutilated, and, as it were, mangled; and so it was, until they returned from exile. For he would have said this to no purpose, *We shall set up for ourselves*, if there had been an unbroken succession of regular government; he could not have said in that case, After Assur shall come into our land, we shall set up princes; but, There shall be princes when Assur shall come. The word *set up* denotes then what I have stated,—that the Church would be for a time without any visible head. Christ indeed has always been the Head of the Church; but as he designed himself to be then seen in the family of David as in an image or picture, so the Prophet shows here, that though the faithful would have to see the head cut off and the Church dead, and like a dead body cast aside, when torn from its head; yea, that though the Church would be in this state dreadfully desolated, there is yet a promise of a new resurrection. *We shall* then *set up*, or choose for ourselves shepherds.

If any one raises an objection and says, that it was God's office to make shepherds for his people,—this indeed I allow to be true: but this point has not been unwisely mentioned by the Prophet; for he extols here the favour of God, in granting again their liberty to his people. In this especially consists the best condition of the people, when they can choose, by common consent, their own shepherds: for when any one by force usurps the supreme power, it is tyranny; and when men become kings by hereditary right, it seems not consistent with liberty.[1] *We shall* then *set up for ourselves princes*, says the Prophet; that is, the Lord will not only give breathing time to his Church, and will also cause that she may set up a fixed and a well-ordered government, and that by the common consent of all.

By *seven* and *eight*, the Prophet no doubt meant a great number. When he speaks of the calamities of the Church, it is said, 'There shall not be found any to govern, but children shall rule over you.' But the Prophet says here that there would be many leaders to undertake the care of ruling and defending the people. The governors of the people shall therefore be seven shepherds and eight princes; that is, the Lord will endue many by his Spirit, that they shall be suddenly wise men: though before they were in no repute, though they possessed nothing worthy of great men, yet the Lord will enrich them with the spirit of power, that they shall become fit to rule. The Prophet now adds—

6. And they shall waste the land of Assyria with the sword, and the land of Nimrod in the entrances thereof: thus shall he deliver *us* from the Assyrian, when he cometh into our land, and when he treadeth within our borders.

6. Et pascent terram Assur (*hoc est*, vastabunt; *nam metaphoricè hic* pascere *accipitur pro* perdere *quemadmodum dicuntur pecora pascere agrum, hoc est, quum denudant herba sua; atque ita pastorum ingluviem notat in vorando populo; et alludit ad nomen illud quo usus fuerat: dixerat enim* רועים *septem pastores; nunc dicit* רעה; *Videmus ergo Prophetam alludere ad nomen illud quod posuerat: pascent ergo* terram Assur) gladio, et terram Nimrod in gladiis suis: et liberabit ab Assur, ubi venerit in terram nostram, et ubi calcaverit in finibus nostris.

In this verse the Prophet says, that the shepherds, chosen

[1] It is by no means a safe rule, to draw a conclusion from the spiritual government as to what a temporal government should be. The subjects are guided by very different principles; and the same sort of government will not suit countries under different degrees of civilization. To theorize on this subject, as on many others, leads often to wrong conclusions. An hereditary sovereignty may seem to trench on liberty; but our own country exhibits an example where both exist to an extent unknown in the present or in any former age. Under no democracy has liberty ever been so freely and so fully enjoyed as in this land, which has been so wonderfully favoured by a kind and gracious Providence. We owe, perhaps, far more than we are aware to an hereditary sovereignty.—*Ed.*

by the Church, after it had been miserably oppressed by the tyranny of its enemies, would have a twofold office. They shall first *feed;* that is, nourish the Church of God;—and, secondly, they shall *feed;* that is, destroy the *land of Asshur,* so that nothing may remain there whole and entire. God will then arm these shepherds with warlike courage; for they must fight boldly and courageously against their enemies: he says, *They shall feed on the land of Nimrod with their swords.* Nimrod, we know, reigned in Chaldea; and we know also that the ten tribes were led away by Shalmanezer, and that the kingdom of Israel was thus demolished: when the Chaldeans obtained the empire, the kingdom of Judah was also laid waste by them. Now the import of the words is, that these shepherds would be sufficiently strong to oppose all the enemies of the Church, whether they were the Babylonians or the Assyrians. And he names the Assyrians and Babylonians, because they had then a contest with the people of God; and this continued to the coming of Christ, though it is certain that they suffered more troubles from Antiochus than from others: but as he was one of the successors of Alexander, the Prophet here, taking a part for the whole, means, by the Assyrians and Chaldeans, all the enemies of the Church, whoever they might be. *Waste,* he says, *shall these shepherds the land of Asshur by the sword,* and *the land of Nimrod,* and that *by their swords.*[1]

But this shall not be until the Chaldeans and the Assyrians *shall penetrate into our land, and tread in our borders.* The Prophet again reminds the faithful, that they stood in need of patience, and that they were to know that God had not

[1] בפתחיה, in its openings or entrances: so most render the word. Εντος πολων αυτης—within its gates.—*Symmachus.* *Marckius, Newcome,* and *Henderson,* agree with our version. Calvin has, in this instance, followed Kimchi and Aben-Ezra: but the affix ה prevents us from adopting this meaning; besides, the word itself is nowhere found in this sense.

This verse is connected with the preceding, and ought to be separated from it only by a semicolon, and may be thus rendered:—

And they shall waste the land of the Assyrian by the sword,
And the land of Nimrod at its entrances:
Thus shall he cause a deliverance from the Assyrian,
When he shall come into our land,
And when he shall tread in our borders.—*Ed.*

made a vain promise. The import of the whole is, that no deliverance was to be expected from God's hand until the faithful yielded their necks to his yoke, and patiently sustained the evils which were then approaching. The Prophet then mentions the intervening time between that state in which the Jews gloried and their deliverance. Why so? Because they were soon after to be smitten heavily by God's hand; but this, as we have seen, they did not think would take place. Hence he says,—"Since you cannot yet be made to believe that merited punishment is nigh you, experience shall be your teacher. In the meantime, let the faithful provide themselves with courage, and, with a meek heart, patiently to submit to God, the righteous Judge: but, at the same time, let them expect a sure deliverance, when they shall have gone through all their evils; for when the ripened time shall come, the Lord will look on his Church; but she must be first afflicted."

PRAYER.

Grant, Almighty God, that as thou hast from the beginning so defended thy Church, that thou hast never wholly forsaken her, and though it had nearly rejected thee by its defections, yet it has been thy pleasure to stand firm to thy covenant, and to show to it thy favour through all ages, until at length the everlasting Redeemer of the whole world appeared,—O grant, that we may experience the same favour at this day, and though we have in various ways provoked thy wrath against us, yet do thou so humble us, that thou mayest sustain us by thy word; and may we so recumb on those promises which we find in Scripture, that we may at length by our patience overcome our enemies, and in patience possess our souls, until thou raisest up thine hand, and showest that invincible power which thou hast given to thy only-begotten Son, that he might repress the devil and all the wicked, and preserve us safe and secure from all injuries. Amen.

Lecture Ninety-second.

7. And the remnant of Jacob shall be in the midst of many people as a dew from the Lord, as the showers upon the grass, that tarrieth not for man, nor waiteth for the sons of men.

8. And the remnant of Jacob shall be among the Gentiles in the midst of many people as a lion among the beasts of the forest, as a young lion among the flocks of sheep: who, if he go through, both treadeth down, and teareth in pieces, and none can deliver.

7. Et erit residuum Jacob in gentibus, in medio populorum multorum (*vel*, magnorum,) sicut ros â Jebova, sicut stillæ super herbam, quæ non expectat hominem, neque sperat in filiis hominum.

8. Et erit residuum Jacob in gentibus, in medio populorum multorum (*vel*, magnorum, *ut diximus*,) sicut leo inter animalia sylvæ, sicut leunculus inter greges ovium, qui si transierit et discerpserit et repuerit, nemo eripiet.

Micah promises here two things as to the future state of the Church,—that God shall defend it without the help and aid of men,—and that he will supply it with strength, so that it will become superior to all enemies. In the first place, to show that the preservation of the Church depends on the mere favour of God, and that there is no need of any earthly aids, he makes use of a most suitable similitude; he says, that the people of God are like a dewy meadow. The Prophet speaks not what is strictly correct; for what he says of the rain and dew is to be applied to the grass or the meadow.[1] *The residue of Jacob*, he says, *shall be as dew from Jehovah, and drops of rain on the grass*. This cannot be applied according to the design of the Prophet, except you take the dew, as I have already said, for the dewy meadow, or for the grass, which draws moisture and vigour from the rain. The sense indeed is by no means obscure, which is,—that God will make his people to grow like the grass, which is fed only by celestial dew, without any culture or labour on the part of men: and this is also what the Prophet expressly

[1] There seems to be no necessity for this supposed inaccuracy in this comparison; it indeed changes the obvious meaning of the passage. The Jews are compared to the dew and rain, through which the grass grows; and then it is said, that the growth of the grass, not the dew or the rain, is not dependant on man, but on the dew or rain. The comparison is thus in every way suitable.—*Ed.*

mentions; for he says, that the grass of which he speaks waits not for men, nor grows through men's care, but grows through the dew of heaven.

But that we may better understand the Prophet's intention, I shall briefly notice the words. *There shall be*, he says, *the residue of Jacob*. He shows here that the whole people would not be preserved; for he had before spoken of their destruction. We hence see that this promise is to be confined to the seed, which God had wonderfully preserved in the calamitous state of the Church, yea, even in its almost total destruction. Then this promise belongs not to the whole body of the people, but to a small number; and hence he uses, as before, the word שארית, *sharit*, a remnant or residue. *There shall* then *be the residue of Jacob;*[1] that is, though the people shall nearly all perish, yet there shall be some residue.

He then adds, *Among great* or many *nations*. There is here a contrast between the remnants and great nations: and the Prophet has not unnecessarily added the expression בקרב, *bekoreb*, in the midst. There are then three things to be observed here,—that God does not promise deliverance to the whole people, but to a residue only,—and then, that he promises this deliverance among powerful or many nations, as though he said,—"Though the Church of God shall not excel in number, nay, so great may be the number of its enemies, as to be sufficient to overwhelm it, yet God will cause it to grow and to propagate: in a word, its enemies, though many in number, and strong in forces and power, shall not yet hinder the Lord, that he should not increase his Church more and more;"—and the third particular is what the expression, *in the midst*, intimates, and that is, that the people of God shall be besieged on every side. When enemies come upon us only from one part, it is not so very distressing, but when they surround us, being in front, and behind, and on both sides, then our condition seems miserable indeed; for when they thus press on us on all sides, they

[1] We have the residue or remnant of Joseph in Amos v. 15,—the remnant of Israel in Micah ii. 12,—and here and in the following verse, the remnant of Jacob.—*Ed.*

hardly allow us time to draw our breath. But the Prophet declares, that though surrounded on all sides by enemies, yet the Church would be safe.

He now adds, כטל מאת יהוה, *cathel meat Ieve, As a dew from Jehovah;* that is, it shall be, as I have said, as the grass, which is nourished and grows by means of dew from heaven, and as grass, which flourishes, not through the culture or labour of men, but which God himself makes to grow. He might have merely said, *as the dew*, but he adds, *from Jehovah*, that he might make a distinction between God and man, and show that the power of God is alone sufficient to support and sustain the Church, though men brought no assistance. And this is expressed more clearly in the next clause, when he says, *As drops of rain on the grass, which wait not for man, nor tarry for the sons of men.* We now then see that the faithful have their attention called to God alone, that they may understand that they are to be safe through his favour, —that if all helps on earth failed, they ought not to fear, since they can be effectually sustained by the power of God alone: for God makes grass to grow on mountains and in meadows without the help and labour of man; and thus he can defend his Church without any foreign aid, but by his own hidden, and, so to speak, his own intrinsic power.

Then follows this promise,—that God will arm his people with invincible and irresistible power, that they may be superior to all their enemies. Hence he says, that *the residue of Israel shall be like a lion among the beasts of the forest, and like a young lion among a flock of sheep.* As a strong lion then is superior to other beasts, and as a young lion dares ferociously to attack a flock of sheep; so he says the people of Israel shall be; they shall be like lions, filling their enemies with terror, yea, and plundering and scattering them, so that no one will dare to resist them. The Prophet, by speaking thus, does not mean, that the people of God would be cruel and sanguinary: for we know that when the Prophets use similes of this kind, they express something not strictly suitable; for who would be so foolish as to select every thing that belongs to a lion, and apply it to the Church of God. Then the reason for this similitude must be observed; it was to show, that the faithful shall be endued with a power so superior to that of their enemies, that they shall be a terror to them. It does not hence follow that they shall be cruel.

But we must, at the same time, see what the Lord promises to his Church. Though God then recommends to his children the spirit of meekness, yet the faithful may still be a dread to their enemies; they ought, however, to observe what is just towards them, and to keep themselves within proper bounds. And yet Micah says, that they shall be endued with such power that they shall drive their enemies afar off; yea, that they shall plunder and tear them in pieces, while no one will be able to resist them.[1] But these two things are necessary as to the preservation of the Church, that God may make it grow; for except it be miraculously increased, it can never grow; and then it has need of a strong and powerful defence against her enemies; for we know that there are always wicked men who oppose the Church, yea, who apply all their powers to destroy it: it is therefore necessary that it should be supplied by the Lord with invincible strength, as our Prophet declares here. Let us proceed—

9. Thine hand shall be lifted up upon thine adversaries, and all thine enemies shall be cut off.	9. Exaltabitur manus tua super hostes tuis, et cuncti, adversarii tui excidentur.

He confirms what is said in the last verse, and expresses in other words what he meant, and what we have explained,—that though the Church must contend with many strong and violent enemies, it will not yet fail, for the Lord will supply it with strength from heaven. *Exalted*, he says, *shall be thy hand, that all thine enemies may be cut off.* He promises not that the Church shall be in a quiet state, but victorious, and declares also that there will never be wanting enemies. This promise, then, ought to arm us for enduring patiently, as we cannot conquer except by fighting. As then there will be

[1] "They shall be bold as a lion in witnessing against the corruptions of the times and places they live in, and strong as a lion in the strength of the Lord, to resist and overcome their spiritual enemies. *The weapons of their warfare* are *mighty through God, to the pulling down of strongholds*, 2 Cor. x. 4, 5. They shall have courage which all their adversaries shall not be able to resist, Luke xxi. 15."—*Henry.*

always enemies to oppose the Church of God; yea, to attempt its ruin, the Prophet says here, *Exalted shall be thy hand above thine enemies.*

But it may be asked, When has this promise been fulfilled? For we know that since the people had been led away into the Babylonian exile, they had always been either tributaries, or kept under cruel tyranny, or at least had been unequal to their enemies. But this principle ought ever to be remembered,—that the faithful ought to be satisfied with victory,—that however hard they may be pressed, and however constant may be the contests which they have to carry on, and however wearisome, this one thing ought still to be sufficient for them—that they shall not wholly perish. And it appears evident, that God's people have always been preserved by his invincible hand, however numerous have been their opposing enemies. We must also keep in mind what we have just heard,—that the promise here is not made to the whole people, but to a residue only. And it surpasses the expectation of the whole world, that even a small number could have survived so many slaughters, by which they might have been swallowed up a hundred times. Now then we see that it had not been without reason promised to the faithful,—that they should be made conquerors over all their enemies. But this has not been really fulfilled, except under the conflict of the cross. It now follows—

10. And it shall come to pass in that day, saith the Lord, that I will cut off thy horses out of the midst of thee, and I will destroy thy chariots:	10. Et accidet in die illo, dicit Jehova, excidam equos tuos è medio tui, et perdam quadrigas tuas;
11. And I will cut off the cities of thy land, and throw down all thy strong holds:	11. Et excidam urbes terræ tuæ, et evertam cunctas munitiones tuas;
12. And I will cut off witchcrafts out of thine hand; and thou shalt have no *more* soothsayers:	12. Et excidam angures (*vel,* divinos) è manu tua; et præstigiatores non erunt tibi (*hæc lengenda sunt in uno contextu;*)
13. Thy graven images also will I cut off, and thy standing images out of the midst of thee; and thou shalt no more worship the work of thine hands.	13. Et excidam scuptilia tua et statuas tuas è medio tui; et non adorabis amplius opus manuum tuarum;
14. And I will pluck up thy	14. Et delebo lucos tuos è medio

groves out of the midst of thee: so will I destroy thy cities.

15. And I will execute vengeance in anger and fury upon the heathen, such as they have not heard.

tui, et detraham hostes tuos *(vel, urbes tuas; utroque enim verti potest;)*

15. Et faciam in ira et furore vindictam in gentibus quæ non audierunt *(vel,* quam non audierunt; *dicam de utroque.)*

There is introduced here a most necessary admonition, in order that the faithful may know, how they are to be preserved by the hand and favour of God, even when they shall be stripped of all their helps, yea, even when God shall take away all those impediments, which would otherwise close up the way against his favour. The sum of the whole then is,—that the Church shall not otherwise be saved by God's kindness, than by being deprived of all her strength and defences, and also by having her obstacles removed by God, even those which in a manner prevented his hand from being put forth to save his people. For the Prophet mentions here cities, then fortified places, he mentions horses and chariots. These, we know, are not in themselves to be condemned: but he means, that as the people foolishly placed confidence in earthly things, the salvation of God could not otherwise come to them than by stripping them of all vain and false confidence. This is one thing. Then, on the other hand, he mentions groves, he mentions carved images and statues, he mentions augurs and diviners: these were corruptions, which closed the door against the favour of God; for a people, given to idolatry, could not call upon God nor hope in him as the author of salvation. We now then perceive the Prophet's design. It now remains for me to run over the words.

He says first, *It shall be in that day, saith Jehovah, that I will cut off thine horses.*[1] Here the Prophet enumerates those things which could not in themselves be ascribed to any thing wrong: for as God has created horses for the use of

[1] As a curious instance of ingenuity and extravagance in allegorizing, practised by some of the Fathers, *Jerome's* interpretation of this verse may be mentioned: the *horses* were lascivious lusts; the *chariots*, sins joined together in which the wicked, as it were, ride and triumph; the *cities*, such as that built by Cain, not like the heavenly Jerusalem; and the *strongholds*, were riches and the pomps of the world, the eloquence of orators and the tenterhooks of dialecticians!—*Ed.*

men, so also he allows them to be for our service. Why then does the Prophet say, that the Church could not be delivered, except horses were taken away? It was owing to an accidental fault; for when men abound in forces, they instantly fix their hope on them. As then such an abuse of God's gifts had prevailed among the people of Israel, it was necessary that horses should be taken away. God indeed could have humbled their minds or withdrawn their confidence from their horses and chariots: but it hence appears how deep are the roots of presumption in the hearts of men, that they cannot be otherwise torn up, than by having the things themselves cut off. To have horses and to have chariots is the bounty of God: for how can we have chariots and horses and other things, except through God's kindness? And yet God cannot find a way by which he can do us good, except by taking away his former gifts. Here then Micah touches the hearts of the people much more sharply than before, when he says, that salvation cannot proceed from the Lord, except their horses were destroyed; as though he said,—"Ye see how great is your wickedness; God has hitherto dealt bountifully with you, since he has enriched you, and has also given you horses. Now as he sees that you abuse these gifts, he complains that all ways of access to you are closed up, as ye do not receive his kindness. Inasmuch as your horses and your chariots engross your attention, ye in a manner drive God far away from you. That he may therefore come to you, he will open a way for himself, by removing all the obstacles and hinderances."

We hence learn, that though all God's benefits ought to raise us up to heaven, serving as kinds of vehicles, they are yet turned, through our wickedness, to another purpose, and are made intervening obstacles between us and God. Hereby then is our ingratitude proved; and hence it comes, that God, when he intends to make his salvation known to us, is in a manner constrained to take away and remove from us his benefits. We now then understand what the Prophet had in view when he mentioned horses and chariots. For he does not threaten here, as some think, that the people would be merely deprived of all God's gifts, that they might see in their destitution and want only signs of a curse; by no means, but it is rather a promise, that is, that God will turn aside all impediments by which he was for a time prevented from bringing help to his people. This doctrine ought at the same time to avail for bringing no ordinary comfort. It is hard and bitter to the flesh to be brought down. Hence the people of Israel were little able at first to bear their lot with submission, when they saw themselves stripped of God's benefits: but the Prophet sets before them a compensation, which was capable of soothing all their grief,—"This," he says, "shall be for your chief good—that God will deprive you of horses and chariots; for the way which your horses and chariots now occupy shall be cleared. While ye are replenished with abundant forces, ye drive away God far from you, and there is no way open for him. He will therefore prepare a way for himself; and this will be the case when your land shall be made naked, when nothing will intervene to prevent him from coming to you."

He afterwards subjoins, *I will cut off the cities of thy land*, and I will destroy all *thy fortresses*. This verse is to be taken in the same sense. That the people dwelt in fortified cities, and had defences and fortified places, was not of itself displeasing to God. But as the people habituated themselves to a false confidence, and as t we re hardened themselves in it, so that this evil could not be remedied without taking away those things to which it is attached, the Prophet says here, *I will cut off the cities of your land*, and then, I will cut off your defences and fortified places. Is it that they may be plundered with impunity by their enemies? By no means, but that the favour of God may be made glorious in their deliverance. For they could not ascribe it to their cities that they kept off enemies, but were constrained to acknowledge the hand of God, and to confess him to have been their only deliverer; for they were exposed to enemies, and there was no aid for them in the land. God then will thus render more evident his favour, when their cities and fortified places shall be cut off. We hence learn that the faithful at this day have no cause to murmur if they are without great riches, and if they are not formidable for the multitude of their horses, nor for the number and strength of their men. —Why so? Because it is the Lord's will that we should be like sheep, that we might depend wholly on his power, and know that we cannot be otherwise safe than under his protection. This reason then ought to comfort us, that it may not be grievous to us, when we find that we are in the midst of wolves, and that we have no equal strength to contend with them; for even this destitution hardly extorts from us a real confession that our safety is in the hand of God. We are always proud. How would it be, were the Church at this day in a flourishing state and all enemies subdued, were there no danger, no fear? Surely earth and heaven could not bear the foolish self-confidence of men. There is therefore no wonder that God thus holds us in, and that while he supports us by his grace, he deprives us of all earthly helps and aids, that we may learn that he alone is the author of our salvation.

This truth ought to be carefully contemplated by us. Whenever we see that the Church of God, though not possessing any great power, is yet diminished daily, yea, and becomes, so to speak, like a naked land, without any defences, —it so happens, in order that the protection of God may be alone sufficient for us, and that he may wholly tear away from our hearts all haughtiness and pride, and dissipate all those vain confidences by which we not only obscure the glory of God, but, as far as we can, entirely cover it over. In short, as there is nothing better for us than to be preserved by the hand of God, we ought to bear patiently the removal of all those impediments which close up the way against God, and, in a manner, keep off his hand from us, when he is ready to extend it for the purpose of delivering us. For when our minds are inflated with foolish self-confidence, we neglect God; and thus a wall intervenes, which prevents him to help us. Who would not wish, seeing himself in extreme danger and help not far distant, that an intercepting wall should immediately fall down? Thus God is near at hand, as he has promised; but there are many walls and many obstacles, from the ruin of which, if we would be safe, we must desire and seek, that God may find an open and free way, in order that he may be able to afford us aid.

The Prophet comes now to the second kind of impediments. We have already said that some things become impediments, as it were, accidentally, when, through our wickedness and misapplication, we turn God's benefits to an end contrary to what he has designed. If, for instance, horses and chariots are given us, to possess them is not in itself an evil, but becomes so through our blindness, that is, when we, blinded by earthly possessions, think ourselves safe, and thus neglect God. But there are other impediments, which are, in their nature, and in themselves, vicious. To these the Prophet now leads us.

I will cut off, he says, *the sorcerers*, כשפים, *cashephim.*[1] Some render the word jugglers, and others, augurs or diviners. We cannot know of a certainty what kind of superstition it was, nor the other which immediately follows:[2] for the Prophet mentions here two words which mean nearly the same thing. There is no doubt but that some, in that age, were called augurs or diviners, and others called jugglers or astrologers, who are now called fortune-tellers. But on this subject there is no necessity of much labour; for the Prophet simply shows here that the people could not be preserved by God, unless they were cleansed from these defilements. These superstitions, we know, were forbidden and condemned by God's Law: but the Law was not able to restrain the wickedness of that people; for they continually turned aside to these evils. God then here shows, that until they had purged the Church, it could not continue safe. Now, in these

[1] From כשף. "In Arabic," says Parkhurst, "the verb signifies to *discover, disclose, reveal*, and is always in the Hebrew Bible applied to some species of *conjuring*." The Septuagint render the word here φαρμακα, drugs or charms. They were inchanters or sorcerers, who applied drugs to magical purposes. See 2 Chron. xxxiii. 6.—*Ed.*

[2] The word here is מעוננים, from ענן, a cloud. Parkhurst renders it *cloudmongers*, who looked upwards to the clouds either on the flight of birds, or on the stars, or on meteors, and thereby pretended to foretell future things. Αποφθεγγομενους—oraclers—*Sept. Theodoret* renders it μαντεις—soothsayers; and *Cyril* ψευδομαντεις—false prophets. Some derive it from ענה, to answer; and others from עין, the eye; and hence, eyers or observers, either of times, or of dreams, or of stars, or of birds. —*Ed.*

words, the Prophet reminds the Jews, and also the Israelites, for their benefit, that it was, and had been, through their own fault, that they laboured under constant miseries, and were not helped by the hand of God.—How so? Because there was no room, as God shows here, for the exercise of his favour; for they were full of auguries, and divinations, and of other diabolical arts. "How," he says, "can I help you, for I have no agreement with Satan? As you are wholly given to wicked superstitions, my favour is rejected by you."[1]

One thing is, that the Prophet intended to humble the people, so that every one might know that it had been through their fault, that God had not brought them help as they wished: but there is another thing,—God promises a cleansing, which would open a way for his favour,—*I will take away*, he says, *all the diviners*. Let us then know, that it ought to be deemed the greatest benefit when God takes away from us our superstitions and other vices. For since a diminution, however hard and grievous it may be at first, is useful to us, as we see, when we wilfully and openly drive away God from us; is it not a singular favour in God when he suffers us not to be thus separated from him, but prepares a way for himself to be connected with us, and has ever his hand extended to bring us help? Thus much as to these two kinds of impediments.

He now adds, *I will cut off thy graven images and thy statues from the midst of thee; and thou shalt not hereafter bend down before the work of thine hands*. This verse is plain and contains nothing new: for the Prophet teaches that God cannot become propitious to his Church, to keep and make her safe, until he purges her from her filth, even from idolatry and other vices, by which the worship of God was corrupted, or even entirely subverted. *I will*, therefore, *cut off thy graven images and statues*[2] *from the midst of thee*. We see that God

[1] "Many of them depended much upon the conduct and advice of their conjurors, diviners, and fortune-tellers, and these God will cut off, not only as weak things, and insufficient to relieve them, but as wicked things, and sufficient to ruin them."—*Henry*.

[2] מצבות, rather pillars or columns than statues; τας στηλας in the *Sept*. The pillar of stone which Jacob set up is called by this name, Gen. xxviii. 18. They were commemorative pillars at which the Canaanites,

anticipates us by his gratuitous goodness, not only by forgiving us, but also by calling us back, when wandering, into the right way. Since then we have deviated from the right way, and God thus withdraws his hand that it might appear that he has cast us away, it is certain that we ought not only to pray him to have mercy on us, but also to ascribe to him a higher favour, inasmuch as he takes away the very impediments which separate us from him, and suffer him not to come nigh us. We hence see that God is not only inclined to pardon when men repent, but that it is his peculiar office to remove the obstacles.

This ought to be carefully noticed, that we may know that our salvation, from the first beginning, proceeds from the mere favour of God,—and that we may also learn, that all those things, of which the Papists vainly talk respecting preparations, are mere figments.

He then adds, *Thou shalt not bend hereafter before the work of thine hands.* God expresses here the cause why he so much abominates idols, even because he sees that his honour is transferred to them: this is one thing. He further arraigns the Jews as guilty, while he makes evident their defection: for surely nothing could have been more shameful, than to take away from God his honour and worship, and to transfer them to dead things; and he says here by way of reproach, that they were the work of their hands. What can be more insane, than for men to ascribe divinity to their own inventions, or to believe that it is in the power of men to make a god from wood or stone? This is surely monstrous in the extreme. Then the Prophet by this form of speaking aggravates the sin of the people of Israel, that is, when he says that they bowed the head before the work of their own hands.

He afterwards subjoins, *I will take away thy groves.* The groves, we know, formed a part of their idolatry: they are therefore mentioned here as an addition by the Prophet. For he speaks not simply of trees, but refers to the wicked prac-

and afterwards the Jews, offered idolatrous worship. There was a pillar of this kind in the house of Baal, 2 Kings x. 26, 27. They were not altars, though altars might have been reared by them, for both are mentioned together in Deut. xii. 3. The word is derived from יצב, to set, to fix firmly. The noun is rendered by *Parkhurst a standing pillar.—Ed.*

tices of the people : for wherever there were high and lofty trees, they thought that something divine was hid under their shade ; hence their superstition. When therefore the Prophet mentions groves, it must be understood of vicious and false modes of worship ; for they thought that those places acquired a sort of sanctity from the trees ; as they also thought that they were nearer to God when they were on a hill. We hence see that this verse is to be connected with the last ; as though the Prophet had said, that the Church could not be in safety and recover her pristine vigour, without being well cleansed from all the filth of idolatry. For we indeed know that some pious kings, when they took away idols did not cut down the groves ; and this exception to their praise is added, that they worshipped God, but that the high places were suffered to stand. We see that the Holy Spirit does not fully commend those kings who did not destroy the groves.—Why ? Because they were the materials of corruption. And further, had the Jews been really penitent, they would have exterminated those groves, by which they had so shamefully abused and profaned the worship of God. The sum of the whole then is, that when God shall have well cleansed his Church and wiped away all its stains, he will then become the unfailing preserver of its safety.[1]

He afterwards subjoins, And *I will destroy thy enemies.* עריך, *orik*, may be rendered, enemies, and many so render it : but others translate it, cities ; and the word, cities, would be the most suitable, were it not that the Prophet had previously mentioned cities. I do not therefore see that it would be proper to render it here by this term. The word עריך, *orik*, then, ought doubtless to be rendered, thy enemies. Let us inquire why the Prophet says, that the enemies of the Church were to be destroyed. This sentence ought to be thus explained, (I leave the former ones, and take only this the last,) *And I will demolish thy groves from the midst of thee,*

[1] *Scott*, speaking of the latter part of this chapter, says, "The reformation of the Jews after their return from Babylon might be alluded to ; but the purification of the Christian Church from all antichristian corruptions of faith and worship, and all idolatry and superstition, seems more immediately to be predicted."—*Ed.*

that I may destroy thine enemies:[1] the copulative is then to be considered as a final particle; and this meaning is the most suitable; as though the Prophet had said, as I have already often stated, that the door was closed against God, so that he could bring no aid to his Church, and deliver it from enemies, as long as it held to false confidence, and was attached to the filth of idolatry, which was still worse. "That I may then destroy thine enemies, it is necessary first that every thing in thee that prevents or hinders my favour should be taken away and removed."

At last he adds, *And I will execute vengeance in wrath and in fury.* He goes on with what I have just said of enemies; *I will then execute vengeance in wrath and in fury on the nations.* Here God mentions his wrath and his fury, that the faithful might feel greater confidence, that though now their enemies poured forth grievous threatenings, yet this could not prevent God from aiding his people.—How so? Because, if we compare the wrath and fury of God with all the terrors of men, doubtless the threats of men would appear as nothing but smoke. We now perceive the Prophet's meaning in these words. And he says, in the last place, I will execute vengeance on the *nations who have not heard.* Almost all interpreters join the relative, אשר, *asher,* with the preceding word, גוים, *guim,*—I will then take vengeance on the nations who have not heard, that is, who have been rebellious against God: not to hear, as they explain, is obstinately to despise the power of God, and not to be moved by his promises or by his threatenings. But a fitter sense may perhaps be elicited, if we refer אשר, *asher,* to vengeance,—I will then execute vengeance on the nations which they have not heard, that is, I will take vengeance on all the nations in a manner unheard of and incredible: and by nations, he understands indiscriminately all the enemies of the Church, as we have elsewhere seen.

[1] *Newcome* renders the word עריך, thine enemies, and not, thy cities, though he connects the verse differently,—more with the last than with the former portion of this,—

I will also destroy thine enemies:
15. And I will execute vengeance, in anger and in fury,
Upon the nations which have not hearkened *unto me.*

PRAYER.

Grant, Almighty God, that since thou so kindly invitest us to thyself, and promisest that thy aid should never be wanting to us, provided we do not close the door against thee,—O grant, that though many earthly benefits may be granted to us, we may not yet trust in them and depart from thee, but, on the contrary, recumb on thy grace only: and then should it happen to us to be deprived of all helps, that our minds may be awakened, and that we may thus learn to hasten to thee, may nothing impede our course, that we may not, with the greatest haste and ardent desire, long to deliver up and devote ourselves wholly to thee, that we may be made safe under the care and protection of thy only-begotten Son, whom thou hast appointed to be the guardian of our safety. Amen.

Lecture Ninety-third.

CHAPTER VI.

1. Hear ye now what the Lord saith; Arise, contend thou before the mountains, and let the hills hear thy voice.	1. Audite nunc (*vel*, quæso) quod dicit Jehova,—Surge, litiga coram montibus, et colles audiant vocem tuam:
2. Hear ye, O mountains, the Lord's controversy, and ye strong foundations of the earth: for the Lord hath a controversy with his people, and he will plead with Israel.	2. Audite montes disceptationem Jehovæ, et fortia fundamenta terræ: quia disceptatio Jehovæ cum populo suo, et cum Israele contendet.

Here the Prophet avowedly assumes, that the people were sufficiently proved guilty; and yet they resisted through a hardiness the most obdurate, and rejected all admonitions without shame, and without any discretion. He is therefore commanded to direct his discourse to the mountains and to the hills; for his labour had now for a long time been useless as to men. The meaning then is, that when the Prophet had spent much labour on the people and derived no fruit, he is at length bidden to call the mountains and the hills to bear their testimony to God; and thus before the elements is made known and proved the ungodliness and the obstinacy of the people. But before he relates what had been committed to him, he makes a preface, in order to gain attention.

Hear ye what Jehovah says. The Prophets are wont, on very serious subjects, to make such a preface as is here made by Micah: and it is indeed sufficiently evident from the passage, that he has here no ordinary subject for his teaching, but that, on the contrary, he rebukes their monstrous stupidity; for he had been addressing the deaf without any advantage. As then the Prophet was about to declare no common thing, but to be a witness of a new judgment,—this is the reason why he bids them to be unusually attentive. Hear, he says, what Jehovah saith. What is it? He might have added, "Jehovah has very often spoken to you, he has tried all means to bring you to the right way; but as ye are past recovery, vengeance alone now remains for you: he will no more spend labour in vain on you; for he finds in you neither shame, nor meekness, nor docility." The Prophet might have thus spoken to them; but he says that another thing was committed to his charge by the Lord, and that is, to contend or to plead before the mountains. And this reproach ought to have most acutely touched the hearts of the people: for there is here an implied comparison between the mountains and the Jews; as though the Prophet said,—"The mountains are void of understanding and reason, and yet the Lord prefers to have them as witness of his cause rather than you, who exceed in stupidity all the mountains and rocks." We now then perceive the design of God.

Some take mountains and hills in a metaphorical sense for the chief men who then ruled: and this manner of speaking very frequently occurs in Scripture: but as to the present passage, I have no doubt but that the Prophet mentions mountains and hills without a figure; for, as I have already said, he sets the hardness of the people in opposition to rocks, and intimates, that there would be more attention and docility in the very mountains than what he had hitherto found in the chosen people. And the particle את, *at*, is often taken in the sense of *before*: it means also *with*; but in this place I take it for ל, *lamed*, before or near, as many instances might be cited. But that this is the meaning of the Prophet it is easy to gather from the next verse, when he says—

Hear, ye mountains, the controversy of Jehovah,[1] how? *and ye strong foundations of the earth,* he says. He speaks here no more of hills, but summons the whole world; as though he said, "There is not one of the elements which is not to bear witness respecting the obstinacy of this people; for the voice of God will penetrate to the farthest roots of the earth, it will reach the lowest depths: these men will at the same time continue deaf." And he says not, the Lord threatens you, or denounces judgment on you; but Jehovah has a contention with his people. We now then see that there is no metaphor in these words; but that the Prophet merely shows how monstrous was the stupor of the people, who profited nothing by the celestial doctrine delivered to them, so that the very mountains and the whole machinery of earth and heaven, though destitute of reason, had more understanding than these men. And it is not unusual with the Prophets, we know, to turn their discourse to mute elements, when there remains no hope of success from men. But our Prophet does not abruptly address mountains and hills as Isaiah does, (Isa. i. 2,) and as also Moses had done, 'Hear, ye heavens, what I shall say, let the earth hear the words of my mouth,' (Deut. xxxii. 1:) but he prefaces his discourse by saying, that it had been specially commanded to him to summon the mountains and hills to God's judgment. By saying then, "Hear ye what Jehovah saith," he prepares, as I have said, the Jews to hear, that they might know that something uncommon and altogether unusual was to be announced,—that the Lord, in order more fully to convict them of extreme impiety, intended to plead his cause before the mountains.

Arise, then, *and plead before the mountains, and let the hills hear thy voice.* What sort of voice was this? They who think that the judges are here figuratively pointed out may be easily refuted; for Micah in the next verse mentions the substance of this pleading, namely, that the Lord expostulated

[1] *Henry* says, "Sin begets a controversy between God and man. The righteous God has an action against every sinner, an action of debt, an action of trespass, an action of slander."

with his people. We hence see that God had no contention with the mountains, but that, on the contrary, the mountains were summoned, that they might understand God's pleading, not against them, but against the people. Hear then, ye mountains, Jehovah's controversy, and ye strong foundations of the earth, that is, the very rocks. There is nothing so hard in the world, he says, that shall not be made to hear; for this pleading shall reach the lowest depths. *Jehovah* then *has a controversy with his people, and he will plead*, or contend, *with Israel.* It follows—

3. O my people, what have I done unto thee? and wherein have I wearied thee? testify against me.	3. Popule mi, quid feci tibi? et in quo exhibui tibi molestiam? Testificare contra me.

Here God, in the first place, offers to give a reason, if he was accused of any thing. It seems indeed unbecoming the character of God, that he should be thus ready as one guilty to clear himself: but this is said by way of concession; for the Prophet could not otherwise express, that nothing that deserved blame could be found in God. It is a personification, by which a character, not his own, is ascribed to God. It ought not therefore to appear inconsistent, that the Lord stands forth here, and is prepared to hear any accusation the people might have, that he might give an answer, *My people! what have I done?* By using this kind expression, *my people*, he renders double their wickedness; for God here descends from his own elevation, and not only addresses his people, in a paternal manner, but stands as it were on the opposite side, and is prepared, if the people had anything to say, to give answer to it, so that they might mutually discuss the question, as it is usually done by friends. Now the more kindly and indulgently the Lord deals with his people, the more enhanced, as I have said, is their sin.

He says first, *What have I done to thee?* that is, what hast thou to accuse me with? He adds, *In what have I caused trouble*[1]

[1] The verb is, הלאתיך, I have wearied, or caused thee to be weary. *Quo fatigavi te*—In what have I wearied thee? *Jun.* and *Trem.* τι ελυπησα σε—how have I caused thee to grieve? *Sept.* *Quo labore te pressi*—with what labour have I oppressed thee? *Jerome.* This last contains the full meaning.—*Ed.*

to thee? or, In what have I been troublesome to thee? *Testify,* he says, *against me.* This testifying was to be made to the mountains and hills; as though he said, "I am ready to plead my cause before heaven and earth; in a word, before all my creatures." Some render the passage, "Answer me:" and ענה, *one,* is also to answer; but the context requires the former meaning; for God conceded so much liberty to the Jews, that they might bring forward against him any fault they had to allege. *Testify,* he says, *against me;* that is, there are witnesses present; make public now thy case by stating particulars, I am ready for the defence. We hence see the truth of what I have before stated,—that a character, not his own, is ascribed to God: but this is done by way of concession. He afterwards adds—

4. For I brought thee up out of the land of Egypt, and redeemed thee out of the house of servants; and I sent before thee Moses, Aaron, and Miriam.	4. Certè (*vel,* quia, *vel,* nempe quòd) ascendere te feci è terra Ægypti, et ex domo servorum redemi te, et misi coram te Mosen, Aaron, et Mariam.

God, having testified that he had in nothing been troublesome to the people, now states with how great and with how many benefits he had bound them to himself. But we may prefer taking the words as explanatory and somewhat ironical, that he records his benefits in the place of trouble or vexation; though, in my judgment, it is better to read the two clauses apart. *I have brought thee,* he says, *from the land of Egypt,* from that miserable bondage; and then he says, *I have redeemed thee.*[1] By the word, redeem, he expresses more clearly and more fully illustrates his kindness. Then he adds, *I have set over thee as leaders Moses,* and Aaron, and Miriam, the sister of them both. Benefits, we know, are often accompanied with injuries; and he who obliges another destroys

[1] The complete sentence is, "from the house of servants," or rather, slaves: for they were not properly what we call servants, but slaves, in Egypt. The Septuagint has εξ οικου δουλειας—from the house of slavery. "The house of slaves," is the version both of Newcome and of Henderson. They are the same words as we find in Exod. xx. 2, rendered, "out of the house of bondage;" which ought to be translated slavery rather than bondage, if we depart from the literal rendering—the house of slaves. —*Ed.*

all his favour, when he turns kindness, as it often happens, into reproach. It is hence frequently the case, that he who has been kind to another brings so serious an injury, that the memory of his kindness ought not to continue. God mentions here these two things,—that he had conferred vast benefits on the people,—and yet that he had in nothing been burdensome to them; as though he said, "Many are those things which I can, if necessary, on my part bring forward, by which I have more than a hundred times made thee indebted to me; now thou canst not in thy turn bring anything against me; thou canst not say that I have accompanied my benefits with wrongs, or that thou hast been despised, because thou wert under obligations to me, as it is often the case with men who proudly domineer, when they think that they have made others bound to them. I have not then thought proper to accompany my great favours with anything troublesome or grievous to thee." We now understand why the Prophet expressly mentions these two things,—that God had in nothing been vexatious to his people,—and that he had brought them up from the land of Egypt.

That redemption was so great, that the people ought not to have complained, had it been the will of God to lay on their shoulders some very heavy burdens: for this answer might have been ever readily given,—"Ye have been delivered by me; ye owe to me your life and your safety. There is therefore no reason why any thing should be now burdensome to you; for the bondage of Egypt must have been bitterer to you than hundred deaths; and I redeemed you from that bondage." But, as the Lord had treated his redeemed people so kindly and so humanely, yea, with so much indulgence, how great and how intolerable was their ingratitude in not responding to his great kindness? We now more fully understand the Prophet's meaning in these words.

I have made thee to ascend, he says, from Egypt; and then, I have redeemed thee. He goes on, as we have said, by degrees. He afterwards adds, I have sent before thy face Moses, Aaron, and Miriam. God means here that it had not been a momentary kindness; for he continued his favour towards the Jews, when he set over them Moses, and Aaron, and Miriam, which was an evidence of his constant care, until he had completed his work of delivering them. For Moses was a minister of their deliverance in upholding civil order, and Aaron as to the priesthood and spiritual discipline. With regard to Miriam, she also performed her part towards the women ; and as we find in the fifteenth chapter of Exodus, she composed a song of thanksgiving after passing through the Red Sea : and hence arose her base envy with regard to Moses ; for being highly praised, she thought herself equal to him in dignity. It is at the same time right to mention, that it was an extraordinary thing, when God gave authority to a woman, as was the case with Deborah, that no one may consider this singular precedent as a common rule. It now follows—

5. O my people, remember now what Balak king of Moab consulted, and what Balaam the son of Beor answered him from Shittim unto Gilgal ; that ye may know the righteousness of the Lord.

5. Popule mi, recordare nunc (*vel*, quæso, *est eadem particula*) quid cogitaverit Balak, rex Moab, et quid responderit ei Balaam, filius Beor, à Sittim usque ad Gilgal, ut cognosceres (*vel*, cognoscas) justitias Jehovæ.

God briefly records here what happened in the desert,—that the people had need of some extraordinary help in addition to the many benefits which he had conferred on them. For though the people lived safely in the desert as to the Egyptians, though they were fed by manna, and water from the rock flowed for them, though the cloud by day protected them from the heat of the sun, and the pillar of fire shone on them during the night, yet the stream of God's mercy seemed to have been stopped when Balaam came forth, who was a Prophet, and then, as one armed with celestial weapons, fought against the people and opposed their deliverance. Now, had God permitted Balaam to curse the people, what could have taken place, but that they must have been deprived of all their blessings ? This is the reason why the Prophet specifically refers to this history,—that the cursing of Balaam was miraculously turned into a blessing, even through the secret purpose of God. Micah might indeed have referred to all those particulars, by which God could have proved the ingratitude of the people ; but he deemed it sufficient to touch on the fact of their redemption, and also to mention by the way this extraordinary instance of God's kindness.

Remember, he says, *what Balak devised*, that is, how crafty was his counsel: for the verb יעץ, *iots*, is to be taken here in a bad sense, and is very emphatical; as though the Prophet had said, that there was more danger in this fraud than in all the violence of enemies; for Balak could not have done so much harm, had he prepared a great army against the Israelites, as by hiring a Prophet to curse the people. For certain it is, that though Balaam was an impostor and full of deceits, as it is probable that he was a man given to profane superstitions, he was yet endued with the gift of prophecy. This was the case no doubt; and we know that God has often so distributed the gifts of his Spirit, that he has honoured with the prophetic office even the ungodly and unbelieving: for it was a special gift, distinct from the grace of regeneration. Balaam then was a Prophet. Now when Balak saw that he was unequal in power to oppose the people, he thought of this expedient—to get some Prophet to interpose for the purpose of exciting the wrath of God against the people. This is the reason why it is here said, Remember what Balak consulted against thee; that is, "Thou wert then in the greatest danger, when a Prophet came, hired for the purpose, that he might in God's name pronounce on thee a curse."

It may be asked, Whether Balaam could really curse the people of Israel? The answer is easy: the question here is not what might have been the effect, without God's permission; but Micah here regards only the office with which Balaam was honoured and endued. As then he was God's Prophet, he could have cursed the people, had not God prevented him. And no doubt Balak was wise enough to know, that the Israelites could not be resisted by human power, and that, therefore, nothing remained for him but the interposition of God; and as he could not bring down God from heaven, he sent for a Prophet. God puts his own power in his word, —as God's word resided in Balaam, and as he was, as it were, its depositary, it was no wonder that Balak thought that he would become the conqueror of the people of Israel, provided they were cursed by Balaam's mouth; for this would have been, as it were, the announcement of God's wrath.

He now subjoins, *And what Balaam, the son of Beor, answered him.* There is here shown, on the one hand, a danger, because Balaam was craftier than all the other enemies of the people, for he could have done more by his artifice than if he had armed against them the whole world: here then was the danger. But, on the other hand, we know what he answered; and it is certain that the answer of Balaam did not proceed from himself, but, on the contrary, from the Spirit of God. As Balaam spoke by the secret influence of the Spirit, contrary to the wish of his own heart, God thus proved that he was present at that very time, when the safety of the people was endangered. Think, then, or remember, what Balaam answered; as though he said,—"Balaam was very nigh cursing thee, for his mouth was opened: for he had sold himself to an ungodly king, and nothing could have pleased him more than to have poured forth many anathemas and many curses: but he was constrained to bless your fathers. What did this mean? Did not the wonderful favour of God shine forth in this instance?" We now perceive the Prophet's design, and what a large meaning there is in these words.

He afterwards adds generally, *From Shittim even to Gilgal.* This is not connected with the last clause; for Balaam did not follow the people from Shittim to Gilgal; but a verb is to be understood,[1] as though he said,—"Thou knowest what things happened to thee from Shittim to Gilgal, from the beginning to the end; at the time when thou didst enter the wilderness, thou hadst begun to provoke the wrath of God." And we know that even in Shittim the Israelites fell away into idolatry; and that defection, in a manner, alienated

[1] Various have been the ways to complete this evidently defective sentence; and there is no assistance from any MSS., or from the Septuagint. Shittim was in the land of Moab, and Gilgal was beyond Jordan, in the land of Canaan. *Grotius* and many others repeat the word "Remember," and supply, "what I have done," or, "what happened." This is a sort of omission, which we can hardly think a writer would have made. It is far more probable that a word or words have been somehow left out: and the *Targum*, though generally no safe guide, has so given the passage as to countenance this conjecture. "Were not great things

them from God. Hence God shows here that he, in his goodness and mercy, had contended with the ungodly ways of the people even to Gilgal; that is, "Thou hast never ceased to provoke me." We indeed know that the people continually excited against themselves the displeasure of God, and that their defections were many and various. In short, then, the Prophet shows that God had so mercifully dealt with the people, that he had, in a most astonishing manner, overcome their wickedness by his goodness.

He at length subjoins, *That thou mayest know the righteousnesses of Jehovah.* By righteousnesses he means acts of kindness, as the sense of the word is in many other passages: for the righteousness of God is often taken not only for uprightness, but also for the faithfulness and truth which he manifests towards his people. It betokens therefore the relation between God and his Church, whenever the word, righteousness, is to be understood in this sense. *That thou mayest* then *know the righteousnesses of Jehovah;* that is, that experience itself may prove to thee how faithful, how beneficent, how merciful has God ever been towards your race.[1] Since then the righteousness of God was conspicuous, the people must surely have been mute, and had nothing for which they could justly expostulate with God: what remained, but that their extreme impiety, fully detected before heaven and earth and all the elements, exposed them to his judgment? It now follows—

6. Wherewith shall I come before the Lord, *and* bow myself before the high God? shall I come before him with burnt-offerings, with calves of a year old?	6. In quo occurram Jehovæ? incurvabo me coram Deo excelso? occurramnè ei in holocaustis? in vitulis anniculis?

done for you," is the supplement of the Targum. "And what I did," seems to be the most natural addition: such words as ומה עשיתי appear to have been left out by transcribers. I would then render the verse thus:—

My people, remember, I pray,
What did Balak, the king of Moab, consult,
And what did Balaam, the son of Beor, answer him,
(And what I did) from Shittim even to Gilgal,
That ye may know the faithful dealings of Jehovah.—*Ed.*

1 "His justice in destroying the Canaanites, his goodness in giving rest to his people Israel, and his faithfulness to his promises made unto the Fathers."—*Henry.*

7. Will the Lord be pleased with thousands of rams, *or* with ten thousands of rivers of oil? shall I give my first-born *for* my transgression, the fruit of my body *for* the sin of my soul?

8. He hath shewed thee, O man, what *is* good; and what doth the Lord require of thee, but to do justly, and to love mercy, and to walk humbly with thy God?

7. An complacitum erit Jehovæ in millibus arietum? in decem millibus vallium olei (*vel*, pinguedinis?) An dabo primogenitum peccatum meum (*hoc est*, piaculum peccati mei?) fructum ventris mei, piaculum sceleris animæ mea?

8. Indicavit tibi, homo, quid bonum; et quid Jehova quærit abs te, nisi facere judicium et deligere clementiam (*vel*, bonitatem,) et humiliari ut ambules cum Deo tuo.

The Prophet now inquires, as in the name of the people, what was necessary to be done: and he takes these two principles as granted,—that the people were without any excuse, and were forced to confess their sin,—and that God had hitherto contended with them for no other end and with no other design, but to restore the people to the right way; for if his purpose had only been to condemn the people for their wickedness, there would have been no need of these questions. But the Prophet shows what has been often stated before,—that whenever God chides his people, he opens to them the door of hope as to their salvation, provided those who have sinned repent. As this then must have been well known to all the Jews, the Prophet here asks, as with their mouth, what was to be done.

He thus introduces them as inquiring, *With what shall I approach Jehovah, and bow down before the high God?*[1] *Shall I approach him with burnt-offerings,*[2] *with calves of a year old?* But at the same time there is no doubt, but that he indirectly refers to that foolish notion, by which men for the most part deceive themselves; for when they are proved guilty, they indeed know that there is no remedy for them, except they reconcile themselves to God: but yet they pretend by circuitous courses to approach God, while they desire to be ever far away from him. This dissimulation has always prevailed in the world, and it now prevails: they see that they whom God convicts and their own conscience condemns, cannot

[1] Literally, "the God of the height," that is, of heaven, אלהי מרום. See Ps. lxviii. 18.

[2] This clause is omitted in my Latin copy; and viewing it as an accidental omission, I have supplied it.—*Ed.*

rest in safety. Hence they wish to discharge their duty towards God as a matter of necessity; but at the same time they seek some fictitious modes of reconciliation, as though it were enough to flatter God, as though he could be pacified like a child with some frivolous trifles. The Prophet therefore detects this wickedness, which had ever been too prevalent among them; as though he said,—"I see what ye are about to say; for there is no need of contending longer; as ye have nothing to object to God, and he has things innumerable to allege against you: ye are then more than condemned; but yet ye will perhaps say what has been usually alleged by you and always by hypocrites, even this,—'We wish to be reconciled to God, and we confess our faults and seek pardon; let God in the meantime show himself ready to be reconciled to us, while we offer to him sacrifices.'" There is then no doubt, but that the Prophet derided this folly, which has ever prevailed in the hearts of men: they ever think that God can be pacified by outward rites and frivolous performances.

He afterwards adds, *He has proclaimed to thee what is good.* The Prophet reproves the hypocrisy by which the Jews wilfully deceived themselves, as though he said,—"Ye indeed pretend some concern for religion when ye approach God in prayer; but this your religion is nothing; it is nothing else than shamelessly to dissemble; for ye sin not either through ignorance or misconception, but ye treat God with mockery." —How so? "Because the Law teaches you with sufficient clearness what God requires from you; does it not plainly enough show you what is true reconciliation? But ye close your eyes to the teaching of the Law, and in the meantime pretend ignorance. This is extremely childish. God has already proclaimed what is good, even *to do judgment, to love kindness, and to walk humbly with God.*" We now perceive the design of the Prophet.

As then he says here, With what shall I appear before God? we must bear in mind, that as soon as God condescends to enter into trial with men, the cause is decided; for it is no doubtful contention. When men litigate one with another, there is no cause so good but what an opposite party can darken by sophistries. But the Prophet intimates that men lose all their labour by evasions, when God summons them to a trial. This is one thing. He also shows what deep roots hypocrisy has in the hearts of all, for they ever deceive themselves and try to deceive God. How comes it that men, proved guilty, do not immediately and in the right way betake themselves to God, but that they ever seek windings? How is this? It is not because they have any doubt about what is right except they wilfully deceive themselves, but because they dissemble and wilfully seek the subterfuges of error. It hence appears that men perversely go astray when ever they repent not as they ought, and bring not to God a real integrity of heart. And hence it also appears, that the whole world which continues in its superstitions is without excuse. For if we scrutinize the intentions of men, it will at length come to this,—that men carefully and anxiously seek various superstitions, because they are unwilling to come before God, and to devote themselves to him, without some dissembling and hypocrisy. Since it is so, certain it is, that all who desire to pacify God with their own ceremonies and other trifles cannot by any pretext escape. What is said here is at the same time strictly addressed to the Jews, who had been instructed in the teaching of the Law: and such are the Papists of this day; though they spread forth specious pretences to excuse their ignorance, they may yet be refuted by this one fact,—that God has prescribed clearly and distinctly enough what he requires: but they wish to be ignorant of this; hence their error is at all times wilful. We ought especially to notice this in the words of the Prophet; but I cannot proceed farther now.

PRAYER.

Grant, Almighty God, that as thou hast made known to us thy Law, and hast also added thy Gospel, in which thou callest us to thy service, and also invitest us with all kindness to partake of thy grace,—O grant, that we may not be deaf, either to thy command or to the promises of thy mercy, but render ourselves in both instances submissive to thee, and so learn to devote all our faculties to thee, that we may in truth avow that a rule of a holy and religious life has been delivered to us in thy law, and that we may also firmly adhere to thy promises, lest through any of the allurements of the world, or through the flatteries and crafts of Satan, thou shouldest suffer our minds to be drawn away from that love which thou hast once manifested to us in thine only-begotten Son, and in which thou daily confirmest us by the teaching of the Gospel, until we at length shall come to the full enjoyment of this love in that celestial inheritance, which has been purchased for us by the blood of thy only Son. Amen.

Lecture Ninety-fourth.

We have seen in the last lecture that hypocrites inquire how God is to be pacified, as though they were very solicitous about the performance of their duty; and that in the meantime these are mere disguises; for by circuitous windings they turn here and there, and never wish to come directly to God. The way might have been easily known by them; but they closed their eyes, and at the same time pretended that they had some concern for religion. And this is also very commonly the case in our day; and common experience, if any one opens his eyes, clearly proves this,—that the ungodly, who deal not sincerely with God, profess a very great concern, as though they were wholly intent on serving God, and yet turn aside here and there, and seek many bypaths, (*diverticula,*) that they may not be constrained to present themselves before God. We have already seen, that this false pretence is fully exposed, inasmuch as God has enough, and more than enough, demonstrated in his Law, what he approves and what he requires from men. Why then do hypocrites, as still uncertain, make the inquiry? It is because they are wilfully blind at mid-day; for the doctrine of the Law ought to have been to them as a lamp to direct their steps; but they smother this light, yea, they do what they can wholly to extinguish it: they ask, as though perplexed, How can we pacify God?

But it ought also to be observed, (for the Prophet says, *Shall I give my first-born, and the fruit of my loins, as an ex-*

piation for my soul?[1]) that hypocrites will withhold nothing, provided they are not to devote themselves to God. We see the same thing under the Papacy at this day; they spare no expense, nor even the greatest toils: provided the ungodly have always a freedom to live in sin, they will easily grant to God all other things. For through a false conceit they make a sort of agreement with God: if they mortify themselves, and toil in ceremonies, and if they pour forth some portion of their money, if they sometimes deprive nature of its support, if with fastings and by other things they afflict themselves, they think that by these means they have fully performed their duties. But these are frivolous trifles; for in the meantime they consider themselves exempt from the duty of obeying God. Being yet unwilling to be regarded as alienated from God, they, at the same time, obtrude on him their meritorious works, to prevent his judgment, and to exempt themselves from the necessity of doing the principal thing, that which he especially requires—to bring a sincere heart. Thus then hypocrites wish to divide things with God, that they may remain within such as they are; and they spread forth outwardly many frivolous things for the purpose of pacifying him. And this is the reason why the Prophet says now, *Shall I give my first-born?* for hypocrites wish to appear as though they were burning with the greatest zeal,—"Rather than that God should remain angry with me, I would not spare the life of my first-born; I would rather be the executioner of my own son: in short, nothing is so valuable to me, which I would not be ready to part with, that God may be propitious to me." This indeed is what they boast with their mouth; but at the same time they will not offer their heart as a sacrifice to

[1] The substance of the two lines is given here, not their literal version. He evidently gives somewhat a different meaning from our translation; and probably the original admits better of the construction adopted here. If פשע, a transgression or trespass, be taken for a trespass-offering, and חטאח, for a sin-offering, as it is often, then the rendering would be this,—

Shall I make my first-born my trespass-offering,
The fruit of my loins a sin-offering for my soul?

The verb נתן is not only to give, to present, to offer, but also to make, to constitute, to appoint. But if the first be rendered transgression, the law of parallelism requires that the second should be rendered sin.—*Ed.*

God: and as they deal dishonestly with God, we see that all is nothing but dissimulation.

If any one objects and says,—that the other rites, of which the Prophet speaks here, had been enjoined by God's Law, the answer is easy; but I shall not now but briefly touch on what I have elsewhere more largely handled: The Prophet denies, that sacrifices avail any thing for the purpose of propitiating God. This may seem inconsistent with the teaching of the Law; but in fact it altogether agrees with it. God indeed wished sacrifices to be offered to him; and then this promise was always added, "Iniquity shall be atoned." But the object must be noticed; for God did not command sacrifices, as though they were of themselves of any worth; but he intended to lead the ancient people by such exercises to repentance and faith. It was therefore his design to remind the Jews that they did no good, except they themselves became sacrifices; and it was also his will that they should look to the only true sacrifice, by which all sins are expiated. But hypocrites, like falsifiers of documents, abused the command of God, and adulterated the sacrifices themselves. It was then a profane sacrilege for them to think that God would be propitious to them, if they offered many oxen and calves and lambs. It was the same thing as if one asked the way, and after having known it, rested quietly and never moved a foot. God had shown the way, by which the Jews might come to repentance and faith: and they ought to have walked in it; but they wickedly trifled with God; for they thought that it would be a satisfaction to his justice, if they only performed outward rites. Whenever then the Prophets in God's name repudiate sacrifices, the abuse, by which God's Law was corrupted, is ever to be considered, that is, when the Jews brought sacrifices only, and had no respect to the end in view, and did not exercise themselves in repentance and faith. It is for this reason that our Prophet declares, that all sacrifices were of no account before God, but were vain things: they were so, when they were separated from their right end.

He then says, that God had shown by his Law *what is good;* and then he adds what it is, *to do justice, to love mercy,* or kindness, *and to be humbled before God.* It is evident that, in the two first particulars, he refers to the second table of the Law; that is, *to do justice, and to love mercy.*[1] Nor is it a matter of wonder that the Prophet begins with the duties of love; for though in order the worship of God precedes these duties, and ought rightly to be so regarded, yet justice, which is to be exercised towards men, is the real evidence of true religion. The Prophet, therefore, mentions justice and mercy, not that God casts aside that which is principal—the worship of his name; but he shows, by evidences or effects, what true religion is. Hypocrites place all holiness in external rites; but God requires what is very different; for his worship is spiritual. But as hypocrites can make a show of great zeal and of great solicitude in the outward worship of God, the Prophets try the conduct of men in another way, by inquiring whether they act justly and kindly towards one another, whether they are free from all fraud and violence, whether they observe justice and show mercy. This is the way our Prophet now follows, when he says, that God's Law prescribes *what is good*, and that is, *to do justice*—to observe what is equitable towards men, and also to perform the duties of mercy.

He afterwards adds what in order is first, and that is, *to humble thyself to walk with God:*[2] it is thus literally, "And to be humble in walking with thy God." No doubt, as the name of God is more excellent than any thing in the whole

[1] The expression is remarkable—*to love mercy*, or benevolence, beneficence, or kindness; it is not only to show mercy or kindness, but to *love* it, so as to take pleasure and delight in it.—*Ed.*

[2] The words are, והצנע לכת עם־אלהיך. The verb צנע occurs nowhere else but as a passive participle in Prov. xi. 2; but its meaning there is evident, for it is opposed to pride, זדון, which means a swelling pride, such as fills one with high notions of one's self. Then the opposite of this is to be humble from a sense of one's own emptiness. As it is here in the infinitive Hiphil, its literal meaning is what Calvin assigns to it—to humble one's self. And the best rendering of this line would be—"And to humble thyself to walk with God." The Septuagint renders it ετοιμον ειναι—to be ready; Theodotion, ασφαλιζου; Vulgate, *solicitum.* But these seem not to have understood the word. The *Welsh* version is exactly and literally the Hebrew—*Ac ymostwng i rodio gyda 'th Dduw. Gostwng* is to humble, and by adding *ym*, and dropping the *g*, the verb has exactly the meaning of the Hiphil in Hebrew—to humble one's self. There are, indeed, *some* verbs in *Welsh* which admit of all the modifications of the Hebrew verbs, being active, passive, causative, and reflective. —*Ed.*

world, so the worship of him ought to be regarded as of more importance than all those duties by which we prove our love towards men. But the Prophet, as I have already said, was not so particular in observing order; his main object was to show how men were to prove that they seriously feared God and kept his Law: he afterwards speaks of God's worship. But his manner of speaking, when he says, that men ought to be humble, that they may walk with their God, is worthy of special notice. Condemned, then, is here all pride, and also all the confidence of the flesh: for whosoever arrogates to himself even the least thing, does, in a manner, contend with God as with an opposing party. The true way then of walking with God is, when we thoroughly humble ourselves, yea, when we bring ourselves down to nothing; for it is the very beginning of worshipping and glorifying God when men entertain humble and low opinion of themselves. Let us now proceed—

9. The Lord's voice crieth unto the city, and *the man of* wisdom shall see thy name: hear ye the rod, and who hath appointed it.

9. Vox Jehovæ ad civitatem (*vel*, ad expergefaciendum) clamat (*ad verbum*, clamabit;) et vir intelligentiæ videbit nomen tuum: audite virgam, et quis testificetur eam.

The Prophet complains here that he and other teachers did but little, though their cry resounded and was heard by the whole people. He therefore says, that the *voice* of God *cried;* as though he had said, that there was no excuse for ignorance, for God had indiscriminately exhorted them all to repentance. Now, since what was taught was common to them all, the Prophet deplores their perverseness, for very few were attentive; and the fable was sung, according to the proverb, to the deaf. We must then notice the word *cry; the voice* of God, he says, *crieth.* God did not whisper in the ear of one or two, but he designed his voice to be heard by all from the least to the greatest. The Prophets then did cry loud enough, but there were no ears to hear them.

We may take the word לָעִיר, *laoir,* in two ways. עִיר, *oir,* means a city. But some derive it from עוּר, *our,* and render it as if it were written לְהָעִיר, *laeoir.* If ה, *he,* is put in, it must be rendered, "To rouse;" and the letter ה, *he,* may be concealed under the point *chamets;* and this sense would be the most suitable, *The voice of Jehovah crieth to arouse* or awaken; that is, though the people are torpid, and as it were overpowered with sleep, for they indulged themselves in their sins; yet the voice of God ought to be sufficient to arouse them all: however sleepy they might have been, there was yet power enough in the doctrine of the Law, which the Prophet daily proclaimed. But still this voice, by which the whole people ought to have been awakened, was not heard!

The man of understanding, he says, *will see thy name.* The word תושיה, *tushie,* means properly understanding, as it is clear from many other passages; but the Prophet means that there was a very small number who were teachable; and he calls them men of understanding. At the same time, he indirectly reproves the sottishness of the people, though they all boasted that they were wise, and boasted also that they were the learners of the Law. The Prophet shows here by implication, that understanding was a rare thing among that people; for few hearkened to the voice of God. And thus we see what his object was; for he wished to touch the Jews to the quick, that they might acknowledge that they were without mind and understanding, because they had hardened themselves against God, so that his voice did not reach their hearts. He therefore shows that they were all besides themselves; for had they any right understanding, they would have hearkened to God speaking to them, as they were his disciples. What indeed could have been more strange, nay more inhuman, than for men to reject the doctrine of their salvation, and to turn aside from hearing even God himself? Thus the madness of the people was reproved; for though the voice of God sounded in the ears of them all, it was not yet listened to.

If one prefers reading, *In the city,* then no doubt the Prophet means, that the voice of God was proclaimed through all the cities: for to confine it, as some interpreters do, to Jerusalem, or to Samaria, appears frigid. We must then understand a change of number, and take city for any large concourse of people; as though he had said, that there was no city in which God did not cry, and yet that there were ears no-where.

It afterwards follows, *Shall see thy name.* Some render it, *Shall fear*,[1] as though it was from ירא, *ira;* but it comes, on the contrary, from ראה, *rae;* and rules of grammar will not allow it to be viewed otherwise. And the Prophet speaks in a striking manner, when he says, that the *intelligent man seeth the name of God.* For whence proceeded the contempt of wicked men, so that they disregarded the voice of God, except from this—that his majesty had no effect on them; that is, they did not acknowledge that they had to do with God? For if they really understood what I have said,—that God spoke to them, his majesty would have immediately come to view, it would have arrested all their thoughts. God then would have constrained even the most heedless to fear him, had it not been, that they imagined the voice which sounded in their ears was that of man. Significantly then does the Prophet say, that it was the act of singular prudence to see the name of God, that is, to understand from whom the doctrine proceeded. For as soon as we hearken to God, his majesty, as I have said, must so penetrate all our thoughts, as to humble us before him, and to constrain us to do him

[1] And so *Newcome* renders it, and there are a few copies in favour of this reading, in which יראי is found: but a fact of this kind is not sufficient to make a change, except there be other reasons. And then in the next line there is a change made, without the authority of one MS. Indeed, these two lines are rendered as though the Archbishop had another text; and indeed it is another: his version is this,—

And *there is* a sound wisdom with them that fear his name:
Hear, O ye tribes, him that testifieth.

This version is partly derived from the Septuagint; which could not have been wholly followed, as it differs so widely from the Hebrew, and hardly presents any meaning. There is far more correspondence in the passage, as it is rendered in our version, and by *Calvin,* and also by *Henderson;* and the Hebrew is closely followed. *Drusius* and others agree with *Calvin*, that תושיה, which is rendered often "sound wisdom," is to be taken here as a concrete, signifying a wise man. מטה is evidently the rod of correction, and is used in this sense in Isa. x. 5, 24; and it is more consistent with the whole passage to consider יעדה as a future, construed, as in the present tense, with an affix, from עד, to testify, than from יעד, to appoint,—"Hear ye the rod," the chastening rod, "and who testifies of it." *Newcome* viewed it as being this verb; but he takes no notice of its affix ה, which refers to the rod, by which chastisement is signified.—*Ed.*

homage. The contempt then of spiritual doctrine, and also the perverseness of ungodly men, proceed from this,—that they see not the name of God, that they understand not that it is his name.

He afterwards adds, *Hear ye the rod, and* him *who proclaims it to you.* By *rod* he means threatenings; as though he said, —"Your arrogance in mocking God shall not go unpunished, as though his voice were an empty sound: there is then no reason for you to deceive yourselves with the hope of impunity; for God will avenge the contempt of his word." Now the Prophet's design was, to denounce an approaching vengeance on those who came not willingly to God, and received not his word with genuine docility of mind. Whenever, then, men despise the voice of God, as though it proceeded only from a mortal being, on such Micah denounces an impending vengeance; for the contempt of his word is a thing intolerable to God. This is the reason why he immediately adds, after having complained of the contempt of his word, that vengeance was not afar off; *Hear ye* then *the rod, and who declares* or testifies *concerning it.*

This last clause ought to be especially noticed; for the ungodly are not terrified when God declares that he will be an avenger, because they think not that they must give an account of their life, or they look only on mortal man,—"Ah! who speaks? Is he indeed our God? Is he armed with celestial power? Do we not see a mortal man and one like ourselves?" We daily see that the ungodly do thus cast away every fear, and wilfully harden themselves against God's judgments. It is not then without reason that the Prophet bids the Jews seriously to consider *who testifies* of the rod; as though he said,—"I indeed confess that I am a mortal man, but remember who hath sent me; for I go not forth as a private individual, nor have I presumptuously intruded into this office; but I am armed with God's command; nay, God himself speaks through my mouth. If then ye despise me, the Lord is present, who will vindicate his own commands; for he will not suffer himself to be despised in his servants: though they may be contemptible according to the flesh, he will yet have the reverence which it deserves to be paid to his word." We now perceive the real meaning of the Prophet. It now follows—

10. Are there yet the treasures of wickedness in the house of the wicked, and the scant measure *that is* abominable?	10. Adhuc an sunt in domo impii thesauri impietatis? et modius macilentus detestabilis (*vel*, provocans iram?)
11. Shall I count *them* pure with the wicked balances, and with the bag of deceitful weights?	11. An justificabo stateras impietatis, et sacculum ponderum doli?

Interpreters differ as to the word האש, *eash:* some think that it ought to be read האיש, *eaish,* with an addition of two letters, and render it, "Is it yet man?" But this would render the passage abrupt. Others translate, "Is there yet fire?" As though it was אש, *ash;* and they suppose that wealth, wickedly and unjustly got, is so called, because it consumes itself. But as this is against what grammar requires, I am more inclined to take their view, who think that האש, *eash,* is to be taken here for היש, *eish,*[1] *aleph* being put for *jod:* and they rightly consider that the sentence is to be read as a question, *Are there yet the treasures of wickedness in the house of the ungodly?* If this view be approved, then we must consider the Prophet as proposing a question respecting a thing really monstrous,—"How can it be that treasures, gathered by plunder and wickedness, still remain with you, since ye have been so often warned, and since God daily urges you to repentance? How great is your hardness, that no fear of God lays hold on your minds?" But the meaning would not be unsuitable were we to regard God as a Judge examining them concerning a matter unknown, "Are there still the treasures of impiety in the house of the ungodly?" that is, "I will see whether the ungodly and wicked hide their treasures:" for God often assumes the character of earthly judges; not that any thing escapes his knowledge, but that

[1] One MS. has היש, which no doubt is the true reading. The Septuagint has μηπυϱ, which seems to have no sense whatever. Many copies have האיש, and this is the reading followed by *Junius* and *Tremelius*, and their version is this,—

Has any one still the house of a dishonest *man?*
The treasures of dishonesty?
And the small detestable ephah?—*Ed.*

we may know that he is not precipitant in deciding a question. This view, then, is by no means inappropriate, that is, that God here assumes the character of an earthly judge, and thus speaks, "I will see whether there are still treasures concealed by the ungodly; I will search their houses; I will know whether they have as yet repented of their crimes." Thus, then, may be understood the words of the Prophet, *Are there yet the treasures of wickedness in the house of the ungodly?* For God, as I have already said, shows that he would know respecting the plunders and the various kinds of cruelty which they had exercised.

He then adds, Is there *the bare measure*, that is, a measure less than it ought to be, *which is detestable?*[1] Then he says, *Shall I justify, &c.?*[2] This verse is connected with the last, and is added as an explanation. For God having come forth as a Judge, now shows what sort of Judge he is, even one who is not biassed by favour, who does not change his judgment, who shows no respect of persons. But men, for the most part, greatly deceive themselves, when they transform God according to their own will, and promise to themselves that he will be propitious to them, provided they only make false pretensions to him. God then here declares, that he differs widely from earthly judges, who now incline to one side and then to another, who are changeable, and often deviate from the right course: but, on the contrary, he says here, *Shall I justify wicked balances? shall I justify weights of fraud*, or deceitful? that is, "Shake off all those delusions by which ye are wont to deceive yourselves; for I do not change either my nature or my purpose; but according to the true teaching of my Law, I will punish all the wicked without any respect of persons: wherever wickedness and iniquity are found, there punishment will be inflicted."

[1] Literally it is, "And the ephah of detestable scantiness?" *Marckius* renders the words, "Et ephah tenuitatis abominabilis?" *Henderson*, "And the accursed *scanty ephah?*"

[2] האזכה. It is not true what *Henderson* says, that the verb זכה is not used transitively. See Ps. lxxiii. 13; Prov. xx. 9. *Jerome* renders the phrase, *numquid justificabo? Junius* and *Tremelius*, *an purum haberem? Grotius, numquid approbabo?* Our own version is no doubt correct. —*Ed.*

We now then understand how these two verses harmonise together. God shows that he will be a judge, and then, that he differs from men, who often change, as it has been said, in their decisions.

I will mention another meaning, which will perhaps be preferred by some. The question, after the manner of the Hebrews, may be taken as an affirmation, as though he had said, that within a short time, (for עוד, *oud*, means sometimes a short time,) the treasures of iniquity would not be found, for they would be taken away: then follows a confirmation, for frauds and robberies by false measures and deceitful weights could not escape God's judgment. The meaning then would be, that as God must necessarily, according to his own office, punish thefts, it cannot be that he will suffer men, who cheat by false weights, to continue always unpunished. It now follows—

12. For the rich men thereof are full of violence, and the inhabitants thereof have spoken lies, and their tongue *is* deceitful in their mouth.

12. Quia (*sic enim verto; nam qui putant esse relativum, frigidè exponunt*, cujus divites ejus impleverunt rapinis; *potius est*, quia; *nam* אשר *sæpe loco causalis particulæ accipitur*, quia[1] *ergo*) divites ejus impleverunt (*vel seipsos, vel domos suas, subaudiendum est*) חמס, rapina (*vel*, violentia;) et incolæ ejus locuti sunt fallaciam, et lingua eorum fallax (*vel*, fraudulenta) in ore ipsorum.

The Prophet means that the people were so given to avarice and plunder, that all the riches they had heaped together had been got by iniquitous robberies or by wicked gain. He now addresses the citizens of Jerusalem: for though iniquity then prevailed through the whole of Judea, there was yet a reason why he should distinctly accuse the inhabitants of

[1] There is nothing in what goes before for which a reason is given here: hence this אשר cannot be rendered as here proposed.. It is an instance of a peculiarity in Hebrew, when a double pronoun is used. Literally it is, "Which the rich men of hers;" the reference is to the city mentioned in verse 9. *Grotius*, *Newcome*, and *Henderson*, render the words thus, "Whose rich men," &c. The *Welsh* is very nearly the same, which no more than the Hebrew can with propriety be literally rendered in English or in the learned languages,—*Yr hon y mae ei chyvoethogion yn llawn trais*—The which her rich men are full of violence. But this mode of speaking has a more distinct and fuller reference to what is gone before than the simple relative "whose:" the connection is made more evident. —*Ed.*

Jerusalem; for they must have led the way by their example, and they were also worse in wickedness than the rest of the people: they were at least more obstinate, as they daily heard God's Prophets.

Hence he says, *her rich men gather not their wealth* except by violence. It is indeed certain, that the rich were not then alone guilty before God; but this evil has too much prevailed, —that the more liberty any one possesses, the more he employs it to do wrong. Those indeed who have not the power refrain, not because they are not inclined to do harm, but because they are as it were restrained; for poverty is often a bridle to men. As then the rich could spread their snares, as they had power to oppress the poor, the Prophet addresses his words to them, not that the rest were without fault or guilt, but because iniquity was more conspicuous in the rich, and that, because their wealth, as I have already said, gave them more power.

He afterwards extends his address to all the inhabitants, *They all*, he says, *speak falsehood*, that is, they have no sincerity, no uprightness; they are wholly given to frauds and deceits. *And their tongue is false in their mouth.* This mode of speaking seems apparently absurd; for where can the tongue be except in the mouth? It appears then a sort of redundancy, when he says that their tongue was deceitful in their mouth. But it is an emphatical mode of speaking, by which the Hebrews mean, that men have falsehoods in readiness as soon as they open their mouth. It is then the same as though the Prophet had said, that no pure word and free from guile could come from them, for as soon as they opened their mouth, falsehoods instantly came forth; their tongue was fraudulent, so that none could expect from these men any truth or faithfulness.—How so? Because as soon as they began to speak, they instantly discovered some guile, there was ever in readiness some falsehood to circumvent the simple.

We now then see that not a few men were summoned before God's tribunal, but that all without exception were condemned; as though the Prophet had said, that there was no more any integrity in the city, and that corruptions prevailed everywhere, for all were intent on deceiving one another. It follows—

13. Therefore also will I make *thee* sick in smiting thee, in making *thee* desolate because of thy sins.

14. Thou shalt eat, but not be satisfied; and thy casting down *shall be* in the midst of thee; and thou shalt take hold, but shalt not deliver; and *that* which thou deliverest will I give up to the sword.

13. Et ego etiam affligam te percutiendo, et te disperdam super peccatis tuis (secundum tua scelera.)

14. Tu comedes, et non satiaberis; et dejectio tua in medio tui; et apprehendes, et non servabis; et quod servaveris gladio tradam.

God, after having declared that he would be the Judge of the people, speaks now more clearly of their punishment. He says therefore that he was armed with vengeance: for it often happens, when a judge, even one who hates wickedness, is not able to punish, for he dreads the fierceness of those whom he thinks himself unequal to restrain. Hence God intimates here, that there will not be wanting to him a power to punish the people, *I will afflict thee*, he says, *by striking* or wounding *thee;* for so some render the words.[1] The sum of what is said is,—that nothing would be an obstacle to prevent God from inflicting punishment on the people, for there would be no want of power in his case. There is therefore no reason for men to promise themselves any escape when God ascends

[1] *Newcome* renders this line differently,—

Wherefore I will begin to smite thee.

Following a few MSS. and the Septuagint, he takes the verb here to be החלתי, which means, to begin; but the rendering seems flat, and suits not the passage; and it is not true, for the Lord had often smitten them before. The verb is in the past tense, and this has created a difficulty. The verbs in the following verse, which is connected with this, are all in the future tense, referring to a coming judgment. To remove this difficulty I propose the following version,—

But even I, *who* have made *thee* to grieve by striking thee,
Will make *thee* wholly desolate on account of thy sins:

Then the threatened desolation is specified. The verb השמם, making desolate, is evidently a participle connected with אני, I, at the beginning of the verse, the rest being an intervening clause: and when a participle follows a nominative case, which often occurs in Hebrew, the auxiliary verb must be supplied in a translation, which in its tense must be regulated by the context, and here by the verse which follows. *Piscator* renders it *Desolabo*, and says, that it is an infinitive put for the future. Grief or sorrow had already been produced, but now entire desolation is threatened.—*Ed.*

his tribunal; for were they fortified by all possible means they could not ward off the hand of God.

And he points out what sort of punishment it would be; and he mentions even two kinds in this verse. He says first, *Thou shalt eat, and shalt not be satisfied.* One of God's plagues, we know, is famine: and so the Prophet here declares, that the people would be famished, but not through the sterility of the fields. God indeed brings a famine in two ways: now the land yields no fruit; the corn withers, or being smitten with hail, gives no fruit; and thus God by the sterility of the fields often reduces men to want and famine: then, another mode is adopted, by which he can consume men with want, namely, when he breaks the staff of bread, when he takes away from bread its nourishing virtue, so that it can no more support men, whatever quantity they may swallow; and this is what experience proves, if only we have eyes to observe the judgments of God. We now see the meaning of this clause, when he says, *Thou shalt eat, and shalt not be satisfied;* as though he said, "I can indeed, whenever it pleases me, deprive you of all food; the earth itself will become barren at my command: but that ye may more clearly understand that your life is in my hand, a good supply of fruit shall be produced, but it shall not satisfy you. Ye shall then perceive that bread is not sufficient to support you; for by eating ye shall not be able to derive from bread any nourishment."

He then adds, *And thy dejection*[1] *shall be in the midst of thee;* that is, though no man from without disturb or afflict thee, yet thou shalt pine away with intestine evils. This is the real meaning; and interpreters have not sufficiently considered what the Prophet means, through too much negligence. But the passage ought to be noticed: for the Prophet, after having threatened a famine, not from want, but from the

[1] *Newcome*, without the authority of a single MS., but following the Septuagint and *Houbigant*, has changed ישחך into יחשך, "it shall be dark." Though the meaning of the passage is not thus materially affected, it is an alteration without sufficient reasons, there being no MS. in its favour, and no necessity arising from the passage itself: indeed, dejection or depression, or casting down, is more suitable to the context, and more emphatical.—*Ed.*

secret curse of God, now adds, *Thy dejection shall be in the midst of thee;* that is, "Though I should rouse against thee no enemies, though evidences of my wrath should not appear, so as to be seen at a distance, yea, though no one should disturb thee, yet thy dejection, thy calamity, shall be in the midst of thee, as though it were cleaving to thy bowels; for thou shalt pine away through a hidden malady, when God shall pronounce his curse on thee."

He now subjoins another kind of punishment, *Thou shalt take hold,*[1] *but shalt not deliver, and what thou shalt deliver, I will give up to the sword.* Some read, "A woman shall lay hold," that is, conceive seed, "and shall not preserve it;" and then, "though she may bring forth in due time, I will yet give up what may be born to the sword." But this meaning is too strained. Others apply the words to fathers, "Thou, father, shalt lay hold;" that is, thou shalt endeavour to preserve thy children, "and thou shalt not preserve" them. But I wonder that interpreters have thus toiled in vain in a matter so simple and plain. For he addresses here the land, or he addresses the city: as though he said, "The city shall take hold," or embrace, as every one does who wishes to preserve or keep any thing; for what we wish to keep safe, we lay hold on it, and keep it as it were in our arms; "*and what thou shalt preserve, I will give up to the sword:* thou wilt try all means to preserve thyself and thy people, but thou shalt not succeed: thou shalt then lose all thy labour, for though thou shouldest preserve some, yet the preserved shall not escape destruction."

If any one prefers to refer what is said to women, with regard to conception, as the third person of the feminine gender is used, let him have his own opinion; for this sense may certainly be admitted, that is, that the Lord would render the women barren, and that what they might bring forth

[1] The verb is תסג, which *Henderson* considers to be in Hiphil, the י being left out, which is sometimes the case: with *Drusius* and others, he renders it, "remove," that is, not *goods*, as he says, but wives and children; for if any were for a time removed to a place of safety, they were afterwards to be given up to the sword. Several copies have ש instead of ס, which makes it to be the verb נשג, and this has the meaning of laying hold or apprehending. But either meanings will suit the context. —*Ed.*

would be given up to the slaughter, inasmuch as the Lord would at length destroy with the sword both the parents and their children.

PRAYER.

Grant, Almighty God, that as thou canst find in us cause enough to execute not only one kind of vengeance, but innumerable kinds of vengeance, so as to destroy us at length altogether,—O grant, that we may of our own accord anticipate thy judgment, and with true humility so abhor ourselves, that there may be kindled in us a genuine desire to seek what is just and right, and thus endeavour to devote ourselves wholly to thee, that we may find thee to be propitious to us: and since we in so many ways offend thee, grant, that in true and sincere faith we may raise up all our thoughts and affections to thy only-begotten Son, who is our propitiation, that thou being appeased, we may lay hold on him, and remain united to him by a sacred bond, until thou at length gatherest us all into that celestial kingdom, which he has procured for us by his own blood. Amen.

Lecture Ninety-fifth.

15. Thou shalt sow, but thou shalt not reap; thou shalt tread the olives, but thou shalt not anoint thee with oil; and sweet wine, but shalt not drink wine.

15. Tu seres, et non metes; tu calcabis (*vel*, premes) oleum, et non unges te oleo; et mustum, et non bibes vinum.

The Prophet adds another kind of punishment, which was to follow the calamity threatened in the last verse. He had said, that those who escaped would at length be destroyed by the sword; he says now, that the whole land would become a prey to enemies: and he took his words from Moses; for it was usual with the Prophets, when they wished to secure greater authority to themselves, to quote literally the curses contained in the Law, as in the present instance: see Deut. xxviii. and Lev. xxvi. Now it is well known, that God denounced this punishment, with others, on the people,—that when they sowed their fields, another would reap,—that when they cultivated with great labour their vineyards, others would become the vintagers. The meaning is, that whatever fruit the land produced, would come into the hands of enemies, for all things would be exposed to plunder. Now it is a very grievous thing, when we see not only our provisions consumed by enemies, but also the fruit of our labour; which is the same as though they were to drink our blood: for the labour of man is often compared to blood, for labour occasions perspiration. It now follows—

16. For the statutes of Omri are kept, and all the works of the house of Ahab, and ye walk in their counsels; that I should make thee a desolation, and the inhabitants thereof an hissing: therefore ye shall bear the reproach of my people.

16. Et observata sunt edicta Amri, et omne opus domus Ahab; et ambulabitis consiliis eorum, ut tradam te in excidium (*vel*, vastitatem,) et incolas ejus in sibilum; et opprobrium populi mei portabitis.

Some read the words in the future tense, "And they will observe the statutes of Omri," &c., and gather this meaning,—that the Prophet now foresees by the Spirit, that the people would continue so perverse in their sins, as to exclude every hope that they could be reformed by any punishments. The meaning then would be,—"The Lord hath indeed determined to punish sharply and severely the wickedness of this people; but they will not repent; they will nevertheless remain stupid in their obstinacy, and go on in their superstitions, which they have learned from the kings of Israel." There is however another view, and one more generally approved, and that is,—that the Jews, having forsaken God, and despised his Law, had turned aside to the superstitions of the kingdom of Israel. Hence he says, that *observed were the decrees of Omri, and every work of the house of Ahab.* Omri was the father of Ahab, who was made king by the election of the soldiers, when Zimri, who had slain the king, was rejected. When Omri bought Samaria, he built there a city; and to secure honour to it, he added a temple; and hence idolatry increased. Afterwards his son Ahab abandoned himself to every kind of superstition. Thus matters became continually worse. Hence the Prophet, by mentioning here king Omri and his posterity, (included in the words, "the house of Ahab,") clearly means, that the Jews, who had purely worshipped God, at length degenerated, and were now wholly unlike Israelites, as they had embraced all those abominations which Omri and his son Ahab had devised. True religion as yet prevailed in the tribe of Judah, though the kingdom of Israel was become corrupt, and filthy superstitions had gained the ascendancy: but in course of time the Jews became also implicated in similar superstitions. Of this sin the Prophet now accuses them; that is, that they made themselves associates with the Israelites: *Observed*[1] then *are the edicts of Omri, and the whole work of the house of Ahab: Ye walk*, he says, (the future here means a continued act, as often elsewhere,) *ye walk in their counsels.*

It must be observed, that the Prophet here uses respectable terms, when he says that חקות, *chekut*, statutes or decrees, were observed; and when he adds, "the counsels" of the kings of Israel: but yet this is in no way stated as an excuse for them; for though men may not only be pleased with, but also highly commend, their own devices, yet the Lord abominates them all. The Prophet no doubt designedly adopted these words, in order to show that those pretences were frivolous and of no account, which superstitious men adduce, either to commend or to excuse their own inventions. They ever refer to public authority,—"This has been received by the consent of all; that has been decreed; it is not the mistake of one or two men; but the whole Church has so determined: and kings also thus command; it would be a great sin not to show obedience to them." Hence the Prophet, in order to show how puerile are such excuses, says, "I indeed allow that your superstitions are by you honourably distinguished,

[1] The verb, ישתמר, is in the singular, and is followed by its nominative case, which is in the plural number. Grammarians are at a loss to account for this, and hence propose several modes of construction. But it is evidently an anomalous idiom, somewhat similar to that in Greek, when plural neuters take a verb in the singular number. As it has been already observed, such a construction as we find here, is very common in the *Welsh* language. The verb is in Hithpael, the reflective mood, the ת, as is often the case, changing place with the first letter of the verb. It is not always that this mood is reflective, but is sometimes passive, as we find to be the case with סתר, in Isa. xxix. 14, and עבר, in Deut. iii. 26. And so here it does not retain its reflective meaning. But it may be, that intensity, diligence, or earnestness, is intended to be conveyed; that is, that the statutes of Omri were diligently and carefully observed.—*Ed.*

for they are approved by the edicts of your kings, and are received by the consent of the many, and they seem not to have been inconsiderately and unadvisedly, but prudently contrived, even by great men, who were become skilful through long experience." But how much soever they might have boasted of their statutes and counsels, and however plausibly they might have referred to prudence and power in order to disguise their idolatries, yet all those things were of no account before God. By counsels, the Prophet no doubt meant that false kind of wisdom which always shines forth in the traditions of men; and by statutes, he meant the kingly authority.

We hence see that it is a vain thing to colour over what is idolatrous, by alleging power on the one hand in its favour, and wisdom on the other.—How so? Because God will not allow dishonour to be done to him by such absurd things; but he commands us to worship him according to what is prescribed in his Word.

And now a denunciation of punishment follows, *That I should deliver thee to desolation*, and its inhabitants, &c. There is a change of person; the Prophet continually addresses the land, and under that name, the people,—*that I should* then *deliver thee to exile*, or desolation, *and thine inhabitants to hissing*. It is a quotation from Moses: and by *hissing* he means the reproach and mockery to which men in a miserable state are exposed.

At last he adds, *Ye shall bear the reproach of my people.* Some take the word, people, in a good sense, as though the Prophet had said here, that God would punish the wrongs which the rich had done to the distressed common people; but this view, in my judgment, is too confined. Others understand this by the reproach of God's people,—that nothing would be more reproachful to the Jews, than that they had been the people of God; for it would redound to their dishonour and disgrace, that they, who had been honoured by such an honourable name, were afterwards given up to so great miseries. But the passage may be otherwise explained: we may understand by the people of God the Israelites; as though the Prophet said, "Do ye not perceive how the

Israelites have been treated? Were they not a part of my people? They were descendants from the race of Abraham as well as you; nor can you boast of a higher dignity: They were then equal to you in the opinion of all; and yet this privilege did not hinder my judgment, did not prevent me from visiting them as they deserved." Such a view harmonises with the passage: but there is, as I think, something ironical in the expression, "my people;" as though he said, "The confidence, that ye have been hitherto my people, hardens you: but this false and wicked boasting shall increase your punishment; for I will not inflict on you an ordinary punishment, as on heathens and strangers; but I shall punish your wickedness much more severely; for it is necessary, that your punishment should bear proportion to my favour, which has been so shamefully and basely despised by you." Hence, by the reproach of God's people I understand the heavier judgments, which were justly prepared for all the ungodly, whom God had favoured with such special honour, as to regard them as his people: for the servant, who knew his master's will, and did it not, was on that account more severely corrected,[1] Luke xii. 47. Let us now proceed—

CHAPTER VII.

1. Woe is me! for I am as when they have gathered the summer fruits, as the grape-gleanings of the vintage: *there is* no cluster to eat: my soul desired the first-ripe fruit.

2. The good *man* is perished out of the earth: and *there is* none upright among men: they all lie in wait for blood; they hunt every man his brother with a net.

1. Væ mihi (*alii deducunt* à ילל, ululare meum; *sed est particula dolentis apud Hebræos;* Væ mihi *ergo*,) quia fui sicut collectiones æstatis (*sic est ad verbum*,) et sicuti racemi vindemiæ; nullus botrus ad comedendum; maturos fructus (*vel*, primitias frugum) desideravit anima mea.

2. Periit humanus (*vel*, mansuetus) è terra, et rectus in hominibus nemo est; et omnes sanguinibus insidiantur, quisque fratrem suum venatur reti (*alii*, ad perniciem; *et* חרם, *etiam Hebræis interdum est occisio.)*

[1] There is another view mentioned by *Drusius*,—that is, the *reproach* which God had previously denounced on his people, in case they sinned and continued in their perverseness. Reproach in this sense would mean punishment.—*Ed.*

The meaning of the first verse is somewhat doubtful: some refer what the Prophet says to punishment; and others to the wickedness of the people. The first think that the calamity, with which the Lord had visited the sins of the people, is bewailed; as though the Prophet looked on the disordered state of the whole land. But it may be easily gathered from the second verse, that the Prophet speaks here of the wickedness of the people, rather than of the punishment already inflicted. I have therefore put the two verses together, that the full meaning may be more evident to us.

Woe then *to me!* Why? *I am become as gatherings.* Too free, or rather too licentious is this version,—"I am become as one who seeks to gather summer-fruits, and finds none;" so that, being disappointed of his hope, he burns with desire. This cannot possibly be considered as the rendering of the Prophet's words. There is indeed some difficulty in the expressions: their import, however, seems to be this,—that the land, which the Prophet undertakes here to represent and personify, was like to a field, or a garden, or a vineyard, that was empty. He therefore says, that the land was stripped of all its fruit, as it is after harvest and the vintage. So by *gatherings* we must understand the collected fruit. Some understand the gleanings which remain, as when one leaves carelessly a few clusters on the vines: and thus, they say, a few just men remained alive on the land. But the former comparison harmonises better with the rest of the passage, and that is, that the land was now stripped of all its fruit, as it is after the harvest and the vintage. *I am become* then *as the gatherings of summer*, that is, as in the summer, when the fruit has been already gathered; *and as the clusters of the vintage*, that is, when the vintage is over.[1]

[1] *Newcome* renders the verse somewhat different, and makes the comparison more clear,—

> "Woe is me! for I am become
> As the gatherers of late figs,
> As the gleaners of the vintage:
> *There is* no cluster to eat;
> My soul desireth the first ripe fig."

Substantially the same is the version of *Dathius* and of *Henderson* "Late figs" is not strictly the meaning of קיץ, which is properly summer

There is no cluster, he says, *to eat.* The Prophet refers here to the scarcity of good men; yea, he says, that there were no longer any righteous men living. For though God had ever preserved some hidden seed, yet it might have been justly declared with regard to the whole people, that they were like a field after gathering the corn, or a vineyard after the vintage. Some residue, indeed, remains in the field after harvest, but there are no ears of corn; and in the vineyard some bunches remain, but they are empty; nothing remains but leaves. Now, this personification is very forcible, when the Prophet comes forth as though he represented the land itself; for he speaks in his own name and person, *Woe is to me,* he says, *for I am like summer-gatherings!* It was then the same thing, as though he deplored his own nakedness and want, inasmuch as there were not remaining any upright and righteous men.

In the second verse he expresses more clearly his mind, *Perished,* he says, *has the righteous*[1] *from the land, and there is none upright*[2] *among men.* Here now he does not personify the land. It was indeed a forcible and an emphatic language when he complained at the beginning, that he groaned as though the land was ashamed of its dearth: but the Prophet now performs the office of a teacher, *Perished,* he says, *has the righteous from the land; there is no one upright among men; all lay in wait for blood; every one hunts his brother as with a net.* In this verse the Prophet briefly shows, that all were

or summer-fruit; yet, as the early or first ripe fig is mentioned in the last line, which forms a contrast with this, what is meant, no doubt, is the late figs. Then the word for "gleaners," עללת, is properly, gleanings; but here it is evidently to be taken as a concrete, gleaners, to correspond with gatherers, though *Newcome* considers the women-gleaners to be intended. The four last lines form a parallelism, in which the first and the last correspond, and the second and the third,—the summer-fruit and the early fig,—the vintage and the cluster.—*Ed.*

[1] *Justus*, rendered in the text *humanus*, vel, *mansuetus*. The Hebrew is חסיד, rendered by the Septuagint "ευσεϐης—godly, pious,"—by *Marckius*, "benignus—kind, benignant,"—by *Newcome*, "the good man,"—and by *Henderson*, "the pious." It is sometimes rendered holy; but its meaning is, kind, benevolent, merciful, actively good, beneficent. In Ps. xii. 1, it is rendered "godly," and in Isa. lvii. 1, "merciful."—*Ed.*

[2] *Rectus*, ישר, rendered by the Septuagint, "κατορθων—one going straight to an object,"—by *Newcome* and *Henderson*, "upright." It is one who proceeds in a straight course according to the rule of the law, without making any windings or turning aside into any devious path.—*Ed.*

full both of cruelty and perfidy, that there was no care for justice; as though he said, "In vain are good men sought among this people; for they are all bloody, they are all fraudulent." When he says, that they *all did lay in wait for blood*, he no doubt intended to set forth their cruelty, as though he had said, that they were thirsting for blood. But when he adds, that each did lay in wait for their brethren, he alludes to their frauds or to their perfidy.

We now then perceive the meaning of the Prophet: and the manner he adopts is more emphatical than if God, in his own name, had pronounced the words: for, as men were fixed, and as though drowned, in their own carelessness, the Prophet introduces here the land as speaking, which accuses its own children, and confesses its own guilt; yea, it anticipates God's judgment, and acknowledges itself to be contaminated by its own inhabitants, so that nothing pure remained in it. It follows—

3. That they may do evil with both hands earnestly, the prince asketh, and the judge *asketh* for a reward; and the great *man*, he uttereth his mischievous desire: so they wrap it up.

3. Super malitia manuum suarum ad beneficiendum; princeps postulat, et judex in mercede (*ego transfero ad verbum*,) et magnus loquitur pravitatem animæ suæ ipse; et complicant (*vel, ut alii vertunt*, confirmant; *sed propriè est* complicari; *et metaphora aptè convenit contextui, ut statim videbimus.*)

This verse is properly addressed to the judges and governors of the people, and also to the rich, who oppressed the miserable common people, because they could not redeem themselves by rewards. The Prophet therefore complains, that corruptions so much prevailed in judgments, that the judges readily absolved the most wicked, provided they brought bribes. The sum of what is said then is, that any thing might be done with impunity, for the judges were venal. This is the Prophet's meaning.

But as interpreters differ, something shall be said as to the import of the words. על הרע כפים, *ol ero caphim*, *For the evil of their hands* to do good. Some give this explanation, "Though they are openly wicked, yet they make pretences, by which they cover their wickedness:" and the sense would be this,—that though they had cast aside every care for what was right, they yet had become so hardened in iniquity, that they wished to be deemed good and holy men; for in a disordered state of things the wicked always show an iron front, and would have silence to be observed respecting their shameful deeds. Some interpreters therefore think that the Prophet here complains, that there was now no difference between what was honourable and base, right and wrong; for wicked men dared so to disguise their iniquities, that they did not appear, or, that no one ventured to say any thing against them. Do you, however, examine and consider, whether what the Prophet says may be more fitly connected together in this way, *That they may do good for the wickedness of their hands*, that is, to excuse themselves for the wickedness of their hands, they agree together; *for the prince asks, the judge is ready to receive a bribe.* Thus, the rich saw that exemption might have been got by them, for they had the price of redemption in their hands: they indeed knew that the judges and princes could be pacified, when they brought the price of corruption. And this is the meaning which I approve, for it harmonises best with the words of the Prophet. At the same time, some give a different explanation of the verb להיטיב, *laeithib;* that is, that they acted vigorously in their wickedness: but this exposition is frigid. I therefore embrace the one I have just stated, which is,—that corruptions so prevailed in the administration of justice, that coverings were ready for all crimes; for the governors and judges were lovers of money, and were always ready to absolve the most guilty, but not without a reward. *For the wickedness then of their works, that they may do good*, that is, that they may obtain acquittance, *the prince* only *asks;* he examines not the case, but only regards the hand; *and the judge*, he says, *judges for reward:* the judges also were mercenary. They did not sit to determine what was right and just; but as soon as they were satisfied by bribes, they easily forgave all crimes; and thus they turned vices into virtues; for they made no difference between white and black, but according to the bribe received.[1]

[1] This clause, though the general sense is allowed by most to be the

This view is consistent with what the Prophet immediately subjoins, *The great*, he says, *speaks of the wickedness of his soul*, even *he*. By the great, he does not mean the chief men, as some incorrectly think, but he means the rich, who had money enough to conciliate the judges. They then who could bring the price of redemption, dared to boast openly of their wickedness: for so I render the word הוּת, *eut*, as it cannot be suitable to translate it here, corruption. *Speak* then *of the wickedness of his soul does the great*; there was then nothing, neither fear nor shame, to restrain the rich from doing wrong. —How so? For they knew that they had to do with mercenary judges, and could easily corrupt them. They hence dared to *speak of the wickedness of their soul*: they did not cloak their crimes, as it is the case when some fear of the Law prevails, when justice is exercised: but as no difference was made between good and evil, the most guilty boasted openly of his wickedness. And the pronoun הוּא, *eva*, he himself, is also emphatical; and this has not been observed by interpreters. *He* then *himself* speaks of the wickedness of his soul; he did not wait until others accuse him of doing wrong, but he shamelessly dared to glory in his crimes; for

same, is yet variously rendered. *Drusius* says, "Locus hic diu me multumque torsit." The original is,—

על הרע כפים להיטיב :

The most satisfactory rendering is that which is offered by *Marckius*, which is this,—

Propter malefaciendum volæ pro benefaciendum,—
For doing evil [*are* their] hands instead of doing good.

Rabbi *Jonathan*, as quoted by *Marckius*, gives substantially the same rendering, though not literally,—

Malum faciunt manibus suis, et non bonum faciunt,—
Evil they do with their hands, and they do no good.

Our version is that of *Junius* and *Tremelius*, and is substantially followed by *Newcome*; and *Henderson's* version is,—

For evil their hands are well prepared;

which is nearly that of the Septuagint,—

Επι το κακον τας χειρας αυτων ετοιμαζουσι.

But the following would be as literal a translation as that of *Marckius*,—

For doing evil *are* their hands, to do *it* thoroughly.

The last verb means not only to do good, but also to make a thing good or complete, fully to execute it.—*Ed.*

impunity was certain, as he could close the mouth of the judges by bringing a bribe. *Speak* then *of the wickedness of his soul does he himself.*[1]

And further, *they fold up* wickedness; which means, that raging cruelty prevailed, because the governors, and those who wished to purchase liberty to sin, conspired together, as though they made ropes, and thus rendered firm their wickedness. For the great man, that is, the rich and the monied, agreed with the judge, and the judge with him; and so there was a collusion between them. It hence happened, that wickedness possessed, as it were, a tyrannical power; for there was no remedy. We now apprehend the real design of the Prophet, at least as far as I am able to discover. It now follows—

4. The best of them *is* as a brier: the most upright *is sharper* than a thorn hedge: the day of thy watchmen *and* thy visitation cometh; now shall be their perplexity.	4. Bonus inter eos quasi paliurus, rectus præ spineto (*aliquid subaudiendum est,* asperior est spineto;) dies speculatorum tuorum, visitatio tua venit; tunc erit confusio ipsorum (*vel,* perplexitas, *ut alii vertunt.*)

The Prophet confirms what he had previously said,—that the land was so full of every kind of wickedness, that they who were deemed the best were yet thorns and briers, full of bitterness, or very sharp to prick; as though he said, "The best among them is a thief, the most upright among them is a robber." We hence see, that in these words he alludes to their accumulated sins, as though he said, "The condition of the people cannot be worse; for iniquity has advanced to its extreme point: when any one seeks for a good or an up-

[1] The whole verse may be rendered thus,—

For doing evil *are* their hands, to execute it fully:
The prince asks, and the judge *also*, for reward;
When the great man speaks of oppression,
That it *is* his desire, then they contrive it together,
or, *literally*, intwine it.

To render הות נפשו הוא, "the wickedness of his soul," as *Newcome* does, is to leave out wholly the last word; and *Henderson* does the same. *Piscator* gives the form of the words, "ærumnam, quam expetit—the mischief, which he desires." The two last words literally are, "his desire it *is*."—*Ed.*

right man, he only finds thorns and briers; that is, he is instantly pricked." But if the best were then like thorns, what must have been the remainder? We have already seen that the judges were so corrupt that they abandoned themselves without feeling any shame to any thing that was base. What then could have been said of them, when the Prophet compares here the upright and the just to thorns; yea, when he says, that they were rougher than briers? Though it is an improper language to say, that the good and the upright[1] among them were like briers; for words are used contrary to their meaning, as it is certain, that those who inhumanly pricked others were neither good nor just: yet the meaning of the Prophet is in no way obscure,—that there was then such license taken in wickedness, that even those who retained in some measure the credit of being upright were yet nothing better than briers and thorns. There is then in the words what may be deemed a concession.

He then adds, *The day of thy watchmen, thy visitation comes.* He here denounces the near judgment of God, generally on the people, and especially on the rulers. But he begins with the first rank, and says, *The day of thy watchmen;* as though he said, "Ruin now hangs over thy governors, though they by no means expect it." *Watchmen* he calls the Prophets, who, by their flatteries, deceived the people, as well as their rulers: and he sets the Prophets in the front, because they were the cause of the common ruin. He does not yet exempt the body of the people from punishment; nay, he joins together these two things,—the visitation of the whole people, and the day of the watchmen.

And justly does he direct his discourse to these watchmen,

[1] It is better, as it is done here, to take the words simply as they are, and not to make superlatives of them: nor is there any change necessary in the second line as proposed by *Dathius*, *Newcome*, and others, by taking the מ from one word and attaching it to another. There is no MS. in its favour, and it is done only on the authority of the Targum. The two lines are these,—

Their good *man* is like a brier,
The upright worse than a thorny hedge.

The preposition מ is often rendered "rather than;" but it may, in many places, be rendered "better than," or "worse than," according to the import of the passage.—*Ed.*

who, being blind, blinded all the rest; and who, being perverted, led astray the whole people. This is the reason why the Prophet now, in an especial manner, threatens them; but, as I have already said, the people were not on this account to be excused. There may seem indeed to have been here a fair pretence for extenuating their guilt: the common people might have said that they had not been warned as they ought to have been; nay, that they had been destroyed through delusive falsehoods. And we see at this day that many make such a pretence as this. But a defence of this kind is of no avail before God; for though the common people are blinded, yet they go astray of their own accord, since they lend a willing ear to impostors. And even the reason why God gives loose reins to Satan as well as to his ministers, and why he gives, as Paul says, (2 Thess. ii. 11,) power to delusion, is this,—because the greater part of the world ever seeks to be deceived. The denunciation of the Prophet then is this,—that as the judges and the Prophets had badly exercised their office, they would be led to the punishment which they deserved, for they had been, as it has been elsewhere observed, the cause of ruin to others: in the meantime, the common people were not excusable. The vengeance of God then would overtake them all, from the least to the greatest, without any exception. *Thy visitation* then *cometh.*

He afterwards speaks in the third person, *Then shall be their confusion,* or perplexity, or they shall be ashamed. The Prophet here alludes indirectly to the hardness of the people; for though the Prophets daily threatened them, they yet remained all of them secure; nay, we know that all God's judgments were held in derision by them. As then the faithful teachers could not have moved wicked men either with fear or with shame, the Prophet says, *Then confusion shall come to them;* as though he said, "Be hardened now as much as ye wish to be, as I see that you are stupid, yea, senseless, and attend not to the word of the Lord; but the time of visitation will come, and then the Lord will constrain you to be ashamed, for he will really show you to be such as ye are; and he will not then contend with you in words as he does now; but the announced punishment will divest you of all your false pretences; and he will also remove that waywardness which now hardens you against wholesome doctrine and all admonitions."

PRAYER.

Grant, Almighty God, that seeing that we are born in a most corrupt age, in which such a license is taken to indulge in wickedness, that hardly a spark of virtue appears,—O grant, that we may yet continue upright in the midst of thorns; and do thou so constantly keep us under the guidance of thy Word, that we may cultivate true piety, and also what is just towards our neighbours: and as there is in us no power to preserve ourselves safe, grant that thy Son may so protect us by the power of the Holy Spirit, that we may continue to advance towards the end of our course, until we be at length gathered into that celestial kingdom, which he has procured for us by his own blood. Amen.

Lecture Ninety-sixth.

5. Trust ye not in a friend, put ye not confidence in a guide: keep the doors of thy mouth from her that lieth in thy bosom.

6. For the son dishonoureth the father, the daughter riseth up against her mother, the daughter-in-law against her mother-in-law; a man's enemies *are* the men of his own house.

5. Ne fidatis amico, ne speretis in consiliario (*vel*, duce ;) ab ea quæ dormit in sinu tuo custodi aperturas oris tui:

6. Quia filius contumeliâ afficit patrem, filia surgit contra matrem suam, nurus contra socrum suam; inimici viri domestici ejus (homines domus ejus, *ad verbum.*)

The Prophet pursues the subject we discussed yesterday, —that liberty, in iniquity, had arrived to its highest point, for no faithfulness remained among men; nay, there was no more any humanity; for the son performed not his duty towards his father, nor the daughter-in-law towards her mother-in-law; in short, there was then no mutual love and concord. He does not here speak of that false confidence, by which many deceive themselves, who rely on mortals, and transfer to them the glory which belongs to God. Those, therefore, without any reason, philosophise here, who say, that we ought not to trust in men; for this was not the design of the Prophet.

But our Prophet complains of his times according to the tenor of Ovid's description of the iron age, who says,—

"———A guest is not safe from his host;
Nor a brother-in-law from a son-in-law; and brotherly love is rare:
A husband seeks the death of his wife, and she, of her husband;
Cruel stepmothers mingle the lurid poison;
The son, before the day, inquires into the years of his father." [1]

So also our Prophet says, that there was no regard to humanity among men; for the wife was ready to betray her husband, the son treated his father with reproach; in short, they had all forgotten humanity or natural affection. We now then understand what the Prophet means by saying, *Trust not a friend;*[2] that is, if any one hopes for any thing from a friend, he will be deceived; for nothing can be found among men but perfidy.

Put no faith in a counsellor. So I render the word אלוף, *aluph;* some translate it, an elder brother; but there is no necessity to constrain us to depart from the proper and true meaning of the word. As then the Prophet had spoken of an associate or a friend, so he now adds a counsellor. And it proves what he had in view, when he says in the next clause, that no enemies are worse than domestics. We hence see that the Prophet simply means, that the men of his age were not only avaricious and cruel to one another, but that without any regard to human feelings the son rebelled against

[1] See *Ov. Met.* Lib. i. 144-148.

[2] *Ne fidatis amico:* it is rather, Believe not in a friend, that is, in what he says, אל-תאמינו ברע. The next expression is that which signifies reliance, trust, or confidence. אלוף, is a leader; ηγουμενος in Sept., one who leads the way. *Diodati* gives its true meaning,—"A conductor, the most trusty friend, who is one's usual counsellor in every difficulty and perplexity.' *Jerome* refers to scriptural instances as to the persons here mentioned: the *friend*, Ahitophel and Judas,—the *counsellor*, Abimelek, who was made king by the men of Sichem, and oppressed them,—*domestics*, Absalom and the wives of Esau. The word used for "dishonouring" is very strong; מנבל, one who counts a thing worthless or abominable; it means not only to dishonour, but to regard with disdain and contempt. "The contempt and violation of the laws of domestic duties," *Henry* justly observes, "are a sad symptom of an universal corruption of manners. Those are never likely to come to good who are undutiful to their parents, and study to be provoking to them and cross them."—*Ed.*

his father, and thus subverted the whole order of nature; so that they had none of those affections, which seem at the same time to be incapable of being extinguished in men. Let us now proceed—

7. Therefore I will look unto the Lord; I will wait for the God of my salvation: my God will hear me.	7. Ego autem ad Jehovam respiciam, expectabo ad Deum salutis meæ; exaudiet me Deus meus.

The Prophet points out here the only remedy, to preserve the faithful from being led away by bad examples, and that is, to fix their eyes on God, and to believe that he will be their deliverer. Nothing is more difficult than to refrain from doing wrong, when the ungodly provoke us; for they seem to afford us a good reason for retaliation. And when no one injures us, yet custom is deemed almost a law: thus it happens that we think that to be lawful which is sanctioned by the manners and customs of the age; and when success attends the wicked, this becomes a very strong incentive. Thus it happens, that the faithful can hardly, and with no small difficulty, keep themselves within proper bounds: when they see that wickedness reigns everywhere, and that with impunity; and still more, when they see the abettors of wickedness increasing in esteem and wealth, immediately the corrupt lust of emulation creeps in. But when the faithful themselves are provoked by injuries, there seems then to be a just reason for doing wrong; for they say that they wilfully do harm to no one, but only resist an injury done to them, or retaliate fraud with fraud: this they think is lawful. The Prophet, in order to prevent this temptation, bids the faithful to look to God. The same sentiment we often meet with in Psalm cxix.: its import is, that the faithful are not to suffer themselves to be led away by bad examples, but to continue ever obedient to God's word, however great and violent the provocations they may receive. Let us now consider the words of the Prophet.

To Jehovah, he says, *will I look.* The verb צפה, *tsaphe*, properly means to look on, to behold, (*speculari;*) it is sometimes taken in the sense of expecting; but I am inclined to retain its proper meaning, *I will look*, he says, *on God;* that is, I will do the same as though the only true God were before my eyes. How indeed does it happen, that even the good indulge themselves while living among the wicked and ungodly, except that they are too much occupied with things around them? If then we desire to maintain integrity, while the world presents to us nothing but examples of sin, let us learn to pass by these temptations as with closed eyes. This may be done, if we direct our eyes to God alone. *I will look*, he says, *to Jehovah.*

He then adds, *I will wait for the God of my salvation.* The Prophet says nothing new here, but only explains more clearly the last clause, defining the manner of the looking of which he had spoken; as though he said,—"Patiently will I bear, while God helps me:" for when the wicked harass us on every side, we shall no doubt soon turn away our eyes from God, except we be armed with patience. And how comes patience, unless we be fully persuaded that God will be our deliverer, when the suitable time shall come? We now perceive the intention of the Prophet. He shows that the godly cannot otherwise continue constant in their integrity, except they turn their eyes to the only true God. Then he adds, that they cannot be preserved in this contemplation, unless they wait patiently for God, that is, for his help.

And he calls him *the God of his salvation;* by which he intimates that, relying on his word, he thus perseveres in enduring injuries: for it cannot be but that every one will submit himself to God, and surrender himself to be protected by him, if this truth be first fixed in his mind—that God will never forsake his own people. This then is the reason why he calls him *the God of* his *salvation.* But this title must be referred to his present circumstances, as though he said,—"Though God's hand does not now appear to help or to bring me aid, I yet feel assured of his favour, and I know that my salvation is secured by it."

He then adds, *Hear me will my God.* He here confirms what we have already said,—that, being supported by the promises of God, he thus composes his mind to patience; for patience would often vanish or would be shaken off by temptations, unless we were surely persuaded that God provides for our salvation, and that we shall not hope in him in vain. Nor is it to no purpose that he says, that God was *his God.* He was one of his people; and this seems to have been the common privilege of all the Jews: yet the Prophet no doubt connects God with himself here in a peculiar manner; for men in general had fallen away into ungodliness. They all indeed gloried in the name of God, but absurdly and falsely. Hence the Prophet intimates, that he was under his protection in a manner different from the rest: for when any one allows himself the liberty of doing evil, he, at the same time, renounces God and his protection. Therefore, the Prophet no doubt alludes indirectly to the irreligion of the people. For though the vain boasting, that they had been adopted by God, that they were the holy race of Abraham, was everywhere in the mouth of all, yet hardly one in a hundred had any regard for God. But it is also of importance to notice, that the Prophet, by saying, *Hear me will God,* gives a testimony, at the same time, respecting his own faith,—that he would always apply to God for help, and exercise himself in prayer whenever necessity urged him; for God hears not except when he is called upon. The Prophet then recommends here, by his example, an attention to prayer.

Now this verse shows to us in general that there is no excuse for us if we suffer ourselves to be led away, as it is daily the case, by bad examples. And then to look to God is especially needful, when all excesses of wickedness prevail in the world: when the lusts of men become the rule and the law, we ought then to renounce in a manner the society of men, that they may not implicate us in their wickedness. They, therefore, who allege for themselves the examples of others, employ a frivolous excuse, as many do in the present day, who set up the shield of custom: though they are clearly condemned by the word of God, yet they think it a sufficient defence, that they follow others. But we see how frivolous is this confidence; for the Prophet no doubt prescribes here a law for all the children of God as to what they ought to do, when the devil tempts them to sin by the bad examples and shameful deeds of the majority. Let us go on—

8. Rejoice not against me, O mine enemy: when I fall, I shall arise; when I sit in darkness, the Lord *shall be* a light unto me.	8. Ne gaudeas de me, inimica mea; quia ceciderim, surgam (*vel,* quamvis ceciderim, surgam;) quum sedebo in tenebris, Jehova erit lux mihi.

Here the Prophet assumes the character of the Church, and repels a temptation, which proves very severe to us in adversities; for there is not so much bitterness in the evil itself, as in the mockery of the wicked, when they petulantly insult us and deride our faith. And to noble minds reproach is ever sharper than death itself: and yet the devil almost always employs this artifice; for when he sees that we stand firm in temptations, he suborns the wicked and sharpens their tongues, to speak evil of us, and to wound us with slanders. This is the reason why the Prophet directs his discourse now to the enemies of the Church. But as God calls the Church his spouse, and as she is described to us under the character of a woman, so also he compares here the enemies of the holy people to a petulant woman. As, therefore, when there is emulation between two women, she, who sees her enemy pressed down by evils and adverse events, immediately raises up herself and triumphs; so also the Prophet says respecting the enemies of the Church; they sharpened their tongues, and vomited forth their bitterness, as soon as they saw the children of God in trouble or nearly overwhelmed with adversities. We now then understand the design of the Prophet,—that he wished to arm us, as I have said, against the taunts of the ungodly, lest they should prevail against us when God presses us down with adversities, but that we may stand courageously, and with composed and tranquil minds, swallow down the indignity.

Rejoice not over me, he says, *O my enemy.* Why not? He adds a consolation; for it would not be enough for one to repel with disdain the taunts of his enemy; but the Prophet says here, *Rejoice not, for should I fall, I shall rise;* or though I fall, I shall rise: and the passage seems to harmonise better when there is a pause after *Rejoice not over me;* and then to add, *Though I fall, I shall rise, though I sit in darkness, Jeho-*

vah shall be a light to me.[1] The Prophet means, that the state of the Church was not past hope. There would be ample room for our enemies to taunt us, were it not that this promise cannot fail us,—seven times in the day the just falls, and rises again, (Prov. xxiv. 16.)—How so? For God puts under him his own hand. We now perceive the meaning of this passage. For if God deprived us of all hope, enemies might justly deride us, and we must be silent: but since we are surely persuaded that God is ready at hand to restore us again, we can boldly answer our enemies when they annoy us with their derisions; *though I fall, I shall rise:* "There is now no reason for thee to triumph over me when I fall; for it is God's will that I should fall, but it is for this end—that I may soon rise again; and though I now lie in darkness, yet the Lord will be my light."

We hence see that our hope triumphs against all temptations: and this passage shows, in a striking manner, how true is that saying of John,—that our faith gains the victory over the world, (1 John v. 4.) For when sorrow and trouble take possession of our hearts, we shall not fail if this comes to our mind—that God will be our aid in the time of need. And when men vomit forth their poison against us, we ought to be furnished with the same weapons: then our minds shall never succumb, but boldly repel all the taunts of Satan and of wicked men. This we learn from this passage.

Now, from what the Prophet says, *Though I fall, I shall rise again,* we see what God would have us to expect, even a happy and joyful exit at all times from our miseries; but

[1] This is not exactly the Hebrew. The verb for rising, as well as that for falling, is in the past tense. The verse, literally rendered, is the following:—

> Rejoice not, my enemy, on my account;
> Though I have fallen, I have risen;
> Though I shall sit in darkness,
> Jehovah *will be* a light to me.

There are no copies which give a different reading as to the verb "I have risen." *Newcome* follows the Septuagint, and thinks that a conversive ו is left out. It ought rather perhaps to be considered as the language of faith, realizing the event before it arrived. The fall and "the darkness" refer no doubt to the outward calamities of the Church, its troubles and afflictions.—*Ed.*

on this subject I shall have to speak more copiously a little farther on. As to the latter clause, *When I sit in darkness, God will be my light*, it seems to be a confirmation of the preceding sentence, where the Prophet declares, that the fall of the Church would not be fatal. But yet some think that more is expressed, namely, that in the very darkness some spark of light would still shine. They then distinguish between this clause and the former one, which speaks of the fall and the rise of the faithful, in this manner,—that while they lie, as it were, sunk in darkness, they shall not even then be without consolation, for God's favour would ever shine on them. And this seems to be a correct view: for it cannot be that any one will expect the deliverance of which the Prophet speaks, except he sees some light even in the thickest darkness, and sustains himself by partaking, in some measure, of God's goodness: and a taste of God's favour in distresses is suitably compared to light; as when one is cast into a deep pit, by raising upward his eyes, he sees at a distance the light of the sun; so also the obscure and thick darkness of tribulations may not so far prevail as to shut out from us every spark of light, and to prevent faith from raising our eyes upwards, that we may have some taste of God's goodness. Let us proceed—

9. I will bear the indignation of the Lord, because I have sinned against him, until he plead my cause, and execute judgment for me: he will bring me forth to the light, *and* I shall behold his righteousness.

9. Iram Jehovæ feram, quia peccavi ei, donec disceptet causam, meam et faciat judicium meum (*vel*, asserat jus meum;) educet me in lucem, cernam justitiam ejus.

Here the Church of God animates and encourages herself to exercise patience, and does so especially by two arguments. She first sets before herself her sins, and thus humbles herself before God, whom she acknowledges to be a just Judge; and, in the second place, she embraces the hope of the forgiveness of her sins, and from this arises confidence as to her deliverance. By these two supports the Church sustains herself, that she fails not in her troubles, and gathers strength, as I have already said, to endure patiently.

First then he says, *The wrath*[1] *of Jehovah will I bear*, for *sinned have I against him.* This passage shows, that when any one is seriously touched with the conviction of God's judgment, he is at the same time prepared to exercise patience; for it cannot be, but that a sinner, conscious of evil, and knowing that he suffers justly, will humbly and thankfully submit to the will of God. Hence when men perversely clamour against God, or murmur, it is certain that they have not as yet been made sensible of their sins. I allow indeed that many feel guilty who yet struggle against God, and fiercely resist his hand as much as they can, and also blaspheme his name when he chastises them: but they are not touched hitherto with the true feeling of penitence, so as to abhor themselves. Judas owned indeed that he had sinned, and freely made such a confession, (Matth. xxvii. 3.) Cain tried to cover his sin, but the Lord drew from him an unwilling confession, (Gen. iv. 13.) They did not yet repent; nay, they ceased not to contend with God; for Cain complained that his punishment was too heavy to be borne; Judas despaired. And the same thing happens to all the reprobate. They seemed then to have been sufficiently convinced to acknowledge their guilt, and, as it were, to assent to the justice of God's judgment; but they did not really know their sins, so as to abhor themselves, as I have said, on account of their sins. For true penitence is ever connected with the submission of which the Prophet now speaks. Whosoever then is really conscious of his sins, renders himself at the same time obedient to God, and submits himself altogether to his will. Thus repentance does ever of itself lead to the bearing of the cross; so that he who sets himself before God's tribunal allows himself to be at the same time chastised, and bears punishment with a submissive mind: as the ox, that is tamed, always takes the yoke without any resistance, so also is he prepared who is really touched with the sense of his sins, to bear any punishment which God may be pleased to inflict on him. This then is the first thing which we ought

[1] *Iram*, זעף, which means a stormy anger or displeasure, which agitates and raises tempests, and such were the calamities which came on the Jewish nation.

to learn from these words of the Prophet, *The wrath of Jehovah will I bear, for sinned have I against him.*

We also learn from this passage, that all who do not patiently bear his scourges contend with God; for though they do not openly accuse God, and say that they are just, they do not yet ascribe to him his legitimate glory, by confessing that he is a righteous judge.—How so? Because these two things are united together and joined by an indissoluble knot—to be sensible of sin—and to submit patiently to the will of the Judge when he inflicts punishment.

Now follows the other argument, *Until he decides my cause, and vindicates my right; he will bring me forth into the light, I shall see his righteousness.* Here the Church leans on another support; for though the Lord should most heavily afflict her, she would not yet cast aside the hope of deliverance; for she knew, as we have already seen, that she was chastised for her good: and indeed no one could even for a moment continue patient in a state of misery, except he entertained the hope of being delivered, and promised to himself a happy escape. These two things then ought not to be separated, and cannot be,—the acknowledgment of our sins, which will humble us before God,—and the knowledge of his goodness, and a firm assurance as to our salvation; for God has testified that he will be ever propitious to us, how much soever he may punish us for our sins, and that he will remember mercy, as Habakkuk says, in the midst of his wrath, (Hab. iii. 2.) It would not then be sufficient for us to feel our evils, except the consolation, which proceeds from the promises of grace, be added.

The Prophet shows further, that the Church was innocent, with regard to its enemies, though justly suffering punishment. And this ought to be carefully observed; for whenever we have to do with the wicked, we think that there is no blame belonging to us. But these two things ought to be considered,—that the wicked trouble us without reason, and thus our cause as to them is just,—and yet that we are justly afflicted by God; for we shall ever find many reasons why the Lord should chastise us. These two things, then, ought to be both considered by us, as the Prophet seems to intimate here: for at the beginning of the verse he says,

"The wrath of God will I bear, for sinned have I against him;" and now he adds, "The Lord will yet vindicate my right," literally, "will debate my dispute," that is, plead my cause. Since the Church is guilty before God, nay, waits not for the sentence of the judge, but anticipates it, and freely confesses herself to be worthy of such punishment, what does this mean,—that the Lord will decide her quarrel, that he will undertake her cause? These two things seem to militate the one against the other: but they agree well together when viewed in their different bearings. The Church had confessed that she had sinned against God; she now turns her eyes to another quarter; for she knew that she was unjustly oppressed by enemies; she knew that they were led to do wrong by cruelty alone. This then is the reason why the Church entertained hope, and expected that God would become the defender of her innocence, that is, against the wicked: and yet she humbly acknowledged that she had sinned against God. Whenever, then, our enemies do us harm, let us lay hold on this truth,—that God will become our defender; for he is ever the patron of justice and equity: it cannot then be, that God will abandon us to the violence of the wicked. He will then at length *plead our pleading*, or undertake our cause, and be its advocate. But, in the meantime, let our sins be remembered by us, that, being truly humbled before God, we may not hope for the salvation which he promises to us, except through gratuitous pardon. Why then are the faithful bidden to be of good comfort in their afflictions? Because God has promised to be their Father; he has received them under his protection, he has testified that his help shall never be wanting to them. But whence is this confidence? Is it because they are worthy? Is it because they have deserved something of this kind? By no means: but they acknowledge themselves to be guilty, when they humbly prostrate themselves before God, and when they willingly condemn themselves before his tribunal, that they may anticipate his judgment. We now see how well the Prophet connects together these two things, which might otherwise seem contradictory.

Now follow the words, *He will bring me to the light, I shall see his righteousness.*[1] The Church still confirms herself in the hope of deliverance: and it is hence also manifest how God is light to the faithful in obscure darkness, because they see that there is prepared for them an escape from their evils; but they see it at a distance, for they extend their hope beyond the boundaries of this life. As then the truth of God diffuses itself through heaven and earth, so the faithful extend their hope far and wide. Thus it is, that they can see light afar off, which seems to be very remote from them. And having this confidence, the Prophet says, The Lord *will bring me into the light.* They have, in the meantime, as I have already said, some light; they enjoy a taste of God's goodness in the midst of their evils: but the Prophet now refers to that coming forth which we ought to look for even in the worst circumstances.

He then adds, *I shall see his righteousness.* By God's righteousness is to be understood, as it has been elsewhere stated, his favour towards the faithful; not that God returns for their works the salvation which he bestows, as ungodly men foolishly imagine; for they lay hold on the word righteousness, and think that whatever favours God freely grants us are due to our merits.—How so? For God in this way shows his own righteousness. But far different is the reason for this mode of speaking. God, in order to show how dear and precious to him is our salvation, does indeed say, that he designs to give an evidence of his justice in delivering us: but there is a reference in this word righteousness to something else; for God has promised that our salvation shall be the object of his care; hence he appears just whenever he delivers us from our troubles. Then the righteousness of God is not to be referred to the merits of works, but, on the contrary, to the promise by which he hath bound himself to us; and so also in the same sense God is often said to be faithful. In a word, the righteousness and faithfulness of God mean the same thing. When the Prophet says now in the person of the Church, *I shall see his righteousness,* he means, that though God concealed his favour for a

[1] "I shall see the equity of his proceedings concerning me, and the performance of his promises to me."—*Henry.*

time, and withdrew his hand, so that no hope of aid remained, it could not yet be, as he is just, but that he would succour us: *I shall see* then *his righteousness*, that is, God will at length really show that he is righteous. It now follows—

10. Then *she that is* mine enemy shall see *it*, and shame shall cover her which said unto me, Where is the Lord thy God? mine eyes shall behold her: now shall she be trodden down as the mire of the streets.	10. Et videbit inimica mea, et operiet eam pudor, quæ dixit mihi (*vel*, de me,) Ubi Jehova Deus tuus? oculi mei videbunt, et nunc erit in conculcationem sicuti lutum platearum.

But I cannot finish the subject now.

PRAYER.

Grant, Almighty God, that seeing we are at this day surrounded by so many miseries, yea, wherever we turn our eyes, innumerable evils meet us everywhere, which are so many evidences of thy displeasure,—O grant, that we being truly humbled before thee, may be enabled at the same time to raise up our eyes to the promises of thy free goodness and paternal favour, which thou hast made to us in thine own Son, that we may not doubt, but that thou wilt be propitious to us, inasmuch as thou hast adopted us as thy people: and while our enemies, fully armed, rage and ferociously rise even daily against us, may we not doubt, but that thou wilt be our protection, as thou knowest that we are unjustly troubled by them; and may we thus go on, trusting in thy goodness, seeing that we ever groan under the burden of our sins, and daily confess that we are worthy of thousand deaths before thee, wert not thou pleased in thine infinite mercy always to receive and restore us to favour, through thy Son our Lord. Amen.

Lecture Ninety-seventh.

In the last lecture I repeated the tenth verse of the last chapter, in which the Prophet adds, as a cause of the greatest joy, that the enemies of the Church shall see granted, to their great mortification, the wonderful favour of which the Prophet had been speaking. But he describes these enemies under the character of an envious woman, as the Church of

God is also compared to a woman: and this mode of speaking is common in Scripture. He then calls Jerusalem his rival, or Babylon, or some city of his enemies.

And he says, *Covered shall she be with shame.* We know that the ungodly grow insolent when fortune smiles on them: hence in prosperity they keep within no bounds, for they think that God is under their feet. If prosperity most commonly has the effect of making the godly to forget God and even themselves, it is no wonder that the unbelieving become more and more hardened, when God is indulgent to them. With regard then to such a pride, the Prophet now says, *When my enemy shall see, shame shall cover her;* that is, she will not continue in her usual manner, to elate herself with her own boastings: nay, she will be compelled for shame to hide herself; for she will see that she had been greatly deceived, in thinking that I should be wholly ruined.

He afterwards adds, *Who said to me, Where is Jehovah thy God?* The Church of God in her turn triumphs here over the unbelieving, having been delivered by divine power; nor does she do this for her own sake, but because the ungodly expose the holy name of God to reproach, which is very common: for whenever God afflicts his people, the unbelieving immediately raise their crests, and pour forth their blasphemies against God, when yet they ought, on the contrary, to humble themselves under his hand. But since God executes his judgments on the faithful, what can be expected by his ungodly despisers? If God's vengeance be manifested in a dreadful manner with regard to the green tree, what will become of the dry wood? And the ungodly are like the dry wood. But as they are blind as to God's judgments, they petulantly deride his name, whenever they see the Church afflicted, as though adversities were not the evidences of God's displeasure: for he chastises his own children, to show that he is the judge of the world. But, as I have already said, the ungodly so harden themselves in their stupor, that they are wholly thoughtless. The faithful, therefore, after having found God to be their deliverer, do here undertake his cause; they do not regard themselves nor their own character, but defend the righteousness of God. Such is this triumphant language, *Who said, Where is now Jehovah thy God?* "I can really show that I worship the true

God, who deserts not his people in extreme necessity: after he has assisted me, my enemy, who dared to rise up against God, now seeks hiding-places."

She shall now, he says, *be trodden under foot as the mire of the streets; and my eyes shall see her.* What the Prophet declares in the name of the Church, that the unbelieving shall be like mire, is connected with the promise, which we already noticed; for God so appears as the deliverer of his Church, as not to leave its enemies unpunished. God then, while he aids his own people, leads the ungodly to punishment. Hence the Church, while embracing the deliverance offered to her, at the same time sees the near ruin, which impends on all the despisers of God. But what is stated, *See shall my eyes,* ought not to be so taken, as though the faithful exult with carnal joy, when they see the ungodly suffering the punishment which they have deserved; for the word *to see* is to be taken metaphorically, as signifying a pleasant and joyful sight, according to what it means in many other places; and as it is a phrase which often occurs, its meaning must be well known. *See* then *shall my eyes,* that is, "I shall enjoy to look on that calamity, which now impends over all the ungodly." But, as I have already said, carnal joy is not what is here intended, which intemperately exults, but that pure joy which the faithful experience on seeing the grace of God displayed and also his judgment. But this joy cannot enter into our hearts, until they be cleansed from unruly passions; for we are ever excessive in fear and sorrow, as well as in hope and joy, except the Lord holds us in, as it were, with a bridle. We shall therefore be only then capable of this spiritual joy, of which the Prophet speaks, when we shall put off all disordered feelings, and God shall subdue us by his Spirit: then only shall we be able to retain moderation in our joy. The Prophet proceeds—

11. *In* the day that thy walls are to be built, *in* that day shall the decree be far removed.	11. Dies ad ædificandum parietes tuos; dies iste procul abiget edictum.
12. *In* that day *also* he shall come even to thee from Assyria, and *from* the fortified cities, and from the fortress even to the river, and from sea to sea, and *from* mountain to mountain.	12. Die isto etiam ad te veniet ab Assur, et urbibus munitionis, et à munitione etiam ad fluvium, et ad mare â mari, et à monte ad montem.

Micah pursues the subject on which he had previously spoken,—that though the Church thought itself for a time to be wholly lost, yet God would become its deliverer. He says first, that *the day was near, in which they were to build the wall.* The word גדר, *gidar,* means either a mound or a wall; so it ought to be distinguished from a wall, that is, a strong fortress. He then intimates that the time would come, when God would gather his Church, and preserve it, as though it were defended on every side by walls. For we know that the scattering of the Church is compared to the pulling down of walls or fences: as when a person pulls down the fence of a field or a vineyard, or breaks down all inclosures; so when the Church is exposed as a prey to all, she is said to be like an open field or a vineyard, which is without any fence. Now, on the other hand, the Prophet says here, that the time would come, when the faithful shall again build walls, by which they may be protected from the assaults and plunder of enemies, *A day* then *to build thy walls.*

Then he adds, *This day shall drive afar off the edict;* some render it tribute; but the word properly means an edict, and this best suits the passage; for the Prophet's meaning is, that the people would not, as before, be subject to the tyranny of Babylon. For after the subversion of Jerusalem, the Babylonians, no doubt, triumphed very unfeelingly over the miserable people, and uttered dreadful threatenings. The Prophet, therefore, under the name of edict, includes that cruel and tyrannical dominion which the Babylonians for a time exercised. We know what God denounces on the Jews by Ezekiel, 'Ye would not keep my good laws; I will therefore give you laws which are not good, which ye shall be constrained to keep; and yet ye shall not live in them,' (Ezek. xx. 25.) Those laws which were not good were the edicts of which the Prophet now speaks. *That day* then *shall drive far away the edict,* that the Jews might not dread the laws of their enemies. For the Babylonians no doubt forbad, under the severest punishment, any one from building even a single house in the place where Jerusalem formerly was; for they wished that place to remain desolate, that the people might know that they had no hope of restoration.

That day then *shall put afar off,* or drive to a distance, *the edict;* for liberty shall be given to the Jews to build their city; and then they shall not tremblingly expect every hour, until new edicts come forth, denouncing grievous punishments on whomsoever that would dare to encourage his brethren to build the temple of God.

Some draw the Prophet's words to another meaning: they first think that he speaks only of the spiritual kingdom of Christ, and then they take רחק, *rechek,* in the sense of extending or propagating, and consider this to be the Gospel which Christ, by the command of the Father, promulgated through the whole world. It is indeed true that David uses the word decree in Ps. ii., while speaking of the preaching of the Gospel; and it is also true, that the promulgation of that decree is promised in Ps. cx., 'The rod of his power will Jehovah send forth from Zion.' But this passage ought not to be thus violently perverted; for the Prophet no doubt means, that the Jews would be freed from all dread of tyranny when God restored them to liberty; and רחק, *rechek,* does not mean to extend or propagate, but to drive far away. *That day* then *shall drive away the decree,* so that the faithful shall be no more subject to tyrannical commands. We now perceive the true meaning of the Prophet.

The faithful doubtless prayed in their adversities, and depended on such prophecies as we find in Ps. cii., 'The day is now come to show mercy to Zion, and to build its walls; for thy servants pity her stones.' Nor did the faithful pray thus presumptuously, but taking confidence, as though God had dictated a form of prayer by his own mouth, they dealt with God according to his promise, "O Lord, thou hast promised the rebuilding of the city, and the time has been prefixed by Jeremiah and by other Prophets: since then the time is now completed, grant that the temple and the holy city may again be built."

Some render the words, "In the day in which thou shalt build (or God shall build) thy walls—in that day shall be removed afar off the decree." But I doubt not but that the Prophet promises here distinctly to the faithful both the restoration of the city and a civil freedom; for the sentence is in two parts: the Prophet intimates first, that the time was now near when the faithful would build their own walls, that they might not be exposed to the will of their enemies,—and then he adds, that they would be freed from the dread of tyranny; for God, as it is said by Isaiah, would break the yoke of the burden, and the sceptre of the oppressor, (Isa. ix. 4;) and it is altogether the same kind of sentence.

He afterwards adds, *In that day also to thee shall* they *come from Asshur*. There is some obscurity in the words; hence interpreters have regarded different words as being understood: but to me the meaning of the Prophet appears not doubtful. *In that day*, he says, *to thee shall* they *come from Asshur, and cities of the fortress, and from the fortress even to the river, and from sea to sea, and from mountain to mountain*; but some think הר, *er*, to be a proper name, and render the last clause, "And from mount Hor:" and we know that Aaron was buried on this mount. But the Prophet, no doubt, alludes here to some other place; and to render it mount Hor is a strained version. I doubt not, therefore, but that the Prophet repeats a common name, as though he said, "From mountains to mountains."

Let us now see what the Prophet means. With regard to the passage, as I have said, there is no ambiguity, provided we bear in mind the main subject. Now the Prophet had this in view,—That Jerusalem, when restored by God, would be in such honour among all nations, that there would be flowing to her from all parts. He then says, that the state of the city would be very splendid, so that people from all quarters would come to it: and therefore the copulative ו, *vau*, is to be taken twice for *even* for the sake of emphasis, *In that day, even to thee*, and then, *even to the river*; for it was not believed that Jerusalem would have any dignity, after it had been entirely destroyed, together with the temple. It is no wonder then that the Prophet so distinctly confirms here what was by no means probable, at least according to the common sentiments of men,—that Jerusalem would attract to itself all nations, even those far away. *Come*, then, *shall they*, (for the verb יבוא, *ibua*, in the singular number must be taken indefinitely as having a plural meaning,) *Come*, then, *shall they from Asshur even to thee.* But the Assyrians had previously destroyed every land, overturned the kingdom of Israel, and almost blotted out its name; and they had also laid waste the kingdom of Judah; a small portion only remained. They came afterwards, we know, with the Chaldeans, after the seat of empire was translated to Babylon, and destroyed Nineveh. Therefore, by naming the Assyrians, he no doubt, taking a part for the whole, included the Babylonians. *Come*, then, *shall they from Asshur*, and then, *from the cities of the fortress*, that is, from every fortress. For they who take צור, *tsur*, for Tyre are mistaken; for מצור, *metsur*,[1] is mentioned twice, and it means citadels and strongholds. And then, *even to the river*, that is, to utmost borders of Euphrates; for many take Euphrates, by way of excellence, to be meant by the word river; as it is often the case in Scripture; though it might be not less fitly interpreted of any or every river, as though the Prophet had said, that there would be no obstacle to stop their course who would hasten to Jerusalem. *Even to the river* then, *and from sea to sea*, that is, they shall come in troops from remote countries, being led by the celebrity of the holy city; for when it shall be rebuilt by God's command, it shall acquire new and unusual honour, so that all people from every part shall assemble there. And then, *from mountain to mountain*, that is, from regions far asunder. This is the sum of the whole.

[1] It is somewhat singular that *Newcome* renders the first "fenced" and the second "Egypt:" but Henderson renders both "Egypt." It is not the common name for Egypt, which is מצרים; the places referred to, 2 Kings xix. 24, and Isa. xix. 6, do not justify this application. The word "day" in three instances is here without a preposition: it may therefore be regarded as the nominative absolute, or the verb, is nigh, or approaches, as Jerome proposes, is understood. I would give this version of the two verses,—

11. The day for building thy walls!
That day! removed far shall be the decree:
12. That day! even to thee shall they come,
From Assyria and cities of fortress,
And from the fortress even to the river,
And *from* sea to sea, and *from* mountain to mountain,
or, *word for word*,
And from the fortress even to the river and the sea,
From the sea and the mountain of the mountain.

The last expression seems to mean, "every mountain."—*Ed.*

The Prophet then promises what all men deemed as fabulous,—that the dignity of the city Jerusalem should be so great after the return of the Jews from exile, that it would become, as it were, the metropolis of the world. One thing must be added: They who confine this passage to Christ seem not indeed to be without a plausible reason; for there follows immediately a threatening as to the desolation of the land; and there seems to be some inconsistency, except we consider the Prophet here as comparing the Church collected from all nations with the ancient people. But these things will harmonize well together, if we consider, that the Prophet denounces vengeance on the unbelieving who then lived, and that he yet declares that God will be merciful to his chosen people. But the restriction which they maintain is too rigid; for we know that it was usual with the Prophets to extend the favour of God from the return of the ancient people to the coming of Christ. Whenever, then, the Prophets make known God's favour in the deliverance of his people, they make a transition to Christ, but included also the whole intermediate time. And this mode the Prophet now pursues, and it ought to be borne in mind by us. Let us go on—

13. Notwithstanding the land shall be desolate because of them that dwell therein, for the fruit of their doings.	13. Et erit terra in desolationem propter incolas suos, à fructu operorum ipsorum.

The Prophet, as I have already said, seems to be inconsistent with himself: for after having spoken of the restoration of the land, he now abruptly says, that it would be deserted, because God had been extremely provoked by the wickedness of the people. But, as I have stated before, it was almost an ordinary practice with the Prophets, to denounce at one time God's vengeance on all the Jews, and then immediately to turn to the faithful, who were small in number, and to raise up their minds with the hope of deliverance. We indeed know that the Prophets had to do with the profane despisers of God; it was therefore necessary for them to fulminate, when they addressed the whole body of the people: the contagion had pervaded all orders, so that they were all become apostates, from the highest to the lowest, with very few exceptions, and those hidden amidst the great mass, like a few grains in a vast heap of chaff. Then the Prophets did not without reason mingle consolations with threatenings; and their threatenings they addressed to the whole body of the people; and then they whispered, as it were, in the ear, some consolation to the elect of God, the few remnants,—"Yet the Lord will show mercy to you; though he has resolved to destroy his people, ye shall yet remain safe, but this will be through some hidden means." Our Prophet then does, on the one hand, as here, denounce God's vengeance on a people past remedy; and, on the other, he speaks of the redemption of the Church, that by this support the faithful might be sustained in their adversities.

He now says, *The land shall be for desolation.*[1] But why does he speak in so abrupt a manner? That he might drive hypocrites from that false confidence, with which they were swollen, though God addressed not a word to them: but when God pronounced any thing, as they covered themselves with the name of Church, they then especially laid hold of any thing that was said to the faithful, as though it belonged to them: "Has not God promised that he will be the deliverer of his people?" as though indeed he was to be their deliverer, who had alienated themselves by their perfidy from him; and yet this was a very common thing among them. Hence the Prophet, seeing that hypocrites would greedily lay hold on what he had said, and by taking this handle would become more audacious, says now, *The land shall be for desolation,* that is, "Be ye gone; for when God testifies that he will be the deliverer of his Church, he does not address you; for ye are the rotten members; and the *land shall be reduced to a waste* before God's favour, of which I now speak, shall appear." We now then perceive the reason for this passage, why the Prophet so suddenly joined threatenings to promises: it was, to terrify hypocrites.

[1] The copulative ו, rendered *et, and,* in the text, is not noticed here. *Newcome* renders it *For,* connecting this with the former verse, and applying it to heathen lands. But *Dathius* and *Henderson* render it, as an adversative, *But, Nevertheless,* and consider, with Calvin, that the land of Israel is here meant.—*Ed.*

He says, *On account of its inhabitants, from the fruit*, or, on account of the fruit *of their works*. Here the Prophet closes the door against the despisers of God, lest they should break forth, according to their custom, and maintain that God was, as it were, bound to them: "See," he says, "what ye are; for ye have polluted the land with your vices; it must therefore be reduced to desolation." And when the land, which is in itself innocent, is visited with judgment, what will become of those despisers whose wickedness it sustains? We hence see how emphatical was this mode of speaking. For the Prophet summons here all the unbelieving to examine their life, and then he sets before them the land, which was to suffer punishment, though it had committed no sin; and why was it to suffer? because it was polluted, as I have said, by their wickedness. Since this was the case, we see, that hypocrites were very justly driven away from the false confidence with which they were inflated, while they yet proudly despised God and his Word. It now follows—

14. Feed thy people with thy rod, the flock of thine heritage, which dwell solitarily *in* the wood, in the midst of Carmel: let them feed *in* Bashan and Gilead, as in the days of old.

14. Pasce populum tuum in virga tua (*vel*, pædo tuo) gregem hæreditatis tuæ, habitantes in solitudine (*vel*, seorsum) in sylva, in medio Carmeli; pascentur in Basan et Gilead, secundum dies antiquos.

Here the Prophet turns to supplications and prayers; by which he manifests more vehemence, than if he had repeated again what he had previously said of the restoration of the Church; for he shows how dreadful that judgment would be, when God would reduce the land into solitude. This prayer no doubt contains what was at the same time prophetic. The Prophet does not indeed simply promise deliverance to the faithful, but at the same time he doubly increases that terror, by which he designed to frighten hypocrites; as though he said, "Most surely, except God will miraculously preserve his own people, it is all over with the Church: there is then no remedy, except through the ineffable power of God." In short, the Prophet shows, that he trembled at that vengeance, which he had previously foretold, and which he did foretell, lest hypocrites, in their usual manner, should deride him. We now see why the Prophet had recourse to this kind of comfort, why he so regulates his discourse as not to afford immediate hope to the faithful, but addresses God himself. *Feed* then *thy people;* as though he said,—"Surely that calamity will be fatal, except thou, Lord, wilt be mindful of thy covenant, and gather again some remnant from the people whom thou hast been pleased to choose: *Feed thy people.*"

The reason why he called them the people of God was, because they must all have perished, unless it had been, that it was necessary that what God promised to Abraham should be fulfilled,—'In thy seed shall all nations be blessed,' (Gen. xii. 3.) It was then the adoption of God alone which prevented the total destruction of the Jews. Hence he says emphatically,—"O Lord, these are yet thy people;" as though he said,—"By whom wilt thou now form a Church for thyself?" God might indeed have collected it from the Gentiles, and have made aliens his family; but it was necessary that the root of adoption should remain in the race of Abraham, until Christ came forth. Nor was there then any dispute about God's power, as there is now among fanatics, who ask, Can God do this? But there was reliance on the promise, and from this they learnt with certainty what God had once decreed, and what he would do. Since then this promise, 'By thy seed shall all nations be blessed,' was sacred and inviolable, the grace of God must have ever continued in the remnant. It is indeed certain, that hypocrites, as it has been already stated, without any discrimination, abused the promises of God; but this truth must be ever borne in mind, that God punished the ungodly, though relying on their great number, they thought that they would be always preserved. God then destroyed *them,* as they deserved; and yet it was his purpose, that some remnant should be among that people. But it must be observed, that this destruction ought not to be extended to all the children of Abraham, who derived their origin from him according to the flesh, but to be applied to the faithful, that is, to the remnant, who were preserved according to the gratuitous adoption of God.

Feed then thy people *by thy crook.*[1] He compares God to a shepherd, and this metaphor often occurs. Though שבט, *shebeth,* indeed signifies a sceptre when kings are mentioned, it is yet taken also for a pastoral staff, as in Ps. xxiii. and in many other places. As then he represents God here as a Shepherd, so he assigns a crook to him; as though he said, "O Lord, thou performest the office of a Shepherd in ruling this people." How so? He immediately confirms what I have lately said, that there was no hope of a remedy except through the mercy of God, by adding, *the flock*[2] *of thine heritage;* for by calling them the flock of his heritage, he does not consider what the people deserved, but fixes his eyes on their gratuitous adoption. Since, then, it had pleased God to choose that people, the Prophet on this account dares to go forth to God's presence, and to plead their gratuitous election,—"O Lord, I will not bring before thee the nobility of our race, or any sort of dignity, or our piety, or any merits." What then? "We are thy people, for thou hast declared that we are a royal priesthood. We are then thine heritage." How so? "Because it has been thy pleasure to have one peculiar people sacred to thee." We now more clearly see that the Prophet relied on God's favour alone, and opposed the recollection of the covenant to the trials which might have otherwise made every hope to fail.

He afterwards adds, *Who dwell apart,* or alone. He no doubt refers here to the dispersion of the people, when he says, that they dwelt alone. For though the Jews had been scattered in countries delightful, fertile and populous, yet they were everywhere as in a desert and in solitude, for they were a mutilated body. The whole of Chaldea and of Assyria was then really a desert to the faithful; for there they dwelt

1 "The crook signifies God's peculiar care for his people."—*Grotius.*

2 "He compares the elect people," says *Marckius,* "to a flock of sheep, because they resemble them in weakness, in innocency, in meekness, in usefulness, in fruitfulness, and in close union. See Ps. xcv. 7; Isa. xl. 11; Ezek. xxxiv. 12; Zech. ix. 16, x. 3; John x. 16, &c." "They are thy sheep, thy peculiar property, who hear thee, who need thy guidance and feeding, for they are weak and helpless, and liable to go astray without the preserving care of their Shepherd."—*Cocceius.*

not as one people, but as members torn asunder. This is the dispersion intended by the words of the Prophet. He also adds, that dwell *in the forest.* For they had no secure habitation except in their own country; for they lived there under the protection of God; and all other countries, as I have already said, were to them like the desert.

He adds, *In the midst of Carmel.* The preposition כ, *caph,* is to be understood here, *As in the midst of Carmel, they shall be fed in Bashan and Gilead, as in ancient days;*[1] that is, though they are now thy solitary sheep, yet thou wilt gather them again that they may feed as on Carmel, (which we know was very fruitful,) and then, *as in Bashan and Gilead.* We know that there are in those places the richest pastures. Since then the Prophet compares the faithful to sheep, he mentions Bashan, he mentions Carmel and Gilead; as though he said, "Restore, O Lord, thy people, that they may dwell in the heritage once granted them by thee." Why he says that they were solitary, I have already explained; and there is a similar passage in Psalm cii. 17; though there is there a different word, ערער, *oror;* but the meaning is the same. The faithful are there said to be solitary, because they were not collected into one body; for this was the true happiness of the people,—that they worshipped God together, that they were under one head, and also that they had one altar as a sacred bond to cherish unity of faith. When therefore the faithful were scattered here and there, they were justly said to be solitary, wherever they were.

[1] These two lines are better arranged by *Newcome*, and the necessity of a preposition understood is obviated, while the original is more strictly rendered,—

In the midst of Carmel let them feed,
In Bashan and Gilead, as in the days of old.

It is also better to render "feed" as a prayer than in the future tense, to correspond in tenor with the beginning of the verse. *Henderson* connects "Carmel" with the former line, and thinks that "dwelling alone in the wood" refers to the condition of the Jews when restored, and quotes the prophecy of Balaam in Num. xxiii. 9. But this seems to be a far-fetched exposition; and the word "wood," which means generally a dreary place, renders it wholly inadmissible. A state of destitution and misery is evidently intended. "They were now," says *Henry*, "a desolate people; they were in the land of their captivity as sheep in a forest, in danger of being lost and made a prey of to the beasts of the forest."—*Ed.*

He afterwards adds, *according to ancient days.* Here he places before God the favours which he formerly showed to his people, and prays that he would, like himself, go on to the end, that is, that he would continue to the end his favours to his chosen people. And it availed not a little to confirm their faith, when the faithful called to mind how liberally had God dealt from the beginning with the posterity of Abraham: they were thus made to feel assured, that God would be no less kind to his elect, though there might be, so to speak, a sad separation: for when God had banished the Jews into exile, it was a kind of divorce, as though they were given to utter destruction. Yet now when they recollect that they had descended from the holy fathers, and that a Redeemer had been promised them, they justly entertain a hope of favour in future from the past benefits of God, because he had formerly kindly treated his people.

PRAYER.

Grant, Almighty God, that since we have so provoked thy displeasure by our sins, that a dreadful waste and solitude appear everywhere,—O grant, that a proof of that favour, which thou hast so remarkably exhibited towards thy ancient people, may shine upon us, so that thy Church may be raised up, in which true religion may flourish, and thy name be glorified: and may we daily solicit thee in our prayers, and never doubt, but that under the government of thy Christ, thou canst again gather together the whole world, though it be miserably dispersed, so that we may persevere in this warfare to the end, until we shall at length know that we have not in vain hoped in thee, and that our prayers have not been in vain, when Christ shall exercise the power given to him for our salvation and for that of the whole world. Amen.

Lecture Ninety-eighth.

15. According to the days of thy coming out of the land of Egypt will I shew unto him marvellous *things*.	15. Secundum dies egressus tui è terra Ægypti, ostendam ei mirabilia.

The Prophet here introduces God as the speaker; and he so speaks as to give an answer to his prayer. God then promises that he will be wonderful in his works, and give such evidences of his power, as he exhibited when he brought up his people from the land of Egypt. We now see that there is more force in this passage, than if the Prophet had at first said, that God would become the deliverer of his people: for he interposed entreaty and prayer; and God now shows that he will be merciful to his people; and at the same time the faithful are reminded, that they must be instant in prayer, if they desire to be preserved by God.

Now God says, that *he will show wonderful things*, as when the people formerly came out of Egypt.[1] That redemption, we know, was a perpetual monument of God's power in the preservation of his Church; so that whenever he designs to give some hope of deliverance, he reminds the faithful of those miracles, that they may feel assured that there will be no obstacles to prevent them from continuing in a state of safety, provided God will be pleased to help them, for his power is not diminished.

And this deserves to be noticed; for though we all allow the omnipotence of God, yet when we struggle with trials, we tremble, as though all the avenues to our preservation had been closed up against God. As soon then as any impediment is thrown in our way, we think that there is no hope. Whence is this? It is because we make no account of God's power, which yet we confess to be greater than that of the whole world.

This is the reason why God now refers to the miracles which he wrought at the coming forth of the people. They ought to have known, that God ever continues like himself, and that his power remains as perfect as it was formerly; and there is in him sufficient support to encourage the hope of assistance. We now perceive the object of the Prophet. He indeed changes the persons; for in the beginning he

[1] "The Prophet prayed that God would feed them, and do kind things for them; but God answers, that he will show them marvellous things, will outdo their hopes and expectations.—Their deliverance from Babylon shall be a work of wonder and grace, not inferior to their deliverance out of Egypt, nay, it shall eclipse the lustre of that, Jer. xvi. 14, 15.—God's former favours to his Church are patterns of future favours, and shall again be copied out as there is occasion."—*Henry*.

addresses the people, *according to the days of thy going forth*, and then he adds, ארְאֶנּוּ, *aranu*, 'I will make him to see;' but this change does not obscure the meaning, for God only means, that his power was sufficiently known formerly to his people, and that there was a memorable proof of it in their redemption, so that the people could not have doubted respecting their safety, without being ungrateful to God, and without burying in oblivion that so memorable a benefit, which God once conferred on their fathers. It follows—

16. The nations shall see and be confounded at all their might: they shall lay *their* hand upon *their* mouth, their ears shall be deaf.	16. Videbunt gentes et pudefient ab omni fortitudine sua; ponent manum super os, aures eorum surdescent:
17. They shall lick the dust like a serpent, they shall move out of their holes like worms of the earth: they shall be afraid of the Lord our God, and shall fear because of thee.	17. Lingent pulverem quasi serpens, quasi reptilia terræ frement (*vel*, movebunt) à latibulis suis; ad Jehovam Deum nostrum pavebunt, et metuent sibi abs te.

Here again the Prophet shows, that though the Church should be assailed on every side and surrounded by innumerable enemies, no doubt ought yet to be entertained respecting the promised aid of God; for it is in his power to make all nations ashamed, that is, to cast down all the pride of the world, so as to make the unbelieving to acknowledge at length that they were elated by an empty confidence. Hence he says, that the *nations shall see;* as though he said, "I know what makes you anxious, for many enemies are intent on your ruin; and when any help appears, they are immediately prepared fiercely to resist; but their attempts and efforts will not prevent God from delivering you."

They shall then *see and be ashamed of all their strength.*[1] By these words the Prophet means, that however strongly armed the unbelieving may think themselves to be to destroy the Church, and that how many obstacles soever they may have in their power to restrain the power of God in its behalf, yet

[1] "They shall be ashamed of the strength in which they trusted,"—*Drusius;* or, as *Grotius* says, "of all their strength which had been so suddenly destroyed;" or, as another author says, "of all their strength when found ineffectual for the purpose of destroying the people of God."—*Ed.*

the whole will be in vain, for God will, in fact, prove that the strength of men is mere nothing.

He adds, *They shall lay their hand on their mouth;* that is, they shall not dare to boast hereafter, as they have hitherto done; for this phrase in Hebrew means to be silent. Since then the enemies of the Church made great boastings and exulted with open mouth, as though the people of God were destroyed, the Prophet says, that when God would appear as the Redeemer of his people, they should become, as it were, mute. He subjoins, *their ears shall become deaf;*[1] that is, they shall stand astounded; nay, they shall hardly dare to open their ears, lest the rumour, brought to them, should occasion to them new trembling. Proud men, we know, when matters succeed according to their wishes, not only boast of their good fortune with open mouths, but also greedily catch at all rumours; for as they think they are all so many messages of victories,—"What is from this place? or what is from that place?" They even expect that the whole world will come under their power. The Prophet, on the other hand, says, *They shall lay the hand on the mouth, and their ears shall become deaf;* that is, they shall tremblingly shun all rumours, for they shall continually dread new calamities, when they shall see that the God of Israel, against whom they have hitherto fought, is armed with so much power.

Some apply this to the preaching of the Gospel; which I readily allow, provided the deliverance be made always to begin with the ancient people: for if any one would have this to be understood exclusively of Christ, such a strained and remote exposition would not be suitable. But if any one will consider the favour of God, as continued from the return of the people to the restoration effected by Christ, he will rightly comprehend the real design of the Prophet. Really fulfilled, then, is what the Prophet says here, when God spreads the doctrine of his Gospel through the whole world: for those who before boasted of their own inventions, begin then to close their mouth, that, being thus silent, they may become his disciples; and they also close their ears, for now

[1] "Malice," says *Jerome*, "not only blinds the eyes, but also deafens the ears."—*Ed.*

they give not up themselves, as before, to foolish and puerile fables, but consecrate their whole hearing to the only true God, that they may attend only to his truth, and no more vacillate between contrary opinions. All this, I allow, is fulfilled under the preaching of the Gospel; but the Prophet, no doubt, connected together the whole time, from the return of the people from the Babylonian exile, to the manifestation of Christ.

He afterwards adds, *They shall lick the dust as a serpent.* He intimates, that however the enemies of the Church may have proudly exalted themselves before, they shall then be cast down, and lie, as it were, on the ground; for to lick the dust is nothing else but to lie prostrate on the earth. They shall then be low and creeping like serpents; and then, *They shall move themselves as worms and reptiles of the ground.* The verb רגז, *regez,* as it has been stated elsewhere, means to raise an uproar, to tumultuate, and it means also to move one's self; and this latter meaning is the most suitable here, namely, that they shall go forth or move themselves from their inclosures; for the wcrd סגר, *sager,* signifies to close up: and by *inclosures* he means hiding-places, though in the song of David, in Psalm xviii., the word is applied to citadels and other fortified places,—'Men,' he says, 'trembled from their fortresses;' though they occupied well-fortified citadels, they yet were afraid, because the very fame of David had broken down their boldness. But as the Prophet speaks here of worms, I prefer this rendering,—'from their lurking-places;' as though he said, "Though they have hitherto thought themselves safe in their inclosures, they shall yet move and flee away like worms and reptiles; for when the ground is dug, the worms immediately leap out, for they think that they are going to be taken; so also, when any one moves the ground, the reptiles come forth, and tremblingly run away in all directions." And the Prophet says that, in like manner, the enemies of the Church, when the Lord shall arise for its help, shall be smitten with so much fear, that they shall in every direction run away. And this comparison ought to be carefully noticed, that is, when the Prophet compares powerful nations, well exercised in wars, who before were audaciously raging, and were swollen with great pride—when he compares them to worms and reptiles of the ground, and also to serpents: he did this to show, that there will be nothing to hinder God from laying prostrate every exalted thing in the world, as soon as it shall please him to aid his Church.

And hence the Prophet adds, *On account of Jehovah our God they shall dread, and they shall fear because of thee.* Here the Prophet shows, that the faithful ought not to distrust on account of their own weakness, but, on the contrary, to remember the infinite power of God. It is indeed right that the children of God should begin with diffidence,—sensible that they are nothing, and that all their strength is nothing; but they ought not to stop at their own weakness, but, on the contrary, to rise up to the contemplation of God's power, that they may not doubt but that, when his power shall appear, their enemies shall be soon scattered. This is the reason why the Prophet here mentions the name of God, and then turns to address God himself. *Tremble* then *shall they at Jehovah our God*, that is, on account of Jehovah our God; and then, *Fear shall they because of thee.*[1] It now follows—

18. Who *is* a God like unto thee, that pardoneth iniquity, and passeth by the transgression of the remnant of his heritage? he retaineth not

18. Quis Deus sicut tu, tollens iniquitatem, et transiens super scelus, erga reliquias hæreditatis suæ? Non retinebit in perpetuum iram suam (*aliivertunt*, non roboravit; *nam* חזק *hoc interdum significat;*

[1] *Dathius* renders these two lines differently, "Jovam Deum nostrum timebunt eumque reverebuntur—Jehovah our God they shall fear, and him will they reverence." But this is neither consistent with the passage, nor with the form in which the words appear. פחד is not commonly, if ever, a transitive verb, and to dread, or to be afraid, and not to fear, is its usual meaning: and ירא, when it means the fear of reverence, is generally construed without a preposition, and with את before Jehovah. The literal rendering is no doubt that which is given by Calvin. The distich is capable of being rendered in *Welsh* exactly as in Hebrew, in the same form and with the same prepositions; and, when thus rendered, the meaning is what is given here,—

Oherwydd Jehova ein Duw yr arswydant,—
Ac ovnant rhagddot.

To fear because of thee, and to fear thee, are two distinct things. You will have the first form in Josh. x. 8; xi. 6; and the second in Deut. xxxi. 12. The first refers to the fear of the Canaanites, the dread of their power; the second, to the fear of Jehovah.—*Ed.*

his anger for ever, because he delighteth *in* mercy.

sed potius hic vertendum est, non reticebit;) quia placet ei clementia (*vel,* diligit misericordiam.[1])

The Prophet here exclaims that God ought to be glorified especially for this—that he is merciful to his people. When he says, *Who is God as thou art?* he does not mean that there are other gods; for this, strictly speaking, is an improper comparison. But he shows that the true and only God may be distinguished from all idols by this circumstance—that he graciously forgives the sins of his people and bears with their infirmities. It is indeed certain, that all nations entertained the opinion, that their gods were ready to pardon; hence their sacrifices, and hence also their various kinds of expiations. Nor has there been any nation so barbarous as not to own themselves guilty in some measure before God; hence all the Gentiles were wont to apply to the mercy of their gods; while yet they had no firm conviction: for though they laid hold on this first principle,—that the gods would be propitious to sinners, if they humbly sought pardon; yet they prayed, we know, with no sure confidence, for they had

[1] *Cocceius* calls this verse the *doxology* of the Church. *Jerome* renders the first words,—*Quis Deus similis tui?* which is literally the original, מי־אל כמוך—What God like thee? that is, Jehovah, mentioned in the preceding verse. Τις Θεος ωσπερ συ; *Sept.* Thinking that the verse will admit of somewhat different arrangement, and of a more literal rendering, I give the following,—

What God *is* like thee?
Taking away iniquity, and passing over transgression!—
Against the remnant of his heritage,
He retaineth not for ever his anger,
For a lover of mercy *is* He.

There is a transition after the second line from the second to the third person; hence I make here the division. Besides, the construction of the third with the second has ever been found awkward by all critics; but its construction with the fourth verse is perfectly natural. נשא, "taking away," or removing, conveys the idea of a burden being lifted up and removed. "Passing over" seems to allude to the angel passing over the houses of the Israelites in Egypt. "Iniquity," עון, is guilt and inward depravity; and "Transgression," פשע, is an overt act of sin, an outward violation of the law. "A lover," חפץ; the Septuagint renders it, θελητης ελεους—the wisher of mercy; which is too weak, for the word means delight. It may be rendered, "For one who delights in mercy *is* He." The *Targum* reads, *Amat enim benefacere*—for he loves to do good. —*Ed.*

no certain promise. We hence see that what the Prophet means is this,—that the God of Israel could be proved to be the true God from this circumstance—that having once received into favour the children of Abraham, he continued to show the same favour, and kept his covenant inviolably, though their sins had been a thousand times a hinderance in the way. That God then in his goodness surmounted all the wickedness of the people, and stood firm in his covenant, which had been so often violated by vices of the people—this fact may be brought as an evidence, that he is the true God: for what can be found of this kind among idols? Let us suppose that there is in them something divine, that they were gods, and endued with some power; yet with regard to the gods of the Gentiles, it could not be known that any one of them was propitious to his own people. Since then this can apply only to the God of Israel, it follows that in this instance his divinity shines conspicuously, and that his sovereignty is hence sufficiently proved. We also learn, that all the gods of heathens are vain; yea, that in the religion of heathens there is nothing but delusions: for no nation can with confidence flee to its god to obtain pardon, when it has sinned. This is the sum of the whole. I shall now come to the words of the Prophet.

Who is a God like thee, taking away iniquity, and passing by wickedness? By these two forms of expression, he sets forth the singular favour of God in freely reconciling himself to sinners. To take away sins is to blot them out; though the verb נשא, *nusha,* often means to raise on high; yet it means also to take, or, to take away. To pass by wickedness, is to connive at it, as though he said, "God overlooks the wickedness of his people, as if it escaped his view:" for when God requires an account of our life, our sins immediately appear, and appear before his eyes; but when God does not call our sins before his judgment, but overlooks them, he is then said to pass by them.

This passage teaches us, as I have already reminded you, that the glory of God principally shines in this,—that he is reconcileable, and that he forgives our sins. God indeed manifests his glory both by his power and his wisdom, and by all the judgments which he daily executes; his glory, at the same time, shines forth chiefly in this,—that he is propitious to sinners, and suffers himself to be pacified; yea, that he not only allows miserable sinners to be reconciled to him, but that he also of his own will invites and anticipates them. Hence then it is evident, that he is the true God. That religion then may have firm roots in our hearts, this must be the first thing in our faith,—that God will ever be reconciled to us; for except we be fully persuaded as to his mercy, no true religion will ever flourish in us, whatever pretensions we may make; for what is said in Ps. cxxx. is ever true, 'With thee is propitiation, that thou mayest be feared.' Hence the fear of God, and the true worship of him, depend on a perception of his goodness and favour; for we cannot from the heart worship God, and there will be, as I have already said, no genuine religion in us, except this persuasion be really and deeply seated in our hearts,—that he is ever ready to forgive, whenever we flee to him.

It hence also appears what sort of religion is that of the Papacy: for under the Papacy, being perplexed and doubtful, they ever hesitate, and never dare to believe that God will be propitious to them. Though they have some ideas, I know not what, of his grace; yet it is a vain presumption and rashness, as they think, when any one is fully persuaded of God's mercy. They therefore keep consciences in suspense; nay, they leave them doubtful and trembling, when there is no certainty respecting God's favour. It hence follows, that their whole worship is fictitious; in a word, the whole of religion is entirely subverted, when a firm and unhesitating confidence, as to his goodness, is taken away, yea, that confidence by which men are enabled to come to him without doubting, and to receive, whenever they sin and confess their guilt and transgressions, the mercy that is offered to them.

But this confidence is not what rises spontaneously in us; nay, even when we entertain a notion that God is merciful, it is only a mere delusion: for we cannot be fully convinced respecting God's favour, except he anticipates us by his word, and testifies that he will be propitious to us whenever we flee to him. Hence I said at the beginning, that the Prophet here exhibits the difference between the God of Israel and all the idols of the Gentiles, and that is, because he had promised to be propitious to his people. It was not in vain that sacrifices were offered by the chosen people, for there was a promise added, which could not disappoint them: but the Gentiles ever remained doubtful with regard to their sacrifices; though they performed all their expiations, there was yet no certainty; but the case was different with the chosen people. What then the Prophet says here respecting the remission of sins, depends on the testimony which God himself has given.

We must now notice the clause which immediately follows, *as to the remnant of his heritage*. Here again he drives away the hypocrites from their vain confidence: for he says that God will be merciful only to a remnant of his people; and, at the same time, he takes away an offence, which might have grievously disquieted the weak, on seeing the wrath of God raging among the whole people,—that God would spare neither the common nor the chief men. When therefore the fire of God's vengeance flamed terribly, above and below, this objection might have greatly disturbed weak minds,—"How is this? God does indeed declare that he is propitious to sinners, and yet his severity prevails among us.—How can this be?" The Prophet meets this objection and says, "God is propitious to the remnant of his heritage;" which means, that though God would execute terrible vengeance on the greater part, there would yet ever remain some seed, on whom his mercy would shine; and he calls them the remnant of his heritage, because there was no reason, as it was stated yesterday, why God forgave the few, except that he had chosen the posterity of Abraham.

He also adds, *He will not retain his wrath perpetually*. By this second consolation he wished to relieve the faithful: for though God chastises them for a time, he yet forgets not his mercy. We may say, that the Prophet mentions here two exceptions. He had spoken of God's mercy; but as this mercy is not indiscriminate or common to all, he restricts what he teaches to the remnant. Now follows another exception,—that how much soever apparently the wrath of God would rage against his elect people themselves, there would yet be some moderation, so that they would remain safe, and that their calamities would not be to them fatal. Hence he says, God retains not wrath; for though, for a moment, he may be angry with his people, he will yet soon, as it were, repent, and show himself gracious to them, and testify that he is already reconciled to them;—not that God changes, but that the faithful are made for a short time to feel his wrath; afterwards a taste of his mercy exhilarates them, and thus they feel in their souls that God has in a manner changed. For when dread possesses their minds, they imagine God to be terrible, but when they embrace the promises of his grace, they call on him, and begin to entertain hope of pardon; then God appears to them kind, gentle, and reconcileable; yea, and altogether ready to show mercy. This is the reason why the Prophet says, that *God retains not his wrath.*

Then follows the cause, *for he loveth mercy.* Here the Prophet more clearly shows, that the remission of sins is gratuitous, and that it has no foundation but in the nature of God himself. There is then no reason, since Scripture declares God to be reconcileable, why any one should seek the cause in himself, or even the means by which God reconciles himself to us: for He himself is the cause. As God then by nature loves mercy, hence it is, that he is so ready to forgive sinners. Whosoever then imagines that God is to be propitiated by expiations or any satisfactions, subverts the doctrine of the Prophet; and it is the same thing as to build without a foundation: for the only prop or support that can raise us up to God, when we desire to be reconciled to him, is this,—that he loves mercy. And this is the reason why God so much commends his mercy, why he says, that he is merciful to thousand generations, slow to wrath, and ready to pardon. For though the unbelieving harden themselves against God, yet when they feel his wrath, there is nothing so difficult for them as to believe that God can be pacified. Hence this reason, which is not in vain added by the Prophet, ought to be especially noticed.

Let us now see to whom God is merciful. For as Satan could not have obliterated from the hearts of men a conviction of God's mercy, he has yet confined mercy to the unbelieving, as though God should forgive sinners only once, when they are admitted into the Church. Thus the Pelagians formerly thought, that God grants reconciliation to none but to aliens; for whosoever has been once received into the Church cannot, as they imagined, stand otherwise before God than by being perfect. And this figment led Novatus and his disciples to create disturbances in the Church. And there are at this day not only deluded men, but devils, who, by the same figment, or rather delirious notions, fascinate themselves and others, and hold, that the highest perfection ought to exist in the faithful; and they also slander our doctrine, as though we were still continuing in the Alphabet or in the first rudiments, because we daily preach free remission of sins. But the Prophet declares expressly that God not only forgives the unbelieving when they sin, but also *his heritage* and his elect. Let us then know, that as long as we are in the world, pardon is prepared for us, as we could not otherwise but fall every moment from the hope of salvation, were not this remedy provided for us: for those men must be more than mad who arrogate to themselves perfection, or who think that they have arrived at that high degree of attainment, that they can satisfy God by their works. It now follows—

19. He will turn again, he will have compassion upon us; he will subdue our iniquities; and thou wilt cast all their sins into the depths of the sea.	19. Revertetur, miserebitur nostri; calcabit iniquitates nostras, et projiciet in profunditates maris cuncta scelera eorum.

The Prophet now prescribes to the faithful a form of glorying, that they may boldly declare that God will be pacified towards them. Since then God loves mercy, *he will return, he will have mercy on us.* The context here ought to be observed by us; for it would avail us but little to understand, I know not what, concerning God's mercy, and to preach in general the free remission of sins, except we come to the application, that is, except each of the faithful believed that God, for his own sake, is merciful, as soon as he is called upon. This conclusion, then, is to be borne in mind,—"God forgives the remnant of his heritage, because he is by nature inclined to show mercy: he will *therefore* be merciful to us, for we are of the number of his people." Except we lay hold on this conclusion, "He will therefore show mercy to us," whatever we have heard or said respecting God's goodness will vanish away.

This then is the true logic of religion, that is, when we are persuaded that God is reconcileable and easily pacified, because he is by nature inclined to mercy, and also, when we thus apply this doctrine to ourselves, or to our own peculiar benefit,—"As God is by nature merciful, I shall therefore know and find him to be so." Until then we be thus persuaded, let us know that we have made but little progress in the School of God. And hence it appears very clear from this passage, that the Papacy is a horrible abyss; for no one under that system can have a firm footing, so as to be fully persuaded that God will be merciful to him; for all that they have are mere conjectures. But we see that the Prophet reasons very differently, "God loves mercy; he will therefore have mercy on us:" and then he adds, *He will return;*[1] and this is said lest the temporary wrath or severity of God should disquiet us. Though God then may not immediately shine on us with his favour, but, on the contrary, treat us sharply and roughly, yet the Prophet teaches us that we are to entertain good hope.—How so? *He will return*, or, as he said shortly before, He will not retain perpetually his wrath: for it is for a moment that he is angry with his Church; and he soon remembers mercy.

The Prophet now specifies what sort of mercy God shows to the faithful, *For he will tread down our iniquities;* he had said before that he passes by the wickedness of his elect people. *He will* then *tread down our iniquities; and he will*

[1] *Grotius*, *Dathius*, and *Henderson*, consider that this verb, placed before another, without a conjunction, expresses only a reiteration; and they render it adverbially, "again." But, in this place, it would be better to give it its proper meaning; for as God is said to depart from his people, Hosea ix. 12, so he may be said also to return. The Septuagint renders it επιστρεψει—He will return. *Drusius* reads, *convertetur*, scil. ab ira sua—*He will turn*, that is, from his anger. *Newcome's* version is, "He will turn again."—*Ed.*

cast[1] *into the depth of the sea all their sins;* that is, Our sins shall not come in remembrance before him. We hence learn what I have said before—that God cannot be worshipped sincerely and from the heart until this conviction be fixed and deeply rooted in our hearts, that God is merciful, not in general, but toward us, because we have been once adopted by him, and are his heritage. And then, were the greater part to fall away, we should not fail in our faith; for God preserves the remnant in a wonderful manner. And, lastly, let us know, that whenever we flee to God for mercy, pardon is ever ready for us, not that we may indulge in sin, or take liberty to commit it, but that we may confess our faults, and that our guilt may appear before our eyes: let us know, that the door is open to us; for God of his own good will presents himself to us as one ready to be reconciled.

It is also said, *He will cast our sins into the depth of the sea.*

[1] There is a mistake as to this verb; it is the *second* person, as are all the verbs which follow. The Prophet resumes here his address to God, which he commenced in the two first lines of the last verse. To show the difference between what he speaks *to* and what he speaks *of* God, the whole passage shall be here given,—

18. What God *is* like thee!
Taking away iniquity, and passing over transgression!—
Against the remnant of his heritage
He retains not for ever his anger;
For a lover of mercy *is* He;
19. He will return, he will pity us,
He will subdue our iniquities;—
Yea, thou wilt cast into the depths of the sea all their sins;
Thou wilt show faithfulness to Jacob, mercy to Abraham,
Which thou swarest to our fathers in the days of old.

"Pity," רחם, is tender compassion; the noun in the plural number is used to designate the bowels. "Subdue," or trample under foot, is rendered "cover" by *Newcome*, on the ground of this being the meaning of כבש in Chaldee. This wholly destroys the striking character of the passage. Our sins are here represented as our enemies; God subdues them; and then in the next line the simile is continued, they are to be drowned like Pharaoh and his hosts in the depths of the sea. *Henderson's* remarks on this point are very excellent. "There is no ground," he says, "for rejecting the radical idea of *trampling under foot as enemies.* Sin must ever be regarded as hostile to man. It is not only contrary to his interests, but it powerfully opposes and combats the moral principles of his nature, and the higher principles implanted by grace; and but for the counteracting energy of divine influence, must prove victorious. Without the subjugation of evil propensities, pardon would not be a blessing." —*Ed.*

We hence learn that there is a full remission of sins, not half, as the Papists imagine, for God, they say, remits the sin, but retains the punishment. How frivolous this is the thing itself clearly proves. The language of the Prophet does however import this, that our sins are then remitted when the records of them are blotted out before God. It follows—for I will run over this verse, that I may to-day finish this Prophet—

20. Thou wilt perform the truth to Jacob, *and* the mercy to Abraham, which thou hast sworn unto our fathers from the days of old.	20. Dabis veritatem Jacob, misericordiam Abrahæ, quas jurasti patribus nostris à diebus antiquis.

The faithful confirm here the former truth, that God had deposited his covenant with them, which could not be made void: and hence also shines forth more clearly what I have said before, that the faithful do not learn by their own understanding what sort of Being God is, but embrace the mercy which he offers in his own word. Except God then speaks, we cannot form in our own minds any idea of his grace but what is uncertain and vanishing; but when he declares that he will be merciful to us, then every doubt is removed. This is now the course which the Prophet pursues.

He says, *Thou wilt give truth to Jacob, mercy to Abraham, which thou hast sworn to our fathers;* as though he said, "We do not presumptuously invent any thing out of our own minds, but receive what thou hast once testified to us; for thy will has been made known to us in thy word: relying then on thy favour, we are persuaded as to thy gratuitous pardon, though we are in many respects guilty before thee." We now then understand the design of the Prophet.

As to the words, it is not necessary to dwell on them, for we have elsewhere explained this form of speaking. There are here two expressions by which the Prophet characterizes the covenant of God. Truth is mentioned, and mercy is mentioned. With respect to order, the mercy of God precedes; for he is not induced otherwise to adopt us than through his goodness alone: but as God of his own will has with so great kindness received us, so he is true and faithful in his covenant. If then we desire to know the character of

God's covenant, by which he formerly chose the Jews, and at this day adopts us as his people, these two things must be understood, that God freely offers himself to us, and that he is constant and true, he repents not, as Paul says, as to his covenant: "The gifts and calling of God," he says, "are without repentance," (Rom. xi. 29;) and he refers to the covenant, by which God adopted the children of Abraham.

He says now, *Thou wilt give*, that is, show in reality; for this, to give, is, as it were, to exhibit in effect or really. *Thou wilt* then *give*, that is, openly show, that thou hast not been in vain so kind to us and ours, in receiving them into favour. How so? Because the effect of thy goodness and truth appears to us.

Thou hast then *sworn to our fathers from the days of old.* The faithful take for granted that God had promised to the fathers that his covenant would be perpetual; for he did not only say to Abraham, "I will be thy God," but he also added, "and of thy seed for ever." Since, then, the faithful knew that the covenant of God was to be perpetual and inviolable, and also knew that it was to be continued from the fathers to their children, and that it was once promulgated for this end, that the fathers might deliver it as by the hand to their children; they therefore doubted not but that it would be perpetual. How so? *for thou hast sworn to our fathers;* that is, they knew that God not only promised, but that having interposed an oath, by which God designed to confirm that covenant, he greatly honoured it, that it might be unhesitatingly received by the chosen people. As then the faithful knew that God in a manner bound himself to them, they confidently solicited him, really to show himself to be such as he had declared he would be to his own elect.

PRAYER.

Grant, Almighty God, that as we abound in so many vices, by which we daily provoke thy wrath, and as by the testimony o our consciences, we are justly exposed to everlasting death, yea, and deserve a hundred and even a thousand deaths,—O grant, that we may strive against the unbelief of our flesh, and so embrace thine infinite mercy, that we may not doubt but that thou wilt be propitious to us, and yet not abuse this privilege by taking liberty to sin, but with fear, and true humility, and care, so walk according to thy word, that we may not hesitate daily to flee to thy mercy, that we may thereby be sustained and kept in safety, until having at length put off all vices, and being freed from all sin, we come to thy celestial kingdom, to enjoy the fruit of our faith, even that eternal inheritance which has been obtained for us by the blood of thy only-begotten Son. Amen.

END OF THE COMMENTARIES ON MICAH.

THE

COMMENTARIES OF JOHN CALVIN

ON THE

PROPHET NAHUM.

CALVIN'S PREFACE TO NAHUM.

The time in which Nahum prophesied cannot with certainty be known. The Hebrews, ever bold in conjectures, say that he discharged his office of teaching under Manasseh, and that the name of that king was suppressed, because he was unworthy of such an honour, or, because his reign was unfortunate, as he had been led into captivity. When any one asks the Jews a reason, they only say, that it appears so to them. As then there is no reason for this conjecture, we must come to what seems probable.

They who think that he prophesied under Jotham, are no doubt mistaken, and can easily be disproved; for he here threatens ruin to the city Nineveh, because the Assyrians had cruelly laid waste the kingdom of Israel; and it is for these wrongs that he denounces vengeance: but under Jotham the kingdom of Israel had not been laid waste. We indeed know that the Assyrians were suborned by Ahaz, when he found himself unequal to resist the attacks of two neighbouring kings, the king of Syria, and the king of Israel. It was then that the Assyrians penetrated into the land of Israel; and in course of time, they desolated the whole kingdom. At this period it was that Nahum prophesied; for it was his object to show, that God had a care for that kingdom, on account of his adoption or covenant; though the Israelites had perfidiously separated themselves from the people of God, yet God's covenant remained in force. His design then was to show, that God was the father and protector of that kingdom. As this was the Prophet's object, it is certain that he taught either after the death of Ahaz under Hezekiah, or about that time.[1]

He followed JONAH at some distance,[2] as we may easily learn. Jonah, as we have already seen, pronounced a threatening on the city NINEVEH; but the punishment was remitted, because the Ninevites humbled themselves, and suppliantly deprecated the punishment which had been announced. They afterwards returned to their old ways, as it is usually the case. Hence it was, that God became less disposed to spare them. Though indeed they were aliens, yet God was pleased to show them favour by teaching them through the ministry and labours of JONAH: and their repentance was not altogether feigned. Since then they were already endued with some knowledge of the true God, the less excusable was their cruelty, when they sought to oppress the kingdom of Israel. They indeed knew, that that nation was sacred to God: what they did then was in a manner an outrage against God himself.

We now understand at what time it is probable that NAHUM performed his office as a teacher; though nothing certain, as I have said at the beginning, can be known: hence it was, that I condemned the Rabbins for rashness on the subject; for they are bold enough to bring any thing forward as a truth, respecting which there is no certainty.

I have already in part stated the design of the Prophet. The sum of the whole is this: When the Assyrians had for some time disturbed the kingdom of Israel, the Prophet arose and exhorted the Israelites to patience, that is, those who continued to be the servants of God; because God had not wholly forsaken them, but would undertake their cause, for

[1] "I conclude from chap. ii. 2, that Nahum prophesied after the captivity of the ten tribes. Josephus places him in the reign of Jotham, and says that his predictions came to pass one hundred and fifteen years afterwards. *Ant.* IX. xi. 3. According to our best chronologers, this date would bring us to the year in which Samaria was taken. And I agree with those who think that Nahum uttered this prophecy in the reign of Hezekiah, and not long after the subversion of the kingdom of Israel by Shalmaneser."—*Newcome.*

[2] The distance is supposed by chronologers to have been about 150 years.—*Ed.*

they were under his protection. This is the substance of the whole.

With regard to NINEVEH, we have already stated that it was the capital of the empire, as long as the Assyrians did bear rule: for BABYLON was a province; that is, Chaldea, whose metropolis was Babylon, was one of the provinces of the empire. The kingdom was afterwards taken away from Meroc-baladan. Some think that Nabuchodonosor was the first monarch of Chaldea. But I bestow no great pains on this subject. It may be, that Meroc-baladan had two names, and this was very common; as we know that the kings of Egypt were called Pharaohs; so the Assyrians and Chaldeans, though otherwise called at first, might have taken a common royal name. Now NINEVEH was so celebrated, that another kingdom could not have been established by the Babylonians without demolishing that city. We indeed know that it was very large, as we have stated in explaining Jonah. It was, as profane writers have recorded, nearly three days' journey in circumference. Then its walls were one hundred feet high, and so wide, that chariots could pass one another without coming in contact: there were one thousand and five hundred towers. We hence see that it was not without reason that this city was formerly so celebrated.

They say that NINUS was its founder; but this is proved to be a mistake by the testimony of Moses in Gen. x. They also imagine that SEMIRAMIS was the first queen of Babylon, and that the city was built by her: but this is a fable. It may have been that she enlarged the city; but it was BABYLON many ages before she was born. So also NINUS may have increased and adorned NINEVEH; but the city was founded before his birth. Profane authors call it NINUS, not Nineveh; probably the Hebrew name was corrupted by them, as it is often the case. However this may be, it is evident, that when Meroc-baladan, or his son, who succeeded him, wished to fix the seat of the empire at Babylon, he was under the necessity of destroying NINEVEH to prevent rivalry. It thus happened, that the city was entirely demolished. Of this destruction, as we shall see, NAHUM prophesied.

COMMENTARIES

ON

THE PROPHET NAHUM

Lecture Ninety-ninth

CHAPTER I

1. The burden of Nineveh. The book of the vision of Nahum the Elkoshite.

Though a vision of Nahum is here delivered to the Israelites and to the Jews, he yet calls it the burden of Nineveh, as that which it principally contains; he calls it, the Book of the Vision of Nahum. Of the word משא, *massa*, we have spoken elsewhere; that the Prophets call their prediction a burden, when they denounce any grievous and dreadful vengeance: and as they often threatened the Jews, it hence happened, that they laid it, by way of ridicule, a prophecy [illegible] burden. But yet the import of the word is well established. It is the same thing as though Nahum had said, that he was sent by God as a herald, to proclaim war to Nineveh, [illegible] the sake of the observation, [illegible] may have learnt how true and accurate God was [illegible]

[1] The word [illegible] [illegible] message [illegible] [illegible]

COMMENTARIES

ON

THE PROPHET NAHUM.

Lecture Ninety-ninth.

CHAPTER I.

1. The burden of Nineveh. The book of the vision of Nahum the Elkoshite.

1. Onus Nineveh: Liber visionis Nahum Helkosi:

Though a part of what is here delivered belongs to the Israelites and to the Jews, he yet calls his Book by what it principally contains; he calls it, *the burden of Nineveh.* Of this word משא, *mesha,* we have spoken elsewhere. Thus the Prophets call their predictions, whenever they denounce any grievous and dreadful vengeance of God: and as they often threatened the Jews, it hence happened, that they called, by way of ridicule, all prophecies by this name משא, *mesha,* a burden.[1] But yet the import of the word is suitable. It is the same thing as though Nahum had said, that he was sent by God as a herald, to proclaim war on the Ninevites for the sake of the chosen people. The Israelites may have hence learnt how true and unchangeable God was in his covenant;

[1] The word comes from נשא, to bear, to carry. Some regard it as the message *carried* or *borne* by the Prophets from God to the people, and hence the same as Prophecy. Others consider it to be the judgment to be *borne* by the people respecting whom it was announced. The latter seems to be its meaning here, where it is said, "the burden of Nineveh." It was the judgment laid on them, and which that city was to bear, endure, and undergo.—*Ed.*

for he still manifested his care for them, though they had by their vices alienated themselves from him.

He afterwards adds, ספר חזון, *sapher chezun, the book of the vision.* This clause signifies, that he did not in vain denounce destruction on the Ninevites, because he faithfully delivered what he had received from God. For if he had simply prefaced, that he threatened ruin to the Assyrians, some doubt might have been entertained as to the event. But here he seeks to gain to himself authority by referring to God's name; for he openly affirms that he brought nothing of his own, but that this burden had been made known to him by a celestial oracle: for חזה, *cheze,* means properly to see, and hence in Hebrew a vision is called חזון, *chezun.* But the Prophets, when they speak of a vision, do not mean any fantasy or imagination, but that kind of revelation which is mentioned in Num. xiv., where God says, that he speaks to his Prophets either by vision or by dream. We hence see why this was added—that the burden of Nineveh was a vision; it was, that the Israelites might know that this testimony respecting God's vengeance on their enemies was not brought by a mortal man, and that there might be no doubt but that God was the author of this prophecy.

Nahum calls himself an Elkoshite. Some think that it was the name of his family. The Jews, after their manner, say, that it was the name of his father; and then they add this their common gloss, that Elkos himself was a Prophet: for when the name of a Prophet's father is mentioned, they hold that he whose name is given was also a Prophet. But these are mere trifles: and we have often seen how great is their readiness to invent fables. Then the termination of the word leads us to think that it was, on the contrary, the proper name of a place; and Jerome tells us that there was in his time a small village of this name in the tribe of Simeon. We must therefore understand, that Nahum arose from that town, and was therefore called "the Elkoshite."[1] Let us now proceed— .

[1] "It has been thought, and not without reason, by some, that Capernaum, Heb. כפר נחום, most properly rendered, *the village of Nahum,* derived its name from our Prophet having resided in it."—*Henderson.*

2. God *is* jealous, and the Lord revengeth; the Lord revengeth, and *is* furious; the Lord will take vengeance on his adversaries, and he reserveth *wrath* for his enemies.	2. Deus æmulator *(sic vertunt,)* et ulciscens Jehova; ulciscens Jehova, et Dominus iræ *(vel,* possidens iram ;) ulciscens Jehova hostes suos, et servans (*vel*, reponens) idem (*vel*, ipse) inimicis suis.

Nahum begins with the nature of God, that what he afterwards subjoins respecting the destruction of Nineveh might be more weighty, and produce a greater impression on the hearers. The preface is general, but the Prophet afterwards applies it to a special purpose. If he had only spoken of what God is, it would have been frigid, at least it would have been less efficacious; but when he connects both together, then his doctrine carries its own force and power. We now apprehend the design of the Prophet. He might indeed have spoken of the fall of the city Nineveh: but if he had referred to this abruptly, profane men might have regarded him with disdain; and even the Israelites would have been perhaps less affected. This is the reason why he shows, in a general way, what sort of Being God is. And he takes his words from Moses; and the Prophets are wont to borrow from him their doctrine:[1] and it is from that most memorable vision, when God appeared to Moses after the breaking of the tables. I have therefore no doubt but that Nahum had taken from Exod. xxxiv. what we read here: he does not, indeed, give literally what is found there; but it is sufficiently evident that he paints, as it were, to the life, the image of God, by which his nature may be seen.

He says first, that *God is jealous*, (*æmulus*—emulous;) for the verb קנא, *kona*, means to irritate, and also to emulate, and to envy. When God is said to be קנוא, *konua*, the Greeks render it jealous, (ζηλωτὴν,) and the Latins, emulous,

[1] How far this language is right, may be questioned. The Prophets, under the immediate direction of the Divine Spirit, can hardly be said to *borrow* from a previous writer. They have no doubt announced the same sentiments, and, in some instances, used the same words, as those found in the writings of Moses; but they derived them not from those writings, but from Divine inspiration: and, as *Calvin* has often observed, they adduced nothing but what they received from God. But this language is not peculiar to *Calvin:* he adopted it from the fathers.—*Ed.*

(*æmulatorem.*) But it properly signifies, that God cannot bear injuries or wrongs. Though God then for a time connives at the wickedness of men, he will yet be the defender of his own glory. He calls him afterwards the avenger, and he repeats this three times, *Jehovah avengeth, Jehovah avengeth and possesseth wrath, he will avenge.* When he says that God *keeps for his enemies*, he means that vengeance is reserved for the unbelieving and the despisers of God. There is the same mode of speaking in use among us, *Je lui garde, et il la garde à ses ennemis.* This phrase, in our language, shows what the Prophet means here by saying, that God keeps for his enemies. And this awful description of God is to be applied to the present case, for he says that he proclaims war against the Ninevites, because they had unjustly distressed the Church of God: it is for this reason that he says, that God is jealous, that God is an avenger; and he confirms this three times, that the Israelites might feel assured that this calamity was seriously announced; for had not this representation been set before them, they might have thus reasoned with themselves,—"We are indeed cruelly harassed by our enemies; but who can think that God cares any thing for our miseries, since he allows them so long to be unavenged?" It was therefore necessary that the Prophet should obviate such thoughts, as he does here. We now more fully understand why he begins in a language so vehement, and calls God a jealous God, and an avenger.

He afterwards adds, that God *possesses wrath.* I do not take חמה, *cheme*, simply for wrath, but the passion or heat of wrath. We ought not indeed to suppose, as it has been often observed, that our passions belong to God; for he remains ever like himself. But yet God is said to be for a time angry, and for ever towards the reprobate, for he is our and their Judge. Here, then, when the Prophet says, that *God is the Lord of wrath*, or that he possesses wrath, he means that he is armed with vengeance, and that, though he connives at the sins of men, he is not yet indifferent, nor even delays, because he is without power, or because he is idle and careless, but that he retains wrath, as he afterwards repeats the same thing, *He keeps for his enemies.*[1] In short, by these forms of speaking the Prophet intimates, that God is not to be rashly judged of on account of his delay, when he does not immediately execute his judgments; for he waits for the seasonable opportunity. But, in the meantime, there is no reason for us to think that he forgets his office when he suspends punishment, or for a season spares the ungodly. When, therefore, God does not hasten so very quickly, there is no ground for us to think that he is indifferent, because he delays his wrath, or retains it, as we have already said; for it is the same thing to retain wrath, as to be the Lord of wrath, and to possess it. It follows—

3. The Lord *is* slow to anger, and great in power, and will not at all acquit *the wicked:* the Lord *hath* his way in the whirlwind and in the storm, and the clouds *are* the dust of his feet.

3. Jehova tardus iris *(ad verbum, sed,* tardus ad iram) et magnus robore; et purgando non purgabit; Jehova in turbine et tempestate via ejus, et nubes pulvis pedum ejus.

The Prophet goes on with the same subject; and still longer is the preface respecting the nature of God, which however is to be applied, as I have said, to the special object, which hereafter he will state. He says here that God is *slow to wrath.* Though this saying is taken also from Moses, yet the Prophet speaks here for the purpose of anticipating an objection; for he obviates the audacity of the ungodly, who

[1] The following may be proposed as the literal rendering of this verse,—

A God jealous and an avenger *is* Jehovah;
Avenger *is* Jehovah, and one who has indignation;
Avenger *is* Jehovah on his adversaries,
And watch does he for his enemies.

God is said to be *jealous* in the second commandment, being one who will not allow his own honour to be given to another. *Avenger,* נקם, is a vindicator of his own rights; and he is said to have indignation, or hot wrath, or great displeasure; בעל חמה, possessor, holder, or keeper of indignation. *His adversaries,* צריו, rather, his oppressors; the oppressors of his people were his own oppressors. נוטר means to watch, rather than to keep. Its meaning here is to watch the opportunity to take vengeance on his enemies. The description is remarkable, and exactly adapted to the oppressive state of the Jews. The dishonour done to God's people was done to him. He is jealous, a defender of his own rights, full of indignation, and watches and waits for a suitable time to execute vengeance, to vindicate his own honour.—*Ed.*

daringly derided God, when any evil was denounced on them, —"Where is the mercy of God? Can God divest himself of his kindness? He cannot deny himself." Thus profane men, under the pretence of honouring God, cast on him the most atrocious slander, for they deprive him of his own power and office: and there is no doubt but that this was commonly done by many of the ungodly in the age of our Prophet. Hence he anticipates this objection, and concedes that God is slow to wrath. There is then a concession here; but at the same time he says that God is *great in strength*, and this he says, that the ungodly may not flatter and deceive themselves, when they hear these high attributes given to God—that he is patient, slow to wrath, merciful, full of kindness. "Let them," he says, "at the same time remember the greatness of God's power, that they may not think that they have to do with a child."

We now then see the design of the Prophet: for this declaration—that God hastens not suddenly to wrath, but patiently defers and suspends the punishment which the ungodly deserve. This declaration would not have harmonised with the present argument, had not the Prophet introduced it by way of concession; as though he said,—"I see that the world everywhere trifle with God, and that the ungodly delude themselves with such sophistries, that they reject all threatenings. I indeed allow that God is ready to pardon, and that he descends not to wrath, except when he is constrained by extreme necessity: all this is indeed true; but yet know, that God is armed with his own power: escape then shall none of those who allow themselves the liberty of abusing his patience, notwithstanding the insolence they manifest towards him."

He now adds, *By clearing he will not clear*. Some translate, "The innocent, he will not render innocent." But the real meaning of this sentence is the same with that in Exod. xxxiv.; and what Moses meant was, that God is irreconcileable to the impenitent. It has another meaning at the end of the third chapter of Joel, where it is said, 'I will cleanse the blood which I have not cleansed.' On that text interpreters differ, because they regard not the change in the tense of the verb; for God means, that he would cleanse the filth and defilements of his Church, which he had not previously cleansed. But Moses means, that God deals strictly with sinners, so as to remit no punishment. By clearing then I will not clear; that is, God will rigidly demand an account of all the actions of men; and as there is nothing hid from him, so every thing done wickedly by men must come forth, when God ascends his tribunal; he will not clear by clearing, but will rigidly execute his judgment.

There seems to be some inconsistency in saying,—that God is reconcileable and ready to pardon,—and yet that by clearing he will not clear. But the aspect of things is different. We have already stated what the Prophet had in view: for inasmuch as the ungodly ever promise impunity to themselves, and in this confidence petulantly deride God himself, the Prophet answers them, and declares, that there was no reason why they thus abused God's forbearance, for he says, By clearing he will not clear, that is, the reprobate: for our salvation consists in a free remission of sins; and whence comes our righteousness, but from the imputation of God, and from this—that our sins are buried in oblivion? yea, our whole clearing depends on the mercy of God. But God then exercises also his judgment, and by clearing he clears, when he remits to the faithful their sins; for the faithful by repentance anticipate his judgment; and he searches their hearts, that he may clear them. For what is repentance but condemnation, which yet turns out to be the means of salvation? As then God absolves none except the condemned, our Prophet here rightly declares, that *by clearing he will not clear*, that is, he will not remit their sins, except he tries them and discharges the office of a judge; in short, that no sin is remitted by God which he does not first condemn. But with regard to the reprobate, who are wholly obstinate in their wickedness, the Prophet justly declares this to them,—that they have no hope of pardon, as they perversely adhere to their own devices, and think that they can escape the hand of God: the Prophet tells them that they are deceived, for God passes by nothing, and will not blot out one sin, until all be brought to mind.

He afterwards says, that *the way of God is in the whirlwind and the tempest;* that is, that God, as soon as he shows himself, disturbs the whole atmosphere, and excites storms and tempests: and this must be applied to the subject in hand; for the appearance of God is in other places described as lovely and gracious: nay, what else but the sight of God exhilarates the faithful? As soon as God turns away his face, they must necessarily be immersed in dreadful darkness, and be surrounded with horrible terrors. Why then does the Prophet say here, that the *way of God is in the whirlwind and storms?* Even because his discourse is addressed to the ungodly, or to the despisers of God himself, as in Ps. xviii.; where we see him described as being very terrible,—that clouds and darkness are around him, that he moves the whole earth, that he thunders on every side, that he emits smoke from his nostrils, and that he fills the whole world with fire and burning. For what purpose was this done? Because David's object was to set forth the judgments of God, which he had executed on the ungodly. So it is in this place; for Nahum speaks of the future vengeance, which was then nigh the Assyrians; hence he says, *The way of God is in the whirlwind and tempest;* that is, when God goes forth, whirlwinds and tempests are excited by his presence, and the whole world is put in confusion.

He adds, that *the clouds are the dust of his feet.* When any one with his feet only moves the dust within a small space, some dread is produced: but God moves the dust, not only in one place,—what then? he obscures, and thus covers the whole heaven, *The clouds* then *are the dust of his feet.*[1] We

[1] I offer the following translation of this verse,—

> Jehovah is slow to wrath, though great in power;
> Absolving, Jehovah will not absolve:
> In the whirlwind and in the storm *is* his way;
> And the cloud is the dust of his feet.

The second line presents some difficulty. It is evidently an imperfect sentence; most supply the word, *guilty;* but rather the "enemies" mentioned before are to be understood. The meaning appears to be this,—Jehovah is slow to wrath, that is, to execute his vengeance, though he is great in power, capable of doing so; but though he delays, he will not eventually clear or absolve his enemies. With the Septuagint I connect "Jehovah" with the second and not with the third line, and

now apprehend the whole meaning of the Prophet, and the purpose for which this description is given. Of the same import is what follows—

4. He rebuketh the sea, and maketh it dry, and drieth up all the rivers: Bashan languisheth, and Carmel, and the flower of Lebanon languisheth.	4. Increpat mare et arefaciet illud (*hoc est*, simulac mare increpuerit, arefaciet;) et omnia flumina exiccat, infirmatur (*vel*, aboletur) Basan et Carmelus, et germen Libani aboletur (*vel*, infirmatur, *est idem verbum.*)

Nahum continues his discourse,—that God, in giving proof of his displeasure, would disturb the sea or make it dry. There may be here an allusion to the history, described by Moses; for the Prophets, in promising God's assistance to his people, often remind them how God in a miraculous manner brought up their fathers from Egypt. As then the passage through the Red Sea was in high repute among the Jews, it may be that the Prophet alluded to that event, (Exod. xiv. 22.) But another view seems to me more probable. We indeed know how impetuous an element is that of the sea; and hence in Jer. v., God, intending to set forth his own power, says, that it is in his power to calm the raging of the sea, than which nothing is more impetuous or more violent. In the same manner also is the majesty of God described in Job xxviii. The meaning of this place, I think, is the same, —that *God by his chiding makes the sea dry*,[1] and that he can *dry up the rivers*. That the Prophet connects rivers with the

agreeably with the idiom of the Hebrew; the verb generally precedes its nominative. The order of the words in Welsh would be exactly the same,—

Gan ddieuogi ni ddieuoga Jehova.—Ed.

[1] Literally, "chiding the sea, he even made it dry." The ו here, though conversive, must be rendered, "even," for the first verb is a participle. By taking the words in their poetical order, the whole verse may be thus rendered,—

Chiding the sea, he even made it dry;
And all the rivers he dried up:
Wither did Bashan and Carmel,
And the bud of Lebanon withered.

The verbs in this, and in the following verse, are in the past tense; reference is made to the past works of God, and in some instances to those performed in the wilderness.—*Ed.*

sea, confirms what I have just said,—that the passage through the Red Sea is not here referred to; but that the object is to show in general how great is God's power in governing the whole world.

To the same purpose is what he adds, *Bashan shall be weakened, and Carmel, and the branch of Lebanon shall be weakened*, or destroyed. By these words he intimates, that there is nothing so magnificent in the world, which God changes not, when he gives proofs of his displeasure; as it is said in Ps. civ., 'Send forth thy Spirit, and they shall be renewed;' and again, 'Take away thy Spirit,' or remove it, 'and all things will return to the dust;' yea, into nothing. So also Nahum says in this place, "As soon as God shows his wrath, the rivers will dry up, the sea itself will become dry, and then the flowers will fade and the grass will wither;" that is, though the earth be wonderfully ornamented and replenished, yet all things will be reduced to solitude and desolation whenever God is angry. And he afterwards adds—

5. The mountains quake at him, and the hills melt, and the earth is burned at his presence, yea, the world, and all that dwell therein.

5. Montes concutientur ab eo (*vel*, contremiscent, *quanquam notat continuum actum; sensus est igitur*, montes contremiscere ad nutum ejus,) et colles dissolvent se (*hoc est*, solvuntur, *vel*, liquefiunt,) et ardet terra à facie ejus, et orbis et omnes qui habitant in eo.

Nahum continues still on the same subject,—that when God ascended his tribunal and appeared as the Judge of the world, he would not only shake all the elements, but would also constrain them to change their nature. For what can be less consonant to nature than for mountains to tremble, and for hills to be dissolved or to melt? This is more strange than what we can comprehend. But the Prophet intimates, that the mountains cannot continue in their own strength, but as far as they are sustained by the favour of God. As soon, then, as God is angry, the mountains melt like snow, and flow away like water. And all these things are to be applied to this purpose, and are designed for this end,—that the wicked might not daringly despise the threatenings of God, nor think that they could, through his forbearance, escape the punishment which they deserved: for he will be their Judge, however he may spare them; and though God is ready to pardon, whenever men hate themselves on account of their sins, and seriously repent; he will be yet irreconcileable to all the reprobate and the perverse. *The mountains*, then, *before him tremble, and the hills dissolve* or melt.

This useful instruction may be gathered from these words, —that the world cannot for a moment stand, except as it is sustained by the favour and goodness of God; for we see what would immediately be, as soon as God manifests the signals of his judgment. Since the very solidity of mountains would be as snow or wax, what would become of miserable men, who are like a shadow or an apparition? They would then vanish away as soon as God manifested his wrath against them, as it is said in Ps. xxxix., that men pass away like a shadow. This comparison ought ever to be remembered by us whenever a forgetfulness of God begins to creep over us, that we may not excite his wrath by self-complacencies, than which there is nothing more pernicious. *Burned*,[1] then, *shall be the earth, and the world, and all who dwell on it.*

PRAYER.

Grant, Almighty God, that as thou settest before us here as in a mirror how dreadful thy wrath is, we may be humbled before thee, and of our ownselves cast ourselves down, that we may not be laid prostrate by thy awful power,—O grant, that we may by this instruction be really prepared for repentance, and so suppliantly deprecate that punishment which we daily

[1] This sense has been given to the verb by the Rabbins, which is inconsistent with it as found here without any variations, and with the Greek versions. תשא is either from נשא, to lift up, or from שאה, to be laid waste, or to be confounded, the final ה being dropped; and this is what *Newcome* adopts. *Marckius* and *Henderson* take the former meaning in the sense of being raised up or heaving. "Ανεσταλη, was removed," *Sept.*; "Εκινηθη, was moved," *Symmachus*; "Εφριξεν, trembled," *Aquila*. The idea of being confounded or laid waste harmonises best with all parts of the sentence; for the idea of heaving does not apply well to the inhabitants. We see here that all the Greek versions have the verb in the past tense; and so are the previous verbs in the verse as given in the Septuagint, and agreeably with the Hebrew.

Mountains have shaken through him,
And hills have melted away;
And confounded has been the earth at his presence,
Yea, the world and all its inhabitants.

deserve through our transgressions, that in the meantime we may be also transformed into the image of thy Son, and put off all our depraved lusts, and be cleansed from our vices, until we shall at length appear in confidence before thee, and be gathered among thy children, that we may enjoy the eternal inheritance of thy heavenly kingdom, which has been obtained for us by the blood of thy Son. Amen.

Lecture One Hundredth.

6. Who can stand before his indignation? and who can abide in the fierceness of his anger? his fury is poured out like fire, and the rocks are thrown down by him.	6. Coram indignatione ejus quis stabit? et quis consistet in furore iræ ejus? furor ejus effunditur tanquam ignis, et rupes solvuntur ab eo.

The Prophet shows here why he gave in the part noticed in the last lecture, such an awful description of God; it was that men might know, that when they shall come before his tribunal, no one will be able to stand unless supported by his favour. Of the Prophet's main object we have sufficiently spoken, nor is it necessary to repeat here what has been stated. It is enough to bear this in mind,—that as the enemies of the Church relied on their power, and daringly and immoderately raged against it, the judgment of God is here set before them, that they might understand that an account was to be rendered to him, whose presence they were not able to bear. But the question has more force than if the Prophet had simply said, that the whole world could not stand before God: for he assumes the character of one adjuring. After having shown how terrible God is, he exclaims, *Who shall stand before his indignation? and who shall be able to bear his wrath?*[1] for his indignation, he says, is poured

[1] And who shall rise up in his hot anger?—*Newcome.*

And who can subsist in the heat of his anger?—*Henderson.*

Neither of these versions convey the meaning. The verb קום, with a ב after it, signifies to rise up against or to resist. Τις αντιστησεται—Who shall resist?—*Sept.* So the line should be thus rendered,—

And who can resist the burning of his wrath?

This line conveys the same idea as the former, only in stronger terms. For displeasure or anger we have here the burning of his wrath, and for

forth as fire. The Hebrew interpreters have here toiled in vain: as the verb נתך, *nutac*, means to pour forth, it seems to them an inconsistent expression, that the wrath of God should be poured forth as fire; for this would be more suitably said of some metal than of fire. But to be poured forth here is nothing else than to be scattered far and wide. *Poured forth* then *is thy wrath as fire;* that is, it advances every moment, as when a fire seizes a whole forest; and when it grows strong, we know how great is its violence, and how suddenly it spreads here and there. But if a different meaning be preferred, I do not much object to it, "His wrath, which is like fire, is poured out."

Some think that the Prophet alludes to lightnings, which, as it were, melt through the air, at least as they appear to us. But as the meaning of the Prophet is sufficiently evident, there is no need of anxiously inquiring how fire is poured out: for I have already mentioned, that the Prophet means no other thing than the wrath of God spreads itself, so that it immediately takes hold, not only of one city, but also of the widest regions and of the whole world, and is therefore like fire, for it passes through here and there, and that suddenly.

He then says, that *rocks are* also *broken* or dissolved *before him.* We must be aware how great our brittleness is. Since there is no hardness which melts not before God, how can men, who flow away of themselves like water, be so daring as to set themselves up against him? We hence see that the madness of men is here rebuked, who, trusting in their own strength, dare to contend even with God, because they forget their own frailty. This is the import of the whole. It now follows—

standing we have resisting. *Can* is better than *will;* the Hebrew future ought often to be thus rendered. With the view of giving the words here used their distinctive character, I offer the following version of the whole verse,—

> Before his anger who can stand?
> And who can resist the burning of his wrath?
> His indignation has been poured forth like fire;
> And rocks have been broken in pieces by him.

The two last verbs are in the past tense, and are more expressive when so rendered.—*Ed.*

7. The Lord *is* good, a strong hold in the day of trouble; and he knoweth them that trust in him.

7. Bonus Jehova ad fortitudinem in die angustiæ, et cognoscens sperantes in se.

The Prophet expresses more clearly here what we referred to in our last lecture,—that God is hard and severe toward refractory men, and that he is merciful and kind to the teachable and the obedient,—not that God changes his nature, or that like Proteus he puts on various forms; but because he treats men according to their disposition.[1] As then the Prophet has hitherto taught us, that God's wrath cannot be sustained by mortals; so now, that no one might complain of extreme rigour, he, on the other hand, shows that God favours what is right and just, that he is gentle and mild to the meek, and therefore ready to bring help to the faithful, and that he leaves none of those who trust in him destitute of his aid.

First, by saying that *God is good*, he turns aside whatever might be objected on the ground of extreme severity. There is indeed nothing more peculiar to God than goodness. Now when he is so severe, that the very mention of his name terrifies the whole world, he seems to be in a manner different from himself. Hence the Prophet now shows, that whatever he had hitherto said of the dreadful judgment of God, is not inconsistent with his goodness. Though God then is armed with vengeance against his enemies, he yet ceases not to be like himself, nor does he forget his goodness. But the Prophet does here also more fully confirm the Israelites and the Jews in the belief, that God is not only terrible to the ungodly, but that, as he has promised to be the guardian of his Church, he would also succour the faithful, and in time alleviate their miseries. *Good* then *is Jehovah;* and it is added, *for help*. The intention of the Prophet may be hence more clearly understood, when he says that he is for strength in the day of distress; as though he said,—"God is ever ready to bring help to his people:"[2] And he adds, *in the day*

[1] "This glorious description of the Sovereign of the world, like the pillar of cloud and of fire, has a bright side towards Israel, and a dark side towards the Egyptians."—*Henry*.

[2] This is no doubt the right view. The object here is not to assert generally that God is good, but that he is good for aid and help in the

of distress, that the faithful may not think that they are rejected, when God tries their patience by adversities. How much soever then God may subject his people to the cross and to troubles, he still succours them in their distress.

He lastly adds, *He knows them who hope in him.* This, to *know*, is no other thing than not to neglect them. Hence God is said to know them who hope in him, because he always watches over them, and takes care of their safety: in short, this knowledge is nothing else but the care of God, or his providence in preserving the faithful. The Prophet, at the same time, distinguishes the godly and sincere worshippers of God from hypocrites: when God leaves many destitute who profess to believe in him, he justly withholds from them his favour, for they do not from the heart call on him or seek him.

We now then understand the Prophet's meaning. He shows, on the one hand, that God is armed with power to avenge his enemies; and, on the other, he shows that God, as he has promised, is a faithful guardian of his Church. How is this proved? He sets before us what God is, that he is good; and then adds, that he is prepared to bring help. But he does not in vain mention this particular,—that he takes care of the faithful, who truly, and from the heart, hope in him; it is done, that they may understand that they are not neglected by God, and also, that hypocrites may know that they are not assisted, because their profession is nothing else but dissimulation, for they hope not sincerely in God, however they may falsely boast of his name. It now follows—

8. But with an overrunning flood he will make an utter end of the place thereof, and darkness shall pursue his enemies.	8. Et cum inundatione (*vel*, per inundationem) transiens consumptionem faciet locoejus; et inimicos ejus persequentur tenebræ (*vel*, persequi faciet inimicos suos à tenebris.)

day of distress. The versions then both of *Newcome* and *Henderson* are faulty; for they divide into two clauses what is one in the original,—

Good *is* Jehovah for protection in the day of distress;
And he knoweth them who trust in him.

The word מעין is from עז, strength, and having the formative מ, it attains a causative sense, and means that which affords or gives strength,—a fortress, a stronghold, or protection.—*Ed.*

The Prophet goes on with the same subject,—that God can easily preserve his people, for he is armed with power sufficient to overcome the whole world. But the Prophet now includes the two things which have been mentioned: Having spoken in general of God's wrath, and of his goodness towards the faithful, he now applies his doctrine to the consolation of his chosen people. It is then a special application of his doctrine, when he says, *By inundation, he, passing through, will make a consummation in her place.* There is a twofold interpretation of this verse.

Some make this distinction,—that God, as it were, in passing through, would consume the land of Israel and Judah, but that perpetual darkness would rest on his enemies. Hence they think, that the distress of the chosen people is distinguished from the overthrow of the kingdom of Asshur, for God would only for a time punish his own people, while he would give up profane and reprobate men to endless destruction. Then, by *passing through*, must be understood, according to these interpreters, a temporary distress or punishment; and by *darkness*, eternal ruin, or, so to speak, irreparable calamities. But the Prophet, I doubt not, in one connected sentence, denounces ultimate ruin on the Assyrians. *By inundation*, then, *he, in passing, will make a consummation in her place;* that is, God will suddenly overwhelm the Assyrians as though a deluge should rise to cover the whole earth. He intimates, that God would not punish the Assyrians by degrees, as men sometimes do, who proceed step by step to avenge themselves, but suddenly. God, he says, will of a sudden thunder against the Assyrians, as when a deluge comes over a land. Hence this passing of God is opposed to long or slow progress; as though he said,—"As soon as God's wrath shall break forth or come upon the Assyrians, it will be all over, for a consummation will immediately follow: by inundation, he, passing through, will make a consummation in her place."[1] By place he means the

[1] The first words in this line are better rendered in our version, "With an overrunning flood," or, as by *Newcome*, "With an overflowing torrent," or, as by *Henderson*, "With an overflowing inundation." The remaining part has occasioned a variety. The text as it is, and there

ground; as though he had said, that God would not only destroy the face of the land, but would also destroy the very ground, and utterly demolish it. A feminine pronoun is here added, because he speaks of the kingdom or nation, as it is usual in Hebrew. But it ought especially to be noticed, that the Prophet threatens the Assyrians, that God would entirely subvert them, that he would not only demolish the surface, as when fire or waters destroy houses, but that the Lord would reduce to nothing the land itself, even the very ground.

He adds, *And pursue his enemies shall darkness.* He has designated the Assyrians only by a pronoun, as the Hebrews are wont to do; for they set down a pronoun relative or demonstrative, and it is uncertain of whom they speak; but they afterwards explain themselves. So does the Prophet in this place; for he directs his discourse to the Israelites and the Jews, and he begins by announcing God's vengeance on Nineveh and its monarchy; but now he speaks as of a thing sufficiently known, and adds, *Pursue shall darkness the enemies* of God. By this second clause he intimates that the ruin of that kingdom would be perpetual. As then he had said that its destruction would be sudden, as God would, as it were, in a moment destroy the whole land; so now he cuts off from them every hope, that they might not think that they could

are no different readings, is this, "A full end he will make of her place;" or, as Henderson renders it, "He will effect a consummation of her place." The only difficulty is, that "her" has no near antecedent; but it is not unusual with the Prophets to allow the general context to supply this. As the vision is the "burden of Nineveh," that city is no doubt referred to. *Newcome*, following the Greek versions, excepting that of Symmachus, translates thus,—"He will make a full end of those who rise up against him." But it is better to follow the Hebrew text; for the many *evident* instances of mistake which are to be found in those versions forbid us to put any great confidence in them. The following may be viewed as a literal version:—

And with inundation overflowing
A full end he will make of her place;
And darkness shall his enemies pursue.

How completely has this prophecy been fulfilled! *Lucian*, a Greek heathen author of the second century, has these remarkable words,—Η Νινος μεν απολωλεν ηδη, και ουδεν ιχνος ετι λοιπον αυτης, ουδ' αν ειπης οπου ποτ' ην—"Nineveh has already been destroyed, and there is no vestige of it remaining, nor can you say where formerly it was." *Bochart* enumerates different conjectures which various authors have made as to its situation, most of them differing from one another.—*Ed.*

within a while gather strength and rise again, as it is the case with the wicked, who ever contend against God. The Prophet then shows that evil which God would bring on them would be without remedy. Some render the verb ירדף, *iredaph*, transitively in this form, "He will pursue his enemies by darkness:" but as to the meaning of the Prophet there is but little or no difference; I therefore leave the point undecided. On the subject itself there is nothing ambiguous; the import of what is said is,—that God would, by a sudden inundation, destroy his enemies,—and that he would destroy them without affording any hope of restoration, for perpetual darkness would follow that sudden deluge. He afterwards adds—

9. What do ye imagine against the Lord? he will make an utter end: affliction shall not rise up the second time.	9. Quid cogitatis contra Jehovam? consumptionem ipse facit; non consurget iterum afflictio.

Some interpreters so consider this verse also, as though the Prophet had said, that the calamity of the chosen people would not be a destruction, as God would observe some moderation and keep within certain limits. The unbelieving, we know, immediately exult, whenever the children of God are oppressed by adverse things, as though it were all over with the Church. Hence the Prophet here, according to these interpreters, meets and checks this sort of petulancy, "What imagine ye against God? He will indeed afflict his Church, but he will not repeat her troubles, for he will be satisfied with one affliction." They also think that the kingdom of Judah is here compared with the kingdom of Israel: for the kingdom of Israel had been twice afflicted: for, first, four tribes had been led away, and then the whole kingdom had been overturned. As then one calamity had been inflicted by Shalmanezar, and another by Tiglathpilezar, they suppose that there is here an implied comparison, as though the Prophet said, "God will spare the kingdom of Judah, and will not repeat his vengeance, as it happened to the kingdom of Israel." But this meaning is forced and too far-fetched. The Prophet then, I doubt not, continues here his discourse, and denounces perpetual ruin on the enemies of the Church. He says first, *What imagine ye against Jehovah?* He exults over the Assyrians, because they thought that they had to do only with mortals, and also with a mean people, and now worn out by many misfortunes. For we know that the kingdom of Judah had been weakened by many wars before the Assyrians made an irruption into the land: they had suffered two severe and grievous attacks from their neighbours, the king of Israel and the king of Syria; for then it was that they made the Assyrians their confederates. When therefore the Assyrians came against Judea, they thought that they would have no trouble in obtaining victory, as they engaged in war with an insignificant people, and as we have said, worn out by evils. But the Prophet shows here that the war was with the living God, and not with men, as they falsely thought. *What* then *imagine ye against Jehovah?* as though he said, "Know ye not that this people are under the care and protection of God? Ye cannot then attack the kingdom of Judah without having God as your opponent. As it is certain that this people are defended by a divine power, there is no reason for you to think that you will be victorious." At the same time, I know not why the Prophet's words should be confined to the tribe of Judah, since the purpose was to comfort the Israelites as well as the Jews.

Now this is a very useful doctrine; for the Prophet teaches us in general, that the ungodly, whenever they harass the Church, not only do wrong to men, but also fight with God himself; for he so connects us with himself, that all who hurt us touch the apple of his eye, as he declares in another place, (Zech. ii. 8.) We may then gather invaluable comfort from these words; for we can fully and boldly set up this shield against our enemies,—that they devise their counsels, and make efforts against God, and assail him; for he takes us under his protection for this end, that whenever we are injured, he may stand in the middle as our defender. This is one thing.

Now in the second clause he adds, that he will make a complete end, *Rise up again shall not distress;* that is, God is able to reduce you to nothing, so that there will be no need to assail you the second time. This passage, we know, has been turned to this meaning,—that God does not punish men twice, nor exceed moderation in his wrath: but this is wholly foreign to the mind of the Prophet. I have also said already that I do not approve of what others have said, who apply this passage to the Church, and especially to the kingdom of Judah. For I thus simply interpret the words of the Prophet,—that God can with one onset, when it seems good to him, so destroy his enemies, that there will be no need of striving with them the second time: *Il n'y faudra plus retourner*, as we say in our language. God then will make a full end; that is, he will be able in one moment to demolish his enemies, and the ruin will be complete, that is, the wasting will be entire. There will be no *distress again* or the second time; for it will be all over with the enemies of God; not that God observes always the same rule when he punishes his enemies, nor does Nahum here prescribe any general rule; but he simply means, that God, whenever it pleases him, instantly destroys his enemies. He afterwards adds—

10. For while *they be* folden together *as* thorns, and while they are drunken *as* drunkards, they shall be devoured as stubble fully dry.

10. Qui ad spinas perplexas et tanquam potatione sua ebrios (*vel*, et ebrios ubi inebriati fuerint; *potest enim duplex sensus; postea)* devorabuntur tanquam stipulæ ariditatis plenæ *(vel*, quasi stipula ariditatis in plenitudine, *vel*, arida in plenitudine.)

He goes on with this same subject,—that God, when he pleases to exercise his power, can, with no difficulty, consume his enemies: for the similitude, which is here added, means this,—that nothing is safe from God's vengeance; for by perplexed thorns he understands things difficult to be handled. When thorns are entangled, we dare not, with the ends of our fingers, to touch their extreme parts; for wherever we put our hands, thorns meet and prick us. As then prickings from entangled thorns make us afraid, so none of us dare to come nigh them. Hence the Prophet says, they who are as *entangled thorns ;* that is, " However thorny ye may be, however full of poison, full of fury, full of wickedness, full of frauds, full of cruelty, ye may be, still the Lord can with one fire consume you, and consume you without any difficulty." They were then as entangled thorns.

And then, *as drunken by their own drinking*. If we read so, the meaning is,—God or God's wrath will come upon you as on drunken men; who, though they exult in their own intemperance, are yet enervated, and are not fit for fighting, for they have weakened their strength by extreme drinking. There seems indeed to be much vigour in a drunken man, for he swaggers immoderately and foams out much rage; but yet he may be cast down by a finger; and even a child can easily overcome a drunken person. It is therefore an apt similitude,—that God would manage the Assyrians as the drunken are wont to be managed; for the more audacity there is in drunken men, the easier they are brought under; for as they perceive no danger, and are, as it were, stupified, so they run headlong with greater impetuosity. "In like manner," he says, "extreme satiety will be the cause of your ruin, when I shall attack you. Ye are indeed very violent; but all this your fury is altogether drunkenness: *Come*, he says, *to you shall the vengeance of God as to those drunken with their own drinking*."[1]

Some render the last words, "To the drunken according to their drinking;" and this sense also is admissible; but as the Prophet's meaning is still the same, I do not contend about words. Others indeed give to the Prophet's words a different sense: but I doubt not but that he derides here that haughtiness by which the Assyrians were swollen, and compares it to drunkenness; as though he said, "Ye are indeed more than enough inflated, and hence all tremble at your strength; but this your excess rather debilitates and

[1] *Newcome*, on the sole authority of the Syriac and the Targum, changes "thorns" into "princes," and thus wholly destroys the propriety of the simile of dry stubble at the end of the verse. *Henderson* says justly, that this change is on no account to be adopted.

Though like thorns, intwined,
And as with their drinking drunken,
They shall be consumed as stubble fully dry.

The particle עד, before "thorns," is to be here taken as in 1 Chron. iv. 27, as designating likeness.—*Ed.*

weakens your powers. When God then shall undertake to destroy you as drunken men, your insolence will avail you nothing; but, on the contrary, it will be the cause of your ruin as ye offer yourselves of your own accord; and the Lord will easily cast you down, as when one, by pushing a drunken man, immediately throws him on the ground."

And these comparisons ought to be carefully observed by us: for when there seems to be no probability of our enemies being destroyed, God can with one spark easily consume them. How so? for as fire consumes thorns entangled together, which no man dares to touch, so God can with one spark destroy all the wicked, however united together they may be. And the other comparison affords us also no small consolation; for when our enemies are insolent, and throw out high swelling words, and seem to frighten and to shake the whole world with their threatenings, their excess is like drunkenness; there is no strength within; they are frantic but not strong, as is the case with all drunken men.

And he says, *They shall be devoured as stubble of full dryness.* מלא, *mela*, means not only to be full, but also to be perfect or complete. Others render the words, "As stubble full of dryness," but the sense is the same. He therefore intimates, that there would be nothing to prevent God from consuming the enemies of his Church; for he would make dry their whole vigour, so that they would differ nothing from stubble, and that very dry, which is in such a state, that it will easily take fire. It follows—

11. There is *one* come out of thee, that imagineth evil against the Lord, a wicked counsellor.	11. Ex te egressus est cogitans (*vel*, consultans) contra Jehovam malum, consultor Beliiaal (*hoc est*, impius, *vel*, perversus; *alii vertunt*, Nihili.)

The Prophet now shows why God was so exceedingly displeased with the Assyrians, and that was, because he would, as a protector of his Church, defend the distressed against those who unjustly oppressed them. The Prophet then designed here to give the Jews a firm hope, so that they might know that God had a care for their safety; for if he had only threatened the Assyrians without expressing the reason, of what avail could this have been to the Jews? It is indeed gratifying and pleasing when we see our enemies destroyed; but this would be a cold and barren comfort, except we were persuaded that it is done by God's judgment, because he loves us, because he would defend us, having embraced us with paternal love; but when we know this, we then triumph even when in extreme evils. We are indeed certain of our salvation, when God testifies, and really proves also, that he is not only propitious to us, but that our salvation is an object of his care. This is the Prophet's design when he thus addresses Nineveh.

From thee has gone forth a deviser of evil against Jehovah, an impious adviser. The manner of speaking is much more emphatical, when he says, that the Assyrians consulted against God, than if he had said, that they had consulted against the Jews, or consulted against the chosen people of God.

But though this was said of the Jews, let us yet remember that it belongs also to us. The Prophet confirms the doctrine which I lately alluded to, that whenever the ungodly cause trouble to us, they carry on war with God himself, that whenever they devise any evil against us, they run headlong against him. For God sets up himself as a shield, and declares, that he will protect under the shadow of his wings all those who commit themselves to his protection. If we then lie hid under the guardianship of God, and flee to him in all our adversities, and while patiently enduring all wrongs, implore his protection and help, whosoever then will rise up against us will have God as his enemy. Why so? because he consults against him. And this reason shows, that whatever the Prophet has hitherto said against the Assyrians ought to be extended indiscriminately to all the enemies of the Church. For why did God threaten the Assyrians with a sudden inundation and with perpetual darkness? The reason is here subjoined,—because they consulted against him and his Church. The same thing then will also happen to our enemies, provided we remain quiet, as it has been said, under the protection of God.

But when he says, that he *had gone forth from that city who contrived evil against Jehovah*,—this ought not to be confined to Sennacherib, but must rather be viewed as common to all the Assyrians; as though he said, "Thou producest the fruit which thou shalt eat; for from thee will arise the cause of thy ruin. There is no reason for thee to expostulate with God, as though he cruelly raged against thee; for *from thee has gone forth he who devised evil against Jehovah:* thou reapest now the reward worthy of thy bringing forth; for where have originated counsels against the Church of God, except in thine own bosom, and in thine own bowels? The evil then which has proceeded from thee shall return on thine own head."

He then adds, *An impious consulter*, or counsellor, יועץ בליעל, *ivots beliol.* Respecting the word בליעל, *beliol*, the Hebrews themselves are not agreed. There are those who suppose it to be a compound word, בל יעל, It profits not; and they think that it is applied to designate things of nought as well as men of nought.[1] There are others who, like *Jerome*, render it, Without a yoke, but without reason. Then *Beliol* is properly a vain thing, which is wholly unsubstantial; and so it designates a man in whom there is no integrity. It is also applied to all the wicked, and to their crimes: hence a thing or work of Belial is said to be any heinous sin or a detestable crime; and the man who acts perversely and wickedly is called Belial. And Paul takes Belial simply for the very pravity of Satan, and of all the wicked; for he opposes Belial to Christ, (2 Cor. vi. 15.) We now then understand the meaning of the Prophet to be this,—that God denounces war on the Assyrians, because they made war unjustly on his people, and consulted not only against the Jews, but also against God, who had taken them, as it has been stated, under his own keeping and protection. It follows—

[1] "From בל, *not*, and יעל, *profit:*—As an abstract noun, *unprofitableness, worthlessness, wickedness:*—As an adjective, *worthless, wicked, good for nothing.*"—*Parkhurst.* "It alludes to *Baal*, the common idol of the natives bordering upon the Jews, whom the penmen of Scripture changing some letters by way of scorn called *Belial:* to express a further hatred to this idol they applied this name to the devil, 2 Cor. vi. 15; which word is derived either from a root that signifieth *not to profit*, or, *not to mount upward*, because he seeks the fall of mankind, and to keep those that are fallen into his snares, 2 Tim. ii. 26. *Jerome* fetcheth it from a root, which, with another word, signifieth *without a yoke*, or, *lawless;* therefore, the Septuagint commonly translate it, παρανομος."—*Leigh.*

12. Thus saith the Lord, Though *they be* quiet, and likewise many, yet thus shall they be cut down, when he shall pass through. Though I have afflicted thee, I will afflict thee no more.	12. Sic dixit Jehovah, Si tranquilli fuerint, utcunque fuerint multi (*vel*, potentes;) sic etiam tollentur et transibit: et si afflixerim te, non affligam te amplius.

The Prophet pursues here the same subject; but expresses more clearly what might have been doubtful,—that whatever strength there might be in the Assyrians, it could not resist the coming of God's vengeance. For *thus saith Jehovah, Though they be quiet and also strong, &c.* I cannot now finish this subject, but will only say this,—The Prophet intimates that though Nineveh promised to itself a tranquil state, because it was well fortified, and had a wide and large extent of empire, yet this thy peace, he says, or this thy confidence and security, shall not be an impediment, that the hand of God should not be extended to thee. *Though*, then, they be many or strong, &c.; for we can render רבים, *rebim*, strong as well as many; but either would suit this place; for we understand the Prophet's meaning to be, that all God's enemies would be cut off, however secure they might be, while depending on their own strength and fortresses. The rest to-morrow.

PRAYER.

Grant, Almighty God, that inasmuch as thou seest thy enemies at this day raging with cruel, yea, with diabolic fury against thy Church, we may find thee to be the same as the faithful in all former ages had found thee, even a defender of the safety of those who truly, and with a sincere heart, called on thee, and sought thee in extreme necessity; and do thou, at this day, stretch forth thine hand, and so restrain the fury which thou seest is against all thy servants and thy children, that the wicked may at length really find, even to their ruin, that they fight not with miserable mortals, disheartened and without defence, but with thine ineffable power, that they may be confounded, though not ashamed, and that, however they may clamour against thee and thine invincible hand, they may yet become an example and a manifest evidence, that thou art not only faithful in thy promises, but also armed with power, by which thou canst execute whatsoever thou hast promised respecting the preservation of thy Church, until thou at length gatherest us into that blessed rest, which has been provided for us by the blood of thy Son. Amen.

Lecture One Hundred and First.

We stated yesterday what the Prophet meant by these words, that *though* the Assyrians *were quiet and many*, they would yet be suddenly *cut off* by the Lord. He clearly intimates, that the wicked are never so fortified by their own forces or by the help of others, but that the Lord can, without any difficulty, destroy them.

As to the words, some connect the particle כן, *can*, with what he had said, "Though they be quiet," and give this version, "Though they be quiet and in like manner many," that is, though they be secure, thinking themselves safe from all danger, and so also trust in their own number, "yet they shall be removed." But the repetition of כן, *can*, in Hebrew is common; and the sentence may be thus explained, "Though they be quiet, and how many soever they may be, yet thus shall they be removed." וכן, וכן, *ucan, ucan*, that is, "As they are many, so also the many shall be destroyed." With regard to the verb גוז, *guz*, (but some, though not correctly, derive it from גזז, *gezaz*,) I take it in the sense of removing from the middle, of destroying: it properly means in Hebrew to remove to a distance, though almost all interpreters render it, "They are shorn," which ought rather to be, "They shall be shorn:" and both the verbs, גוז, *guz*, as well as גזז, *gizaz*, mean to clip or shear: but as the other sense suits the form of the Prophet's discourse better, I hesitate not thus to render it, "They shall be taken away," or destroyed. What the Prophet next adds, ועבר, *uober*, and he shall pass, is applied by some to the angel, by whom the army of Sennacherib was destroyed. Others think that a temporary pestilence is meant; as though he had said, that it would only pass through. But the Prophet seems to refer to a former clause, where he said, that God would suddenly destroy the Assyrians as it were with a sudden and unexpected deluge. This, then, is the most suitable meaning, that however much the Assyrians excelled in number of men and in strength, they would yet be suddenly destroyed; for the Lord would pass through, that is, the Lord would by one onset reduce them to nothing.[1]

Then it follows, *Though* (*and,* literally) *I have afflicted thee, yet afflict thee will I no more.* But this sentence must be thus rendered, 'Though thee have I afflicted, I will not afflict thee any more.' The Prophet meets a doubt, which might have laid hold on the perplexed minds of the faithful; for they saw that God had been hitherto angry with them. They might then have succumbed under their grief, had it not been added, that they had indeed been afflicted for a time, but that God would now put an end to his severity, for he would no longer afflict them. It is indeed certain, that they were often afflicted afterwards; but this ought to be confined to what the Assyrians had done; for we know that our Prophet directed his predictions chiefly against that monarchy: and then the monarchy of Babylon succeeded; but it was necessary that Nineveh should be first subverted, and that the government should be transferred to the Chaldeans, that the Israelites as well as the Jews might know, that that monarchy had been overthrown, because it rebelled against God himself by distressing his own people.

We now then perceive the intention of the Prophet: after having threatened the Assyrians, he now turns his discourse to the Israelites, *Though I have afflicted thee, I will no more afflict thee;* that is, There is no reason for the faithful to despond, because they have been hitherto severely treated by

[1] The best and the most literal version of these two lines, with the exception of the last word, is that of *Dr Wheeler*, as given by *Newcome*,—

Though they are at peace, and also mighty,
Still shall they be cut off, and pass away.

The last verb is in the singular number, ועבר, "and he shall pass through" or away, that is, the wicked counsellor mentioned in the preceding verse. *Newcome's* own version is that of a new text, which he has himself formed, from a mere hint derived from the Septuagint. *Henderson's* version is the following,—

Though they are complete and so very numerous,
Yet in this state they shall be cut off,
And he shall pass away.

The word שלמים means, no doubt, entire, complete, perfect, as well as to be at peace, secure, quiet; and may be referred, as the author says, to the complete condition of the Assyrian army: but what seems to be intended is the character of the nation.—*Ed.*

God; let them on the contrary remember, that these scourges are temporary, and that God's displeasure with his elect people and his Church is such, that he observes moderation; for this must ever be fulfilled,—'In the moment of mine indignation I smote thee; but I will show thee perpetual mercies,' (Isa. liv. 8.) This promise has been once given to the Church; and it is now in force, and will be in force to the end of the world. Thus we see that the Prophet obviated a doubt, lest the faithful should think that there was no hope for them, because they had found God so severe towards them; for he says that God was satisfied with the punishment which he had inflicted, and that he would no longer afflict his people. It follows—

13. For now will I break his yoke from off thee, and will burst thy bonds in sunder.	13. Et nunc conteram (*vel*, confringam) jugum ejus ab te, et vincula tua disrumpam.

He confirms what the former verse contains,—that God would now cease from his rigour; for he says, that the deliverance of this chosen people was nigh, when God would break down and reduce to nothing the tyranny of that empire. This verse clearly shows, that a clause in the preceding verse ought not to be so restricted as it is by some interpreters, who regard it as having been said of the slaughter of the army of Sennacherib. But the Prophet addresses here in common both the Israelites and the Jews, as it is evident from the context; and this verse also sufficiently proves, the Prophet does not speak of the Jews only; for they had not been so subdued by the Assyrians as the Israelites had been. I indeed allow that they became tributaries; for when they had broken their covenant, the Assyrian, after having conquered the kingdom of Israel and the kingdom of Syria, extended his arms at length to Judea. It is then certain, that they had been in some measure under the yoke; but it was not so hard a servitude that the words of the Prophet could be applied to it. I therefore take the expression generally, that God would free from the tyranny of Nineveh his own people, both the Israelites and the Jews. If any one objects and says, that the Israelites were never delivered.

This indeed is true; but as to Nineveh, they were delivered when the empire was transferred to the Chaldeans, and Babylon became the seat of the empire.

We now then see, that the meaning of our Prophet is simply this,—that though God by the Assyrians chastised his people, he yet did not forget his covenant, for the Assyrians were punished. It was then sufficient for his purpose to say that the Jews as well as the Israelites were no longer under the yoke of Nineveh, how much soever they might have afterwards suffered under other tyrants. And what is said about the yoke being broken, belongs also in some measure to the Jews; for when we extend this to both, the Israelites and also the Jews, it would not be unsuitable to say, that they were both under the yoke and bound with chains. For though the servitude of Israel was hard, yet the Jews had also been deprived of their liberty. It is then right that this which is said should be taken generally, *I will now break his yoke from thee, and thy bonds will I burst.*

Now this verse teaches us, that the people were not so subdued by the tyranny of their enemies, but that their deliverance was always in the hand and power of God. For how came it, that the Assyrians prevailed against the Israelites, and then subjugated the Jews, except that they were as a rod in the hand of God? So Isaiah teaches us in the tenth chapter. Though they armed themselves, they were yet but as the weapons and arms of God, for they could not have made any movement, except the Lord had turned their course, wherever he pleased, as when one throws a javelin or a dart with his hand. It follows—

14. And the Lord hath given a commandment concerning thee, *that* no more of thy name be sown: out of the house of thy gods will I cut off the graven image and the molten image: I will make thy grave; for thou art vile.

14. Et mandavit super te Jehova, Ne seminetur ex nomine tuo posthac; è domo (*vel*, è templo) deorum tuorum excidam sculptile et conflatile; ponam sepulchrum tuum, quia execrabilis es (*aut*, vilis factus es.)

Nahum explains more clearly, and without a figure, what he had previously said of darkness,—that the kingdom of Nineveh would be so overturned, that it could never recruit its strength and return again to its pristine state. He indeed addresses the king himself, but under his person he includes no doubt the whole kingdom.

Commanded then *has Jehovah*, he says, *respecting thee, let there not be sown of thy name;* that is, God has so decreed, that the memory of thy name shall not survive: for to sow from the name of one, is to extend his fame. When, therefore, God entirely exterminates a race from the world, or when he obliterates a nation, he is said to command that there should not be sown of such a name; that is, that there should be no propagation of that name. In short, our Prophet denounces on the Assyrians a ruin, from which they were never to rise again. And when such a command is ascribed to God, it means, that by the sole bidding of God both nations and kingdoms are propagated, and are also abolished and destroyed: for what is said of individuals ought to be extended to all nations, 'Seed, or the fruit of the womb,' as it is said in the Psalms, 'is the peculiar gift of God,' (Ps. cxxvii.) For how comes it, that many are without children, while others have a large and a numerous family, except that God blesses some, and makes others barren? The same is to be thought of nations; the Lord propagates them and preserves their memory; but when it seems good to him, he reduces them to nothing, so that no seed remains. And when the Prophet testifies, that this is the command of Jehovah, he confirms the faith of the Israelites and of the Jews, that they might not doubt, but that the Assyrians would perish without any hope of restoration; for it was so decreed by Heaven.

He afterwards adds, *From the house*, or from the temple, *of thy gods will I cut off graven images.* It is probable, and it is the commonly received opinion, that the Prophet alludes here to Sennacherib, who was slain in the temple of his idol by his own sons, shortly after his return from Judea, when the siege of the holy city was miraculously raised through the instrumentality of an angel. As then he was slain in the temple, and it was by his murder profaned, I am inclined to receive what almost all others maintain, that there is here a reference to his person: but, at the same time, the Prophet no doubt describes, under the person of one king, the destruction and ruin of the whole kingdom. God, indeed, did at that time make known what he had determined respecting the empire of Nineveh and all the Assyrians; for from this event followed also the change, that Nebuchodonosor transferred the empire to Babylon, and that the whole race, and every one who assumed power, became detestable. When, therefore, the Assyrians were torn by intestine discords, it was an easy matter for the Chaldeans to conquer them. Hence the Prophet does not here predict respecting one king only; but as his murder was, as it were, a prelude of the common ruin, the Prophet relates this history as being worthy of being remembered,—that the temple would be profaned by the murder of Sennacherib, and that then the monarchy would be soon transferred to the Chaldeans.

When he says, *I will appoint thy sepulchre,* he connects this clause with the former; for how was it that idols were cut off from that temple, except that that tragic deed rendered the place detestable? For there is no one who feels not a horror at such a base crime as that of children killing their father with their own hands. We know when a proud woman at Rome ordered her chariot to be drawn over the dead body of her father, the road was counted polluted. So also the temple was no doubt viewed as polluted by the murder of the king. Then these two clauses ought to be read together, —that God would cut off idols and graven images from the temple,—and then, that the sepulchre of Sennacherib would be there.

He adds, *For thou art execrable.*[1] I have rendered קלות, *kolut*, a thing to be abominated. It may indeed be referred to that history; but I take it by itself as meaning, that Sennacherib was to be abominable, and not he alone, but also the whole royal family, and the monarchy of Nineveh. For it is not consistent, as we have said already, to say, that all these things refer to the person of Sennacherib; for the Pro-

[1] For thou art become vile.—*Newcome.*
Because thou art worthless.—*Henderson.*
Execrable, or, accursed, which the word sometimes means, seems most suitable to the context.—*Ed.*

phet speaks of the destruction of the city and nation, and that generally; at the same time, this does not prevent him from referring, as it were, in passing, to the person of Sennacherib.

It must, at the same time, be noticed, that the vain confidence, which the Assyrian kings placed in their idols and graven images, is here indirectly reproved; for we know that idolaters not only confide in their own strength, but that a part of their hope is also founded on their superstitions. Hence the Prophet says, that their temple was to be profaned by God, so that no aid would remain to the Assyrians, to the kings themselves any more than to the whole people. Let us proceed—

15.[1] Behold upon the mountains the feet of him that bringeth good tidings, that publisheth peace! O Judah, keep thy solemn feasts, perform thy vows: for the wicked shall no more pass through thee; he is utterly cut off.

15. Ecce super montes pedes annunciantis, promulgantis pacem: celebra Jehudah solennitates tuas, redde vota tua; quia non adjiciet posthac ad transeundum in te, impius (Beliiaal) in totum excisus est.

The Prophet again teaches us, that whatever he prophesied respecting the destruction of the city Nineveh, was for this end,—that God, by this remarkable evidence, might show that he had a care for his people, and that he was not unmindful of the covenant he had made with the children of Abraham. This prophecy would have otherwise produced no salutary effect on the Israelites; they might have thought that it was by chance, or by some fatal revolution, or through some other cause, that Nineveh had been overthrown. Hence the Prophet shows, that the ruin of the city, and of the monarchy of Nineveh, would be a proof of the paternal love of God towards his chosen people, and that such a change was to be made for the sake of one people, because God, though he had for a time punished the Israelites, yet purposed that some seed should remain; for it would have been inconsistent, that the covenant, which was to be inviolate, should be entirely abolished. We now then understand the Prophet's

[1] This forms the first verse of the second chapter in Hebrew. Most versions have followed the division of the Septuagint.—*Ed.*

object, and how this verse is to be connected with the rest of the context.

Behold, he says, *on the mountains the feet of him who announces peace.*[1] Some think that the Prophet alludes to the situation of Jerusalem. We indeed know that mountains were around it: but the Prophet speaks more generally,—that heralds of peace shall ascend to the tops of mountains, that their voice might be more extensively heard: *Behold*, he says, *on the mountains the feet of him who announces peace;* for all the roads had been before closed up, and hardly any one dared to whisper. If any one inquired either respecting peace or war, there was immediate danger lest he should fall under suspicion. As then the Assyrians, by their tyrannical rule, had deprived the Israelites of the freedom of speech, the Prophet says now, that the feet of those who should announce peace would be on the mountains; that is, that there would be now free liberty to proclaim peace on the highest places. By *feet*, he means, as we have explained, coming; and Isaiah speaks a similar language, 'How beautiful are the feet of those who announce peace, who announce good things!' (Isa. lii. 7.) Arise, then, he says, shall heralds of peace everywhere: and the repetition in other words seems to express this still more clearly; for he says, *of him who announces and causes to hear.* He might have simply said מבשר, *mebesher*, but he adds משמיע, *meshemio;* not only, he says, he will announce peace, but also with a clear and loud voice, so that his preaching may be heard from the re-

[1] *Calvin* gives to מבשר only the sense of announcing or declaring. To spread or to bring news or tidings is its meaning; for it is used to designate bad as well as good tidings. See 1 Sam. iv. 17; 2 Sam. i. 20; and 2 Sam. iv. 10; Isa. lii. 7. It is commonly rendered εναγγελιζεσθαι by the Septuagint. It may be regarded here as a participle in the same predicament with the participle which follows. The same mode of construction we find in Isa. lii. 7; where it evidently appears that the word means strictly to bring or to declare tidings, for *good* is added to it. That passage is as follows:—

How beautiful on the mountains
Are the feet of him who announceth,
Who proclaimeth peace,—
Of him who announceth good, (מבשר טוב,)
Who proclaimeth salvation!
Saying to Zion, Reign doth thy God.—*Ed.*

motest places. We now perceive what the Prophet had in view, and what his words import.

Now he adds, *Celebrate, Judah, thy festal days.* It is indeed a repetition of the same word, as if we were to say in Latin, *Festiva festivitates,* feast festivities; but this has nothing to do with the meaning of the passage. I am disposed to subscribe to the opinion of those who think, that there is here an intimation of the interruption of festal days; for so disordered were all things at Jerusalem and in the country around, that sacrifices had ceased, and festal days were also intermitted; for sacred history tells us, that the Passover was celebrated anew under Hezekiah, and also under Josiah. This omission no doubt happened, owing to the wars by which the country had been laid waste. Hence the Prophet now intimates, that there would be quietness and peace for the chosen people, so that they might all without any fear ascend to Jerusalem, and celebrate their festal days, and give thanks to the Lord, and rejoice before him, according to the language often used by Moses. At the same time, the Prophet no doubt reminds the Jews for what end the Lord would break off the enemy's yoke, and exempt them from servile fear, and that was, that they might sacrifice to God and worship him, while enjoying their quiet condition. And that he addresses Judah is not done without reason; for though the kingdom of Israel was not as yet so rejected, that God did not regard them as his people, yet there were no legitimate sacrifices among them, and no festal days which God approved: we indeed know that the worship which prevailed there was corrupt and degenerated. Inasmuch then as God repudiated the sacrifices which were offered in Israel, Nahum addresses here his discourse to Judah only; but yet he intimates, that God had been thus bountiful to the Israelites, that they, remembering their deliverance, might give him thanks.

Let us then know, that when the Lord grants us tranquillity and preserves us in a quiet state, this end ought ever to be kept in view,—that it is his will, that we should truly serve him. But if we abuse the public peace given us, and if pleasures occasion a forgetfulness of God, this ingratitude will by no means be endured. We ought, indeed, in extreme necessities, to sacrifice to God, as we have need then especially of fleeing to his mercy; but as we cannot so composedly worship him in a disturbed state of mind, he is pleased to allow us peaceable times. Now, if we misapply this leisure, and indulge in sloth, yea, if we become so heedless as to neglect God, this, as I have said, will be an intolerable evil. Let us then take notice of the Prophet's words in setting forth the design of God,—that he would free his people from the power of the Assyrians, that they might celebrate their festal days.

He adds, *Pay thy vows.* He not only speaks here of the ordinary sacrifices and of the worship which had been prescribed; but he also requires a special proof of gratitude for having been then delivered by the hand of God; for we know what paying of vows meant among the Hebrews: they were wont to offer peace-offerings, when they returned victorious from war, or when they were delivered from any danger, or when they were relieved from some calamity. The Prophet therefore now shows, that it was right to pay vows to God, inasmuch as he had dealt so bountifully with his people; as it is said in Ps. cxvi. 'What shall I return to the Lord for all his benefits, which he hath bestowed on me? The cup of salvation will I take, and on the name of the Lord will I call.' We also find it thus written in Hosea, 'The calves of thy lips to me shalt thou render,' (Hosea xiv. 13.) We now perceive what Nahum substantially meant,—that when peace was restored, the people were not to bury so great and so remarkable a kindness of God, but to pay their vows; that is, that the people were to testify that God was the author of their deliverance, and that the redemption which they had obtained was the peculiar work of God.

It follows, *Add no more to pass through thee shall Belial, for utterly is he cut off.* This passage must not be explained in a general sense; for we know that the Chaldeans became more grievous to the Jews than the Assyrians had been; but the Prophet here refers especially to the Ninevites, that is, to the Assyrians, whose metropolis, as it has been said, was Nineveh. *That wicked one* then *shall not add any more to pass* through thee.—Why? for *he is entirely cut off*. This reason given by the Prophet clearly proves, that he speaks not of the wicked generally, but that he especially points out the Assyrians. Now follows—

CHAPTER II.

1. He that dasheth in pieces is come up before thy face: keep the munition, watch the way, make *thy* loins strong, fortify *thy* power mightily.

2. For the Lord hath turned away the excellency of Jacob, as the excellency of Israel: for the emptiers have emptied them out, and marred their vine branches.

1. Ascendit destructor coram facie tua; custodi munitionem, respice viam, robora lumbos, fortifica vires valdè:

2. Quia abstulit (*alii vertunt*, recedere fecit; *alii*, quiescere fecit) Jehova fortitudinem (*alii*, superbiam) Jacob, sicuti fortitudinem (*vel*, superbiam, *est idem nomen)* Israel; quia evacuarunt evacuantes, et palmites eorum succiderunt.

The waster spoken of here by the Prophet, some consider him to have been Sennacherib, and others, Nebuchodonosor. The verb עלה, *ole*, is also variously explained: it is often taken metaphorically in Hebrew for vanishing, as we say in French, *Il s'en va en fumee;* for smoke ascends, and this is the reason for the metaphor. They then elicit this meaning,—that a destroyer had ascended before the face of the chosen people, that is, openly; so that it was evidently the work of God, that the Assyrians vanished, who had come to lay waste the whole land: Vanished then has the destroyer; and then *before thy face*, that is, manifestly, and before thine eyes. נצור מצורה, *nutsur metsure, guard the fortress;* that is, let every one return to his own city, and keep watch, as it is usually done; for the country shall be left without men; and *watch the way*, that is, look out which way Sennacherib took in coming to assail the holy city; that way shall be now free from enemies; and then, keep *firm* or strengthen *the loins*, for חזק, *chesek*, sometimes means to keep firm,—keep firm then or strengthen the loins, that thou mayest not relax as before, but stand courageously, for there is no one who can terrify thee; and, lastly, *fortify strength greatly*, that is, doubt not but thou shalt be hereafter strong enough to retain thy position; for cut off shall be that monarchy, which has been an oppression to thee. But others take a different view and say,—that the destroyer had ascended, that is, that Sennacherib had come; and what follows, they think, was intended to strike terror, as though the Prophet said, "Now while ye are besieged, keep watch, and be careful to preserve your fortresses and strengthen all your strongholds; but all this will avail nothing.—Why? Because God hath taken away the pride of Jacob as he has the pride of Israel." This is the second explanation. Others again think, that the Prophet addresses here the Assyrians, and that Nebuchodonosor is here called a waster, by whom the empire was removed, and Nineveh, as it has often been stated, was destroyed. According to these interpreters, the Prophet here denounces ruin on the Assyrians in this manner, —"The destroyer now ascends before thy face." The Assyrians might indeed have regarded such threatenings with disdain, when they were surrounded by many provinces and had cities well fortified:—"It will not be," he says, "according to your expectation; the waster will yet come before thy face; and how much soever thou mayest now guard thy fortresses, watch thy ways, and carefully look around to close up every avenue against thy enemies, thou wilt yet effect nothing; strengthen the loins as much as thou pleasest and increase thy power, yet this shall be useless and vain." If this view be approved, it will be in confirmation of what has been previously said,—that God had now determined to destroy the city Nineveh and the empire possessed by the Assyrians. This meaning then is not unsuitable; but if we receive this view, something additional must also be stated, and that is,—that God now designed to destroy Nineveh and its monarchy, because it had humbled more than necessary his people, the kingdom of Judah, as well as the ten tribes. I cannot proceed farther now.

PRAYER.

Grant, Almighty God, that since we are daily chastised by thy scourges, we may know that we are justly punished by thee, and so examine our whole life, that with true and sincere confession we may humbly flee to thy mercy, which is offered to us by thy gospel in Christ our Lord; and since thou dost also show us so many favours, may we not be ungrateful, and may no forgetfulness of thy grace creep over us, but may we especially exercise ourselves through our whole life in the worship of thy name and in giving thanks to thee, and so offer to thee, with our tongues, the sacrifices of praise, that our whole life may be consistent, and thus glorify thy name on earth, that at length we may be gathered into thy celestial kingdom, through the same Christ Jesus our Lord. Amen.

Lecture One Hundred and Second.

We said yesterday that some interpreters regard these words of the Prophet, *Ascended has the destroyer before thy face, guard the fortress*, as having a reference to Sennacherib; that is, that God had taken him away, and made him like mist to disappear. We also said, that some elicit this meaning,—that Sennacherib ascended into Judea and filled the whole country with terror, and that he had at length laid it wholly waste. But I am disposed to take their view, who think that this is said of Nebuchodonosor, the waster of Nineveh: as he had been raised up by God to overturn the tyranny of that city, the Prophet ridicules all the efforts and preparations made by the Ninevites (as it is usual when a country is invaded) to oppose him. He therefore says, *guard the fortress, watch the way, confirm the loins, and strengthen thy courage greatly*. But these are ironical expressions; as though he said, "Whatever the Ninevites may contrive to defend themselves against the assault of their enemies will be all in vain."[1]

[1] That the Babylonian power is meant by "the destroyer," or disperser, or scatterer, is the opinion of *Jerome*, *Drusius*, *Grotius*, *Marckius*, and *Newcome*. But *Kimchi*, *Dathius*, *Henderson*, and some others, regard the "destroyer" as the king of Assyria. What agrees best with the context is the former opinion. Having in the preceding verse announced the release of the people of Israel from the rule of Assyria, the Prophet now introduces its destroyer, and then proceeds with the main object of his prophecy, and describes the fall of Nineveh. *Marckius* considers the whole verse as addressed to the Babylonian power under the person of the king, while *Calvin* regards it, with the exception of the first line or clause, as addressed ironically to Nineveh. The verbs are either participles or preterites indicative; but they are construed by the former as gerunds; most regard them as imperatives. נצור is rendered as a passive parti-

What is now subjoined has been added, in my view, in reference to what had already taken place, that is, that God *had taken away the pride of Jacob, as the pride of Israel.* Some give this rendering, "God has made to return, or to rest;" and they take גאון, *gaun,* in a good sense, as meaning courage or glory. The sense, according to these, would be,—that God, having routed the army of Sennacherib, or destroyed the Assyrians, would make the ancient glory of his people to return; for both kingdoms had fallen. They then understand this to have been said respecting the restoration of the whole people; and they who translate, "he will make to rest," think that continual peace is here promised to the Israelites, as well as to the Jews. But, on the contrary, it appears to me, that the Prophet shows, that it was the ripened time for the destruction of the city Nineveh, for God had now humbled his people. *He had* then *taken away the pride of Jacob, as the pride of Israel;* that is, God, having first corrected the pride of Israel, had also applied the same remedy to Judah: thus the whole people were humbled, and had left off their extreme height; for גאון, *gaun,* for the most part, is taken in a bad sense, for haughtiness or pride. This then is the reason why God now declares, that the ruin of Nineveh was nigh at hand; it was so, because the Jews and the Israelites had been sufficiently brought down. This sense is the most suitable.

And then for the same purpose is the next clause,—that *the emptiers had emptied,* that is, that robbers had pillaged them, and left nothing to remain for them. There is a

ciple by the Septuagint, and so it appears to be, and the three which follow, as imperatives. But in two copies it is without the ו; then all the verbs in the verse appear to be in the same form, and may be considered to be either preterites indicative or participles; and participles are often used in Hebrew to express the present tense: and the Prophet may be considered as seeing the Babylonian ascending and laying siege to Nineveh, for מצורה means a siege as well as a fortress: then the rendering would be as follows,—

> Ascend does the waster before thee;
> He watches the siege, guards the way,
> Makes firm the loins, exerts strength mightily.

But if "fortress" be preferred to "siege," it may be adopted consistently with the context.—*Ed.*

passage in Isaiah which corresponds with this, where it is said,—that when the Lord had completed his work on mount Zion and in Jerusalem, he would then turn his vengeance against the Assyrians, (Isa. x. 12:) but why were they not sooner destroyed? Because the Lord designed to employ them for the purpose of chastising the Jews. Until then the whole work of God was completed, that is, until he had so corrected their pride, as wholly to cast it down, it was not his purpose to destroy the Ninevites; but they were at length visited with destruction. The same thing does our Prophet now teach us here,—that Nebuchodonosor would come to demolish Nineveh, when the Lord had taken away the haughtiness of his people.[1]

What follows, *And they have destroyed their shoots*, or their branches, I take metaphorically, because the Israelites, as to outward appearances, had been pulled up by the roots; for before the eyes of their enemies they were reduced to nothing, and their very roots were torn up, so that they perceived nothing left. The Lord indeed always preserved a hidden remnant; but this was done beyond the perceptions of men. But what the Prophet says metaphorically of the ruined branches, is to be understood of what was apparent.

3. The shield of his mighty men is made red, the valiant men *are* in scarlet: the chariots *shall be* with flaming torches in the day of his preparation, and the fir-trees shall be terribly shaken.	3. Clypeus fortium ejus rubefactus est, viri potentiæ ejus vermiculati (*hoc est*, rubro etiam colore;) in igne lampadum (*vel*, tædarum) currus in die expeditionis ejus, et abietes tremefactæ sunt.

[1] *Drusius* confessed that he did not understand this verse. The view given of it by *Calvin* seems plain, and *Marckius* takes the same view of it: but *Newcome*, as well as *Henderson*, differ widely, and give a rendering which seems not to comport with the context. It is like that of *Drusius*, which no doubt made him to say that he did not understand the passage.

For Jehovah restoreth the excellency of Jacob,
As the excellency of Israel.

In this connection, this can have no meaning. The version of *Henderson* is the same, only he puts the verb in the future tense. The verb שב has the meaning of turning away, as well as of restoring, and *Marckius* renders it *avertit*, he turned away. Then גאון, rising, swelling, *elatio*, is more commonly taken in a bad than in a good sense, as meaning pride, haughtiness. The latter part of the verse sets before us distinctly the means which had been adopted to take away this pride. The passage is evidently parenthetic.—*Ed.*

The Prophet describes here how dreadful the Chaldeans would be when prepared against the Assyrians. He says, *The shield of his brave men*[1] *is made red.* Some think that their shields were painted red, that blood might not appear; and that the soldiers had on red garments, that they might not be frightened in case they were wounded; and this is what history records of the Lacedemonians. But as the habits of these nations are not much known to us, it is enough for us to know, that their warlike appearance is here described; as though he had said, that the Chaldeans would come against Nineveh with violent and terrible power. Hence he says, that *the men of his strength*[2] *would be clad in scarlet;* he refers no doubt to the colour of their dress. Some expound this of the Assyrians, and say that their shame is here designated; but this is too strained. The Prophet, I have no doubt, describes here the Chaldeans, and shows that they would be so armed that even their very appearance would put to flight their enemies, that is, the Assyrians.

For the same purpose he afterwards adds, *With fire of torches,*[3] or lamps, *is the chariot in the day of his expedition.* The word פלדות, *peladut,* occurs no where else; and the Jews think that the letters are inverted, and that it should be לפידות, as this word is afterwards used by the Prophet in the next verse, and in the same sense. It is certainly evi-

[1] גבוריהו, of his heroes,—" heroum."—*Dathius.*

[2] אנשי־חיל, men of war,—" warriors," *Henderson;* " the valiant men." —*Newcome.*

[3] The most satisfactory explanation of this word is what is offered by *Parkhurst,* and adopted by *Henderson.* He says that פלד, in Arabic, is to *cut,* or *cut in pieces,* and that פלדות may have been the *scythes* or cutting instruments with which the chariots were armed. Then in eight or nine MSS. the ב, *beth,* before אש, is כ, *caph.* If this reading be adopted, and the poetical singular number be retained as to the word chariot, the clause may be thus translated :—

Like fire *are* the scythes of the chariot,
In the day of his preparation.

To which shall be added the line which follows,—

And the fir-trees (spears) tremulously shake.

Fir-trees are rendered " cypresses " by *Henderson;* and *Newcome,* following the Septuagint, changes the word into what signifies " horsemen." The figure is bold, but it is no unusual thing in poetry to call an instrument by the name of the material of which it is made.—*Ed.*

dent from the context that either torches or lamps are meant by the Prophet. His chariot then is with the fire of lamps, that is, his chariots drive so impetuously that they appear as flames of fire, when wheels roll with such velocity.

And *the fir-trees*, he says, *are terribly shaken.* Some translate, "are inebriated," or, "stunned;" and they apply this to the Assyrians,—that their great men (whom they think are here compared to fir-trees, or are metaphorically designated by them) were stunned through amazement. Astonished then shall be the principal men among the Assyrians; for the very sight of their enemies would render them, as it were, lifeless; for the verb רעל, *rol*, is taken by some in the sense of infecting with poison, or of stupifying. But their opinion is more correct who think that fir-trees are to be taken for lances, though they do not sufficiently express the meaning of the Prophet; for he means, I have no doubt, that such would be the concussion among the lances, that it would be like that of fir-trees, tossed here and there in the forest. For lances, we know, are made of fir-trees, because it is a light wood and flexible, as when any one says in our language, *les lances branslent.* The lances then trembled, or shook in the hands of the soldiers, as fir-trees shake. Thus we see that the Prophet here continues to describe the terrible appearance of the Chaldeans. Let us go on—

4. The chariots shall rage in the streets, they shall justle one against another in the broad ways: they shall seem like torches, they shall run like the lightnings.	4. In compitis insanient per currus *(est hic nomen singulare*, currus, *ideo quidam subaudiunt viros currus, sed possumus aliter intelligere, quòd insaninient in suis curribus; deinde)* properabunt in plateis *(alii vertunt*, congregabuntur; *potest deduci tam à* שקק, *quàm à* שוק, *sed hic significat properare;)* aspectus eorum quasi lampades *(hoc est*, lampadum,) quasi fulgura discurrent.

He still goes on with the same subject,—that they shall be furious in the streets, that is, that they shall be so turbulent, as though they were out of their minds: as furious men are wont to be who are impetuously carried away beyond all reason and moderation, so shall they also become mad in their tumult. He then says, *They shall hasten.* The verb is derived from the hips; for he who hastens shakes the hips, and moves them with a quick motion; and if it be lawful to coin a word, it is, they shall hip; *Ils remueront les hanches.* This is what the Prophet meant. And then, *Their appearance*[1] shall be *as lamps.* He refers here to the chariots. They shall then be like lamps; that is, they will dazzle the eyes of beholders with their brightness. All these things are intended to set forth what is terrific. He says also, *as lightning* they shall run here and there.

In short, he intimates, that the impetuosity of the Chaldeans would be so violent as to surpass what is commonly witnessed among men, that it would be, as it were, a species of fury and madness, sent down from above. Thus, then, they were to be like lightning and flames of fire, that they might exceed every thing human. But these forms of speech, though they are hyperbolical, were not yet used without reason; for we may easily conjecture how great was then the security of the city Nineveh, and how incredible was the event of its ruin. That monarchy was then pre-eminent over every other in the whole world, and no one could have thought that it could ever be assailed. Since then it was difficult to persuade the Jews that ruin was nigh the Assyrians, it was necessary for the Prophet to accumulate these various forms of expressions, by which he sets forth the power of God in the destruction of the Assyrians. It afterwards follows—

5. He shall recount his worthies: they shall stumble in their walk; they shall make haste to the wall thereof, and the defence shall be prepared.

5. Recordabitur fortium suorum, impingent in itinere suo *(vel,* itineribus suis, *si legamus plurali numero;)* festinabunt ad murum ejus, parabitur integumentum.

Some interpreters explain this also of the Chaldeans: The king of Babylon then shall remember his mighty men; that is, shall recount his forces and whatever strength he will have under his power; all this he will collect to make war with Nineveh and the Assyrians. Others think that there is here a transposition in the words, (which is too strained,) "Mighty men shall remember," as though it were a change of number. But I take the words of the Prophet simply as they are,—

[1] מראיהן, three MSS. have the masculine suffix הם.—*Ed.*

that he will remember mighty men: but this, as I think, refers to the Assyrians. He then, that is, either the king of Nineveh, or the people, will remember the mighty men; that is, he will gather from every quarter his forces, and will omit nothing which may avail for defence; as it is usually done in great danger and in extremities: for they were noted then as warlike men; and every one who had any skill, every one who was endued with courage, every one who was trained up in arms, all these were mustered, that they might give help. So then the Prophet says, that such would be the dread in the land of Assyria, that they would collect together whatever force they had, to defend themselves against their enemies. The king then *shall remember his mighty men*, that is, he will muster all the subsidies within his reach.

Then he says, *They shall stumble in their march;* that is, the mighty men, when gathered, shall tremble and stumble like the blind: and this will be occasioned by fear; so that like men astounded, they will move to and fro, and have no certain footing. The Prophet then declares here two things, that the Assyrians would be diligent in gathering forces to repel the assault of their enemies,—but that yet they would effect nothing, for trembling would seize the minds of all, so that mighty men would stumble in their marches. They shall stumble, and then it is said, they *shall hasten to its wall*, that is, they shall ascend the wall; and it is added, *Prepared shall be the covering*, as it is usual in defending cities. Some apply this to the Chaldeans; prepared shall be the covering, that is, when they shall come to the wall. It was indeed usual, as it is well known from histories, for those who approached a wall to defend themselves either with turrets or hurdles. But the Prophet, I doubt not, intimates, that the Assyrians would come with great trembling to meet their enemies, but without any success. However then they might defend themselves, their enemies would yet prevail.[1] He therefore subjoins—

[1] This verse is applied by *Grotius* and *Newcome* to the Babylonian and not to the Assyrian king. The last clause seems to favour this opinion, but the second, the other. To render יכשלו as a Hiphil, "They cast down," without an objective case, cannot be approved; but they may

6. The gates of the rivers shall be opened, and the palace shall be dissolved.

6. Portæ fluviorum apertæ sunt, et palatium solutum est.

By the gates of the rivers the Prophet means that part of the city which was most fortified by the river Tigris; for the Tigris flowed close by the city. As then the Tigris was like the strongest defence, (for we know it to have been a most rapid river,) the Prophet ridicules the confidence of the Ninevites, who thought that the access of enemies could be wholly prevented in that part where the Tigris flowed. *The gates* then *of the rivers are opened;* that is, your river shall not prevent your enemies from breaking through and penetrating into your city.

We hence see, that the Prophet removes all the hinderances which might have seemed available to keep off enemies; and he did so, not so much for the sake of Nineveh as for the sake of his chosen people, that the Israelites and Jews might know, that that city was no less in the power of God than any other; for God can no less easily pass through rivers than go along the plain, where there is no obstacle. We now see why the Prophet says, that the gates of the rivers were opened: and then he adds, *The palace is dissolved;* that is, there will be no impediment to prevent the approach of enemies; for all the fortresses will melt away, and that of themselves, as though they were walls of paper, and the stones, as though they were water. He afterwards adds—

7. And Huzzab shall be led away captive, she shall be brought up, and her maids shall lead *her* as with the voice of doves, tabering upon their breasts.

7. Et quæ stabat solida (*vel,* firma) ejecta est in exilium (*vel,* quæ stabat occulta, patefacta est, jussa est ascendere;) et ancillæ ejus ducentes tanquam in voce columbarum, plangentes super pectora sua.

There is some ambiguity in these words, and many interpreters think that הצב, *etsab,* to be the name of the queen. The queen then, they say, of the name of הצב, *etsab,* is drawn away into exile; she is bidden to ascend, that she

have been said to "stumble," as the word means, from their great haste, afterwards mentioned. *Piscator*, *Marckius*, and *Henderson*, agree in the view given here.—*Ed.*

might migrate to a hostile land. But this view is too strained; nor was there any reason to suppose the word to be a proper name, except that there was a wish to say something, and that there was no other conjecture more probable. But I regard their opinion more correct, who refer this to the state of the kingdom; and there is here, I have no doubt, a personification, which is evident if we attend to the meaning. If any one prefers to regard the queen as intended, it would yet be better to take הצב, *etsab*, in its proper and real meaning,—that the queen, previously hid in her palace, and hardly able, through being so delicate, to move a step,—that she was brought forth to the light; for גלה, *gele*, means to uncover, and also to cast out. If we render it, "was made manifest," the Prophet alludes to hiding-places, and means that the queen did not go forth to the light, but was like delicate women who keep themselves within their chambers: but if we render it, "Who is drawn forth into exile," it would be more suitable to one who was previously fixed in her dwelling. The word comes from יצב, *itsab*, to stand; but it is here in Hophal, הוצב, *eutsab:* it then signifies one who was before fixed and firmly settled, that is, in her concealment; she is drawn, he says, into exile. If then any one chooses to refer this to the person of the queen, the most suitable meaning would be,—that the queen, who before sat in the midst of her pleasures, shall be violently drawn into exile, and carried away to another country. And it is probable that the Prophet speaks of the queen, because it immediately follows, *Her handmaids lead* her as *with the voice of doves, and smite on their breasts;* that is, her maids, who before flattered her, shall lament, and with sighing and tears, and mourning, shall lead away, as a captive, their own mistress. Thus the context would harmonise.

But, as I have said, their opinion seems right, who think that under the person of a woman the state of the kingdom is here described. She then, who before stood, or remained fixed, shall be drawn into captivity; or she, who before sat at leisure, shall be discovered; that is, she shall no more lie hid as hitherto in her retirement, but shall be forced to come abroad. And then, *she shall ascend;* that is, vanish away, for the verb is to be here taken metaphorically; *she shall* then *vanish away*, or be reduced to nothing. And as the Prophet sets a woman here before us, what follows agrees with this idea,—Her handmaids shall weep and imitate the doves in their moaning; that is, the whole people shall bewail the fate of the kingdom, when things shall be so changed, as when handmaids lead forth their own mistress, who had been before nourished in the greatest delicacies.[1]

Now this accumulation of words was by no means in vain; for it was necessary to confirm, by many words, the faith of the Israelites and of the Jews respecting the near approach of the destruction of the city Nineveh, which would have

[1] Various have been the opinions respecting the construction of this verse. The Rabbins have generally considered the first word as the name of the queen of Nineveh: but this opinion has been adopted but by a few. *Newcome* joins the word with the last verse, and changes it into מצב, on no authority but that of conjecture, and renders it "fortress." What *Henderson* has adopted seems the best: he also joins it to the last verse, but makes no change in it, only he gives the ו an adversative meaning, which it often has. The evident gender, as he rightly says, of הצב proves its connection with the former verse, it being masculine, while the verbs in this verse are feminines. His version of the two verses is the following,—

7. The floodgates are opened,
And the palace is dissolved,
Though firmly established.
8. She is made bare, she is carried up,
While her handmaids moan like doves,
And smite upon their hearts.

With the exception of the word הצב, this version is liable to several objections. The verb גלה is often used in Kal intransitively, "is removed;" and this meaning enables us better to understand that of the next verb, "she is made to ascend," that is, into captivity, even into Babylon, the seat of empire, being ever considered as the highest place. מנהגות is a word which in some form or another often occurs in Hebrew, and has never the meaning here given to it. Here it is a participle in Hophal, and "carried away" is its evident meaning, and is rendered *ηγουτο*, led away, by the Septuagint. "Like," or, as "the voice of doves," are literally the words which follow this verb. However connected, they must be considered as elliptical—"as *with* the voice, or, with a voice as that of doves." They might then be construed with the next line. The whole verse would then be this,—

She is removed, she is made to ascend;
Yea, her handmaids are led away,
Who with a voice as that of doves, tabour on their breasts.

They were accompanying the tabering with a voice like that of doves. "Tabour" is literally the original, and "on their breasts" is an English diom, as "on their hearts" is a Hebrew idiom.—*Ed.*

been otherwise incredible; and of this we can easily form a judgment by our own experience. If any one at this day were to speak of mighty kings, whose splendour amazes the whole world,—if any one were to announce the ruin of the kingdom of one of them, it would appear like a fable. This then is the reason why the Prophet, by so many figures, sets forth an event which might have been expressed in few words, and confirms it by so many forms of speech, and even by such as are hyperbolical. He at length subjoins—

8. But Nineveh *is* of old like a pool of water: yet they shall flee away. Stand, stand, *shall they cry;* but none shall look back.

8. Atqui Nineveh quasi piscina aquarum à diebus (*hoc est*, à longo tempore) fuit; ipsi autem fugiunt; state, state; et nemo respicit.

The Prophet here anticipates a doubt which might have weakened confidence in his words; for Nineveh not only flourished in power, but it had also confirmed its strength during a long course of time; and antiquity not only adds to the strength of kingdoms, but secures authority to them. As then the imperial power of the city Nineveh was ancient, it might seem to have been perpetual: "Why! Nineveh has ever ruled and possessed the sovereign power in all the east; can it be now shaken, or can its strength be now suddenly subverted? For where there is no beginning, we cannot believe that there will be any end." And a beginning it had not, according to the common opinion; for we know how the Egyptians also fabled respecting their antiquity; they imagined that their kingdom was five thousand years before the world was made; that is, in numbering their ages they went back nearly five thousand years before the creation. The Ninevites, no doubt, boasted that they had ever been; and as they were fixed in this conceit respecting their antiquity, no one thought that they could ever fail. This is the reason why the Prophet expressly declares, that *Nineveh had been like a pool of waters from* ancient *days;*[1] that is, Nineveh had

[1] The original is in a singular form, מימי היא, "from the days of it," or, of her. *Henderson* says, that "it is an antiquated mode of expressing the feminine pronominal affix—the absolute form of the pronoun being retained instead of the fragmental ה." The verse may be thus rendered:—

been, as it were, separated from the rest of the world; for where there is a pool, it seems well fortified by its own banks, no one comes into it; when one walks on the land he does not enter into the waters. Thus, then, had Nineveh been in a quiet state not only for a short time, but for many ages. This circumstance shall not, however, prevent God from overturning now its dominion. How much soever, then, Nineveh took pride in the notion of its ancientness, it was yet God's purpose to destroy it.

He says then, *They flee:* by fleeing, he means, that, though not beaten by their enemies, they would yet be overcome by their own fear. He then intimates, that Nineveh would not only be destroyed by slaughter, but that all the Assyrians would flee away, and despair would deliver them up to their enemies. Hence the Chaldeans would not only be victorious through their courage and the sword, but the Assyrians, distrusting their own forces, would flee away.

It afterwards follows, *Stand ye, stand ye, and no one regards.* Here the Prophet places, as it were, before our eyes, the effect of the dread of which he speaks. He might have given a simple narrative,—that though one called them back they would not dare to look behind; and that, thinking that safety alone was in flight, they would pursue their course. The Prophet might have formed this sort of narrative: this he has not done; but he assumes the person of one calling back the fugitives, as though he saw them fleeing away, and tried to bring them back: *No one*, he says, *regards.* We now see what the Prophet meant.

But from this passage we ought to learn that no trust is to be put in the number of men, nor in the defences and

Though Nineveh *has been* like a pool of water during her days,
Yet they flee;——" Stand, stand;"
But none is looking back.

Newcome's version of the first line is as follows,—

And the waters of Nineveh are as a pool of water:

And he says, that the pronoun sometimes is at the end of a clause: but it cannot be so considered here, because היא is in *regimine* with מימי. It is to be noticed, that the Prophet throughout represents the whole transaction as an eye-witness, as it had been shown to him in a vision. —*Ed.*

strongholds of cities, nor in ancientness; for when men excel in power, God will hence take occasion to destroy them, inasmuch as pride is almost ever connected with strength. It can hardly be but that men arrogate too much to themselves when they think that they excel in any thing. Thus it happens, that on account of their strength they run headlong into ruin; not that God has any delight, as profane men imagine, when he turns upside down the face of the earth, but because men cannot bear their own success, nor keep themselves within moderate bounds, but madly triumph against God: hence it is that human power recoils on the head of those who possess it. The same thing must also be said of ancientness: for they who boast of their antiquity, know not for how long a time they have been provoking the wrath of God; for it cannot be otherwise but that abundance of itself generates licentiousness, or that it at least leads to excess; and further, they who are the most powerful are the most daring in corrupting others. Hence the increase of putridity; for men are like the dead when not ruled by the fear of God. A dead body becomes more and more fetid the longer it continues putrifying; and so it is with men. When they have been for a long time sinning, and still continue to sin, the fetidness of their sins increases, and the wrath of God is more and more provoked. There is then no reason why ancientness should deceive us. And if, at any time, we are tempted to think that men are sufficiently fortified by their own strength, or by numerous auxiliaries, or that they are, as it were, sacred through their own ancientness, let what is said here come to our minds,—that Nineveh had been like a pool of waters from the ancient days; but that, when it was given up to destruction, it fled away; and that, when their enemies did not rout them, they yet, being driven by their own fear, ran away and would not stop, though one called them to return.

PRAYER.

Grant, Almighty God, that as thou constantly remindest us, in thy word, and teachest us by so many examples, that there is nothing permanent in this world, but that the things which seem the firmest tend to ruin, and instantly fall and of themselves vanish away, when by thy breath thou shakest that strength in which men trust,—O grant, that we being really subdued and humbled, may not rely on earthly things, but raise up our hearts and our thoughts to heaven, and there fix the anchor of our hope ; and may all our thoughts abide there, until at length, when thou hast led us through our course on earth, we shall be gathered into that celestial kingdom, which has been obtained for us by the blood of thy only-begotten Son. Amen.

Lecture One Hundred and Third.

9. Take ye the spoil of silver, take the spoil of gold: for *there is* none end of the store *and* glory out of all the pleasant furniture.

9. Diripite argentum, diripite aurum ; et non finis (quia non est, *copula debet resolvi in causalem particulam ;* quia nullus finis) præparationis ejus (*sic vertunt, sed propriè* תכונה significat locum ;) gloria ex omni vase desiderabili.

Here the Prophet, as it were, by the command and authority of God, gives up Nineveh to the will of its enemies, that they might spoil and plunder it. Some think that this address is made in the name of a general encouraging his soldiers ; but we know that the Prophets assume the person of God, when they thus command any thing with authority ; and it is a very emphatical mode of speaking. It is adopted, that we may know that the Prophets pour not forth an empty sound when they speak, but really testify what God has determined to do, and what he in due time will execute. As then we know, that this manner of speaking is common to the Prophets, there is no reason to apply this to the person of Nebuchadnezzar or of any other. God then shows here that Nineveh was given up to ruin ; and therefore he delivered it into the hands of enemies.

It is indeed certain, that the Babylonians, in plundering the city, did not obey God's command ; but yet it is true, that they punished the Assyrians through the secret influence of God : for it was his purpose to visit the Ninevites for the cruelty and avarice for which they had been long notorious, and especially for having exercised unexampled barbarity toward the Jews. This is the reason why God now gives them up to the Babylonians and exposes them to plunder. But as I have spoken at large elsewhere of the secret judgments of God, I shall only briefly observe here,—that God does not command the Babylonians and Chaldeans in order to render them excusable, but shows by his Prophet, that Nineveh was to be destroyed by her enemies, not by chance, but that it was his will to avenge the wrongs done to his people. At the same time, we must bear in mind what we have said elsewhere,—that the Prophets thus speak when the execution is already prepared; for God does not in vain or without reason terrify men, but he afterwards makes it manifest by the effect: as he created the world from nothing by his word, so also by his word he executes and fulfils his judgments. It is then no wonder, that the Prophet does here, as though he ruled the Chaldeans according to his will, thus address them, *Take ye away, take ye away*. But this must be viewed as having a reference to the faithful; for the Babylonians, in plundering the city Nineveh, did not think that they obeyed God, nor did they give to God the praise due for the victory; but the faithful were thus reminded, that all this was done through the secret providence of God, and that it was also a clear, and, as it were, a visible evidence of God's paternal love towards his Church, when he thus deigned to undertake the cause of his distressed people.

It then follows, *There is no end of preparations:* Some render תכונה, *tacune*, treasure, or hidden wealth, and derive it from כון, *cun*, which is to prepare; but תכונה, *tacune*, is almost always taken for a measure. תכנות, *tacanut*, from תכן, *tacun*, means a sum, for תכן, *tacan*, is to number or to count; and this meaning suits the passage.[1] But there is no

[1] *Buxtorf* derives the word from כון, to prepare, and *Parkhurst* from תכן, to regulate, to measure. It is rendered "store" by *Newcome* and *Henderson*. What is meant is evidently the vast treasure amassed by the Assyrians. The next words are more variously rendered. *Newcome* connects the word כבד with "store," and renders the two lines thus,—

And there is no end of the glorious store,
Because of all *kinds* of pleasant vessels.

But more consistent with the character of the language, and agreeably to what *Dr Wheeler* suggests, is this,—

need of labouring much about this word; if we take it simply for place, the meaning would be, that there was no plot of ground in that city which was not as it were a gulf filled up; for it had amassed all the wealth of the nations: and this sense would harmonise well with the subject of the Prophet,—that the soldiers were to plunder until they were satiated; for the place was, as it were, a deep abyss.

He afterwards adds, *There is glory from every desirable vessel.* Those who think *mem*, מ, a particle of comparison in this place are much mistaken, and misapply the meaning of the Prophet; their rendering is, "In comparison with every desirable vessel;" but this, as all must see, is very frigid. The Prophet, I have no doubt, declares that the wealth of Nineveh consisted of every desirable vessel; for they had for a long time heaped together immense wealth, and that of every kind. The Hebrews call what is precious a desirable thing; and their vessels we include under the term furniture. We now then perceive what the Prophet means. Some take כבד, *cabed*, as a participle, and give this version, "It is burdened," or adorned, (for it means both,) "with every desirable vessel." But the simpler mode of speaking is what we have explained,—that its glory was from every desirable vessel.

And here the Prophet condemns what the Assyrians had done in heaping together so much wealth from all quarters; for they had committed indiscriminate plunder, and gathered for themselves all the riches of the nations. They had indeed plundered all their neighbours, yea, and wholly stripped them. The Prophet now shows, in order to expose them to ridicule, that other robbers would be made rich, whom the Lord would raise up against them. The same is said by Isaiah, 'O thou plunderer, shalt not thou also be exposed to plunder?' (Isa. xxxiii. 1.) So also the Prophet shows in this passage, that men foolishly burn with so much avidity for money, and with so much anxiety heap together great

And there is no end to her store,
It is more precious than all desirable vessels.

The preposition מ, after כבד, may be viewed as the comparative degree.
—*Ed.*

wealth; for God will find out some who in their turn will plunder those who have plundered. It follows—

10. She is empty, and void, and waste: and the heart melteth, and the knees smite together, and much pain *is* in all loins, and the faces of them all gather blackness.

10. Exinanita et exinanita est, et nudata; et cor liquefactum, et collisio genuum, et terror in omnibus lumbis; et facies omnium contraxerunt nigredinem (*vel*, splendorem, *ut alii vertunt.*)

The Prophet here confirms what the last verse contains; for he shows why he had called the Chaldeans to take away the spoil,—because it was to be so. He did not indeed (as I have already said) command the Chaldeans in such a way as that their obedience to God was praiseworthy: but the Prophet speaks here only of His secret counsel. Though then the Chaldeans knew not that it was God's decree, yet the Prophet reminds the faithful that the Ninevites, when made naked, suffered punishment for their cruelty, especially for having so hostilely conducted themselves towards the Jews: and hence he declares, that Nineveh is *emptied, is emptied, and made naked.*[1] By repeating the same word, he intimates the certainty of the event: Emptied, emptied, he says, as when one says in our language, *videe et revidee.* We hence see that by this repetition what the Prophet meant is more distinctly expressed, that the faithful might not doubt respecting the event: and then for the same purpose he adds, She is made *naked.*

We now then perceive the Prophet's design. As in the last verse he shows that he had power given him from above to send armies against Nineveh, and to give up the city to them to be spoiled and plundered; so he now shows that he had not so commanded the Chaldeans, as though they were

[1] The three words in Hebrew form a very striking alliteration; and they present another peculiarity,—they increase in length or in syllables, somewhat similar to what follows,—

She is made void, and empty, and desolate:

or,

She is empty, and emptied, and desolated.

בוקה ומבוקה ומבלקה

Buke, umebuke, umebelake.

Some consider the words as nouns, but they are evidently participles.—*Ed.*

the legitimate servants of God, and could pretend that they rendered service to Him. He therefore points out for what end he had commanded the Chaldeans to plunder Nineveh; and that was, because God had so decreed; and he had so decreed and commanded, because he would not bear the many wrongs done to his people whom he had taken under his protection. As then Nineveh had so cruelly treated God's chosen people, it was necessary that the reward she deserved should be repaid to her. But the repetition, which I have noticed, ought to be especially observed; for it teaches us that God's power is connected with his word, so that he declares nothing inconsiderately or in vain.

He then adds, that *knees smite together*, and every *heart is dissolved*, or melted, and also, that *all loins tremble*. We hence learn, that there is in men no courage, except as far as God supplies them with vigour. As soon then as He withdraws his Spirit, those who were before the most valiant become faint-hearted, and those who breathed great ferocity are made soft and effeminate: for by the word heart is meant inward boldness or courage; and by the knees and loins the strength of body is to be understood. There is indeed no doubt but the Assyrians, while they ruled, were a very courageous people, as power ever generates boldness; and it is also probable that they were a warlike people, since all their neighbours had been brought under their power. But the Prophet now shows, that there would be no vigour in their hearts, and no strength in their loins, or in any part of their body. *The heart*, then, he says, *is melted*. And hence we learn how foolishly men boast of their courage, while they seem to be like lions; for God can in a moment so melt their hearts, that they entirely lose all firmness. Then as to external vigour, we see that it is in God's hand; *there will be*, he says, *a confriction*, or the knees will knock one against another, as they do when they tremble. And he says afterwards, *And trembling shall be in all loins.*[1]

[1] These three lines are literally as follows,—

And the heart is melted,
And *there is* tottering of the knees,
And anguish in all loins.

The word חלחלה is not trembling, but violent pain, pang, or anguish, as that of a woman in travail.—*Ed.*

He at last adds, *And the faces of all shall gather blackness.* The word פארור, *parur*, some derive from פאר, *par;* and so the rendering would be, "all faces shall draw in or withdraw their beauty," and so also they explain Joel ii. 6, for the sentence there is the same. But they who disapprove of this meaning say, that קבץ, *kobets*, cannot mean to draw in or to withdraw; and so they render the noun, blackness. But this is a strained explanation. פארור, *parur*, [they say,] does not mean a black colour but a pot: when therefore a caldron or a kettle contracts blackness from smoke, it is then called פארור, *parur:* but in this place these interpreters are constrained to take it metaphorically for that colour; which is, as I have said, strained and far-fetched. I am therefore inclined to adopt their opinion who render the sentence, all faces shall withdraw their beauty, or their brightness: but as to the import of the passage, there is little or no difference; let then every one have his free choice.[1] With regard to the Prophet's design, he evidently means, that the faces of all would be sad, for the Lord would fill their minds and thoughts with dread. The withdrawing then of beauty signifies an outward appearance of sorrow, or paleness, or whatever may appear in the countenance of men, when dejected with grief. In short, the Prophet means, that how much soever the Assyrians might have hitherto raised on high their crests, and breathed great swelling words, and conducted themselves insolently, they would now be dejected; for the Lord would prostrate their courage and melt their strength: he would, by casting down their high spirits, constrain them to undergo shame. This is the import of the whole. It now follows—

[1] *Parkhurst* and others agree with *Calvin*, as to the construction of this line. The idea adopted seems to have been first suggested by *Aben-Ezra*, as it appears from *Marckius*, but was strongly opposed by *Kimchi*, and on apparently a good ground—the meaning of the verb here used. קבץ, as a verb and as a noun, in all its variations, has invariably the idea of collecting or gathering, and in no instance that of withdrawing, except, as it is said, in this sentence, and in Joel. *Dathius*, *Marckius*, and *Newcome*, retain the idea contained in our version; and consistent with this is the paraphrase of the clause given by the Septuagint, "*και το προσωπον* (*τα προσωπα*, compl.) *παντων ως προσκαυμα χυτρας*—and the face (or, the faces) of all as the burning on the pot." This idea is much more expressive and striking than the other.—*Ed.*

11. Where *is* the dwelling of the lions, and the feeding-place of the young lions, where the lion, *even* the old lion, walked, *and* the lion's whelp, and none made *them* afraid?	11. Ubi domicilium leonum, et locus pascui leonibus, quò veniebant leo, leo, catulus leonis, et nemo exterrens?
12. The lion did tear in pieces enough for his whelps, and strangled for his lionesses, and filled his holes with prey, and his dens with ravin.	12. Leo rapiebat quantum sufficeret catulis suis, et strangulabat leænis suis, et replebat rapina speluncas suas et lustra sua præda.

Here the Prophet triumphs over the Assyrians, because they thought that the city Nineveh was remote from every danger: as lions, who fear nothing, when they are in their dens, draw thither their prey in their claws or in their mouths: so also was the case with the Assyrians; thinking themselves safe, while Nineveh flourished, they took the greater liberty to commit plunders everywhere. For Nineveh was not only the receptacle of robbers, but was also like a den of lions. And the Prophet more fully expresses the barbarous cruelty of the Assyrians by comparing them to lions, than if he had simply called them lions. We now then see what he means, when he says, *Where is the place of lions?* And he designedly speaks thus of the Assyrians: for no one ever thought that they could be touched by even the least injury; the fear of them had indeed so seized all men, that of themselves they submitted to the Assyrians. As then no one dared to oppose them, the Prophet says, *Where?* as though he had said, that though all thought it incredible that Nineveh could be overthrown, it would yet thus happen. But he assumes the character of one expressing his astonishment, in order to intimate, that when the Lord should execute such a judgment, it would be a work of wonder, which would fill almost all with amazement. This question then proves that those are very foolish who form a judgment of God's vengeance, of which the Prophet speaks, according to the appearance of things at the time; for the ruin of Nineveh and of that empire was to be the incomprehensible work of God, and which was to fill all minds with astonishment.

He says first, *Where is the place of lions?* The feminine gender is indeed here used; but all agree that the Prophet speaks of male lions.[1] He then adds, *the place of feeding for lions?* כפרים, *caphrim,* mean young lions, as we shall hereafter see; and אריות, *ariut,* are old lions. He afterwards adds, *Where* אריה, *arie, came:* and then comes לביא, *labia,* which some render, lioness; but לביא, *labia,* properly means an old lion; the Prophet, no doubt, uses it in the next verse in the feminine gender for lionesses. I therefore do not deny, but that we may fitly render the terms here, lion and lioness; afterwards, *and the whelp of lions, and none terrifying.* He then adds, *Seize did the lion* (the word is אריה, *arie*) *for his whelps to satiety,* that is, sufficiently; and strangle *did he for his lionesses,* ללבאתיו, *lalabatiu.* Here no doubt the Prophet means lionesses; there would otherwise be no consistency in the passage. He afterwards says, *And filled has he with prey his dens and his recesses with ravin;* it is the same word with a different termination, טרף, *thereph,* and טרפה, *therephe.*

Now the repetition, made here by the Prophet, of lion, young lion, and lioness, was not without its use; for he meant by this number of words to set forth the extreme ferocity of the Assyrians, while they were dominant. He no doubt compares their kings, their counsellors, and their chief men, to lions: and he calls their wives lionesses, and their children he calls young lions or whelps of lions. The sum of the whole is, that Nineveh had so degenerated in its opulence, that all in power were like ferocious wild beasts, destitute of

[1] It is better to retain the gender as it is in Hebrew: and this makes the passage more consistent, and corresponds better with the "feeding-place" in the next line. The recesses of the lionesses and the whelps are here mentioned, and in the next verse is stated what the lions did for them :—

11. Where *is* the haunt of the lionesses,
And the feeding-place, *even* that for the whelps,
Where did go the lion, the lioness, the cub of the lion,
And none made *them* afraid?
12. The lion ravined for the supply of his cubs,
And strangled for his lionesses,
And filled with ravin his dens,
And his haunts by ravining.

"The allegory," says *Newcome,* "is beyond measure beautiful. Where are the inhabitants of Nineveh, who were strong and rapacious like lions?"—*Ed.*

every kind feeling. And I wish that this could have only been said of one city and of one monarchy! But here, as in a mirror, the Prophet represents to us what we at this day observe, and what has always and in all ages been observed in great empires; for where great power exists, there great licentiousness prevails; and when kings and their counsellors become once habituated to plunder, there is no end of it; nay, a kind of fury is kindled in their hearts, that they seek nothing else but to devour and to tear in pieces, to rend and to strangle. The Prophet indeed wished here to console both the Israelites and the Jews, by showing, that the injustice of their enemies would not go unpunished: but at the same time he intended to show how great, even to the end of the world, would be the cruelty of those who would rule tyrannically: and as I have said, experience proves, that there are too many like the Ninevites. It is indeed unquestionable, that the Prophet does not without reason speak so often here of lions and lionesses.

Hence he says, 'Come thither did the lion, the lioness, and the whelp of the lion.' He means, that when justice was sought in that city, it was found to be the den of cruel beasts; for the king had put off all humanity, as well as his counsellors; their wives were also like lionesses, and their children and domestics were as young lions, or the whelps of lions. And cruelty creeps in, somewhat in this manner: When a king takes to himself too much liberty, his counsellors follow him; and then every one follows the common example, as though every thing received as a custom was lawful. This is the representation which the Prophet in these words sets before us; and we with our own eyes see the same things. Then he adds, 'The lion did tear what sufficed his whelps, and strangled for his lionesses; he filled with prey his dens and his recesses with plunder.' He goes on with the same subject,—that the Assyrians heaped for themselves great wealth by unjust spoils, because they had no regard for what was right. The lion, he says, did tear for his whelps: as lions accustom their whelps to plunder, and when they are not grown enough, so as to be able to attack innocent animals, they provide a prey for them, and also bring some to the lionesses; so also, as the Prophet informs us, was the case at Nineveh; the habits of all men were formed for cruelty by the chief men and the magistrates. By the word בְּדֵי, *bedi*, sufficiency, he means not that the Ninevites were satisfied with their prey, for they were insatiable; but it rather refers to the abundance which they had. And he says, that the lion strangled for his lionesses: I wish there were no lionesses to devour at this day; but we see that there are some who surpass their husbands in boldness and cruelty. But the Prophet says here what is natural,—that the lion strangles the prey and gives it afterwards to his lionesses. He then adds, that the Ninevites were not satisfied with daily rapines, as many robbers live for the day; but he says, that their plunder was laid up in store. Hence they filled their secret places and dens with their booty and spoils. Still further, though the Prophet speaks not here so plainly, as we shall see he does in what follows, it is yet certain, that the reason is here given, why God visited the Ninevites with so severe a vengeance, and that was, because they had ceased to be like men, and had degenerated into savage beasts. It follows—

13. Behold, I *am* against thee, saith the Lord of hosts, and I will burn her chariots in the smoke, and the sword shall devour thy young lions: and I will cut off thy prey from the earth, and the voice of thy messengers shall no more be heard.

13. Ecce Ego ad te, dicit Jehova exercituum, et comburam in fumo currum ejus, et leunculos tuos comedet gladius, et excidam è terra prædam tuam, et non audietur amplius vox nunciorum tuorum (*aut*, dentium molarium.)

To give more effect to what he says, the Prophet introduces God here as the speaker. *Behold*, he says, *I* am *against thee*. He has been hitherto, as it were, the herald of God, and in this character gave an authoritative command to the Chaldeans to plunder Nineveh: but when God himself comes forward, and uses not the mouth of man, but declares himself his own decrees, it is much more impressive. This then is the reason why God now openly speaks: *Behold, I am*, he says, *against thee*. We understand the emphatical import of the demonstrative particle, *Behold;* for God, as if awakened from sleep, shows that it will be at length his work, to undertake the cause of his people, and also to punish the world for its wickedness, *Behold, I am against thee,* he says. We have elsewhere seen a similar mode of speaking; there is therefore no need of dwelling on it here.

I will burn, he says, *with smoke her chariots.* Here by smoke some understand a smoky fire; but the Prophet, I think, meant another thing,—that at the first onset God would consume all the chariots of Nineveh; as though he had said, that as soon as the flame burst forth, it would be all over with all the forces of Nineveh; for by chariots he no doubt means all their warlike preparations; and we know that they fought then from chariots: as at this day there are employed in wars horsemen in armour, so there were then chariots. But the Prophet, by taking a part for the whole, includes all warlike forces: *I will burn* then *the chariots.*[1]—How? By smoke alone, that is, as soon as the first flame begins to emerge; for the smoke rises before the fire appears or gathers strength: in short, the Prophet shows that Nineveh would be, as it were, in a moment, reduced to nothing, as soon as it pleased God to avenge its wickedness.

He then adds in the third person, *And thy young lions shall the sword devour.* He indeed changes the person here; but the discourse is more striking, when God manifests his wrath in abrupt sentences. He had said, *Behold, I am against thee;* then, *I will burn her chariots,* he now hardly deigns to direct his speech to Nineveh; but afterwards he returns to her, *and thy young lions shall the sword devour.* Then God, by speaking thus in broken sentences, more fully expresses the dreadful vengeance which he had determined to execute on the Ninevites. He then says, *And I will exterminate from the earth thy prey;* that is, it will not now be allowed thee to go on as usual; for I will put a stop to thy inhuman cruelty. Thus *prey* may be taken for the act itself; or it may be fitly explained of the spoils taken from the nations, for the Ninevites, by their tyrannical ravening, had everywhere plundered; and thus it may be applied to the pillaging of the city. *I*

[1] *Jerome* renders the clause, " Succendam usque ad fumum—I will burn to smoke" the chariots: and the version of *Henderson* is the same. But the most natural supposition is, that smoke here is mentioned instead of fire. And so *Dathius* renders it—" igni—with fire."—*Ed.*

will then *exterminate* from the land, that is, from thy country, those riches which have been hitherto heaped together, as though a lion had been everywhere gathering a prey.

And heard no more shall be the voice of thy messengers. They who understand מלאכים, *melakim*, to be messengers, apply the word to the heralds, by whom the Assyrians were wont to proclaim wars on neighbouring nations. As then they sent here and there their heralds to announce war, and as their terrible voice sounded everywhere, the words of the Prophet have this meaning given them,—that God would at length produce silence, so that they should not hereafter disturb all their neighbouring countries with the clamour of war. But as this explanation is strained, I am inclined to adopt what others think,—that the grinding teeth are here intended. The word is not written, if it be taken for messengers, according to grammar; it is מלאככה, *melakke;* there ought not to have been the ה, *he*, at the end, and י, *jod*, ought to have been inserted before the last letter but one: and if it be deemed as meaning the king, it ought then to have been written מלכך, *melkak.* All then confess, that the word is not written according to the rule of grammar; and as the Persians call the grinders מלאככה, *melakke*, we may give this version, which well suits the context, 'No more shall be heard the sound of grinders.' For since lions seize the prey with their teeth, and also break the bones, and thus make a great noise when they tear an animal or a man with their teeth, this rendering seems to be the most suitable, *Heard no more shall be the sound of teeth*,[1] that is, heard shall not be the noise made by thy teeth; for when thou now tearest thy prey, thy teeth make a noise. No more heard then shall the noise from that breaking, or the clashing or the crashing of the

[1] The context undoubtedly favours this rendering. The Septuagint has "τα εργα σου—thy works," which cannot consist with the word, "voice," which precedes, though *Newcome*, following the Septuagint, renders it, "the fame of thy deeds." There is but one different reading, except as to points, and that is, מלאככם, "their messenger," in two copies, and this comes nearest to the received text of any that has been conjectured: and to render "messenger" in the singular number comports better with the usual style of the Prophets, than in the plural. Perhaps the ה may be deemed redundant at the end of the sentence; and then it would be literally, "thy messenger," taken in a collective sense.—*Ed.*

teeth. But as to the chief point, this is no matter of importance.

The Prophet simply teaches us here that it could not be, but that God would at length restrain tyrants; for though he hides himself for a time, he yet never forgets the groans of those whom he sees to be unjustly afflicted: and particularly when tyrants molest the Church, it is proved here by the Prophet that God will at length be a defender; and hence we ought to consider well these words, *Behold, I am against thee.* For though God addresses these words only to the Assyrians, yet as he points out the reasons why he rises up with so much displeasure against them, they ought to be extended to all tyrants, and to all who exercise cruelty towards distressed and innocent men. But this is more clearly expressed in the following verse.

CHAPTER III.

1. Woe to the bloody city! it *is* all full of lies *and* robbery; the prey departeth not.	1. O urbs sanguinaria! tota mendacio (*vertunt*) rapina plena est; non recedit præda (*vel*, non recedet præda.)

The Prophet, as I have said, more clearly expresses here the reason why the vengeance of God would be so severe on the Ninevites,—because they had wholly given themselves up to barbarous cruelty; and hence he calls it the bloody city. *Bloody city!* he says. The exclamation is emphatical. Though הוי, *eu*, sometimes means Woe; yet it is put here as though the Prophet would have constrained Nineveh to undergo its punishment, *O sanguinary city!* then, *the whole of it is full of* כחש, *cachesh:* the word signifies leanness, and the Prophet no doubt joins here together two words, which seem to differ widely, and yet they signify the same thing. For פרק, *perek*, means to lay by; and כחש, *cachesh*, is taken for a lie or vanity, when there is nothing solid in what is said: but the Prophet, I doubt not, means by both words the spoils of the city Nineveh. It was then full of leanness, for it had consumed all others; it was also full of spoils, for it had filled itself. But the meaning of the Prophet is in no way dubious; for at length he adds, *Depart shall not the prey;* that is, as some think, it shall not be withdrawn from the hands of conquerors; but others more correctly think that a continued liberty in plundering is intended, that the Assyrians were constantly employed in pillaging and kept within no bounds.

We hence see that the Prophet now shows why God says, that he would be an adversary to the Ninevites, because he could not endure its unjust cruelty. He bore with it indeed for a time; for he did not immediately execute his judgment; but yet he never forgot his own people.

As, then, God has once declared by the mouth of his Prophet that he would be the avenger of the cruelty which the Assyrians had exercised, let us know that he retains still his own nature; and whatever liberty he may for a time grant to tyrants and savage wild beasts, he yet continues to be a just avenger. It is our duty calmly to bear injuries, and to groan to him; and as he promises to be at length our helper, it behoves us to flee to him, and to ask him to succour us, so that seeing his Church oppressed, and tyrants exercising licentiously their power, he may hasten the time to restrain them. If then we were at all times to continue thus resigned under God's protection, there is no doubt but that he would be ready even at this day to execute a similar judgment to that which the city Nineveh and its people had to endure.

PRAYER.

Grant, Almighty God, that as we have now heard of punishments so dreadful denounced on all tyrants and plunderers, this warning may keep us within the limits of justice, so that none of us may abuse our power to oppress the innocent, but, on the contrary, strive to benefit one another, and wholly regulate ourselves according to the rule of equity: and may we hence also receive comfort whenever the ungodly molest and trouble us, and doubt not but that we are under thy protection, and that thou art armed with power sufficient to defend us, so that we may patiently bear injuries, until at length the ripened time shall come for thee to help us, and to put forth thy power for our preservation; nor let us cease to bear our evils with patience, as long as it may be thy will to exercise us in our present warfare, until having gone through all our troubles, we come to that blessed rest which has been provided for us in heaven by Christ Jesus our Lord. Amen.

Lecture One Hundred and Fourth.

2. The noise of a whip, and the noise of the rattling of the wheels, and of the prancing horses, and of the jumping chariots.

3. The horseman lifteth up both the bright sword and the glittering spear: and *there is* a multitude of slain, and a great number of carcases; and *there is* none end of *their* corpses; they stumble upon their corpses:

2. Sonitus flagelli, et sonitus commotionis rotæ, et equus concutiens, et quadriga exultans;

3. Eques ascendere faciens, et flamma gladii, et fulgur lanceæ, et multitudo occisi *(est mutatio numeri*, occisorum,) et pondus cadaverum *(hoc est* etiam multitudo,) et nullus finis cadaveribus ejus; impingent in cadavera ejus:

The Prophet represents here, as in a lively picture, what was nigh the Assyrians; for he sets forth the Chaldeans their enemies with all their preparations and in their quick movements.[1] *The sound of the whip*, he says; the whips

[1] It appears from *Marckius* that *Theodoret* and *Cyril* regarded this verse, with *Calvin*, as a description of the Chaldean army after having invaded Nineveh, but that *Jerome* and *Cocceius* viewed it as a delineation of the state of Nineveh in the Prophet's time; and with the last *Newcome* agrees, while *Henderson* coincides with the former. The version given by them all is nearly the same. It seems certainly more consistent with the order of the poem to regard the verse as describing the state of Nineveh at the time, for the sacking of Nineveh had been before very minutely delineated. Having done this, the Prophet may be supposed to give here a reason for the dreadful catastrophe which he had mentioned. Entertaining this view, and differing from others as to the meaning of some of the clauses, I offer the following version of the three verses,—

1. Oh! the city of blood! all of it deceit;
   Of plunder it is full, none can search out the spoil:—
2. The sound of the whip, and the sound of the rattling wheel!
   And the horse prancing, and the chariot bounding!
   The horseman mounting,
   And the flaming of the sword and the glittering of the spear!
   And a multitude dancing, and a mass inactive!
   And no end to her people!
   Who are fallen, with their nations,
3. Through the many fornications of the harlot,
   That exults in beauty, *and* possesses enchantments;
   Who sells nations by her fornications,
   And tribes by her enchantments.

ימיש, "search out," I derive from מש, which is to feel for the purpose of

made a noise in exciting the horses: *the sound of the rattling of the wheel;* that is, great shall be the haste and celerity, when the horses shall be forced on by the whip; *the horse* also *shaking* the earth, *and the chariot bounding; the horseman making it to ascend;* and then, *the flame of the sword and the lightning of the spear.* He then says, that there would be such a slaughter, that the whole place would be full of dead bodies.

We now then understand what the Prophet means: for as Nineveh might have then appeared impregnable, the Prophet confirms at large what he had said of its approaching ruin, and thus sets before the eyes of the Israelites what was then incredible.

As to the words, some interpreters connect what we have rendered, *the horseman makes to ascend,* with what follows, that is, he makes to ascend *the flame of the sword and the lightning of the spear.* But as a copulative comes between, it seems rather to be an imperfect sentence, meaning, that the horseman makes to ascend or mount, that is, his horses, by urging them on. With regard to the word להב, *leb,* it means, I have no doubt, a flame. By this word, I know, is also understood metaphorically the brightness of swords, which appears like a flame: but the Prophet immediately adds *lightning.* As then he says that spears lighten, I doubt not but that for the same reason he meant to say that swords flame. All these things were intended for the purpose of fully convincing the Israelites that Nineveh, however much it was supplied with wealth and power, was yet approaching its ruin, for its enemies would prevail against it: and therefore he adds, that all the roads would be full of dead bodies, that the enemies could not enter without treading on them everywhere. It follows—

exploring, and then, to explore or search out; see Gen. xxxi. 34. The second verse contains a simple enumeration of what the city exhibited. רב חלל, "a multitude dancing" or piping, the ו being dropped in חלל, as it is in חללים, pipers, 1 Kings i. 40. Then as a contrast comes the dead, heavy, inactive mass, כבד פגר. "To her people" or nations, לגויה, τοις εθνεσιν αυτης.—*Sept.* In the word בנויתם, I take that ת is a mistake for ה. If taken for carcases, it wants a ו before ת; see Ps. cx. 6. The third verse must be connected with the second, as it has otherwise no grammatical construction.—*Ed.*

4. Because of the multitude of the whoredoms of the well-favoured harlot, the mistress of witchcrafts, that selleth nations through her whoredoms, and families through her witchcrafts.	4. Ob multitudinem scortationum meretricis pollentis gratia, magistræ veneficiorum, vendentis gentes in scortationibus suis, et nationes in suis veneficiis.

The Prophet mentions again the cause why God would execute so dreadful a vengeance on that city, which yet procured by its splendour so much glory and respect among all people : and God seems in a manner to have but little regard for the order of the world when he thus overturns great cities. For since he is the Creator of the whole world, it seems to be his proper office to protect its various parts, especially those which excel in beauty, for they seem to deserve a higher regard. When therefore any splendid city is demolished, such thoughts as these occur to us,—That God is either delighted with the ruin of the world, or is asleep in heaven, and that thus all things revolve by chance and contingency. Therefore the Prophet shows, that God had just reasons for decreeing the ruin of Nineveh, and for deforming that beauty, that it might not deceive the eyes of men. Hence he compares Nineveh to a harlot. The similitude seems not to be very suitable : but yet if we take a nearer view of things, the Prophet could not have more fitly nor more strikingly set forth the condition of that city. He had before mentioned its barbarous cruelty, and said, that it was the den of lions, and that savage and bloody wild beasts dwelt there. He now begins to speak of the frauds and crafty artifices by which the kings of this world attain for themselves both wealth and power. The Prophet then makes the city Nineveh to be like a harlot for this reason,—because it had not only brought under its power neighbouring nations by threats and terrors, and also by cruelty, but because it had ensnared many by oblique arts and fraudulent means, by captious dealings and allurements. This is the reason why it is now called a *harlot* by the Prophet.

The Prophets of God seem indeed to speak but with little reverence of great cities and empires : but we know that it rightly belongs to the Spirit of God, that in exercising his own jurisdiction, he should uncover the base deeds of the whole world, which otherwise would lie concealed, and even under the appearance of virtues, deceive the eyes and senses of the simple: and as men so much flatter themselves, and are inebriated with their own delusions, it is necessary that those who are too self-indulgent and delicate should be roughly handled. As then kings ever set up their own splendour that they may dazzle the eyes of the simple, and seem to have their own greatness as a beautiful covering, the Spirit of God divests them of these masks. This then is the reason why the Prophet speaks here, in no very respectful terms, of that great monarchy which had attracted the admiration of all nations. For when the Spirit of God adopts a humble and common mode of speaking, men, blinded by their vices, will not acknowledge their own baseness; nay, they will even dare to set up in opposition those things which cover their disgraceful deeds: but the Spirit of God breaks through all these things, and dissipates those delusions by which men impose on themselves.

Such is the reason for this similitude; *On account of the multitude*, he says, *of the whoredoms of the harlot, who excels in favour*. It is said by way of concession that Nineveh was in great favour, that is, that by her beauty she had allured to herself many nations, like a harlot who attains many lovers: and thus the Prophet allows that Nineveh was beautiful. But he adds, that she was *the mistress of sorceries*. כשף, *casheph*, means sorcery, and also juggling: we may then render כשפים, *cashaphim*, used here, juggleries, (*præstigias*—sleights of hand.) But the Prophet seems to allude to filters or amatory potions, by which harlots dementate youths. As then harlots not only attract notice by their beauty and bland manners and other usual ways; but they also in a manner fascinate unhappy youths, and use various arts and delusions; so the Prophet under this word comprehends all the deceits practised by harlots; as though he said, "This harlot was not only beautiful, but also an enchantress, who by her charms deceived unhappy nations, like a strumpet, who dementates unhappy youths, who do not take care of themselves."

He afterwards adds, *Who sells nations by her whoredoms, and tribes by her sorceries.* Though Nahum still carries on the same metaphor, he yet shows more clearly what he meant by whoredoms and sorceries,—even the crafts of princes, by which they allure their neighbours, and then reduce them to bondage. Then all the counsels of kings (which they call policies[1]) are here, by the Spirit of God, called sorceries or juggleries, and also meretricious arts. This reproof, as I have already said, many deem to have been too severe; for so much majesty shone forth then in the Assyrians, that they ought, as they think, to have been more respectfully treated. But it behoved the Spirit of God to speak in this forcible language: for there is no one who does not applaud such crafty proceedings. Were any one, without mentioning princes, to ask, Is it right to deceive, and then by lies, deceptions, perjuries, cavils, and other arts, to make a cover for things?—were this question asked, the prompt answer would be, that all these things are as remote as possible from virtue, as nothing becomes men more than ingenuous sincerity. But when princes appear in public, and make this pretence, that the world must be ruled with great prudence, that except secret counsels be taken, all kingdoms would immediately fall into ruin,—this veil covers all their shameful transactions, so that it becomes lawful for them, and even praiseworthy, to deceive one party, to circumvent another, and a third to oppress by means of deception. Since then princes are praised for their craftiness, this is the reason why the Prophet here takes away, as it were by force, the mask, under which they hide their base proceedings; "They are," he says, "meretricious arts, and they are sorceries and juggleries."

It is of one city, it is true, that he speaks here; but the Prophet no doubt describes in this striking representation how kingdoms increase and by what crafty means,—first, by robberies,—and then by artful dealings, such as would by no means become honest men in the middle class of life. But

[1] *Practicas*, used here evidently in a sense not classical, meaning the crafty tactics of politicians. The word *practic*, in English, was, at one time, used in a bad sense, signifying what was *sly* and *artful*, or *crafty:* and *practice* too was employed to designate a *trick*, or a *stratagem.—Ed.*

princes could never succeed, except they practised such artifices. We yet see how they are described here by the Spirit of God,—that they are like strumpets, given to juggleries, and to other base and filthy arts, which he calls whoredoms. But I have said, that the meaning of the Prophet can be more clearly elicited from the second clause of the verse, when he says that the Ninevites made a merchandise of the nations. We see indeed even at this day that princes disturb the whole world at their pleasure; for they deliver up innocent people to one another, and shamefully sell them, while each hunts after his own advantage, without any shame; that he may increase his own power, he will deliver others into the hand of an enemy. Since then there are crafty proceedings of this kind carried on too much at this day, there is no need that I should attempt to explain at any length the meaning of the Prophet. I wish that examples were to be sought at a distance. Let us proceed—

5. Behold, I *am* against thee, saith the Lord of hosts; and I will discover thy skirts upon thy face, and I will show the nations thy nakedness, and the kingdoms thy shame.

6. And I will cast abominable filth upon thee, and make thee vile, and will set thee as a gazingstock.

5. Ecce Ego ad te, inquit Jehova exercituum, et retegam fimbrias tuas super faciem tuam, et ostendam gentibus nuditatem tuam, et regnis fœditatem tuam:

6. Et projiciam super te sordes (*vel,* inquinamenta) et ignominia afficiam te, et ponam te quasi stercus (*alii vertunt; alii autem,* quasi exemplum; *dicam postea de ipsa voce.*)

The Prophet confirms here what he has said of the fall of Nineveh; but, as it was stated yesterday, he introduces God as the speaker, that his address might be more powerful. God then testifies here to the Assyrians, that they should have no strife or contention with any mortal being, but with their own judgment; as though he said, "There is no reason for thee to compare thy forces with those of the Chaldeans; but think of this—that I am the punisher of thy crimes. The Chaldeans indeed shall come; chariots shall make a noise and horses shall leap, and horsemen shall shake the earth; they shall brandish the flaming swords, and their spears shall be like lightning; but there is no reason for thee to think that the Chaldeans will, of themselves, break in upon thee: for I guide them by my hidden providence, as it is my purpose to destroy thee; and now the time is come when I shall execute on thee my judgment."

I am, he says, *Jehovah of hosts*. The epithet צבאות, *tsabaut*, must be referred to the circumstance of this passage; for God declares here his own power, that the Assyrians might not think that they could by any means escape. He then adds, *I will disclose thy extremities on thy face*. He alludes to the similitude which we have lately observed; for harlots appear very fine, and affect neatness and elegance in their dress; they not only put on costly apparel, but also add disguises. Though then this fine dress conceals the baseness of strumpets, yet, were any to take the clothes of a harlot and throw them over her head, all her beauty would disappear, and all men would abhor the sight: to see her concealed parts disclosed would be a base and filthy spectacle. So God declares that he would strip Nineveh of its magnificent dress, that she might be a detestable sight, only exhibiting her own reproach. We now then apprehend the Prophet's meaning; as though he said, "Nineveh thinks not that she is to perish.—How so? Because her own splendour blinds her: and she has wilfully deceived herself, and, by her deceits, has dazzled the eyes of all nations. As then this splendour seems to be a defence to the city Nineveh, *I the Lord*, he says, *will disclose her hidden parts*; I will deprive the Assyrians of all this splendour in which they now glory, and which is in high esteem and admiration among other nations."

And this passage ought to be especially noticed; for, as I have said, true dignity is not to be found in the highest princes. Princes ought, indeed, to seek respect for themselves by justice, integrity, mercy, and a magnanimous spirit: but they only excel in mean artifices; then they shamelessly deceive, lie, and swear falsely; they also flatter, even meanly, when circumstances require; they insinuate themselves by various crafty means, and by large promises decoy the simple. Since then their true dignity is not commonly regarded by princes, this passage ought to be observed, so that we may know that their elevation, which captivates the minds of men, is an abomination before God; for they do not discern things, but are blind, being dazzled by empty splendour.

Disclose, then, he says, *will I thy shame.* He says first, *Disclose will I thy fringes on thy face;* and then, *I will show to the nations thy nakedness.* And the nakedness of great kings is shown to the nations when the Lord executes his vengeance: for then even the lowest of the low will dare to pass judgment,—"He deserved to perish with shame; for he exercised tyranny on his own subjects, and spared not his own neighbours; he never was a good prince; nay, he only employed deceits and perjuries." When, therefore, princes are cast down, every one, however low, becomes a judge, and ascends, as it were, the tribunal to burden and load them with reproaches. And hence the Prophet says, in the person of God, *Disclose will I thy fringes on thy face, and will show to the nations thy nakedness, and to kingdoms thy filthiness.*

He afterwards adds, *I will besprinkle thee with filth*, or defilements. The Prophet still alludes to the similitude of a harlot, who is well and sumptuously adorned, and by her charms captivates the eyes of all: but when any one takes mire and filth from the middle of the road, and bespatters her with it, there is then no one who will not turn away his eyes from so filthy an object. But we have already explained the import of this. God is indeed said to besprinkle kingdoms with defilements, when he casts them down; for then all begin freely to express their opinion: and those who before pretended great admiration, now rise up and bring forth many reproachful things. Then it is, that the Lord is said to besprinkle great kingdoms with filth and defilements.

He then adds, *I will disgrace thee.* נבל, *nubel*, is to fall, and it is applied to dead bodies; but it means also to disgrace, as it is to be taken here. *I will make thee as the dung.* Some think רואי, *ruai*, to be dung, or some thing fœtid: but as it comes from ראה, *rae*, to see, and is in many parts of Scripture taken for vision or view, they are more correct, in my judgment, who render it thus, *I will make thee an example;* so Jerome renders it; as though he said, "Thou shalt be a spectacle to all nations."[1] And Nineveh is said to be made

[1] The *Septuagint* favours this meaning, "εις παραδειγμα—for an example." In this sense *Grotius* and *Piscator* take the word. *Henderson*, with less propriety, renders it "gazingstock," the word of our version. *Newcome* translates it "dung," according to the Rabbins.—*Ed.*

an example, because its ruin was more memorable than that of any other which had previously happened. *Thou shalt* then *be a spectacle;* that is, the calamity which I now denounce shall attract the observation of all. It afterwards follows—

7. And it shall come to pass, *that* all they that look upon thee shall flee from thee, and say, Nineveh is laid waste: who will bemoan her? whence shall I seek comforters for thee?

7. Et accidet ut quisquis te viderit recedat abs te, et dicat, Vastata est Nineveh: quis condolebit ei? unde quæram consolatores tibi?

When he says, כל־ראיך, *cal-raik*, 'whosoever seeth thee,' we hence learn again that ראי, *ruai*, at the end of the last verse, is to be taken for example or spectacle; for the Prophet proceeds with the same subject: *I will make thee*, he says, *an example*, or a spectacle.—For what purpose? *that whosoever seeth thee may depart from thee.*[1] And it was an evidence of horror, though some think it to have been a reward for her cruelty, that no one came to Nineveh, but that she was forsaken by all friends in her desolation. And they take in the same sense what follows, *Who will condole with her? and whence shall I seek comforters for thee?* For they think that the Ninevites are here reproached for their cruelty, because they made themselves so hated by all that they were unworthy of sympathy; for they spared none, they allowed themselves full liberty in injuring others, they had gained the hatred of all the world. Hence some think that what is here intimated is, that the Ninevites were justly detested by all, so that no one condoled with them in so great a calamity, inasmuch as they had been injurious to all: *It shall* then *happen, that whosoever seeth thee shall go far away from thee, and shall say, Wasted is Nineveh; who will condole with her? Whence shall I call comforters to her?*

But I know not whether this refined meaning came into the Prophet's mind. We may explain the words more simply, —that all would flee far away as a proof of their horror, and that the calamity would be such, that no lamentation would

[1] Literally, "Every one of thy seers shall hasten from thee."—*Ed.*

correspond with it. Who will be able to condole with her? that is, were the greatness of her calamity duly weighed, though all were to weep and utter their moanings, it would not yet be sufficient: all lamentations would be far unequal to so great a calamity. The Prophet seems rather to mean this. *Who* then *shall condole with her? and whence shall I seek comforters?* as though he said, "The ruin of so splendid a city will not be of an ordinary kind, but what cannot be equalled by any lamentations." It then follows—

8. Art thou better than populous No, that was situate among the rivers, *that had* the waters round about it, whose rampart *was* the sea, *and* her wall *was* from the sea?

9. Ethiopia and Egypt *were* her strength, and *it was* infinite; Put and Lubim were thy helpers.

10. Yet *was* she carried away, she went into captivity: her young children also were dashed in pieces at the top of all the streets: and they cast lots for her honourable men, and all her great men were bound in chains.

8. An melior es quam No (*id est,* Alexandria,) Amon (*vertunt quidam,* populosum; *alii putant esse nomen Regis; an igitur* melior es quam Alexandria populosa,) quæ habitabat in fluviis? mare in circuitu ejus, cujus fossa erat mare, et à mari murus ejus;

9. Æthiopia fortitudo ejus et Ægyptus; et nullus finis; Aphrica et Libyæ fuerunt in auxilium ejus.

10. Etiam ipsa in transmigrationem abiit ad captivitatem; etiam parvuli ejus allisi sunt in capite omnium platearum; et super proceres ejus (*vel,* honorabiles, *ad verbum*) jecerunt sortem, et magnetes ejus vincti sunt compedibus.

The Prophet, in order to gain credit to his prophecy, produces here the example of Alexandria. It is indeed certain, from many testimonies of Scripture, that Alexandria is called No, which was a very ancient city, situated on the confines of Africa, and yet in Egypt. It might, at the same time, be, that the Alexandrians formerly had their own government, at least their own kings: and this is probable; for the Prophet says here, that Egypt and Ethiopia, as well as Africa and the Lybian nations, were the confederates of this city. It may hence then be concluded, that Alexandria was not then a part of Egypt, but had its own government, and was in alliance with the Egyptians, as with the other nations. But as Egypt, after the death of our Prophet, was in part overthrown by the Assyrians, and in part by the Chaldeans, some interpreters think, that the Prophet speaks of a ruin which had not yet taken place.[1] But this would not harmonise with his design; for the Prophet shows here, as in a mirror, that the chief empires fall according to the will of God, and that cities, the richest and the best fortified, come to nothing, whenever it pleases God. Unless, then, the destruction of Alexandria was notorious and everywhere known, the Prophet could not have suitably adduced this example: I therefore doubt not but that Alexandria had been then demolished. It is no matter of wonder that it afterwards returned to its former state and became rich; for the situation of the city was most commodious, not so much on account of the fertility of the land, as on account of its traffic; for ships from the Mediterranean sailed up near to it. It had, indeed, on one side, the lake Mareotis, which is not very healthy; and then the sea fortified it; and Pharos was a neighbouring island: but yet the city was inhabited by many, and adorned with splendid buildings; for the advantage of traffic drew together inhabitants from all quarters. It was afterwards built again by Alexander of Macedon. But it is evident enough that it had been already an opulent city: for Alexander did not build a new city but enlarged it.[2] Let us now come to the words of the Prophet.

Shall it be better to thee than to Alexandria? The word אמון, *amun*, some render populous; and I am inclined to adopt this meaning, which has been received nearly by the consent of all. Others have supposed it to be the name of a king; but as proof fails them, I leave to themselves their own conjecture. *Shall it* then *be better to thee than to Alexandria?* For *it stood*, he says, *between the rivers.* Alexandria had the Nile, as it were, under its own power; for it was then divided into many

[1] So does *Newcome*, but with no countenance from the passage. The verb in the 10th verse, which refers to the captivity of No, is in the past tense. Most commentators regard the event having passed.—*Ed.*

[2] Opinions differ as to No. *Bochart* supposed it to be *Diospolis*, near Mendes, in Lower Egypt. *Henderson* says, that later commentators are in favour of *Thebes*, the ancient capital of Upper Egypt. It is of no consequence to the present purpose which it was. It was some celebrated city in Egypt, whose ruin was well known in the Prophet's time. Both the Rabbins and early Fathers thought that it was what was afterwards called Alexandria. But most probably it was a city which had lost its name and existence from the catastrophe that is here mentioned.—*Ed.*

parts, so that it intersected the city in various places. So then he says, that Alexandria dwelt between the rivers; for it divided the Nile, as it suited its convenience, into several streams.

Then he says, *The sea was around her:* for it was surrounded on one side by the sea, and protected by the island Pharos, which had a tower, not only for the sake of defence, but that ships, coming in from the Mediterranean, might have a signal, by which they might direct their course straight to the harbour. *The sea* then *was around her;* for the sea encircled more than half of the city; and then the lake Mareotis was on the other side to the south. He afterwards adds, *And its wall* or moat *was the sea.* The word is written with י, *iod,* חיל, *chil;* but it means a wall or a moat, though Latins render *antemurale*—a front-work: for they were wont formerly to fortify their cities with a double wall, as old buildings still show. According to these interpreters, חיל, *chil,* is the inner wall, and so they render it, front-work: and there was also an outer wall towards the sea. But we may take חיל, *chil,* for a moat or a trench; and it is easy to find from other passages that it was a trench rather than a front-work. It is said that the body of Jezebel was torn by dogs in the trench, and the word there is חיל, *chil.* As to the object of the Prophet, he evidently intended to show, that Alexandria was so well fortified, that Nineveh had no reason to think herself to be in a safer state; for its fortress was from the sea, and also from *Ethiopia,* on account of the munitions which he has mentioned. Then he speaks of *Africa* and *Egypt,* and the *Lybian* nations,[1] and says, in short, that there was *no end* of her strength; that is, that she could seek the help of many friends and confederates: many were ready to bring aid, even Africa, Ethiopia, and the Lybians.

Yet, he says, *she departed into captivity a captive;* that is, the

[1] The original names in this verse are כוש, supposed to be Ethiopia,—מצרים, Egypt, here, either Upper or Lower,—פוט, Put, a country to the west of Lower Egypt, its inhabitants the descendants of Ham, Gen. x. 6,—לובים, Lybians, who occupied the region between Put and Numidia. —*Ed.*

inhabitants of Alexandria have been banished, and the city become as it were captive, for its inhabitants were driven here and there. *Dashed*, he says, *have been their little ones at the head of every street.* The Prophet means, that so great a power as that of Alexandria did not prevent the conquerors to exercise towards her the most barbarous cruelty; for it was a savage act to dash little children against stones, who ought, on account of their tender age, to have been spared. There was indeed no reason for raging against them, for they could not have been deemed enemies. But yet the Prophet says that Alexandria had been thus treated; and he said this, that Nineveh might not trust in her strength, and thus perversely despise God's judgment, which he now denounced on it. He adds, *They cast lots on her princes*, and *bound were her great men with fetters.* In saying that lots were cast, he refers to an ancient custom; for when there was any dispute respecting a captive, the lot was cast: as for instance, when two had taken one man, to prevent contention, it was by lot determined who was to be his master. So then he says, that lots were cast on their princes. This usually happened to the common people and to the lowest slaves; but the Prophet says that the conquerors spared not even the princes. They were therefore treated as the lowest class; and though they were great princes, they were led into captivity and bound with chains, in the same manner with the meanest and the lowest of the people. They were not treated according to their rank; and there was no difference between the chief men and the most degraded of the humbler classes; for even the very princes were so brought down, that their lot differed not from that of the wretched; for as common people are usually treated with contempt, so were the chiefs of Alexandria treated by their enemies.

PRAYER.

Grant, Almighty God, that since by thy awful judgments thou dost show thy displeasure at the pride of this world, we may be ruled by the spirit of meekness, and in such a manner humble ourselves willingly under thy hand, that we may not experience thy dreadful power in our destruction, but being, on the contrary, supported by thy strength, we may keep ourselves in our own proper station and in true simplicity, and, at the same time, relying on thy protection, we may never doubt, but thou wilt sustain us against all the assaults of our enemies, however violent they may be, and thus persevere in the warfare of the cross which thou hast appointed for us, until we be at length gathered into that celestial kingdom, where we shall triumph together with thy Son, when his glory shall shine in us, and all the wicked shall be destroyed. Amen.

Lecture One Hundred and Fifth.

11. Thou also shalt be drunken: thou shalt be hid, thou also shalt seek strength because of the enemy.	11. Etiam tu inebriaberis, tu eris abscondita; etiam tu quæres robur (*vel*, suppetias) ab hoste (*vel*, propter hostem.)

Nahum, after having adduced the example of Alexandria, now shows that nothing would be able to resist God, so that he should not deal with Nineveh in the same manner; and he declares that this would be the case, *Thou also*, he says, *shalt be inebriated*. Well known is this metaphor, which often occurs in Scripture: for the Prophets are wont frequently to call punishment a cup, which God administers. But when God executes a heavy punishment, he is said to inebriate the wicked with his cup. The Prophet says now, that the chastisement of Nineveh would make her like a drunken man, who, being overcome with wine, lies down, as it were, stupified. Hence by this metaphor he intended to set forth a most severe punishment: *Thou* then *shalt be also inebriated*. The particle גם, *gam*, is here emphatical; it was introduced, that the Ninevites might know, that they could not possibly escape the punishment which they deserved; for God continues ever like himself. *Thou* then *shalt be also inebriated*. This would not be consistent, were not God the judge of the world to the end. There is then a common reason for this proceeding; hence it necessarily follows,—since God punished the Alexandrians, the Assyrians cannot escape his hand, and be exempt from punishment.

He adds, *Thou shalt be hidden*. Some refer this to shame,

as though the Prophet had said,—"Thou indeed showest thyself now to be very proud, but calamity will force thee to seek hiding-places, in which to conceal thyself." But I am more inclined to this meaning,—that Nineveh would vanish away, as though it never had been; for to be hidden is often taken in Hebrew in the sense of being reduced to nothing.

He afterwards says, *Thou shalt also seek strength*, or supplies, *from the enemy*. The words מעוז מאויב, *meouz meavib*, may admit of two meanings,—either that she will humbly solicit her enemies,—or that on account of her enemies she will flee to some foreign aid; for the preposition מ, *mem*, may be taken in both senses. If we adopt the first meaning, then I think that the Prophet speaks not of the Babylonians, but of the other nations who had been before harassed by the Assyrians. Thou shalt now then humbly pray for the aid of those who have been hitherto thine enemies,—not because they had provoked thee, but because thou hast as an enemy treated them. Now it is an extreme misery, when we are constrained to seek the help of those by whom we are hated, and hated, because we have by wrongs provoked them. But the other sense is more approved, for it is less strained: *Thou shalt also seek aids on account of the enemy*; that is, as strength to resist will fail thee, thou wilt seek assistance from thy neighbours.[1] It follows—

12. All thy strongholds *shall be like* fig-trees with the first-ripe figs: if they be shaken, they shall even fall into the mouth of the eater.	12. Omnes munitiones tuæ ficus cum maturis (fructibus;) si moveantur, cadunt super os comedentis.

The Prophet here declares that the strongholds of the Assyrians would avail them nothing; whether they trusted in the number of their men, or in their walls, or in other defences, they would be disappointed; for all things, he says, will of themselves fall, even without being much assailed. And he employs a very apposite similitude, "Thy fortifications," he says, "which thou thinkest to be very strong, shall

[1] Thou shalt seek a refuge from the enemy.—*Newcome.* But מעוז is rather a defence, aid, assistance, that which affords strength.—*Ed.*

be like figs; for when the fruit is ripe, and any comes to the tree, as soon as he touches it or any of the branches, the figs will fall off themselves." We indeed know that there is not much firmness in that fruit; when it is ripe, it immediately falls to the ground, or if it hangs on the branches, a very little shaking will bring it down. We now see the design of the Prophet.

And hence an useful doctrine may be deduced: whatever strength men may seek for themselves from different quarters, it will wholly vanish away; for neither forts, nor towers, nor ramparts, nor troops of men, nor any kind of contrivances, will avail any thing; and were there no one to rise against them, they would yet fall of themselves. It afterwards follows—

13. Behold, thy people in the midst of thee *are* women: the gates of thy land shall be set wide open unto thine enemies: the fire shall devour thy bars.	13. Ecce populus tuus mulieres in medio tui; inimicis tuis aperiendo aperientur portæ terræ tuæ; vorabit ignis vectès tuos.

The Prophet declares here, that the hearts of them all would become soft and effeminate when God would proceed to destroy Nineveh. We have said before that the hearts of men are so in the hand of God, that he melts whatever courage there may be in them, whenever he pleases: and God prepares men for ruin, when he debilitates their hearts, that they cannot bear the sight of their enemies. God indeed can leave in men their perverseness, so that they may ever run furiously into ruin, and not be able, with a courageous heart, to repel the attacks of their enemies; but he often softens their hearts and deprives them of power, that he may make more evident his judgment: God does not, however, always work in the same way; for variety in his judgments is calculated to do us good, for thereby our minds are more powerfully awakened. Were his proceedings uniformly the same, we could not so well distinguish the hand of God, as when he acts now in this way, and then in another. But, as I have already said, it is what is well known, that God enervates men and strips them of all courage, when he gives them over to destruction.

So now the Prophet speaks of the Ninevites, *Behold*, he says, *thy people are women.*[1] The demonstrative particle, *Behold*, is here emphatical: for the Assyrians, no doubt, ridiculed, as a fable, the prediction of the Prophet; and it was what the Israelites found it difficult to believe. This is the reason why the Prophet pointed out, as by the finger, what surpassed the comprehensions of men. By saying, *in the midst of thee*, he intimates, that though they should be separated from their enemies and dwell in a fortified city, they should yet be filled with trembling. This amplification deserves to be noticed: for it is nothing wonderful, when an onset frightens us, when enemies join battle with us, and when many things present themselves before our eyes, which are calculated to deprive us of courage; but when we are frightened by report only concerning our enemies, and we become fainthearted, though walls be between us, it then appears evident, that we are smitten by the hand of God; for when we see walls of stone, and yet our hearts become brittle like glass, is it not evident, that we are inwardly terrified by the Lord, as it were, through some hidden influence, rather than through intervening and natural causes? We now then perceive the Prophet's meaning, when he says, that *the people would become women*, or effeminate, *in the midst* of the city, in its very bowels; as though he had said, that they would not cease to tremble, even while they were dwelling in a safe place.

By opening, opened shall be thy gates, he says, *to thy enemies*. He shows again, that though the Assyrians were fortified, every access would be made open to their enemies, as though there was no fortress. By saying, *the gates of thy land*, it is probable that he speaks not only of the city, but of all their strongholds. The Assyrians, no doubt, fortified many cities, in order to keep afar off the enemy, and to preserve the chief seat of the empire free from danger and fear. I therefore understand the Prophet as referring here to many cities, when he says, *By opening, opened shall be the gates of thy land to thine enemies, and fire shall consume thy bars.* He means,

[1] Both *Homer* and *Virgil* have this comparison. "Αχαιιδες, ουκ ετ' Αχαιοι—Grecian women, not Grecians."—"O! vere Phrygiæ, neque enim Phryges—O truly Phrygian women, but not Phrygians."

that though they had before carefully fortified the whole land around, so that they thought themselves secure from all hostile invasion, yet all this would be useless; for the fire would consume all their bars. By fire, the Prophet understands metaphorically the judgment of God. For as we see that so great is the vehemence of fire, that it melts iron and brass, so the Prophet means, that there would be no strength which could defend Nineveh and its empire against the hand of God. It follows—

14. Draw thee waters for the siege, fortify thy strong holds: go into clay, and tread the mortar, make strong the brick-kiln.

15. There shall the fire devour thee; the sword shall cut thee off, it shall eat thee up like the cankerworm: make thyself many as the cankerworm, make thyself many as the locusts.

14. Aquas obsidionis hauri tibi, robora munitiones tuas, ingredere in lutum, calca cæmentum, fortifica fornacem (*vel*, laterem; *alii vertunt*, tene, *vel*, apprehende.)

15. Illic vorabit te ignis, exterminabit te gladius, comedet te quasi bruchus (*alii vertunt*, quasi bruchum;) multiplicari (*ad verbum*, *vel*, multiplicando; *est* כירק *quasi bruchus*,) multiplicare quasi locusta.

The Prophet goes on with the same subject,—that the Ninevites would labour in vain, while striving anxiously and with every effort to defend themselves against their enemies. The meaning then is, "That though thou remittest no diligence, yet thou shalt lose all thy labour; for thou wilt not be able to resist the vengeance of God; and thou deceivest thyself if thou thinkest that by the usual means thou canst aid thyself; for it is God who attacks thee by the Babylonians. How much soever then thou mayest accumulate of those things which are usually employed to fortify cities, all this will be useless." *Draw for thyself*, he says, *waters for the siege;* that is, lay up provisions for thyself, as it is usually done, and have water laid up in cisterns; *strengthen thy fortresses*, that is, renew them; *enter into the clay* for the sake of treading the mortar: *fortify*, or cement, or join together, *the brick-kiln*, (for what some think that חזק, *chezek*, means here is to hold, or to lay hold, is wholly foreign to the Prophet's meaning:) to *fortify* then the *brick-kiln*, that is, the bricks which come forth from the kiln, is nothing else than to construct and join them together, that there might be a solid building: for we know that buildings often fall, or are overturned, because they are not well joined together: and he refers to the mode of building which historians say was in use among the Assyrians. For as that country had no abundance of stones, they supplied the defect by bricks. We now then understand the intention of the Prophet.

But he adds, *There shall the fire consume thee.* There is much importance in the adverb of place, *there*, which he uses: *there* also, he says, *shall the fire eat thee up:* for he expresses more than before, when he said, that the Assyrians would weary themselves in vain in fortifying their city and their empire; for he says now, that the Lord would turn to their destruction those things in which they trusted as their defences; *There* then *shall the fire consume thee.* We now then see what the Prophet means.

We must at the same time observe, that he mentions water; as though he said, "However sparingly and frugally thy soldiers may live, being content with water as their drink, (for it is necessary, when we would firmly resist enemies, to undergo all indulgences, and if needs be to endure want, at least the want of delicate meat and drink,)—though thy soldiers be content with water, and seek not water fresh from the spring or the river, but drink it from cisterns, and though thy fortresses be repaired, and thy walls carefully joined together in a solid structure, by bricks well fitted and fastened, —yet *there shall the fire consume thee;* that is, thy frugality, exertion, and care, not only will avail thee nothing, but will also turn out to thy ruin; for the Lord pronounces accursed the arrogance of men, when they trust in their own resources."

He afterwards adds, *Exterminate thee shall the sword;* that is, the Lord will find out various means by which he will consume thee. By the fire, then, and by the sword, will he waste and destroy thee. He then says, *He will consume thee as the chafer.* We may read the last word in the nominative as well as in the objective case—He as a chafer will consume thee. If we approve of this rendering, then the meaning would be,—"As chafers in a short time devour a meadow or standing corn, so thy enemies shall soon devour thee as with one mouthful." We indeed know, that these little animals are so hurtful, that they will very soon eat up and consume all the fruit; and there is in these insects an astonishing voracity. But as the Prophet afterwards compares the Assyrians to chafers and locusts, another sense would be more suitable, and that is,—that God's judgment would consume the Assyrians, as when rain, or a storm, or a change of season, consumes the chafers; for as these insects are very hurtful, so the Lord also exterminates them whenever he pleases.[1] He afterwards adds, *to be multiplied;* which is, as I have said, a verb in the infinitive mood. But the sentence of the Prophet is this, *by multiplying as the chafer, to multiply as the locusts:* but why he speaks thus, may be better understood from the context; the two following verses must be therefore added—

16. Thou hast multiplied thy merchants above the stars of heaven: the cankerworm spoileth, and fleeth away.

16. Multiplicasti negotiatores tuos quasi stellas cœlorum; bruchus prædatus est et avolat.

17. Thy crowned *are* as the locusts, and thy captains as the great grasshoppers which camp in the hedges in the cold day, *but* when the sun ariseth they flee away, and their place is not known where they *are*.

17. Principes tui (*vel,* coronati; *deducitur enim à* נזר, *quod significat coronam; sed malo vertere,* egregios, *vel,* præstantissimos quosque; principes *ergo* tui, *vel,* eximii tui) quasi locusta, et duces tui quasi locusta locustarum (*est quidem aliud nomen, sed non possumus certò distinguere inter illas species, quemadmodum dictum est Jœlis* 1. *capite,)* quæ castramentantur (*id est,* considunt) in maceriis (*id est,* clausuris) in die frigoris: sol exortus est, et migrârunt; et non cognoscitur locus earum ubi.

From these words we may learn what the Prophet before meant, when he said that the Assyrians were like locusts or chafers; as though he said,—"I know that you trust in your great number; for ye are like a swarm of chafers or locusts; ye excel greatly in number; inasmuch as you have assembled your merchants and traders as the stars of heaven." Here he

[1] *Grotius* agrees in this view, though *Newcome* takes the former, explaining, "as the locust," that is, in a manner equally unsparing.—*Ed.*

shows how numerous they were. But when he says, *The chafer hath spoiled, and flies away*, he points out another reason for the comparison; for it is not enough to lay hold on one clause of the verse, but the two clauses must be connected; and they mean this,—that the Assyrians, while they were almost innumerable, gloried in their great number,—and also, that this vast multitude would vanish away. He then makes an admission here and says, by multiplying thy merchants, thou hast multiplied them; but when he says, as chafers and as locusts, he shows that this multitude would not continue, for the Lord would scatter them here and there. As then the scattering was nigh, the Prophet says that they were chafers and locusts.

We now understand the design of the Prophet: He first ridicules the foolish confidence with which the Assyrians were inflated. They thought, that as they ruled over many nations, they could raise great armies, and set them in any quarter to oppose any one who might attack them: the Prophet concedes this to them, that is, that they were very numerous, *by multiplying thou hast multiplied;* but what will this avail them? They shall be locusts, they shall be chafers. —How so? A fuller explanation follows, *Thou hast multiplied thy merchants as the stars of heaven:* but this shall be temporary; for thou shalt see them vanishing away very soon; they shall be like the chafers, who, being in a moment scattered here and there, quit the naked field or the meadow. But by merchants or traders some understand confederates; and this comparison also, as we have before seen, frequently occurs in the Prophets: and princes at this day differ nothing from traders, for they outbid one another, and excel in similar artifices, as we have elsewhere seen, by which they carry on a system of mutual deception. This comparison then may be suitable, *Thou hast multiplied thy traders,—tes practiciens.* But the meaning of the Prophet may be viewed as still wider; we may apply this to the citizens of Nineveh; for the principal men no doubt were merchants: as the Venetians of the present day are all merchants, so were the Tyrians, and the Ninevites, and also the Babylonians. It is then nothing strange, that the Prophet, by taking a part for the whole, should include under this term all the rich, *Thou hast* then *multiplied thy merchants.*[1]

He has hitherto allowed them to be very numerous; but he now adds, *The chafer has spoiled, and flies away.* The verb means sometimes to spoil, and it means also to devour: The chafer then has devoured, and flies away; that is, "Thy princes, (as he afterwards calls them,) or thy principal men, have indeed devoured; they have wasted many regions by their plunders, and consumed all things on every side, like the chafers, who destroy the standing corn and all fruits: thou hast then been as a swarm of chafers." For as chafers in great numbers attack a field, so Nineveh was wont to send everywhere her merchants to spoil and to denude the whole land. "Well," he says, "the chafer has devoured, but he flies away, he is scattered; so it shall happen," says the Prophet, "to the citizens of Nineveh." And hence he afterwards adds, *And thy princes are as locusts:* this refers to the wicked doings, by which they laid waste almost the whole earth. As then the locusts and chafers, wherever they come, consume every kind of food, devour all the fields, leave nothing, and the whole land becomes a waste; so also have been *thy princes;* they have been *as locusts, and thy leaders as the locusts of locusts,* that is, as very great locusts; for this form, we know, expresses the superlative degree in Hebrew. Their leaders were then like the most voracious locusts, for the whole land was made barren by them, as nothing was capable of satisfying their avarice and voracity.

The Prophet then adds, They are locusts, who *dwell in the*

[1] The latter clause of the last verse and this verse and the following are evidently connected. The first, התכבד, hath י added to it in ten or more copies, and may be deemed an imperative as well as the other, and in the feminine gender; *Calvin* takes it an infinitive. This would be literal rendering—

Increase thyself as the chafer,
Increase thyself as the locust,
16. Multiply thy merchants more than the stars of heaven:
The chafer spoils, and flies away:
17. Thy crowned ones *shall be* as the locusts,
And thy rulers as the gibbous caterpillar;
Which lodge in the fences in the cold day;
The sun rises and they flit away,
And not known is the place where they *are.—Ed.*

mounds during the time of cold; but when the sun rises, not known any more is their place. He now shows, that it would not be perpetual, that the Ninevites would thus devour the whole earth, and that all countries would be exposed to their voracity; "for as the locusts," he says, "hide themselves in caverns, and afterwards fly away, so it shall happen to thy princes." But this passage may be taken to mean,—that the Ninevites concealed themselves in their hiding-places during the winter, and that when the suitable time for plundering came, they betook themselves in different directions, and took possession of various regions, and brought home plunder from the remotest parts. This meaning may be elicited from the words of the Prophet; and the different clauses would thus fitly coalesce together, that when the Ninevites left their nests, they dispersed and migrated in all directions. I do not at the same time disapprove of the former meaning: they are then like locusts, who *lodge in mounds during the time of cold; but when the sun rises,*—that is, when the season invites them, (for he speaks not of the winter sun,) but when the heat of the sun prevails and temperates the air,—then, he says, the locusts go forth and *fly away, and known no more is their place.* He means, in short, that the Ninevites plundered, and that they did so after the manner of locusts; and that a similar end also was nigh them; for the Lord would destroy them, yea, suddenly consume them, so that no trace of them could be found. It follows—

18. Thy shepherds slumber, O king of Assyria: thy nobles shall dwell *in the dust:* thy people is scattered upon the mountains, and no man gathereth *them.*

18. Dormitaverunt pastores tui, rex Assur; jacuerunt fortes tui; dispersus est populus tuus super montes, et nemo congregans.

He confirms the preceding verse, and says that there would be no counsel nor wisdom in the leading men: for the *shepherds* of the king of Assyria were his counsellors, in whose wisdom he trusted, as we know that kings usually depend on their counsellors: for they think that there is in them prudence enough, and therefore they commit to them the care of the whole people. But the Prophet ridicules the confidence of the king of Assyria, because the shepherds would not have so much vigilance as to take care of themselves, and of the people, and of the whole kingdom. He speaks in the past tense, either to show the certainty of the prediction, or because the change of tenses is common in Hebrew. *Lie still,* he says, *shall thy mighty men;*[1] that is, they shall remain idle; they shall not be able to sally out against their enemies, to stop their progress. *They shall* then *lie still:* and then he says, *Scattered are thy people.* פוש, *push,* is not to scatter; hence I doubt not, but that there is a change of letter, that ש, *schin,* is put for צ, *tzaddi:* and I am surprised that some derive the verb from פוש, *push,* when, on the contrary, it is from פוץ, *puts,* and the change of these two letters is common in Hebrew. *Thy people* then *are dispersed on the mountains, and there is no one to assemble them.*

By these words the Prophet means, that such would be the scattering of the whole kingdom, that there would be no hope of restoration; *There will* then *be none to assemble them.* He had said before that the chiefs or mighty men would be still. Though it would be needful to go forth to check the progress of their enemies; yet he says, *They shall idly lie down:* He refers here to their sloth. But the people who ought to be quiet at home, as being weak and feeble, *shall be dispersed on the mountains, and no one will be there to gather them.* It follows—

19. *There is* no healing of thy bruise; thy wound is grievous: all that hear the bruit of thee shall clap the hands over thee: for upon whom hath not thy wickedness passed continually?

19. Non est contractio (*vel,* cicatrix) fracturæ tuæ; dolore est plena plaga tua; omnes qui audierint famam tuam (*id est,* de te) percutient manum super te; quia super quem non transiit malitia tua jugiter?

[1] *Fortes tui,* אדיריך, thy eminents, thy nobles. "The shepherds," the governors of the people, נמו, slumber; and the nobles, the princes, ישכנו, rest, sit still, without making any effort: then it follows,—

Dispersed are thy people on the mountains,
And *there is* no gatherer.

Calvin is mistaken as to the meaning of the verb פוש: it means more properly, than the other, a dispersed state. It is applied in Lev. xiii. 5, and in other places, to the *spreading* of leprosy. When so used, it is in Kal. It is here, and here only, in Niphal.—*Ed.*

The Prophet shows here more clearly, that when the empire of Nineveh should be scattered, it would be an incurable evil, that every hope of a remedy would be taken away. Though the wicked cannot escape calamity, yet they harbour false expectations, and think that they can in a short time gather new strength. Hence, in order to take from them this hope, the Prophet says, that there would be no *contraction of the fracture.*[1] And this is a striking similitude; for he compares the ruin of Nineveh to a wound which cannot be seamed and healed. *There is* then *no contraction;* some render it, a wrinkle, but improperly. *There is* then *no contraction:* and he adds, *Thy stroke is full of pain;*[2] that is, the pain of thy stroke cannot be allayed. This is one thing,—that the ruin of Nineveh would be irreparable.

Then he says, *Whosoever shall hear the report, shall strike the hand on thy account.* Many give this rendering, They shall clap the hand over thee, or with the hands; and they think that the singular is put for the plural number. But as in Hebrew to strike the hand is a token of consent, it would not be unsuitable to say, that the Prophet means, that wherever the report of this calamity would be heard, all would express their approbation, "See, God has at length proved himself to be the just avenger of so much wickedness." To strike the hand is said to be done by those who make an agreement, or when any one pledges himself for another.[3] As then in giving pledges, and in other compacts, men are said to strike the hand; so also all shall thus give their assent to God's judgment in this case, "O how rightly is this done! O how justly has God punished these tyrants, these plunder-

[1] אין־כהה לשברך—No stopping or restraining to thy breach. The word is applied to the restraint put on men's wickedness, 1 Sam. iii. 13, and to the checking and restraining of the spread of leprosy, Lev. vi. 28. The breach or breaking was such that there was no stopping of it from becoming entire and complete. The Septuagint gives the meaning—"ουκ εστιν ιασις τη συντριβη σου—there is no healing to thy breach."—*Ed.*

[2] Rather, "grievous is thy stroke." The verb is נחלה, from חלה, to be languid, and sometimes, to make languid, grievous or afflictive, and then in Niphal, as here, to be grievous. See the same clause in Jer. x. 19. As a noun it is rendered "grief" in Isa. xvii. 11.—*Ed.*

[3] The phrase here used, תקע כף, is found in three other places, Ps. xlvii. 1; Prov. xvii. 18; xxii 26. In the first it is a symptom of joy; and in the two other places, in the sense here mentioned.—*Ed.*

ers!" *They will* then *strike the hand on thy account;* that is, "This thy ruin will be approved;" as though he said, "Not only before God art thou, Nineveh, accursed, but also according to the consent of all nations." And thus he intimates, that Nineveh would perish in the greatest dishonour and disgrace. It sometimes happens that an empire falls, and all bewail the event: but God here declares, that he would not be satisfied with the simple destruction of the city Nineveh without adding to it a public infamy, so that all might acknowledge that it happened through his righteous judgment.

He afterwards adds, *For upon whom hath not thy wickedness passed continually?* This is a confirmation of the last clause; and this reason will suit both the views which have been given. If we take the striking of the hand for approbation, this reason will be suitable.—How? For all nations will rejoice at thy destruction, because there is no nation which thou hast not in many ways injured. So also, in token of their joy, all will congratulate themselves, as though they were made free; or they will clap their hands, that is, acknowledge that thou hast been destroyed by the judgment of God, because all had experienced how unjustly and tyrannically thou hast ruled. As then thy wickedness has been like a deluge, and hast nearly consumed all the earth, all will clap or shake their hands at thy ruin.

And he says, *continually*, to show that God's forbearance had been long exercised. Hence, also, it appears, that the Assyrians were inexcusable, because, when God indulgently spared them, they did not repent, but pursued their wicked ways for a long course of time. As then to their sinful licentiousness they added perverseness, every excuse was removed. But the Prophet does, at the same time, remind the Israelites, that there was no reason for them to be cast down in their minds, because God did not immediately execute punishment; for by the word תמיד, *tamid*, he intimates, that God would so suspend for a time his judgment as to Nineveh, that his forbearance and delay might be an evidence of his goodness and mercy. We hence see that the Prophet here opposes the ardour of men, for they immediately grow angry or complain when God delays to execute vengeance on their enemies.

He shows that God has a just reason for not visiting the wicked with immediate punishment; but yet the time will come when it shall appear that they are altogether past recovery,—the time, I say, will come, when the Lord shall at length put forth his hand and execute his judgment.

PRAYER.

Grant, Almighty God, that as we are not able to keep a firm footing in the way of justice and uprightness,—O grant, that, being governed by thy Spirit, we may restrain ourselves from doing any harm, and thus abstain from all evil deeds, and that we may labour to do good to all, so that we may, by experience, find that all are protected by thee, who so conform themselves to the rule of thy Law, that they take no advantage of the simple, either for the purpose of ruining or of injuring them, but who, being content with their own small portion, know that there is nothing better than to be wholly subject to thee, and to thy guidance: and may we thus live in forbearance and justice towards our neighbours, that we may, at the same time, rely on thy mercy, by which alone we can be defended, and made safe against so many assaults of Satan and of the wicked, until, having at length completed the course of our warfare, we shall come into that blessed rest which has been prepared for us in heaven by Christ Jesus our Lord. Amen.

END OF THE COMMENTARIES ON NAHUM.

A TRANSLATION

OF

CALVIN'S VERSION

OF

THE BOOK OF JONAH,

AS MODIFIED BY

HIS COMMENTARIES.

A TRANSLATION

OF

CALVIN'S VERSION

OF

THE BOOK OF JONAH.

CHAPTER I.

1 And the word of Jehovah came to Jonah the son of
Amittai, saying,
2 "Arise, go to Nineveh, to that great city, and cry against
it; for their wickedness has ascended before my face."
3 But Jonah rose up to flee to Tarshish from the presence
of Jehovah, and went down to Joppa, and found a ship,
which was going to Tarshish; and he paid the fare, and
went down into it, that he might go with them to Tar-
shish from the presence of Jehovah. 4 And Jehovah sent
a strong wind on the sea, and a great tempest arose in
the sea, and the ship was thought to be breaking: 5 And
the mariners feared, and cried every one to his god, and
cast out the wares, which were in the ship, into the sea, that
it might be lightened of them; but Jonah had gone down to
the sides of the ship; and he lay down and slept. 6 And
the pilot came to him, and he said to him,—"What meanest
thou, O sleeper? Arise, call on thy God, if so be that God
will show himself propitious to us, that we may not perish."
7 And they said each to his friend,—"Come and let us

cast lots, that we may know for what cause *is* this evil *come*
upon us." And they cast lots, and the lot fell upon Jonah.
8 And they said to him,—"Tell us now why has this evil
happened to us, what is thy work, and whence comest thou,
what is thy country, and from what people art thou?" 9 And
he said to them,—"I am an Hebrew, and I fear Jehovah,
the God of heaven, who made the sea and the dry *land*."
10 And the men feared with great fear, and said to him,—
"Why hast thou done this?" (52) For the men knew that
he was fleeing from the presence of Jehovah, because he had
told them. 11 And they said to him,—"What shall we do
to thee, that the sea may be still to us?" for the sea was
going and was tempestuous. 12 And he said to them,—
"Take me and cast me into the sea, and the sea will be still
to you; for I know that on my account is this great tempest
come upon you."

13 But the men toiled to bring back the ship, (59) and
they could not; for the sea was going and was tempestuous
against them. 14 And they cried to Jehovah, and said,—
"We beseech, Jehovah, we pray, that we perish not for the
life of this man, and lay not on us innocent blood; for thou,
Jehovah, hast done as it has seemed good to thee." (62)
15 Then they took Jonah, and cast him into the sea; and the
sea stopped from its raging. 16 And with great fear, the men
feared Jehovah, and sacrificed a sacrifice to Jehovah, and
vowed vows.

17 And Jehovah provided a great fish to swallow up Jonah;
and Jonah was in the bowels of the fish three days and three
nights.

CHAPTER II.

1 And Jonah prayed to Jehovah his God from the belly of
the fish, 2 And said,—

I cried in my distress to Jehovah, and he heard me; (75)
From the belly of the grave I cried, thou didst hear my voice.

3 But cast me hadst thou into the deep,
Into the midst of the seas, and the flood surrounded me;
All thy billows and waves over me passed:
4 Then I said,—"I am driven from the sight of thine eyes;
But I would again see the temple of thy holiness."
5 Beset me did the waters even to the soul,
The deep on every side surrounded me,
The sedge was wrapped around my head:
6 To the roots of mountains I descended,
The earth with its bars was around me for ever:
But to ascend hast thou made my life from the grave,
O Jehovah, my God.
7 When fail did my soul within me,
Jehovah did I remember,
And enter did my prayer into the temple of thy holiness.

8 They who observe lying vanities,
Their own mercy forsake: (87)
9 But I, with the voice of praise, will sacrifice to thee;
What I have vowed will I pay:
To Jehovah *belongs* salvation.

10 And Jehovah commanded the fish, and it cast forth Jonah on the dry land.

CHAPTER III.

1 And the word of Jehovah came to Jonah the second time,
saying,—2 "Arise, go to Nineveh, to that great city, and
proclaim to it the proclamation which I command thee." (92)
3 And Jonah arose, and went to Nineveh, according to the
command of Jehovah.
4 Now Nineveh was a very great city, a journey of three
days. And Jonah began to enter a journey of one day, and
cried and said, "Yet forty days, and Nineveh shall be over-
thrown." 5 And the men of Nineveh believed God, and
proclaimed a fast, and put on sackcloth, from the greatest
of them even to the least of them: 6 For word had come to

the king of Nineveh, and he arose from his throne, and cast
aside his splendid robe from him, and put on sackcloth and
sat on ashes; 7 And it was proclaimed and published through
Nineveh, by the counsel of the king and his nobles, saying,—
"Man and beast! ox and sheep! let them taste nothing,
let them not be fed, and let them not drink water; 8 And let
man and beast put on sackcloth, and cry to God mightily;
(107) and return let every one from his evil way, and from
the plunder that is in their hands. 9 Who knows, whether
God will change and repent, and turn away from the fury of
his wrath, that we perish not?"

10 And God saw their works, that they turned from their
evil way; and God repented of the evil which he had de-
clared that he would do to them, and did *it* not.

CHAPTER IV.

1 And Jonah was grievously displeased, and he was very
angry; (116) and he prayed to Jehovah, and said,—2 "I
pray thee, Jehovah, was not this my word, when I was yet
in my own land? I therefore hastened to flee to Tarshish;
for I knew that thou art a God full of grace, and merciful,
slow to wrath, great in kindness, and who repentest of evil.
3 And thou, Jehovah, take, I pray, my life from me; for better
it is for me to die than to live." 4 And Jehovah said to him,
—"Doest thou well in being angry?" (129)

5 And Jonah went out of the city, and sat on the east
over against the city, and made there for himself a tent, and
sat under it in the shade, until he saw what might be in the
city. 6 And Jehovah God prepared a gourd, and made it to
come up for Jonah, that it might be a shade over his head,
and free him from his distress; and Jonah rejoiced for the
gourd with great joy. 7 God also prepared a worm, when
the morning rose the next day, which smote the gourd, and
it withered: 8 And it was, when the sun arose, that God pre-
pared an impetuous wind, and the sun smote the head of
Jonah, and he fainted, and wished for himself that he might
die, and said, "Better is my death than my life." 9 And God

said to Jonah,—"Doest thou well in being angry for the gourd?" and he said,—"I do well in being angry even unto death."

10 And Jehovah said,—"Thou wouldest have spared the gourd, for which thou hast not laboured, and which thou hast not raised up; the daughter of a night it was,[1] and *as* the daughter of a night it has passed away; 11 And should I not spare Nineveh, this great city, in which there are twelve times ten thousand men, every one of whom knows not his right hand from his left, and also many animals?"

[1] It is literally, "the son of a night," but as *cucurbita*, gourd, is feminine, *Calvin* adopted *filia* instead of *filius*.—*Ed.*

END OF NEW TRANSLATION OF JONAH.

A TRANSLATION

OF

CALVIN'S VERSION

OF

THE PROPHECIES OF MICAH.

CHAPTER I.

1 THE word of Jehovah, which came to Micah, the Moras-
thite, in the days of Jotham, Ahaz, Hezekiah, kings of Judah,
which he saw concerning Samaria and Jerusalem:

2 Hear, all ye people,
Give ear, O earth, and its fulness; (155)
And the Lord Jehovah shall be against you a witness,
Even the Lord from the temple of his holiness:
3 For, behold, Jehovah goeth forth from his place,
And will descend and tread on the heights of the earth;
4 And melt shall the mountains under him,
And rent shall be the valleys;
As wax before the fire,
As waters rolling into a lower place. (160)

5 For the wickedness of Jacob is all this,
And for the transgressions of the house of Israel:
What is the wickedness of Jacob?
Is it not Samaria?
And what are the high places of Judah?
Are they not *those of* Jerusalem? (162)
6 I will therefore make Samaria
A heap of the field, a plantation for vineyards;

And I will roll into the valley its stones,
And its foundations will I discover;
7 And all her graven images shall be broken down,
And all her rewards shall be burnt in the fire,
And all her idols will I lay desolate;
For from the reward of a harlot hath she gathered,
And to the reward of a harlot shall they return.

8 For this will I wail and howl,
I will go spoiled and naked;
I will make wailing as the dragons,
And mourning as the daughters of the ostrich: (170)
9 For grievous is her stroke,
For it has come to Judah,
It has reached the gate of my people—even Jerusalem.

10 In Gath tell ye it not; weeping, weep not;
In the house of Ophrah, roll thyself in the dust.
11 Pass over also, thou inhabitant of Saphir,
Naked and in shame;
Go forth shall not the inhabitant of Zaanan,
In the mourning of Beth-ezel;
She will take from you her station. (176)
12 Verily, grieved for good has the inhabitant of Maroth;
For come down has evil from Jehovah
To the gate of Jerusalem.
13 Tie the chariot to the dromedary,
Thou inhabitant of Lachish;
The beginning of sin has she been to the daughter of Zion;
For in thee have been found the transgressions of Israel.
14 Thou shalt therefore send presents,
For Moresheth-gath, to the sons of Achzib, (180)
Who have been a deception to the kings of Israel.
15 Yet a possessor will I send to thee, inhabitant of Mareshah;
Even to Adullam, the glory of Israel, shall he come.
16 Make bald, and poll thyself,
For the children of thy delicacies;
Enlarge thy baldness as the eagle,
Inasmuch as they have migrated from thee.

CHAPTER II.

1 Woe to those who devise iniquity,
And contrive wickedness on their beds!
When the morning shines, they execute it;
For to do it their hand is ready.
2 And they covet fields, and forcibly take them;
And houses, and they take them away:
And they oppress a man and his house,
A man and his heritage. (187)

3 Therefore, thus saith Jehovah,—
Behold, I am devising against this family an evil,
From which ye shall not remove your necks;
And ye shall not walk in your height,
For an evil time will it be.
4 In that day shall they take up against thee a proverb,
And bewail with a lamentable lament,
And say, "Wasted, we are laid waste;
The portion of my people has he changed;
How he takes away from me instead of restoring!
Our fields he divides." (191)
5 There shall not therefore be for thee
One to cast a line for lot in the assembly of Jehovah.

6 "Prophesy not, ye who prophesy;"—
They shall not prophesy for them;—
He will not take reproaches. (195)
7 O thou who art called the house of Jacob!
Is the Spirit of Jehovah straitened?
Are these his works?
Are not my words good to him
Who walks uprightly? (201)
8 And they who were heretofore my people,
Have risen up as an enemy against me;
The robe of beauty they plunder
From those who pass by securely,
As those who return from war. (203)
9 The women of my people have ye expelled

From the house of their delights;
From their children have ye taken away
My ornament for ever. (204)
10 Arise, depart, for this is not *your* rest;
Because it has been polluted: (206)
He will scatter *you* with a violent scattering.

11 If a man, walking in the spirit, and lying deceitfully, says,
"I will prophesy to thee of wine and of strong drink,"
He shall be the prophet of this people. (208)
12 Gathering, I will gather the whole of thee Jacob,
Assembling, I will assemble the residue of Israel;
I will set them together as the sheep of Bozrah,
As a flock in the midst of its fold;
They shall make a noise on account *of the number* of men.
13 Ascend shall a breaker before them,
They shall break through and pass the gate;
Yea, they shall go out through it;
And pass shall their king before them,
And Jehovah at their head. (215.)

CHAPTER III.

1 And I said, "Hear, I pray, ye princes of Jacob;
And ye rulers of the house of Israel:
Is it not for you to know judgment?"
2 But they hate good and love evil;
They pull off the skin from them,
And the flesh from their bones:
3 Yea, they devour the flesh of my people,
And their skin they strip from them,
And their bones they break,
And make them small as for the pot,
And their flesh for the cauldron.

4 They shall then cry to Jehovah,
And he will not answer them,
But he will hide his face from them at that time,
As they have acted perversely in their doings.

5 Thus saith Jehovah to the Prophets,
Who deceive my people,
And bite with their teeth, and cry, "Peace;"
And when any one putteth not in their mouth,
Against him they declare war:
6 Night shall therefore be to you instead of a vision,
And darkness shall be to you instead of divination;
And set shall the sun on the Prophets,
And darkened over them shall be the day: (227)
7 And ashamed shall be the seers,
And confounded shall be the diviners;
And they shall all cover their lips,
For there will be no answer from God.

8 But I indeed am filled with power,
By the Spirit of Jehovah, yea, with judgment and courage,
To declare to Jacob his wickedness,
And to Israel his sin.
9 Hear this, I pray, ye princes of the house of Jacob,
And ye rulers of the house of Israel,
Who abominate judgment,
And all rectitude pervert; (237)
10 Who build Zion by blood,
And Jerusalem by iniquity.
11 Its princes judge for reward,
And its priests for wages teach,
And its prophets for money divine;
And on Jehovah they lean, saying,
"Is not Jehovah in the midst of us?
Come upon us shall no evil."
12 Therefore for you Zion as a field shall be plowed,
And Jerusalem shall be a heap,
And the mount of the house as the heights of a forest.

CHAPTER IV.

1 But it shall be in the last days,
That the mount of the house of Jehovah
Shall be set in order on the top of the mountains,

And elevated shall it be above the hills;
And assemble there shall nations; (252)
2 And go shall many nations and say,—
"Come and let us ascend to the mount of Jehovah,
And to the house of the God of Jacob;
And he will teach us of his ways,
And we will walk in his paths:"
For from Zion shall go forth a law,
And the word of Jehovah from Jerusalem;
3 And he will rule among many people,
And convince strong nations afar off; (260)
And beat their swords shall they into plowshares,
And their spears into pruninghooks;
And lift up shall not a nation against a nation a sword,
And they shall learn war no more;
4 And they shall sit every one under his own vine,
And under his own fig-tree;
And none will there be to terrify them;
For *thus* hath the mouth of Jehovah of hosts spoken.
5 For all people shall walk,
Every one in the name of his god; (271)
But we will walk
In the name of Jehovah our God for ever.

6 In that day, saith Jehovah,
I will assemble the lame,
And the driven out will I gather,
And her whom I have afflicted:
7 And I will make the lame a remnant,
And the driven out a strong nation;
Reign over them shall Jehovah on mount Zion,
From henceforth, even for ever.
8 And thou tower of the flock,
The fortress of the daughter of Zion,
To thee it shall come;
Yea, come shall the former dominion;
The kingdom, to the daughter of Jerusalem.

9 Why dost thou now cry with a loud crying?

Is there no king in thee?
Has thy counsellor perished?
For seized thee has pain as one in travail.
10 Be in pain, and groan, O daughter of Zion,
As a woman in travail;
For go forth shalt thou from the city,
And thou shalt dwell in the field,
Yea, thou shalt go as far as Babylon;
There shalt thou be delivered,
There shall Jehovah redeem thee
From the hand of thy enemies.
11 And now gathered against thee are many nations,
Who say, "Let her be condemned,
And look shall our eye on Zion." (284)
12 But they know not the thoughts of Jehovah,
And understand not his counsel;
For he shall gather them as a handful to the floor.
13 Arise, and thrash, thou daughter of Zion;
For thy horn will I make iron,
And thy hoofs will I make brass;
And thou shalt tear in pieces strong nations;
And consecrate to Jehovah their wealth,
And their substance to the Lord of the whole earth.

CHAPTER V.

1 Assemble now thyself, thou daughter of a troop;
A siege has he set against us: (294)
With a rod shall they smite on the cheek the judge of Israel.
2 And thou, Bethlehem Ephratah,
Art small to be among the thousands of Judah!
From thee shall to me come forth
One to be a ruler in Israel;
And his goings forth *are* from the beginning,
From the days of ages.
3 He will therefore give them up till the time,
When she who travails shall bring forth,
And return to the children of Israel
Shall the residue of his brethren:

4 And he shall stand and feed in the power of Jehovah,
In the majesty of the name of Jehovah his God;
And they shall quietly dwell,
For he shall be now magnified to the ends of the earth.

5 And he shall be *our* peace;
When the Assyrian shall come into our land,
And when he shall tread in our palaces,
Then we shall set up against him seven shepherds,
And eight princes of men;
6 And they shall lay waste
The land of the Assyrian by the sword,
And the land of Nimrod by their swords; (311)
And he will deliver us from the Assyrian,
When he shall come into our land,
And when he shall tread in our borders.
7 And the residue of Jacob shall be,
Among the nations, in the midst of many people,
As a dew from Jehovah, as drops of rain on the grass;
Which tarries not for man, nor waits for the sons of men.
8 The residue of Jacob shall also be,
Among the nations, in the midst of many people,
As a lion among the beasts of the forest,
As a young lion among a flock of sheep,
Who, when he passes through, tears and carries away,
And no one can deliver.
9 Exalted shall be thy hand above thine enemies,
And all thine adversaries shall be cut off.
10 And it shall be in that day, saith Jehovah,
That I will cut off thy horses from the midst of thee,
And will destroy thy chariots;
11 And cut off will I the cities of thy land,
And will overthrow all thy fortresses;
12 And I will cut off diviners from thine hand,
And soothsayers shall not be to thee;
13 And cut off will I thy graven images,
And thy statues from the midst of thee,
And thou shalt no more bow down
Before the work of thy hands;

14 And I will demolish thy groves from the midst of thee,
That I may destroy thine enemies;
15 And in anger and fury will I execute on the nations
A vengeance, which they have not heard.

CHAPTER VI.

1 Hear ye now what Jehovah saith,—
"Arise, contend before the mountains,
And let the hills hear thy voice."
2 Hear, ye mountains, the controversy of Jehovah,
And ye strong foundations of the earth;
For Jehovah has a controversy with his people,
And with Israel he will contend:—
3 "My people! what have I done to thee?
And in what have I molested thee?
Testify against me.
4 I have indeed made thee to ascend from Egypt,
And from the house of servants I redeemed thee;
I sent before thee Moses, Aaron, and Miriam.
5 My people! remember now
What Balak, the king of Moab, consulted,
And what Balaam, the son of Bosor, answered him,
And what happened from Shittim even to Gilgal,
That thou mayest know the righteousness of Jehovah."(336)

6 "Wherewith shall I approach Jehovah?
And bow down myself before the high God?
Shall I approach him with burnt-sacrifices?
With calves a year old?
7 Will Jehovah be pleased with thousands of rams?
With ten thousands of rivers of oil?
Shall I give my first-born as my sin-offering?
The fruit of my loins as an expiation
For the wickedness of my soul?"—
8 He hath declared to thee, O man, what is good:
And what does Jehovah require from thee,
But to do justice, and to love mercy,
And to humble thyself to walk with thy God?

9 The voice of Jehovah crieth to arouse;
And the man of understanding will see his name:
Hear ye the rod, and who testifies of it.
10 Are there still in the house of the wicked
The treasures of iniquity,
And the scanty detestable measure?
11 Shall I justify balances of wickedness,
And the bag of deceitful weights?
12 For her rich men have filled themselves by violence,
And her inhabitants have spoken falsehood,
And their tongue is deceitful in their mouth.
13 And I also by smiting will afflict thee,
And thee will I destroy for thy sins: (352)
14 Thou shalt eat and not be satisfied,
And thy casting down shall be in the midst of thee;
And thou shalt lay hold, and not deliver,
And what thou deliverest will I give up to the sword:
15 Thou shalt sow and not reap,
Thou shalt press the oil, and not anoint thyself with oil,
And the new wine, and not drink wine.
16 For observed are the statutes of Omri,
And every work of the house of Ahab;
And ye walk in their counsels,
That I should make thee a desolation,
And her inhabitants an hissing;
And the reproach of my people ye shall bear.

CHAPTER VII.

1 Woe is me! for I am as the ingatherings of summer,
And as the bunches of the vintage:
There is no cluster to eat;
The ripe fruits my soul hath desired. (360)
2 Perished has the meek from the land,
And upright among men there is none;
For all lie in wait for blood,
Every one hunts his brother with a net.
3 To effect the wickedness of their hands,
The prince asketh, and the judge also, for reward,

And the great man speaks himself
Of the mischief of his soul; and they wrap it up. (365)
4 The good among them is like a brier,
The upright is worse than a thorn-hedge:
The day of thy watchmen, thy visitation, is coming;
Then shall be their confusion.

5 Trust not a friend, put no faith in a counsellor;
From her who sleepeth in thy bosom,
Guard the openings of thy mouth:
6 For the son dishonours his father,
The daughter rises up against her mother,
The daughter-in-law against her mother-in-law;
Enemies to man are his own domestics.

7 But I to Jehovah will look,
I will wait for the God of my salvation;
Hear me will my God.
8 Rejoice not thou over me, my enemy; (374)
Though I have fallen, I shall rise again;
When I sit in darkness, Jehovah will be my light.
9 The wrath of Jehovah will I bear,
(For I have sinned against him,)
Until he plead my cause,
And execute judgment for me;
He will bring me to light,
I shall see his righteousness:
10 And see shall my enemy,
And cover her shall shame, who said to me,—
"Where is Jehovah thy God?"
Mine eyes shall see her;
And now trodden shall she be as the mire of the street.

11 The day to build thy walls!
That day shall remove far the decree:
12 And in that day to thee shall they come
From Assyria and the cities of the fortress,
From the fortress also to the river, (386)
And from sea to sea, and from mountain to mountain.—

13 But the land shall become a desolation,
On account of its inhabitants,
For the fruit of their works.

14 Feed thy people by thy crook,
The flock of thy heritage,
Who dwell in solitude, in the wood,
As in the midst of Carmel;
They shall be fed in Bashan and Gilead,
As in the days of old. (392)
15 As in the days of thy going forth from the land of Egypt,
I will show to him wonderful things.
16 See shall the nations,
And be ashamed of all their might;
They shall lay their hand on their mouth,
Their ears shall become deaf;
17 They shall lick the dust as a serpent,
As reptiles of the earth shall they move from their holes;
Jehovah our God shall they dread,
And they shall be afraid of thee.

18 What God is like thee,
Taking away iniquity,
And passing over transgression,
As to the remnant of his heritage?
He will not retain for ever his anger,
For he loveth mercy:
19 He will return, he will have mercy on us;
He will tread down our iniquities,
And cast into the depths of the sea all their sins:
20 Thou wilt grant truth to Jacob,
Mercy to Abraham;
Which thou hast sworn to our fathers
In the days of old.

END OF NEW TRANSLATION OF MICAH.

A TRANSLATION

OF

CALVIN'S VERSION

OF

THE PROPHECIES OF NAHUM.

CHAPTER I.

1 The burden of Nineveh,—the book of the vision of Nahum the Elkoshite:

2 A God jealous, and an avenger is Jehovah;
Avenger is Jehovah, and a retainer of wrath;
Take vengeance does Jehovah on his enemies,
And keep *it* for his adversaries: (421)
3 Jehovah is slow to wrath, and great in power,
And by clearing he will not clear:
Jehovah! in the whirlwind and tempest is his way,
And the cloud is the dust of his feet: (424)
4 He chides the sea, and it becomes dry;
And all the rivers he dries up;
Languish do Bashan and Carmel,
And the flower of Lebanon languishes:
5 Mountains tremble at him, and hills melt;
And burn does the earth before his face,
Yea, the world, and all who dwell in it. (427)
6 Before his indignation who can stand?

And who can bear the fierceness of his wrath? (429)
His fury is poured out like fire,
And rocks dissolve before him.
7 Good is Jehovah for strength in the day of distress;
And he knoweth them who hope in him.
8 But with an inundation, he, passing through,
Will make a consummation in her place; (433)
And pursue shall darkness his enemies.

9 What do ye imagine against Jehovah?
A consummation he makes!
Not rise again shall affliction.
10 They who are like entangled thorns,
And drunken as with their own drinking—
Devoured shall they be as stubble fully dry. (437)
11 From thee has gone forth a contriver of evil
Against Jehovah, a wicked counsellor.

12 Thus saith Jehovah,—
Though they are secure, and though they are many,
They shall *yet* be cut off, and he shall pass through: (443)
And though I have afflicted thee, I will afflict thee no more;
13 For now will I break off from thee his yoke,
And his bonds will I burst asunder.

14 And a command respecting thee hath Jehovah given,—
"Let none be sown hereafter of thy name;"
From the house of thy gods will I cut off
The graven and the molten image;
I will make thy grave, for thou art execrable.

15 Behold on the mountains the feet of him
Who announceth, who publisheth peace!
Celebrate thou, Judah, thy solemnities,
Perform thy vows; for pass through thee
Shall the wicked one no more,—he is wholly cut off.

CHAPTER II.

1 Come up is the destroyer before thy face;
Watch the fortress, guard the way, (455)
Make strong the loins, fortify mightily thy strength:
2 (For taken away hath Jehovah the pride of Jacob,
As he had done as to the pride of Israel;
For emptied them have the emptiers,
And their branches have they cut down:)
3 The shield of his mighty ones are made red,
The men of his strength are clad in scarlet;
With the fire of torches is the chariot,
In the day of his expedition;
And the fir-trees tremulously shake:
4 In the wide places they madden with their chariots,
They hurry away through the streets,
The appearance of them is that of lamps,
As lightnings they run here and there.

5 He will remember his valiant men,
They shall stumble in their march,
They shall hasten to her wall,
And prepared will be the defence.
6 The gates of the rivers are opened,
And the palace is dissolved;
7 And she which stood firm is cast into exile,
And her maids lead her as with the voice of doves,
Beating on their breasts. (463)
8 And yet Nineveh has been
As a pool of waters from *ancient* days;
But now they flee—"Stand ye, stand;"
And no one regards.
9 Take ye away the silver, take away the gold;
For there is no end of her preparations;
Her glory is from every desirable vessel. (468)
10 Emptied and emptied is she, and denuded;
And the heart is melted;

And there is a knocking of the knees,
And trembling in all loins,
And the faces of all withdraw their brightness. (472)

11 Where is the abode of lions?
And the place of feeding for young lions?
Where came the lion, the lioness, the cub of the lion;
And none terrified them. (474)
12 The lion tare what sufficed his whelps,
And strangled for his lionesses,
And filled with ravin his caves,
And his dens with prey.
13 Behold, I am against thee, saith Jehovah of hosts,
And I will burn with smoke her chariot,
And thy young lions shall the sword devour,
And I will cut off from the land thy prey,
And the sound of thy teeth shall no more be heard.

CHAPTER III.

1 Oh bloody city! the whole is full of deceit, *and* of ravin;
From it the prey departs not.
2 The sound of the whip!
The sound of the rattling of the wheel!
And the horse prancing, and the chariot bounding!
3 The horseman urging onward!
And the flame of the sword, and the lightning of the spear!
And the number of the slain, and the mass of carcases!
And there is no end to her dead bodies,
They stumble on their carcases!
4 *This is* for the multitude of the fornications
Of the harlot who excels in beauty,
The mistress of sorceries,
Who sells nations by her fornications,
And tribes by her sorceries. (481)

5 Behold, I am against thee, saith Jehovah of hosts;
And I will throw thy skirts over thy face,

And show to the nations thy nakedness,
And to kingdoms thy filthiness;
6 And I will cast on thee filth, and disgrace thee,
And I will make thee an example:
7 And it shall be, that whosoever seeth thee
Shall flee away from thee, and say,—
"Wasted is Nineveh! who will condole with her?
Whence shall I seek comforters for thee?"

8 Art thou better than populous No,
Which dwelt among the rivers? the sea was around her;
Whose mound was the sea, and the sea was her wall;
9 From Ethiopia was her strength, and from Egypt,
And there was no end *to it;*
Africa and Lybia were her auxiliaries:
10 Even she migrated, she went into captivity;
And her infants were dashed at the head of every street,
And on her chief men did they cast lots,
And her nobles were bound in chains.
11 Thou also shalt be inebriated, thou shalt be hid;
And thou shalt seek strength from the enemy.
12 All thy fortresses shall be like fig-trees with ripe fruit;
If they be shaken, they fall into the mouth of the eater.
13 Behold, thy people shall be women in the midst of thee;
To thine enemies shall be opened the gates of thy land,
Devour shall the fire thy bars.

14 Waters for the siege draw for thyself,
Strengthen thy fortresses,
Enter into the clay, tread the mortar,
Make strong the brick-kiln:
15 There shall the fire devour you,
Exterminate thee shall the sword,
It shall devour thee as the chafer.
Increase as the chafer, increase as the locust;
16 Thou hast multiplied thy merchants
More than the stars of heaven;—
The chafer has spoiled, and flies away.
17 Thy princes are as locusts,

And thy captains are as the largest locusts ;
Which encamp in the fences in the cold day ;
The sun rises, and they fly away,
And not known is the place where they are. (502)

18 Slept have thy shepherds, king of Assyria ;
Lie down did thy mighty men :
Dispersed is thy people on the mountains,
And no one gathers them.
19 There is no binding for thy fracture,
Altogether grievous is thy wound ;
All who shall hear a report of thee,
Shall, on thy account, strike the hand ;
For upon whom hath not passed
Thy wickedness continually ?

END OF NEW TRANSLATION OF NAHUM.

EDINBURGH :
THE EDINBURGH PRINTING COMPANY,
12, South St David Street.

ERRATA.

VOL. III.

Page 48, line 35,	populi	*ought to be*	populo.
... 154, ... 20,	tuæ		suæ.
... 177, ... 17,	the most suitable		very suitable.
... 190, note 5,	gravitaque		graviterque.
... 194, line 1,	to those who distil		who distil.
... 195, note 9,	thou shalt prophesy		those shall prophesy.
... ... 29,	to thee		to these.
... 277, line 27,	went forth from		went forth ; from.
... 280, note 1,	תה		עתה.
... 303, line 2,	So the children		To the children.
... 315, ... 14,	which wait		which waits.
... ... 15,	nor tarry		nor tarries.
... 390, ... 35,	destruction		distinction.
... 399, note 18, 19,	פש, ון		פשע, עון.